Frommer's®

Washington, D.C. 2005

IN THIS TEMPLE
S IN THE HEARTS OF THE PEOPLE
OR WHOM HE SAVED THE UNION
E MEMORY OF ABRAHAM LINCOLN
IS ENSHRINED FOREVER

D1418163

This moving testament to one of the nation's greatest presidents is a neoclassical temple-like structure, housing Daniel Chester French's timeless and powerful 19-foot-high seated statue of Lincoln. See chapter 7. © Robert Shafer/Folio, Inc.

The Supreme Court and the Capitol, two prime examples of Washington, D.C.'s grand neoclassical architecture. See chapter 7. © Kelly/Mooney Photography.

Viewing this stark memorial to America's Vietnam War dead is a powerful and poignant experience. See chapter 7. © Wolfgang Kaehler Photography.

Washington is at its most beautiful in the spring, when delicate pink and white blossoms from thousands of cherry trees burst into bloom along the Tidal Basin. The trees bloom for a little less than two weeks in March or early April, an event that's heralded by a festival with a major parade. See chapter 7. © John Skowronski/Folio, Inc.

The Folger Shakespeare Library houses the world's largest collection of the Bard's printed works. See chapter 7. © Catherine Karnow Photography.

Painstakingly restored to its former glory, stunning Union Station is not only a gateway for trains to and from D.C., but an attraction in itself, with great dining and shopping. See chapters 6, 7, and 8. © Catherine Karnow Photography.

The dignified simplicity of Arlington National Cemetery, which is the resting place for luminaries such as President John F. Kennedy, Thurgood Marshall, and President William Howard Taft, also contains graves for more than 260,000 war dead, veterans, and dependents as well as The Tomb of the Unknowns. See chapter 7. © Christie Parker/Houserstock, Inc.

The domed Main Reading Room of the Library of Congress is the epicenter of the world's largest library. Visit it to admire its exquisite architecture or to peruse one of its 113 million items. See chapter 7. © Jake Rajs/Getty Images.

Lincoln was sitting in this box at Ford's Theatre when he was shot by John Wilkes Booth on April 14, 1865. See chapter 7.
© Catherine Karnow Photography.

The streets extending out from Dupont Circle are jumping with all-night bookstores, great restaurants and nightspots, movie theaters, and Washingtonians at play. See chapters 6 and 9. © Michael Ventura/Folio, Inc.

The memorial to America's third president and its original Renaissance man, Thomas Jefferson, is especially beautiful at night. See chapter 7. © Robert Shafer/Getty Images.

Frommer's®

Washington, D.C.

2005

by Elise Hartman Ford

Here's what the critics say about Frommer's:

"Amazingly easy to use. Very portable, very complete."
—*Booklist*

"Detailed, accurate, and easy-to-read information for all price ranges."
—*Glamour Magazine*

"Hotel information is close to encyclopedic."
—*Des Moines Sunday Register*

"Frommer's Guides have a way of giving you a real feel for a place."
—*Knight Ridder Newspapers*

WILEY

Wiley Publishing, Inc.

About the Author

Elise Hartman Ford has been a freelance writer in the Washington, D.C. area since 1985. Her writing has appeared in the *Washington Post, Washingtonian* magazine, the London-based *Bradman's North America Guide, The Essential Guide to Business Travel, Ladies' Home Journal,* and other national, regional, and trade publications. In addition to this guide, she is the author of *Frommer's Washington, D.C., from $80 a Day, Frommer's Memorable Walks in Washington, D.C.,* and *Unique Meeting, Wedding, and Party Places in Greater Washington.*

Published by:

Wiley Publishing, Inc.

111 River St.
Hoboken, NJ 07030-5774

ISBN 0-7645-7290-3

Editor: Elizabeth Heath
Production Editor: Blair J. Pottenger
Cartographer: Roberta Stockwell
Photo Editor: Richard Fox
Production by Wiley Indianapolis Composition Services

Front cover photo: Woman at the Vietnam Veterans Memorial
Back cover photo: Lincoln Memorial illuminated at night

For information on our other products and services or to obtain technical support, please contact our Customer Care Department within the U.S. at 800/762-2974, outside the U.S. at 317/572-3993 or fax 317/572-4002.

Wiley also publishes its books in a variety of electronic formats. Some content that appears in print may not be available in electronic formats.

Manufactured in the United States of America

5 4 3

Contents

List of Maps   v

What's New in Washington, D.C.   1

1   The Best of Washington, D.C.   4

1 Frommer's Favorite D.C.
Experiences 4

2 Best Hotel Bets 7

3 Best Dining Bets 10

Site Seeing: The Best
Washington, D.C. Websites 12

2   Planning Your Trip to Washington, D.C.   16

1 Visitor Information 16

2 Money 17

Destination: Washington,
D.C.—Red-Alert Checklist 18

3 When to Go 20

Washington, D.C. Calendar
of Events 21

4 Travel Insurance 26

5 Health & Safety 27

6 Specialized Travel Resources 28

7 Planning Your Trip Online 33

Frommers.com: The Complete
Travel Resource 35

8 The 21st-Century Traveler 35

9 Getting There 37

Flying with Film & Video 46

10 Recommended Reading 48

3   For International Visitors   49

1 Preparing for Your Trip 49

2 Getting to the United States 56

3 Getting Around the
United States 56

Fast Facts: For the International
Traveler 57

4   Getting to Know Washington, D.C.   62

1 Orientation 62

The Neighborhoods in Brief 69

2 Getting Around 71

Fast Facts: Washington, D.C. . . .78

5   Where to Stay   80

1 Capitol Hill/The Mall 82

2 Downtown, East of
16th Street NW 88

Family-Friendly Hotels 89

3 Downtown, 16th Street
NW & West 96

4 Adams-Morgan 101

5 Dupont Circle 104

6 Foggy Bottom/West End 109

7 Georgetown 112

8 Woodley Park 115

6 Where to Dine   118

1 Restaurants by Cuisine 119
2 Capitol Hill 121
   Dining at Sightseeing
   Attractions 122
3 Downtown, East of
   16th Street NW 125
   Vegetarian Times 130
   Family-Friendly Restaurants . . .135
4 Downtown, 16th Street
   NW & West 138

5 U Street Corridor 144
6 Adams-Morgan 145
7 Dupont Circle 148
8 Foggy Bottom/West End 153
9 Georgetown 156
   A Spot of Tea 162
10 Glover Park 163
11 Woodley Park & Cleveland
    Park 164

7 Exploring Washington, D.C.   166

   Call Ahead 167
   Suggested Itineraries 170
   Openings and Closings 171
1 The Three Houses
   of Government 171
2 The Major Memorials 180
3 The Smithsonian Museums 188
   Museum Exhibits Scheduled
   for 2005 194
4 Elsewhere on the Mall 200
5 Other Government Agencies . . .204

6 More Museums 206
   Museums of Special Interest . . .210
7 Other Attractions 215
8 Just Across the Potomac:
   Arlington 218
9 Parks & Gardens 221
10 Especially for Kids 226
    Favorite Children's
    Attractions 226
11 Organized Tours 227
12 Outdoor Activities 230

8 Shopping   232

1 The Shopping Scene 232
2 Great Shopping Areas 232

3 Shopping A to Z 234
   Emergency Shopping 247

9 Washington, D.C., After Dark   250

1 The Performing Arts 251
2 The Club & Music Scene 258
   D.C. Boogie 261
   Late-Night Bites 264

3 The Bar Scene 266
   Cheap Eats: Happy Hours
   to Write Home About 269
   Arlington Row 270

10 Side Trips from Washington, D.C.   273

1 Mount Vernon 273
2 Alexandria 276

   Biking to Old Town Alexandria
   & Mount Vernon 281

Appendix: Washington, D.C., in Depth   289

1 History 101 290   *Dateline* 290

Index   298

General *Index* 298   Restaurant *Index* 306
Accommodations *Index* 306

List of Maps

D.C. Metropolitan Area   39

Washington, D.C., at a Glance   66

Major Metro Stops   72

Washington, D.C., Accommodations   84

Adams-Morgan, Dupont Circle & West End Accommodations   103

Capitol Hill, Downtown & Foggy Bottom Dining   126

Adams-Morgan & Dupont Circle Dining   147

Georgetown Dining   157

Washington, D.C., Attractions   168

Capitol Hill   173

The White House Area   177

The Mall   181

Arlington National Cemetery   219

Rock Creek Park Area   223

Washington, D.C., After Dark   252

Old Town Alexandria   277

To Jim, Caitlin and Lucy

An Invitation to the Reader

In researching this book, we discovered many wonderful places—hotels, restaurants, shops, and more. We're sure you'll find others. Please tell us about them, so we can share the information with your fellow travelers in upcoming editions. If you were disappointed with a recommendation, we'd love to know that, too. Please write to:

Frommer's Washington, D.C. 2005
Wiley Publishing, Inc. • 111 River St. • Hoboken, NJ 07030-5774

An Additional Note

Please be advised that travel information is subject to change at any time—and this is especially true of prices. We therefore suggest that you write or call ahead for confirmation when making your travel plans. The authors, editors, and publisher cannot be held responsible for the experiences of readers while traveling. Your safety is important to us, however, so we encourage you to stay alert and be aware of your surroundings. Keep a close eye on cameras, purses, and wallets, all favorite targets of thieves and pickpockets.

Other Great Guides for Your Trip:

Frommer's Memorable Walks in Washington, D.C.
Frommer's Washington, D.C., from $80 a Day
Frommer's Irreverent Guide to Washington, D.C.
Frommer's Portable Washington, D.C.
The Unofficial Guide to Washington, D.C.
Frommer's Washington, D.C. with Kids

Frommer's Star Ratings, Icons & Abbreviations

Every hotel, restaurant, and attraction listing in this guide has been ranked for quality, value, service, amenities, and special features using a **star-rating system.** In country, state, and regional guides, we also rate towns and regions to help you narrow down your choices and budget your time accordingly. Hotels and restaurants are rated on a scale of zero (recommended) to three stars (exceptional). Attractions, shopping, nightlife, towns, and regions are rated according to the following scale: zero stars (recommended), one star (highly recommended), two stars (very highly recommended), and three stars (must-see).

In addition to the star-rating system, we also use **seven feature icons** that point you to the great deals, in-the-know advice, and unique experiences that separate travelers from tourists. Throughout the book, look for:

Finds	Special finds—those places only insiders know about
Fun Fact	Fun facts—details that make travelers more informed and their trips more fun
Kids	Best bets for kids and advice for the whole family
Moments	Special moments—those experiences that memories are made of
Overrated	Places or experiences not worth your time or money
Tips	Insider tips—great ways to save time and money
Value	Great values—where to get the best deals

The following **abbreviations** are used for credit cards:

AE	American Express	DISC	Discover	V	Visa
DC	Diners Club	MC	MasterCard		

Frommers.com

Now that you have the guidebook to a great trip, visit our website at **www.frommers.com** for travel information on more than 3,000 destinations. With features updated regularly, we give you instant access to the most current trip-planning information available. At Frommers.com, you'll also find the best prices on airfares, accommodations, and car rentals—and you can even book travel online through our travel booking partners. At Frommers.com, you'll also find the following:

- Online updates to our most popular guidebooks
- Vacation sweepstakes and contest giveaways
- Newsletter highlighting the hottest travel trends
- Online travel message boards with featured travel discussions

What's New in Washington, D.C.

This year, 2005, is an inaugural year and Washington, D.C., as usual, has taken great pains to look its best to the world during the president's swearing-in ceremonies and celebrations. There's a slight problem, however: The capital is in a state of dramatic renewal, which means construction equipment is everywhere. Enormous and unsightly cranes hover over the grounds of the Capitol, as they have for years now, digging out a Visitors Center beneath the building. Originally planned to be complete in 2005, the Visitors Center has taken on a life of its own, as Congressional members lay claim to new office space. The due date is now spring of 2006, and I'm afraid that ugly construction equipment will be around just as long.

And so it goes at the Washington Monument, where vehicle security barriers are being installed, and at the Lincoln Memorial, where the streets are being torn up and re-paved, and at the Kennedy Center, where the complex is undergoing a huge expansion. Washington, D.C., is a beautiful and thriving city, but beauty requires constant maintenance, symbols of freedom need protection, and success demands more and more room and ways to satisfy, it seems.

GETTING THERE All of a sudden, airlines with fun names like Ted and JetBlue and Independence Air are flying into D.C. airports. As it happens, the airlines with these uncommon names are discount airlines, so find out whether **Ted** (© **800/CALL-TED;** www.flyted.com) and **Independence Air** (© **800/FLY-FLYI;** www.flyi.com) or **JetBlue** (© **800/538-2583;** www.jetblue.com) fly into your city, and hop one of their planes to Washington, cause if you can, it's going to be cheaper. And if not, consider one you already know—Southwest Airlines, which flies into Baltimore-Washington International Airport, is always a good deal.

GETTING AROUND Less than a year after the Washington Metropolitan Area Transit Authority (WMATA) raised its base fares for bus and rail service by 10¢, to $1.20, it proposed another increase, this time by 15 cents, to $1.35 for its base fare, with $3.75 the maximum you would pay for travel to the furthest destination. By the time you read this, the new fare will surely be in effect.

Scheduled to be in place by the start of the National Cherry Blossom Festival on March 26th, is a **"Circulator"** shuttle bus system. The District and federal governments and downtown businesses teamed up to pay for and operate the service, whose buses run every 5 minutes along two east-west routes between Union Station and Georgetown and two north-south routes between the D.C. Convention Center and the waterfront in southwest D.C. Similar in service and purpose to the successful Georgetown Shuttle, the Circulator is intended to ease the city's congested streets while providing quick, easy, and cheap (50¢ one-way) access to well-traveled spots around town. Proponents of the system expect residents, tourists, and federal workers to use the buses, which supplement Metro's rail and bus transportation.

ACCOMMODATIONS A number of new hotels are opening around town in 2005, including two offering much needed affordable lodging in the downtown area: a **Hampton Inn** at 6th Street and Massachusetts Avenue NW, not far from the MCI Center, the International Spy Museum, the new Koshland Science Museum (see description, below), and restaurants; and an **Embassy Suites** hotel at 1000 K St., within walking distance of the convention center, the City Museum, and other attractions. The two hotels creating the biggest buzz currently, though, are the 400-room luxury **Mandarin Oriental, Washington DC,** 1330 Maryland Ave. SW (© 202/554-8588; www.mandarinoriental.com), at 12th Street SW, on the Washington Channel, but just 2 blocks from Smithsonian museums, and the **Residence Inn Capitol**, near the Mall (at 4th and E sts. SW). The **Mandarin,** which debuted in spring 2004, is startlingly lush inside, with great views of the water and the city; its signature restaurant opened in August 2004 and has as its chef Eric Ziebold, who most recently worked at the renowned French Laundry restaurant, in California's Napa Valley. The **Residence Inn Capitol** opened just in time for the inaugural on January 20, 2005. Its location ties in with that of the nearby Smithsonian National Museum of the American Indian; four Native American tribes are partners with local developers in the hotel, whose features incorporate Native designs and materials.

DINING The idea of making a meal from small plates of food has

been around for a while in D.C., starting perhaps with Spanish tapas, introduced to Washington diners by **Jaleo,** 480 7th St. NW (© **202/628-7949**), when the restaurant opened in 1993. Jaleo, by the way is still going strong. Lately, the culinary trend in Washington seems to be that restaurants of all stripes now offer affordable small plates of food. Most noteworthy are those restaurants of the highest caliber that serve these dishes: at **Palena,** 3529 Connecticut Ave. NW (© **202/537-9250;** www.palenarestaurant.com) in Cleveland Park, you can sit at the bar and dine on exquisite versions of burgers and fries, Caesar salad, and pastas, each item priced under $9. Come to **Galileo,** 1110 21st St. NW (© **202/293-7191;** www.robertodonna.com) for lunch at the bar and you can choose from dishes such as lasagne Bolognese or fusilli tossed with asparagus and proscuitto, each dish costing between $4 and $12. (Contrast that to dinners here, where you can choose one of three fixed price menus: $65, $75, or $85.) Finally, consider a seat in the pretty wine bar on the second floor of Georgetown's **Bistrot Lepic,** 1736 Wisconsin Ave. NW (© **202/333-0111;** www.bistrotlepic.com), where nightly you can choose from a list of 16 items, each under $12, and including a homemade foie gras terrine and a fresh onion tart.

SIGHTSEEING The **White House** (© **202/456-7041**) has reopened for public tours. You must contact your congressperson or senator to reserve a spot, months in advance, and you must be part of a group of 10 people, minimum, but your congressional office will help you sort all that out. (See the section in chapter 7 that talks about touring the White House.) The **U.S. Capitol,** at the east end of the Mall (© **202/225-6827**), is open to public tours, but you can no longer go through self-guided, nor can you arrange reserve tickets ahead of time, as you could in the past. Again, see chapter 7 for details.

As noted earlier, construction continues on a comprehensive underground **Capitol Visitor Center,** with completion scheduled for 2006. The new visitor center is being created directly beneath the plaza where people traditionally lined up for tours on the east side of the Capitol, which means that you must now stand in line at the southwest corner of the Capitol, the side facing the Mall, at the intersection of 1st Street and Independence Avenue SW.

The construction that is underway around the Lincoln Memorial, the Washington Monument, and the Kennedy Center may interfere with easy access but all three remain fully open to the public. Renovation work winds up at the FBI Building (© 202/324-3447; www.fbi.gov), which is due to re-open for public tours sometime in 2005, but call to confirm. Remaining closed for renovation throughout 2005 are the Smithsonian's **American Art Museum** and **National Portrait Gallery.** The **Kennedy Center for the Performing Arts** is going on with all shows, though the place looks like construction-central, as it will for the coming decade while its grand expansion, including a pedestrian plaza, is in production.

The big news in Washington these days has to do with the debut of Smithsonian's much-heralded **National Museum of the American Indian,** 4th Street and Independence Avenue SW (© 202/633-1000; www.nmai.si.edu) which opened on the National Mall on September 21, 2004, and the installation on the National Mall of the **National World War II Memorial,** 17th Street and Constitution Avenue NW (© 202/426-6841; www.wwii memorial.com), whose dedication ceremony took place on May 29, 2004. The American Indian Museum includes three permanent exhibit halls displaying up to 8,000 objects from the museum's 800,000-piece collection, as well as a theater and an outdoor performance space. So many people want to visit this new museum that the Smithsonian has established a free, timed entry pass system, just like the one in place at the Washington Monument, to control the numbers of visitors. You won't need passes to visit the World War II Memorial. In April 2004, the National Academy of Sciences opened the **Marian Koshland Science Museum,** at 6th and E streets NW (© 202/334-1202; www.koshlandsciencemuseum. org), whose exhibits on global warming, DNA sequencing, and other wonders of science are sure to interest science lovers—over the age of 13, the museum advises; admission is $5 adults, $3 for those under 18 and older than 65.

The Best of Washington, D.C.

In the White House, our nation's most-recently elected president presides, having been inaugurated in January. Three miles east of the White House, at the U.S. Capitol, the 109th Congress gets underway, and an expansive visitor center, set to open in early 2006, takes shape beneath the building. Across the street, the Supreme Court deliberates over a new caseload. Down the hill from the Capitol, the final Smithsonian museum, the National Museum of the American Indian, is only months old but already a smashing success. Further along on the Mall, the National World War II Memorial, dedicated Memorial Day Weekend 2004, attracts crowds eager to honor all those who served in that Great War. Alongside the Potomac River, the Kennedy Center for the Performing Arts grows bigger with every breath, as a decade-long expansion makes the nation's theater ever more accessible and inclusive. Welcome to Washington, D.C., in 2005.

At any given time, in any given year, so much is happening in the nation's capital. From the new science museum downtown (the Marian Koshland Museum) to the spectacularly luxurious new hotel near the Mall (the Mandarin Oriental) to the new petting farm at the National Zoo, this joint is jumping.

Within its city limits (67 sq. miles), Washington teems with history, made and in the making; the arts; cosmopolitan culture; magnificent parks, gardens, and architecture. Put it all together and you have a world hub of power, diplomacy, beauty, and intellect. So much to do, so much to see. If you don't know where to begin your trip planning, you've come to the right source. Read on and enjoy.

1 Frommer's Favorite D.C. Experiences

- **Sipping Afternoon Tea at the Top of Washington National Cathedral.** On Tuesday and Wednesday afternoons at 1:30pm, you can tour the world's sixth largest cathedral, then indulge in tea, scones, and lemon tarts served on the seventh floor of the West tower, whose arched windows overlook the city and beyond to Sugarloaf Mountain in Maryland. It's $22 per person; reserve as far in advance as possible (© 202/537-8993). See p. 217.
- **Visiting the Lincoln Memorial After Dark.** A must. During the day, be prepared to run interference with hordes of schoolchildren

and tour groups; at night, the experience is amazing. See p. 184.
- **Taking a Monument and Memorials Walking Tour.** Have a hearty breakfast, then take the Metro to Foggy Bottom, and when you exit turn right on 23rd Street NW and follow it to Constitution Avenue NW. Cross the avenue, make a left, walk past Henry Bacon Drive, and follow the signs to the Vietnam and Lincoln memorials; cross Independence Avenue and follow the cherry tree-lined Tidal Basin path to the FDR Memorial and further to the Jefferson Memorial; circle around the other side of the Tidal Basin and carefully re-cross

Independence Avenue to view the National World War II Memorial; then traverse the grounds of the Washington Monument to finish your tour there. This is a long but beautiful hike; afterward, head up 15th Street NW for a strength-restoring meal at one of the many excellent downtown restaurants. See chapters 6 and 7.

• **Rambling Through Rock Creek Park.** A paved bike/walking path extends 11 miles from the Lincoln Memorial to the Maryland border. You can hop on the trail at many spots throughout the city—it runs past the National Zoo, behind the Omni Shoreham Hotel in Woodley Park, near Dupont Circle, and across from the Watergate/Kennedy Center complex. You can rent a bike from **Big Wheel Bikes** at 1034 33rd St. NW (© **202/337-0254**) in Georgetown, and from **Thompson's Boat Center** (© **202/333-4861**), located on the path across from the Kennedy Center. For a really long bike ride, trek to the Lincoln Memorial, get yourself across the busy stretch that connects the parkway to the Arlington Memorial Bridge, and cross the bridge to the trail on the other side; this path winds 19 miles to Mount Vernon. See chapters 7 and 10.

• **Spending the Day in Alexandria.** Just a short distance (by Metro, car, or bike) from the District is George Washington's Virginia hometown. Roam the quaint cobblestone streets, browse charming boutiques and antiques stores, visit the 18th-century houses and other historic attractions, and dine in one of Alexandria's fine restaurants. See chapter 10.

• **Weighing in Judgment.** If you're in town when the Supreme Court is in session (Oct to late Apr; call © **202/479-3211** for details), you can observe a case argued; it's thrilling to see this august institution at work. See p. 175.

• **Admiring the Library of Congress.** The magnificent Italian Renaissance–style Thomas Jefferson Building of the Library of Congress—filled with murals, mosaics, sculptures, and allegorical paintings—is one of America's most notable architectural achievements. The LOC also displays exhibits of American treasures, from Thomas Jefferson's rough draft of the Declaration of Independence to the piano and other belongings used by American composers Ira and George Gershwin. See p. 205.

• **Attending a Millennium Stage Performance at the Kennedy Center.** Every evening at 6pm, the Kennedy Center presents a free 1-hour concert performed by local, up-and-coming, national or international musicians. This is a winner. Call the Kennedy Center (© **800/444-1324** or 202/467-4600), or check its website at **www.kennedy-center.org** to see the schedule of upcoming acts. See p. 251.

• **Spending a Morning on the Mall.** Take the Metro to the Smithsonian station early in the morning (about 8am is early enough), when the Mall is magical and tourist-free. Walk toward the Capitol Building along Jefferson Drive to the Smithsonian Information Center (the Castle) and stroll through the magnolia-lined parterres of the beautiful Enid A. Haupt Garden. Return to Jefferson Drive, walk farther east to the Hirshhorn, ducking in, on your way, for a look at the lovely Ripley Garden, before crossing the street to tour the Hirshhorn's sunken Sculpture Garden. Climb back to street level and cross the Mall to the enchanting National Gallery Sculpture Garden, at 7th Street and Madison Drive. See chapter 7.

• **Debarking at Union Station.** Noted architect Daniel H. Burnham's turn-of-the-20th-century beaux arts railway station is worth a visit even if you're not trying to catch a train. Dawdle and admire its coffered 96-foot-high ceilings, grand arches, and great halls, modeled after the Baths of Diocletian and the Arch of Constantine in Rome. Then shop and eat: The station's 1988 restoration filled the trilevel hall with everything from Ann Taylor and Crabtree & Evelyn to a high-quality food court and the refined B. Smith's restaurant. See chapters 7 and 8.

• **Enjoying an Artful Evening at the Phillips Collection.** Thursday evenings year-round, from 5 to 8:30pm, you pay $8 to tour the mansion-museum rooms filled with Impressionist, post-Impressionist, and modern art. Your tour ends up in the paneled Music Room, where you'll enjoy jazz, blues, or other musical combinations performed by fine local musicians, topped off by an artful lecture. It's a popular mingling spot for singles (there's a cash bar and sandwich fare). Call ℂ **202/ 387-2151** for information. See chapter 7 for complete details on the Phillips Collection. See chapter 9 for more nightlife.

• **Strolling Along Embassy Row.** Head northwest on Massachusetts Avenue from Dupont Circle. It's a gorgeous walk along tree-shaded streets lined with beaux-arts mansions. Built by fabulously wealthy magnates during the Gilded Age, most of these palatial precincts are occupied today by foreign embassies. See chapter 7 for more information.

• **People-Watching at Dupont Circle.** One of the few "living" circles, Dupont's is the all-weather hangout for mondo-bizarre biker-couriers, chess players, street musicians, and lovers. Sit on a bench and be astounded by the passing scene. See chapter 4.

• **Viewing Washington from the Water.** Cruise the Potomac River aboard one of several sightseeing vessels and relax from foot-weary travels. River cruises not only offer a pleasant interval for catching a second wind, they treat you to a marvelous perspective of the city. See chapter 7.

• **Cutting a Deal at the Georgetown Flea Market.** Pick up a latte and spend a pleasant Sunday browsing through the castoffs of wealthy Washingtonians, hand-painted furniture by local artists, and a hodgepodge of antiques and collectibles. Everybody shops here at one time or another, so you never know who you'll see or what you'll find. Wisconsin Avenue NW at S Street NW in Georgetown; open year-round, Sunday from 9am to 5pm. See chapter 8 for more shopping.

• **Shopping at Eastern Market.** Capitol Hill is home to more than government buildings; it's a community of old town houses, antiques shops, and the veritable institution, Eastern Market. Here, the locals barter and shop every Saturday and Sunday for fresh produce and baked goods, and flea-market bargains. At 7th Street SE, between North Carolina Avenue and C Street SE.

• **Ordering Drinks on the Sky Terrace of the Hotel Washington.** Posher bars exist, but none with this view. The experience is almost a cliché in Washington: When spring arrives, make a date to sit on this outdoor rooftop terrace,

Impressions

My God! What have I done to be condemned to reside in such a city!
                                        —A French diplomat in the early days

sip a gin and tonic, and gaze at the panoramic view of the White House, Treasury Building, and monuments. Open from the end of April to October for drinks and light fare, it's located at 515 15th St. NW, at Pennsylvania Avenue NW (② **202/638-5900**). See p. 93.

• **Chilling to the Sounds of Live Jazz in the Sculpture Garden.** Friday evenings in the summer at the National Gallery of Art Sculpture Garden, dip your toes in the fountain pool and chill, as live jazz groups serenade you, from 5 to 8pm. The garden's Pavilion Café sells tapas and wine and beer, by the way. See chapter 7.

• **Ice Skating on the Mall.** The National Gallery of Art Sculpture Garden pool turns into an ice-skating rink in winter. So visit the Gallery, finishing up at the Sculpture Garden, where you can rent skates and twirl around on the ice, admiring sculptures as you go. Treat yourself to hot chocolate and sandwiches at the Pavilion Café in the garden. 7th Street and Madison Drive. See chapter 7.

2 Best Hotel Bets

• **Best Historic Hotel:** The grande dame of Washington hotels is the magnificent **Renaissance Mayflower,** 1127 Connecticut Ave. NW (② **800/468-3571** or 202/347-3000; www.renaissance hotels.com/wassh), which, when it was built in 1925, was considered not only the last word in luxury and beauty, but also "the second-best address" in town. Harry S Truman preferred it to the White House. See p. 97.

• **Best Historic-into-Hip Hotel:** Hotel Monaco, 700 F St. NW (② **800/649-1202** or 202/628-7177; www.monaco-dc.com), with its mid-19th-century neoclassical architecture, looks stately and historic. Step inside, though, and you'll marvel over the way the hotel cleverly marries contemporary decor with original, century-and-a-half-old features. See p. 89.

• **Best Location: Willard Inter-Continental,** 1401 Pennsylvania Ave. NW (② **800/827-1747** or 202/628-9100; www.washington. interconti.com), is within walking distance of the White House, museums, theaters, downtown offices, good restaurants, and the Metro; and in this, an inaugural year, it's prime position puts it right on the parade route. It's also a quick taxi ride to Capitol Hill. A top contender in the best historic hotel category, as well. See p. 91.

• **Best Place for Hipsters:** It's a toss up between the **Hotel Rouge,** 1315 16th St. NW (② **800/368-5689** or 202/232-8000; www. rougehotel.com), where the color red rules in the decor, Bloody Marys are complimentary in the morning, and Red Bull is found in the in-room minibar; and the **Topaz Hotel,** 1733 N St. NW (② **800/424-2950** or 202/ 393-3000; www.topazhotel.com), where the decor is all New Agey, the complimentary morning drinks are energy potions, and guest room offerings include "yoga" rooms, which come with yoga mat and instructional tapes, and "energy" rooms, which come with a piece of exercise equipment and fitness magazines. Each of the hotels has an exotically decorated bar that serves wild drinks and delicious food. See p. 99 and 106.

- **Best Place for a Romantic Getaway:** The posh **Jefferson,** 1200 16th St. NW (© **800/235-6397** or 202/347-2200; www.the jeffersonhotel.com), is just enough off the beaten track, but still conveniently downtown, to feel like you've really escaped. Because the service, bar, and restaurant (see chapter 6) are outstanding, you have no need to leave the premises. The restaurant has one of the most romantic nooks in the city. Just up the street at 16th and K streets is another excellent choice, the **The St. Regis,** 923 16th St. NW (© **800/562-5661** or 202/638-2626; www.stregis. com), with its luxurious guest rooms, an opulent lobby that resembles an Italian palazzo, and a cozy paneled bar. See p. 97 and 98.

- **Best Moderately Priced Hotel: Embassy Suites Hotel Downtown,** 1250 22nd St. NW (© **800/EMBASSY** or 202/857-3388; www.embassysuitesdcmetro. com), is located downtown, within easy walking distance of the White House, Dupont Circle, and Foggy Bottom. Its rates are a good value ($149–$309) for its newly refurbished two-room suites with kitchenettes. The hotel has its own fitness center, sauna, and indoor pool, and serves a complimentary full breakfast and evening reception daily. See p. 106.

- **Best Inexpensive Hotel:** The **Jurys Normandy Inn,** a boutique hotel at 2118 Wyoming Ave.

NW (© **800/424-3729** or 202/ 483-1350; www.jurysdoyle.com), charges $89 to $185 for personable service and rooms that are small but charming. Extras like an exercise room, a pool, and a restaurant are available at its sister hotel around the corner. See p. 102.

- **Best Inn:** The charming **Morrison-Clark Historic Inn,** 1015 L St. NW (© **800/332-7898** or 202/898-1200; www. morrisonclark.com), housed in two beautifully restored Victorian town houses, has lovely rooms and a good restaurant. See p. 94.

- **Best B&B: Swann House,** 1808 New Hampshire Ave. NW (© **202/265-4414;** www.swann house.com), is remarkably pretty and comfortable, and in a great neighborhood (Dupont Circle). See p. 105.

- **Best Service:** The staff at **The Ritz-Carlton,** 1150 22nd St. NW (© **800/241-3333** or 202/835-0500; www.ritzcarlton.com), is engaging but not overbearing; service is solicitous and quick, whether you've ordered a glass of wine in the lounge or room service. A 24-hour concierge will handle anything you request, and the nightly turndown maid places a freshly baked brownie upon your pillow instead of a mint. Likewise, the **Four Seasons Hotel,** 2800 Pennsylvania Ave. NW (© **800/ 332-3442** or 202/342-0444; www.fourseasons.com), pampers you relentlessly and greets you by name. The hotel also offers an "I Need It Now" program that delivers any of 100 or more left-at-home essentials (tweezers, batteries, cuff links, electric hair curlers, and so on) to you in 3 minutes, at no cost. And finally, the new **Mandarin Oriental,** 1330 Maryland Ave. SW

(© **866/526-6567** or 202/554-8588; www.mandarinoriental. com), where the staff speak in hushed tones, almost bowing; the spa features something called an amethyst steam room; and the very design of the hotel follows the principles of feng shui, and is intended to attract good fortune. See p. 110, 112, and 83.

- **Best for Pets: The Jefferson,** 1200 16th St. NW (© **800/235-6397** or 202/347-2200; www.the-jeffersonhotel.com), is known for its pet perks, which include pet place mats and toys and treats in the room, information about nearby dog-walking routes and veterinarians, and the availability of pet-walking and pet-sitting services. See p. 97.

- **Best Place to Hide If You're Embroiled in a Scandal:** Lovely as it is, the **Jurys Normandy Inn,** 2118 Wyoming Ave. NW (© **800/424-3729** or 202/483-1350; www.jurysdoyle.com), remains unknown to many Washingtonians—a plus if you need to lie low. The neighborhood teems with embassies, in case your trouble is of the I-need-a-foreign-government-to-bail-me-out variety. (And it's a bargain to boot.) See p. 102.

- **Best for Business Travelers:** If money's no object, the **Four Seasons Hotel,** 2800 Pennsylvania Ave. NW (© **800/332-3442** or 202/342-0444; www.fourseasons. com), is a standout, offering complimentary sedan service weekdays within the District, high-speed Internet access in every room, and

soundproofed rooms, each with an office equipped with a fax machine and portable telephones. Transmitters installed throughout the entire hotel afford you wireless connection to the Internet on your laptop, wherever you go in the hotel. Finally, the hotel has started up a "Travel Light" program, which allows guests who stay there frequently to store personal belongings at the hotel; you then find your possessions waiting for you in your room, upon your return. See p. 112.

Business travelers on a budget should try the **Four Points Sheraton, Washington, D.C. Downtown,** 1201 K St. NW (© **888/481-7191** or 202/289-7600; www. fourpointswashingtondc.com). You'll get a great central downtown location near both convention centers, weekday rates as low as $99, and services that include high-speed Internet access in all rooms, a 24-hour fitness center, and an excellent on-site restaurant for business entertaining. See p. 94.

- **Best Hotel Restaurant:** My vote goes to **Michel Richard Citronelle,** in the Latham Hotel, 3000 M St. NW (© **202/625-2150;** www.citronelledc.com), for creative French fare; this hotel is not included in this year's edition of the book, though its sister hotel, the **Georgetown Inn,** 1310 Wisconsin Ave. NW, (© **202/333-8900**) is for great American fare. Another top pick is the **Melrose,** in the Park Hyatt, 1201 24th St. NW (© **202/419-6755;**

Impressions

I know of no other capital in the world which stands on so wide and splendid a river. But the people and the mode of life are enough to take your hair off!

—Henry James

www.washington.parkhyatt.com), for New American cuisine. See p. 156 and 153.

- **Best Health Club:** The **Ritz-Carlton,** 1150 22nd St. NW (© 800/241-3333 or 202/835-0500; www.ritzcarlton.com), has the best fitness center in the city. Its two-level, 100,000-square-foot Sports Club/LA boasts state-of-the-art weight-training equipment and free weights, two regulation-size basketball courts and four squash courts, an indoor heated swimming pool and aquatics pool with sun deck, exercise classes, personal trainers, the full-service Splash Spa and Roche Salon, and its own restaurant and cafe. See p. 110.

- **Best Views:** The **Hay-Adams,** One Lafayette Square, 16th and H streets NW (© 800/853-6807 or 202/638-6600; www.hayadams.com), has such a great, unobstructed view of the White House that the Secret Service comes over regularly to do security sweeps of the place. See p. 96.

- **Best for Travelers with Disabilities:** The **Omni Shoreham Hotel,** 2500 Calvert St. NW (© 800/843-6664 or 202/234-0700; www.omnihotels.com), has 41 specially equipped rooms for guests with disabilities, about half with roll-in showers; vibrating door knockers and pillows, TTYs, and flashing lights to alert guests when fire alarms are sounding (all of these devices are available, but you must ask for them); and the hotel carries copies of disabilityguide.org's *Access Entertainment* guide, which offers detailed information about how to travel around and enjoy D.C., if you have disabilities. See p. 116.

- **Best for Packages:** The **St. Gregory Luxury Hotel and Suites,** 2033 M St. NW (at 21st St.; © 800/829-5034 or 202/530-3600; www.stgregoryhotelwdc.com), is distinctly lovely, which makes its packages distinctly good values. One example: posted on its website in 2004 was the One Dollar Clearance Sale, which offered you an overnight stay for $169, with the second night for $1. The package was available on an ongoing basis, with rates fluctuating between $169 and $209, on Friday and Saturday nights, or Saturday and Sunday nights. (If this package is no longer available, look for others on the website.) See p. 105

- **Best for Deluxe-Deluxe:** The **Mandarin Oriental,** 1330 Maryland Ave. SW; © 888/888-1788 or 202/554-8588; www.mandarinoriental.com), is new, just opened in April 2004, but it's giving the Four Seasons and Ritz-Carltons a run for their money by providing sublime service, almost decadent spa features ("a haven of holistic rejuvenation and tranquility"), heavenly guest rooms (Fili D'Oro linens, flat-screen TVs), and what promise to be two of the best restaurants in town: the Café MoZu and a signature restaurant (yet unnamed), whose chef most recently worked at the world-renowned French Laundry restaurant, in California.

3 Best Dining Bets

- **Best Spot for a Romantic Dinner:** Butterfield 9, 600 14th St. NW (© 202/BU9-8810), woos you with its award-winning cuisine and its romantic, stylized black-and-white photos of handsome men and women dressed in fashions of the 1930s, '40s, and '50s. See p.125.

- **Best Spot for a Business Lunch: La Colline,** 400 N. Capitol St. NW (© **202/737-0400**), conveniently located near Capitol Hill, has a great bar, four private rooms, high-backed leather booths that allow for discreet conversations, and, last but not least, consistently good food. A perfect spot for the Washington breakfast meeting or fundraiser. And then there's **The Caucus Room,** 401 9th St. NW (© **202/393-1300**), where there's always a whole lot of handshaking going on. See p. 124 and 128.
- **Best Spot for a Celebration: Café Atlantico,** 405 8th St. NW (© **202/393-0812**), will give you reason to celebrate even if you didn't arrive with one. The restaurant is pure fun, with charming waiters, seating on three levels, colorful wall-size paintings by Latin and Caribbean artists, fantastic cocktails, and unusual but not trendy South American food. Other good choices: **Teatro Goldoni,** 1909 K St. NW (© **202/955-9494**); and **Kinkead's,** 2000 Pennsylvania Ave. NW (© **202/296-7700**). See p. 130, 141, and 155.
- **Best Decor:** The **Taberna del Alabardero,** 1776 I St. NW (© **202/429-2200**), is so elegant and Old World, with its red-tufted banquettes, green-satin-covered chairs, and ornate wall decorations. (Consider this another contender in the "Most Romantic" category.) See p. 140.
- **Best View:** The awning-covered sidewalk at **Les Halles,** 1201 Pennsylvania Ave. NW (© **202/ 347-6848**), is open in summer, enclosed in winter—a fine spot for viewing the sights along Pennsylvania Avenue all year-round. The dining room at **Charlie Palmer Steak,** 101 Constitution Ave. NW (© **202/547-8100**), offers views of the Capitol, much better in winter than in summer, though. See p. 135 and 121.
- **Best Wine List:** At **Michel Richard Citronelle,** in the Latham Hotel, 3000 M St. NW (© **202/625-2150**), the extensive, 8,000-bottle wine cellar is on display behind glass in the dining room. If you're serious about wine, come here; but check your wallet first. Citronelle is one of the city's most expensive restaurants and wines with three-digit prices predominate. The food is excellent. See p. 156.
- **Best for Kids: Famous Luigi's Pizzeria Restaurant,** 1132 19th St. NW (© **202/331-7574**), serves up some of the best pizza in town, in an already rowdy atmosphere. The long menu also features kids' favorites, like spaghetti and meatballs. Plus, the place is loud and indestructible. See p. 144.
- **Best American Cuisine: Cashion's Eat Place,** 1819 Columbia Rd. NW (© **202/797-1819**), is as welcoming as can be. Chef-owner Ann Cashion serves creative American food with a homey touch—she's unafraid to put onion rings next to something like a finely grilled black bass filet. Desserts are prepared with care. See p. 145.
- **Best Chinese Cuisine: Tony Cheng's Seafood Restaurant,** 619 H St. NW (© **202/371-8669**), in the heart of Chinatown, specializes in Cantonese, Szechuan, and Hunan cuisine, like the roasted duck on display in a case in the dining room. If you want to enjoy your surroundings as well as the food, head to Dupont Circle's **City Lights of China,** 1731 Connecticut Ave. NW (© **202/265-6688**). See p. 138 and 151.
- **Best French Cuisine:** Top of the line and extremely expensive is **Gerard's Place,** 915 15th St. NW

Site Seeing: The Best Washington, D.C. Websites

- **www.washingtonpost.com**: This is the *Washington Post*'s site, a most helpful source for up-to-date information on restaurants, attractions, shopping, and nightlife (as well as world news).
- **www.washington.org**: The Washington, D.C. Convention and Tourism Corporation operates this site, which gives a broad overview of what to see and do in D.C., and provides travel updates on security issues. Click on "Visitor Information" for tips on where to stay, dine, shop, and sightsee.
- **www.washingtonian.com**: The print magazine of the same name posts some of its articles here, including "What's Happening," a monthly guide to what's on at museums, theaters, and other cultural showplaces around town, and a directory of reviews of Washington restaurants. The magazine really wants you to buy the print edition, though—for sale at bookstores, drugstores, and grocery stores throughout the area.
- **www.fly2dc.com**: In addition to its extensive information about airline travel in and out of Washington (and ground transportation from each airport), this site also offers fun articles about restaurants and things to do in D.C. The monthly print magazine version, "Washington Flyer," is available free at Washington National and Dulles airports.
- **www.opentable.com**: This site allows you to make reservations at some of the capital's finest restaurants.
- **www.dcaccommodations.com**: This nicely designed site recommends hotels suited for families, women, sightseers, or business travelers.
- **www.hotelsdc.com**: Capitol Reservations, a 21-year-old company, represents more than 100 hotels in the Washington area, each of which has been screened for cleanliness, safety, and other factors. You can book your room online.
- **www.bnbaccom.com**: For those who prefer to stay in a private home, guesthouse, inn, or furnished apartment, this service offers more than 30 for you to consider.
- **www.si.edu**: This is the Smithsonian Institution's home page, which provides information about visiting Washington and leads you to the individual websites for each Smithsonian museum.
- **www.kennedy-center.org**: Find out what's playing at the Kennedy Center and listen to live broadcasts through the Net.
- **www.mountvernon.org**: Click on "Visit" for daily attractions at Mount Vernon and a calendar of events, as well as information on dining, shopping, and school programs. For a sneak preview, click on

(© 202/737-4445), which boasts the only Michelin two-star chef working in the United States: Gerard Pangaud, whose cooking expertise is considered an art

form. Also consider **Michel Richard Citronelle,** in the Latham Hotel in Georgetown, 3000 M St. NW (© **202/625-2150**), where Richard ebulliently

"Virtual Mansion Tour" to see images of the master bedroom, dining room, slave memorial, and the Washingtons' tomb.

- **www.nps.gov**: This National Park Service site includes links to some dozen memorials and monuments. (Click on "Parks and Recreation," then click on "Washington, D.C.") Among the links: the World War II Memorial, the Washington Monument, Jefferson Memorial, National Mall, Ford's Theatre, FDR Memorial, Lincoln Memorial, and Vietnam Veterans Memorial.
- **www.house.gov**: Once you're in the U.S. House of Representatives site, click on "Visiting D.C." to learn more about touring the Capitol building. From here, click on "The House Chamber," where you can get a view of the chamber where the House meets and learn whether the House is in session. The site also connects you with the Web pages for each of the representatives; you can use this site to e-mail your representative.
- **www.senate.gov**: In the U.S. Senate site, click on "Visitors" for an online virtual tour of the Capitol building and information about touring the actual Senate Gallery. It takes a few seconds for the images to download, but it's worth the wait to enjoy the panoramic video tour. Also, find out when the Senate is in session. The site connects you with the Web pages for each of the senators; you can use this site to e-mail your senator.
- **www.whitehouse.gov**: Click on "History & Tours" to learn about visiting the White House and upcoming public events. You'll find all sorts of links here, from a history of the White House, to archived White House documents, to an e-mail page you can use to contact the president or vice president.
- **www.dc.gov**: This is the city of Washington's website, full of details about both federal and local D.C., including history and tourism. Every day, the site lists a calendar of what's going on around town. Also helpful is a link to Cultural Tourism (you can also connect directly to it by going to www.culturaltourismdc.org), which lists tours available and other useful info.
- **www.metwashairports.com**: Ground transport, terminal maps, flight status, and airport facilities for Washington Dulles International and Ronald Reagan Washington National airports.
- **www.bwiairport.com**: Ground transport, terminal maps, flight status, and airport facilities for Baltimore-Washington International Airport.
- **www.wmata.com**: Timetables, maps, fares, and more for the Metro buses and subways that serve the Washington, D.C., metro area.

works in his open kitchen, creating sumptuous, constantly changing dishes. For French classics, with a hint of southwestern France influence, dine at **Bistrot D'Oc,** 518 10th St. NW (② **202/393-5444**), where dishes like cassoulet and filet mignon pepper steak are on the menu. For Parisian atmosphere, bistro food and spirit, try **Bistrot du Coin,** 1738 Connecticut Ave. NW (✆ **202/234-6969**). See p. 129, p. 156, p. 129, and 151.

- **Best Italian Cuisine:** Roberto Donna's **Galileo,** 1110 21st St. NW (✆ **202/293-7191**), does fine Italian cuisine best, preparing exquisite pastas, fish, and meat dishes with savory ingredients. Also see listing below for "Best of the Best." **Tosca,** 1112 F St. NW (✆ **202/367-1990**), is another winner, serving fine and unusual dishes derived from the chef's northern Italian upbringing. At **Obelisk,** 2029 P St. NW (✆ **202/ 872-1180**), chef-owner Peter Pastan crafts elegantly simple and delicious food in a pleasantly spare room. See p. 138, 133, and 148, respectively.

- **Best Seafood:** You could eat at **Kinkead's,** 2000 Pennsylvania Ave. NW (✆ **202/296-7700**), every day and never go wrong. See p. 155.

- **Best Southern Cuisine:** At **Vidalia,** 1990 M St. NW (✆ **202/ 659-1990**), chef Jeff Buben calls his cuisine "regional American"— it's a euphemism for fancy fare that includes cheese grits and biscuits in cream gravy. See p. 142.

- **Best Mexican Cuisine: Lauriol Plaza,** 1835 18th St. NW (✆ **202/ 387-0035**), isn't completely Mexican (it's also Salvadoran and Cuban). But it's all delicious and well priced, and worth standing in line for, since the restaurant does not take reservations. For more contemporary, more sophisticated Mexican cuisine, try **Andale,** 401 7th St. NW (✆ **202/783-3133**). See p. 145 and 134.

- **Best Steakhouse: The Prime Rib,** 2020 K St. NW (✆ **202/ 466-8811**), is considered by steakhounds in-the-know to be the top place for top cuts of beef.

Also consider **The Palm,** 1225 19th St. NW (✆ **202/293-9091**). Still going strong after 33 years, this classy joint serves some of the best beef in town, despite some awesome competition. See p. 139.

- **Best Spanish Cuisine:** No contest here. The elegant **Taberna del Alabardero,** 1776 I St. NW (✆ **202/429-2200**), is famous for its paellas, as well as tapas. See p. 140.

- **Best Pizza:** At **Pizzeria Paradiso,** 2029 P St. NW (✆ **202/223- 1245**), peerless chewy-crusted pies are baked in an oak-burning oven and crowned with delicious toppings; you'll find great salads and sandwiches on fresh-baked focaccia here, too. If you like thick, old-fashioned pizzas, head to **Luigi's,** 1132 19th St. NW (✆ **202/331-7574**). See p. 152 and 144.

- **Best for Vegetarians:** Consider the **Bombay Club,** 815 Connecticut Ave. NW (✆ **202/659- 3727**), whose menu features one whole page of vegetarian main courses. See p. 142.

- **Best Healthy Meal:** At **Legal Sea Foods,** 2020 K St. NW (✆ **202/ 496-1111**), follow up a cup of light clam chowder (made without butter, cream, or flour) with an entree of grilled fresh fish and vegetables and a superb sorbet for dessert. It's fabulous guilt-free dining. The restaurant has several other locations throughout the area. See p. 143.

- **Best Late-Night Dining:** For comfortable surroundings and good old American cuisine, try the **Old Ebbitt Grill,** 675 15th St. NW (✆ **202/347-4801**), whose kitchen stays open until 1am on weekends. Open even later is **Ben's Chili Bowl,** 1213 U St. NW (✆ **202/667-0909**): until

4am on weekends, until 2am other nights. See p. 136 and 144.

- **Best for a Bad Mood:** At **Al Tiramisu,** 2014 P St. NW (© **202/467-4466**), the waiters, the owner, the conviviality, and the Italian food gently coax that smile back onto your face. See p. 149.

- **Best Brunch:** Go to **Georgia Brown's,** 950 15th St. NW (© **202/393-4499**), Sunday from 10:30am to 2:30pm to enjoy live jazz and a part buffet/part a la carte menu featuring such dishes as biscuit-batter French toast with maple-pecan syrup, country ham, buttermilk-fried chicken, omelets made to order, and a host of other items. This brunch ($27 per person) is popular, so be sure to make a reservation. See p. 132.

- **Best for Pretheater Dinner:** Head for **701,** at 701 Pennsylvania Ave. NW (© **202/393-0701**). How could you do better than 701's $25 three-course bargain and its prime location (right around the corner from the Shakespeare Theatre and a few blocks from the National and Warner theaters)? More expensive, but still a deal, is **Marcel's,** 2401 Pennsylvania Ave. NW (© **202/296-1166**),

pretheater dinner: For $48 you might dine on arugula salad, pan-seared salmon, and crème brûlée. Marcel's even throws in free shuttle service to the Kennedy Center. See p. 133 and 153.

- **Best for "Taste of Washington" Experience:** Eat lunch at **The Monocle,** 107 D St. NE (© **202/ 546-4488**), and you're bound to see a Supreme Court justice, congressman, or senator dining here, too. For some down-home and delicious Washington fun, sit at the counter at **Ben's Chili Bowl,** 1213 U St. NW (© **202/667-0909**), and chat with the owners and your neighbor over a chili dog or plate of blueberry pancakes; the place is an institution, and open for breakfast, lunch, and dinner. See p. 124 and 144.

- **Best of the Best:** Few can deny that Roberto Donna's **Laboratorio del Galileo,** inside the restaurant Galileo, 1110 21st St. NW (© **202/331-0880**), is a sublime experience. In this private dining area enclosed by glass, Donna prepares a 10- to 12-course tasting menu and entertains the 30 diners lucky enough to have snagged a table. See p. 139.

2

Planning Your Trip to Washington, D.C.

Planning can be the most intimidating part about taking a trip. The task of organizing oneself, and assorted loved ones, to depart one location without forgetting anything (Did we stop the newspapers? Close the windows? Remember the camera?) and arrive at another location, luggage intact, loved ones still loved, is not a small task. The master planner has a stressful job, in my opinion. But perhaps you are reading this chapter in the hotel, two days into your trip, wondering what the big deal is about planning. If such is the case, then congratulations on being remarkably able and adaptable. Now I encourage you to stop wasting time, tuck this book under your arm and go back to sightseeing!

But if the job has fallen to you to plan a trip to Washington and you're still in the sorting-it-all-out, not-sure-where-to-begin stage, keep reading. These pages cover the essentials about what to bring, the weather you can expect, what's going on in D.C. throughout the year, how to get here, how to plan your trip online, and other salient points. This chapter also refers you to a number of helpful sources for additional and timely information.

But don't stop with this chapter: The rest of the book aims to assist you in selecting lodging, dining, shopping, entertainment, and sightseeing preferences.

1 Visitor Information

Before you leave, contact the **Washington, D.C. Convention and Tourism Corporation (WCTC),** 901 7th St. NW, Washington, DC 20001-3719 (© **800/422-8644** or 202/789-7000; www.washington.org), and ask for a free copy of the *Washington, D.C. Visitors Guide,* which details hotels, restaurants, sights, shops, and more, and is updated twice yearly. At the 202/789-7000 number, you can speak directly to a staff "visitor specialist" and get answers to your specific questions about the city. You should also consult the WCTC website, which provides the latest information, including upcoming exhibits at the museums and anticipated closings of tourist attractions.

For additional information about Washington's most popular tourist spots, check out the National Park Service website, **www.nps.gov/nacc** (the Park Service maintains Washington's monuments, memorials, and other sites), and the Smithsonian Institution's **www.si.edu**.

Also helpful is the *Washington Post* site, **www.washingtonpost.com**, which gives you up-to-the-minute news, weather, visitor information, restaurant reviews, and nightlife insights. Another good source is *Washington Flyer* magazine available for free at the airports, or browse it online in advance (at **www.fly2dc. com**), since it often covers airport and airline news and profiles upcoming events in Washington—things you might want to know before you travel. The site also allows you to subscribe to its free weekly e-mail newsletter for the latest information. The Metropolitan Washington Airports Authority publishes the magazine, which carries comprehensive airport maps of Ronald Reagan Washington National and Washington Dulles International airports in each issue. If you don't have Internet access, you can subscribe to the bimonthly by calling ℂ 202/331-9393; the rate is $15 for six issues, or $3 for one.

2 Money

Perhaps because so many of Washington's attractions (the Smithsonian museums, the monuments, even nightly concerts at the Kennedy Center) are either free or inexpensive, it may come as a shock to see the high price of lodging or a meal at a fine restaurant.

It makes sense to have some cash on hand to pay for incidentals, but it's not necessary to carry around large sums. After all, even some Metro farecard machines accept credit cards now. See the "Money" section in chapter 3 for additional information.

ATMs

ATMs (automated teller machines) are everywhere, from the National Gallery of Art gift shop, to Union Station, to the bank at the corner. ATMs link local banks to a network that most likely includes your bank at home. **Cirrus** (ℂ 800/424-7787; www. mastercard.com) and **PLUS** (ℂ 800/843-7587; www.visa.com) are the two most popular networks in the United States; call or check online for ATM locations at your destination. Be sure you know your four-digit PIN before you leave home and be sure to find out your daily withdrawal limit before you depart. Keep in mind that many banks impose a fee, usually $1.50 to $2, every time you use a card at an ATM in a different city or bank. On top of this, the bank from which you withdraw cash may charge its own fee. You may be able to use your ATM card as a debit card, withdrawing money directly from your account to pay for a purchase. You can also get cash advances on your credit card at an ATM, although credit card companies try to protect themselves from theft by limiting the funds one can withdraw away from home. Call your credit card company before you leave and let a rep know where you're going and how much you plan to spend.

TRAVELER'S CHECKS

ATMs have made traveler's checks all but obsolete. But if you still prefer the security of traveler's checks over carrying cash (and you don't mind showing identification every time you want to cash one), you can get them at almost any bank, paying a service charge that usually ranges from 1% to 7%. **American Express** offers denominations of $20, $50, $100, $500, and (for cardholders only) $1,000. You can also get **American Express** traveler's checks online at www.americanexpress.com, over the phone by calling ℂ 800/221-7282, or in person at any American Express Travel Service location.

(Tips Small Change

When you change money, ask for some small bills or loose change. Petty cash will come in handy for tipping and public transportation. Consider keeping the change separate from your larger bills, so it's readily accessible and you'll be less of a target for theft.

Destination: Washington, D.C.—Red-Alert Checklist

- Have you packed a photo ID? You'll need one to board a plane, of course, but even if you are not flying, you will probably be asked for photo ID once you're here. As a result of the September 11, 2001, terrorist attacks, some hotels require some type of photo ID at check in. Government buildings might also require a photo ID for entry.
- And while we're on the subject of IDs: Did you bring ID cards that may entitle you to discounts? Proof of AAA, AARP, or other membership, or of your status as a student can gain you special treatment or rates.
- Have you booked theater and restaurant reservations? If you're hoping to dine at a hot new restaurant or return to an old favorite, or if you're keen on catching a performance scheduled during your stay, why not play it safe by calling in advance? Two weeks is realistic to reserve a table, and you can't book theater tickets too early.
- Have you checked to make sure your favorite attraction is open? Some sites, such as the Pentagon, remain closed indefinitely to public tours, for security reasons. Other attractions, such as the National Portrait Gallery, are closed for renovations. Call ahead for opening and closing hours, and again on the day of your visit to an attraction, to confirm that it is open.
- Would you like to avoid the wait of a long line or the ultimate disappointment of missing a tour altogether? A number of sightseeing attractions permit you to reserve a tour slot in advance. The Supreme Court, the Library of Congress, and the Kennedy Center all direct you to your senator or representative's office to request advance reservations for "congressional" tours at each of their sites. (Advance tickets

Both **Visa** (www.visa.com; ✆ **800/227-6811**) and Mastercard (www.mastercard.com; ✆ **800/223-9920**) sell traveler's checks at financial institutions nationwide. Checks come in denominations of $20, $50, $100, $500, and $1,000.

AAA members can obtain Visa checks (in denominations of $20, $50, and $100) without a fee at most AAA offices. (AAA has a downtown Washington office, open weekdays, 8:30am–5pm, at 701 15th St. NW [✆ **202/331-3000**], not far from the White House.)

CREDIT CARDS

Credit cards are invaluable to travelers. They are a safe way to carry money and provide a convenient record of all your expenses. You can also withdraw cash advances from your credit cards at any bank (though you'll start paying hefty interest on the advance the moment you receive the cash). At most banks, you don't even need to go to a teller; you can get a cash advance at the ATM if you know your PIN. If you've forgotten yours, or didn't even know you had one, call the number on the back of your credit card and ask the bank to send it to you. It usually takes 5 to 7 business days, though some banks will provide the number over the phone if you tell them your mother's maiden name or pass some other security clearance.

for congressional tours are not necessary to tour an attraction; they just preclude a long wait.) Specify the dates you plan to visit and the number of tickets you need. Your Congress member's allotment of tickets for each site is limited, so there's no guarantee you'll secure them.

The switchboard for the Senate is ✆ **202/224-3121**; for the House switchboard, call ✆ **202/225-3121.** You can also correspond by e-mail; check out the websites www.senate.gov and www.house.gov for e-mail addresses, individual member information, legislative calendars, and much more. Or you can write for information. Address requests to representatives as follows: name of your congressperson, U.S. House of Representatives, Washington, DC 20515; or name of your senator, U.S. Senate, Washington, DC 20510. Don't forget to include the exact dates of your Washington trip.

- If you purchased traveler's checks, have you recorded the check numbers, and stored the documentation separately from the checks?
- Did you pack your camera and an extra set of camera batteries, and purchase enough film? If you packed film in your checked baggage, did you invest in protective pouches to shield film from airport X-rays?
- Do you have a safe, accessible place to store money?
- Did you bring emergency drug prescriptions and extra glasses and/or contact lenses?
- Do you have your credit card PIN?
- If you have an E-ticket, do you have documentation?
- Did you leave a copy of your itinerary with someone at home?

WHAT TO DO IF YOUR WALLET GETS STOLEN

Be sure to block charges against your account the minute you discover a card has been lost or stolen. Then be sure to file a police report.

Almost every credit card company has an emergency toll-free number to call if your card is stolen. The company may be able to wire you a cash advance off your credit card immediately, and in many places, deliver an emergency credit card in a day or two. The issuing bank's toll-free number is usually on the back of your credit card—though, of course, if your card has been stolen, that won't help you unless you recorded the number elsewhere.

Citicorp Visa's U.S. emergency number is ✆ **800/336-8472.** American Express traveler's check holders should call ✆ **800/221-7282** and credit card holders should call ✆ **800/528-4800.** MasterCard holders should call ✆ **800/307-7309.** Otherwise, call the toll-free number directory at ✆ **800/555-1212.**

Odds are that if your wallet is gone, the police won't be able to recover it for you. However, it's still worth informing the authorities. Your credit card company or insurer may require a police report number or record of the theft.

If you choose to carry traveler's checks, be sure to keep a record of their serial numbers separate from your checks. You'll get a refund faster if you know the numbers.

If you need emergency cash over the weekend when all banks and American Express offices are closed, you can have money wired to you from **Western Union** (© **800/325-6000;** www.westernunion.com). You must present a valid, government-issued ID to pick up the cash at the Western Union office. However, in most countries, you can pick up a money transfer even if you don't have valid identification, as long as you can answer a test question provided by the sender. Be sure to let the sender know in advance that you don't have ID. If you need to use a test question instead of ID, the sender must take cash to his or her local Western Union office, rather than transferring the money over the phone or online.

3 When to Go

The city's peak seasons generally coincide with two activities: the sessions of Congress and springtime, starting with the appearance of the cherry blossoms along the Potomac. Specifically, when Congress is "in," from about the second week in September until Thanksgiving, and again from about mid-January through June, hotels are full with guests whose business takes them to Capitol Hill or to conferences. Mid-March through June traditionally is the most frenzied season, when families and school groups descend upon the city to see the cherry blossoms and enjoy Washington's sensational spring. This is also a popular season for protest marches. Hotel rooms are at a premium and airfares tend to be higher.

If crowds turn you off, consider visiting Washington at the end of August/early September, when Congress is still "out," and families return home to get their children back to school, or between Thanksgiving and mid-January, when Congress leaves again and many people are ensconced in their own holiday-at-home celebrations. Hotel rates are cheapest at this time, too, and many hotels offer attractive packages.

If you're thinking of visiting in July and August, be forewarned: The weather is very hot and humid. Many of Washington's performance stages go dark in summer, although outdoor arenas and parks pick up some of the slack by featuring concerts, festivals, parades, and more (see chapter 9 for details about performing arts schedules). And, of course, Independence Day (July 4th) in the capital is a spectacular celebration.

THE WEATHER

Check the *Washington Post*'s website (**www.washingtonpost.com**) or the Washington, D.C. Convention and Tourism Corporation website (**www.washington.org**) for current and projected weather forecasts.

Season by season, here's what you can expect of the weather in Washington:

Fall: This is my favorite season. The weather is often warm during the day—in fact, if you're here in early fall, it may seem entirely *too* warm. But it cools off, even getting a bit crisp, at night. All the greenery that Washington is famous for dons the brilliant colors of fall foliage, and the stream of tourists tapers off.

Winter: People like to say that Washington winters are mild—and sure, if you're from Minnesota, you'll find Washington warmer, no doubt. But D.C. winters can be unpredictable: bitter cold one day, an ice storm the next, followed by a couple of days of sun and higher temperatures. Pack for all possibilities.

Spring: Spring weather is delightful, and, of course, there are those cherry blossoms. Late spring is especially lovely, with mild temperatures and intermittent days of sunshine, flowers and trees colorfully erupting in gardens and parks all over town. Washingtonians, restless after having been cooped inside for months, sweep outdoors to stroll the National Mall, sit on a park bench, or laze away an afternoon at an outdoor cafe. This is a good time to enjoy D.C.'s outdoor attractions. But this is when the city is most crowded with visitors and school groups.

Summer: Throngs remain in summer, and anyone who's ever spent August in D.C. will tell you how hot and steamy it can be. Though the buildings are air-conditioned, many of Washington's attractions, like the memorials, monuments, and organized tours, are outdoors and unshaded, and the heat can quickly get to you. Make sure you stop frequently for drinks (vendors are everywhere), and wear a hat and/or sunscreen.

Average Temperatures (°F/°C) & Rainfall (in inches) in Washington, D.C.

	Jan	Feb	Mar	Apr	May	June	July	Aug	Sept	Oct	Nov	Dec
Avg. High	44/7	46/8	54/12	66/19	76/25	83/29	87/31	85/30	79/26	68/20	57/14	46/8
Avg. Low	30/-1	29/-1	36/2	46/8	57/14	65/19	69/20	68/20	61/16	50/10	39/4	32/0
Rainfall	3.21	2.63	3.6	2.71	3.82	3.13	3.66	3.44	3.79	3.22	3.03	3.05

WASHINGTON, D.C. CALENDAR OF EVENTS

Washington's most popular annual events are the Cherry Blossom Festival in spring, the Fourth of July celebration in summer, the Taste of D.C. food fair in the fall, and the lighting of the National Christmas Tree in winter. But there's some sort of special event almost daily. For the latest schedules, check www.washington.org.

In the calendar below, I've done my best to accurately list phone numbers for more information, but they seem to change constantly. If the number you try doesn't get you the details you need, call the **Washington, D.C. Convention and Tourism Corporation** at © 202/789-7000.

Once you're in town, grab a copy of the *Washington Post,* especially the Friday "Weekend" section. The **Smithsonian Information Center,** 1000 Jefferson Dr. SW (© 202/357-2700), is another good source of information.

For annual events in Alexandria, see p. 278.

January

Presidential Inauguration. On the steps of the U.S. Capitol. After the swearing-in, crowds line the sidewalks as the newly elected president of the United States proceeds by motorcade, and if he feels like it, on foot, down Pennsylvania Avenue to the White House. Parades, concerts, parties, inaugural balls, and other festivities herald the occasion. For details, call © **202/789-7000.** January 20.

Martin Luther King Jr.'s Birthday. Events include speeches by prominent civil rights leaders and politicians; readings; dance, theater, concerts and choral performances; prayer vigils; a wreath-laying ceremony at the Lincoln Memorial (call © **202/619-7222**). Many events take place at the Martin Luther King Jr. Memorial Library, 901 G St. NW (© **202/727-0321**). Third Monday in January.

February

Black History Month. Features numerous events, museum exhibits, and cultural programs celebrating the contributions of African Americans to American life, including a celebration of abolitionist Frederick Douglass's birthday. For details, check the *Washington Post* or call © **202/357-2700.** For additional activities at the Martin Luther King Jr. Library, call © **202/727-0321.**

Chinese New Year Celebration. A friendship archway, topped by 300 painted dragons and lighted at night, marks Chinatown's entrance at 7th and H streets NW. The celebration begins the day of the Chinese New Year and continues for 10 or more days, with traditional firecrackers, dragon dancers, and colorful street parades. Some area restaurants offer special menus. For details, call ℂ **202/789-7000.** Early February.

Abraham Lincoln's Birthday. Marked by a wreath-laying and reading of the Gettysburg Address at noon at the Lincoln Memorial. Call ℂ **202/619-7222.** February 12.

George Washington's Birthday. Similar celebratory events to Lincoln's birthday, centered around the Washington Monument. Call ℂ **202/619-7222** for details; the Washington Monument remains open though its grounds may be off limits because of ongoing construction of security barriers. See chapter 7's write-up of the Washington Monument for more information. Both presidents' birthdays also bring annual citywide sales. February 22. See chapter 10, "Side Trips from Washington, D.C.," for information about the bigger celebrations held at Mount Vernon and in Old Town Alexandria, on the third Monday in February.

International Tourist Guide Day. A 3½-hour motor coach and 1-hour walking tour of Washington during this 16th annual event, departing from a downtown location, with stops at historic spots throughout the city. Each year's tour usually embraces a different theme; in 2004, the tours embraced the theme "200 years of black history in the capital." The World Federation of Tourist Guide Associations sponsors International Tourist Guide Day, whose members offer educational tours in major cities throughout the world. In Washington, it's the Guild of Professional Tour Guides that conducts the tours, which are free on this day, though space is limited. Call ℂ **202/298-9425.** Late February.

March

Women's History Month. Various institutions throughout the city stage celebrations of women's lives and achievements. For the schedule of Smithsonian events, call ℂ **202/357-2700;** for other events, check the *Washington Post.*

St. Patrick's Day Parade. A big parade on Constitution Avenue NW, from 7th to 17th streets, with floats, bagpipes, marching bands, and the wearin' o' the green. For parade information, call ℂ **202/789-7000.** The Sunday before March 17.

Smithsonian Kite Festival. A delightful event if the weather cooperates—an occasion for a trip in itself. Throngs of kite enthusiasts fly their unique creations on the National Mall grounds and compete for ribbons and prizes. The parkland encircling the Washington Monument is traditionally the site for the kite festival, but ongoing construction of security barriers at the Washington Monument required the festival be staged elsewhere in 2004—on the grounds in front of the Smithsonian's National Air and Space Museum. It's possible that construction at the Monument continues to prohibit the staging of the kite festival and other events there, so be sure to call ℂ **202/357-2700** or 202/357-3030 for details. Then, to compete, it's just a matter of showing up at the designated spot with your kite and registering between 10am and noon. A

Saturday in mid- or late March, or early April.

April

Cherry Blossom Events. Washington's best-known annual event: the blossoming of more than 3,700 famous Japanese cherry trees by the Tidal Basin in Potomac Park. Festivities include a major parade at the end of the festival with floats, concerts, celebrity guests, and more. There are also special ranger-guided tours departing from the Jefferson Memorial. For information, call ✆ **202/547-1500** or go to www.nps.gov/nacc/cherry. See p. 222 for more information about the cherry blossoms. Late March or early April (national and local news programs monitor the budding).

White House Easter Egg Roll. The biggie for little kids. This year's White House Easter Egg Roll continues a tradition begun in 1878. In past years, entertainment on the White House South Lawn and the Ellipse has included clog dancers, clowns, Ukrainian egg-decorating exhibitions, puppet and magic shows, military drill teams, an egg-rolling contest, and a hunt for 1,000 or so wooden eggs, many of them signed by celebrities, astronauts, or the president. *Note:* Children of all ages are welcome, as long as a child age 7 or younger, and an adult, are in your group. You may obtain a maximum of five tickets. The hourly timed tickets are issued at the National Parks Service Ellipse Visitors Pavilion just behind the White House at 15th and E streets NW beginning at 7:30am on the Saturday before Easter, and again on Easter Monday. Call ✆ **202/208-1631** for details. Easter Monday between 10am and 2pm; enter at the southeast gate on East Executive Avenue, and arrive early to make sure you get in, and also to allow for increased security procedures. One other precaution: Strollers are not permitted.

African-American Family Day at the National Zoo. This tradition extends back to 1889, when the zoo opened. The National Zoo celebrates African-American families the day after Easter with music, dance, Easter egg rolls, and other activities. Free. Call ✆ **202/357-2700** for details. Easter Monday.

Thomas Jefferson's Birthday. Celebrated at the Jefferson Memorial with wreaths, speeches, and a military ceremony. Call ✆ **202/619-7222** for time and details. April 13.

White House Spring Garden Tours. These beautifully landscaped creations are open to the public for free tours, 2 days only. Call ✆ **202/208-1631** for details. Two days in mid-April.

Shakespeare's Birthday Celebration. Music, theater, children's events, food, and exhibits are all part of the afternoon's hail to the bard at the Folger Shakespeare Library. Call ✆ **202/544-7077.** Free admission. Mid-April.

Filmfest DC. This annual film festival presents as many as 75 works by filmmakers from around the world. Screenings are staged throughout the festival at movie theaters, embassies, and other venues. Tickets are usually $9 per movie and go fast; some events are free. Call ✆ **202/789-7000** or check the website, www.filmfestdc.org. Two weeks in April.

Smithsonian Craft Show. Held in the National Building Museum, 401 F St. NW, this juried show features one-of-a-kind limited-edition crafts by more than 100 noted artists from all over the country. There's an entrance fee of about $12 per adult, free for children under 12, each day. No strollers. For details, call ✆ **202/357-4000** (TDD 202/357-1729). Four days in late April.

May

Georgetown Garden Tour. View the remarkable private gardens of one of the city's loveliest neighborhoods. Admission (about $25) includes light refreshments. Some years there are related events such as a flower show at a historic home. Call ✆ **202/789-7000** or browse the website, www.gtowngarden.org for details. Early to mid-May.

Washington National Cathedral Annual Flower Mart. Now in its 66th year, the flower mart takes place on cathedral grounds, featuring displays of flowering plants and herbs, decorating demonstrations, ethnic food booths, children's rides and activities (including an antique carousel), costumed characters, puppet shows, and other entertainment. Admission is free. Call ✆ **202/537-6200** for details. First Friday and Saturday in May, rain or shine.

Memorial Day. At 11am, a wreath-laying ceremony takes place at the Tomb of the Unknowns in Arlington National Cemetery, followed by military band music, a service, and an address by a high-ranking government official (sometimes the president); call ✆ **703/695-3175** for details. There are ceremonies at the World War II and Vietnam Veterans Memorial, including a wreath-laying, speakers, and the playing of taps (✆ **202/619-7222** for details), and activities at the U.S. Navy Memorial (✆ **202/737-2300**). On the Sunday before Memorial Day, the National Symphony Orchestra performs a free concert at 8pm on the West Lawn of the Capitol to officially welcome summer to Washington; call ✆ **202/619-7222** for details.

June

Dupont-Kalorama Museum Walk Day. This is an annual celebration of collections by six or more museums and historic houses in this charming neighborhood. Free food, music, tours, and crafts demonstrations. Call ✆ **202/667-0441.** Early June.

Shakespeare Theatre Free For All. This free theater festival presents a different Shakespeare play each year for a 2-week run at the Carter Barron Amphitheatre in upper northwest Washington. Tickets are required, but they're free. Call ✆ **202/334-4790.** Evenings in mid-June.

Smithsonian Festival of American Folklife. A major event with traditional American music, crafts, foods, games, concerts, and exhibits, staged the length of the National Mall. All events are free; most events take place outdoors. Call ✆ **202/357-2700,** or check the listings in the *Washington Post* for details. For 5 to 10 days, always including July 4.

July

Independence Day. There's no better place to be on the Fourth of July than in Washington, D.C. The festivities include a massive National Independence Day Parade down Constitution Avenue, complete with lavish floats, princesses, marching groups, and military bands. A morning program in front of the National Archives includes military demonstrations, period music, and a reading of the Declaration of Independence. In the evening, the National Symphony Orchestra plays on the west steps of the Capitol with guest artists (for example, Leontyne Price). And big-name entertainment also precedes the fabulous fireworks display behind the Washington Monument. You can also attend a free 11am organ recital at Washington's National Cathedral. Consult the *Washington Post* or call ☏ **202/789-7000** for details. July 4, all day.

Bastille Day. This Washington tradition honors the French Independence Day with live entertainment and a race by tray-balancing waiters and waitresses from Les Halles Restaurant to the U.S. Capitol and back. Free, *mais bien sur.* Twelfth Street and Pennsylvania Avenue NW. Call ☏ **202/296-7200.** July 14.

September

Labor Day Concert. West Lawn of the Capitol. The National Symphony Orchestra closes its summer season with a free performance at 8pm; call ☏ **202/619-7222** for details. Labor Day. (Rain date: Same day and time at Constitution Hall.)

Kennedy Center Open House Arts Festival. A day-long festival of the performing arts, featuring local and national artists on the front plaza and river terrace (which overlooks the Potomac), and throughout the stage halls of the Kennedy Center. Past festivals have featured the likes of Los Lobos, Mary Chapin Carpenter, and Washington Opera soloists. Kids' activities usually include a National Symphony Orchestra "petting zoo," where children get to bow, blow, drum, or strum a favorite instrument. Admission is free, although you may have to stand in a long line for the inside performances. Check the *Washington Post* or call ☏ **800/444-1324** or 202/467-4600 for details. A Sunday in early to mid-September, noon to 6pm.

Black Family Reunion. Performances, food, and fun are part of this celebration of the African-American family and culture, held on the Mall. Free. Call ☏ **202/737-0120.** Mid-September.

Hispanic Heritage Month. Various museums and other institutions host activities celebrating Hispanic culture and traditions. Call ☏ **202/789-7000.** Mid-September to mid-October.

Washington National Cathedral's Open House. Celebrates the anniversary of the laying of the foundation stone in 1907. Events include demonstrations of stone carving and other crafts utilized in building the cathedral; carillon and organ demonstrations; and performances by dancers, choirs, strolling musicians, jugglers, and puppeteers. This is the only time visitors are allowed to ascend to the top of the central tower to see the bells; it's a tremendous climb, but you'll be rewarded with a spectacular view. For details, call ☏ **202/537-6200.** A Saturday in late September or early October.

October

White House Fall Garden Tours. For 2 days, visitors have an opportunity to see the famed Rose Garden and South Lawn. Admission is free. A military band provides music. For details, call ☏ **202/208-1631.** Mid-October.

Marine Corps Marathon. More than 16,000 runners compete in this 26.2-mile race (the 4th-largest marathon in the United States). It begins at the Marine Corps Memorial (the Iwo Jima statue) and passes major monuments. Call ☏ **800/RUN-USMC** or 703/784-2225 for details. Anyone can enter; register online at www.marinemarathon.com. Fourth Sunday in October.

Halloween. There's no official celebration, but costumed revels seem to get bigger every year. Giant block parties take place in the Dupont Circle area and Georgetown. Check

> **Tips   Quick ID**
>
> Tie a colorful ribbon or piece of yarn around your luggage handle, or slap a distinctive sticker on the side of your bag. This makes it less likely that someone will mistakenly appropriate it. And if your luggage gets lost, it will be easier to find.

the *Washington Post* for special parties and activities. October 31.

November

Veterans Day. The nation's war dead are honored with a wreath-laying ceremony at 11am at the Tomb of the Unknowns in Arlington National Cemetery followed by a memorial service. The president of the United States or a very high-ranking government personage officiates. Music is provided by a military band. Call © **202/685-2951** for information. At the Vietnam Veterans Memorial (© **202/619-7222**), observances include speakers, wreath placement, a color guard, and the playing of taps; a wreath laying is among the ceremonies performed at the World War II Memorial. November 11.

December

Christmas Pageant of Peace/ National Tree Lighting. At the northern end of the Ellipse, the president lights the national Christmas tree to the accompaniment of orchestral and choral music. The lighting inaugurates the 4-week Pageant of Peace, a tremendous holiday celebration with seasonal music, caroling, a nativity scene, 50 state trees, and a burning yule log. Call © **202/208-1631** for details. A select Wednesday or Thursday in early December at 5pm.

4 Travel Insurance

Check your existing insurance policies and credit-card coverage before you buy travel insurance. You may already be covered for lost luggage, cancelled tickets, or medical expenses. The cost of travel insurance varies widely, depending on the cost and length of your trip, your age, health, and the type of trip you're taking.

TRIP-CANCELLATION INSUR-ANCE Trip-cancellation insurance helps you get your money back if you have to renege on a trip, if you have to go home early, or if your travel supplier goes bankrupt. Allowed reasons for cancellation can range from sickness to natural disasters to the State Department declaring your destination unsafe for travel. (Insurers usually won't cover vague fears, though, as many travelers discovered who tried to cancel their trips in Oct 2001 because they were wary of flying.) In this unstable world, trip-cancellation insurance is a good buy if you're getting tickets well in advance—who knows what the state of the world, or of your airline, will be in 9 months? Insurance policy details vary, so read the fine print—and especially make sure that your airline or cruise line is on the list of carriers covered in case of bankruptcy. For information, contact one of the following insurers: **Access America** (© **866/807-3982;** www.accessamerica.com); **Travel Guard International** (© **800/826-4919;** www.travelguard.com); **Travel Insured International** (© **800/243-3174;** www.travelinsured.com); and **Travelex Insurance Services** (© **888/457-46022;** www.travelexinsurance.com).

MEDICAL INSURANCE Most health insurance policies cover you if you get sick away from home—but check, particularly if you're insured by an HMO. If you require additional medical insurance, try **MEDEX International** (℡ 800/527-0218 or 410/453-6300; www.medexassist. com) or **Travel Assistance International** (℡ 800/821-2828; www.travel assistance.com; for general information on services, call the company's Worldwide Assistance Services, Inc., at ℡ 800/643-5525).

LOST-LUGGAGE INSURANCE
On domestic flights, checked baggage is covered up to $2,500 per ticketed passenger. On international flights (including U.S. portions of international trips), baggage is limited to approximately $9.07 per pound, up to approximately $635 per checked bag. If you plan to check items more valuable than the standard liability, see if your valuables are covered by your homeowner's policy, get baggage insurance as part of your comprehensive travel-insurance package, or buy Travel Guard's (℡ 800/826-4919) "BagTrak" product, a 24-hour bag tracking service that locates lost luggage and sends it directly to you. The best thing about this kind of insurance, if you travel a lot, is that the insurance covers you for a year, not just for one trip. Don't buy insurance at the airport, as it's usually overpriced. Be sure to take any valuables or irreplaceable items with you in your carry-on luggage, as items such as books, money, and electronics aren't covered by airline policies.

If your luggage is lost, immediately file a lost-luggage claim at the airport, detailing the luggage contents. For most airlines, you must report delayed, damaged, or lost baggage within 24 hours of arrival. The airlines are required to deliver luggage, once found, directly to your house or destination free of charge.

5 Health & Safety

WHAT TO DO IF YOU GET SICK AWAY FROM HOME

In most cases, your existing health plan will provide the coverage you need. But double-check; you may want to buy **travel medical insurance** instead. (See the section on insurance, above.) Bring your insurance ID card with you when you travel.

If you suffer from a chronic illness, consult your doctor before your departure. For conditions like epilepsy, diabetes, or heart problems, wear a **Medic Alert Identification Tag** (℡ 800/825-3785; www.medicalert. org), which will immediately alert doctors to your condition and give them access to your records through Medic Alert's 24-hour hot line.

Pack **prescription medications** in your carry-on luggage, and carry prescription medications in their original containers, with pharmacy labels—otherwise they won't make it through airport security. Also bring along copies of your prescriptions in case you lose your pills or run out. Don't forget an extra pair of contact lenses or prescription glasses. Carry the generic name of prescription medicines, in case a local pharmacist is unfamiliar with the brand name.

If you get sick, consider asking your hotel concierge to recommend a local doctor—even his or her own. You can also try the emergency room at a local hospital; many have walk-in clinics for emergency cases that are not life-threatening. (See the entry for "Hospitals" in "Fast Facts: Washington, D.C.," on p. 78, in chapter 4.)

STAYING SAFE

The first thing you want to do is get on the Internet and access the Washington, D.C. Convention and Tourism Corporation's website, www. washington.org, which publishes travel updates, often on a daily basis. The travel updates alert you to the general state of affairs in D.C. and to new security and touring procedures around town, and refers you to other sections of its website for information about restaurants, hotels, and attractions.

In the years following the September 11, 2001, terrorist attack on the Pentagon, the federal and D.C. governments, along with agencies such as the National Park Service, have continued to work together to increase security, not just at airports, but around the city, including government buildings, tourist attractions, and the subway. You will notice vehicle barriers in place at a wider radius around the Capitol building and the White House, and new vehicle barriers and better lighting installed at the Washington Monument and at the Lincoln and Jefferson memorials. Self-guided tours of the Capitol are no longer possible, and public guided tours are less comprehensive than they used to be. Greater numbers of police and security officers are on duty around and inside government buildings, the monuments, and the Metro. By the time you read this, a new, tightly secured underground visitors center will have opened at the Capitol.

Just because there are so many police around, you shouldn't let your guard down. Washington, like any urban area, has a criminal element, so it's important to stay alert and take normal safety precautions.

Ask your hotel front-desk staff or the city's tourist office if you're in doubt about which neighborhoods are safe.

For more safety tips, see "General Safety Suggestions," in chapter 3.

6 Specialized Travel Resources

TRAVELERS WITH DISABILITIES

Washington, D.C., is one of the most accessible cities in the world for travelers with disabilities. The best overall source of information about accessibility at specific Washington hotels, restaurants, shopping malls, and attractions is the nonprofit organization **Access Information.** You can read the information (including restaurant reviews) online at www.disabilityguide. org, or order a free copy of the *Washington, DC Access Guide* by calling ℂ **301/528-8664,** or by writing to Access Information, 21618 Slidell Rd., Boyds, MD 20841.

The **Washington Metropolitan Transit Authority** publishes accessibility information on its website **www.wmata.com**, or you can call ℂ **202/962-1245** with questions about Metro services for travelers with disabilities, including how to obtain a Disabled ID card that entitles you to discounted fares. (Make sure that you call at least 3 weeks ahead to allow enough time to obtain an ID card.) For up-to-date information about how Metro is operating on the day you're using it, for instance, to verify that the elevators are operating at the stations you'll be traveling to, call ℂ **202/962-1212.**

Each Metro station is equipped with an elevator (complete with Braille number plates) to train platforms, and rail cars are fully accessible. Metro has installed 24-inch sections of punctuated rubber tiles leading up to the granite-lined platform edge to warn visually impaired Metro riders that they're nearing the tracks. Unfortunately, a 1- to 3-inch gap between the train platform and the subway car can make it difficult for those in powered wheelchairs to board the train. Train operators make station and onboard announcements of train destinations and stops, although the noise of the train and a less-than-perfect audio system often make these announcements unintelligible. Most of the District's Metrobuses have wheelchair lifts and kneel at the curb (the number will increase as time goes on). The TTY number for Metro information is © **202/638-3780.**

Regular **Tourmobile** trams (p. 227) are accessible to visitors with disabilities. The company also operates special vans for immobile travelers, complete with wheelchair lifts. Tourmobile recommends that you call a day ahead to ensure that the van is available for you when you arrive. For information, call © **202/554-5100,** or go to www.tourmobile.com.

Major Washington museums, including all **Smithsonian museum buildings** are accessible to wheelchair visitors. A comprehensive free publication called "Smithsonian Access" lists all services available to visitors with disabilities, including parking, building access, sign-language interpreters, and more. To obtain a copy, call © **202/357-2700** or TTY 202/357-1729, or find the information online, at www.si.edu/opa/accessibility. You can also use the TTY number to get information on all Smithsonian museums and events.

Likewise, all of the memorials, including the **Lincoln, Jefferson, Franklin Delano Roosevelt, Vietnam, Korea, and World War II memorials** and the **Washington Monument** are each equipped to accommodate visitors with disabilities and keep wheelchairs on the premises. There's limited parking for visitors with disabilities on the south side of the Lincoln Memorial. Call ahead to other sightseeing attractions for accessibility information and special services.

Call your senator or representative to arrange wheelchair-accessible tours of the **Capitol;** they can also arrange special tours for the blind or deaf at both the Capitol and at the **White House.** The **White House** is accessible to those in wheelchairs and requires no advance notice or special tour instructions for wheelchair-bound tourists. For further information about Capitol tours, call © **202/224-4048.** The TDD phone number for the Members of Congress Visitors Office is © **202/456-2121.**

Washington theaters are handily equipped. Among the most accessible are the following three.

The **John F. Kennedy Center for the Performing Arts** is fully accessible. The center provides headphones to hearing-impaired patrons at no charge. A wireless, infrared listening-enhancement system is available in all theaters. Some performances offer sign language and audio description. A public TTY is located at the Information Center in the Hall of States as well as on parking lot level A. Large-print programs are available at every performance; a limited number of Braille programs are available from the house manager. All theaters in the complex are wheelchair accessible. To reserve a wheelchair, call © **202/416-8340.** For other questions regarding patrons with disabilities, including information about half-price tickets (you will need to submit a letter from your doctor stating that your disability is permanent), access the center's website, www.kennedy-center.org, or call the Office for Accessibility © **202/416-8727.** The TTY number is © **202/416-8728.**

The **Arena Stage** (© **202/488-3300;** www.arenastage.org) offers audio description and sign interpretation at designated performances as well as infrared and audio loop assisted-listening devices for the hearing impaired, plus program books in Braille and large print. The TTY box office line is © **202/484-0247.** You can also call ahead to reserve handicapped parking spaces for a performance.

The **National Theatre** is wheelchair accessible and features special performances of its shows for visually and hearing-impaired theatergoers. To obtain amplified-sound earphones for narration, simply ask an usher before the performance (you'll need to provide an ID). The National also offers a limited number of half-price tickets to patrons with disabilities, who have obtained a Special Patron card from the theater, or who can provide a letter from a doctor certifying disability; seating is in the orchestra section and you may receive no more than two half-price tickets. For details, call ℭ **202/628-6161,** or go the website, www.nationaltheatre.org.

Many travel agencies offer customized tours and itineraries for travelers with disabilities. **Flying Wheels Travel** (ℭ **507/451-5005;** www. flyingwheelstravel.com) offers escorted tours and cruises that emphasize sports and private tours in minivans with lifts. **Accessible Journeys** (ℭ **800/846-4537** or 610/521-0339; www.disabilitytravel.com) caters specifically to slow walkers and wheelchair travelers and their families and friends.

Organizations that offer assistance to disabled travelers include the **Moss Rehab Hospital** (www.mossresource net.org), which provides a library of accessible-travel resources online; the **Society for Accessible Travel and Hospitality** (ℭ **212/447-7284;** www. sath.org; annual membership fees: $45 adults, $30 seniors and students), which offers a wealth of travel resources for all types of disabilities and informed recommendations on destinations, access guides, travel agents, tour operators, vehicle rentals, and companion services; and the **American Foundation for the Blind** (ℭ **800/232-5463;** www.afb.org), which provides information on traveling with Seeing Eye dogs.

For more information specifically targeted to travelers with disabilities,

the community website **iCan** (www. icanonline.net/channels/travel/index. cfm) has destination guides and several regular columns on accessible travel. Also check out the quarterly magazine *Emerging Horizons* ($14.95 per year, $19.95 outside the U.S.; www.emerginghorizons.com); and *Open World Magazine,* published by the Society for Accessible Travel and Hospitality (see above; subscription: $13 per year, $21 outside the U.S.).

GAY & LESBIAN TRAVELERS

Washington, D.C., has a strong gay and lesbian community, and clearly welcomes gay and lesbian visitors, as evidenced by the fact that the Washington, D.C. Convention and Tourism Corporation includes on its website, www.washington.org, a link to information for gay and lesbian tourists: click on "Pride in DC," which appears on the site's home page. You can also order the WCTC's publication, "The Gay, Lesbian, Bisexual and Transgender Travelers Guide to Washington, D.C.," by calling ℭ **202/789-7000.**

While in Washington, you'll want to get your hands on the *Washington Blade,* a comprehensive weekly newspaper distributed free at many locations in the District. Every issue provides an extensive events calendar and a list of hundreds of resources, such as crisis centers, health facilities, switchboards, political groups, religious organizations, social clubs, and student activities; it puts you in touch with everything from groups of lesbian bird-watchers to the Asian Gay Men's Network. Gay restaurants and clubs are also listed and advertised. You can subscribe to the *Blade* for $90 a year, check out **www.washingtonblade.com**, or pick up a free copy at Olsson's Books/ Records, 1307 19th St. NW; Borders, 18th and L streets; and Kramerbooks, 1517 Connecticut Ave. NW, at Dupont Circle. Call the *Blade* at ℭ **202/797-7000** for other locations.

Washington's gay bookstore, **Lambda Rising,** 1625 Connecticut Ave. NW (© 202/462-6969), also informally serves as an information center for the gay community, which centers in the Dupont Circle neighborhood.

The International Gay & Lesbian Travel Association (IGLTA) (© 800/448-8550 or 954/776-2626; www.iglta.org) is the trade association for the gay and lesbian travel industry, and offers an online directory of gay- and lesbian-friendly travel businesses; go to their website and click on "Members."

Many agencies offer tours and travel itineraries specifically for gay and lesbian travelers. **Above and Beyond Tours** (© 800/397-2681; www.abovebeyondtours.com) is the exclusive gay and lesbian tour operator for United Airlines. **Now, Voyager** (© 800/255-6951; www.nowvoyager.com) is a well-known San Francisco–based gay-owned and operated travel service.

The following travel guides are available at most travel bookstores and gay and lesbian bookstores, and online at www.amazon.com: *Out and About* (© 800/929-2268 or 415-834-6411; www.outandabout.com), which offers guidebooks and a newsletter 10 times a year packed with solid information on the global gay and lesbian scene; *Spartacus International Gay Guide* and *Odysseus, the International Gay Travel Planner* both good, annual English-language guidebooks focused on gay men; and the *Damron* guides, with separate, annual books for gay men and lesbians.

SENIOR TRAVEL

Always mention the fact that you're a senior citizen when you make your travel reservations, on the chance that you may be eligible for a discount. Several domestic and foreign airlines offer discounts to "mature" travelers, including America West, Frontier,

Southwest, USAirways, Air Canada, and Air France, all of which fly to Washington, D.C. America West's discount program is typical: anyone who is 62 or older is eligible for a 10% discount off the published airfare; a companion of any age traveling with the older passenger may receive the 10% discount, too. You'll want to do some research, however, since cheaper rates may be available through a discount booking agency or an airline's own special program. Many hotels, especially chain hotels such as the Hilton offer senior discounts.

In Washington, you'll find discounted admission prices for seniors at theaters, at those few museums that charge for entry, and for discounted travel on Metro, although the designated "senior" age differs slightly from place to place. For instance, discount eligibility requires that you must be 60 or older at Arena Stage, 62 or older at the Phillips Collection, and 65 or older for the Metro. Some places, such as Arena Stage, take you at your word that you qualify for a discount, so you may order your tickets over the phone, then show proof of your age on your photo ID when you pick up your tickets. To obtain discounted fare cards to ride the Metro, you must visit a Metro sales office—there's one in the Metro Center subway station at 13th and G streets NW—flash your photo ID with your birthdate on it, and pay half-price for your fare card; call © 202/962-1245 for more information.

Members of **AARP** (formerly known as the American Association of Retired Persons), 601 E St. NW, Washington, DC 20049 (© 888/687-2277 or 202/434-2277; www.aarp.org), get discounts on hotels, airfares, and car rentals. AARP offers members a wide range of benefits, including *AARP, The Magazine* and a monthly newsletter. Anyone over 50 can join; annual membership is $12.50.

Many reliable agencies and organizations target the 50-plus market. **Elderhostel** (© **877/426-8056**; www.elderhostel.org) arranges study programs for those aged 55 and over (and a spouse or companion of any age) in the U.S. and in more than 90 countries around the world. Most courses last 5 to 7 days in the U.S. (2–4 weeks abroad), and many include airfare, accommodations in university dormitories or modest inns, meals, and tuition. In 2004, Elderhostel sponsored 10 programs in Washington, D.C.

Recommended publications offering travel resources and discounts for seniors include the quarterly magazine *Travel 50 & Beyond* (www.travel50andbeyond.com) and the brochure *101 Tips for Mature Travelers,* available from Grand Circle Travel (© **800/221-2610** or 617/350-7500; www.gct.com). Books include *The 50+ Traveler's Guidebook* (St. Martin's Press) and *Unbelievably Good Deals and Great Adventures That You Absolutely Can't Get Unless You're Over 50* (McGraw Hill), both available online at www.amazon.com.

FAMILY TRAVEL

Field trips during the school year and family vacations during the summer keep Washington, D.C., crawling with kids all year long. More than any other city, perhaps, Washington is crammed with historic buildings, arts and science museums, parks, and recreational sites to interest young and old alike. Some museums, like the National Museum of Natural History and the Daughters of the American Revolution (DAR) Museum, have hands-on exhibits for children. Many more sponsor regular, usually free, family-oriented events, such as the Corcoran Gallery of Art's "Family Days" and the Folger Shakespeare Library's seasonal activities. It's worth calling or checking websites in advance for schedules from the attractions you're thinking of

visiting (see chapter 7 for attractions and activities that appear with a "Kids" icon in the title, to indicate they are especially recommended for children). The fact that so many attractions are free is a boon to the family budget.

Hotels, more and more, are doing their part to make family trips affordable, too. At many lodgings, children under a certain age (usually 12) sleep free in the same room with their parents (I've noted these policies in all the listings in chapter 5). Hotel weekend packages often offer special family rates. See the "Family-Friendly Hotels" box on p. 89 for a rundown of the hotels that are most welcoming to young travelers.

Restaurants throughout the Washington area are growing increasingly family friendly. Many provide kids' menus or charge less for children's portions. The best news, though, is that families are welcome at all sorts of restaurants these days and need no longer stick only to burger joints. See the "Family-Friendly Restaurants" box on p. 135 for a list of places kids will especially love.

Washington, D.C., is easy to navigate with children. The Metro covers the city and it's safe. Children 4 and under ride free.

Once you arrive, get your hands on a copy of the most recent *Washington Post* "Weekend" section, published each Friday. The section covers all possible happenings in the city, with a weekly feature, "Saturday's Child," and a column, "Carousel," devoted to children's activities.

You can find good family-oriented vacation advice on the Internet from sites like the **Family Travel Network** (www.familytravelnetwork.com); **Family Travel Forum** (© **888/383-6786**; www.familytravelforum.com), which has as its motto "Have Family, Still Travel," and offers helpful information and travel discounts for families planning trips; and **Family Travel Files** (www.thefamilytravelfiles.com), which offers an online magazine and a directory of off-the-beaten-path tours and tour operators for families.

Also look for *Frommer's Washington, D.C., with Kids* (Wiley Publishing, Inc.), which makes an excellent companion piece to this book, providing in-depth coverage of sightseeing with children in Washington.

STUDENT TRAVEL

When it comes to admission discounts in Washington, students rule. The one caveat: You must have a valid ID, although your current school ID should be good enough. For benefits that extend beyond reduced admission to D.C. attractions, you may want to consider obtaining an International Student Identity Card (ISIC).

STA Travel (© **800/781-4040;** www.statravel.com) is the largest student travel agency in the world, catering especially to young travelers, although their bargain-basement prices are available to people of all ages. From STA, you can purchase the $22 ISIC, good for cut rates on rail

passes, plane tickets, and other discounts. It also provides you with basic health and life insurance, and a 24-hour help line. If you're no longer a student but are still under 26, you can get a **GO 25 card** from the same people, which entitles you to insurance and some discounts (but not on museum admissions). In Washington, STA has three offices: in Georgetown, at 3301 M St. NW (© **202/337-6464**); on the George Washington University campus, in the Marvin Center, at 800 21st St. NW (© **202/994-7800**); and on the American University campus, 4400 Massachusetts Ave. NW (© **202/244-7330**). STA has offices all over the world; for the location of an office nearest you, check out STA's website, but also call the main number, since the website did not provide all D.C. locations when I reviewed its information.

Studentuniverse.com (www.studentuniverse.com) is an online student travel agency in partnership with airlines and other travel agencies, consistently offering great discounts on airfares to students and faculty.

7 Planning Your Trip Online

SURFING FOR AIRFARES

The "big three" online travel agencies, **Expedia.com**, **Travelocity**, and **Orbitz** sell most of the air tickets bought on the Internet. (Canadian travelers should try expedia.ca and travelocity.ca; U.K. residents can go to expedia.co.uk and opodo.co.uk.) Each has different business deals with the airlines and may offer different fares on the same flights, so it's wise to shop around. Expedia and Travelocity will also send you **e-mail notification** when a cheap fare becomes available to your favorite destination. Of the smaller travel agency websites, **SideStep** (www.sidestep.com) has gotten the best reviews from Frommer's authors. It's a browser add-on that

purports to "search dozens of sites at once," but in reality only beats competitors' fares as often as other sites do.

Also remember to check **airline websites,** especially those for low-fare carriers such as Southwest, JetBlue, and AirTran, whose fares are often misreported or not posted on travel agency websites. Even with major airlines, you can often shave a few bucks from a fare by booking directly through the airline and avoiding a travel agency's transaction fee. But you'll get these discounts only by **booking online:** Most airlines now offer online-only fares that even their phone agents know nothing about. For the websites of airlines that fly to and from your destination, go to "Getting Here," later in this chapter.

Great **last-minute deals** are available through free weekly e-mail services provided directly by the airlines. Most of these are announced on Tuesday or Wednesday and must be purchased online. Most are only valid for travel that weekend, but some (such as Southwest's) can be booked weeks or months in advance. Sign up for weekly e-mail alerts at airline websites or check mega-sites that compile comprehensive lists of last-minute specials, such as **Smarter Living** (smarterliving.com). For last-minute trips, **site59.com** in the U.S. and **lastminutetravel.com** in Europe often have better deals than the major-label sites.

If you're willing to give up some control over your flight details, use an **opaque fare service** like **Priceline** (www.priceline.com; www.priceline.co.uk for Europeans) or **Hotwire** (www.hotwire.com). Actually, Priceline now offers you the choice of picking your flights, times, and airlines, or going the opaque route; the opaque service continues to capture the better rate. So let's assume you're negotiating opaque services. Here's how it works: Both Priceline and Hotwire offer rock-bottom prices in exchange for travel on a "mystery airline" at a mysterious time of day, often with a mysterious change of planes en route. The mystery airlines are all major, well-known carriers—and the possibility of being sent from Philadelphia to Chicago via Tampa is remote; the airlines' routing computers get better and better. But your chances of getting a 6am or 11pm flight are pretty high. Hotwire tells you flight prices before you buy; Priceline usually has better deals than Hotwire, but you must play the "name your price" game. Priceline and Hotwire are great for flights within North America and between the U.S. and Europe.

For much more about airfares and savvy air-travel tips and advice, pick up a copy of *Frommer's Fly Safe, Fly Smart* (Wiley Publishing, Inc.).

SURFING FOR HOTELS

Hotel marketing experts figure that online hotel bookings account for as much as 15% of hotel reservations—and the number continues to increase. One of the best sites is **Expedia.com,** thanks to its long list of special deals. **Travelocity** (www.travelocity.com), **Quikbook** (www.quikbook.com), **Orbitz** (www.orbitz.com), and hotel specialist sites, such as **hotels.com** and **hoteldiscounts.com,** are also reliable. An excellent free, downloadable program, **TravelAxe** (www.travelaxe.net), can help you search as many as 20 hotel sites at once. Each site has its own, sometimes off-putting, features, however. For instance, Expedia seems to have an agreement with many of its hotels to book reservations only for travelers staying more than 1 night; try to book just 1 night at these hotels and you often get the message, "minimum 2 night" or "minimum 3 night" stay required.

You should also check out the individual websites of Washington hotels; the two, free online reservation services for Washington hotels: **Capitol Reservations,** www.hotelsdc.com, and **DC Accommodations,** www.dcaccommodations.com (see chapter 5 for more information about these services); as well as the website for the **Washington, D.C. Convention and Tourism Corporation (WCTC),** www.washington.org, which includes a hotel booking option. I compared rates offered by Expedia, Capitol Reservations, the WCTC, and the hotel websites for the hotels I had chosen: the Hotel George, on Capitol Hill, and the Jurys Washington Hotel, at Dupont Circle. My month-in-advance request for a double room for

Frommers.com: The Complete Travel Resource

For an excellent travel-planning resource, we highly recommend **Frommers.com** (www.frommers.com). We're a little biased, of course, but we guarantee that you'll find the travel tips, reviews, monthly vacation giveaways, and online-booking capabilities thoroughly indispensable. Among the special features are our popular **Message Boards,** where Frommer's readers post queries and share advice (sometimes even our authors show up to answer questions); **Frommers.com Newsletter,** for the latest travel bargains and insider travel secrets; and **Frommer's Destinations Section,** where you'll get expert travel tips, hotel and dining recommendations, and advice on the sights to see for more than 3,000 destinations around the globe. When your research is done, the **Online Reservations System** (www.frommers.com/book_a_trip) takes you to Frommer's preferred online partners for booking your vacation at affordable prices.

a Thursday night in May turned up the same rate of $269 through the online reservations services of Expedia, Capitol Reservations, and the hotel's own site for the Hotel George, with the WCTC site telling me it was unable to find the property and to try again later; and the same rate of $185 from all four sources, for the Jurys Washington Hotel. I recommend you use this book to help you figure out your desired neighborhood and hotel, and then try Expedia and the individual website for the hotel you've chosen. As helpful as the WCTC is in other respects, its hotel information isn't always accurate, comprehensive . . . or thrifty.

SURFING FOR RENTAL CARS

For booking rental cars online, the best deals are usually found at rental-car company websites, although all the major online travel agencies also offer rental-car reservations services. Priceline and Hotwire work well for rental cars, too; the only "mystery" is which major rental company you get, and for most travelers the difference between Hertz, Avis, and Budget is negligible.

8 The 21st-Century Traveler

INTERNET ACCESS AWAY FROM HOME

Travelers have any number of ways to check e-mail and access the Internet on the road. Of course, using your own laptop—or even a PDA (personal digital assistant) or electronic organizer with a modem—gives you the most flexibility. But you may be able to leave your laptop at home, if you want, since other computer options may be available.

WITHOUT YOUR OWN COMPUTER

Increasingly, hotels provide guests computer and Internet access on one or more computers in the hotel business center. In some cases, the hotel provides this as a free service. In Washington, the Embassy Suites Hotel Downtown is one such property, availing to guests complimentary use of three computers in its business center. (See the hotel's listing in chapter 5.)

Washington, D.C., has at least two cybercafes: Cyberlaptops.com, on the second floor at 1636 R St. NW (© 202/462-7195), providing Internet access and also laptop repairs; and Cyberstop Café, 1513 17th St. NW (© 202/234-2470). For other listings, as well as the locations of **Internet kiosks** throughout the D.C. area, check the website, **www.cybercaptive. com**.

All three of Washington's airports offer some variation of Internet access. Each of National's 150 public phones has a data jack to which you can connect your laptop for the price of a phone call—50¢. Dulles has only six such kiosks, and the connection charge is $3.50, plus $4 per 10 minutes. BWI has three locations where high-speed wireless Internet access is available; you can borrow for a short period or purchase, for 25¢ per minute or $7.95 for unlimited daily access, a network card to plug into your laptop to connect you. Elsewhere, you may see Internet kiosks in shopping malls, hotel lobbies, and tourist information offices around the city, which give you basic Web access for a per-minute fee that's usually higher than cybercafe prices.

To retrieve your e-mail, ask your **Internet Service Provider (ISP)** if it has a Web-based interface tied to your existing e-mail account. If your ISP doesn't have such an interface, you can use the free **mail2web** service (www. mail2web.com) to view (but not reply to) your home e-mail. For more flexibility, you may want to open a free, Web-based e-mail account with **Yahoo! Mail** (http://mail.yahoo.com). (Microsoft's Hotmail is another popular option, but Hotmail has severe spam problems.) Your home ISP may be able to forward your e-mail to the Web-based account automatically.

If you need to access files on your office computer, look into a service called **GoToMyPC** (www.go tomypc.com). The service provides a Web-based interface for you to access and manipulate a distant PC from anywhere—even a cybercafe—provided your "target" PC is on and has an always-on connection to the Internet (such as with Road Runner cable). The service offers top-quality security, but if you're worried about hackers, use your own laptop rather than a cybercafe to access the GoToMyPC system.

WITH YOUR OWN COMPUTER

Major Internet Service Providers (ISP) have **local access numbers** around the world, allowing you to go online by simply placing a local call. Check your ISP's website or call its toll-free number and ask how you can use your current account away from home, and how much it will cost.

If you're traveling outside the reach of your ISP, the **iPass** network has dial-up numbers in most of the world's countries. You'll have to sign up with an iPass provider, who will then tell you how to set up your computer for your destination(s). For a list of iPass providers, go to www.ipass. com and click on "Reseller Locator." Under "Select a Country" pick the country that you're coming from, and under "Who is this service for?" pick "Individual." One solid provider is **i2roam** (www.i2roam.com; © 866/ 874-0495 or 920/233-5863).

Wherever you go, bring a **connection kit** of the right power and phone adapters, a spare phone cord, and a spare Ethernet network cable. Electricity in Washington is standard 110-volt power; European appliances will require a voltage transformer.

Just about every hotel in Washington offers dataports for laptop modems, and most now offer high-speed Internet access using an Ethernet network cable. You'll have to bring your own cables either way, so **call your hotel in advance** to find out what the options are.

Many business-class hotels in the U.S. also offer a form of computer-free Web browsing through the room TV set. We've successfully checked Yahoo! Mail and Hotmail on these systems.

If you have an 802.11b/**Wi-fi** card for your computer, several commercial companies have made wireless service available in airports, hotel lobbies, and coffee shops, primarily in the U.S. **T-Mobile Hotspot** (www.t-mobile. com/hotspot) serves up wireless connections at more than 38 Starbucks coffee shops in the D.C. area, and in downtown Borders Bookstores and Kinkos office supply stores. **Boingo** (www.boingo.com) and **Wayport** (www.wayport.com) have set up networks in airports and high-class hotel lobbies. IPass providers (see above) also give you access to a few hundred wireless hotel lobby setups. Best of all, you don't need to be staying at the Four Seasons to use the hotel's network; just set yourself up on a nice couch in the lobby. Unfortunately, the companies' pricing policies are byzantine, with a variety of monthly, per-connection, and per-minute plans.

Community-minded individuals have also set up **free wireless networks** in major cities around the world. These networks are spotty, but you get what you (don't) pay for. Each network has a home page explaining how to set up your computer for their particular system; start your explorations at www.personaltelco.net/index.cgi/WirelessCommunities.

USING A CELLPHONE ACROSS THE U.S.

Just because your cellphone works at home doesn't mean it'll work elsewhere in the country (thanks to our nation's fragmented cellphone system), although it's a good bet that your phone will work here in D.C. But take a look at your wireless company's coverage map on its website before heading out.

If you're not from the U.S., you'll be appalled at the poor reach of our **GSM (Global System for Mobiles) wireless network,** which is used by much of the rest of the world (see below). Your phone will probably work in most major U.S. cities; it definitely won't work in many rural areas. (To see where GSM phones work in the U.S., check out www.t-mobile. com/coverage/national_popup.asp.) And you may or may not be able to send SMS (text messaging) home. Assume nothing—call your wireless provider and get the full scoop. In a worst-case scenario, you can always rent a phone; **InTouch USA** (© **800/ 872-7626;** www.intouchglobal.com) delivers to hotels. Washington Dulles International Airport has a **Rent-a-Cellular kiosk,** if you're flying into that airport.

---

9 Getting There

BY PLANE

Domestic airlines with scheduled flights into all three of Washington, D.C.'s airports, Washington Dulles International (Dulles), Ronald Reagan Washington National (National), and Baltimore–Washington International (BWI), include **American** (© 800/ 433-7300; www.aa.com), **Continental** (© 800/525-0280; www.continental. com), **Delta** (© 800/221-1212; www.delta.com), **Northwest** (© 800/ 225-2525; www.nwa.com), **United** (© 800/241-6522; www.united.com), and **US Airways** (© 800/428-4322; www.usairways.com).

For a list of international airlines with scheduled flights into all three area airports, see chapter 3, "For International Visitors."

Low-fare airlines seem to be most successful and dependable these days.

Two of the newest to arrive in Washington are United Airline's subsidiary **Ted Airlines** (✆ 800/225-5833; www.flyted.com), which debuted in April 2004, and **Independence Air** (www.flyi.com), which got off the ground in June 2004. Both airlines fly into and out of Dulles, with Ted's flights traveling to and from cities in Florida and to Las Vegas, and Independence Air's flights not specified at the time of this writing, the airline is planning 300(!) daily flights. With the addition of Ted and Independence Air flights, Dulles Airport now becomes a national hub for discount travel; other bargain airlines serving Dulles include **Delta Express** (✆ 800/325-5205; www.flydlx.com), **America West** (✆ 800/235-9292; www.americawest. com), **AirTran** (✆ 800/247-8726; www.airtran.com), **JetBlue** (✆ 800/ 538-2583; www.jetblue.com), and **Frontier** (✆ 800/432-1359; www. frontierairlines.com).

Meanwhile, **Southwest Airlines** (✆ 800/435-9792; www.southwest. com) anchors BWI Airport with its roster of flights to more than 35 cities; AirTran, America West, and Frontier also use BWI.

Five discount airlines use National Airport: Frontier, **American Trans Air (ATA)** (✆ 800/435-9282; www. ata.com), America West, and **Spirit** (✆ 800/772-7177; www.spiritair. com).

SHUTTLE SERVICE FROM NEW YORK, BOSTON & CHICAGO

Delta and US Airways continue to dominate the lucrative D.C.–East Coast shuttle service. Between the two of them, the airlines operate hourly or almost hourly shuttle service between Boston's Logan Airport and Washington, and New York's La Guardia Airport and Washington. The **Delta Shuttle** (✆ 800/933-5935) travels daily between New York and Washington, while the **US Airways Shuttle** (✆ 800/428-4322) operates daily between Boston and Washington, and New York and Washington. Both airlines fly into and out of Ronald Reagan Washington National Airport. Discount airline **Southwest** (see details above) offers nearly hourly service daily between BWI and Chicago's Midway Airport, Providence, Hartford, Long Island, Manchester (New Hampshire), Orlando, and Nashville.

D.C.'S AREA AIRPORTS

General information follows that should help you determine which airport is your best bet; for details about individual airport services, see "Visitor Information," in chapter 4.

Note: At these three airports, as at all American airports now, only ticketed passengers are permitted to go through security to the gates, which

---

Travel in the Age of Bankruptcy

At press time, two major U.S. airlines were struggling in bankruptcy court and most of the rest weren't doing very well either. To protect yourself, **buy your tickets with a credit card,** as the Fair Credit Billing Act guarantees that you can get your money back from the credit card company if a travel supplier goes under (and if you request the refund within 60 days of the bankruptcy). **Travel insurance** can also help, but make sure it covers against "carrier default" for your specific travel provider. And be aware that if a U.S. airline goes bust mid-trip, a 2001 federal law requires other carriers to take you to your destination (albeit on a space-available basis) for a fee of no more than $25, provided you rebook within 60 days of the cancellation.

D.C. Metropolitan Area

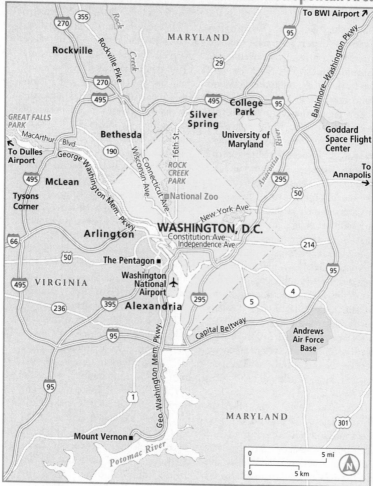

means that if people are meeting you at the airport they will no longer be allowed to greet you at the gate; you should agree beforehand on some other designated rendezvous site. If you are arriving in Washington from another country, you should tell your friends or relatives to meet you at the International Arrivals gate, the area where all international travelers emerge into the main terminal. That's easy. But for everyone else arriving from some other city in the U.S: Don't

have your party wait just outside the security clearance areas to greet you, since this section gets pretty crowded, and you may have trouble spotting each other; you may not even be sure that you are both at the same security clearance gates. Your best plan is to arrange to rendezvous at the baggage claim area. Monitors always post the designated baggage claim carousel for each arriving flight, so, for the time being, at least, this zone remains the best spot for reunions—even if you haven't checked your luggage. Eventually, airports may provide waiting rooms.

Ronald Reagan Washington National Airport (everyone still calls it simply "National") lies across the Potomac River in Virginia, a few minutes by car, 15 to 20 minutes by Metro from downtown in non-rush-hour traffic. Its proximity to the District and its direct access to the Metro rail system are reasons why you might want to fly into National. National's security procedures add certain precautions not in place at other airports, like the "30-minute rule:" Passengers must stay in their seats for the 30 minutes prior to landing at National, and for the 30 minutes after their plane takes off from National.

Approximately 22 major airlines and shuttles serve this airport, which has flights to 67 U.S. cities and three Canadian/Caribbean cities. Nearly all nonstop flights are to and from cities located within 1,250 miles from Washington. The exceptions are flights between National and Phoenix, Denver, Las Vegas, Seattle and, as of 2004, Los Angeles.

While Washington's two other airports remain in the midst of extensive renovations, National is up to date with certain enhancements that may still be in the works at Dulles and BWI: a new terminal; ticket counters that provide access to passengers with disabilities; more than 100 restaurants and shops; more parking space; and climate-controlled pedestrian bridges that connect the terminal directly to the Metro station, whose Blue and Yellow lines stop here. National's airport code is DCA. The Metropolitan Washington Airports Authority oversees both National and Dulles airports, so the website is the same for the two facilities: www.metwashairports.com. Check there for airport information, or call (✆) **703/417-1806.** For Metro information, call (✆) **202/637-7000.**

Washington Dulles International Airport (Dulles) lies 26 miles outside the capital, in Chantilly, Virginia, a 35- to 45-minute ride to downtown in non-rush-hour traffic. Of the three airports, Dulles handles more daily flights and its airlines fly to more destinations, about 69 U.S. and 37 foreign cities. And though the airport is not as convenient to the heart of Washington as National, it's more convenient than BWI, thanks to an uncongested airport access road that travels half the distance toward Washington. A decades-long expansion has so far added two new concourses, a parking garage, and as of late 2004, a pedestrian walkway between the main terminal and concourse B that offers travelers an option over the mobile lounges. Eventually, the airport will more than triple its annual passenger traffic to 55 million, add a runway, another pedestrian walkway, and an underground airport train system that will completely replace those inconvenient and unwieldy mobile lounges that transport most travelers to and from the main and midfield terminals. Fifteen major domestic, eight regional, and 20 international carriers use Dulles. As stated earlier, Dulles now has nine discount airlines operating here, including a new one, Independence, which plans a roster of 300 flights; this will make Dulles the national hub for discount travel. The airport's airport code is IAD, its website is www.metwashairports.com, and its information line is (✆) **703/572-2700.**

Last but not least is **Baltimore–Washington International Airport (BWI),** which is located about 45 minutes from downtown, a few miles outside of Baltimore. One factor especially recommends BWI to travelers: Southwest Airlines, with its bargain fares, commands a major presence here, pulling in nearly half of BWI's business. BWI destinations via Southwest total at least 31, and you should find out whether your city is one of them, if you want to save some money. (A couple of other low-fare airlines operate here as well; see the "By Plane" section earlier in this chapter.)

Call ✆ **800/435-9294** for airport information, or point your browser to www.bwiairport.com. The airport code for BWI is just that: BWI.

GETTING INTO TOWN FROM THE AIRPORT

Each of the three airports offers the following options for getting into the city. In each case, you follow the signs to "ground transportation" in your airport, and look there for the banners or a staff representative of the service you desire. All three airports could really use better signage, especially since their ground transportation desks always seem to be located quite a distance from the gate at which you arrive. Keep trudging, and follow baggage claim signs, too, since ground transportation operations are always situated near baggage carousels.

TAXI SERVICE   For a trip to downtown D.C., you can expect a taxi to cost anywhere from $8 to $15 for the 10- to 15-minute ride from National Airport; $44-plus for the 30- to 40-minute ride from Dulles Airport; and $55 for the 45-minute ride from BWI.

SUPERSHUTTLE   Vans (✆ **800/258-3826**; www.supershuttle.com) offer shared-ride, door-to-door service between the airport and your destination, whether in the District or in a suburban location. You can't reserve space on the van for a ride from the airport, which means that you probably will have to wait 15 to 30 minutes before boarding, so that your driver can fill his van with other passengers, to make his trip worthwhile. This also means that you're going to be taken to your destination in rather a roundabout way, as the driver drops off other passengers en route. If you arrive

after midnight, you can summon a van by calling the toll-free number above from National Airport, ✆ **703/416-7884** from Dulles, and ✆ **888/826-2700** from BWI. The 24-hour service bases its fares on zip code, so, to reach downtown, expect to pay about $10, plus $8 for each additional person from National; $22, plus $10 per additional person from Dulles; and $26 to $32, plus $8 per additional person from BWI. If you're calling the SuperShuttle for a ride from a D.C. area location to one of the airports, you must reserve a spot at least 24 hours in advance.

LIMOUSINES   Limousine service is the most costly of all options, with prices starting at $25 at National, $42 at Dulles, and $95 at BWI, for private car transportation to downtown D.C. For pickup from BWI, reserve passage by calling ✆ **301/912-0000** or 800/878-7743; for pickup from National or Dulles, try **Red Top Executive Sedan** (✆ **800/296-3300** or 202/882-3300—see "When You Want to Travel in Style," below) or consult the Yellow Pages.

Free hotel/motel shuttles operate from all three airports to certain nearby properties. Best to inquire about such transportation when you book a room at your hotel.

Individual transportation options at each airport are as follows:

FROM RONALD REAGAN WASHINGTON NATIONAL AIRPORT   If you are not too encumbered with luggage, you should take **Metrorail** (✆ **202/637-7000**) into the city. Metro's Yellow and Blue lines stop at the airport and connect via an enclosed walkway to level two, the concourse level, of the main terminal, adjacent to terminals B and C. If yours is one of the airlines that still uses the "old" terminal A (Spirit, Air Tran, Midway, Northwest, Alaska, and ATA), you will have a longer walk to reach the Metro station. Signs pointing the way can be confusing, so ask an airport employee if you're headed in the right direction; or, better yet, head out to the curb and hop a shuttle bus to the station, but be sure to ask the driver to let you know when you've reached the Metro (it may not be obvious, and drivers don't always announce the stops). **Metrobuses** (© 202/637-7000) also serve the area, should you be going somewhere off the Metro route. But Metrorail is fastest, a 15- to 20-minute non-rush-hour ride to downtown. It is safe, convenient, and cheap, costing $1.20 during non-rush hours, $1.50 during rush hour.

If you're renting a car from on-site **car-rental agencies, Avis** (© 703/419-5815), **Budget** (© 703/419-1021), **Dollar** (© 703/519-8701), **Hertz** (© 703/419-6300), or **National** (© 703/419-1032), go to level two, the concourse level, follow the pedestrian walkway to the parking garage, find garage A, and descend one flight. You can also take the complimentary Airport Shuttle (look for the sign posted at the curb outside the terminal) to parking garage A. If you've rented from off-premises agencies **Alamo** (© 703/684-0086), **Enterprise** (© 703/553-7744), or **Thrifty** (© 877/283-0898), head outside the baggage claim area of your terminal, and catch the shuttle bus marked for your agency. See appendix B at the back of this book for toll-free numbers and websites.

To get downtown by car, follow the signs out of the airport for the George Washington Parkway. Stay on the GW Parkway until you see signs for I-395 north to Washington. Take the I-395 north exit to the 12th Street exit, which puts you at 12th Street and Constitution Avenue NW; ask your hotel for directions from that point. Or, take the more scenic route, always staying to the left on the GW Parkway

as you follow the signs for Memorial Bridge. You'll be driving alongside the Potomac River, with the monuments in view across the river; then, as you cross over Memorial Bridge, you're greeted by the Lincoln Memorial. Stay left coming over the bridge, swoop around to the left of the Memorial, take a left on 23rd Street NW, a right on Constitution Avenue, and then left again on 15th Street NW (the Washington Monument will be to your right), if you want to be in the heart of downtown.

FROM WASHINGTON DULLES INTERNATIONAL AIRPORT

The **Washington Flyer Express Bus** runs between Dulles and the West Falls Church Metro station, where you can board a train for D.C. Buses to the West Falls Church Metro station run daily, every 30 minutes, and cost $8 one-way. (By the way, **"Washington Flyer"** is also the name under which the taxi service operates at Dulles.)

More convenient is the **Metrobus** service that runs between Dulles and the L'Enfant Plaza Metro station, located near Capitol Hill and within walking distance of the National Mall and Smithsonian museums. The bus departs hourly, daily, costs only $2.50, and takes about 45 to 50 minutes.

If you are renting a car at Dulles, head down the ramp near your baggage claim area, and walk outside to the curb to look for your rental car's shuttle bus stop. The buses come by every 5 minutes or so en route to nearby rental lots. These include **Alamo** (© 703/260-0182), **Avis** (© 703/661-3505), **Budget** (© 703/437-9373), **Dollar** (© 866/434-2226), **Enterprise** (© 703/661-8800), **Hertz** (© 703/471-6020), **National** (© 703/471-5278), and **Thrifty** (© 877/283-0898). See appendix B at the back of this book for these companies' toll-free numbers and websites.

To reach downtown Washington from Dulles by car, exit the airport

Tips When You Want to Travel in Style

So you don't want to wait in line for a cab at the airport, or share a ride with fellow passengers aboard a shuttle van? You can call in advance to reserve a **Red Top Executive Sedan** (© 800/296-3300 or 202/882-3300; www.redtopcab.com), which will be waiting for you at the curb outside your airline's baggage-claim area. Your chauffeur tracks the status of your flight to know of delays or early arrivals so he can be there when you are. It's more expensive than regular cab service (for instance, from National Airport to downtown you'll pay at least $25, plus 15% tip, versus cab fare of about $10, plus gratuity), but the relief of being able to step right into a comfortable and spacious private car after a tiring trip may be worth the extra money to you. The service is available 24 hours.

and stay on the Dulles Access Road, which leads right into I-66 east. Follow I-66 east, which takes you across the Theodore Roosevelt Memorial Bridge and onto Constitution Avenue. Ask your hotel for directions from this point.

FROM BALTIMORE–WASHINGTON INTERNATIONAL AIRPORT

BWI offers an Express Metro Bus service that runs between the Greenbelt Metro station and the airport. In the airport, look for "Public Transit" signs to find the service, which operates daily, departs every 40 minutes, and costs $2.50. At the Greenbelt Metro station, you purchase a Metro fare card and board a Metro train, which takes you into the city.

You also have the choice of taking either an **Amtrak** (© 800/872-7245) or a **Maryland Rural Commuter** (**MARC;** © 800/325-7245) train into the city. Both trains travel between the BWI Railway Station (© 410/672-6167) and Washington's Union Station (© 202/484-7540), about a 30-minute ride. Amtrak's service is daily (ticket prices range from $13 to $36 per person, one-way, depending on time and train type), while MARC's is weekdays only ($6 per person, one-way). A courtesy shuttle runs every 10 minutes or so between the airport and the train station; stop at the desk near the baggage-claim

area to check for the next departure time of both the shuttle bus and the train. Trains depart about once per hour.

BWI opened a brand-new, offsite, car rental facility in late 2003. From the ground transportation area, you board a shuttle bus that transports you to the lot. Rental agencies include **Avis** (© 410/859-1680), **Alamo** (© 410/850-5011), **Budget** (© 410/859-0850), **Dollar** (© 800/800-4000), **Hertz** (© 410/850-7400), **National** (© 410/859-8860), and **Thrifty** (© 410/859-1136). For these companies' toll-free numbers and websites, consult appendix B at the back of this book.

Here's how you reach Washington: Look for signs for I-195 and follow I-195 west until you see signs for Washington and the Baltimore–Washington Parkway (I-295); head south on I-295. Get off I-295 when you see the signs for Route 50/New York Avenue, which leads into the District, via New York Avenue. Ask your hotel for specific directions from New York Avenue NE.

GETTING THROUGH THE AIRPORT

With the federalization of airport security, security procedures at U.S. airports are more stable and consistent than ever. Generally, you'll be fine if you arrive at the airport **1 hour** before a domestic flight and **2 hours** before an international flight.

Bring a **current, government-issued photo ID** such as a driver's license or passport, and if you've got an E-ticket, print out the **official confirmation page;** you'll need to show your confirmation at the security checkpoint, and your ID at the ticket counter or the gate. (Children under 18 do not need photo IDs for domestic flights, but the adults checking in with them need them. Also keep in mind that teenagers younger than 18 often look older, so it's probably a good idea to have your teenager bring a school photo ID or driver's license, to avoid any hassles.)

Security lines can sometimes take a long time to clear. If you have trouble standing for extended periods, tell an airline employee; the airline will provide a wheelchair. Speed up security by **not wearing metal objects** such as big belt buckles or clanky earrings. If you've got metallic body parts, a note from your doctor can prevent a long chat with the security screeners. Keep in mind that only **ticketed passengers** are allowed past security.

Federalization has stabilized **what you can carry on** and **what you can't.** The general rule is that sharp things are out, nail clippers are okay, and food and beverages must be passed through the X-ray machine—but that security screeners can't make you drink from your coffee cup. Bring food in your carry-on rather than checking it, as explosive-detection machines used on checked luggage have been known to mistake food (especially chocolate, for some reason) for bombs. Travelers in the U.S. are allowed one carry-on bag, plus a "personal item" such as a purse, briefcase, or laptop bag. Carry-on hoarders can stuff all sorts of things into a laptop bag; as long as it has a laptop in it, it's still considered a personal item. The Transportation Security Administration (TSA) reports that laptops are the item most frequently forgotten at security, so be sure to label your laptop in a singularly identifiable way, to make it easier to claim should you forget it. The TSA has issued a list of restricted items; check its website (www.tsa.gov/public/index.jsp) for details.

In 2003, the TSA phased out **gate check-in** at all U.S. airports. Passengers with E-tickets and without checked bags can still beat the ticket-counter lines by using **electronic kiosks** or even **online check-in.** Ask your airline which alternatives are available, and if you're using a kiosk, bring the credit card you used to book the ticket. If you're checking bags, you will still be able to use most airlines'

(Tips Don't Stow It—Ship It

If ease of travel is your main concern and money is no object, you can ship your luggage with one of the growing number of luggage-service companies that pick up, track, and deliver your luggage (often through couriers such as Federal Express) with minimum hassle for you. Traveling luggage-free may be ultra-convenient, but it's not cheap: One-way overnight shipping can cost from $100 to $200, depending on what you're sending. Still, for some people, especially the elderly or the infirm, it's a sensible solution to lugging heavy baggage. Specialists in door-to-door luggage delivery are **Virtual Bellhop** (www.virtualbellhop.com), **SkyCap International** (wwww.skycapinternational.com), and **Luggage Express** (www.usxpluggageexpress.com).

kiosks; again call your airline for up-to-date information. **Curbside check-in** is also a good way to avoid lines, although a few airlines still ban curbside check-in entirely; call before you go.

The TSA also recommends that you **not lock your checked luggage** so screeners can search it by hand if necessary. The agency says to use plastic "zip ties" instead, which can be bought at hardware stores and can be easily cut off.

FLYING FOR LESS: TIPS FOR GETTING THE BEST AIRFARE

Passengers sharing the same airplane cabin rarely pay the same fare. Travelers who need to purchase tickets at the last minute, change their itinerary at a moment's notice, or fly one-way often get stuck paying the premium rate. Here are some ways to keep your airfare costs down.

- Passengers who can book their ticket **long in advance,** who can **stay over Saturday night,** or who **fly midweek** or **at less-trafficked hours** will pay a fraction of the full fare. If your schedule is flexible, say so, and ask if you can secure a cheaper fare by changing your flight plans.
- You can also save on airfares by keeping an eye out in local newspapers for **promotional specials** or **fare wars,** when airlines lower prices on their most popular routes. You rarely see fare wars offered for peak travel times, but if you can travel in the off-months, you may snag a bargain.
- Search **the Internet** for cheap fares (see "Planning Your Trip Online").
- **Consolidators,** also known as bucket shops, are great sources for international tickets, although they usually can't beat the Internet on fares within North America.

Start by looking in Sunday newspaper travel sections, like the *New York Times, Los Angeles Times,* and *Miami Herald.* **Beware:** Bucket shop tickets are usually nonrefundable or rigged with stiff cancellation penalties, often as high as 50% to 75% of the ticket price, and some put you on charter airlines with questionable safety records. Protect yourself by paying with a credit card rather than cash. You should always do comparison shopping by contacting the airlines directly before buying from a consolidator.

Several reliable consolidators are worldwide and available on the Net. **STA Travel** is the world's leader in student travel, but also offers good fares for travelers of all ages. **Flights.com** (✆ 312/332-0090; www.flights.com) started in Europe and has excellent fares worldwide. It also has "local" websites in quite a few countries. **Fly-Cheap** (✆ 800/FLY-CHEAP; www.1800flycheap.com) is owned by Priceline.com and so has especially good access to discount fares. **Air Tickets Direct** (✆ 800/778-3447; www.airticketsdirect.com) is based in Montreal and leverages the Canadian dollar for low fares.

- Join **frequent-flier clubs.** Accrue enough miles, and you'll be rewarded with free flights and elite status. It's free, and you'll get the best choice of seats, faster response to phone inquiries, and prompter service if your luggage is stolen, your flight is canceled or delayed, or if you want to change your seat. You don't need to fly to build frequent-flier miles—**frequent-flier credit cards** can provide thousands of miles for doing your everyday shopping.
- For many more tips about air travel, including a rundown of the

major frequent-flier credit cards, pick up a copy of *Frommer's Fly Safe, Fly Smart* (Wiley Publishing, Inc.).

BY CAR

Major highways approach Washington, D.C., from all parts of the country. Specifically, these are I-270, I-95, and I-295 from the north; I-95 and I-395, Route 1, and Route 301 from the south; Route 50/301 and Route 450 from the east; and Route 7, Route 50, I-66, and Route 29/211 from the west.

No matter which road you take, there's a good chance you will have to navigate some portion of the **Capital Beltway** (I-495 and I-95) to gain entry to D.C. The Beltway girds the city, 66 miles around, with 56 interchanges or exits, and is nearly always congested, but especially during weekday morning and evening rush hours, roughly between 6 to 9:30am and 3 to 7pm. Commuter traffic on the Beltway now rivals that of major L.A. freeways, and drivers can get a little crazy, weaving in and out of traffic.

If you're planning to drive to Washington, get yourself a good map before you do anything else. The **American Automobile Association (AAA;** ✆ **800/763-9900** for emergency road service and for connection to the mid-Atlantic office; www.aaa. com) provides its members with maps and detailed Trip-Tiks that give precise directions to a destination, including up-to-date information about areas of construction. AAA also provides towing services should you have car trouble during your trip. If you are driving to a hotel in D.C. or its

Flying with Film & Video

Never pack film—developed or undeveloped—in checked bags, as the new, more powerful scanners in U.S. airports can fog film. The film you carry with you can be damaged by scanners as well. X-ray damage is cumulative; the slower the film, and the more times you put it through a scanner, the more likely the damage. Film under 800 ASA is usually safe for up to five scans. If you're taking your film through additional scans, U.S. regulations permit you to demand hand inspections. In international airports, you're at the mercy of airport officials. Highly trafficked attractions are X-raying visitors' bags with increasing frequency.

Most photo supply stores sell protective pouches designed to block damaging X-rays. The pouches fit both film and loaded cameras. They should protect your film in checked baggage, but they also may raise alarms and result in a hand inspection.

An organization called **Film Safety for Traveling on Planes, FSTOP** (✆ **888/301-2665**; www.f-stop.org), can provide additional tips for traveling with film and equipment.

Carry-on scanners will not damage **videotape** in video cameras, but the magnetic fields emitted by the walk-through security gateways and handheld inspection wands will. Always place your loaded camcorder on the screening conveyor belt or have it hand-inspected. Be sure your batteries are charged, as you will probably be required to turn the device on to ensure that it's what it appears to be.

suburbs, contact the establishment to find out the best route to the hotel's address and other crucial details concerning parking availability and rates. See "Getting Around," in chapter 4 for information about driving in D.C.

The District is 240 miles from New York City, 40 miles from Baltimore, 700 miles from Chicago, nearly 500 miles from Boston, and about 630 miles from Atlanta.

BY TRAIN

Amtrak (© 800/USA-RAIL; www. amtrak.com) offers daily service to Washington from New York, Boston, Chicago, and Los Angeles (you change trains in Chicago). Amtrak also travels daily from points south of Washington, including Raleigh, Charlotte, Atlanta, cities in Florida, and to New Orleans.

Metroliner service—which costs a little more but provides faster transit and roomier, more comfortable seating than regular trains—is available between New York and Washington, D.C., and points in between. *Note:* Metroliner fares are substantially reduced on weekends. The most luxurious way to travel is First Class Club Service, available on all Metroliners as well as some other trains. For a hefty additional fee, passengers enjoy more spacious and refined seating in a private car; complimentary meals and beverage service; and Metropolitan Lounges (in New York, Chicago, Philadelphia, and Washington), where travelers can wait for trains in a comfortable setting while enjoying free snacks and coffee.

Even faster, roomier, and more expensive than Metroliner service are Amtrak's high-speed **Acela** trains. The trains, which travel as fast as 150 miles per hour, navigate the Northeast Corridor, linking Boston, New York, and Washington. Acela Express trains travel between New York and Washington in 2 hours and 43 minutes (about 15 minutes faster than the Metroliner), and between Boston and Washington in about 6 hours and 30 minutes. Acela Regional trains travel between New York and Washington in 3 hours and 40 minutes, and between Boston and Washington in about 8 hours. Amtrak continues to refine the design and production of the Acela cars, which have proved problematic since they were introduced in late 2000. Amtrak hopes eventually to run a total of 19 Acela round-trips daily between New York and Washington, replacing Metroliner service between those two cities.

Amtrak trains arrive at historic **Union Station,** 50 Massachusetts Ave. NE (© **202/371-9441;** www.union-stationdc.com), a short walk from the Capitol, across the circle from several hotels, and a short cab or Metro ride from downtown. Union Station is a turn-of-the-20th-century beaux arts masterpiece that was magnificently restored in the late 1980s. Offering a three-level marketplace of shops and restaurants, this stunning depot is conveniently located and connects with Metro service. There are always taxis available there. (For more on Union Station, see chapters 4, 7, and 8.)

Like the airlines, Amtrak offers several discounted fares; although not all are based on advance purchase, you have more discount options by reserving early. The discount fares can be used only on certain days and hours of the day; be sure to find out exactly what restrictions apply. Tickets for children ages 2 to 15 cost half the price of a regular coach fare when the children are accompanied by a fare-paying adult. Amtrak's website features a weekly bargain fares service, Rail SALE, which allows you to purchase tickets for one-way designated coach seats at great discounts. This program is only available on **www.amtrak.com** when you charge your tickets by credit card.

Also inquire about money-saving packages that include hotel accommodations, car rentals, tours, and so on with your train fare. Call Amtrak Vacations at ℂ **800/321-8684** for details.

10 Recommended Reading

You can put yourself in the mood for a visit to Washington by reading some great novels set in Washington, memoirs and histories by some of the city's more famous residents, and other guidebooks whose topics supplement what you've learned in these pages.

Fiction-lovers might pick up books by Ward Just, including his collection of stories *The Congressman Who Loved Flaubert;* Ann Berne's *A Crime in the Neighborhood;* Marita Golden's *The Edge of Heaven;* Allen Drury's *Advise and Consent;* or one of the growing number of mysteries whose plot revolves around the capital, such as Margaret Truman's series (*Murder at the Smithsonian, Murder at the Kennedy Center,* and so on), or George Pelecanos's hard-core thrillers that take you to parts of Washington you'll never see as a tourist: *Hell to Pay* and *King Suckerman,* to name just two.

If you're keen on learning more about the history of the nation's capital and about the people who have lived here, try Arthur Schlesinger's *The Birth of the Nation,* F. Cary's *Urban Odyssey,* David Brinkley's *Washington at War,* and Paul Dickson's *On This Spot,* which traces the history of the city by revealing exactly what took place at specific locations—"on this spot"—in years gone by, neighborhood by neighborhood. If you like your history leavened with humor, purchase Christopher Buckley's *Washington Schlepped Here: Walking in the Nation's Capital,* to read as a hilarious companion piece to this guidebook. Buckley's book, published in spring 2003, is an irreverent look at the capital's most famous attractions and characters, all of its anecdotes true. Buckley, a Washington insider whose experience includes speechwriting for Vice President George Bush during the first Reagan administration, has also written a couple of funny, Washington-based novels, *The White House Mess* and *No Way to Treat a First Lady.*

Two memoirs are musts for finding out how the powerful operate in Washington: *Personal History,* by the late Katharine Graham, who for many years was publisher of the *Washington Post,* and *Washington,* by Graham's close friend and colleague, Meg Greenfield, a columnist and editor at the *Washington Post* for more than 30 years.

Finally, to find out more about the architecture of Washington, pick up a copy of the *AIA Guide to the Architecture of Washington, D.C.,* by Christopher Weeks; to discover information about Washington's parks, hiking trails, and other green spaces, look for *Natural Washington* by Richard Berman and Deborah Gerhard; for another humorous read, put your hands on Dave Barry's *Dave Barry Hits Below the Beltway,* and for a book that may send chills up your spine, purchase a copy of *Ghosts: Washington's Most Famous Ghost Stories* by John Alexander.

3

For International Visitors

More than 30 international airlines fly into Washington, D.C., area airports, including Aer Lingus, Alitalia, Aeroflot, Ethiopian, Icelandair, KLM, and three different British airlines: British Airways, British Midland, and Virgin Atlantic. Stricter security procedures are in place at airports, it's true, but judging by the latest tourism figures, travelers are getting used to them: the Washington, D.C. Convention and Tourism Corporation reports that in 2003, more than 1 million international travelers visited D.C., which is close to pre-September 11, 2001 statistics. So, welcome to Washington, we're glad you're here.

1 Preparing for Your Trip

ENTRY REQUIREMENTS

Check the **U.S. State Department**'s website, **www.state.gov**, for current information, including the address of your closest U.S. embassy or consulate. You can then go in person to the embassy or consulate to obtain your application and other information or you can continue online at the State Department's website, at **www.travel.state.gov**. In Washington, D.C., the State Department's Visa Services public information phone number is ✆ **202/663-1225.** You'll hear taped instructions, with the option to speak to an officer.

VISAS The U.S. State Department has a **Visa Waiver Program (VWP)** allowing citizens of certain countries to enter the United States without a visa for stays of up to 90 days. These include Andorra, Australia, Austria, Belgium, Brunei, Denmark, Finland, France, Germany, Iceland, Ireland, Italy, Japan, Liechtenstein, Luxembourg, Monaco, the Netherlands, New Zealand, Norway, Portugal, San Marino, Singapore, Slovenia, Spain, Sweden, Switzerland, and the United Kingdom. If you are a citizen of a VWP country, you must have the following items to enter the United States:

1. A machine-readable passport valid for 6 months beyond the dates of your intended visit.

2. A round-trip transportation ticket issued on a carrier that has signed an agreement with the United States government to participate in the VWP, and you must arrive in the U.S. aboard such a carrier. An exception is made for citizens of participating VWP countries who apply for entry into the U.S. from Canada or Mexico, at a land border crossing point: in such cases, you need not present round-trip transportation tickets, nor must you enter aboard a carrier that has signed an agreement with the U.S. to participate in the Visa Waiver Program.

3. A completed and signed Nonimmigrant Visa Waiver Arrival-Departure Record, form I-94W, waiving the right of review or appeal of an immigration officer's determination about admissibility,

or deportation. Forms are available from participating carriers, travel agents, and land-border ports of entry.

4. A record free of visa ineligibilities, meaning, if you have been refused a visa in the past, have a criminal record, or are otherwise ineligible for entry through the Visa Waiver Program, you must apply for a visa to enter the U.S.

Citizens from Visa Waiver countries who first enter the United States may also visit Mexico and Canada and return to the United States without a visa, as long as the total visit does not exceed 90 days. Further information is available from any U.S. embassy or consulate. Canadian citizens may enter the United States without visas but are required to show proof of citizenship and a photo ID. Citizens of all other countries must have (1) a valid passport that expires at least 6 months later than the scheduled end of their visit to the United States, and (2) a tourist visa, which may be obtained from any U.S. consulate.

To obtain a tourist visa, here's what you must do:

1. Visit the U.S. State Department's website, http://unitedstatesvisas. gov, for thorough and up-to-date information about the process.
2. Contact your nearest U.S. Embassy or Consulate to find out how to obtain application form DS-156, and, if you are a man between the ages of 16 and 45, supplemental form DS-157. Make an appointment and ask about fees, which are nonrefundable and must be paid prior to your appointment. Procedures can vary among embassies and consulates.
3. Gather required documentation: valid passport; completed and signed applications; 2-by-2-inch-square photo; evidence detailing your financial status, including evidence of funds to cover your expenses in the U.S.; documentation supporting the reason for your trip, as well as binding ties to a residence abroad; proof of payment of fees.
4. Submit your application, passport, and supporting documents to your embassy or consulate, which will review the information and issue the visa.

Note: The visa process often takes much longer than it once did, so be sure to allow at least 3 or 4 weeks.

British subjects can obtain up-to-date passport and visa information by calling the **U.S. Embassy Visa Information Line** (© 09055/444-546), or going to the U.S. Embassy Great Britain website (**www.usembassy.org. uk**, then click on "Visas to the U.S." for information and e-mail contact).

Irish citizens can obtain up-to-date passport and visa information through the **Embassy of USA Dublin,** 42 Elgin Rd., Dublin 4, Ireland (© **1580 47 8482**), or by checking the visa website at **http://dublin.usembassy. gov**.

Australian citizens can obtain up-to-date passport and visa information by calling the **U.S. Embassy Canberra,** Moonah Place, Yarralumla, ACT 2600 (© **01800 687 844**), or checking the website's visa page (**http://usembassy-australia.state. gov**).

Citizens of **New Zealand** can obtain up-to-date passport and visa information by calling the **U.S. Embassy New Zealand,** 29 Fitzherbert Terrace, Thorndon, Wellington, New Zealand (© **644/462-6000**) or getting the information directly from the website (**http://usembassy.org.nz**).

DRIVER'S LICENSES Foreign driver's licenses are mostly recognized in the United States, although you may want to get an international driver's license if your home license is not written in English.

PASSPORT INFORMATION

As of October 1, 2004, the U.S. requires that passports be machine readable, which means that the size of the passport and photo, and the arrangement of data fields containing biographical data, meet the standards of the International Civil Aviation Organization, Doc 9303, Part 1 Machine Readable Passports.

Safeguard your passport in an inconspicuous, inaccessible place like a money belt. Make a copy of the critical pages, including the passport number, and store it in a safe place, separate from the passport itself. If you lose your passport while in Washington, visit your country's embassy or consulate as soon as possible for a replacement. Passport applications are downloadable from most government Internet sites, including those listed in the text that follows, for Canada, the United Kingdom, Ireland, Australia, and New Zealand.

Note that the International Civil Aviation Organization (ICAO) has recommended a policy requiring that *every* individual who travels by air have his or her own passport. In response, many countries are now requiring that children must be issued their own passports to travel internationally, where before those under 16 or so may have been allowed to travel on a parent or guardian's passport.

Procedures, fees, and processing times for obtaining or renewing passports vary, of course, from country to country, and requirements can change as governments incorporate more effective security precautions into their procedures. Best to inquire at the closest passport office in your country. Here is a list of central passport offices for the English-speaking countries, Canada, the United Kingdom, Ireland, Australia, and New Zealand.

CANADA

Canada has 29 regional passport offices rather than one central office; call the toll-free number ✆ **800/567-6868,** or check the website, **www.passport. gc.ca,** to find out the location nearest you. Send written inquiries to Passport Office, Department of Foreign Affairs and International Trade, Ottawa, ON K1A 0G3.

UNITED KINGDOM

London Passport Office, Globe House, 89 Eccleston Square, London SW1V 1PN (✆ **0870/521-0410;** www.ukpa.gov.uk).

IRELAND

Passport Office, Setanta Centre, Molesworth Street, Dublin 2 (✆ **353 1/671-1633;** www.irlgov.ie/iveagh/services/abroad).

AUSTRALIA

Australia operates a central Australian Passport Information Phone Service line, ✆ **131 232,** which you may call from anywhere in Australia, or access the website, **www.dfat.gov.au/passports,** for information. The government directs its citizens to one of its 1,700 Australia Post outlets for passport applications and processing; there is no central passport office.

NEW ZEALAND

Department of Internal Affairs, New Zealand Passports, Level 3, Boulcott House, 47 Boulcott St., Wellington (✆ **0800/225-050**). By mail, the address is Department of Internal Affairs, New Zealand Passports, P.O. Box 10-526, Wellington. For information online, go to **www.govt.nz.**

CUSTOMS
WHAT YOU CAN BRING IN

U.S. Customs and Border Protection, whose duties include regulating every aspect of what our government allows travelers to bring in and take out of the country, is now an agency of the U.S. Department of Homeland Security.

Rules are comprehensive, covering everything from the maximum amount of money a foreign tourist is permitted to carry in or take out without having to declare it to Customs ($10,000 in U.S. or foreign currencies), to whether you can bring your cat to the United States (yes, as long as the cat is free of evidence of diseases communicable to humans when the cat is examined at the U.S. port of entry).

If you have any questions about what you may bring to the U.S., the first thing you should do is contact the Commercial Officer at your nearest U.S. Embassy or Consulate, who can give you the list of U.S. Customs regulations. (As earlier mentioned, you can find the address of your closest embassy/consulate on the website, www.state.gov.) You can also go directly to the Customs Service website, www.cbp.gov, and click on "Travel." At that site, you will be able to download brochures, read more about regulations, and contact the U.S. Customs Service by e-mail to obtain answers to specific questions.

Upon arrival by plane in the United States, you can expect to complete an arrival/departure form and be interviewed by a U.S. official at the airport. The Customs Service is working to improve its customer service to international travelers at major U.S. airports. Washington-Dulles International Airport is one of the 20 or so ports of entry where Customs has "Passenger Service Representatives" in place. If you arrive at Dulles, look for posted photos to help you find a rep, who can then assist you in clearing Customs. Customs has also installed kiosks at certain airports (Dulles has several, but only for outbound passengers), that feature touch-screens that you can use to obtain information about Customs regulations.

Visitors arriving by air, no matter what the port of entry, should cultivate patience and resignation before setting foot on U.S. soil. Getting through immigration control can take as long as 2 hours on some days, especially on summer weekends, so be sure to carry this guidebook or something else to read.

People traveling by air from Canada, Bermuda, and certain countries in the Caribbean can sometimes clear Customs and Immigration at the point of departure, which is much quicker.

Finally, if you have further questions while you're here in Washington, you can always call the Customs and Border Protection customer service number, ✆ 202/354-1000, for answers and assistance.

WHAT YOU CAN TAKE HOME

Again, this information will vary from country to country, and in every case, you should determine this information before you leave your own country. Here are the first points of contact for residents of the U.K, Canada, Ireland, Australia, and New Zealand.

U.K. citizens: Contact **HM Customs & Excise** (✆ **0845 010 9000;** www.hmce.gov.uk) for information and the address of the nearest office; from outside the U.K. ✆ **44/208-929-0152.**

Canadian citizens: Contact the **Canada Border Services Agency's Automated Customs Information Service** (✆ **800/461-9999;** www.cbsa-asfc.gc.ca); from outside Canada, call ✆ **506/636-5064.**

Irish citizens: Contact the **Customs and Excise Information Office** (✆ 9010 877 6200; www.revenue.ie). In Washington, you can contact the Irish Embassy, ✆ **202/462-3939.**

Australian citizens: Contact the **Australian Customs Services** (✆ **1 300 363 263;** www.customs.gov.au). Outside of Australia, call ✆ **61 (2) 6275 6666.**

New Zealand residents: Contact New Zealand Customs (© **08004 28 786;** www.customs.govt.nz).

HEALTH INSURANCE

Although it's not required of travelers, health insurance is highly recommended. Unlike many European countries, the United States does not usually offer free or low-cost medical care to its citizens or visitors. Doctors and hospitals are expensive, and in most cases will require advance payment or proof of coverage before they render their services. Policies can cover everything from the loss or theft of your baggage and trip cancellation to the guarantee of bail in case you're arrested. Good policies will also cover the costs of an accident, repatriation, or death. See "Travel Insurance, Health & Safety," in chapter 2 for more information. Packages such as **Europ Assistance** in Europe are sold by automobile clubs and travel agencies at attractive rates. **Worldwide Assistance Services, Inc.** (© **800/ 777-8710;** www.worldwideassistance. com), is the agent for Europ Assistance in the United States. Worldwide Assistance Services has offices in Washington, D.C., at 1133 15th St. NW, Suite 400, Washington, D.C. 20005 (© **202/331-1609**).

Though lack of health insurance may prevent you from being admitted to a hospital in nonemergencies, don't worry about being left on a street corner to die: The American way is to fix you now and bill the living daylights out of you later.

INSURANCE FOR BRITISH TRAVELERS Most big travel agents offer their own insurance, and will probably try to sell you their package when you book a holiday. Think before you sign. **Britain's Consumers' Association** recommends that you insist on seeing the policy and reading the fine print before buying travel insurance. **The Association**

of **British Insurers** (© **020/7600- 3333;** www.abi.org.uk) represents 400 companies. The ABI has also teamed up with the Foreign and Commonwealth Office to provide helpful insurance and other information to travelers; go to **www.fco.gov.uk/knowbefore yougo**. You might also shop around for better deals: Try **Columbus Direct** (© **020 7375-0011;** www.columbus direct.net).

INSURANCE FOR CANADIAN TRAVELERS Canadians should check with their provincial health plan offices or call **Health Canada** (© **613/ 957-2991;** http://hwcweb.hcsc.gc.ca) to find out the extent of their coverage and what documentation and receipts they must take home in case they are treated in the United States.

MONEY

CURRENCY The U.S. monetary system is very simple: The most common **bills** are the $1 (colloquially, a "buck"), $5, $10, and $20 denominations. There are also $2 bills (seldom encountered), $50 bills, and $100 bills (the last two are usually not welcome as payment for small purchases). All the paper money was recently redesigned, adding tints of color and making the famous faces adorning the bills disproportionately large. The old-style bills are still legal tender.

There are seven denominations of coins: 1¢ (1 cent, or a penny); 5¢ (5 cents, or a nickel); 10¢ (10 cents, or a dime); 25¢ (25 cents, or a quarter); 50¢ (50 cents, or a half dollar); the gold "Sacagawea" coin worth $1; and, prized by collectors, the rare, older silver dollar.

CURRENCY EXCHANGE It's best to change money before you arrive in the United States, but if you do need to exchange currency, you can go to the currency-exchange desk at any of the three D.C.-area airports, or to one of the following locations:

the Travelex currency exchange office (© **202/371-9220**) at Union Station, opposite Gate G on the train concourse; the Sun Trust Bank, 1445 New York Ave. NW (© **202/879-6308**); and at three Riggs Bank locations at 1913 Massachusetts Ave. NW, 1503 Pennsylvania Ave. NW, and 800 17th St. NW. (Dial © **301/887-6000** to be connected to the individual locations.)

TRAVELER'S CHECKS Though traveler's checks are widely accepted, make sure that they're denominated in U.S. dollars, as foreign-currency checks are often difficult to exchange. The three traveler's checks that are most widely recognized—and least likely to be denied—are **Visa, American Express,** and **MasterCard.** Be sure to record the numbers of the checks, and keep that information in a separate place in case they get lost or stolen. Most businesses are pretty good about taking traveler's checks, but you're better off cashing them in at a bank (in small amounts, of course) and paying in cash. *Remember:* You'll need identification, such as a driver's license or passport, to change a traveler's check.

CREDIT CARDS & ATMs Credit cards are the most widely used form of payment in the United States: **Visa** (BarclayCard in Britain), **MasterCard** (EuroCard in Europe, Access in Britain, Chargex in Canada), **American Express, Diners Club, Discover,** and **Carte Blanche.** Most Washington establishments accept Visa, Master-Card, and American Express, and many also accept Diners Club, Discover, and Carte Blanche. A handful of stores and restaurants do not take credit cards at all, so be sure to ask in advance. Most businesses display a sticker near their entrance to let you know which cards they accept. (*Note:* Businesses may require a minimum purchase, usually around $10, to use a credit card.)

You should bring at least one major credit card. You must have a credit or charge card to rent a car. Hotels and airlines usually require a credit card imprint as a deposit against expenses, and in an emergency a credit card can be priceless.

You'll find **automated teller machines (ATMs)** on just about every block—at least in almost every town—across the country. Some ATMs will allow you to draw U.S. currency against your bank and credit cards. Check with your bank before leaving home, and remember that you will need your personal identification number (PIN) to do so. Most accept Visa, MasterCard, and American Express, as well as ATM cards from other U.S. banks. Expect to be charged up to $3 per transaction, however, if you're not using your own bank's ATM.

One way around these fees is to ask for cash back at grocery stores that accept ATM cards and don't charge usage fees. Of course, you'll have to purchase something first.

ATM cards with major credit card backing, known as "debit cards," are now a commonly acceptable form of payment in most stores and restaurants. Debit cards draw money directly from your checking account. Some stores enable you to receive "cash back" on your debit-card purchases as well.

SAFETY

GENERAL SAFETY SUGGESTIONS Although tourist areas are generally safe, they are not crime-free. You should always stay alert. Ask your hotel front-desk staff or call the Washington, D.C. Convention and Tourism Corporation (© **202/789-7000**) if you have specific questions about traveling to certain neighborhoods. Read chapter 4's "The Neighborhoods in Brief" section to get a better idea of where you might feel most comfortable.

Tips **Travel Tip**

Be sure to keep a copy of all your travel papers separate from your wallet or purse, and leave a copy with someone at home should you need it faxed in an emergency.

Avoid deserted areas, especially at night, and don't go into public parks at night unless there's a concert or similar occasion that will attract a crowd.

Avoid carrying valuables with you on the street, and don't display expensive cameras or electronic equipment. If you're using a map, consult it inconspicuously—or better yet, try to study it before you leave your room. In general, the more you look like a tourist, the more likely someone will try to take advantage of you. If you're walking, pay attention to who is near you as you walk. If you're attending a convention or event where you wear a nametag, remove it before venturing outside. Hold on to your purse, and place your billfold in an inside pocket. In theaters, restaurants, and other public places, keep your possessions in sight.

Remember also that hotels are open to the public, and in a large hotel, security may not be able to screen everyone entering. Always lock your room door.

Be careful crossing streets, especially in the downtown area, especially at rush hour. Though this may seem like obvious advice, it's worth a mention here, as there's been an alarming increase lately in the number of pedestrians being hit by cars and buses. Drivers in a hurry run red lights, turn corners too quickly, and so on, so be sure to take your time and check for oncoming traffic when crossing streets, and to use the crosswalks. If you're from Great Britain, you'll need to pay special attention, looking to your left, rather than to your right, on two-way streets.

DRIVING SAFETY Question your rental agency about personal safety and ask for a traveler-safety brochure when you pick up your car. Obtain written directions—or a map with the route clearly marked—from the agency showing how to get to your destination. And, if possible, arrive and depart during daylight hours.

If you drive off a highway and end up in a dodgy-looking neighborhood, leave the area as quickly as possible. If you have an accident, even on the highway, stay in your car with the doors locked until you assess the situation or until the police arrive. If you're bumped from behind on the street or are involved in a minor accident with no injuries, and the situation appears to be suspicious, motion to the other driver to follow you. Never get out of your car in such situations. Go directly to the nearest police precinct, well-lit service station, or 24-hour store. You may want to look into renting a cellphone on a short-term basis. (Many agencies now offer the option of renting a cellular phone for the duration of your car rental; check with the rental agent when you pick up the car.) One recommended wireless rental company is **InTouch USA** (© **800/872-7626;** www.intouchusa.com).

Park in well-lit and well-traveled areas whenever possible. Always keep your car doors locked, whether the vehicle is attended or unattended. Never leave any packages or valuables in sight. If someone attempts to rob you or steal your car, don't try to resist the thief/carjacker. Report the incident to the police department immediately by calling © **911.**

2 Getting to the United States

Most international flights to the Washington, D.C., area land at Washington Dulles International Airport, with Baltimore–Washington International Airport handling some, and Ronald Reagan Washington National Airport offering service to only one international carrier. Specific information follows.

The one international airline with scheduled flights into Ronald Reagan Washington National Airport is **Air Canada** (✆ 888/247-2262; www.aircanada.ca).

International airlines with scheduled flights into Baltimore–Washington International airport include **Air Canada** (see above), **British Airways** (✆ 0870/850 9850 in the U.K., or 800/247-9297; www.british-airways.com), and **Aer Lingus** (✆ 800/474-7424; www.aerlingus.com).

International airlines with scheduled flights into Washington Dulles International Airport include **Aeroflot** (✆ 888/340-6400; www.aeroflot.com), **Air Canada** (see above), **Air France** (✆ 800/321-4538; www.airfrance.com), **Alitalia** (✆ 800/223-5730; www.allitalia.com), **ANA Airways** (✆ 800/235-9262; www.svc.ana.co.jp), **British Airways** (see above), **KLM** (✆ 800/225-2525; www.klm.com), **Lufthansa** (✆ 800/645-3880; www.lufthansa.com), **Saudi Arabian Airlines** (✆ 800/472-8342; www.saudiairlines.com), and **Virgin Atlantic** (✆ 0870 380 2007 in the U.K., or 800/862-8621 in the U.S.; www.virgin-atlantic.com).

AIRLINE DISCOUNTS The smart traveler can find numerable ways to reduce the price of a plane ticket simply by taking time to shop around. For example, overseas visitors can take advantage of the APEX (Advance Purchase Excursion) reductions offered by all major U.S. and European carriers. For more money-saving airline advice, see "Getting Here," in chapter 2. For the best rates, compare fares and be flexible with the dates and times of travel.

3 Getting Around the United States

BY PLANE Some large airlines, Northwest, for example, offer travelers on their transatlantic or transpacific flights special discount tickets under the name **Visit USA ("VUSA"),** allowing mostly one-way travel from one U.S. destination to another at very low prices. These discount tickets are not on sale in the United States and must be purchased abroad in conjunction with your international ticket. This system is the best, easiest, and fastest way to see the United States at low cost. You should obtain information well in advance from your travel agent or the office of the airline concerned, since the conditions attached to these discount tickets can be changed without advance notice.

BY TRAIN International visitors (excluding Canada) can also buy a **USA Railpass.** Amtrak sells four kinds of passes, covering different geographic regions. All of the passes allow for 15 or 30 days of unlimited travel on Amtrak (✆ **800/USA-RAIL;** www.amtrak.com). The "Northeast," which includes Washington, D.C., in its coverage from Virginia to Montreal, Canada, also offers a 5-day ($145 off-peak, $170 peak) pass, along with its 15-day ($185–$205), and 30-day ($225–$240) passes. (These are 2004 prices.) USA Railpasses are available through many foreign travel agents. With a foreign passport, you can also buy passes at Amtrak stations and at travel agencies in the United States, including locations in San Francisco, Los Angeles, Chicago, New York, Miami, Boston, and Washington, D.C. Reservations are generally required and should be made for each part of your trip as early as possible.

FAST FACTS: For the International Traveler

Automobile Organizations Auto clubs will supply maps, suggested routes, guidebooks, accident and bail-bond insurance, and emergency road service. The **American Automobile Association (AAA)** is the major auto club (really an organization of regional auto clubs) in the United States. If you belong to an auto club in your home country, inquire about AAA reciprocity before you leave. You may be able to join AAA even if you're not a member of a reciprocal club; to inquire, call the MidAtlantic Region's AAA (© **800/763-9900;** www.aaa.com), which is also the number you would call in the Washington, D.C., area for AAA's emergency road service.

Business Hours Offices are usually open weekdays from 9am to 5pm. Banks are open Monday through Thursday from 9am to 3pm, 9am to 5pm on Friday, and sometimes Saturday mornings. Stores typically open between 9 and 10am and close between 5 and 6pm from Monday through Saturday. Stores in shopping complexes or malls tend to stay open late: until about 9pm on weekdays and weekends, and many malls and larger department stores are open on Sundays.

Currency & Currency Exchange See "Customs" and "Money" under "Preparing for Your Trip," earlier in this chapter.

Electricity Like Canada, the United States uses 110 to 120 volts AC (60 cycles), compared to 220 to 240 volts AC (50 cycles) in most of Europe, Australia, and New Zealand. If your small appliances use 220 to 240 volts, you'll need a 110-volt transformer and a plug adapter with two flat parallel pins to operate them here. Downward converters that change 220 to 240 volts to 110 to 120 volts are difficult to find in the United States, so bring one with you.

Embassies & Consulates All embassies are located in the nation's capital, Washington, D.C. On the Internet, you will find a complete listing, with links to each embassy, at www.embassy.org/embassies/index.html.

Here are several embassy addresses: **Australia,** 1601 Massachusetts Ave. NW (© 202/797-3000; www.austemb.org); **Canada,** 501 Pennsylvania Ave. NW (© 202/682-1740; www.canadianembassy.org); **France,** 4101 Reservoir Rd. NW (© 202/944-6000; www.ambafrance-us.org); **Germany,** 4645 Reservoir Rd. NW (© 202/298-4000; www.germany-info.org); **Ireland,** 2234 Massachusetts Ave. NW (© 202/462-3939; www.irelandemb.org); **Japan,** 2520 Massachusetts Ave. NW (© 202/238-6700; www.embjapan. org); the **Netherlands,** 4200 Linnean Ave. NW (© 202/244-5300; www. netherlands-embassy.org); **New Zealand,** 37 Observatory Circle NW (© 202/ 328-4800; www.nzemb.org); and the **United Kingdom,** 3100 Massachusetts Ave. NW (© 202/588-6500; www.britainusa.com/consular/embassy). You can also obtain the telephone numbers of other embassies and consulates by calling **information** in Washington, D.C. (© **411** within D.C. and its metropolitan area), or consult the phone book in your hotel room.

Emergencies Call ⓒ **911** to report a fire, call the police, or get an ambulance anywhere in the United States. This is a toll-free call. (No coins are required at public telephones.)

If you encounter serious problems, contact the **Traveler's Aid Society International** (ⓒ **202/546-1127**; www.travelersaid.org), a nationwide, nonprofit, social-service organization geared to helping travelers in difficult straits, from reuniting families separated while traveling, to providing food and/or shelter to people stranded without cash, to emotional counseling. Traveler's Aid operates help desks at Washington Dulles International Airport (ⓒ 703/572-8296), Ronald Reagan Washington National Airport (ⓒ 703/417-3975), and Union Station (ⓒ 202/371-1937).

Gasoline (Petrol) Petrol is known as gasoline (or simply "gas") in the United States, and petrol stations are known as both gas stations and service stations. Gasoline costs about half as much here as it does in Europe (about $2.10 per gallon at press time), and taxes are already included in the printed price. One U.S. gallon equals 3.8 liters or .85 imperial gallons.

Holidays Banks, government offices, post offices, and many stores, restaurants, and museums are closed on the following legal national holidays: January 1 (New Year's Day), the third Monday in January (Martin Luther King Jr. Day), January 20 (Inauguration Day), the third Monday in February (Presidents' Day, Washington's Birthday), the last Monday in May (Memorial Day), July 4 (Independence Day), the first Monday in September (Labor Day), the second Monday in October (Columbus Day), November 11 (Veterans' Day/Armistice Day), the fourth Thursday in November (Thanksgiving Day), and December 25 (Christmas). Also, the Tuesday following the first Monday in November is Election Day and is a federal government holiday in presidential-election years (held every 4 years, so this is an election year).

Language Aid **Meridian International Center** provides language assistance via a telephone bank of volunteers who, together, speak 40 different languages. Best of all, this service is free. Call the Center at ⓒ **202/939-5552** or 202/939-5554, Monday through Friday, 9am to 5pm. You may hear a recorded voice asking you to leave a message; you can hit "0" for the operator and explain why you are calling, or leave a message, and someone from Meridian will call you back with the assistance you need. Or you can go to Meridian's website at **www.meridian.org** and e-mail the center from there. In addition, most Washington museums, hotels restaurants, and other attractions boast multilingual staff. Many sights, like the White House, the Kennedy Center, the Library of Congress, and the Smithsonian Institution, offer free brochures in several languages; the Smithsonian also welcomes international visitors at its Information Center with a multilingual slide show and audio phones. The city's Washington Metropolitan Area Transit Authority offers translations on its website, www.wmata.com, of Metrorail system information—just click on the appropriate flag symbolizing the language you speak. You can also download information in many different languages from the website. Or, you can order Metro system maps in French, German, Japanese, Korean, or Spanish in advance by calling ⓒ **202/637-7000**. The Washington, D.C.

Convention and Tourism Corporation has maps, but no visitors guides, in French, Spanish, Portuguese, and German; call © **202/789-7000.**

Legal Aid If you are "pulled over" for a minor infraction (such as speeding), never attempt to pay the fine directly to a police officer; this could be construed as attempted bribery, a much more serious crime. Pay fines by mail, or directly into the hands of the clerk of the court. If accused of a more serious offense, say and do nothing before consulting a lawyer. Here the burden is on the state to prove a person's guilt beyond a reasonable doubt, and everyone has the right to remain silent, whether he or she is suspected of a crime or actually arrested. Once arrested, a person can make one telephone call to a party of his or her choice. Call your embassy or consulate.

Liquor Laws The legal age for purchase and consumption of alcoholic beverages is 21; proof of age is required and often requested at bars, nightclubs, and restaurants, so it's always a good idea to bring an ID when you go out. Liquor stores are closed on Sunday. District gourmet grocery stores, mom-and-pop grocery stores, and 7-11 convenience stores often sell beer and wine, even on Sunday.

Do not carry open containers of alcohol in your car or any public area that isn't zoned for alcohol consumption. The police can fine you on the spot. And nothing will ruin your trip faster than getting a citation for DUI (driving under the influence), so don't even think about driving while intoxicated.

Mail Generally found at intersections, mailboxes are blue with a red-and-white stripe and carry the inscription U.S. MAIL. If your mail is addressed to a U.S. destination, don't forget to add the five-digit postal code (or zip code), after the two-letter abbreviation of the state to which the mail is addressed. This is essential for prompt delivery.

At press time, domestic postage rates were 23¢ for a postcard and 37¢ for a letter. For international mail, a first-class letter of up to 1 ounce costs 80¢ (60¢ to Canada and to Mexico); a first-class postcard costs 70¢ (50¢ to Canada and Mexico); and a preprinted postal aerogramme costs 70¢.

Measurements See the chart on the inside front cover of this book for details on converting metric measurements to U.S. equivalents.

Taxes The United States has no value-added tax (VAT) or other indirect tax at the national level. Every state, county, and city has the right to levy its own local tax on all purchases, including hotel and restaurant checks, airline tickets, and so on.

The sales tax on merchandise is 5.75% in the District, 5% in Maryland, and 4.5% in Virginia. The tax on restaurant meals is 10% in the District, 5% in Maryland, and 4.5% in Virginia.

In the District, you pay 14.5% hotel tax. The hotel tax in Maryland varies by county from 5% to 8%. The hotel tax in Virginia also varies by county, averaging about 9.75%.

Telephone, Telegraph, Telex & Fax The telephone system in the United States is run by private corporations, so rates, especially for long-distance service and operator-assisted calls, can vary widely. Generally, hotel surcharges on long-distance and local calls are astronomical, so you're usually better off using a **public pay telephone,** which you'll find clearly marked in most public buildings and private establishments as well as on the street. Convenience grocery stores and gas stations always have them. Many convenience groceries and packaging services sell **prepaid calling cards** in denominations up to $50; these can be the least expensive way to call home. Many public phones at airports now accept American Express, MasterCard, and Visa credit cards. **Local calls** made from public pay phones in most locales cost either 25¢ or 35¢. Pay phones do not accept pennies, and few will take anything larger than a quarter. You may want to look into leasing a cellphone for the duration of your trip.

Most long-distance and international calls can be dialed directly from any phone. **For calls within the United States and to Canada,** dial 1 followed by the area code and the seven-digit number. **For other international calls,** dial 011 followed by the country code, city code, and the telephone number of the person you are calling.

Calls to area codes **800, 888,** and **877** are toll-free. However, calls to numbers in area codes **700** and **900** (chat lines, bulletin boards, "dating" services, and so on) can be very expensive—usually a charge of 95¢ to $3 or more per minute, and they sometimes have minimum charges that can run as high as $15 or more. You must dial 1 before dialing area codes 800, 888, 877, 700, and 900.

For **reversed-charge or collect calls,** and for person-to-person calls, dial 0 (zero, not the letter O) followed by the area code and number you want; an operator will then come on the line, and you should specify that you are calling collect, or person-to-person, or both. If your operator-assisted call is international, ask for the overseas operator.

For **local directory assistance (information),** dial 411; for long-distance information, dial 1, then the appropriate area code and 555-1212.

Telegraph and telex services are provided primarily by Western Union. You can bring your telegram into the nearest Western Union office (there are hundreds across the country) or dictate it over the phone (✆ **800/325-6000**). You can also telegraph money, or have it telegraphed to you, very quickly over the Western Union system, but this service can cost as much as 15% to 20% of the amount sent.

Most hotels have **fax machines** available for guest use (be sure to ask about the charge to use it). Many hotel rooms are even wired for guests' fax machines. A less expensive way to send and receive faxes may be at stores such as Mail Boxes Etc., a national chain of packing service shops. (Look in the Yellow Pages directory under "Packing Services.")

There are two kinds of telephone directories in the United States. The so-called **White Pages** list private households and business subscribers in alphabetical order. The inside front cover lists emergency numbers for police, fire, ambulance, the Coast Guard, poison-control center, crime-victims hot line, and so on. The first few pages will tell you how to make long-distance and international calls, complete with country codes and area codes. Government numbers are usually printed on blue paper within the White Pages. Printed on yellow paper, the so-called **Yellow Pages** list all local services, businesses, industries, and houses of worship according to activity with an index at the front or back. (Drugstores/pharmacies and restaurants are also listed by geographic location.) The Yellow Pages also include city plans or detailed area maps, postal zip codes, and public transportation routes.

Time The continental United States is divided into **four time zones:** Eastern Standard Time (EST), Central Standard Time (CST), Mountain Standard Time (MST), and Pacific Standard Time (PST). Alaska and Hawaii have their own zones. For example, noon in Washington, D.C. (EST), is 11am in Chicago (CST), 10am in Denver (MST), 9am in Los Angeles (PST), 8am in Anchorage (AST), and 7am in Honolulu (HST).

Daylight savings time is in effect from 1am on the first Sunday in April through 1am on the last Sunday in October, except in Arizona, Hawaii, part of Indiana, and Puerto Rico. Daylight saving time moves the clock 1 hour ahead of standard time. At 1am on the last Sunday in October, clocks are set back 1 hour. For the correct time, call ✆ 202/844-2525.

Tipping Tipping is so ingrained in the American way of life that the annual income tax of tip-earning service personnel is based on how much they should have received in light of their employers' gross revenues. Accordingly, they may have to pay tax on a tip you didn't actually give them.

Here are some rules of thumb:

In hotels, tip **bellhops** at least $1 per bag ($2–$3 if you have a lot of luggage) and tip the **chamber staff** $1 to $2 per day (more if you've left a disaster area for him or her to clean up, or if you're traveling with kids and/or pets). Tip the **doorman** or **concierge** only if he or she has provided you with some specific service (for example, calling a cab for you or obtaining difficult-to-get theater tickets). Tip the **valet-parking attendant** $1 every time you get your car.

In restaurants, bars, and nightclubs, tip **service staff** 15% to 20% of the check, tip **bartenders** 10% to 15%, tip **checkroom attendants** $1 per garment, and tip **valet-parking attendants** $1 per vehicle. Tipping is not expected in cafeterias and fast-food restaurants.

Tip **cab drivers** 15% of the fare.

As for other service personnel, tip **skycaps** at airports at least $1 per bag ($2–$3 if you have a lot of luggage) and tip **hairdressers** and **barbers** 15% to 20%.

Tipping ushers at movies and theaters, and gas-station attendants, is not expected.

Toilets You won't find public toilets or "restrooms" on the streets in most U.S. cities, but they can be found in hotel lobbies, bars, restaurants, museums, department stores, railway and bus stations, and service stations. Large hotels and fast-food restaurants are probably the best bet for good, clean facilities. If possible, avoid the toilets at parks and beaches, which tend to be dirty; some may be unsafe. Restaurants and bars in heavily visited areas may reserve their restrooms for patrons. Some establishments display a notice indicating this. You can ignore this sign or, better yet, avoid arguments by paying for a cup of coffee or a soft drink, which will qualify you as a patron.

4

Getting to Know Washington, D.C.

Washington, D.C., is a city of 572,000 residents, 67 square miles, more than 150 embassies, 60-plus museums, at least 100 hotels, roughly 2,000 restaurants, two major rivers, 3,700 cherry trees, scores of historic monuments and landmarks, and boundless beauty. And that's just to give you an idea. Read this chapter to learn how to navigate the city, before you get out there and go.

1 Orientation

On the one hand, Washington, D.C., is an easy place to get to know. It's a small city, where walking will actually get you places, but also with a model public transportation system that travels throughout D.C.'s neighborhoods, and to most tourist spots. A building height restriction creates a landscape in which the lost tourist can get his bearings from tall landmarks—the Capitol, the Washington Monument—that loom into view from different vantage points.

On the other hand, when you do need help, it's hard to find. The city lacks a single, large, comprehensive, and easy-to-find visitor's center. Signs to tourist attractions and Metro stations, even street signs, are often missing or frustratingly inadequate. In the wake of September 11, touring procedures at individual sightseeing attractions are constantly changing as new security precautions take effect, and these changes can be disorienting.

The District is always in the process of improving the situation, it seems. But in the meantime, you can turn to the following smaller visitors and information centers, helpful publications, and information phone lines.

VISITOR INFORMATION
INFORMATION CENTERS
At the Airports

If you are arriving by plane, you may as well think of your airport as a visitor information center, since all three Washington-area airports offer all sorts of visitor services. See chapter 2 for specific information about each airport's location, flights, designated place to rendezvous when someone is meeting you at the airport, and transportation options into town.

BALTIMORE–WASHINGTON INTERNATIONAL AIRPORT (BWI; ℂ **800/435-9294;** www.bwiairport.com; airport code: BWI). BWI services include two information desks (ℂ **800/435-9294** for information and paging) located on the upper level near the ticket counters and a Maryland Welcome Center (ℂ **410/691-2878**) at Pier C on the lower level near the international arrival gates; several locations for buying insurance and exchanging currency (ℂ **410/859-4466**); several ATMs (at the entrances to Piers C and D on the upper level and at the international gates on the lower level); plenty of public phones throughout the airport, many equipped with dataports and some with TDD services and voice-relay phones; many restrooms, restaurants, shops, and bars; a playroom for kids; and a small aviation museum.

Other useful phone numbers are lost and found (© **410/859-7387**), police (© **410/859-7040**), and parking lots and garage (© **410/468-6294**).

RONALD REAGAN WASHINGTON NATIONAL AIRPORT ("National;" © **703/417-8000;** www.mwaa.com/national; airport code: DCA). You'll arrive on the second level; ticket counters are on the third level, baggage claim and ground transportation on the first level. The second, or concourse, level is where you'll get your questions answered: At either end of the main concourse are both a general information desk and a customer service center (© **703/417-3200** or 703/417-3201), where you can exchange currency, purchase insurance, and recharge batteries. Some pay phones equipped with dataports are located throughout terminals B and C. An enclosed passageway connects the main concourse to "historic terminal A," where a **Traveler's Aid** desk operates (© **703/ 417-3972**). You should seek Traveler's Aid assistance if you need foreign-language or crisis help or to page someone; a second Traveler's Aid desk (© **703/ 417-3974**) operates on the baggage-claim level of the main concourse. You'll find ATMs located near the customer-service centers on the concourse level and next to the Traveler's Aid desk on the baggage-claim level. National Airport has more than 100 shops and restaurants.

Other useful phone numbers are lost and found (© **703/417-8560**), parking lots and garage (© **703/417-7275**), and police (© **703/417-8560**).

WASHINGTON DULLES INTERNATIONAL AIRPORT ("Dulles;" © **703/572-2700;** www.mwaa.com/Dulles; airport code: IAD). Dulles is the most chaotic airport to arrive at, with an ongoing major renovation and heavy traffic. Most flights arrive at midfield terminals, where you follow the crowd to the mobile lounges, which you ride for 7 minutes to the main terminal. As of late 2004, a pedestrian walkway between the main terminal and concourse B offers travelers an option over the mobile lounges. In time, the plan is for an underground rail system to replace these lounges altogether. The satellite terminals are actually rather attractive and offer decent shopping; the main terminal is another story. You can count on getting help from the Traveler's Aid folks (© **703/572-8296,** or 703/260-0175 for TDD service). Phone numbers for other help desks include © **703/572-2536** or 703/572-2537 for the international visitors information desk; © **703/572-2963** or 703/572-2969 for general service, foreign currency exchange, and insurance purchases. There are about 40 eateries, 35 retail shops, seven currency exchanges, and plentiful ATMs, restrooms, stamp vending machines, and phones.

Other useful numbers: police © **703/572-2952;** lost and found © **703/572-2954;** and parking lots and rates information © **703/572-4580.**

Baggage claim areas are at ground level in the main terminal.

At the Train Station

Historic **Union Station** (© **202/371-9441;** www.unionstationdc.com), 50 Massachusetts Ave. NE, offers visitors a pleasant introduction to the capital. The building is both an architectural beauty and a useful stopping place. Here you'll find a three-level marketplace of shops and restaurants, direct access to Metro service (you'll see signs directing you to the Metro's Red Line station even before you reach the main hall of Union Station), and, when you proceed through the grand arcade straight out through the station's front doors, a stellar view of the Capitol Building.

The central information desk is in the main hall at the front of the building. You'll find ATMs in the gate area, another near the side doors of the building (near the outdoor escalator to the Metro), and on the lower level, at the end of the Food Court. In the gate area is a Travelex Currency Exchange office (© **202/ 371-9220**) across from gate G, and a Traveler's Aid desk (© **202/371-1937**) near the McDonald's and gate L. A number of car-rental agencies operate lots here (see "Getting Around," later in this chapter for specific names and phone numbers). For security, lost and found, and other help or information, call the main number, which is © **202/371-9441.**

Around Town

The Washington, D.C., Visitor Information Center (© **866/324-7386** or 202/328-4748; www.dcvisit.com) is a small visitors center inside the immense Ronald Reagan International Trade Center Building, at 1300 Pennsylvania Ave. NW. To enter the federal building, you need to show a picture ID. The visitor center lies on the ground floor of the building, a little to your right as you enter from the Wilson Plaza, near the Federal Triangle Metro. From March 15 through Labor Day, the center is open Monday through Friday, 8:30am to 5:30pm and on Saturday from 9am to 4pm; from Labor Day to March 15, the center is open Monday through Friday 9am to 4:30pm.

Businesses have banded together in at least three D.C. neighborhoods to provide information, safety, and maintenance services for residents and visitors within their individual districts. Right now, the three are the **Downtown DC Business Improvement District (Downtown DC BID),** 1250 H St. NW (© **202/638-3232**; www.downtowndc.org), which covers the territory between Constitution and Massachusetts avenues, and between 16th and First streets; the **Golden Triangle Business Improvement District (Golden Triangle BID),** 1025 Connecticut Ave. NW (© **202/463-3400**; www.gtbid.com), an area bounded by 16th and 21st streets NW and Pennsylvania Avenue and Dupont Circle; and the **Capitol Hill Business Improvement District (Capitol Hill BID),** 20 Massachusetts Ave. NE (© **202/842-3333**; www.capitolhillbid.org), which covers the streets around the U.S. Capitol and Union Station. Look for the patrolling, red uniformed "SAMS" (Downtown DC BID's safety and maintenance workers) downtown, black and gold outfitted hospitality ambassadors in the golden triangle area, and blue and gold attired "STARS" near Capitol Hill, if you need directions, information, or any assistance at all. From March to October the Downtown DC BID also has special information kiosks stationed throughout the downtown.

National Park Service information kiosks are located inside the Jefferson, Lincoln, and FDR memorials and near the Vietnam Veterans, Korean War, and World War II memorials. Park rangers are on hand at the Washington Monument at its ticket booth at the bottom of the hill, at 15th Street NW and Constitution Avenue, inside the monument, and at the Ranger Station, located at the southwest point of the monument grounds, across from the Tidal Basin. © **202/619-7222**; www.nps.gov/ncro.

The **White House Visitor Center,** on the first floor of the Herbert Hoover Building, Department of Commerce, 1450 Pennsylvania Ave. NW (between 14th and 15th sts.; © **202/208-1631,** or 202/456-7041 for recorded information), is open daily (except for Christmas Day, Thanksgiving, and New Year's Day) from 7:30am to 4pm.

The **Smithsonian Information Center,** in the "Castle," 1000 Jefferson Dr. SW ((C) **202/357-2700,** or TTY 202/357-1729; www.si.edu), is open every day but Christmas from 9am to 5:30pm. Call for a free copy of the Smithsonian's "Planning Your Smithsonian Visit," which is full of valuable tips, or stop at the Castle for a copy. A calendar of Smithsonian exhibits and activities for the coming month appears the third Friday of each month in the *Washington Post*'s "Weekend" section.

See chapter 7 for more information about the White House Visitor and Smithsonian Information centers.

The **American Automobile Association (AAA)** has a large central office near the White House, at 701 15th St. NW, Washington, DC 20005-2111 ((C) **202/ 331-3000**). Hours are 9am to 5:30pm Monday through Friday.

PUBLICATIONS

At the airport, pick up a free copy of *Washington Flyer* magazine (www.fly2dc. com), which is handy as a planning tool (see chapter 2).

Washington has two daily newspapers: the *Washington Post* (www.washington post.com) and the *Washington Times* (www.washingtontimes.com). The Friday "Weekend" section of the *Post* is essential for finding out what's going on, recreation-wise. *City Paper,* published every Thursday and available free at downtown shops and restaurants, covers some of the same material but is a better guide to the club and art gallery scene.

Also on newsstands is *Washingtonian,* a monthly magazine with features, often about the "100 Best" this or that (doctors, restaurants, and so on) in Washington; the magazine also offers a calendar of events, restaurant reviews, and profiles of Washingtonians.

HELPFUL TELEPHONE NUMBERS & WEBSITES

- **National Park Service** ((C) **202/619-7222;** www.nps.gov/ncro). You reach a real person and not a recording when you call the phone number with questions about the monuments, the National Mall, national park lands, and activities taking place at these locations.
- **Dial-A-Park** ((C) **202/619-7275**). This is a recording of information regarding park-service events and attractions.
- **Dial-A-Museum** ((C) **202/357-2020;** www.si.edu). This recording offers the locations of the 14 Washington Smithsonian museums and their daily activities.

CITY LAYOUT

Pierre Charles L'Enfant designed Washington's great sweeping avenues, which are crossed by numbered and lettered streets. At key intersections he placed spacious circles. Although the circles are adorned with monuments, statuary, and fountains, L'Enfant also intended them to serve as strategic command posts to ward off invaders or marauding mobs. (After what had happened in Paris during the French Revolution—and remember, that was current history at the time—his design views were quite practical.)

The U.S. Capitol marks the center of the city, which is divided into quadrants: **northwest (NW), northeast (NE), southwest (SW),** and **southeast (SE).** Almost all the areas of interest to tourists are in the northwest. If you look at your map, you'll see that some addresses—for instance, the corner of G and 7th streets—appear in all quadrants. Hence you must observe the quadrant designation (NW, NE, SW, or SE) when looking for an address.

Washington, D.C., at a Glance

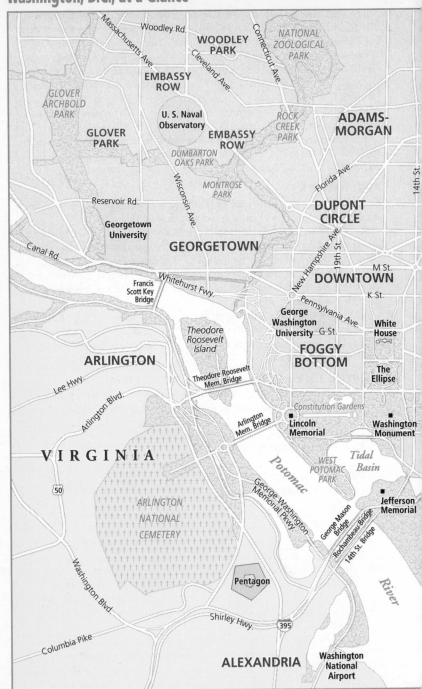

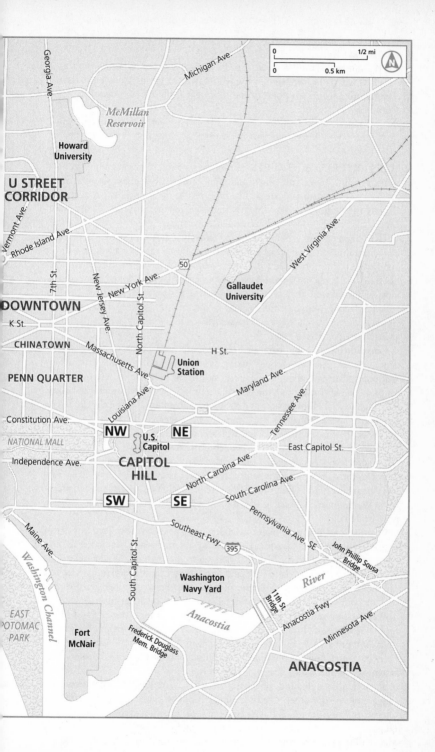

Impressions

If Washington should ever grow to be a great city, the outlook from the Capitol will be unsurpassed in the world. Now at sunset I seemed to look westward far into the heart of the continent from this commanding position.

—Ralph Waldo Emerson

MAIN ARTERIES & STREETS   From the Capitol, North Capitol Street and South Capitol Street run north and south, respectively. East Capitol Street divides the city north and south. The area west of the Capitol is not a street at all, but the National Mall, which is bounded on the north by Constitution Avenue and on the south by Independence Avenue.

The primary artery of Washington is **Pennsylvania Avenue,** scene of parades, inaugurations, and other splashy events. Pennsylvania runs northwest in a direct line between the Capitol and the White House—if it weren't for the Treasury Building, the president would have a clear view of the Capitol—before continuing on a northwest angle to Georgetown, where it becomes M Street.

Pennsylvania Avenue in front of the White House, between 15th and 17th streets NW remains closed to cars for security reasons, but has been re-made into an attractive pedestrian plaza.

Constitution Avenue, paralleled to the south most of the way by Independence Avenue, runs east-west, flanking the Capitol and the Mall. If you hear Washingtonians talk about the "House" side of the Hill, they're referring to the southern half of the Capitol, the side closest to Independence Avenue, and home to Congressional House offices and the House Chamber. Conversely, the Senate side is the northern half of the Capitol, where Senate offices and the Senate Chamber are found, closer to Constitution Avenue.

Washington's longest avenue, **Massachusetts Avenue,** runs parallel to Pennsylvania (a few avenues north). Along the way, you'll find Union Station and then Dupont Circle, which is central to the area known as Embassy Row. Farther out are the Naval Observatory (the vice president's residence is on the premises), Washington National Cathedral, American University, and, eventually, Maryland.

Connecticut Avenue, which runs more directly north (the other avenues run southeast to northwest), starts at Lafayette Square, intersects Dupont Circle, and eventually takes you to the National Zoo, on to the charming residential neighborhood known as Cleveland Park, and into Chevy Chase, Maryland, where you can pick up the Beltway to head out of town. Downtown Connecticut Avenue, with its posh shops and clusters of restaurants, is a good street to stroll.

Wisconsin Avenue originates in Georgetown; its intersection with M Street forms Georgetown's hub. Antiques shops, trendy boutiques, nightclubs, restaurants, and pubs all vie for attention. Wisconsin Avenue basically parallels Connecticut Avenue; one of the few irritating things about the city's transportation system is that the Metro does not connect these two major arteries in the heart of the city. (Buses do, and, of course, you can always walk or take a taxi from one avenue to the other. Overwhelmingly popular is the Georgetown Metro Connection shuttle, which travels between Georgetown and the Foggy Bottom, Dupont Circle, and Rosslyn Metro stations, and costs only $1, or 35¢ with a Metrorail transfer.) Metrorail's first stop on Wisconsin Avenue is in Tenleytown, a residential area. Follow the avenue north, and you land in the affluent Maryland cities of Chevy Chase and Bethesda.

FINDING AN ADDRESS   Once you understand the city's layout, it's easy to find your way around. As you read this, have a map handy.

Each of the four corners of the District of Columbia is exactly the same distance from the Capitol dome. The White House and most government buildings and important monuments are west of the Capitol (in the northwest and southwest quadrants), as are major hotels and tourist facilities.

Numbered streets run north-south, beginning on either side of the Capitol with First Street. Lettered streets run east-west and are named alphabetically, beginning with A Street. (Don't look for a B, a J, an X, a Y, or a Z Street, however.) After W Street, street names of two syllables continue in alphabetical order, followed by street names of three syllables; the more syllables in a name, the farther the street is from the Capitol.

Avenues, named for U.S. states, run at angles across the grid pattern and often intersect at traffic circles. For example, New Hampshire, Connecticut, and Massachusetts avenues intersect at Dupont Circle.

With this in mind, you can easily find an address. On lettered streets, the address tells you exactly where to go. For instance, 1776 K St. NW is between 17th and 18th streets (the first two digits of 1776 tell you that) in the northwest quadrant (NW). *Note:* I Street is often written as "Eye" Street to prevent confusion with 1st Street.

To find an address on numbered streets, you'll probably have to use your fingers. For instance, 623 8th St. SE is between F and G streets (the 6th and 7th letters of the alphabet; the first digit of 623 tells you that) in the southeast quadrant (SE). One thing to remember: You count B as the second letter of the alphabet even though no B Street exists today (Constitution and Independence Aves. were the original B sts.), but since there's no J Street, K becomes the 10th letter, L the 11th, and so on.

THE NEIGHBORHOODS IN BRIEF

Capitol Hill Everyone's heard of "the Hill," the area crowned by the Capitol. When people speak of Capitol Hill, they refer to a large section of town, extending from the western side of the Capitol to the D.C. Armory going east, bounded by H Street to the north and the Southwest Freeway to the south. It contains not only the chief symbol of the nation's capital, but the Supreme Court building, the Library of Congress, the Folger Shakespeare Library, Union Station, and the U.S. Botanic Garden. Much of it is a quiet residential neighborhood of tree-lined streets and Victorian homes. There are a number of restaurants in the vicinity and a smattering of hotels, mostly close to Union Station. Keep to the well-lit, well-traveled streets at night, and don't walk alone, since crime occurs more frequently in this neighborhood than in some other parts of town.

The Mall This lovely, tree-lined stretch of open space between Constitution and Independence avenues, extending for 2½ miles from the Capitol to the Lincoln Memorial, is the hub of tourist attractions. It includes most of the Smithsonian Institution museums and many other visitor attractions. The 300-foot-wide Mall is used by tourists as well as natives —joggers, food vendors, kite-flyers, and picnickers among them. As you can imagine, hotels and restaurants are located on the periphery.

Downtown The area roughly between 7th and 22nd streets NW going east to west, and P Street and Pennsylvania Avenue going north to south, is a mix of the Federal Triangle's government office buildings, K Street (Lawyer's Row), Connecticut Avenue restaurants and shopping, historic hotels, the city's poshest small hotels, **Chinatown,** and the White House. You'll also find the historic **Penn Quarter,** a part of downtown that continues to flourish, since the opening of the MCI Center, trendy restaurants, boutique hotels, and art galleries. (Despite a continuing marketing attempt by the city to promote the name "Penn Quarter," no one I know actually refers to this neighborhood by that title—we tend to say "near the MCI Center" instead, and everyone knows where the MCI Center is.) The total downtown area takes in so many blocks and attractions that I've divided discussions of accommodations (chapter 5) and dining (chapter 6) into two sections: "Downtown, 16th Street NW and West," and "Downtown, East of 16th Street NW." 16th Street and the White House form a natural point of separation.

U Street Corridor D.C.'s avant-garde nightlife neighborhood between 12th and 15th streets NW continues to rise from the ashes of nightclubs and theaters frequented decades ago by African Americans. At two renovated establishments, the Lincoln Theater and the Bohemian Caverns jazz club, where Duke Ellington, Louis Armstrong, and Cab Calloway once performed, patrons today can enjoy performances by leading artists. The corridor offers many nightclubs and several restaurants (see chapter 9 for details). Go here to party, not to sleep—there are no hotels along this stretch.

Adams-Morgan This ever-trendy, multiethnic neighborhood is about the size of a postage stamp, though crammed with boutiques, clubs, and restaurants. Everything is located on either 18th Street NW or Columbia Road NW. You won't find any hotels here, although there are several nearby in the Dupont Circle and Woodley Park neighborhoods (see below). Parking during the day is okay, but forget it at night (although a parking garage did open recently, on 18th St., which helps things a little). But you can easily walk (be alert—the neighborhood is edgy) to Adams-Morgan from the Dupont Circle or Woodley Park Metro stops, or taxi here. Weekend nightlife rivals that of Georgetown and Dupont Circle.

Dupont Circle My favorite part of town, Dupont Circle is fun day or night. It takes its name from the traffic circle minipark, where Massachusetts, New Hampshire, and Connecticut avenues collide. Washington's famous **Embassy Row** centers on Dupont Circle, and refers to the parade of grand embassy mansions lining Massachusetts Avenue and its side streets. The streets extending out from the circle are lively with all-night bookstores, really good restaurants, wonderful art galleries and art museums, nightspots, movie theaters, and Washingtonians at their loosest. It is also the hub of D.C.'s gay community. There are plenty of hotels.

Foggy Bottom The area west of the White House and southeast of Georgetown, Foggy Bottom was Washington's early industrial center. Its name comes from the foul fumes emitted in those days by a coal depot and gasworks, but its original name, Funkstown (for owner Jacob Funk), is perhaps even worse. There's nothing foul (and not much funky) about the area today. This is a low-key part of town, enlivened by the presence of the Kennedy Center, George Washington University, small and medium-size hotels, and a mix of restaurants on the main drag, Pennsylvania Avenue, and residential side streets.

Georgetown This historic community dates from Colonial times. It was a thriving tobacco port long before the District of Columbia was formed, and one of its attractions, the Old Stone House, dates from pre-Revolutionary days. Georgetown action centers on M Street and Wisconsin Avenue NW, where you'll find the luxury Four Seasons hotel and less expensive digs, numerous boutiques (see chapter 8 for details), chic restaurants, and popular pubs (lots of nightlife here). But get off the main drags and see the quiet, tree-lined streets of restored Colonial row houses;

stroll through the beautiful gardens of Dumbarton Oaks; and check out the C&O Canal. Georgetown is also home to Georgetown University. Note that the neighborhood gets pretty raucous on the weekends, which won't appeal to everyone.

Glover Park Mostly a residential neighborhood, this section of town, just above Georgetown and just south of the Washington National Cathedral, is worth mentioning because of the increasing number of good restaurants and bars opening along its main stretch, Wisconsin Avenue NW. Glover Park sits between the campuses of Georgetown and American Universities, so there's a large student presence here.

Woodley Park Home to Washington's largest hotel (the Marriott Wardman Park), Woodley Park boasts the National Zoo, many good restaurants, and some antiques stores. Washingtonians are used to seeing conventioneers wandering the neighborhood's pretty residential streets with their name tags still on.

2 Getting Around

Washington is one of the easiest U.S. cities to navigate, thanks to its comprehensive public transportation system of trains and buses. Ours is the second largest rail transit network and the fifth largest bus network in the country. But because Washington is of manageable size and marvelous beauty, you may find yourself shunning transportation and choosing to walk.

BY METRORAIL

If you travel by Metrorail during rush hour (Mon–Fri 5:30–9:30am and 3–7pm), you may not be so smitten with the system, since delays can be frequent, lines at fare-card machines long, trains overcrowded, and Washingtonians at their rudest. An increasing ridership is overloading the system, maintenance problems are cropping up, and the **Washington Metropolitan Area Transit Authority** (**WMATA;** www.wmata.com) is struggling just to keep pace, much less prevent future crises. Among the solutions are the addition of new trains and the installation of passenger information display boxes on station platforms reporting the number of minutes before the arrival of the next train and any delays or irregularities.

Though it's true that service has deteriorated, Washingtonians were spoiled to begin with. Stations are cool, clean, and attractive. Cars are air-conditioned and

Major Metro Stops

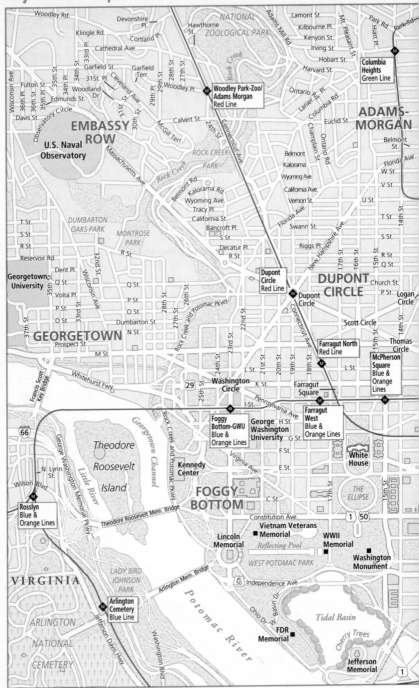

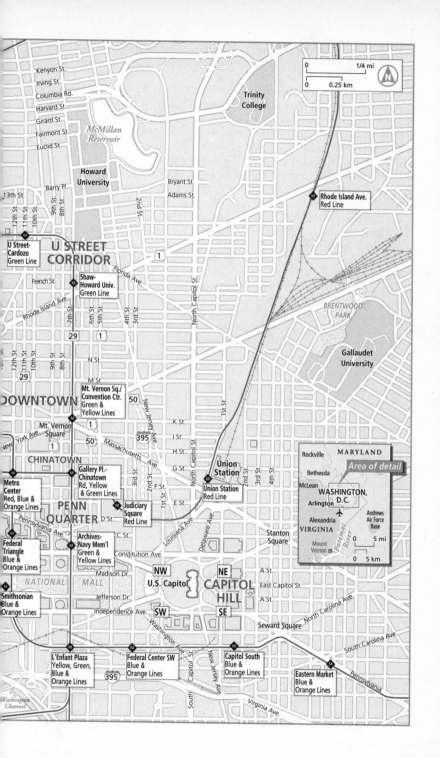

comfortable, fitted with upholstered seats; rides are quiet. You can expect to get a seat during off-peak hours (basically weekdays 10am–3pm, weeknights after 7pm, and all day weekends).

Metrorail's system of 86 stations and 106 miles of track includes locations at or near almost every sightseeing attraction and extends to suburban Maryland and northern Virginia. There are five lines in operation—Red, Blue, Orange, Yellow, and Green. The lines connect at several points, making transfers easy. All but Yellow and Green Line trains stop at Metro Center; all except Red Line trains stop at L'Enfant Plaza; all but Blue and Orange Line trains stop at Gallery Place/Chinatown. The year 2005 sees the extension of the Blue line further into Prince George's County, MD, and the opening of a new station on New York Avenue, between the Union Station and Rhode Island Avenue stops on the Red line. See the color map on the inside cover of this book.

Metro stations are indicated by discreet brown columns bearing the station's name and topped by the letter M. Below the M is a colored stripe or stripes indicating the line or lines that stop there. When entering a Metro station for the first time, go to the kiosk and ask the station manager for a free *Metro System Pocket Guide.* It contains a map of the system, explains how it works, and lists the closest Metro stops to points of interest. The station manager can also answer questions about routing or purchase of fare cards. You can also download a copy of the pocket guide and obtain loads of information, including schedules, from Metro's website, mentioned above, www.wmata.com.

To enter or exit a Metro station, you need a computerized **fare card,** available at vending machines near the entrance. The machines take nickels, dimes, quarters, and bills from $1 to $20; they can return up to $4.95 in change (coins only). The vending machines labeled "Passes/Farecards" accept both cash and credit cards. At this time, the minimum fare to enter the system is $1.20, which pays for rides to and from any point within 7 miles of boarding during nonpeak hours; during peak hours (Mon–Fri 5:30–9:30am and 3–7pm), $1.20 takes you only 3 miles. The maximum you will pay to the furthest destination is $3.60. Metro Authority was contemplating a fare hike as this book was being researched, so it's likely that fares have increased by at least 15¢ since then. If you plan to take several Metrorail trips during your stay, put more value on the fare-card to avoid having to purchase a new card each time you ride. Up to two children ages 4 and under can ride free with a paying passenger. Seniors (65 and older) and people with disabilities (with valid proof) ride Metrorail and Metrobus for a reduced fare.

Discount passes, called "One-Day Rail passes," cost $6 per person and allow you unlimited passage for the day, after 9:30am weekdays, and all day on Saturday, Sunday, and holidays. You can buy them at most stations; at WMATA headquarters, 600 5th St. NW (© **202/637-7000;** www.wmata.com), and at its sales

---

Tips **Metro Etiquette 101**

To avoid risking the ire of commuters, be sure to follow these guidelines: Stand to the right on the escalator so that people in a hurry can get past you on the left; and when you reach the train level, don't puddle at the bottom of the escalator blocking the path of those coming behind you, but move down the platform. Eating, drinking, and smoking are strictly prohibited on the Metro and in stations.

Tips **Getting to Georgetown**

Metrorail doesn't go to Georgetown but a special shuttle bus, called the Georgetown Metro Connection, links three Metro stations, Rosslyn, Foggy Bottom, and Dupont Circle, to Georgetown. The shuttle travels between the three stations and Georgetown every 10 minutes from 7am to midnight Monday through Thursday, 7am to 2am Friday, 8am to 2am Saturday, and 8am to midnight Sunday. One-way fares cost $1, or 35¢ with a Metrorail transfer.

---

office at Metro Center, 12th and G streets NW; or at retail stores, like Giant or Safeway grocery stores. Other passes are available—check out the website or call the main number for further information.

When you insert your card in the entrance gate, the time and location are recorded on its magnetic tape, and your card is returned. Don't forget to snatch it up and keep it handy; *you have to reinsert your fare card in the exit gate at your destination,* where the fare will automatically be deducted. The card will be returned if there's any value left on it. If you arrive at a destination and your fare card doesn't have enough value, add what's necessary at the Exitfare machines near the exit gate.

Metrorail opens at 5:30am weekdays and 7am Saturday and Sunday, operating until midnight Sunday through Thursday, and until 3am Friday and Saturday. Call ✆ **202/637-7000,** or visit www.wmata.com, for holiday hours and for information on Metro routes.

BY BUS

The **Metrobus** system encompasses 12,490 stops on its 1,489-square-mile route (it operates on all major D.C. arteries as well as in the Virginia and Maryland suburbs). You'll know the stops by their red, white, and blue signs. However, the signs tell you only what buses pull into a given stop, not where they go. Furthermore, the bus schedules posted at bus stops are often way out of date, so don't rely on them. Instead, for routing information, call ✆ **202/637-7000.** Calls are taken Monday through Thursday from 6am to 10:30pm, Friday 6am to 11:30pm, Saturday 7am to 11:30pm, and Sunday 7am to 10:30pm. This is the same number you call to request a free map and time schedule, information about parking in Metrobus fringe lots, and for locations and hours of the places where you can purchase bus tokens.

Base fare in the District is $1.20; bus transfers are free and valid for 2 hours from boarding. There may be additional charges for travel into the Maryland and Virginia suburbs. Bus drivers are not equipped to make change, so be sure to carry exact change or tokens. If you'll be in Washington for a while and plan to use the buses a lot, consider buying a 1-week pass ($11), also available at the Metro Center station and other outlets. Buy tokens at the Metro Center Sales Office, at 12th and G streets, the 12th Street entrance.

Most buses operate daily almost around the clock. Service is quite frequent on weekdays, especially during peak hours. On weekends and late at night, service is less frequent.

Up to two children 4 and under ride free with a paying passenger on Metrobus, and there are reduced fares for seniors (✆ **202/637-7000**) and people with disabilities (✆ **202/962-1245** or 202/962-1100; see "Travelers with

---

Tips **Transit Tip**

If you're on the subway and plan to continue your travel via Metrobus, pick up a free transfer at the station when you enter the system (not your destination station). Transfer machines are on the mezzanine levels of most stations. With the transfer, you can subtract 85¢ from your bus fare, which means you'll probably pay 35¢, when you board a bus upon exiting your Metrorail station. There are no bus-to-subway transfers.

Disabilities," in chapter 2 for transit information for travelers with disabilities). If you should leave something on a bus, a train, or in a station, call Lost and Found at © **202/962-1195.**

BY CAR

More than half of all visitors to the District arrive by car; but once you get here, my advice is to park your car and either walk or use Metrorail for getting around. If you must drive, be aware that traffic is always thick during the week, parking spaces are often hard to find, and parking lots are ruinously expensive.

Watch out for **traffic circles.** The law states that traffic already in the circle has the right of way. No one pays any attention to this rule, however, which can be frightening (cars zoom into the circle without a glance at the cars already there). The other thing you will notice is that while some circles are easy to figure out (Dupont Circle, for example), others are nerve-wrackingly confusing (Thomas Circle, where 14th St. NW, Vermont Ave. NW, and Massachusetts Ave. NW come together, is to be avoided at all costs).

Sections of certain streets in Washington become **one-way** during rush hour: Rock Creek Parkway, Canal Road, and 17th Street NW are three examples. Other streets during rush hour change the direction of some of their traffic lanes: Connecticut Avenue NW is the main one. In the morning, traffic in four of its six lanes travels south to downtown, and in late afternoon/early evening, downtown traffic in four of its six lanes heads north; between the hours of 9am and 3:30pm, traffic in either direction keeps to the normally correct side of the yellow line. Lit-up traffic signs alert you to what's going on, but pay attention. Unless a sign is posted prohibiting it, a right-on-red law is in effect.

To keep up with street closings and construction information, grab the day's *Washington Post,* pull out the Metro section, and turn to page three, where the column "Metro, In Brief" tells you about potential traffic and routing problems in the District and suburban Maryland and Virginia. The paper also publishes a regular column in the Metro section called "Dr. Gridlock," which addresses traffic questions. Another helpful source is a page on the D.C. government's website, http://dc.gov/closures, which identifies major street closures and construction in the city.

CAR RENTALS

Outside of the city, you'll want a car to get to most attractions in Virginia and Maryland. All the major car-rental companies are represented here, including Alamo, Avis, Budget, Dollar, Enterprise, Hertz, National, and Thrifty. Consult appendix B at the back of this book for each rental company's toll-free number and website, and refer to the information about area airports at the beginning of this chapter for phone numbers for each company's airport locations. Within the District, car-rental locations include **Avis,** 1722 M St. NW (© 202/467-6585) and 4400 Connecticut Ave. NW (© 202/686-5149); **Budget,** Union Station (© 202/289-5374); **Enterprise,** 3307 M St. NW (© 202/338-0015); **Hertz,** 901 11th St. NW (© 202/628-6174); **National** and **Alamo,** Union Station (same location and phone number: © 202/842-7454); and **Thrifty,** inside the MCI Center, at 7th and G streets NW (© 202/371-0485).

Car-rental rates can vary even more than airfares. Taking the time to shop around and asking a few key questions could save you hundreds of dollars:

- Are weekend rates lower than weekday rates? Ask if the rate is the same for pickup Friday morning, for instance, as it is for Thursday night.
- Is the weekly rate cheaper than the daily rate? Even if you need the car for only 4 days, it may be cheaper to keep it for 5.
- Does the agency assess a drop-off charge if you don't return the car to the same location where you picked it up? Is it cheaper to pick up the car at the airport or at a downtown location?
- Are special promotional rates available? If you see an advertised price in your local newspaper, be sure to ask for that specific rate; otherwise, you may be charged the standard cost. Terms change constantly.
- Are discounts available for members of AARP, AAA, frequent-flier programs, or trade unions?
- How much tax will be added to the rental bill? Local tax? State use tax? Local taxes and surcharges can vary from location to location, even within the same car company, which can add quite a bit to your costs.
- What is the cost of adding an additional driver's name to the contract?
- How many free miles are included in the price? Free mileage is often negotiable, depending on the length of your rental.

Some companies offer "refueling packages," in which you pay for an entire tank of gas up front. The price is usually fairly competitive with local gas prices, but you don't get credit for any gas remaining in the tank. If a stop at a gas station on the way to the airport will make you miss your plane, then by all means take advantage of the fuel purchase option. Otherwise, skip it.

As for **insurance,** see chapter 2.

BY TAXI

At the time of this writing, District cabs continue to operate on a zone system instead of using meters, and the cabbies hope to keep it that way. By law, basic rates are posted in each cab. If you take a trip from one point to another within the same zone, you pay just $5.50 (during non-rush hour) regardless of the distance traveled. So it would cost you $5.50 to travel a few blocks from the U.S. Capitol to the National Museum of American History, but the same $5.50 could take you from the Capitol all the way to Dupont Circle. They're both in Zone 1, as are most other tourist attractions: the White House, most of the Smithsonian, the Washington Monument, the FBI, the National Archives, the Supreme Court, the Library of Congress, the Bureau of Engraving and Printing, the Old Post Office, and Ford's Theatre. If your trip takes you into a second zone, the price is $7.60, $9.50 for a third zone, $11.40 for a fourth, and so on. These rates are based on the assumption that you are hailing a cab. If you telephone for a cab, you will be charged an additional $2. During rush hour, between 7 and 9:30am and 4 and 6:30pm weekdays, you pay a surcharge of $1 per trip, plus a surcharge of $1 when you telephone for a cab, which brings the telephone surcharge to $3.

Other charges might apply, as well: There's a $1 charge for each additional passenger after the first, so a $5.50 Zone 1 fare can become $8.50 for a family of four (though one child under 5 can ride free). Surcharges are also added for luggage (from 50¢ to $2 per piece, depending on size). Try **Diamond Cab Company** (☎ 202/387-6200) or **Yellow Cab** (☎ 202/544-1212).

The zone system is not used when your destination is an out-of-District address (such as an airport); in that case, the fare is based on mileage—$2.65 for the first half-mile or part thereof and 80¢ for each additional half-mile or part. You can call ☎ 202/331-1671 to find out the rate between any point in D.C. and an address in Virginia or Maryland. Call ☎ 202/645-6018 to inquire about fares within the District. For more information about D.C. taxicabs than you could ever even guess was available, check out the D.C. Taxicab Commission's website, www.dctaxi.dc.gov.

It's generally easy to hail a taxi. Unique to the city is the practice of allowing drivers to pick up as many passengers as they can comfortably fit, so expect to share (unrelated parties pay the same as they would if they were not sharing). To register a complaint, note the cab driver's name and cab number and file a written complaint either by fax (☎ 202/889-3604) or mail (Commendations/ Complaints, District of Columbia Taxicab Commission, 2041 Martin Luther King Jr. Ave. SE, Room 204, Washington, DC 20020).

FAST FACTS: Washington, D.C.

American Express There's an American Express Travel Service office at 1150 Connecticut Ave. NW (☎ 202/457-1300).

Area Codes Within the District of Columbia, it's 202. In suburban Virginia, it's 703. In suburban Maryland, it's 301. You must use the area code when dialing any number, even local calls within the District or to nearby Maryland or Virginia suburbs.

Business Hours See "Fast Facts: For the International Traveler," chapter 3.

Car Rentals See "Getting Around," earlier in this chapter.

Climate See "When to Go," in chapter 2.

Congresspersons To locate a senator or congressional representative, call the Capitol switchboard (☎ 202/225-3121). Point your Web browser to www.senate.gov and www.house.gov to contact individual senators and congressional representatives by e-mail, find out what bills are being worked on, the calendar for the day, and more.

Driving Rules See "Getting Around," earlier in this chapter.

Drugstores **CVS,** Washington's major drugstore chain (with more than 40 stores), has two convenient 24-hour locations: 14th Street and Thomas Circle NW, at 1199 Vermont Ave. NW (☎ 202/628-0720), and at Dupont Circle (☎ 202/785-1466), both with round-the-clock pharmacies. Check your phone book for other convenient locations.

Emergencies In any emergency, call ☎ 911.

Hospitals If you don't require immediate ambulance transportation but still need emergency-room treatment, call one of the following hospitals (and be sure to get directions): **Children's Hospital National Medical Center,** 111 Michigan Ave. NW (☎ 202/884-5000); **George Washington**

University Hospital, 23rd St. NW at Washington Circle (© 202/715-4000); **Georgetown University Medical Center,** 3800 Reservoir Rd. NW (© 202/784-2000); or **Howard University Hospital,** 2041 Georgia Ave. NW (© 202/865-6100).

Hot Lines To reach a 24-hour poison-control hot line, call © 800/222-1222; to reach a 24-hour crisis line, call © 202/561-7000.

Internet Access Your hotel should be your first stop, since many hotels now offer free Internet access. Away from the hotel, try **Cyberstop Cafe,** 1513 17th St. NW (© 202/234-2470; www.cyberstopcafe.com), where you can get a bite to eat while you surf one of 11 computers for $6.99 per half hour, $8.99 per hour; the cafe is open from 7am to midnight Monday through Friday, 8am to midnight Saturday and Sunday. In Dupont Circle, the bookstore **Kramerbooks and Afterwords,** 1517 Connecticut Ave. NW (© 202/387-1400), has one computer available for free Internet access, 15-minute limit.

Legal Aid See "Fast Facts: For the International Traveler," in chapter 3.

Liquor Laws See "Fast Facts: For the International Traveler," in chapter 3.

Maps Free city maps are often available at hotels and throughout town at tourist attractions. You can also contact the **Washington, D.C. Convention and Tourism Corporation,** 901 7th St. NW, 4th floor, Washington, DC 20001 (© 202/789-7000).

Newspapers & Magazines See "Visitor Information," earlier in this chapter.

Police In an emergency, dial © 911. For a nonemergency, call © 202/727-1010.

Safety See "Health & Safety," in chapter 2.

Taxes See "Fast Facts: For the International Traveler," in chapter 3.

Time See "Fast Facts: For the International Traveler," in chapter 3.

Weather Call © 202/936-1212.

5

Where to Stay

Washington, D.C., has just about every type of accommodation you can imagine. We have really big hotels, like the 1,349-room Wardman Park Marriott, centered on 16 acres in Woodley Park. And we have elegant little inns, like the 18-room Woodley Park Guest House, which, incidentally, lies just across the street from the Wardman Park.

Boutique hotels are plentiful and varied, from the everything-is-red Hotel Rouge, to the celestial-themed Topaz Hotel. Even more abundant are chain hotels, with Marriott brands at the forefront of a pack that includes Hiltons, Hyatts, and Holiday Inns.

We've got new—the Mandarin Oriental, the Residence Inn Capitol; and we've got historic—the Willard Hotel and the Hotel Washington. Our hotels range from the ultra-expensive Ritz-Carltons and Four Seasons, where you can expect to pay upwards of $400 per night, to the inexpensive Jurys Normandy Hotel or Kalorama Guest House, where it's possible to pay less than $100 for a room.

All together, there are more than 100 in the city of Washington. So the first thing you should do is figure out your preferred neighborhood. Most of Washington's hotels lie downtown or near Dupont Circle, with a handful scattered in Georgetown, on Capitol Hill, and northward on Connecticut Avenue. Each of these communities has a distinct personality, which you should consider in choosing a location in which to base yourself. See "The Neighborhoods in Brief" section of chapter 4 and peruse the following descriptions to help you decide which location best suits you.

If proximity to the capital's major attractions is most important to you, consider hotels near Capitol Hill and the National Mall. Convenient for sightseeing and in the thick of things during the day, these hotels may feel isolated at night and on weekends, when the Hill staff and office workers go home. With the exception of Capitol Hill Suites, the hotels are not located near residential areas, and restaurants and shops are few.

To take the pulse of the city as it goes about its business, stay in a downtown hotel. This is also where you should bunk if you want to be able to walk to good restaurants, bars, and nightclubs. Divided into two sections here, between 7th and 16th streets NW ("Downtown, East of 16th St. NW") and between 16th and 22nd streets NW ("Downtown, 16th St. NW & West"), Washington's downtown is bustling day and night during the week; it's quieter on weekends, but still fairly lively. Hotels in the downtown segment east of 16th Street are close to theaters; properties located on or near Pennsylvania Avenue, like the Willard and the Hotel Washington, are within walking distance of Smithsonian museums and the White House. Downtown hotels west of 16th Street are also within a stroll of the White House, as well as some smaller museums, like National Geographic, Decatur House, and the Renwick and Corcoran galleries.

If you prefer the feel of being in a residential neighborhood, look to hotels in the Dupont Circle and Wood-ley Park areas. For a taste of campus life, you might choose lodging in Foggy Bottom; the accommodations near Pennsylvania Avenue and Washington Circle border George Washington University's widening campus. And if you're a serious shopper, Georgetown should be your top choice, with Dupont Circle as your second pick.

Within each neighborhood heading, this chapter further organizes hotels by rate categories, based on their lowest high-season rates for double rooms: Very Expensive (from about $250 and up), Expensive (from about $185), Moderate (from about $120), and Inexpensive (anything under $100). But these categories are intended as a general guideline only—rates can rise and fall dramatically, depending on how busy the hotel is. It's often possible to obtain a special package or a better rate.

SAVING ON YOUR HOTEL ROOM

The **rack rate** is the maximum rate that a hotel charges for a room. Hardly anybody pays this price, however. Every hotel usually offers ways for customers to pay a lower rate than the published rate. In each hotel write-up, I mention tips for obtaining the best rate as specified by the hotel. These general guidelines also can help lower the cost of your room:

- **Ask about special rates or other discounts.** Always ask whether a room less expensive than the first one quoted is available, or whether any special rates apply to you. You may qualify for corporate, government, student, military, senior, or other discounts, and these can be substantial. Mention membership in AAA, AARP, frequent-flier programs, or trade unions, which may entitle you to special deals as well. Find out the hotel policy on children—do kids stay free in the room or is there a special rate?
- **Dial direct.** When booking a room in a chain hotel, you'll often get a better deal by calling the individual hotel's reservation desk rather than the chain's main number.
- **Book online.** Many hotels offer Internet-only discounts, or supply rooms to Priceline, Travelocity, or Expedia at rates much lower than the ones you can get through the hotel itself. (See chapter 2, "Surfing for Hotels.")
- **Remember the law of supply and demand.** Washington's downtown hotels are busiest during the week, so you can expect the best discounts over the weekend. Most hotels have high-season and low-season prices, and booking the day after high season ends can mean good deals.
- **Look into group or long-stay discounts.** If you come as part of a large group, you should be able to negotiate a bargain rate, since the hotel can then guarantee occupancy in a number of rooms. Likewise, if you're planning a long stay (at least 5 days), you might qualify for a discount. As a general rule, expect 1 night free after a 7-night stay.
- **Avoid excess charges and hidden costs.** D.C. hotels charge unbelievable rates for overnight parking—often more than $25 a night. So if you can avoid driving to D.C., you can save yourself parking expenses, at least. Use your own cellphone, pay phones, or prepaid phone cards instead of dialing direct from hotel phones, which usually have exorbitant rates, as do the room's minibar offerings: Most hotels charge through the nose for water, soda, and snacks. Finally, ask about local taxes and service charges. The D.C. hotel sales tax is a whopping 14.5%, merchandise sales tax is 5.75%, and restaurant tax is 10%, all of which can rapidly increase the cost of a room. If a hotel insists upon tacking on a surprise "energy surcharge" that wasn't mentioned at check-in, you can often make a case for getting it removed.

- **Book an efficiency room.** A room with a kitchenette allows you to shop for groceries and cook your own meals. This is a big money saver, especially for families on long stays.

LANDING THE BEST ROOM

Somebody has to get the best room in the house. It might as well be you. You can start by joining the hotel's frequent-guest program, which may make you eligible for upgrades. A hotel-branded credit card usually gives it owner "silver" or "gold" status in frequent-guest programs for free. Always ask about a corner room. They're often larger and quieter, with more windows and light, and they often cost the same as standard rooms. When you make your reservation, ask if the hotel is renovating; if it is, request a room away from the construction. Ask about nonsmoking rooms, rooms with views, rooms with twin, queen- or king-size beds. If you're a light sleeper, request a quiet room away from vending machines, elevators, restaurants, bars, and discos. Ask for one of the rooms that have been most recently renovated or redecorated. If you aren't happy with your room when you arrive, say so. If another room is available, most lodgings will be willing to accommodate you.

USING A LOCAL RESERVATIONS SERVICE

If you suffer from information overload and would rather someone else do the research and bargaining, you can always turn to one of the following reputable—and free!—local reservations services:

- **Capitol Reservations** (✆ 800/VISIT-DC [800/847-4832] or 202/452-1270; www.hotelsdc.com) will find you a hotel that meets your specific requirements and is within your price range. The 21-year-old service works with about 100 area hotels that have been screened for cleanliness, safe locations, and other desirability factors; you can check rates and book online.
- **Washington D.C. Accommodations** (✆ 800/503-3330 or 202/289-2220; www.dcaccommodations.com) has been in business for 20 years, and, in addition to finding lodgings, can advise you about transportation and general tourist information and even work out itineraries.
- **USA Groups** (✆ 800/872-4777) can help you plan a meeting, convention, or other group function requiring 10 rooms or more; it's a free service representing hotel rooms at almost every hotel in the District and the suburban Virginia-Maryland region, in all price categories.
- **Bed & Breakfast Accommodations, Ltd.** (✆ 877/893-3233 or 413/582-9888; www.bnbaccom.com), in business since 1978, works with more than 30 homes, inns, guesthouses, and unhosted furnished apartments to find visitors lodging. Bookings accepted with American Express, Diners Club, MasterCard, Visa, and Discover.

1 Capitol Hill/The Mall

VERY EXPENSIVE

The Hotel George ★★   The Hotel George is one of Washington's hippest places to stay. With its facade of stainless steel, limestone, and glass; a lobby done in a sleek white, splashed with red, blue, and black furnishings; posters throughout the hotel depicting a modern-day George Washington, sans wig; and clientele tending toward celebs (everyone from Enrique Iglesias to Gov. Arnold Schwarzenegger), the George is in every way a capital establishment. The oversize guest rooms sport a minimalist look, all creamy white and modern. Fluffy vanilla-colored comforters rest on oversize beds; slabs of granite top the desks and bathroom counters; and nature sounds (of the ocean, forest, and wind) emanate from the stereo CD/clock radios. A speaker in the spacious, mirrored, marble bathroom broadcasts TV sounds from the other room; other amenities include cordless phones, umbrellas, and spa robes. All rooms have free high-speed Internet access; eighth-floor rooms also have fax machines, at no extra cost. The hotel has three one-bedroom suites.

Contributing to the hotel's hipness is the presence of its restaurant, Bistro Bis, which serves (duh) French bistro food to hungry lobbyists and those they are lobbying. See chapter 6 for a full review.

15 E St. NW (at N. Capitol St.), Washington, DC 20001. © 800/576-8331 or 202/347-4200. Fax 202/347-4213. www.hotelgeorge.com. 139 units. Weekdays $285–$350 double; weekends from $149 double; $950 suite. Ask about seasonal and corporate rates. Extra person $25. Children under 16 stay free in parent's room. AE, DC, DISC, MC, V. Parking $24, may be increasing in 2005. Metro: Union Station. **Amenities:** Restaurant (French bistro); small 24-hr. fitness center with steam rooms; cigar-friendly billiards room; 24-hr. concierge; business services; room service (7am–11pm); same-day laundry/dry cleaning; VCR rentals; 4 rooms for those w/limited mobility. *In room:* A/C, TV w/pay movies, 2-line phone w/dataport, minibar, coffeemaker, hair dryer, iron, safe, robes, umbrella.

Mandarin Oriental Washington, DC ★★★   I took the Metro to the Mandarin Oriental, which is easy to do, since the 12th Street exit of the Smithsonian Metro station is only a 5-minute walk from the hotel. The Mandarin does not really cater to Metro-riding guests, however. If you stay at this sumptuous hotel, you're more likely to arrive by car, limo, taxi, or perhaps yacht (the Washington waterfront is behind the hotel, across a roadway or two, but a pedestrian footbridge connects the complex with the marina and Tidal Basin). My point is that the Mandarin Oriental is fabulously posh, but its location is odd. The hotel is situated at the end of a concrete peninsula, known as the multipurpose Portals complex, which is set to include offices, retail shops, and restaurants. The government building neighborhood is not attractive and at night you will not be where the action is: These streets are not meant for strolling.

Having said all that, the opening of the Mandarin Oriental in March 2004 upped the ante on luxury in the capital. The service is positively sublime, everyone sweetly gracious. Hotel decor richly combines Asian and American traditions. The two-story lobby is a light-filled, glassed-in rotunda, the circular design used here and throughout the hotel to invite good luck. Each guest room is laid out in accordance with the principles of feng shui (for example, the mirror does not face the entry door, to prevent the reflection of good fortune out of the room), and furnishings include nightstand lamps of contemporary Japanese lantern design, replica pieces from the Smithsonian's Asian art galleries, the Sackler and Freer, and tapestries of hand-woven Thai silk panels. On the thick-mattressed beds are sensuously beautiful linens that make you reach out your hand to touch.

Finally, the setting that separates the hotel from the rest of the city also helps create a feeling that you are away, but not away. You may not want to roam the neighborhood but you can walk around the hotel's property, which includes terraces of landscaped gardens and views of the Tidal Basin and marina, the Jefferson Memorial, the Virginia skyline, and District buildings. Guest rooms offer these same views. And when you are on the inside, looking out from the sound-proofed, very quiet, and elegant refuge of your room, even nearby Interstate 95 appears rather magnificent.

Note: Not open at the time of research, both the restaurant (with a chef coming from the West Coast's acclaimed French Laundry) and the spa are expected to be world-class.

Washington, D.C., Accommodations

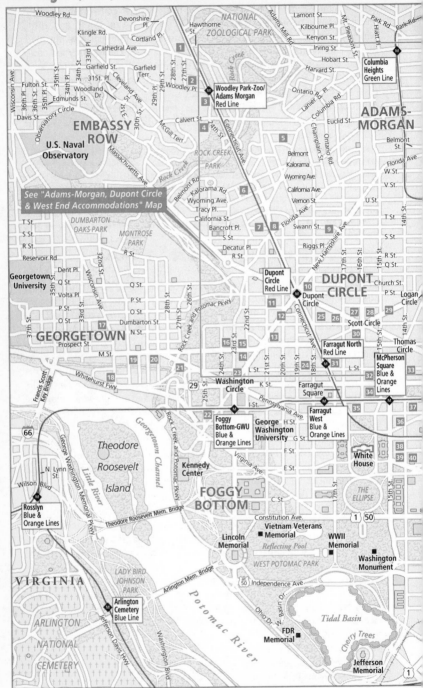

Woodley Rd.
Devonshire Pl.
Klingle Rd.
Cortland Pl.
Cathedral Ave.
Hawthorne St.
NATIONAL ZOOLOGICAL PARK
Lamont St.
Kilbourne Pl.
Kenyon St.
Irving St.
Park Rd.
Park Rd.

Garfield St.
31St. Pl.
Garfield Terr.
Woodley Pl.
Woodley Park-Zoo/ Adams Morgan Red Line
Hobart St.
Harvard St.
Columbia Heights Green Line

EMBASSY ROW
U.S. Naval Observatory

Calvert St.
24th St.
ROCK CREEK PARK
Ontario Pl.

ADAMS-MORGAN

McGill Terr.
Belmont
Kalorama
Wyoming Ave.
California Ave.
Vernon St.
Belmont St.
Florida Ave.
W. St.
V. St.
U St.

Kalorama Rd.
Wyoming Ave.
Tracy Pl.
California St.
Bancroft Pl.
S St.
Decatur Pl.
R St.
Florida Ave.
Swann St.
Riggs Pl.

DUMBARTON OAKS PARK
MONTROSE PARK

Georgetown University

Dent Pl.
Q St.
Volta Pl.
P. St.
O St.
Dumbarton St.
N St.

Dupont Circle Red Line
Dupont Circle

DUPONT CIRCLE
Church St.
P.St.
Logan Circle

Scott Circle
Thomas Circle

GEORGETOWN
Prospect St.
M. St.

Farragut North Red Line

McPherson Square Blue & Orange Lines

Francis Scott Key Bridge
Whitehurst Fwy.

Washington Circle

Farragut Square

Theodore Roosevelt Island

Foggy Bottom-GWU Blue & Orange Lines
George Washington University

Farragut West Blue & Orange Lines

White House

Rosslyn Blue & Orange Lines
N. Lynn St.
Wilson Blvd.

Kennedy Center

FOGGY BOTTOM

THE ELLIPSE

VIRGINIA

LADY BIRD JOHNSON PARK

Arlington Cemetery Blue Line

ARLINGTON NATIONAL CEMETERY

Theodore Roosevelt Mem. Bridge
Arlington Mem. Bridge

Constitution Ave.
Lincoln Memorial
Vietnam Veterans Memorial
Reflecting Pool
WEST POTOMAC PARK
WWII Memorial
Washington Monument

Independence Ave.

Potomac River

FDR Memorial

Tidal Basin
Cherry Trees

Jefferson Memorial

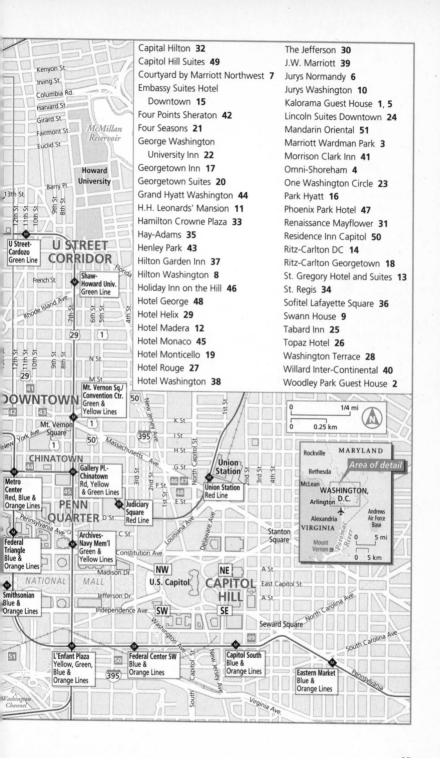

Capital Hilton **32**
Capitol Hill Suites **49**
Courtyard by Marriott Northwest **7**
Embassy Suites Hotel
   Downtown **15**
Four Points Sheraton **42**
Four Seasons **21**
George Washington
   University Inn **22**
Georgetown Inn **17**
Georgetown Suites **20**
Grand Hyatt Washington **44**
H.H. Leonards' Mansion **11**
Hamilton Crowne Plaza **33**
Hay-Adams **35**
Henley Park **43**
Hilton Garden Inn **37**
Hilton Washington **8**
Holiday Inn on the Hill **46**
Hotel George **48**
Hotel Helix **29**
Hotel Madera **12**
Hotel Monaco **45**
Hotel Monticello **19**
Hotel Rouge **27**
Hotel Washington **38**

The Jefferson **30**
J.W. Marriott **39**
Jurys Normandy **6**
Jurys Washington **10**
Kalorama Guest House **1, 5**
Lincoln Suites Downtown **24**
Mandarin Oriental **51**
Marriott Wardman Park **3**
Morrison Clark Inn **41**
Omni-Shoreham **4**
One Washington Circle **23**
Park Hyatt **16**
Phoenix Park Hotel **47**
Renaissance Mayflower **31**
Residence Inn Capitol **50**
Ritz-Carlton DC **14**
Ritz-Carlton Georgetown **18**
St. Gregory Hotel and Suites **13**
St. Regis **34**
Sofitel Lafayette Square **36**
Swann House **9**
Tabard Inn **25**
Topaz Hotel **26**
Washington Terrace **28**
Willard Inter-Continental **40**
Woodley Park Guest House **2**

1330 Maryland Ave. SW (at 12th St.), Washington, DC 20001. © **866/526-6567** or 202/554-8588. Fax 202/554-8999. www.mandarinoriental.com/washington. 400 units. Weekdays $350–$695 double, $950–$8,000 suite; weekends $295–$525 double, $900–$1400 suite. Children under 12 stay free in parent's room. For information about special packages, call the hotel directly or check the website. AE, DC, DISC, MC, V. Parking $34. Metro: Smithsonian. **Amenities:** 2 restaurants (French American, Asian-influenced cafe cuisine); 2 bars; lap pool in spa; fully equipped fitness center; 10,400-sq.-ft. full-service spa; 24-hr. concierge; business center with full Internet access; 24-hour room service; same-day laundry/dry cleaning; club levels; several rooms for those w/limited mobility. *In room:* A/C, TV w/pay movies and HDTV, 3-line phone w/dataports, minibar, coffeemaker, hair dryer, iron, safe, robes, DVD/CD player, high-speed Internet access ($12 per day).

EXPENSIVE

Holiday Inn on the Hill ⭐   A major renovation completed in 2003 took the Bing Crosby out of this traditional Holiday Inn, and garnered a "Renovation of the Year Award" from the hotel's umbrella organization, the Inter-Continental Hotels Group. What you see now is a hotel that's very 21st century, or trying hard to be, anyway. Gone are double beds and family-friendly features, like the Discovery Zone kids program. Gone, too, are the prices that made this hotel a great value for families and business folks on a budget (this hotel used to be listed in the "Inexpensive" category). Instead, you'll find guest rooms done in shades of cobalt blue, with zebra wood armoires, glass-topped desks with ergonomic mesh chairs, and triple-sheeted king-size or two queen-size beds. Rooms are standard size, though bathrooms are larger than expected, with a small vanity ledge just outside the bathroom for overflow counter space.

Every guest room offers free high-speed Internet access, and the restaurant and an area of the lobby allow for wireless Internet access. Some of the hotel's former clientele will be outpriced here, but for others the Capitol Hill location remains unbeatable. Several labor union headquarters are nearby, making the hotel a popular choice among the "labor" folks doing business with one of them. And for families, proximity to the Capitol and other sites, as well as certain amenities, may appeal: the free 24-hour fitness center, seasonal (outdoor) pool, and the "kids 12 and under eat free" restaurant policy.

To get the best deals and perks, ask about summer promotions, the "Great Rates" package, and the hotel's "Priority Club" frequent guest membership.

415 New Jersey Ave. NW (between D and E sts.), Washington, DC 20001. © **800/638-1116** or 202/638-1616. Fax 202/638-0707. www.holidayinnonthehill.com. 343 units. $189–$389 double (Mon and Tues are the most expensive days). Extra person $20. Children under 19 stay free in parent's room. Ask about special promotions and packages. AE, DC, DISC, MC, V. Parking $22. Metro: Union Station. **Amenities:** Restaurant (American), where kids ages 12 and under eat free with an adult; bar; outdoor (unheated) rooftop pool; 24-hr. fitness room; concierge; business center; room service (6am–11pm); same-day laundry/dry cleaning service; 8 rooms for those w/limited mobility, including 4 with roll-in showers. *In room:* A/C, TV w/pay movies and Nintendo, 2-line phone w/dataport, coffeemaker, hair dryer, iron, high-speed Internet access.

Phoenix Park Hotel ⭐   The Phoenix Park is one of a cluster of hotels across from Union Station and 2 blocks from the Capitol. It's distinguished by its popular and authentic Irish pub, The Dubliner, which attempts to set the tone for the entire property. Because of this well-worn, wood-paneled pub, which offers Irish fare, ale, and nightly entertainment (p. 268), the hotel attracts numerous sons and daughters of Erin, stages a number of Ireland-related events in its Connemara marble-accented ballroom, and generally conveys an air of Irish hospitality. The rooms are attractive but rather cramped with furnishings. Reserve a "deluxe" room (about $30 more than a standard) to stay in a room with a view (Union Station, Smithsonian museums, or congressional buildings). Or book a one- or two-story suite, some of which have balconies, working fireplaces, and spiral staircases. The last major renovation was in 1997, when marble was installed in all the bathrooms; more recently, bathroom scales and heat lamps were added. Irish decorative accents include linens and bathrobes, artwork, toiletries, and carpeting. High-speed Internet access is currently available only in deluxe rooms.

520 N. Capitol St. NW (at Massachusetts Ave.), Washington, DC 20001. ℂ **800/824-5419** or 202/638-6900. Fax 202/393-3236. www.phoenixparkhotel.com. 150 units. Weekdays $209–$339 double; weekends $119–$189 double; $299–$699 suite. Extra person $30. Children under 16 stay free in parent's room. AE, DC, DISC, MC, V. Valet parking $25, self-parking $10. Metro: Union Station. **Amenities:** Irish pub; small exercise room; concierge; secretarial services; room service (7am–11pm); same-day dry cleaning; 7 rooms for those w/limited mobility. *In room:* A/C, TV w/pay movies, 2-line phone w/dataport, minibar, coffeemaker, hair dryer, iron.

MODERATE

Capitol Hill Suites ✿ A $3 million renovation completed at this well-run, all-suite property in spring 2000 produced remarkable and lasting results. Bedroom walls are painted cobalt blue, heavy velvet drapes keep out morning sun, lamps and mirrors are from Pottery Barn, desks are long, desk chairs are ergonomically correct, and beds are firm. Bathrooms are tiny, but sparkling. The lobby, which features an enclosed fireplace, leather chairs, and an antique credenza where self-serve coffee is laid out, is inviting enough to linger. (Sit here long enough and you might spy a congressperson or senator—a number of members reserve suites for 100 days at a time.) High-speed Internet access is available in all guest rooms at a charge of about $10 per day.

The location is another plus: Capitol Hill Suites is the only hotel truly *on* the Hill (on the House side of the Capitol). It stands on a residential street across from the Library of Congress, a short walk from the Capitol and Mall attractions, a food market, and more than 20 restaurants (many of which deliver to the hotel).

The term *suite* denotes the fact that every unit has a kitchenette with coffeemaker, toaster oven, microwave, refrigerator, flatware, and glassware. Most units are efficiencies, with the kitchenette, bed, and sofa all in the same room. The best choices are one-bedroom units, in which the kitchenette and living room are separate from the bedroom. A third option is a "studio double," with two queen beds and a kitchenette, but no living room area. Some rooms in each category have pullout sofas.

Guests, no matter their political leanings, have privileges to dine at the Capitol Hill Club, a members-only club for Republicans, and can charge their meals and drinks to their hotel bill.

200 C St. SE (at 2nd St.), Washington, DC 20003. ℂ **800/424-9165** or 202/543-6000. Fax 202/547-2608. www.capitolhillsuites.com. 152 units. $119–$239 double. Weekend and long-term rates may be available. Extra person $20. Rates include continental breakfast. Children under 18 stay free in parent's room. AE, DC, DISC, MC, V. Valet parking $25 plus tax. Metro: Capitol South. **Amenities:** Privileges ($10 a day) at nearby Washington Sports and Health Club; business services; coin-op washer/dryers; same-day laundry/dry cleaning; 8 rooms for those w/limited mobility, all with roll-in showers. *In room:* A/C, TV w/pay movies, 2-line phone w/dataport, fridge, coffeemaker, hair dryer, iron, high-speed Internet access ($10 per day).

Residence Inn Capitol   This brand-new hotel was still under construction at press time; it's due to open in January 2005, in time for the presidential inauguration on January 20. I was anxious to include the hotel, which promises to be remarkable, in this newest edition of the guidebook, despite the fact that some information was not available at the time of my research. Here are some reasons why I think you should check out the hotel: The Residence Inn Capitol is located 3 blocks south of the Smithsonian's fabulous new National Museum of the American Indian. Not only that, but four Native American tribes are 58%

owners of the hotel, which makes this the first multi-tribal partnership with non-tribal partners on land off a reservation. Hotel features mimic the look of the National Museum of the American Indian; for instance, the Kasota limestone, which covers the museum's exterior, is used throughout the first floor of the hotel. The hotel's covetous location, close to the National Mall and to Capitol Hill, endows it with a spectacular view: From the top three floors of the 13-story building, one has breathtaking sights of the Capitol building. Finally, this Residence Inn, like all Residence Inns, offers some attractive amenities for families and business people who are in Washington for more than just a couple of days: The roomy suites all have fully equipped kitchens, which allows for flexible dining options; the hotel hosts a generous hot lunch daily, social hours with food on weeknights, and a barbeque once a week; and the property provides a pool, exercise room, and free high-speed Internet service.

333 E St. SW (at 4th St.), Washington, DC 20024. (℃) 800/331-3131. www.Marriott.com/residenceinn. 233 suites. $179–$209 1-bedroom suite; $269–$309 2-bedroom suite. Weekend and long-term rates available. Rates include hot breakfast daily and "social hour" week nights. AE, DC, DISC, MC, V. Parking $22. Metro: Federal Center Southwest. **Amenities:** Indoor pool; exercise room; grocery shopping service; copy/fax service; laundry valet and self-serve laundry. *In room:* A/C, TV w/pay movies, full kitchen, coffeemaker, hair dryer, iron, safe, free high-speed Internet access.

2 Downtown, East of 16th Street NW

VERY EXPENSIVE

Grand Hyatt Washington ⭐ Until the D.C. Convention Center's on-site hotel, with its 1,000-plus rooms, opens in 2007, the Grand Hyatt is the largest hotel near the convention center.

The Grand Hyatt has a lot of other things going on besides its room count of 900. The vast lobby is in an atrium 12 stories high and enclosed by a glass, mansard-style roof. A baby grand piano floats on its own island in the 7,000-square-foot "lagoon"; waterfalls, catwalks, 22-foot-high trees, and an array of bars and restaurants on the periphery will keep you permanently entertained. Should you get bored, head to the nearby nightspots and restaurants, or hop on the Metro, to which the Hyatt has direct access. The hotel lies between Capitol Hill and the White House, 2 blocks from the MCI Center, and about 3 blocks from the new D.C. Convention Center, at 801 Mount Vernon Place NW.

Guest rooms and corridors underwent a complete renovation in 2003. Features include new showerheads and light-colored marble in the bathrooms and a fresh contemporary look of dark, hardwood furniture and hues of blue and gold in the guest rooms, and updated carpeting everywhere. Nearly half of the rooms offer high-speed Internet access, for a rate of $9.95 per 24 hours. Among the potpourri of special plans and packages available is one for business travelers: Pay an extra $20 and you stay in an eighth- or ninth-floor room equipped with a large desk, fax machine, computer hookup, and coffeemaker; have access to printers and other office supplies on the floor; and are entitled to complimentary continental breakfast and access to the health club. Always ask about seasonal and special offers, and check the website for the best deals.

1000 H St. NW, Washington, DC 20001. (℃) 800/233-1234 or 202/582-1234. Fax 202/628-1641. www.grand washington.hyatt.com. 900 units. Weekdays $350 double; weekends $125–$139 double; $360–$2,200 suite. Extra person $25. Children under 18 stay free in parent's room. Ask about special promotions and packages. AE, DC, DISC, MC, V. Valet parking $26, self-parking $20. Metro: Metro Center. **Amenities:** 4 restaurants (Italian/Asian, Continental, deli); 3 bars; health club with whirlpool, lap pool, steam and sauna rooms, aerobics, and spa services (hotel guests pay $11 for club use); concierge; courtesy car available on a first-come, first-served basis to nearby destinations; business center; room service (6am–1am); in-room and health-club massage; same-day dry cleaning; concierge-level rooms; 24 rooms for those w/limited mobility, some with roll-in showers. *In room:* A/C, TV w/pay movies, 2-line phone w/dataports, minibar, coffeemaker, hair dryer, iron.

Hotel Monaco Washington DC ★★★   Let's cut to the chase: This is where I'd stay if I were a visitor to D.C. The Monaco has been winning awards and great notice ever since it opened, summer of 2002. Museum-like in appearance, the Monaco occupies a four-story, all marble mid-19th-century building, half of which was designed by Robert Mills, the architect for the Washington Monument, the other half designed by Thomas Walter, one of the architects for the U.S. Capitol. The two halves connect seamlessly, enclosing an interior, landscaped courtyard. Jutting into the courtyard from the F Street side of the hotel is its marvelous restaurant, **Poste,** which got off to a rough start, but has finally established itself as a top spot for dining. The hotel takes up an entire block, between 7th and 8th streets, and E and F streets. Superlatives are in order: The hotel is truly magnificent.

The spacious guest rooms, similarly, combine historic and hip. Their vaulted ceilings are high (12 ft.–18 ft.) and windows are long, hung with charcoal and white patterned drapes. Eclectic furnishings include neoclassic armoires and three-legged desks. A color scheme successfully marries creamy yellow walls with periwinkle blue lounge chairs, with orange damask pillows. Interior rooms overlook the courtyard and the restaurant; you'll see the charming arched passageway through which horse and carriage came a century ago. Exterior rooms view the MCI Center and the Smithsonian's National Portrait Gallery on the north side, and downtown sights on the south side. This is a great location: When you stay at the Monaco, you're not just downtown, you're part of the scene.

Need more? The Hotel Monaco gives you a complimentary goldfish at check-in (if you so request); offers specially designed "Tall Rooms" with 18-foot-high ceilings, 96-inch-long beds, and raised showerheads, for tall guests. Go to the hotel's website or call direct to the hotel to obtain lowest available rates. With

---

Kids Family-Friendly Hotels

Embassy Suites Hotel Downtown (p. 106)   You're close to both a Red line and a Blue line Metro station (the zoo is on the Red line; the Smithsonian museums are on the Blue line) and within walking distance of Georgetown. Your kids can sleep on the pullout sofa in the separate living room. You've got some kitchen facilities, but you might not use them, since the complimentary breakfast in the atrium is unbelievable, and the restaurant discounts meals for hotel guests (anywhere from 10% to 20%), and has a special $4.95 kids menu. And there's an indoor pool and a free game room.

Hilton Washington (p. 101)   A large heated outdoor pool, three tennis courts, and a goodie bag at check-in—what more does a kid need?

Omni Shoreham Hotel (p. 116)   Adjacent to Rock Creek Park, the Omni is also within walking distance of the zoo and Metro and is equipped with a large outdoor pool and kiddie pool. The hotel gives children a goodie bag at check-in and the concierge has a supply of board games at the ready (no charge to borrow, just remember to return).

your own laptop, you have free high-speed Internet access in your guest room; otherwise, you pay $10 a day for Web TV access to the Internet.

700 F St. NW (at 7th St.), Washington, DC 20004. © **800/649-1202** or 202/628-7177. Fax 202/628-7277. www.monaco-dc.com. 184 units. Weekdays $239–$349 double, $439–$849 suite; weekends $149–$349 double, $349–$699 suite. Extra person $20. Children under 18 stay free in parent's room. Rates include complimentary Starbucks coffee in morning and wine receptions in evening. AE, DC, DISC, MC, V. Parking $27. Pets allowed—they get VIP treatment, with their own registration cards at check-in, maps of neighborhood fire hydrants and parks, gourmet puppy and kitty treats. Metro: Gallery Place. **Amenities:** Restaurant (modern American); bar; spacious fitness center with flat screen TVs; 24-hr. concierge; full-service business center; 24-hr. room service; same-day laundry/dry cleaning; 9 rooms for those w/limited mobility, 4 with roll-in showers. *In room:* A/C, TV w/pay movies and Nintendo, Web access ($10 per day), 2-line phones w/dataports, minibar, hair dryer, iron, safe, robes, CD player, high-speed Internet access.

JW Marriott Hotel on Pennsylvania Avenue ★

The best thing about this hotel is its prime location on Pennsylvania Avenue, especially in this, a presidential inaugural, year. The parade route goes right by here. By the time you read this, however, the JW will have been booked months in advance for the January 20, 2005 event. The hotel is also adjacent to the National Theatre, 1 block from the Warner Theater, 2 blocks from the White House, and within walking distance of the Washington Monument, the Smithsonian museums, and lots of restaurants. The best rooms on the 7th to 12th, 14th, and 15th floors overlook Pennsylvania Avenue and the monuments (floors 12, 14, and 15 are concierge levels). Corporate types and conventioneers make up much of the clientele, with tourists (including families) filling in the rest on weekends. Guest rooms are looking patriotic these days, decorated in hues of red, white, and blue. They are furnished with desks and armoires, many of them cherry-wood pieces. All rooms are equipped with high-speed Internet access, charged at $9.95 per day.

For the best value, book around the Christmas holidays, any time during the summer, or on weekends. You're more likely to hear about special promotions by calling direct to the hotel or by browsing the hotel's website.

1331 Pennsylvania Ave. NW (at E St.), Washington, DC 20004. © **800/228-9290** or 202/393-2000. Fax 202/626-6991. www.marriott.com. 772 units. Weekdays $289–$359 double; weekends $159–$259 double (but always ask for best available rates); suites from $2,000. Extra person free. AE, DC, DISC, MC, V. Valet parking $25. Metro: Metro Center. **Amenities:** 2 restaurants (both upscale American); complete health club (with indoor swimming pool and whirlpool); concierge (6am–11pm); business center; 24-hr. room service; same-day laundry/dry cleaning; concierge-level rooms; 15 rooms for those w/limited mobility, some with roll-in showers. *In room:* A/C, TV w/pay movies, 2-line phones w/dataports, minibar, coffeemaker, hair dryer, iron, safe, robes, high-speed Internet access ($9.95 per day).

The Madison ★★

Having completed a $40-million plus renovation and reinvention in 2003, The Madison is once again at the top of its game. Not surprisingly, with all of the extra touches offered here (fresh fruit always available, water and fruit waiting for returning morning runners, etc.), the Madison feels like a nice mix of luxury hotel and comfortable home. Having hosted every U.S. president since JFK as well as numerous dignitaries and heads of state, The Madison really knows how to give its customers everything they could need or want (consider a whole floor devoted to those traveling with pets—and there's no size limit nor deposit required to bring Benji along). The Federalist decor is effectively juxtaposed with all the modern amenities you'd expect from a world-class hotel. Though the 2-bedded doubles are a tad on the small side and the beds were a bit firm for my taste, the luxe sheets, Frette duvet covers, helpful staff, shower curtains that curve away from the tub (no more sticking to you—why haven't more places done this?), and the hotel's location all make this a great choice in the area. Be sure to check out the framed and signed presidential correspondences on the wall of Postscript, the hotel's lounge. Funfact: the Madison was the first hotel to introduce the minibar!

15th and M sts. NW, Washington, DC 20005. © **800/424-8577** or 202/862-1600. Fax 202/785-1255. www. madisonhoteldc.com. 353 units. $379 double; $429 suite. No additional charge for children or additional guests. AE, DC, DISC, MC, V. All pets allowed; no deposit required. Parking: $26. Metro: Farragut North. **Amenities:** 2 restaurants, bar; health club and spa treatments; sauna; concierge; courtesy car; business center; 24-hr. room service; massage; laundry service; dry cleaning; nonsmoking rooms. *In-room:* A/C, TV, high-speed Internet access (free), minibar, coffeemaker, hair dryer, iron, safe, CD player.

Sofitel Lafayette Square, Washington, D.C. ★★

The Hay-Adams (p. 96) faces some competition since the 2002 opening of this luxury hotel, which, like the Hay-Adams, borders Lafayette Square and is just minutes from the White House. The Hay-Adams offers White House views, and the Sofitel does not, it's true, but the Sofitel's other appealing features may make up for that.

This handsome, 12-story limestone building was erected in the early 20th century, and its distinctive facade includes decorative bronze corner panels, bas-relief sculptural panels at ground-floor level, and a 12th-floor balcony that travels the length of both the H and 15th street-sides of the structure (decorative, not accessible, alas). Inside, hotel staff dressed in designer uniforms greet you with *"Bonjour!,"* small hints that a French company (Accor Hotels) owns the Sofitel. Noted French designer Pierre-Yves Rochon styled the interior; a Michelin three-star chef is behind the contemporary French cuisine served in Café 15 (p. 128), the hotel's restaurant; and the gift shop sells such specialty items as French plates and porcelain dolls. The Sofitel also has a super bar, Le Bar, which also serves lunch.

Because of its corner location and exceptionally large windows, guest rooms are bright with natural light; second- and third-floor rooms facing 15th or H street bring in more light still, because their windows extend nearly from floor to ceiling. Each room sports elegantly modern decor that includes a long desk, creamy duvet with a colorful throw on a king-size bed (about 17 rooms have two double beds instead of kings), a much-marbled bathroom with tub separate from the shower stall, fresh flowers, and original artwork, including dramatic photographs of Washington landmarks. The 11th floor has been designed with visiting heads of state in mind, and can be easily secured. In each of the 17 suites, the bedroom is separate from the living room.

806 15th St. NW (at H St.), Washington, DC 20005. © **202/737-8800.** Fax 202/730-8500. www.sofitel.com. 237 units. Weekdays $235–$480 double; weekends, call for rates, which can start as low as $139 for a double; from $495 suite. For lowest rates at any time, call directly to the hotel and ask about specials or packages; also check out the website. Extra person $20. Children under 12 stay free in parent's room. AE, DC, DISC, MC, V. Parking $26. Metro: McPherson Square, Farragut West, or Farragut North. Pets allowed with prior approval. **Amenities:** Restaurant (contemporary French); bar; 24-hour state-of-the-art fitness center; 24-hr. concierge; 24-hour business services; 24-hr. room service; same-day laundry/dry cleaning; 8 rooms for those w/limited mobility, all with roll-in showers; library with books about D.C. and Paris. *In room:* A/C, TV w/pay movies and Nintendo, 2-line phones w/dataports, minibar, hair dryer, iron, safe, robes, slippers, CD player, high-speed Internet access ($9.95 per day).

Willard Inter-Continental Washington ★★★

If you're lucky enough to stay here, you'll be a stone's throw from the White House and the Smithsonian museums, in the heart of downtown near plenty of excellent restaurants, down the block from the National Theatre, and down the avenue from the Capitol. The Willard is definitely the classiest hotel in this neighborhood, among the best in the city, and also, naturally, one of the most expensive. Heads of state favor the Willard (the hotel offers one floor as "Secret Service–cleared"), as do visitors from other countries and movie directors (who like to shoot scenes in the famously ornate lobby and restaurant).

A renovation completed in late 2000 spruced up the guest rooms' handsome, if staid, decor, which is heavy on reproduction Federal- and Edwardian-style furnishings. The rooms with the best views are the oval suites overlooking Pennsylvania Avenue to the Capitol and the rooms fronting Pennsylvania Avenue. Rooms facing the courtyard are the quietest. Best of all is the "Jenny Lind" suite, perched in the curve of the 12th floor's southeast corner; its round bull's-eye window captures glimpses of the Washington Monument.

The Willard's designation as a National Historic Landmark in 1974 and magnificent restoration in the 1980s helped revitalize Pennsylvania Avenue and this part of town. Stop in at the Round Robin Bar for a mint julep (introduced here), and listen to bartender and manager Jim Hewes spin tales about the history of the 1901 Willard and its predecessor, the City Hotel, built on this site in 1815.

Always inquire about off-season and weekend packages, when rates are sometimes halved and come with one of several complimentary options, sometimes an upgrade to a suite, valet parking, or a second room at half price.

1401 Pennsylvania Ave. NW (at 14th St.), Washington, DC 20004. ✆ 800/827-1747 or 202/628-9100. Fax 202/637-7326. www.washington.interconti.com. 341 units. Weekdays $480 double; weekends from $209; $850–$4,200 suite. Ask about special promotions and packages. AE, DC, DISC, MC, V. Parking $25. Metro: Metro Center. Small pets allowed. **Amenities:** Restaurant (Modern French-American); cafe; bar; modest-size but state-of-the-art fitness center; children's programs; concierge; business center; 24-hr. room service; babysitting; same-day laundry/dry cleaning; currency exchange; airline/train ticketing. *In-room:* A/C, TV, 2-line phone w/dataport and complimentary wireless Internet access, minibar, hair dryer, iron, safe, robes,

EXPENSIVE

Hamilton Crowne Plaza Washington, DC ⭐ A much needed renovation in 2002 updated the appearance and amenities in the guest rooms, adding handy items like CD players and wireless Internet access (the latter for $9.95 per day), handsome features such as royal blue robes and dark wood armoires and headboards, and comfortable accommodations like the seven-layer bed. Not much they could do about the size of the rooms, though, so those with king-size beds feel a bit tight, those with two double beds a little roomier. K Street–side rooms overlook Franklin Park, which is pleasant, and those on the upper floors offer views of the city skyline. In keeping with the times, the hotel has a designated "women's floor," accessible only to those with a special elevator key. This is a well-placed hotel, sort of central between the two sections of downtown: the K Street side and the section that's fast being revitalized around the MCI Center. The hotel's restaurant is popular with office workers at weekday lunch, thanks to a generous buffet of soups, salads, and rotisserie items, for $15.

1001 14th St. NW (at K St.), Washington, DC 20005. ✆ 800/2-CROWNE or 202/682-0111. Fax 202/682-9525. www.hamiltoncrowneplazawashingtondc.com. 318 units. Weekdays $119–$325 double; suites $300–$600; look for much lower rates on weekends. Extra person $20. Children under 18 stay free in parent's room. AE, DC, DISC, MC, V. Parking $24. Metro: McPherson Square. **Amenities:** Restaurant (American); bar; 24-hr. fitness room; concierge; 24-hr. business center; room service (6am–midnight); same-day laundry/dry cleaning (not on weekend); club level. *In room:* A/C, TV w/pay movies, 2-line speaker phone w/dataport, coffeemaker, hair dryer, iron, safe, robes, CD player/clock radio, wireless high-speed Internet access ($9.95 per day).

Henley Park ⭐ This intimate English-style hotel with 119 gargoyles on its facade was originally an apartment house. Built in 1918, the stunning building retains many of its Tudor-style features, including the lobby's exquisite ceiling, archways, and leaded windows. Its design offers a charming counterpoint to that of the newly opened and modern convention center, whose location is "727 steps" away (according to the Henley Park's director of sales). The hotel's popular restaurant, bar, and parlor received face-lifts in late 2000, while an ongoing renovation recently replaced wallpaper, linens, and other items in all the guest rooms. Guest rooms overlook busy Massachusetts Avenue on one side, or an interior enclosed courtyard on the other side. The decor is old-fashioned, in rooms full of dark wood Hepplewhite-, Chippendale-, and Queen Anne–style furnishings. Televisions are small and lighting fixtures project dim light. Rooms and bathrooms are of standard size. A handful of suites are either one-bedroom or junior (combined living room and bedroom). The hotel puts on a smashing afternoon tea, but even better is the live jazz that plays in the bar Thursday through Saturday (and often Sundays in summer) evenings. If you dine in the restaurant, you'll enjoy the pleasant cosseting of maitre d' Ralph Fredericks, and the music wafting in from the bar. But the food is not great. Look in the Sunday *New York Times* "Travel" section for ads posting low rates.

926 Massachusetts Ave. NW (at 10th St.), Washington, DC 20001. ⓒ 800/222-8474 or 202/638-5200. Fax 202/638-6740. www.henleypark.com. 96 units. Weekdays $185–$245 double; suites from $325; summer and weekends $99–159 double, look for much lower rates for suites on weekends. Extra person $20. Children under 14 stay free in parent's room. AE, DC, DISC, MC, V. Parking $22. Metro: Metro Center, Gallery Place, or Mt. Vernon Square. **Amenities:** Restaurant (New American); pub (with live jazz Thurs–Sat evenings); afternoon tea (daily 4–6pm); access to a fitness room in the Morrison-Clark Historic Inn (see listing below) across the street; 24-hr. concierge; complimentary weekday-morning sedan service to downtown and Capitol Hill; business services; 24-hour room service; same-day laundry/dry cleaning. *In room:* A/C, TV, 2-line speaker phone w/dataport, minibar, coffeemaker, hair dryer, iron, safe, robes.

Hotel Washington ⚐★

Built in 1918, this hotel is the oldest continuously operating hotel in Washington. Renovations throughout the years have played up the historic angle. The wooden moldings and crystal chandeliers in the two-story lobby are reconstructed originals. A remodeling done in 2001 added overstuffed chairs and lots of plants to make the lobby more comfortable. Decor in the small guest rooms is traditional, with lots of mahogany furnishings and historically suggestive print fabrics and wall coverings; a renovation completed in 2004 spruced up the guest rooms with new carpeting, wallpaper, and drapes, but did not change the overall decor. Bathrooms are in marble and include telephones.

With at least four theaters nearby, the Hotel Washington is often home to cast members in current shows. But most of the clientele is a mix of business and leisure travelers, who are attracted to the hotel for its location and views, as well as its rates, which are among the more reasonable in this part of town. From its corner perch at Pennsylvania Avenue and 15th Street, the 12-story hotel surveys the avenue, monuments, the Capitol, and the White House. Ask for a room facing Pennsylvania Avenue for your own private view (these rooms also tend to be a little more spacious). The hotel has 14 suites, all one-bedroom, most with the capability of turning into two-bedroom suites.

No other hotel in town provides a more panoramic spectacle than the Hotel Washington's rooftop Sky Terrace, where from late April through October you can have drinks and light fare. The more formal Sky Room restaurant is also on the top floor.

515 15th St. NW (at Pennsylvania Ave. NW), Washington, DC 20004. ⓒ 800/424-9540 or 202/638-5900. Fax 202/638-4275. www.hotelwashington.com. 340 units. Weekdays $195–$285 double; weekends $145–$285 double; $495–$725 suite. Family and other discount packages available. Extra person $20. Children under 14 stay free in parent's room. AE, DC, MC, V. Parking $25. Metro: Metro Center. Pets under 25 lb. allowed; inquire about policies when you reserve. **Amenities:** 2 restaurants (both American, 1 seasonal); bar; fitness center with sauna; tour desk; business center; salon; room service (6:30am–11pm); same-day laundry/dry cleaning; 12 rooms for those w/limited mobility, 2 with roll-in showers. *In room:* A/C, TV w/pay movies, 2-line phone w/dataport, fridge, coffeemaker, hair dryer, iron, robes.

Morrison-Clark Historic Inn ⭐ This property offers the homey ambience and personable service of an inn, coupled with hotel amenities, such as a first-rate restaurant, phones and TV, and a fitness center. The inn occupies twin 1864 Victorian brick town houses (with a newer wing in converted stables across an interior courtyard) and is listed on the National Register of Historic Places. Guests enter via a turn-of-the-20th-century drawing room, with Victorian furnishings and lace-curtained bay windows. Beyond this room lies a suite of lovely public spaces including the inn's restaurant. Only a couple of years ago, the Morrison-Clark's location was considered out of the way, but with the 2003 opening of the immense convention center a couple of blocks away, the inn is now in the thick of things.

Newly refurbished in 2003, the inn's high-ceilinged guest rooms remain individually decorated with original artworks, sumptuous fabrics, and antique or reproduction 19th-century furnishings, and are graced with fresh flowers. Most popular are the grand Victorian-style rooms, with new chandeliers and bedspreads. Four Victorian rooms have private porches; many others have plant-filled balconies. Guests enjoy a complimentary continental breakfast served daily in the Victorian drawing room. Come the warm weather, you'll want to sip the inn's signature "Steel Magnolia" cocktail on the veranda.

1015 L St. NW (at 11th St. and Massachusetts Ave. NW), Washington, DC 20001. © 800/332-7898 or 202/898-1200. Fax 202/289-8576. www.morrisonclark.com. 54 units. Weekdays $175–$245 double; weekends $99–$159 double. Extra person $20. Rates include continental breakfast. Children under 16 stay free in parent's room. AE, DC, DISC, MC, V. Parking $22. Metro: Metro Center or Mt. Vernon Square. **Amenities:** Restaurant (American-Southern); tiny fitness center; concierge; business services; room service during restaurant hours; same-day laundry/dry cleaning. *In room:* A/C, TV, dataport, minibar, hair dryer, robes.

MODERATE

Four Points Sheraton, Washington, D.C. Downtown ⭐ *Value* This former Days Inn has been totally transformed into a contemporary property that offers all the latest gizmos, from complimentary high-speed Internet access in all the rooms, and wireless Internet access in the lobby and meeting rooms, to a 650-square-foot fitness center. A massive renovation undertaken by a new owner essentially gutted the old building, but the location is still as terrific as ever (close to the Convention Center, MCI Center, and downtown). Best of all, the rates are reasonable, hotel amenities spectacular, which make this a good choice for both business and leisure visitors.

Five types of rooms are available: units with two double beds, with one queen bed, or with one king bed; junior suites; or one-bedroom suites. In 2003, the hotel put "Heavenly Beds" (a custom-designed, multi-layered, pillow-top mattress) in all of the rooms. Corner rooms (there are only about 10) are a little more spacious than others, which are of standard size. While guest rooms offer city views, the rooftop pool and lounge boast a sweeping vista of the city that includes the Capitol. Under separate ownership from the hotel is a recommended restaurant, Corduroy.

1201 K St. NW (at 12th St.), Washington, DC 20005. © 888/481-7191 or 202/289-7600. Fax 202/349-2215. www.fourpointswashingtondc.com. 265 units. In season $149–$275 double; off-season $99–$245 double; from $400 suite. Extra person $20. Children under 18 stay free in parent's room. AE, DC, DISC, MC, V. Parking $26. Metro: McPherson Square or Metro Center. **Amenities:** Restaurant (seasonal American); bar; indoor heated pool on rooftop; fitness center; business center; room service (6am–midnight); same-day laundry/dry cleaning; executive-level rooms; 8 rooms for those w/limited mobility, 3 with roll-in showers. *In room:* A/C, TV w/pay movies, 2-line phone w/dataport, minibar, coffeemaker, hair dryer, iron, safe, robes, high-speed Internet access.

Hilton Garden Inn, Washington, DC, Franklin Square   Located downtown between H and I streets, the Hilton Garden Inn is across the street from Metro's Blue Line McPherson Square station (and three stops from the Smithsonian museums station) and within walking distance of the White House, the new convention center, and the MCI Center. Rooms are spacious with either king-size or double beds, and are designed for comfort—each room has a cushiony chair with ottoman and a large desk with an ergonomic chair and adjustable lighting. Its location and perks make this 4-year-old hotel a good choice for both business and leisure travelers. The hotel's 20 suites are almost apartment size, with a small pullout sofa in the living room, and the bathroom separating the bedroom from the living room. Complimentary high-speed Internet access is now available in all guest rooms, with wireless Internet access in meeting areas.

815 14th St. NW (between H and I sts.), Washington, DC 20005. © 800/HILTONS or 202/783-7800. Fax 202/783-7801. www.hiltongardendc.com. 300 units. Weekdays $139–$289 double; weekends $109–$179 double; $239–$375 suite. Extra person $20. No more than 4 people per room. Children under 18 stay free in parent's room. AE, DC, DISC, MC, V. Parking $24. Metro: McPherson Square. **Amenities:** Restaurant (American); bar with fireplace; small fitness center with indoor pool; business center; room service (6am–10pm); same-day laundry/dry cleaning; 16 rooms for those w/limited mobility, 3 with roll-in showers. In room: A/C, TV w/pay movies, 2-line phone w/dataports, fridge, coffeemaker, hair dryer, iron, high-speed Internet access, microwave.

Hotel Helix ♠   The Helix doesn't so much invite you in, as intrigue you in. The giant, peacock-blue English lawn chairs and the Magritte-like painting out front are just the beginning. Your steps across a mosaic-tiled vestibule trigger an automatic swoosh of curtains, parting to let you inside the hotel. The small lobby is spare, its main furnishings the illuminated "pods," or podiums with flat computer screens for check in. The guest rooms have a minimalist quality to them, too, which is an odd thing to say about a decor that uses such startling colors: cherry-red and royal-blue ottomans, striped green settees, bright orange vanities in bathrooms, metallic-sheen walls, lime-green honor bar/armoires. But rooms are uncluttered and roomy, due to a design that puts the platform bed behind sheer drapes in an alcove (in the king deluxe rooms), leaving the two-person settee, a triangular desk, and the 22-inch flat screen TV on its stainless steel stand, out in the open. Deluxe rooms, without alcoves, feel a little less spacious, but otherwise look the same. Roomiest are the 18 suites, with separate bedroom and, in the living room, slate blue sectional sofas. The Helix, like its sister hotels (see the Madera, Topaz, and Rouge), offers "specialty" rooms which play up particular themes, in this case, "Eats" rooms, which include Italian cafe tables and barstools, and a fully equipped kitchenette; "Bunk" rooms, which have a separate bunk bed area where the TV has a built-in DVD player; and "Zone" rooms, equipped with a plasma screen TV, high-tech stereo system, lava lamp, and lounge chair. Every guest room has a five-disc CD player, complimentary wireless Internet access, and Web TV (for a charge).

1430 Rhode Island Ave. NW (between 14th and 15th sts.), Washington, DC 20006. © 866/508-0658 or 202/462-9001. Fax 202/332-3519. www.hotelhelix.com. 178 units. Weekdays and weekends $119–$239 double; specialty rooms: add $40 to double rate; suites: add $125 to double rate. Best rates usually on Sun and Mon. Extra person $20. Children under 18 stay free in parent's room. Rates include "bubbly hour" (champagne) in evening. AE, DC, DISC, MC, V. Parking $22 plus tax. Metro: McPherson Square. Pets welcome. **Amenities:** Bar/cafe; exercise room; room service (during breakfast and dinner hours); same-day laundry/dry cleaning; 9 rooms for those w/limited mobility, some with roll-in showers. In room: A/C, TV w/pay movies, Nintendo, and Web access (for a fee), CD player, 2-line phones w/dataports, minibar, hair dryer, iron, free wireless Internet access.

Washington Terrace Hotel ✦   For all intents and purposes, this is a new hotel, the 2002 transformation of the former Doubletree property being so utterly complete. Beautifully landscaped terraces front and back help create a buffer for this urban hotel. The flow of the public spaces leading back to the garden courtyard, and abundant use of earth tones and sandstone in decor, accentuate the hotel's theme of "bringing the outdoors in." This theme resonates in the guest rooms—the light golden wall coverings feature an abstract botanical pattern, and the windows are larger than the hotel norm, delivering lots of natural light. Ask for a room at the front of the hotel for a view of Scott Circle, the park across the street, and the city; request a room at the back for a view of the garden terrace. Best rooms are the spacious suites, which come with a small wet bar, a dining table, sleeper sofa, and larger bathroom. Sixth through eighth floor suites offer executive level privileges, such as high-speed Internet access ($14 per 24 hr.). Added to all guest rooms in 2004 were tempurpedic mattresses, the kind that form to your body. Be sure to dine at the hotel's excellent restaurant, 15 Ria (for full review, see chapter 6).

Although the Washington Terrace calls itself an "upscale boutique hotel," I think its large size and its practical amenities, like ergonomic chairs in the guest rooms and extensive conference and party facilities, disqualify it. Still, the guest rooms do have a boutiquey feel, thanks to imaginative touches such as granite-topped desks, circular nightstands, and a blueberry-toned wall behind the bed (the suites feature other colors: aubergine, nectar, and sienna), contrasting with the light toned coverings on the other walls.

1515 Rhode Island Ave. NW (at Scott Circle), Washington, DC 20005. (℗ **866/984-6835** or 202/232-7000. Fax 202/332-8436. www.washingtonterracehotel.com. 220 units. Weekdays $139–$189 double; weekends $119–$149 double; rates for suites usually run $50 higher than doubles. Extra person $30. Children 16 and under stay free in parent's room. AE, DC, DISC, MC, V. Parking $22. Metro: Dupont Circle or McPherson Square. **Amenities:** Restaurant (contemporary American with Southern flair); bar; fitness center; 24-hr. concierge; business services; 24-hr. room service; same-day laundry/dry cleaning; 10 rooms for those w/limited mobility, 2 with roll-in showers. *In room:* A/C, TV w/pay movies, 2-line phones w/dataport, minibar, hair dryer, iron, safe, radio/CD player.

3 Downtown, 16th Street NW & West

VERY EXPENSIVE

Hay-Adams ✦✦   An extensive $18 million renovation completed in spring 2002 was the Hay-Adams's first major refurbishment in its 75-year history. Some improvements, like the new heating and air-conditioning system and structural changes that make the hotel accessible to guests with disabilities, were long overdue. Other improvements, like the modernized kitchen, are invisible to guests. Whether or not you've stayed at the Hay-Adams before, you'll appreciate the hotel's elegant decor of sage green, off-white, beige, and gold tones, the CD players, high-speed and wireless Internet access, custom European linens, new furnishings (the hotel donated its old furniture to local homeless shelters), and thermostats in each room.

But the best of the Hay-Adams remains much the same. The hotel still offers the best views in town. Reserve a room on the sixth through eighth floors on the H Street side of the hotel (or as low as the second floor in winter, when the trees are bare), pull back the curtains from the windows, and *voilà!*—you get a full frontal view of Lafayette Square, the White House, and the Washington Monument in the background. (You'll pay more for rooms with these views.) The view from rooms facing 16th Street isn't bad, either: Windows overlook the yellow-painted exterior of St. John's Episcopal Church, built in 1815, and known as the "church of the presidents."

The Hay-Adams is one in the triumvirate of exclusive hotels built by Harry Wardman in the 1920s (the Jefferson and the St. Regis are the other two). Its architecture is Italian Renaissance and much of the original features, such as ornate plaster moldings and ornamental fireplaces, the walnut-paneled lobby, and high-ceilinged guest rooms, are still in place. The hotel has about 13 one-bedroom suites (the living room and bedroom are separate) and seven junior suites (living room and bedroom are together in one space). Stop in at the Off the Record bar for casual fare at lunch and dinner and the occasional sighting of a big name in the media or administration.

One Lafayette Square (at 16th and H sts. NW), Washington, DC 20006. ℭ 800/853-6807 or 202/638-6600. Fax 202/638-2716. www.hayadams.com. 145 units. Weekdays $385–$595 double; weekends $269–$489 double; from $785 jr suite; from $1,250 1-bedroom suite. Extra person $30. Children under 18 stay free in parent's room. AE, DC, DISC, MC, V. Valet parking $28. Metro: Farragut West or McPherson Square. Pets under 25 lbs. accepted. **Amenities:** Restaurant (American); bar; access to local health club ($15 per day); 24-hr. concierge; complimentary morning car service; secretarial and business services; 24-hr. business center; 24-hr. room service; same-day laundry/dry cleaning; 9 rooms for those w/limited mobility, 3 with roll-in showers. *In room:* A/C, TV w/pay movies, 2-line phone w/dataports, minibar, hair dryer, iron, safe, robes, slippers, umbrella, wireless Internet access, CD player.

The Jefferson, a Loews Hotel ✿✿ Opened in 1923 just 4 blocks from the White House, the Jefferson is one of the city's three most exclusive hotels (along with the Hay-Adams and the St. Regis). Those looking for an intimate hotel, with excellent service, a good restaurant, sophisticated but comfortable accommodations, inviting public rooms (should you want to hang out), and proximity to attractions and restaurants (should you not want to hang out) will find that the Jefferson satisfies on all scores. About one-third of the lodgings are suites: junior, one-, and two-bedroom size. The hotel's largest standard rooms are located in the "carriage house," an attached town house with its own elevator, which you reach by passing through the pub/lounge in the main building. Guest rooms are individually decorated with antiques and lovely fabrics, evoking a European feel. A fine art collection, including original documents signed by Thomas Jefferson, graces the public areas as well as the guest rooms. A renovation in 2004 restored antiques, added sleeper sofas to all of the suites, and installed wireless Internet access in the public areas.

Many local foodies like to dine at the hotel's acclaimed **Restaurant at the Jefferson** ✿✿. And the paneled pub/lounge is another popular stopping place for Washingtonians; here you can sink into a red-leather chair and enjoy a marvelous high tea or cocktails.

1200 16th St. NW (at M St.), Washington, DC 20036. ℭ 800/235-6397 or 202/347-2200. Fax 202/331-7982. www.loewsjefferson.com. 100 units. Weekdays starting at $339 double, $439–$1,500 suite; weekends from $199 double, from $299 suite. Extra person $25. Children under 12 stay free in parent's room. AE, DC, DISC, MC, V. Parking $28. Metro: Farragut North. Pets welcomed and pampered. **Amenities:** Restaurant (American); bar/lounge (serving high tea 3–5pm); 24-hour fitness room; access to health club (with pool) at the University Club across the street ($20 per visit); children's program (care package at check-in); 24-hr. concierge; 24-hr. room service; 24-hr. butler service; in-room massage; babysitting; same-day laundry/dry cleaning; 1 room for those w/limited mobility, has roll-in shower; video and CD rentals. *In room:* A/C, TV w/pay movies and VCR, 2-line phone w/dataport, minibar, hair dryer, safe, robes, CD player, high-speed Internet access (for $11 fee).

Renaissance Mayflower ✿ Superbly located in the heart of downtown, the Mayflower has been the hotel of choice for guests as varied as Kurt Russell and Wynton Marsalis. The lobby, which extends an entire block from Connecticut

Avenue to 17th Street, is always bustling—read chaotic, at check-in/check-out times—since Washingtonians tend to use it as a shortcut in their travels.

The Mayflower is steeped in history: When it opened in 1925, it was the site of Calvin Coolidge's inaugural ball (though Coolidge didn't attend—he was mourning his son's death from blood poisoning). President-elect FDR and family lived in rooms 776 and 781 while waiting to move into the White House, and this is where he penned the words, "The only thing we have to fear is fear itself." A major restoration in the 1980s uncovered large skylights and renewed the lobby's pink marble bas-relief frieze and spectacular promenade.

In 2004, the hotel completed a $9 million, top-to-bottom renovation that transformed the guest rooms into individual refuges of pretty elegance: silvery green bed coverings, embroidered drapes, silk wall coverings, pillow-topped mattresses, and sink-into armchairs are some of the finer touches. Certain gracious appointments remain: Each guest room still has its own marble foyer, high ceiling, mahogany reproduction furnishings (Queen Anne, Sheraton, Chippendale, and Hepplewhite), and Italian marble bathroom. The Mayflower now has a club level on the eighth floor, as well as 74 executive suites.

In the hotel's lovely Café Promenade, lawyers and lobbyists continue to gather for weekday power breakfasts, and a full English tea is served Monday through Saturday afternoons. The clubby, mahogany-paneled Town and Country Lounge is the setting for light buffet lunches and complimentary hors d'oeuvres during cocktail hour. Bartender Sambonn Lek has quite a following, as much for his conversation as for his magic tricks, so the place is jumping.

1127 Connecticut Ave. NW (between L and M sts.), Washington, DC 20036. © **800/468-3571** or 202/347-3000. Fax 202/776-9182. www.renaissancehotels.com/WASSH. 657 units. Weekdays $199–$399 double, suites from $329; weekends $109–$209 double, suites from $259. Rates include complimentary coffee service with wakeup call. No charge for extra person in room. AE, DC, DISC, MC, V. Parking $26. Metro: Farragut North. **Amenities:** Restaurant (Mediterranean); lobby lounge; bar; fitness center; concierge; 24-hr. business center; 24-hr. room service; same-day laundry/dry cleaning; club level; 15 rooms for those w/limited mobility. *In room:* A/C, TV w/pay movies, 2-line phone w/dataport, hair dryer, iron, robes, high-speed Internet access ($9.95 per day).

The St. Regis ⭐⭐ Ah, luxury! Guest rooms are quietly opulent and decorated in tastefully coordinated colors, with duvets on the beds, desks set in alcoves, mirror-covered armoire, creamy silk moiré wall coverings, gilded chandeliers and sconces, and marble bathrooms. On the concierge level (called the "Astor Floor"), a butler unpacks and packs your suitcase, presses two items upon your arrival, and generally sees to your needs. The best rooms (other than those on the Astor Floor) probably are the grand deluxe units, which are oversize traditional rooms with a sitting area. Suites number 13, plus one presidential suite. The hotel has a restaurant on-site, but it's the bar that is the winner here: The Library Lounge might be the best hotel bar in Washington, with a working fireplace and paneled walls lined with bookcases. Recent changes have installed 24-inch flat screen TVs in standard guest rooms, 48-inch plasma screen TVs in the suites, high-speed Internet access in all guest rooms, and wireless Internet service in the lobby, restaurant, and bar.

923 16th St. NW (at K St.), Washington, DC 20006. © **800/562-5661** or 202/638-2626. Fax 202/638-4231. www.stregis.com. 193 units. Weekdays $225–$460 double; weekends $179–$405 double; from $600 suite. For best rates, check the website or call the hotel directly to ask about special promotions. Children under 16 stay free in parent's room. AE, DC, DISC, MC, V. Parking $24. Metro: Farragut West or McPherson Square. Small pets allowed for $25 per night. **Amenities:** Restaurant (American); bar/lounge; 24-hr. state-of-the-art fitness suite (plus access, for $25 fee, to either of 2 nearby health clubs, 1 of which has an indoor lap pool); 24-hr.

concierge; complimentary 1-way transportation within 6 blocks of hotel (7–9:30am weekdays); 24-hr. business center; 24-hr. room service; in-room massage; babysitting; same-day laundry/dry cleaning; concierge-level rooms; 3 rooms for those w/limited mobility, all with roll-in showers. *In room:* A/C, TV w/pay movies, fax 2-line phone w/dataport, minibar, hair dryer, iron, safe, robes, high-speed Internet access ($11 from noon to noon).

EXPENSIVE

Capital Hilton ✷   This longtime Washington hotel attracts locals as well as hotel guests to its Capital City Club fitness center and full-service day spa. The club fronts on K Street, so you can work your buns off while watching the downtown Washington scene. The club doesn't have a pool but does have 60 pieces of exercise equipment, from Lifecycle to treadmills; facials, massages, and other spa services; and personal trainers. Use of the club is free to certain Hilton HHonors guests and $10 per day ($25 maximum, no matter how long your stay) for all others.

The hotel has hosted every American president since FDR, and the annual Gridiron Club Dinner and political roast takes place in its ballroom. The Hilton's central location (2 blocks from the White House) makes it convenient for tourists, and business travelers appreciate the Tower's concierge floors (10, 11, 12, and 14) and extensive facilities.

The rooms are decorated in Federal-period motif with Queen Anne– and Chippendale-style furnishings. Corner rooms on the 16th Street side are the most spacious and offer the best city views. A number of suites are available, including three with outdoor patios. Most of the rooms are on the high end of the price range given below. But always check out the website for best deals. An ongoing promotion is the "Hilton bounce-back" weekend rate, which includes full buffet breakfast for two, and discounts for AAA members, seniors, military, and families.

1001 16th St. NW (between K and L sts.), Washington, DC 20036. ✆ **800/HILTONS** or 202/393-1000. Fax 202/639-5784. www.capital.hilton.com. 544 units. Weekdays $169–$399 double, $30 more for Tower units; weekends from $119 double; from $339 minisuite; $439 1-bedroom suite. Extra person $25. Children 18 and under stay free in parent's room. Weekend packages and other discounts available. AE, DC, DISC, MC, V. Parking $26. Metro: Farragut West, Farragut North, or McPherson Square. **Amenities:** 2 restaurants (steakhouse, American); 2 bars; 10,000-sq.-ft. health club and spa; concierge (6:30am–11pm); tour and ticket desk; business center; salon; room service (until 1am); massage; same-day laundry/dry cleaning; concierge floors; 13 rooms for those w/limited mobility; ATM with foreign currency. *In room:* A/C, TV w/pay movies, 2-line phone w/dataport, minibar, coffeemaker, hair dryer, iron, high-speed Internet access ($10 per day).

MODERATE

Hotel Rouge ✷   High-energy rock music dances out onto the sidewalk. A red awning extends from the entrance. A guest with sleepy eyes and brilliant blue hair sits diffidently upon the white tufted leather sofa in the small lobby. Attractive, casually dressed patrons come and go, while an older couple roosts at a table just inside the doorway of the adjoining Bar Rouge sipping martinis. Shades of red are everywhere: in the staff's funky shiny shirts, in the accent pillows on the retro furniture, and in the artwork. This used to be a Quality Hotel: It's come a long way, baby.

The Kimpton Hotel & Restaurant Group, LLC (known for its offbeat but upscale boutique accommodations) has transformed five old D.C. buildings into these cleverly crafted and sexy hotels (see the Topaz, Helix, Madera, and Hotel Monaco reviews on p. 106, 95, 107, and 89 respectively). In the case of Rouge, this means that your guest room will have deep crimson drapes at the window, a floor-to-ceiling red "pleather" headboard for your comfortable, white-with-red-piping duvet-covered bed, and, in the dressing room, an Orange Crush–colored dresser, whose built-in minibar holds all sorts of red items, such as Hot Tamales candies, red wax lips, and Red Bull. Guest rooms in most boutique hotels are notoriously cramped; not so here, where the rooms are spacious enough to easily accommodate several armchairs and a large ottoman (in shades of red and gold), a number of funky little lamps, a huge, mahogany framed mirror leaning against a wall, and a 10-foot-long mahogany desk. The Rouge has no suites but does offer 15 specialty guest rooms, including "Chill Rooms," which have DVD players and Sony PlayStation, "Chat Rooms," which have computer/printers, and "Chow Rooms," which have a microwave and refrigerator. The hotel embraces the theme of adventure, inviting guests to partake of a complimentary Bloody Mary in the lobby on weekends, 10am to 11am. Weeknights, 5 to 6pm, the hotel serves complimentary red wine and red beer. If that aperitif whets your appetite, you can head to the **Bar Rouge,** settle into one of the thronelike armchairs and slurp a "Brigitte Bardot Martini" (orange vodka, citron, Grand Marnier, and orange juice), or some other exotic concoction, with a plate of seductive bar food to go with it. See p. 266 for more info about Bar Rouge.

1315 16th St. NW (at Massachusetts Ave. NW and Scott Circle), Washington, DC 20036. ⓒ **800/368-5689** or 202/232-8000. Fax 202/667-9827. www.rougehotel.com. 137 units. Weekdays $159–$269 double; weekends $129–$219 double; add $40 to reserve a specialty room, weekdays or weekends. Best rates available on the website and by calling the 800 number and asking for promotional price. Extra person $20. Rates include complimentary Bloody Marys and cold pizza weekend mornings 10–11am and complimentary wine and beer weeknights 5–6pm. Children under 18 stay free in parent's room. AE, DC, DISC, MC, V. Parking $22. Metro: Dupont Circle. Pets are more than allowed, they're pampered here. **Amenities:** Bar/restaurant (American, with a French twist); modest size fitness center; 24-hr. concierge; business center; room service (7am–11pm); same-day laundry/dry cleaning; 6 rooms for those w/limited mobility, 1 with roll-in shower. *In room:* A/C, 27-in. flat-screen TV w/pay movies, 2-line cordless phones w/dataport, minibar, coffeemaker (with Starbucks coffee), hair dryer, iron, robes, CD player, free high-speed Internet access.

Lincoln Suites Downtown ★★ *Value*   This is a little hotel with a big heart. It tries hard to do right by its guests and, judging from feedback I've received from readers who've stayed here, I would say it succeeds. (Check out the website, where the hotel's can-do personality shines through.) Key elements include the hotel's location, in the heart of downtown, near Metro stops, restaurants, and the White House; a congenial staff; the complimentary milk and homemade cookies served each evening; and daily complimentary breakfast (fruit, pastries, muffins, cereals, and sometimes waffles) in the breakfast room. Lincoln Suites also has direct access to **Mackey's,** an Irish pub right next door, and to **Recessions,** a restaurant on the lower level serving American/Mediterranean cuisine. **Famous Luigi's Pizzeria Restaurant** ★, an Italian restaurant and veritable Washington institution (p. 144), located right around the corner, delivers room service for lunch and dinner.

The all-suite 10-story hotel is quite nice, in a nothing-fancy sort of way. Lots of long-term guests bunk here. Suites are large and comfortable; about 28 offer full kitchens, while the rest have wet bars (mini-refrigerator, microwave, and coffeemaker). An ongoing renovation has slowly but surely overhauled the hotel, replacing all the furniture, appliances, carpeting, and wall coverings, so that the overall design is brighter and contemporary. That goes for the lobby, which has been transformed into a hip two-story lobby/lounge. By the time you read this, the hotel will be offering high-speed Internet access and have on-site its own fitness center (most likely, you'll still have the choice to use the nearby larger facility for free).

1823 L St. NW, Washington, DC 20036. (C) **800/424-2970** or 202/223-4320. Fax 202/293-4977. www. lincolnhotels.com. 99 suites. Weekdays $175–$215 peak, $135–$175 non-peak; weekends $115–$155 year-round. Rates include deluxe continental breakfast. Discounts available for long-term stays. Children under 16 stay free in parent's room. AE, DC, DISC, MC, V. Parking $20 (in adjoining garage). Metro: Farragut North or Farragut West. Pets under 25 lb. accepted, second floor only, for $15 a day (the fee may increase in 2005). **Amenities:** Restaurant (American/Mediterranean); bar (Irish); free passes to the well-equipped Bally's Holiday Spa nearby; 24-hr. front desk/concierge; room service (11am–11pm); coin-op washer/dryers; Mon–Sat same-day laundry/dry cleaning; 2 rooms for those w/limited mobility, 1 with roll-in shower. *In room:* A/C, TV w/pay movies, dataport, fridge, coffeemaker, hair dryer, iron, high-speed Internet access, microwave, wet bar.

4 Adams-Morgan

Note: The hotels listed here are situated just north of Dupont Circle, more at the mouth of Adams-Morgan than within its actual boundaries.

EXPENSIVE

Hilton Washington ★ *Kids* This sprawling hotel, built in 1965, occupies 7 acres and calls itself a "resort"—mostly on the basis of having landscaped gardens, tennis courts, and an Olympic-style pool on its premises, unusual amenities for a D.C. hotel. The Hilton caters to corporate groups, some of whom may have families in tow (during the summer, the reception desk gives families a complimentary gift and lends them board games—ask for the "Vacation Station" perk), and is accustomed to coordinating meetings for thousands of attendees. Its vast conference facilities include one of the largest hotel ballrooms on the East Coast (it accommodates nearly 4,000). By contrast, guest rooms are on the small side. A renovation of all guest rooms completed in 2003 installed elegant dark wood furnishings in every room. High-speed Internet access is available in all guest rooms, for a charge of $10 per 24 hours. From the fifth floor up, pool-side, you'll have panoramic views of Washington. The hotel's health club has been thoroughly renovated and expanded, and now offers extensive spa services.

The designated concierge-level rooms usually go for about $30 more than the standard room rate. The hotel has 52 suites, in all kinds of configurations, from the junior executive (in which parlor and bedroom are combined) to the huge Presidential Suite.

The Hilton puts you within an easy stroll of embassies, great restaurants, museums, and the charming neighborhoods of Adams-Morgan, and Woodley Park (all up the hill), and Dupont Circle (down the hill).

1919 Connecticut Ave. NW (at T St.), Washington, DC 20009. (C) **800/HILTONS** or 202/483-3000. Fax 202/232-0438. www.Washington.Hilton.com. 1,119 units. Weekdays $169–$374 double; weekends (and some weekdays and holidays) $119–$314 double; $500–$1,800 suite. Look for deals on the website or by calling Hilton's 800 number. Extra person $25. Children 18 and under stay free in parent's room. AE, DC, DISC, MC, V. Self-parking $21. Metro: Dupont Circle. **Amenities:** 2 restaurants (both American); deli; 2 bars (a pub, and lobby bar occasionally featuring a pianist); Olympic-style heated outdoor pool; 3 lighted tennis courts; extensive health-club facilities; concierge; transportation/sightseeing desk; comprehensive business center; lobby shops; room service (until 2am); same-day laundry/dry cleaning; concierge-level rooms; 28 rooms for those w/limited mobility, some with roll-in showers. *In room:* A/C, TV w/pay movies; 2-line phone w/dataport, coffeemaker, hair dryer, iron, high-speed Internet access ($10 per day).

MODERATE

Courtyard by Marriott Northwest This hotel isn't much to look at from the outside, but inside it has a European feel and a well-heeled appearance. Crystal chandeliers hang in the lobby and in the restaurant, and you may hear an Irish lilt from time to time (the hotel is one of three in Washington owned by Jurys Doyle Hotel Group, an Irish management company). Guests tend to linger in the comfortable lounge off the lobby, where coffee is available all day.

A complete refurbishment in 2004 replaced just about everything in the guest rooms, from TVs to carpeting. Cherry wood furniture, blue carpeting, 25-inch TVs, complimentary high-speed Internet access—all new. Guest rooms are still very comfortable and bright. Accommodations facing the street on the sixth to ninth floors provide panoramic views. Especially nice are the 16 "executive king" rooms, which are a little larger and are equipped with marble bathrooms, trouser presses, and robes.

For the best deals, call direct to the hotel or go to the website.

1900 Connecticut Ave. NW (at Leroy Place), Washington, DC 20009. $\textcircled{C}$ 888/236-2427 or 202/332-9300. Fax 202/319-1793. www.marriot.com. 147 units. $89–$245 double. Extra person $15. Children under 18 stay free in parent's room. Ask about discount packages. AE, DC, DISC, MC, V. Parking $20. Metro: Dupont Circle. **Amenities:** Restaurant (American, open for breakfast and dinner); bar; outdoor pool (seasonal); small exercise room; business center; room service (5–10pm); coin-operated laundry; same-day laundry and dry cleaning; 2 rooms for those w/limited mobility, both with roll-in showers. *In room:* A/C, TV w/pay movies, 2-line phone w/dataport, coffeemaker, hair dryer, iron, safe, complimentary high-speed Internet access.

INEXPENSIVE

Jurys Normandy Inn ★ *Finds*   This gracious hotel is a gem—a small gem, but a gem nonetheless. Situated in a neighborhood of architecturally impressive embassies, the hotel hosts many embassy-bound guests. You may discover this for yourself on a Tuesday evening, when guests gather in the charming Tea Room to enjoy complimentary wine and cheese served from the antique oak sideboard. This is also where you'll find daily continental breakfast (for about $6.50), complimentary coffee and tea after 10am, and cookies after 3pm. You can lounge or watch TV in the conservatory, or, in nice weather, you can move outside to the garden patio.

The six-floor Normandy has small but pretty twin and queen guest rooms (all remodeled in 2003), with tapestry-upholstered mahogany and cherry-wood furnishings in 18th-century style, and pretty floral-print bedspreads covering firm beds. Rooms facing Wyoming Avenue overlook the tree-lined street, while other rooms mostly offer views of apartment buildings. The Normandy is an easy walk from both Adams-Morgan and Dupont Circle, where many restaurants and shops await you. All rooms offer free, high-speed Internet access.

2118 Wyoming Ave. NW (at Connecticut Ave.), Washington, DC 20008. $\textcircled{C}$ 800/424-3729 or 202/483-1350. Fax 202/387-8241. www.jurysdoyle.com. 75 units. $89–$185 double. Extra person $10. Children under 12 stay free in parent's room. AE, DC, DISC, MC, V. Parking $15 plus tax. Metro: Dupont Circle. **Amenities:** Access to the neighboring Courtyard by Marriott Northwest's pool and exercise room; room service at breakfast; coin-op washer/dryers; same-day laundry/dry cleaning (Mon–Sat); 4 rooms for those w/limited mobility, 1 with roll-in shower. *In room:* A/C, TV, 2-line phone w/dataport, mini-fridge, coffeemaker, hair dryer, iron, safe, free high-speed Internet access.

Kalorama Guest House   This San Francisco–style B&B has two locations: in Adams-Morgan, where a Victorian town house at 1854 Mintwood Place NW is the main dwelling, with two other houses on the same street providing additional lodging; and in nearby Woodley Park ($\textcircled{C}$ **202/328-0860;** fax 202/328-8730), where two houses on Cathedral Avenue NW offer a total of 19 guest rooms (see "Woodley Park," later in this chapter for more information about this location).

The cozy common areas and homey guest rooms are furnished with finds from antique stores, flea markets, and auctions. The Mintwood Place town house has a breakfast room with plant-filled windows. There's a garden behind the house with umbrella tables.

Rooms in all the houses generally offer either double or queen-size beds, but the Mintwood Place town house offers larger units in a greater variety of

Adams-Morgan, Dupont Circle & West End Accommodations

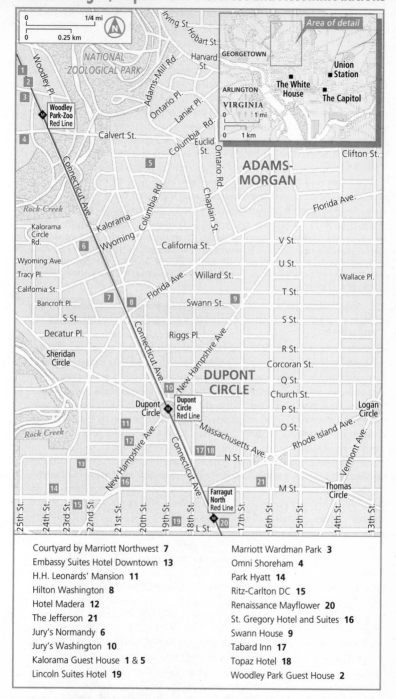

Courtyard by Marriott Northwest **7**
Embassy Suites Hotel Downtown **13**
H.H. Leonards' Mansion **11**
Hilton Washington **8**
Hotel Madera **12**
The Jefferson **21**
Jury's Normandy **6**
Jury's Washington **10**
Kalorama Guest House **1** & **5**
Lincoln Suites Hotel **19**

Marriott Wardman Park **3**
Omni Shoreham **4**
Park Hyatt **14**
Ritz-Carlton DC **15**
Renaissance Mayflower **20**
St. Gregory Hotel and Suites **16**
Swann House **9**
Tabard Inn **17**
Topaz Hotel **18**
Woodley Park Guest House **2**

configurations: There's an efficiency apartment with a kitchen, telephone, and TV; one small two-room apartment with a kitchen, cable TV, and telephone; and four suites (two two-bedroom and two "executive" suites, in which the living room and bedroom are together).

All locations serve a complimentary breakfast of juice, coffee, fruit, bagels, croissants, and English muffins. They also give guests access to laundry and ironing facilities, a refrigerator, a seldom-used TV, and a phone (local calls are free; incoming calls are answered around the clock, so people can leave messages for you). It's customary for the innkeepers to put out sherry daily, adding lemonade and cookies in summer, and tea and cookies in winter. Magazines, games, and current newspapers are available. All of the houses are nonsmoking. At both locations, your fellow guests are likely to be Europeans, tourists, and business people.

The Mintwood Place location is near Metro stations, restaurants, nightspots, and shops. The Cathedral Avenue houses, which are even closer to the Woodley Park–Zoo Metro, offer proximity to Rock Creek Park and the National Zoo.

1854 Mintwood Place NW (between 19th St. and Columbia Rd.), Washington, DC 20009. © 202/667-6369. Fax 202/319-1262. http://yp.washingtonpost.com/yp/kgh. 30 units, 16 with bathroom (6 with shower only). $55–$75 double with shared bathroom; $75–$100 double with bathroom; $105–$145 suite or apt. Extra person $5 in doubles, $10 in suites. Rates include continental breakfast. AE, DC, DISC, MC, V. Limited parking $7. Metro: Woodley Park–Zoo or Dupont Circle. Kids 6 and older only. **Amenities:** Washer/dryer; common fridge; common TV. *In room:* A/C.

5 Dupont Circle

EXPENSIVE

The Mansion on O Street ★★ *Finds*   A legend in her own time, H. H. Leonards operates this Victorian property, made up of four interconnecting, five-story town houses, as a museum with rotating exhibits, an event space, a private club, an art gallery, an antiques emporium, and—oh, yeah—a B&B. The Mansion attracts a lot of celebrities and CEOs, mostly people who crave both luxury and privacy (H won't reveal her guests' names). If you stay here, you may find yourself buying a sweater, a painting, or (who knows?) an antique bed. Everything's for sale.

Guest rooms are so creative they'll blow you away; they're expensive, but simply outrageous. Most breathtaking is the Log Cabin loft suite, with a bed whose headboard encases an aquarium. The Art Deco–style penthouse takes up an entire floor (with a large living room, a bedroom, and a kitchen) and has its own security cameras, elevator, 10 phones, and multiple televisions and DVD systems. The International Room (one room with a queen bed and sitting area) has a nonworking fireplace and four TVs, a combination of Victorian antiques and contemporary furnishings, a sunny sitting area, hand-made prism-glass windows, and a bright bathroom with two-person Jacuzzi. The simplest of the bunch is the Country Room, decorated in blue and white, and with French doors leading to a porch overlooking O Street. All rooms have either king-size or queen-size beds and complimentary high-speed Internet access; most have a whirlpool and a few have kitchens. Elsewhere on the property, there's an outdoor pool, eight office/conference spaces, 28 far-out bathrooms, art and antiques everywhere, and a thousand or so books. Full business services are available.

2020 O St. NW (between 20th and 21st sts.), Washington, DC 20036. © 202/496-2000. Fax 202/659-0547. www.omansion.com. 19 units, all with private bathrooms. $150–$1,000; summer $125–$750. Nonprofit, group, and long-term rates available. Rates include breakfast. AE, MC, V. Parking $15 by reservation. Metro: Dupont Circle. **Amenities:** Small outdoor pool; concierge; state-of-the-art business center; laundry service at no charge. *In room:* A/C, TV, 2-line phone w/dataport, hair dryer, iron, robes, free high-speed Internet access.

St. Gregory Luxury Hotel and Suites ★★ The St. Gregory, open since June 2000, is an affordable luxury property, with marble floors and chandeliers. The hotel is well situated at the corner of 21st and M streets, not far from Georgetown, Dupont Circle, Foggy Bottom, and the White House, and with many good restaurants within a literal stone's throw.

Most of the guest rooms are one-bedroom suites, with a separate living room and bedroom, and with a pullout sofa in the living room. For privacy and views, choose one of the 16 "sky" suites on the ninth floor, each with terrace and city overlooks. Of the 100 suites, 85 have fully appointed kitchens, including microwaves, ovens, and full-size refrigerators (the other 15 suites have no kitchens). In the remaining 54 units are either king or two double beds. Decor throughout the hotel is an attractive mélange of olive green and gold, with un-hotel-like lamps, mirror frames, and fabrics. Three whole floors of the hotel are reserved for club-level rooms. The St. Gregory offers special rates to long-term and government guests, and to those from the diplomatic community. If you don't fall into one of those categories, check the hotel's website for great deals like the often available "One Dollar Clearance Sale": You pay a set price—this can fluctuate, sometimes $159, sometimes $209—the first night and only $1 for the second night, for Friday and Saturday, or Saturday and Sunday stays. To book this discount, you must call the hotel's 800 number.

2033 M St. NW (at 21st St.), Washington, DC 20036. ℂ 800/829-5034 or 202/530-3600. Fax 202/466-6770. www.stgregoryhotelwdc.com. 154 units. Weekdays $189–$269 double or suite; weekends $149–$249 double or suite. Extra person $20. Children under 16 stay free in parent's room. Ask about discounts, long-term stays, and packages. AE, DC, MC, V. Parking $15 weekends, $22 weekdays. Metro: Dupont Circle or Farragut North. **Amenities:** Restaurant and coffee bar (American) with sidewalk seating seasonally; state-of-the-art fitness center, as well as access (for $20 fee) to the nearby and larger Sports Club/LA (p. 110 for full description); concierge; tour desk; business center; room service (6:30am–10:30pm); massage; babysitting; coin-op laundry room; same-day laundry/dry cleaning; concierge-level rooms; 6 rooms for those w/limited mobility, 2 with roll-in showers. *In room:* A/C, TV w/pay movies, 2-line phone w/dataport, fridge, coffeemaker, hair dryer, iron, CD player, high-speed Internet access ($9.95 per day).

Swann House ★ *Finds* At the rate it's going, Swann House may one day be known as "the inn that launched 1,000 marriages," for all of the couples who have become engaged while staying here. This stunning 1883 mansion, poised prominently on a corner 4 blocks north of Dupont Circle, has nine exquisite guest rooms. The coolest unit is the Blue Sky Suite, covered in blue and white toile, with the original rose-tiled working fireplace, a queen-size bed and day bed, a sitting room, a gabled ceiling, and a roof deck. The most romantic room is probably Il Duomo, with Gothic windows, a cathedral ceiling, a working fireplace, and a turreted bathroom with angel murals, a claw-foot tub, and a rain showerhead. The Jennifer Green Room has a queen-size four-poster bed, a working fireplace, an oversize marble steam shower, and a private deck overlooking the pool area and garden. The Regent Room also has a private deck overlooking the pool, as well as a king-size bed in front of a carved working fireplace and a whirlpool. There are three suites. You'll want to spend some time on the main floor of the mansion, which has 12-foot ceilings, fluted woodwork, inlaid wood floors, a turreted living room, a columned sitting room, and a sunroom (where breakfast is served) leading through three sets of French doors to the garden and pool. Free high-speed Internet access is available in the public rooms, and wireless access is available in most guest rooms. No smoking.

1808 New Hampshire Ave. NW (between S and Swann sts.), Washington, DC 20009. ℂ 202/265-4414. Fax 202/265-6755. www.swannhouse.com. 9 units, all with private bathroom (3 with shower only). $140–$295 depending on unit and season. 2-night minimum weekends, 3-night minimum holiday weekends. Extended-stay and government rates available. Extra person $35. Rates include expanded continental breakfast. Limited off-street parking $12. AE, MC, V. Metro: Dupont Circle. No children under age 12. **Amenities:** Outdoor pool; access to nearby health club; business services; in-room massage; same-day dry cleaning. *In room:* A/C, TV, phone w/voicemail and dataport, hair dryer, wireless Internet access (in most rooms).

Topaz Hotel ✪   Like the Hotel Rouge (p. 99 for review), the Topaz is an upscale boutique hotel for those who think young. This hotel seems tamer than the Rouge, but it still has a buzz about it, a pleasant, interesting sort of buzz. The reception area, lobby, and bar flow together, so if you arrive in the evening, you may feel like you've arrived at a party: The **Topaz Bar** and the Bar Rouge have fast become favorite hangouts for the after-work crowd. At the Topaz, they're liking drinks called "Blue Nirvana" (champagne mixed with vodka and blueberry liqueur) and "Pop" (6-oz. single servings of Pommery champagne), the better-than-bar-food cuisine with an Asian accent, and the decor of velvety settees, zebra-patterned ottomans, and a lighting system that fades in and out. (See p. 272 for more information about the Topaz Bar.)

Upstairs are guest rooms appealingly, whimsically decorated with striped lime green wallpaper; a polka dot padded headboard for the down-comforter-covered bed; a bright blue, curved-back settee; a big, round mirror set in a sunburst frame; a light green and yellow painted armoire with fabric panels; and a red, with gold star-patterned cushioned chair. The rooms are unusually large (in its former life as the Canterbury Hotel, these were "junior suites" and held kitch-enettes), and each has an alcove where the desk is placed, and a separate dress-ing room that holds a dressing table and cube-shaped ottoman. The Topaz pursues a sort of New Age wellness motif; do note the spill of smooth stones arranged just so upon your bed. ("Through time people have carried special stones called totems to bring them energy and empowerment . . ." reads a little card accompanying the stones.) You also have the option to book a specialty room: one of four "energy" guest rooms, which include a piece of exercise equip-ment (either a treadmill or a stationary bike), and fitness magazines; or one of three "yoga" rooms, which come with an exercise mat, an instructional tape, padded pillows, special towels, and yoga magazines. Wireless Internet access is available in all guest rooms.

The Topaz lies on a quiet residential street, whose front-of-the-house win-dows overlook picturesque town houses.

1733 N St. NW (right next to the Tabard Inn, see below, between 17th and 18th sts.), Washington, DC 20036. ℭ **800/424-2950** or 202/393-3000. Fax 202/785-9581. www.topazhotel.com. 99 units. Weekdays $209–$279 double, $280 specialty room; weekends $139 double, $169 specialty room. It is very likely that you can get a much lower rate by calling direct to the hotel or by booking a reservation online. Extra person $20. Chil-dren under 16 stay free in parent's room. Rates include complimentary morning energy potions. AE, DC, DISC, MC, V. Parking $24. Metro: Dupont Circle. Pets welcome. **Amenities:** Bar/restaurant (innovative American with an Asian influence); access to nearby health club ($5 per guest); 24-hr. concierge; 24-hour business cen-ter; room service (7am–11pm); same-day laundry/dry cleaning; 5 rooms for those w/limited mobility, 2 with roll-in showers. *In room:* A/C, TV w/pay movies, 2-line cordless phones w/dataports, minibar, hair dryer, iron, safe, robes, wireless Internet access, teapot with exotic teas.

MODERATE

Embassy Suites Hotel Downtown ✪ *Kids*   This hotel offers unbelievable value and a convenient location, within walking distance of Foggy Bottom, Georgetown, and Dupont Circle. You enter into a tropical and glassy eight-story atrium with two waterfalls constantly running. This is where you'll enjoy an ample complimentary breakfast—not your standard cold croissant and coffee, but stations from which you can choose omelets made to order, waffles, bacon, fresh fruit, juices, bagels, and pastries. Tables are scattered in alcoves throughout the atrium to allow for privacy. Each evening, the atrium is the setting for complimentary beverages (including cocktails) and light cold snacks. The hotel's restaurant offers discounts to hotel guests and a children's menu for $4.95.

By February 2005, the hotel will have completed a $4.5 million renovation to give the entire property an "urban-modern, but not chi-chi" look: Dark marble replaces light marble, guest room sofas will be covered in maroon tapestry fabric, and wireless Internet access will be available throughout the hotel (guests pay $9.95 per 24-hours for a computer access card, if needed).

The accommodations remain, as always, nicer than your average hotel room, with better amenities. Every unit is a two-room suite, with a living room that closes off completely from the rest of the suite. The living room holds a queen-size sofa bed, TV, easy chair, and large table with four comfortable chairs around it. The bedroom lies at the back of the suite, overlooking a quiet courtyard of brick walkways or the street. A king-size bed or two double beds, TV, sink, easy chair, and chest of drawers furnish this space. Between the living room and the bedroom are the bathroom, small closet, and a kitchenette. It's worth requesting one of the eighth- or ninth-floor suites with views of Georgetown and beyond, as far as Washington National Cathedral (the hotel will note your request, but won't be able to guarantee you such a suite). For the roomiest quarters, ask for an "executive corner suite," the slightly larger, slightly more expensive suites situated in the corners of the hotel.

1250 22nd St. NW (between M and N sts.), Washington, DC 20037. (℃) 800/EMBASSY or 202/857-3388. Fax 202/293-3173. www.embassysuitesdcmetro.com. 318 suites. $149–$309 double. Rates include full breakfast and evening reception. Ask for AAA discounts or check the website for best rates. Extra person $25 weekdays. Children 18 and under stay free in parent's room. AE, DC, DISC, MC, V. Parking $20. Metro: Foggy Bottom. **Amenities:** Restaurant (northern Italian); state-of-the-art fitness center with indoor pool, whirlpool, sauna; game room; concierge; business center (with free Internet access on 3 computers); room service (11am–11pm); coin-op washer/dryers; same-day laundry/dry cleaning; 8 rooms for those w/limited mobility, 2 with roll-in showers. *In room:* A/C, TV w/pay movies, 2-line phone w/dataport, kitchenette with fridge and microwave, coffeemaker, hair dryer, iron.

Hotel Madera ⭐ The Hotel Madera fancies itself as a kind of *pied-a-terre,* or home away from home, for travelers. But it would be a mistake to think that means the hotel is homey in the traditional sense. This is a boutique hotel, whose sisters, the hotels Rouge, Topaz, Helix, and Monaco, each reviewed elsewhere in this chapter, have all made separate splashes in our fair city. The Madera, likewise, caters to those with avant-garde tastes. The registration desk in the small lobby is covered in leather; a hammered copper mobile of abstract leaflike shapes dangles overhead. The guest rooms are large (this used to be an apartment building), measuring an average 340 square feet. Those on the New Hampshire Avenue side have balconies that offer city views. Rooms at the back of the house, 6th through 10th floors don't have balconies, but do have pretty good views of Rock Creek Park, Georgetown, and the Washington National Cathedral. All rooms are comfortable and furnished with sofas and bed benches, and with beds whose wild-looking headboards are giant dark wood panels inset with a patch of vibrant blue padded mohair. Other fey touches: pillows covered in animal print or satiny fabrics, grass-clothlike wall coverings, and black granite with chrome bathroom vanities. Every guest room has complimentary high-speed Internet access. The "specialty" rooms (a feature of all Kimpton Group hotels) at the Madera include a Nosh Room (studio with kitchenette and grocery shopping service), Flash Room (with personal computer, printer), Strength (has a Nautilus machine) and Cardio (has either a treadmill, exercise bike, or elliptical steps) rooms, and a Screening Room (equipped with a second TV, DVD player, and a library of DVDs).

The Madera has an excellent restaurant, **Firefly,** which I review in chapter 6.

1310 New Hampshire Ave. NW (between N and O sts.), Washington, DC 20036. ℂ **800/368-5691** or 202/296-7600. Fax 202/293-2476. www.hotelmadera.com. 82 units. Weekdays and weekends $159–$259 double; add $40 to the going rate for a specialty room. For best rates, call direct to the hotel or go its website. Extra person $20. Children under 16 stay free in parent's room. Rates include evening wine hour. AE, DC, DISC, MC, V. Parking $24. Metro: Dupont Circle. Pets welcome. **Amenities:** Bar/restaurant (American bistro); access to the posh Sports Club/LA health club at the nearby Ritz-Carlton ($15 per guest per day); 24-hr. concierge; business center; room service (during restaurant hours); same-day laundry/dry cleaning; 6 rooms for those w/limited mobility, all with roll-in showers. *In room:* A/C, TV w/pay movies, 2-line cordless phones w/dataports, minibar, coffeemaker with Starbucks coffee, hair dryer, iron, safe, robes, umbrella, free high-speed Internet access.

Hotel Tabard Inn If you favor the offbeat and the personal over brand names and cookie-cutter chains, this might be the place for you. The Tabard Inn, named for the hostelry in Chaucer's *Canterbury Tales,* is actually three Victorian town houses that were joined in 1914 and have operated as an inn ever since. Situated on a quiet street of similarly old dwellings, the Tabard is a well-worn, funky hotel that's looked after by a chummy, peace-love-and-understanding sort of staff who clearly cherish the place.

The heart of the ground floor is the dark-paneled lounge, with worn furniture, a wood-burning fireplace, the original beamed ceiling, and bookcases. This is a favorite spot for Washingtonians to come for a drink, especially in winter, or to linger before or after dining in the charming **Tabard Inn restaurant** ✦ (p. 150 for a full review).

From the lounge, the inn leads you up and down stairs, along dim corridors, and through nooks and crannies to guest rooms. Can you dig chartreuse? (Ask for room 3.) How about aubergine? (Ask for room 11.) Each is different, but those facing N Street are largest and brightest, and some have bay windows. Furnishings are a mix of antiques and flea-market finds. Perhaps the most eccentric room is the top-floor "penthouse," which has skylights, exposed brick walls, its own kitchen, and a deck accessed by climbing out a window. The inn is not easily accessible to guests with disabilities.

1739 N St. NW (between 17th and 18th sts.), Washington, DC 20036. ℂ **202/785-1277.** Fax 202/785-6173. www.tabardinn.com. 40 units, 27 with private bathroom (6 with shower only). $108–$130 double with shared bathroom; $135–$205 double with private bathroom. Extra person $15. Rates include continental breakfast. AE, DC, DISC, MC, V. Limited street parking, plus 2 parking garages on N St. Metro: Dupont Circle.

Moments **"There's a Small Hotel"**

If you're in Washington on a Sunday night and you're staying at the **Hotel Tabard Inn,** be sure to plant yourself in the paneled parlor by 7:30pm. Even if you're not staying at the Tabard, you might want to get yourself there. From 7:30 to 10:30pm each Sunday, bassist Victor Dvoskin, usually accompanied by a guitarist, plays world-class jazz for free. Order a drink from the bar in the next room, then settle into one of the old chairs or sofas to enjoy the show. "There's a Small Hotel" is the name of a CD released by Dvoskin, in honor of Tabard owners Fritzi Cohen and her late husband, Edward, whose private program, the Capitals Citizens' Exchange, first brought Dvoskin to this country from Russia in 1988.

Small and confined pets allowed ($20 fee). **Amenities:** Restaurant (regional American) with lounge (free live jazz Sun evenings); free access to nearby YMCA (with extensive facilities that include indoor pool, indoor track, and racquetball/basketball courts); laundry service; fax, iron, hair dryer, and safe available at front desk. *In room:* A/C, dataport.

Jurys Washington Hotel *★ Value*   This hotel gets high marks for convenience (it's located right on Dupont Circle), service, and comfort. Open since 2000, the hotel is favored by business groups especially, who like its reasonable rates. Each of the large rooms is furnished with two double beds with firm mattresses, an armoire with TV, a desk, a wet-bar alcove, and a tiny but attractive bathroom. Decor is Art Deco-ish, with lots of light-wood furniture. All guest rooms offer free, high-speed Internet access. Despite its prime location in a sometimes raucous neighborhood, the hotel's rooms are insulated from the noise. Rooms on higher floors offer the best views of the city and of Dupont Circle. An Irish management company owns this hotel (along with two other properties in Washington, D.C.), and the comfortable and attractive hotel pub, Biddy Mulligan's, proudly features a bar imported from the Emerald Isle. Its American restaurant, **Dupont Grille,** opened in spring 2003, and a welcome addition it is to the hotel and the neighborhood (see review, chapter 6). Check the hotel's website for guaranteed lowest rates.

1500 New Hampshire Ave. NW (across from Dupont Circle), Washington, DC 20036. ℂ **866/JDHOTELS** or 202/483-6000. Fax 202/238-3265. www.jurysdoyle.com. 314 units. $89–$245 double; from $600 suite. Extra person $15. Children 17 and under stay free in parent's room. AE, DC, DISC, MC, V. Parking $20. Metro: Dupont Circle. **Amenities:** Restaurant (American); bar; exercise room; 24-hr. concierge; business center; room service (6:30am–midnight); same-day laundry/dry cleaning; 11 rooms for those w/limited mobility, 4 with roll-in showers. *In room:* A/C, TV w/pay movies, 2-line phone w/dataport, minibar, coffeemaker, hair dryer, iron, safe, free high-speed Internet access.

6 Foggy Bottom/West End

VERY EXPENSIVE

Park Hyatt Washington *★★*   This luxury hotel, last renovated in 1998, features large guest rooms with goose-down duvets on the beds, modern furniture, wall coverings, and fabrics. High-speed Internet access is available in all the guest rooms (at the time of this writing, the hotel had not decided whether to charge for this service). Specially commissioned artwork hangs throughout the hotel. More than half of the rooms are suites (meaning the parlor and bedroom are separate), and the remaining rooms are deluxe kings. The suites also have dressing rooms with full vanities. Each bathroom has a TV, a radio, and a telephone, along with the usual amenities. The 17-year-old 10-story hotel hosts big names, royal families (who use the Presidential Suite, with its fireplace and grand piano), lobbyists, and tourists. Rooms are handsome and service is superb. A major renovation scheduled for completion in 2005 will redesign the look of the sleeping rooms.

The bright and lovely **Melrose** dining room offers four-star cuisine with an emphasis on seafood (p. 153 for a full review); the amiable chef, Brian McBride, pops into the dining room personally from time to time to make sure all is well. Adjoining the Melrose is a bar, where there's swing dancing to live jazz every weekend. For the lowest rate, visit the hotel's website.

1201 24th St. NW (at M St.), Washington, DC 20037. ℂ **800/778-7477** or 202/789-1234. Fax 202/419-6795. www.parkhyattwashington.com. 223 units. Weekdays $320–$450 double; weekends $215–$289 double. Extra person $25 (no charge on weekends). Children 18 and under stay free in parent's room. AE, DC, DISC, MC, V. Valet parking $25. Metro: Foggy Bottom or Dupont Circle. Pets allowed. **Amenities:** Restaurant (American); bar/lounge (with live entertainment Fri–Sat); health club with indoor pool, whirlpool, and sauna and steam rooms; spa with hair and skin salon; concierge; business center; 24-hr. room service; in-room massage; same-day laundry/dry cleaning; 10 rooms for those w/limited mobility, 3 with roll-in showers. *In room:* A/C, TV w/pay movies, 2-line phone w/dataport, minibar, hair dryer, iron, safe, robes, high-speed Internet access (fee).

The Ritz-Carlton, Washington, D.C. ★★★ This Ritz-Carlton, which opened in October 2000, surpasses all other Washington hotels for service and amenities. From the cadre of doormen and valet parking attendants who greet you effusively when you arrive, to the graceful young women in long dresses who swan around you serving cocktails in the bar and lounge, the Ritz staff is always looking after you.

The hotel is built around a multi-tiered Japanese garden and courtyard with reflecting pools and cascading waterfall; guest rooms on the inside of the complex overlook the waterfall or terraced garden, while guest rooms on the outside perimeter view landmarks and cityscapes. The woman who showed me to my terrace-view room inadvertently, but appropriately, kept referring to the hotel as the "Rich-Carlton." My standard room was very large, and richly furnished with a firm king-size bed covered in both duvet and bedspread, decorative inlaid wooden furniture, a comfy armchair and ottoman, and very pretty artwork. The marble bathroom was immense, with long counter space, separate bathtub and shower stall, and the toilet in its own room behind a louvered door. The clock radio doubles as a CD player and the phone features a button for summoning the "technology butler" (a complimentary, 24/7 service for guests with computer questions). Other nice touches in the rooms include an umbrella, windows that open, and an outlet for recharging laptops. Don't make the same mistake that I did when I passed up the evening turndown—the maid places a warm, freshly baked brownie upon your pillow instead of the usual mint.

Among the different versions of suites available, most are "executives," which include a sitting room and separate bedroom.

Guests enjoy free use of the hotel's fitness center, the two-level, 100,000-square-foot **Sports Club/LA,** which leaves all other hotel health clubs in the dust with its state-of-the-art weight-training equipment and free weights, two regulation-size basketball courts and four squash courts, an indoor heated swimming pool and an aquatics pool with a sun deck, exercise classes, personal trainers, the full-service Splash Spa and Roche Salon, and a restaurant and cafe.

The Ritz's bar and lounge are also exceptionally inviting, with lots of plush upholstered couches and armchairs, a fire blazing in the fireplace in winter, and a pianist playing every day. Afternoon tea is served in the lounge daily.

1150 22nd St. NW (at M St.), Washington, DC 20037. ℂ 800/241-3333 or 202/835-0500. Fax 202/835-1588. www.ritzcarlton.com. 300 units. $450 double; from $595 suite. No charge for extra person in the room. Ask about discount packages. AE, DC, DISC, MC, V. Valet parking $28. Metro: Foggy Bottom or Dupont Circle. Pets accepted (no fee). **Amenities:** Restaurant (American); lounge; fabulous health club and spa (the best in the city; see above); 24-hr. concierge; business center (open weekdays); salon; 24-hr. room service; in-room massage; babysitting; same-day laundry/dry cleaning with 1-hr. pressing; club level with 5 complimentary food presentations throughout the day (including a chef station each morning to prepare individual requests); 10 rooms for those w/limited mobility, 6 with roll-in showers; 24-hr. fax and currency-exchange services. *In room:* A/C, TV w/pay movies, 2-line phone, minibar/fridge, hair dryer, iron, safe, robes, umbrella, CD player, high-speed Internet access ($10 per day).

EXPENSIVE

George Washington University Inn Rumor has it that this whitewashed brick inn, another former apartment building, used to be a favorite spot for clandestine trysts for high-society types. These days you're more likely to see

Kennedy Center performers and visiting professors. The university purchased the hotel (formerly known as the Inn at Foggy Bottom) in 1994 and renovated it. The most recent refurbishment, in 2001, replaced linens, drapes, and the like in the guest rooms. Free high-speed Internet access was added in 2004.

Rooms are a little larger and corridors are a tad narrower than those in a typical hotel, and each room includes a roomy dressing chamber. More than one-third of the units are one-bedroom suites. These are especially spacious, with living rooms that hold a sleeper sofa and a TV hidden in an armoire (there's another in the bedroom). The suites, plus the 16 efficiencies, have kitchens. The spaciousness and the kitchen facilities make this a popular choice for families and for long-term guests.

This is a fairly safe and lovely neighborhood, within easy walking distance to Georgetown, the Kennedy Center, and downtown. But keep an eye peeled—you have to pass through wrought-iron gates into a kind of cul-de-sac to find the inn.

Off the lobby is the restaurant, **Nectar** (p. 155 for review), which opened in spring 2003.

If it's not full, the inn may be willing to offer reduced rates. Mention your affiliation with George Washington University, if you have one, to receive a special "GWU" rate.

824 New Hampshire Ave. NW (between H and I sts.), Washington, DC 20037. Ⓒ **800/426-4455** or 202/337-6620. Fax 202/298-7499. www.gwuinn.com. 95 units. Weekdays $139–$249 double, $159–$269 efficiency, $179–$289 1-bedroom suite; weekends $119–$189 double; $139–$209 efficiency; $159–$229 1-bedroom suite. Children under 12 stay free in parent's room. AE, DC, MC, V. Limited parking $18. Metro: Foggy Bottom. **Amenities:** Restaurant (upscale contemporary American); complimentary passes to nearby fitness center; room service; coin-op washer/dryers; same-day laundry/dry cleaning; 5 rooms for those w/limited mobility, 1 with roll-in showers. In room: A/C, TV w/pay movies and Nintendo, 2-line phone w/dataport, fridge, coffeemaker, hair dryer, iron, safe, robes, umbrella, CD player, free high-speed Internet access, microwave.

MODERATE

One Washington Circle Hotel ☆   Built in 1960, this building was converted into a hotel in 1976, making it the city's first all-suite hotel property. The George Washington University purchased the hotel in 2001 (see its other property, the George Washington University Inn, above), closed the place down and totally renovated it, reopening in 2002. One Washington Circle gleams now, from its double-paned windows to its contemporary new furniture. Five types of suites are available, ranging in size from 390 to 710 square feet. The one-bedroom suites have a sofa bed and dining area; all rooms are spacious and have walkout balconies, some overlooking the Circle and its centerpiece, the statue of George Washington. But keep in mind that across the Circle is George Washington University Hospital's emergency room entrance, which is busy with ambulance traffic; even with the installation of those double-paned windows, you may still hear sirens, so ask for a suite on the L Street side if you desire a quieter room. Ninety percent of the suites have full kitchens, each with an oven, microwave, and refrigerator.

Clientele is mostly corporate, but families like the outdoor pool, in-house restaurant, prime location near Georgetown and the Metro, and that full kitchen. Call directly to the hotel for best rates and be sure to mention a GWU affiliation if you have one. The well-reviewed **Circle Bistro,** serves bistro food with a Mediterranean influence.

One Washington Circle NW (between 22nd and 23rd sts. NW), Washington, DC 20037. Ⓒ **800/424-9671** or 202/872-1680. Fax 202/887-4989. www.thecirclehotel.com. 151 units. Smallest suites: weekdays $149–$209, weekends $129–$189; largest suites: weekdays $169–$229, weekends $149–$209. Call hotel to get best rates. Extra person: $20. Children under 12 stay free in parent's room. AE, DC, MC, V. Parking $20. Metro: Foggy Bottom. **Amenities:** Restaurant (traditional bistro with Mediterranean flair); bar; outdoor pool; on-site fitness center; concierge; room service (7am–midnight weekends, 7am–11pm weekdays); coin-op washer/dryers; same-day laundry/dry cleaning; 5 rooms for those w/limited mobility, 1 with roll-in showers. *In room:* A/C, TV w/pay movies and Nintendo, 2-line cordless phones, full kitchens (in 90% of suites, w/oven, fridge, microwave), coffeemaker, hair dryer, iron, free high-speed Internet access, CD player.

7 Georgetown

VERY EXPENSIVE

Four Seasons Hotel ★★★　　A renovation started in August 2004 is winding up in early 2005, bringing big changes to this Four Seasons, including the gutting of all of the guest rooms in the hotel's main building. In the end, guest rooms will be fewer, but much larger and feature the design of world-famous interior designer Pierre Yves Rochon, who renovated the landmark Four Seasons Georges V Hotel in Paris. The new decor will include custom designed furniture and color schemes of either celadon or purple.

The hotel's lobby and lower levels, which hold the restaurant, conference room, spa and exercise center, will stay open throughout the renovation, as will the hotel's auxiliary building of 25 rooms and 35 suites. Certain Four Seasons features always hold true: The hotel continues to attract the rich, the famous, and the powerful, people used to being catered to. Staff members are trained to know the names, preferences, and even allergies of guests, and repeat clientele rely on this discreet attention.

The hotel sits at the mouth of Georgetown, backing up against Rock Creek Park and the C&O Canal. The auxiliary building's guest rooms offer state-of-the-art business amenities (each is soundproof and has an office equipped with a fax machine, at least three telephones with two-line speakers, portable telephones, and headsets for private TV listening). Three of the suites have kitchenettes. Original avant-garde artwork from the personal collection of owner William Louis-Dreyfus (yes, Julia's dad) hangs in every room and public space. Transmitters installed throughout the hotel allow you wireless connection to the Internet on your laptop, wherever you go in the hotel. The Four Seasons is always devising new ways to pamper its guests; in 2003 the hotel initiated its "On the Road to Room Service," which allows guests who have been picked up by the hotel's car service, to place a room service order from the limo, and have the meal delivered to their guest room moments after they arrive.

2800 Pennsylvania Ave. NW (which becomes M St. a block farther along), Washington, DC 20007. ⓒ **800/ 332-3442** or 202/342-0444. Fax 202/944-2076. www.fourseasons.com. 257 units. Weekdays $455–$615 double, $695–$5,150 suite; weekends from $295 double, from $550 suite. Extra person $40. Children under 16 stay free in parent's room. AE, DC, MC, V. Parking $26, plus tax. Metro: Foggy Bottom. Pets allowed, up to 15 lb. **Amenities:** Formal restaurant (regional American); lounge (for afternoon tea and cocktails); extensive state-of-the-art fitness club and spa with personal trainers, lap pool, Vichy shower, hydrotherapy, and synchronized massage (2 people work on you at the same time); bike rentals; children's program (various goodies provided, but no organized activities); 24-hr. concierge; complimentary sedan service weekdays within the District; business center; salon; 24-hr. room service; in-room massage; babysitting; same-day laundry/dry cleaning; 7 rooms for those w/limited mobility, some of which have roll-in showers. *In room:* A/C, TV w/pay movies and Web access, minibar, hair dryer, iron, safe, robes, high-tech CD player, high-speed Internet access.

The Ritz-Carlton Georgetown ★★　　Staff at area hotels have taken to calling this hotel the "Baby Ritz," to distinguish it from the other, larger Ritz on 22nd Street. The moniker is the only cute thing about the hotel, however. The Georgetown Ritz is a sophisticated property, exclusively small (only 86 rooms), and designed to feel like a refuge in the middle of wild and woolly Georgetown. The hotel opened in April 2003, after years of construction. Look for the 130-foot-high smokestack to guide you to the hotel, which is built on the site of a historic incinerator and incorporates the smokestack into the design. In fact, you can have a meeting at the bottom of the smokestack, which, obviously, is inoperative. The lobby, whose brick walls are original to the incinerator, always smells of a recently lit fire, even on a summer day. (There's a large fireplace at one end of the lobby.) The restaurant is called "Fahrenheit," the bar is called "Degrees," and the signature drink is the "Fahrenheit 5 Martini." To get to your room, you have to go down one level from the lobby, travel along a wide, cavelike corridor with vaulted brick ceiling, to a special elevator. You must have a key card to operate the elevator, so anyone visiting you at the hotel must either be escorted by a staff person or be met by you. Rooms are very large, decorated in serious colors of moss green, gold, and a burnt red, with lots of dark wood furniture and accents. Ritz-Carlton hotels have the best bathrooms, and this property is no exception: spacious, marble vanities, separate tub and shower, fancy wood shelving.

3100 South St. NW (at 31st St., between K and M sts.), Washington, DC 20007. © **800/241-3333** or 202/912-4100. Fax 202/912-4199. www.ritzcarlton.com. 86 units. Weekdays from $425 double; weekends from $285 double; suites start at $579 weekdays and weekends. No charge for extra person in the room. Check website or 800 number for weekend packages and specials. AE, DC, DISC, MC, V. Valet parking $28. Metro: Foggy Bottom, with Georgetown shuttle bus connection. Small (under 30 lb.) pets accepted (no fee). **Amenities:** Restaurant (seasonal American); lounge; fitness room (complimentary) and spa; 24-hour concierge; 24-hr. room service; in-room massage; babysitting; same-day laundry/dry cleaning; 1-hr. pressing; 3 rooms for those w/limited mobility, all with roll-in showers; fax and some currency-exchange services. *In room:* A/C, TV w/pay movies and Web access, 2-line phone, minibar, hair dryer, iron, safe, robes, umbrella, CD player, high-speed Internet access (about $10 per 24 hours).

EXPENSIVE

Georgetown Inn ★ This hotel is in the thick of Georgetown. Most guests are here on business, but come Memorial Day weekend, the hotel is full of the proud parents of graduating Georgetown University students. (The hotel books up 2 years in advance for graduation weekend.)

A million dollar renovation completed in 2004 refurbished the lobby, corridors, and guest rooms. Guest rooms now have "Heavenly Beds," new upholstery, and drapes. The hotel's general style remains European-handsome, heavy on the dark woods. Half of the rooms hold two double beds, although a couple of rooms have twin single beds, connecting with suites, helpful to families traveling with children. Ask for an "executive room" if you'd like a sitting area with pullout sofa, and extra conveniences like a reading lamp over the bed. Even better are the 10 one-bedroom suites, in which bedroom and large living room are separate. The bathrooms have only showers (some also have bidets), no tub.

The **Daily Grill** has an outpost here, offering the same generous portions of American food served at its original D.C. location, at 1200 18th St. NW (p. 140 for a full review).

1310 Wisconsin Ave. NW (between N and O sts.), Washington, DC 20007. © **800/368-5922** or 202/333-8900. Fax 202/333-8308. www.georgetowninn.com. 96 units. Weekdays $195–$245 double; weekends $139–$245 double; suites from $345. Ask about promotional rates. Extra person $20. Children under 12 stay free in parent's room. AE, DC, DISC, MC, V. Valet parking $25 plus tax. Metro: Foggy Bottom, with a 30-minute walk, or take a cab. **Amenities:** Restaurant (American); bar; access to an outdoor pool; exercise room, plus free access to nearby health club and spa; concierge; room service during restaurant hours; same-day laundry/dry cleaning; 4 rooms for those w/limited mobility, all with roll-in showers. *In room:* A/C, TV w/pay movies and Nintendo, 2-line phones w/dataport, hair dryer, iron, high-speed Internet access ($9.95 per 24 hours).

MODERATE

Georgetown Suites   This hotel was designed to meet the needs of business travelers on extended visits, but its casual atmosphere and kitchen suites work well for families, too. It has two locations, within a block of each other.

The main building, which I prefer, is the one on 30th Street, a quiet residential street that's only steps away from Georgetown's action. This building offers a large lobby for hanging out; it almost feels like a student lounge, with the TV going; games, books, magazines, and daily newspapers scattered across table tops in front of love seats and chairs; and a cappuccino machine on the counter. In the morning, an extensive breakfast, featuring everything from waffles to fresh pastries, is laid out here. By contrast, the property on 29th Street (known as the "Harbor Building") is situated right next to the Whitehurst Freeway, is much noisier, and has a very small lobby (although you can linger outside in the brick courtyard where there are flowering plants and Victorian white wooden benches). Continental breakfast is served here, too, in the lobby.

Accommodations at both locations have living rooms, dining areas, and fully equipped kitchens. All rooms offer high-speed Internet access, at no charge. About half of the units are studios and half are one-bedroom suites. Glass-topped tables, chrome-framed chairs, and pastel-striped fabrics figure prominently in the decor. The biggest and best suites are the three two-level, two-bedroom town houses attached to the main building. The town houses feature modern furnishings, sunken Jacuzzi tubs and double sinks in the bathrooms, TVs with VCRs, CD players, and other deluxe amenities. These town houses have their own doors on 29th Street, through which you may exit only; to enter a town house, you must go through the hotel, as your key will not unlock the 29th Street door. This building also has two penthouse suites, which have their own terraces overlooking the rooftops of Georgetown.

1111 30th St. NW (just below M St.) and 1000 29th St. NW (at K St.), Washington, DC 20007. ☎ **800/348-7203** or 202/298-1600. Fax 202/333-2019. www.georgetownsuites.com. 220 units. Weekdays $155 studio, $215 1-bedroom suite; weekends $155 studio, $185 1-bedroom suite. Penthouse suites from $350, town houses from $425. Rollaways or sleeper sofa $10 extra. Rates include continental breakfast. AE, DC, DISC, MC, V. Limited parking $15. Metro: Foggy Bottom, with a 15-min. walk. **Amenities:** Small exercise room; coin-op laundry; same-day laundry/dry cleaning; 2 rooms for those w/limited mobility, both with roll-in showers. *In room:* A/C, TV, 2-line phone w/dataport, full kitchen (with fridge, coffeemaker, microwave, and dishwasher), hair dryer, iron, free high-speed Internet access.

Hotel Monticello of Georgetown 🌟 *(Value*   This hotel gets a lot of repeat business from both corporate and leisure travelers, who appreciate the intimacy of a small hotel, including personalized service from a staff who greets you by name and protects your privacy. It's also a favorite choice for families celebrating weddings or graduations (both Georgetown and George Washington universities are close by); they sometimes book several suites, or maybe a whole floor. A major renovation in 2000 gutted the whole building and created a more upscale setting (this used to be the Georgetown Dutch Inn). Rooms now bring in much more light, thanks to layout and design changes, better use of windows, and the placement of French doors with frosted glass between rooms. You'll notice that the top sheet on your bed is monogrammed, the sofa in the living room folds out, and those are Hermès bath products in the marble bathrooms. Wireless Internet access is available in all guest rooms, at no extra charge.

Accommodations are medium-size one- and two-bedroom apartment-like suites. Six of the suites are studios, in which the living room and bedroom are joined, and nine of them are duplex penthouses with 1½ bathrooms. Every suite has a wet bar with a microwave and refrigerator. The duplex penthouses have full kitchens. In addition to continental breakfast in the morning, fresh fruit, coffee, and herbal tea are available in the lobby all day.

The hotel is in the heart of Georgetown, surrounded by shops and restaurants. The C&O Canal towpath, just down the block, is ideal for jogging and cycling, though you should be wary at night.

1075 Thomas Jefferson St. NW (just below M St.), Washington, DC 20007. (**C**) **800/388-2410** or 202/337-0900. Fax 202/333-6526. www.monticellohotel.com. 47 suites. Peak-season weekdays $149–$189, off-peak weekdays $129–$149; weekends, peak- and off-peak season, $109–$129. Call the hotel directly for best rates and to find out penthouse suite rates. Extra person $20. Rates include continental breakfast. Children under 14 stay free in parent's room. Promotional rates and discounts may be available. AE, DC, DISC, MC, V. Limited parking $10 (small to mid-size cars only—no SUVs). Metro: Foggy Bottom, with a 20-min. walk, or take the Georgetown Shuttle. Bus: 32, 34, and 36 go to all major Washington tourist attractions. **Amenities:** Free access to nearby fitness center; business center; in-room massage; babysitting; same-day laundry/dry cleaning except Sun; 2 rooms for those w/limited mobility. *In room:* A/C, TV, 2-line phone w/dataport, kitchenette with microwave, fridge, coffeemaker, hair dryer, iron, free wireless Internet access.

8 Woodley Park

VERY EXPENSIVE

Wardman Park Marriott Hotel ⭐ This is Washington's biggest hotel, resting on 16 acres just down the street from the National Zoo and several good restaurants. Its size and location (the Woodley Park–Zoo Metro station is literally at its doorstep) make it a good choice for conventions, tour groups, and individual travelers. (*Warning:* You can get lost here, and I have.) Built in 1918, it is also one of Washington's oldest hotels. A massive $100 million renovation completed in 1999 replaced bed and bath linens, carpeting, and wall coverings in all the guest rooms, upgraded the ballroom and meeting rooms, restructured the outdoor pools, revamped the restaurants, and topped the lobby with a soaring four-story dome. More recently, the hotel remodeled all of the guest room bathrooms, replacing walls, floors, and fixtures. The hotel has also added outdoor seating to Harry's Bar and an outdoor cafe to its Starbucks, set in the center of beds of blooming flowers. Wireless Internet access is available in the Lobby Lounge, Starbucks, and the atrium.

From the outside, the hotel resembles a college campus: There's an old part, whose entrance is draped by stately trees, and a new part, preceded by a great green lawn. The oldest section is the nicest. The 86-year-old redbrick Tower houses 205 guest rooms, each with high ceilings, ornate crown moldings, and an assortment of antique French and English furnishings. This was once an apartment building whose residents included presidents Hoover, Eisenhower, and Johnson, as well as actors like Douglas Fairbanks Jr. and authors such as Gore Vidal.

The hotel has 125 suites in all, ranging in size from one to three bedrooms. Best are the 54 suites in the Wardman Tower, many of which have balconies overlooking the gardens. The size of the hotel enables it to accommodate requests for different setups: two double beds, king beds, and so on. All rooms offer high-speed Internet access, for $9.95 per day.

2660 Woodley Rd. NW (at Connecticut Ave. NW), Washington, DC 20008. (**C**) **800/228-9290** or 202/328-2000. Fax 202/234-0015. www.marriotthotels.com/wasdt. 1,349 units. Weekdays $289 double; weekends $119–$289 double; $350–$2,500 suite. Children under 18 stay free in parent's room. AE, DC, DISC, MC, V. Valet parking $22, self-parking $19. Metro: Woodley Park–Zoo. Pets under 20 lb. permitted but charges may apply; call for details. **Amenities:** 2 restaurants (American, Mediterranean); pub (serves meals); deli/pastry shop (offers to-go gourmet dinners, which you can heat up in the shop's microwave); lobby bar; Starbucks; 2 outdoor heated pools with sun deck; well-equipped fitness center; concierge; business center; salon; room service (6am–1am); in-room massage; babysitting; coin-op washer/dryers; same-day laundry/dry cleaning; concierge-level rooms; 32 rooms for those w/limited mobility, 10 with roll-in showers. *In room:* A/C, TV w/pay movies, 2-line phone w/dataport, coffeemaker, hair dryer, iron, high-speed Internet access ($9.95 per day).

EXPENSIVE

Omni Shoreham Hotel ⚡ *Kids*   This is Woodley Park's *other* really big hotel, although with 836 rooms, the Omni Shoreham is still 500 short of the behemoth Marriott Wardman Park. And it's all the more appealing for it, since it's not quite so overwhelming as the Marriott. Its design—wide corridors, vaulted ceilings and archways, and arrangements of pretty sofas and armchairs in the lobby and public spaces—endows the Shoreham with the air of a grand hotel. A massive $80 million renovation completed in 2000 installed a new air-conditioning system, restructured the pool, upgraded the already excellent fitness center health spa, and restored a traditional, elegant look to guest rooms and the lobby. The spacious rooms remain twice the size of your average hotel room and every guest room is equipped with free wireless high-speed Internet access, added in 2003. Most of the 52 suites are junior suites, with the sitting room and bedroom combined. The hotel sits on 11 acres overlooking Rock Creek Park; park-side rooms are a little smaller but offer spectacular views.

With its 22 meeting rooms and 7 ballrooms (some of which open to terraces overlooking the park!), the hotel is popular as a meeting and convention venue. Leisure travelers, especially families, appreciate the Shoreham for its large outdoor swimming pool; its proximity to the National Zoo, excellent restaurants, and the Woodley Park–Zoo Metro station; and the immediate access to biking, hiking, and jogging paths through Rock Creek Park. Children receive a goodie bag at check-in that includes coloring books, puzzles, playing cards, postcards, and candy. You can walk to the more hip neighborhoods of Adams-Morgan and Dupont Circle from the hotel; the stroll to Dupont Circle, taking you over the bridge that spans Rock Creek Park, is especially nice (and safe at night, too).

Built in 1930, the Shoreham has been the scene of inaugural balls for every president since FDR. Do you believe in ghosts? Ask about Room 870, the haunted suite (available for $3,000 a night).

2500 Calvert St. NW (near Connecticut Ave.), Washington, DC 20008. © **800/843-6664** or 202/234-0700. Fax 202/265-7972. www.omnihotels.com. 836 units. $179–$309 double; from $350–$3,000 suite. Call the hotel directly for best rates. Extra person $20. Children under 18 stay free in parent's room. AE, DC, DISC, MC, V. Valet parking $26, self-parking $22. Metro: Woodley Park–Zoo. **Amenities:** Restaurant (continental; terrace overlooks Rock Creek Park); gourmet carryout; bar/lounge (serves light fare and has live music Thurs–Sat nights); fitness center and spa with heated outdoor pool, separate kids' pool, and whirlpool; children's gifts; concierge; travel/sightseeing desk; business center; shops; 24-hr. room service; massage; same-day laundry/dry cleaning; 41 rooms for those w/limited mobility, half with roll-in showers. *In room:* A/C, TV w/pay movies and Nintendo, 2-line phone w/dataport, coffeemaker, hair dryer, iron, robes, free wireless Internet access.

INEXPENSIVE

In addition to the Woodley Park Guest House, listed below, you might consider the Woodley Park location of the **Kalorama Guest House,** at 2700 Cathedral Ave. NW (entrance on 27th St.; © **202/328-0860;** fax 202/328-8730), which has 19 units, 12 with private bathrooms. Rates are $55 to $75 for a double with a shared bathroom, $75 to $100 for a double with private bathroom, and include continental breakfast. Limited parking is available for $7, and the Woodley Park–Zoo Metro stop is nearby. See p. 102 for the full listing for the main location of the Kalorama Guest House in Adams-Morgan for more information.

Woodley Park Guest House   This charming, 18-room B&B offers clean, comfortable, and cozy lodging, inexpensive rates, super location, and a personable staff: How's that for a recommendation? Four local couples bought the hundred-year-old property in 2000, gutted it, and made the place over. Guests are

---

Finds **Hotel Packages as Pleasant Surprises**

Hotel packages can offer some sweet little deals, special rates combined with intriguing perks that give you a true taste of the hotel's personality. Just go to any hotel website and you'll see what I mean. Here are examples of packages that were offered at three very different hotels in 2004 (all three hotels are reviewed in this chapter):

"The Improv Package": The Lincoln Suites Hotel (p. 100) teamed up with the Improv Comedy Club to offer a deal through September 7, 2004, that included an overnight stay at Lincoln Suites, VIP passes to the Improv, dinner for two before the early show or appetizers for two before the later show, all for $169 on a weekend night.

"Celestial Sensation": In spring 2004, the Topaz Hotel (p. 106) advertised this special, which included accommodations, a psychic reading, a deck of tarot cards, tickets to the Einstein Planetarium at the National Air and Space Museum, and two chocolate MoonPies for $255.

"Grandparents' Package": The Hay-Adams Hotel (p. 96) offered this package, as part of a tribute to "the greatest generation," tied to the Memorial Day dedication on the Mall of the World War II Memorial. The package included overnight accommodations in a standard room, parking, breakfast, a 1-hour private sedan tour of the monuments by day or night, four tickets to the International Spy Museum, a sightseeing goodie bag, and a special amenity for the children in your party, all for $549 for the first night, with a reduced rate for add-on nights.

---

from around the globe, a fact which inspired the owners to add an actual globe to the breakfast room; it's common practice for people sitting across the table from each other in the morning to go over to the globe and point out exactly where they live: the Arctic Circle, Brazil, Seattle—they come from all over, says co-owner Courtney Lodico.

Special features of the guesthouse include a wicker-furnished, tree-shaded front porch; exposed, century-old brick walls; beautiful antiques (mostly purchased from Antique Row in Kensington, MD; see chapter 8 for information about these shops); and breathtaking original art (the innkeepers only buy works from artists who have stayed at the guesthouse, so the art is diffuse rather than profuse, and each piece quite different). Rooms have either two twins, one double, or a queen bed, each covered with a pretty chenille spread or quilt. An intimate alternative to the grand 1,349-room Marriott Wardman Park hotel directly across the street, the guesthouse nevertheless benefits from its proximity to the big hotel, since it's able to offer lodgers quick access to airport shuttles and taxis and views of the Wardman Park's beautifully landscaped gardens. Meanwhile, the Woodley Park–Zoo Metro stop is literally cattycorner to the inn, Connecticut Avenue and its good restaurants 1 block away, and Rock Creek Park and the National Zoo only a few minutes further than that.

2647 Woodley Road NW (at Connecticut Ave. NW), Washington, DC 20008. © **866/667-0218** or 202/667-0218. Fax 202/667-1080. www.woodleyparkguesthouse.com. 18 units, 11 with private bathroom (all with shower only), 7 with shared bath. $80–$90 double with shared bathroom; $100–$160 double with private bathroom. Rates include continental breakfast. AE, MC, V. On-site parking $10. Metro: Woodley Park–Zoo. Children over 12. **Amenities:** Laundry and ironing service; wireless Internet access for $6.95 per day (your laptop must be equipped with access card). *In room:* A/C, phone w/voicemail and dataports.

6

Where to Dine

My husband and I were wandering around Georgetown at 2 in the afternoon on Valentine's Day last year, annoyed with each other for not having called a restaurant in advance to snag a dinner reservation. I don't know what Valentine's Day is like where you live, but in Washington it is the most popular day of the year to eat out. Not having dinner à deux, we were hoping for the next best thing, a Valentine's Day lunch. And every place was booked for lunch, as well. Then we noticed the petite **Ristorante Piccolo,** nestled in a town house on 31st Street, and inquired within to see if the kitchen was still open: just. There we enjoyed a sweet little lunch in this pretty and intimate, nearly empty, almost closed restaurant. The Piccolo is not a restaurant you hear about, and still we were very much taken with our meal of gnocchi, salad, and minestrone, and the decor, which included a balcony and fireplace, and the service, not hurrying us, even though we'd come so late.

Washington, generally, is not the kind of city where you can find a good meal in any restaurant you turn in to. And yet, it can happen to you, as it happened to us. Take your chances, if you dare, and see what you discover. And let me know. (My publisher forwards readers' mail to me.)

But if you'd prefer to make your dining experience more of a sure thing, read this chapter, which presents a variety of the best the capital has to offer, and all vouched for (look for more about Piccolo on p. 161). Then,

if a restaurant sounds irresistible, call ahead for **reservations,** especially for Saturday night. A number of restaurants are affiliated with an online reservation service called **www.opentable. com**, so if you've got Internet access, you might reserve your table online.

If you wait until the last minute to make a reservation, expect to dine really early, say 5:30 or 6pm, or really late (by Washington standards, 9:30pm qualifies as late—this is not a late-night town). Or you can sit at the bar and eat, which can be more of a culinary treat than you might imagine: Some of the best restaurants, including Palena, Bistrot Lepic, and Galileo offer area-sonably priced bar menu.

Better yet, consider a restaurant that doesn't take reservations. This practice seems to be on the upswing and works for places like Johnny's Half Shell and Lauriol Plaza, where the atmosphere is casual, the wait can become part of the experience, and the food is worth standing in line for. At some eateries, like Zaytinya, you receive a beeper, and are free to walk around until you're "buzzed."

Few places require men to wear a jacket and tie; I've made a special note in the listings for those places that do. If you're driving, call ahead to inquire about valet parking, complimentary or otherwise—on Washington's crowded streets, this service can be a true bonus. Finally, if you are meeting chronically late people for dinner, find out if the restaurant has a "full party must be present to be seated" policy, which can really throw a wrench in your plans if you lose a table because someone is late. I've listed the closest Metro station to each restaurant only when it's within walking distance of a restaurant. The closest Metro stop to Georgetown is the Blue Line's Foggy Bottom station, where you can hop on the Georgetown Metro Connection shuttle bus for a short ride to Georgetown. If you need bus-routing information, call © **202/637-7000.**

ABOUT THE PRICES

I've selected a range of menus and prices in almost every Washington neighborhood. Restaurants are grouped first by location, then alphabetically by price

category. Keep in mind that the price categories refer to dinner prices, but some very expensive restaurants offer affordable lunches, early-bird dinners, tapas, or bar meals. (Or consider something totally different, like high tea in the late afternoon—look for "A Spot of Tea," on p. 162, which lists some swell places to swill tea.) The prices within each review refer to the cost of individual entrees, not the entire meal. I've used the following price categories: **Very Expensive,** main courses at dinner average more than $25; **Expensive,** $16 to $25; **Moderate,** $10 to $15; and **Inexpensive,** $10 and under.

1 Restaurants by Cuisine

AMERICAN/NEW AMERICAN

Ben's Chili Bowl (U Street Corridor, $, p. 144)

Butterfield 9 ★★★ (Downtown East, $$$$, p. 125)

Cashion's Eat Place ★★ (Adams-Morgan, $$$, p. 145)

Charlie Palmer Steak ★ (Capitol Hill, $$$$, p. 121)

Clyde's of Georgetown (Georgetown, $$, p. 160)

Daily Grill ★ (Downtown West, Georgetown, $$$, p. 140)

DC Coast ★ (Downtown East, $$$, p. 131)

Dupont Grille ★ (Dupont Circle, $$$, p. 149)

Equinox ★★ (Downtown West, $$$, p. 141)

15 Ria ★ (Downtown East, $$$, p. 131)

Firefly ★ (Dupont Circle, $$$, p. 149)

Kinkead's ★★★ (Foggy Bottom, $$$, p. 155)

Melrose ★★ (Foggy Bottom, $$$$, p. 153)

Mendocino Grille and Wine Bar ★ (Georgetown, $$$, p. 158)

The Monocle ★ (Capitol Hill, $$$, p. 124)

Nectar ★★ (Foggy Bottom, $$$, p. 155)

New Heights ★ (Woodley Park/Cleveland Park, $$$, p. 164)

Nora ★★ (Dupont Circle, $$$$, p. 148)

Occidental Grill ★ (Downtown East, $$$, p. 132)

Old Ebbitt Grill (Downtown East, $$, p. 136)

Oval Room at Lafayette Square ★★ (Downtown West, $$$, p. 141)

Red Sage Grill ★ (Downtown East, $$$$, p. 129)

701 ★ (Downtown East, $$$, p. 133)

1789 ★★ (Georgetown, $$$$, p. 157)

Tabard Inn ★ (Dupont Circle, $$$, p. 150)

Vidalia ★★ (Downtown West, $$$, p. 142)

Zola (Downtown East, $$, p. 137)

Key to Abbreviations: $$$$ = Very Expensive $$$ = Expensive $$ = Moderate $ = Inexpensive

ASIAN FUSION

Asia Nora ✹ (Foggy Bottom, $$$, p. 154)

Café Asia (Downtown West, $, p. 143)

Teaism (Dupont Circle, $, p. 152)

TenPenh ✹✹ (Downtown East, $$$, p. 133)

BARBECUE

Old Glory Barbecue (Georgetown, $$, p. 160)

CHINESE

Ching Ching Cha (Georgetown, $, p. 161)

City Lights of China (Dupont Circle, $$, p. 151)

Tony Cheng's Seafood Restaurant ✹ (Downtown East, $, p. 138)

ETHIOPIAN

Meskerem (Adams-Morgan, $, p. 146)

Zed's (Georgetown, $, p. 162)

FRENCH

Bistro Bis ✹✹ (Capitol Hill, $$$, p. 124)

Bistrot D'Oc ✹✹ (Downtown East, $$$, p. 129)

Bistrot du Coin ✹ (Dupont Circle, $$, p. 151)

Bistrot Lepic ✹✹ (Georgetown, $$, p. 159)

Café 15 ✹✹ (Downtown East, $$$$, p. 128)

Gerard's Place ✹✹✹ (Downtown East, $$$$, p. 129)

La Colline ✹✹ (Capitol Hill, $$$, p. 124)

La Fourchette (Adams-Morgan, $$, p. 145)

Les Halles (Downtown East, $$, p. 135)

Marcel's ✹✹ (Foggy Bottom, $$$$, p. 153)

Michel Richard Citronelle ✹✹✹ (Georgetown, $$$$, p. 156)

Montmartre ✹ (Capitol Hill, $$$, p. 125)

Palena ✹✹ (Woodley Park/Cleveland Park, $$$$, p. 164)

Petits Plats ✹ (Woodley Park/Cleveland Park, $$$, p. 165)

INDIAN

Aditi (Georgetown, $, p. 161)

Bombay Club ✹ (Downtown West, $$, p. 142)

INTERNATIONAL

New Heights ✹ (Woodley Park/Cleveland Park, $$$, p. 164)

701 ✹ (Downtown East, $$$, p. 133)

ITALIAN

Al Tiramisu ✹✹ (Dupont Circle, $$$, p. 149)

Café Milano ✹ (Georgetown, $$$, p. 158)

Coppi's Organic (U Street Corridor, $, p. 144)

Etrusco ✹✹ (Dupont Circle, $$, p. 151)

Famous Luigi's Pizzeria Restaurant (Downtown West, $, p. 144)

Galileo ✹✹✹ (Downtown West, $$$$, p. 138)

Il Radicchio (Capitol Hill, $, p. 125)

I Ricchi ✹ (Downtown West, $$$$, p. 139)

Matchbox (Downtown East, $, p. 138)

Obelisk ✹✹✹ (Dupont Circle, $$$$, p. 148)

Olives ✹ (Downtown West, $$$, p. 141)

Palena ✹✹ (Woodley Park/Cleveland Park, $$$$, p. 164)

Pasta Mia (Adams-Morgan, $, p. 146)

Pizzeria Paradiso ✹ (Dupont Circle, $, p. 152)

Ristorante Piccolo (Georgetown, $$, p. 161)

Teatro Goldoni ✹✹ (Downtown West, $$$, p. 141)

Tosca ✹✹✹ (Downtown East, $$$, p. 133)

JAPANESE

Kaz Sushi Bistro (Foggy Bottom, $$, p. 155)

Sushi-Ko ✹ (Glover Park, $$$, p. 163)

LATIN AMERICAN

Café Atlantico ✹✹ (Downtown East, $$$, p. 130)

Lauriol Plaza ✹ (Adams-Morgan/ Dupont Circle, $$, p. 145)

MEXICAN

Andale ✹ (Downtown East, $$, p. 134)

Lauriol Plaza ✹ (Adams-Morgan/ Dupont Circle, $$, p. 145)

Mixtec (Adams-Morgan, $, p. 146)

MIDDLE EASTERN

Lebanese Taverna (Woodley Park/ Cleveland Park, $$, p. 165)

Zaytinya ✹✹✹ (Downtown East, $$, p. 136)

SEAFOOD

Johnny's Half Shell ✹ (Dupont Circle, $$$, p. 150)

Legal Sea Foods ✹ (Downtown West, $$, p. 143)

Kinkead's ✹✹✹ (Foggy Bottom, $$$, p. 155)

Morton's of Chicago ✹ (Downtown West, Georgetown, $$$$, p. 156)

Oceanaire Seafood Room ✹ (Downtown East, $$$, p. 132)

The Prime Rib ✹✹ (Downtown West, $$$$, p. 139)

Sea Catch ✹ (Georgetown, $$$, p. 159)

Tony Cheng's Seafood Restaurant ✹ (Downtown East, $, p. 138)

SOUTHERN/SOUTHWESTERN

Austin Grill (Glover Park, $, p. 163)

B. Smith's ✹ (Capitol Hill, $$$, p. 123)

Georgia Brown's ✹ (Downtown East, $$$, p. 132)

Red Sage Border Café ✹ (Downtown East, $$$$, p. 129)

Vidalia ✹✹ (Downtown West, $$$, p. 142)

SPANISH

Jaleo ✹ (Downtown East, $$, p. 134)

Lauriol Plaza ✹ (Adams-Morgan/ Dupont Circle, $$, p. 145)

Taberna del Alabardero ✹✹ (Downtown West, $$$$, p. 140)

STEAK

The Caucus Room ✹✹ (Downtown East, $$$$, p. 128)

Charlie Palmer Steak ✹ (Capitol Hill, $$$$, p. 121)

Les Halles (Downtown East, $$, p. 135)

Morton's of Chicago ✹ (Downtown West, Georgetown, $$$$, p. 156)

The Palm ✹ (Downtown West, $$$$, p. 139)

The Prime Rib ✹✹ (Downtown West, $$$$, p. 139)

THAI

Haad Thai (Downtown East, $, p. 137)

Sala Thai (Dupont Circle, $, p. 152)

VIETNAMESE

Miss Saigon (Georgetown, $$, p. 160)

2 Capitol Hill

For information on eating at the Capitol and other government buildings, see the box titled "Dining at Sightseeing Attractions," on p. 122.

VERY EXPENSIVE

Charlie Palmer Steak ✹ STEAKHOUSE   Nothing intimate about Charlie Palmer. It's a place to see and be seen, in big groups, preferably. The ceilings are

Dining at Sightseeing Attractions

With so many great places to eat in Washington, I have a hard time recommending those at sightseeing attractions. Most are overpriced and too crowded, even if they are convenient. But a few places stand out, for their admirable cuisine, noteworthy setting, or both.

Two restaurants within the Capitol building itself may be open to the public, with certain conditions: the **House of Representatives Restaurant** (also called the "Members' Dining Room") in Room H118, at the South end of the Capitol (② **202/225-6300**) and the **Senate Dining Room** (② **202/224-4100**). At the House of Representatives Restaurant, the food is all-American and its prices reasonable: everything from a cup of soup for $1.50, to entree salads for $8.50, to the favorite, crab cake platter, for $19. The Members' Dining Room is open when the House is in session, weekdays 8am to 2:30pm. Tuesday through Thursday lunch (11am–1:45pm), you may dine here only as the guest of a Member. You may dine here unaccompanied by a Member, on Monday and Friday, and on any weekday for breakfast, or between 1:45pm and 2:30pm. The Senate Dining Room's menu features American cuisine and "comfort food," such as meatloaf, grilled salmon, crab Louis (a kind of crab salad), and lots of sandwiches; prices range from $9 to $22. The Senate Dining Room is open only when the Senate is in session and you may dine here weekdays between 1:30pm and 2:30pm. You must dress appropriately, that is, in jacket and tie for men, no jeans or sloppy appearance for men or women, and you must present a letter from your senator confirming his or her invitation to you. Be sure to call and ask about other requirements.

You are always welcome (after you've gone through security, of course) in the eateries located in the Capitol office buildings across the street from the Capitol. You'll be surrounded by Hill staffers, who head to places like the immense, full-service **Rayburn House Office Building Cafeteria** (② **202/225-7109**), which is in the basement of the building, at First Street and Independence Avenue SW. Adjoining the cafeteria is

high, the rooms expansive. The bar and lounge are made for circulating. The most provocative feature is the glass-walled wine storage area, suspended over a shallow pool of water; the inventory stocks 10,000 bottles of exclusively American wines, representing nearly every state. Guests survey the wine list via the eWinebook, a kind of Palm Pilot that allows you to scroll through the selections, while three sommeliers are on hand for consultation. The restaurant advertises that it overlooks the Capitol, but views are seasonal: in winter, you'll see more of the Capitol than you do in summer, when only the Capitol dome and the grounds are visible. Best views are from the rooftop terrace, which is open only for private parties. About a third of the menu's main courses are beef entrees, like the excellent grilled beef filet mignon, with roasted shallot and cabernet sauce. But Charlie Palmer Steak, despite its name, also serves "progressive American" fish and fowl dishes, such as smoked squab with chipotle glaze and seared diver a carryout that sells pizza and sandwiches. At the **Longworth Building Cafeteria,** Independence Avenue and South Capitol Street SE (✆ 202/225-0878), you can grab a bite from a fairly nice food court. By far the best deal for visitors is the **Dirksen Senate Office Building South Buffet Room,** First and C streets NE (✆ 202/224-4249). For just $11 per adult, $8.50 per child under 10, you can choose from a buffet that includes a carving station and eight other hot entrees; the price covers a nonalcoholic drink and dessert, too. The dining room is often crowded, but accepts reservations for parties of more than five. Other options include the Russell Carryout, in the basement of the Russell Building, and the Cannon Carryout, likewise, in the basement of the Cannon Building. All of these eateries are open weekdays only. The carryouts stay open until late afternoon, while the other dining rooms close at 2:30pm.

In the same neighborhood, two institutions offering great deals and fair views (of famous sights or people) at weekday breakfast and lunch are the **Library of Congress**'s Cafeteria and its more formal Montpelier Room (✆ 202/707-8300), where the options usually cost under $10 per person; and the **Supreme Court**'s Cafeteria (✆ 202/479-3246), where you'll likely spy a justice or two enjoying the midday meal.

Among museum restaurants, the ones that shine are the six-story Atrium Cafe in the **National Museum of Natural History** (✆ 202/357-2700); the **National Gallery of Art**'s Sculpture Garden Pavilion Café (✆ 202/289-3360), Garden Café (✆ 202/216-2480), and the Terrace Café (✆ 202/216-5966), which is open only Saturday and Sunday 11am to 3pm, for jazz brunch.

Finally, the newly renovated **Kennedy Center**'s Roof Terrace Restaurant and KC Café (✆ 202/416-8555, for both) offer theater-goers convenient, gourmet dining in glamorous settings. These two restaurants take in dramatic views, since immense windows present a sweeping panorama of the Potomac River and Washington landmarks.

sea scallops with potato crème fraiche foam. The restaurant's opening in April 2003 brought Capitol Hill its first swanky steakhouse.

101 Constitution Ave. NW, at Louisiana Ave. ✆ 202/547-8100. www.charliepalmer.com. Reservations recommended. Lunch main courses $13–$23; dinner main courses $19–$38. AE, DC, MC, V. Mon–Fri 11:30am–2:30pm and 5:30–10pm; Sat 5–10:30pm. Metro: Union Station.

EXPENSIVE

B. Smith's 🖈 *Finds* TRADITIONAL SOUTHERN   This is one of the few upscale restaurants on Capitol Hill, and the only one in Union Station, and even if the restaurant isn't on your route, it's worth coming here—for the food, of course, but also to admire the restaurant's amazing interior. The dramatic dining room once served as a presidential reception room hall, and now its 30-foot-high ceilings, white marble floors, and towering Ionic columns make it a fitting place for lobbyists, senators, and other well-paid Washingtonians to discuss serious business. On weekends, the ambience lightens up and romantic couples and Southern food–loving families dine here. Background music is always mellow (Nat King Cole, Ray Charles, Sarah Vaughan). The restaurant features live jazz on Friday and Saturday evenings and at Sunday brunch.

The restaurant's Southern/Cajun/Creole cuisine and its quality seldom change. On offer are appetizers such as jambalaya or red beans and rice studded with andouille sausage and *tasso* (spicy smoked pork). Standouts among the main dishes are the Southern fried chicken with buttermilk mashed potatoes and something called "Swamp Thing" (seafood served over greens with a mustard sauce). A basket of mini-biscuits, corn and citrus poppy-seed muffins, and sourdough rolls accompanies all dishes. For dessert, try either pecan sweet-potato pie or coconut cake. The wine list features many by-the-glass selections.

In Union Station, 50 Massachusetts Ave. NE. (C) **202/289-6188.** www.bsmith.com. Reservations recommended. Main courses mostly $17–$30. AE, DC, DISC, MC, V. Mon–Thurs 11:30am–3pm and 5–9pm; Fri 11:30am–3pm and 5–10pm; Sat noon–3pm and 5–10pm; Sun 11:30am–9pm. Metro: Union Station.

Bistro Bis 🌟🌟 FRENCH BISTRO   The chic Hotel George is the home of this excellent French restaurant, whose owner-chef, Jeff Buben, and his wife, Sallie, also run Vidalia (p. 142). You can sit at tables in the bar area (which always seem loud, even when it's not that crowded), on the balcony overlooking the bar, or at leather banquettes in the main dining room, where you can watch Buben and staff at work in the glass-fronted kitchen. (In warm weather, there's a sidewalk cafe.) The menu covers French classics like bouillabaisse, pistou, steak *frites,* as well as Buben's own take on grilled salmon (with oyster mushrooms and braised lentils), pan-seared red snapper, and seared scallops provencale with tomatoes, garlic, olives, and an eggplant custard. Many items, including the salmon and the steak frites, appear on both the lunch and dinner menus but are considerably cheaper at lunch. The restaurant has been popular from the day it opened, with hungry movers and shakers intermingling with ordinary folk who just love good food. The wine list is mostly French and American.

15 E St. NW. (C) **202/661-2700.** www.bistrobis.com. Reservations recommended. Breakfast $6.75–$12; lunch main courses $13–$23; dinner main courses $20–$32. AE, DC, DISC, MC, V. Daily 7–10am, 11:30am–2:30pm, and 5:30–10:30pm. Metro: Union Station.

La Colline 🌟🌟 FRENCH   This is the perfect spot for that breakfast fundraiser. Hill people like La Colline for its convenience to the Senate side of the Capitol, the great bar, the four private rooms, the high-backed leather booths that allow for discreet conversations, and, last but not least, the food. You'll always get a good meal here. The regular menu offers an extensive list of French standards, including Salade Niçoise, terrine of foie gras, and fish—poached, grilled, or sautéed. Almost as long is the list of daily specials—the soft-shell crab is superb here in season, and so is the gratin of crayfish. Trout and salmon are smoked in-house—try them. The wine list concentrates on French and California wines; by-the-glass choices change with the season to complement the menu. Don't let the dessert cart roll past you; the apple pie is a winner, as is the restaurant, which has been in business for 23 years.

400 N. Capitol St. NW. (C) **202/737-0400.** www.restaurant.com/lacolline. Reservations recommended. Breakfast $5–$8.75; lunch main courses $12–$19; dinner main courses $12–$24. AE, DC, MC, V. Mon–Fri 7am–10pm; Sat 6–10pm. Metro: Union Station.

The Monocle 🌟 *Finds* AMERICAN   A Capitol Hill institution, the Monocle has been around since 1960. This is a men-in-suits place, where the litter of

briefcases resting against the too-close-together tables can m
navigating. But you might want to take a look at whose br
stumbling over, for its proximity to both the Supreme Court
guarantees that the Monocle is the haunt of Supreme Court jus
bers of Congress. At lunch you'll want to order either the hamb
excellent, the tasty federal salad (field greens and tomatoes tossed
vinaigrette), the penne pasta with tomato-basil sauce and olives, o
bean soup, whenever it's on the menu. At dinner, consider the bake oysters or
the pork-rib chop with pommery mustard sauce. Or you can do what my friend
and Monocle regular, Bob Harris, does, and order "Nick's Dish," which is a rib-
eye steak served with a side of pasta and butter; named after the affable owner,
Nick's Dish is not found on the menu. Don't bother with the crab cakes. Service
is old-style, all-male.

107 D St. NE. ⓒ 202/546-4488. www.themonocle.com. Reservations recommended. Lunch main courses
$9–$18; dinner main courses $15–$29. AE, DC, MC, V. Mon–Fri 11:30am–midnight. Closed 2 weeks preced-
ing Labor Day. Metro: Union Station.

Montmartre ⚝ FRENCH   Montmartre's ambience is warmed by its decor—
pale yellow-orange walls, exposed wood ceiling, cozy bar, and old wooden tables.
The owners are French, and Montmartre is their little French restaurant offering big French pleasures: chicory salad tossed with crisped bacon and duck-giz-
zard confit, pistou, potato gratin, confit of guinea hen with Jerusalem
artichokes, seared tuna with chopped red pepper and olives, hangar steak served
over fingerling potatoes and topped with sautéed shallots and demi-glace sauce,
and calves liver sautéed with smothered onions, bok choy, potato purée, and a
balsamic vinegar sauce. Desserts, like the Alsatian apple tart, don't disappoint.

327 7th St. SE. ⓒ 202/544-1244. www.montmartre.us. Reservations recommended. Lunch main courses
$12–$18; dinner main courses $15–$23. AE, DC, DISC, MC, V. Tues–Sun 11:30am–2:30pm; Sun 5:30–9pm;
Tues–Thurs 5:30–10pm; Fri–Sat 5:30–10:30pm. Metro: Eastern Market.

INEXPENSIVE

Il Radicchio ⟨Value⟩ ITALIAN   What a great idea: Order a replenishable bowl
of spaghetti for the table at a set price of $6.95, and each of you chooses your
own sauce from a long list, at prices that range from $1.95 to $4. Most are standards, like the puttanesca with black olives, capers, garlic, anchovies, and
tomato. My favorite is the radicchio, sausage, red wine, and tomato sauce.

The kitchen prepares daily specials, like a sautéed fresh trout with sautéed
green beans, and garlic and tomato sauce, as well as sandwiches, and an assortment of wood-baked pizzas, with a choice of at least 20 toppings.

Ingredients are fresh and flavorful, the service quick and solicitous. The
restaurant gets a lot of overworked and underpaid Hill staffers, who appreciate
Il Radicchio's heartening food and low prices.

223 Pennsylvania Ave. SE. ⓒ 202/547-5114. www.robertodonna.com. Reservations not accepted. Main
courses $7.95–$19. AE, DC, DISC, MC, V. Mon–Thurs 11am–2:30pm and 4:30–10pm; Fri–Sat 11:30am–11pm;
Sun 5–10pm. Metro: Capitol South.

3 Downtown, East of 16th Street NW
VERY EXPENSIVE

Butterfield 9 ⚝⚝⚝ NEW AMERICAN   This remains a favorite restaurant
of my husband, and he eats at fine establishments nearly every day. In spring
2001, less than a year after opening, Butterfield 9 was chosen by *Condé Nast*

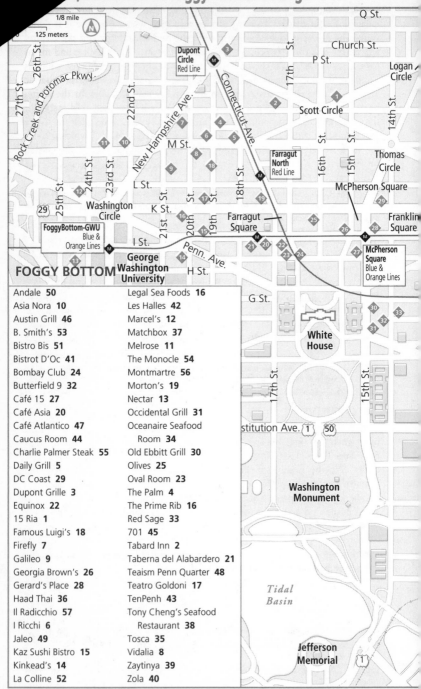

..., Downtown & Foggy Bottom Dining

Andale **50**
Asia Nora **10**
Austin Grill **46**
B. Smith's **53**
Bistro Bis **51**
Bistrot D'Oc **41**
Bombay Club **24**
Butterfield 9 **32**
Café 15 **27**
Café Asia **20**
Café Atlantico **47**
Caucus Room **44**
Charlie Palmer Steak **55**
Daily Grill **5**
DC Coast **29**
Dupont Grille **3**
Equinox **22**
15 Ria **1**
Famous Luigi's **18**
Firefly **7**
Galileo **9**
Georgia Brown's **26**
Gerard's Place **28**
Haad Thai **36**
Il Radicchio **57**
I Ricchi **6**
Jaleo **49**
Kaz Sushi Bistro **15**
Kinkead's **14**
La Colline **52**

Legal Sea Foods **16**
Les Halles **42**
Marcel's **12**
Matchbox **37**
Melrose **11**
The Monocle **54**
Montmartre **56**
Morton's **19**
Nectar **13**
Occidental Grill **31**
Oceanaire Seafood
  Room **34**
Old Ebbitt Grill **30**
Olives **25**
Oval Room **23**
The Palm **4**
The Prime Rib **16**
Red Sage **33**
701 **45**
Tabard Inn **2**
Taberna del Alabardero **21**
Teaism Penn Quarter **48**
Teatro Goldoni **17**
TenPenh **43**
Tony Cheng's Seafood
  Restaurant **38**
Tosca **35**
Vidalia **8**
Zaytinya **39**
Zola **40**

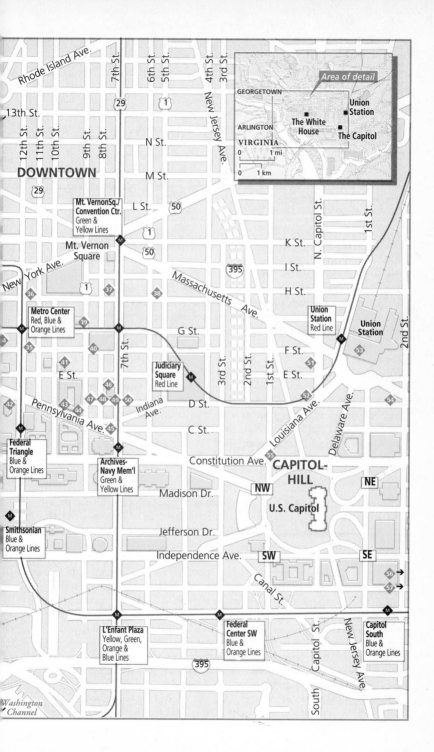

Area of detail

GEORGETOWN

Union
Station

ARLINGTON

The White
House

VIRGINIA

The Capitol

0   1 mi

0   1 km

Rhode Island Ave.

7th St.

6th St.

5th St.

4th St.

3rd St.

New Jersey Ave.

13th St.

12th St.

11th St.

10th St.

9th St.

8th St.

N St.

M St.

DOWNTOWN

29

Mt. VernonSq./
Convention Ctr.
Green &
Yellow Lines

L St.

50

Mt. Vernon
Square

K St.

N. Capitol St.

1st St.

New York Ave.

50

I St.

H St.

Massachusetts Ave.

395

36

37

38

Union
Station
Red Line

Union
Station

2nd St.

Metro Center
Red, Blue &
Orange Lines

39

G St.

53

35

40

7th St.

F St.

Judiciary
Square
Red Line

3rd St.

2nd St.

1st St.

51

41

E St.

E St.

46

47 48 49 50

Indiana
Ave.

D St.

52

Delaware Ave.

54

42

Pennsylvania Ave.

43

45

C St.

Louisiana Ave.

Federal
Triangle
Blue &
Orange Lines

Archives-
Navy Mem'l
Green &
Yellow Lines

Constitution Ave.

55

CAPITOL-
HILL

NW

NE

Madison Dr.

U.S. Capitol

Smithsonian
Blue &
Orange Lines

Jefferson Dr.

Independence Ave.

SW

SE

56

57

Canal St.

L'Enfant Plaza
Yellow, Green,
Orange &
Blue Lines

Federal
Center SW
Blue &
Orange Lines

Capitol
St.

New Jersey Ave.

Capitol
South
Blue &
Orange Lines

395

Washington
Channel

South

Traveler magazine as one of the top 100 new restaurants in the world. We recently enjoyed a tossed salad with baby artichoke hearts; risotto with shrimp, crab, peas, and carrots; venison with a pistachio bread pudding; and the horse-radish-crusted halibut with leek fondue.

The highlight of Butterfield 9's classy decor is a series of large, stylized black-and-white prints of handsome men and women dressed in 1930s, '40s, and '50s fashions. Butterfield 9 is the latest venture of restaurateur Amarjeet (Umbi) Singh, owner of New Heights (p. 164). A bar menu of about nine items priced from $5 to $13 is available all day, featuring items like the soup of the day, a cheese plate with fresh fruit, fried oysters, duck spring rolls, and gnocchi.

600 14th St. NW. ℂ 202/BU9-8810. www.butterfield9.com. Reservations recommended. Lunch main courses $14–$22; dinner main courses $18–$36. AE, DC, DISC, MC, V. Mon–Fri 11:30am–2:30pm; Sun–Thurs 5:30–10pm; Fri–Sat 5:30–11pm. Metro: Metro Center.

Café 15 𝄞𝄞 FRENCH   This hotel restaurant is aimed at those with the most sophisticated palates and deepest pockets. On the menu are items like frog's legs, which are served with sweet onion–filled ravioli; terrine of layered foie gras and free range chicken; and beef tournedos with a red wine glaze, sautéed potatoes, and caramelized onions. Everything is done perfectly and presented expertly. A whirl of servers descends upon your table, places the plates just so, then pulls away, to leave you in admiring contemplation. My entree of scallops was quite scrumptious, but that is what they were, a little plate of scallops. It was all just a little too precious for me, but I'd love to give it another go. My husband Jim is a big fan, dining here for lunch and enjoying sautéed John Dory and vegeta-bles. This is a comfortably small and quiet dining room with high ceilings and big windows. (For more dramatic decor, go across the lobby to Le Bar, which is quite the lounge.) Meals begin and end with complimentary and delicious nib-bles: a tiny taste of foie gras or pea soup as an *amuse boule*, and a little tray of truffles, almond clusters, and chocolate-covered dried fruit bars to complete.

In the Sofitel Lafayette Square, 806 15th St. NW (at H St.). ℂ 202/730-8800. Reservations recommended. Breakfast main courses $6–$17; lunch main courses $19–$26; dinner main courses $27–$33. AE, DC, DISC, MC, V. Daily 6:30–10:30am; Mon–Fri 11:30am–2pm; daily 6–9:30pm. Metro: McPherson Square (White House exit), Farragut North, or Farragut West.

The Caucus Room 𝄞𝄞 STEAK   Washington's powerful people like steak-houses, and that's a fact. Since the Caucus Room is owned by a bipartisan bunch of heavy-hitting politicos and entrepreneurs (Democratic lobbyist Tommy Boggs and former Republican National Committee chairman Haley Barbour, to name but two of the 70 investors), the Caucus Room was almost a guaranteed success even before it opened in August 2000. At lunch and dinner, it's a true Washington scene, with all that that entails: a sprinkling of congressmen and -women, television newscasters, and corporate VIPs throughout the main dining room; lots of backslapping and shaking of hands; and private meetings taking place behind closed doors (the restaurant has a number of private dining rooms).

But I'm here to tell you, the food is good. Haley's chopped salad of diced bell peppers and lettuce, blue cheese, and mustard vinaigrette is a hit. The porter-house steak is juicy, and the bison osso buco is thoroughly delicious. The restau-rant also is known for certain non-meat entrees, such as the crab cakes (the pass/fail test for a D.C. restaurant), which are served here with a smoky bacon succotash. Even side dishes, like the creamed spinach and the horseradish-spiked mashed potatoes, are winners.

When you've finished all that, you can lean back against the leather banquettes and discreetly search for famous faces while you enjoy dessert. I polished off a big slice of coconut cake, but I hear the pecan pie is pretty good, too.

401 9th St. NW (at D St.). 𝄞 **202/393-1300**. www.thecaucusroom.com. Reservations recommended. Lunch items $9–$25; dinner main courses $25–$38. AE, DISC, MC, V. Mon–Fri 11:30am–2:30pm; Mon–Sat 5:30–10:30pm. Metro: Navy/Archives or Gallery Place.

Gerard's Place ✹✹✹ FRENCH   Gerard Pangaud is the only Michelin two-star chef working in this country. His restaurant has been here for quite some time now, and his popularity shows no signs of abating. Though Pangaud changes his menu every 2 weeks, he can be counted on to combine exquisite taste sensations, like Jerusalem artichokes with foie gras and truffles, or curried eggplant soup, cod with sautéed endives, or fricassee of monkfish in a red wine sauce. Every once in a while you'll see his famous lobster with ginger, lime, and sauterne on the menu (for $53), and if you do, order it, for it's justly famous. The dining room itself is small, seating only 50 at a time, and is rather underwhelming in design. And this is a quiet restaurant, not a place to get rowdy. You're here for the food, and quiet conversation. And though Gerard's Place is also very expensive, the restaurant bows to your budget in offering a three-course fixed-price weekday lunch for $30, and by waiving the corkage fee (usually $25) on Monday nights, so feel free to bring your own bottle of wine.

915 15th St. NW. 𝄞 **202/737-4445**. www.restaurant.com/gerardsplace. Reservations recommended. Lunch and dinner main courses $23–$50; fixed-price menu $85. AE, MC, V. Mon–Fri 11:30am–2pm; Mon–Thurs 5:30–9pm; Fri–Sat 5:30–9:30pm. Metro: McPherson Square.

Red Sage Grill/Red Sage Border Café ✹ AMERICAN/SOUTHWESTERN   There's Red Sage, the Grill, which is downstairs, and Red Sage, the Border Café, upstairs: two different chefs and two menus, but the same decor, which conjures up a whimsical Wild West fantasy. Downstairs, the main dining room is a warren of cozy, candlelit alcoves under a curved ponderosa-log-beamed ceiling. The menu dares you to try something different, like the elk loin topped with dried fruit mostarda, but also offers tamer dishes, such as fresh Casco Bay cod on garlicky polenta. You should like things spicy, for Red Sage is famous for entrees like the roasted red chile pecan-crusted chicken. I prefer and highly recommend the more casual Border Café ✹✹ and its inexpensive light fare, especially the sweetish State of the Union chili, which features red beans and bits of bacon; the salmon tacos, for which the salmon has been marinated and grilled; and the hickory-grilled chicken quesadillas. The margaritas are superb.

605 14th St. NW (at F St.). 𝄞 **202/638-4444**. www.redsage.com. Reservations recommended for main dining room, not accepted for Border Café. Lunch main courses $10–$17; dinner main courses $25–$38; Border Café main courses $6–$15. AE, DISC, MC, V. Restaurant Mon–Thurs 11:30am–2pm and 5:30–10pm; Fri 11:30am–2pm and 5:30–10:30pm; Sat 5–10:30pm; Sun 5:30–10pm. Border Café Mon–Sat 11:30am–11:30pm; Sun 4:30–11pm. Metro: Metro Center.

EXPENSIVE

Bistrot D'Oc ✹✹ FRENCH   Fans of Bernard and Thasanee Grenier, who for 20 years owned the French restaurant, La Miche, in the Maryland suburb of Bethesda, have followed the family to this French bistro, which the Greniers opened in Spring 2003. Business has been brisk at Bistrot D'Oc from the start, and we were among the first to delight in the hangar steak and pommes frites, mussels in cream sauce, bouillabaisse, and a special salad of haricots verts, avocado, and tomato, with a mustard vinaigrette. The cuisine represents the tastes

Vegetarian Times

You know when a restaurant called The Prime Rib lists a "vegetable plate entree" on its dinner menu that vegetarianism has officially entered the mainstream of American eating habits. And it's clear that restaurants are ready to accommodate non-meat-eaters, recognizing that vegetarians like to dine out as much as carnivores. In addition to The Prime Rib's entree (which, by the way, is a spread of fresh asparagus, broccoli, spinach, whole tomato gratiné, and baked potato), here are some other restaurants whose menus cater to vegetarians. See individual listings within this chapter for full descriptions of each establishment.

On the upscale end of the spectrum is **Nora** (p. 148). At Nora, restaurateur Nora Pouillon's passion for organic ingredients means that her menus always include at least one fresh vegetarian entree, like the wild-mushroom and asparagus risotto described on a recent menu. Nora also offers a vegetarian tasting menu for $58, which recently listed an artichoke tart with goat cheese and olives and a spring risotto with roasted cauliflower and grilled asparagus.

Georgia Brown's (p. 132) is another fine restaurant to consider; its menu presents three vegetarian entrees, including "vegetarian chicken croquettes," which are patties made of minced celery, onion, and garlic, served with garlicky mashed potatoes, sautéed spinach, and blackened tomato coulis. And then there's the fabulous and fun **Café Atlantico's** (p. 130) Latino dim sum "all you can eat" brunch on Saturday and Sunday, 11:30am to 2:30pm, a favorite for vegetarians, since the brunch offers a vegetarian tasting menu of close to 20 dishes, from avocado with corn nuts to spinach with pumpkin seeds. The price is $25 per person.

Indian restaurants are always a good bet for vegetarians. The **Bombay Club** (p. 142) offers a full page of nine vegetarian entrees, everything from a mixed-vegetable curry to spinach and lentil dumplings simmered in a yogurt and herb sauce. Other ethnic restaurants worth checking out are the inexpensive Italian cafe **Pasta Mia** (p. 146), Ethiopian restaurant **Meskerem** (p. 146), and the **Lebanese Taverna** (p. 165), great options all.

of Bernard's native Languedoc, in southwestern France, and the red and yellow washed walls call to mind the colors found in that part of the country. An extensive wine list includes selections from the Languedoc region.

518 10th St. NW (between E and F sts. NW). ℂ 202/393-5444. Reservations recommended. Lunch main courses $13–$18; dinner main courses $13–$22. AE, DC, DISC, MC, V. Mon–Fri 11:30am–2:30pm; Sat–Sun 11:30am–4:30pm (brunch); Mon–Thurs 5:30–10pm; Fri–Sat 5:30–11pm; Sun 4:30–8:30pm. Metro: Metro Center.

Café Atlantico ⋆⋆ *Finds* LATIN AMERICAN This place rocks all week long, but especially on weekend nights, it's a favorite hot spot in Washington's still-burgeoning downtown. The colorful three-tiered restaurant throbs with Latin, calypso, and reggae music, and everyone is having a fiesta—including, it seems, the waiters. If the place is packed, try to snag a seat at the second-level bar, where you can watch the genial bartender mix the potent drinks for which Café Atlantico is famous: the *caipirinha*, made of limes, sugar, and *cachacha* (sugar-cane liqueur); the *mojito*, a rum and crushed mint cocktail; or the passion-fruit cocktail, a concoction of passion-fruit juice, ginger, and jalapeño mixed with mandarin orange–flavored vodka. But take a gander at the remarkable, award-winning wine list, too—it boasts 110 selections, mostly from South America, with many bottles priced under $30.

Seated at the bar or table, you'll watch as your waiter makes fresh guacamole right before your eyes. As for the main dishes, you can't get a more elaborate meal for the price. Check out the ceviche, duck confit, and seared scallops with coconut crispy rice and ginger, squid, and squid ink oil, (though the menu changes, you're sure to find these or their equivalent listed), and tropical side dishes and pungent sauces produce a burst of color on the plate. Feel free to ask your friendly waiter for guidance.

For adventurous gourmands: make a reservation at the Minibar at Café Atlantico, where chef Jose Andres concocts a $65 per person, prix fixe menu of 30 to 40 small dishes, from foie gras in a cocoon of cotton candy to pineapple raviolis, for six people per seating, Tuesday to Saturday, at 6pm and 8:30pm.

405 8th St. NW. ⓒ 202/393-0812. www.cafeatlanticodc.com. Reservations recommended. Lunch main courses $9–$15; dinner main courses $18–$24; pretheater menu $22 (5–6:30pm); Latino dim sum: you can choose a la carte ($2–$9 each) items, or pay $25 for a vegetarian all you can eat meal, or $35 for a deluxe version (Sat 11:30am–2:30pm). AE, DC, DISC, MC, V. Mon–Fri 11:30am–2:30pm; Sat–Sun brunch 11:30am–2pm; Sun–Thurs 5–10pm; Fri–Sat 5–11pm. The bar stays open late on weekends. Metro: Archives–Navy Memorial and Gallery Place/MCI Center.

DC Coast ⍟ AMERICAN   The dining room is sensational: two stories high, with glass-walled balcony, immense oval mirrors hanging over the bar, and a full-bodied stone mermaid poised to greet you at the entrance. Gather at the bar first to feel a part of the loud and trendy scene; while you're there, why not nosh on something from the bar menu, perhaps the crispy fried calamari or maybe a luscious pork spring roll? This continues to be one of the city's most popular restaurants, so call way ahead to book a reservation. Chef Jeff Tunks is famous for his Chinese-style smoked lobster with crispy fried spinach—you'll almost always find it on the menu here. Other entrees that I recommend include the pan-seared sea scallops, and the fish filet encrusted with portobello paste and served with truffled potatoes and porcini broth. Seafood is a big part of the menu, but there are a handful of meat dishes, too. **TenPenh** is another popular Tunks restaurant (p. 133).

1401 K St. NW. ⓒ 202/216-5988. www.dccoast.com. Reservations recommended. Lunch main courses $14–$19; dinner main courses $19–$29; light fare $7–$11. AE, DC, DISC, MC, V. Mon–Fri 11:30am–2:30pm; Mon–Thurs 5:30–10:30pm; Fri–Sat 5:30–11pm (light fare Mon–Thurs 2:30–10:30pm, Fri 2:30–11pm, Sat 5:30–11pm). Metro: McPherson Square.

15 Ria ⍟ AMERICAN   If you're staying at the Washington Terrace, the hotel in which this restaurant is located, you will want to dine here, but even if you're not an overnight guest, the restaurant is a good choice. Fifteen Ria (the acronym for the address: Rhode Island Avenue) serves dressed up comfort food: sirloin crusted in blue cheese, a burger on brioche, Caesar salad alternating layers of romaine with bacon and cherry tomatoes, and the beef short ribs sweetened with molasses. The restaurant is known for its nightly specials and for its bar, where drinks are concocted with fresh fruit and juices and the bar menu features some of the best onion rings, popcorn shrimp, and calamari in town.

1515 Rhode Island Ave. NW (at Scott Circle and 15th St.). © 202/232-7000. www.15ria.com. Reservations recommended. Lunch main courses $9–$19; dinner main courses $12–$30. AE, DC, DISC, MC, V. Mon–Fri 6:30–11am; Sat–Sun 7am–noon; Sun brunch 11am–4pm; Mon–Fri 11:30am–2:30pm; Sun–Thurs 6–10:30pm; Fri–Sat 6–11:30pm (light fare Mon–Fri 2:30–6pm, Sat 1–6pm, Sun 4–6pm). Metro: Dupont Circle or McPherson Square.

Georgia Brown's ✦ SOUTHERN   In Washington restaurants, seldom do you find such a racially diverse crowd. The harmony may stem from the waiters, whose obvious rapport results in gracious service, and certainly extends from the open kitchen, where the chef directs his multicultural staff. But in this large, handsome room, whose arched windows overlook McPherson Square, the food might capture all of your attention. A plate of corn bread and biscuits arrives, to be slathered with butter that's been whipped with diced peaches and honey. The menu is heavily Southern, with the emphasis on the Low Country cooking of South Carolina and Savannah: collards, grits, and lots of seafood, especially shrimp dishes. The Charleston *perlau* is a stewlike mix of duck, spicy sausage, jumbo shrimp, and rice, topped with toasted crumbs and scallions. It has bite but isn't terribly spicy. For something totally decadent, try the buttermilk batter-fried chicken. Georgia Brown's is famous for its Sunday brunch, lively with the sounds of jazz and conversation, and luscious with the tastes of country sausage, omelets made to order, creamy grits, and many other dishes.

950 15th St. NW. © 202/393-4499. www.gbrowns.com. Reservations recommended. Lunch main courses $7–$20; dinner main courses $17–$23; Sun jazz brunch $27. AE, DC, DISC, MC, V. Mon–Thurs 11:30am–10:30pm; Fri 11:30am–11:30pm; Sat 5:30–11:30pm; Sun 10am–2:30pm (brunch) and 5:30–9pm. Metro: McPherson Square.

Occidental Grill ✦ NEW AMERICAN   The Occidental has always been a place to go for atmosphere as much as food. Dark-wood paneling, a classic bar, and walls lined with booths give the place a clubby feel, making it a favorite spot for business lunches and dinners. (Its proximity to National Theatre also makes it convenient for theater-goers.) On the walls hang more than 2,600 autographed photographs of famous customers, from Buffalo Bill Cody (the original restaurant opened in 1906, closed in 1972, then reopened in 1986), to more recent celebs like Steven Spielberg, Colin Powell, Hillary Clinton, and Oprah Winfrey. In pleasant weather, you can sit at the outdoor patio on Pennsylvania Avenue, where you have a grand view of the Capitol. The upstairs dining room is more formal, with larger booths, a smaller bar, and no photos.

For a while, food was secondary to atmosphere, but Chef Patrick Bazin has rescued the menu, updating the traditional meat-and-potatoes fare with elegant sauces and sophisticated accents. So now, look for braised lobster with applewood smoked bacon; grilled lamb chop with mint pesto; and seared salmon with lobster mashed potatoes. The potato dishes are always good.

1475 Pennsylvania Ave. NW. © 202/783-1475. www.occidentaldc.com. Reservations recommended. Lunch items $10–$25; dinner main courses $20–$40. AE, DC, MC, V. Mon–Thurs 11:30am–10:30pm; Fri–Sat 11:30am–11:30pm; Sun 11am–9:30pm (brunch 11am–4pm). Metro: Metro Center or Federal Triangle.

Oceanaire Seafood Room ✦ SEAFOOD   The Oceanaire is a good spot for a lively party, with its red-leather booths, Art Deco–ish decor, long bar, and festive atmosphere. It would be hard to get romantic or serious about business here—there's just too much to distract you, like the sight of mile-high desserts en route to another table. Oceanaire serves big portions of everything (including cocktails, another reason to bring a bunch of friends here). On a menu that proclaims, "Fresh fish flown in daily from around the world!" you'll read intriguing names of fish on offer that day: grilled Hawaiian Opah moonfish, Tasmanian steelhead trout, Ecuadorian mahimahi, and so on. These are usually served simply grilled or broiled. The waitstaff excel at explaining the tastes and textures of everything on the menu, so don't hesitate to ask. Two of the best entrees are not hard to figure at all: the crab cakes, which are almost all lump crab meat, and the fisherman's platter, a fresh, fried selection of oysters, scallops, shrimp, and other seafood, with hot matchstick fries alongside it all. The dozen varieties of oysters are fresh and plump, but if you want to start with a salad, consider the BLT, which is exactly as it sounds, like eating a bacon-lettuce-tomato sandwich without the toast.

1201 F St. NW. ☎ 202/347-2277. www.theoceanaire.com. Reservations recommended. Lunch and dinner main courses $9.95–$40. AE, DISC, MC, V. Mon–Thurs 11:30am–10pm; Fri 11:30am–11pm; Sat 5–11pm; Sun 5–9pm. Metro: Metro Center.

701 ⭐ AMERICAN/INTERNATIONAL   701 is known for its vodka selections and sophisticated American fare. For starters, try the foie gras raviolis. Other recommendable dishes are the medallions of venison with sweet potatoes, gala apples, and lemon-orange whiskey sauce, and the crabmeat-stuffed, Serrano-ham wrapped cod. Artful presentation makes the food all the more enticing. Portions are generous and service is marvelous.

This restaurant is literally steps away from the Archives–Navy Memorial Metro stop and a short walk from several theaters. Its plate-glass windows allow you to watch commuters, theatergoers, and tourists scurrying along Pennsylvania Avenue. Walls, glass partitions, and columns in the dining room create pockets of privacy throughout. Live jazz plays nightly.

701 Pennsylvania Ave. NW. ☎ 202/393-0701. www.701restaurant.com. Reservations recommended. Lunch main courses $8.95–$18; dinner main courses $15–$28; pretheater dinner (5:30–6:45pm) $25. AE, DC, MC, V. Mon–Fri 11:30am–3pm; Mon–Thurs 5:30–10:30pm; Fri–Sat 5:30–11:30pm; Sun 5–9:30pm. Metro: Archives–Navy Memorial.

TenPenh ⭐⭐ ASIAN FUSION   We'd heard that the service was excellent here, and in its early days this proved to be true: Our waiter actually split a glass of wine for me and my friend, when we both wanted a little more, but not an entire additional glass. The same waiter checked out someone we thought was Rob Lowe in the bar, reporting back to us, alas, that it was not he. But service is not what it used to be, or so it seemed when we dined here recently, and waited quite a while for dinner to arrive. The atmosphere is still lively, however, and the food is still stellar. TenPenh has a separate, loungy, hard-to-leave bar, but the dining room itself is inviting, with soft lighting, comfortable booths, and an open kitchen. In this, his second restaurant (DC Coast is his other), Jeff Tunks presents translations of dishes he's discovered in travels throughout Asia: smoked salmon and crisp wonton napoleon (which actually had too much salmon); 5-spice pecan-crusted halibut; Chinese-style smoked lobster (also available at DC Coast); wok-seared calamari; and dumplings filled with chopped pork and crab. We finished with a trio of crème brûlée, the best of which was the coffee-crème.

1001 Pennsylvania Ave. NW (at 10th St.). ☎ 202/393-4500. www.tenpenh.com. Reservations recommended. Lunch main courses $13–$18; dinner main courses $13–$28. AE, DISC, MC, V. Mon–Fri 11:30am–2:30pm; Mon–Thurs 5:30–10:30pm; Fri–Sat 5:30–11pm. Metro: Archives–Navy Memorial.

Tosca ⭐⭐⭐ NORTHERN ITALIAN   Washington probably has more Italian restaurants than any other kind of ethnic eatery, yet this central part of downtown has almost no Italian fare. In fact, since it opened in spring 2001, Tosca remains the standout fine *ristorante italiano* between Capitol Hill and the western edge of downtown, a range of at least 20 blocks. Tosca's interior design of pale pastels in the thick carpeting and heavy drapes creates a hushed atmosphere, a suitable foil to the rich food.

The menu, meanwhile, emphasizes the cooking of chef Cesare Lanfranconi's native Lake Como region of Italy. A good example of a traditional pasta dish is the *scapinasch,* a ravioli of aged ricotta and raisins (or sometimes it's made with amaretto cookies) with butter and sage sauce. Lanfranconi's take on a rack of veal is to marinate and grill the meat, serving it with Yukon gold and roasted garlic potato purée and local asparagus timbale. Tosca has something for everyone, including simply grilled fish accompanied by organic vegetables for the health conscious, tiramisu and citrus cannoli for those with a sweet tooth. No wonder the restaurant is always full. But even when there's a crowd, Tosca doesn't get too noisy—the restaurant's designers kept acoustics in mind.

1112 F St. NW. ℂ 202/367-1990. www.toscadc.com. Reservations recommended. Lunch main courses $9–$18; dinner main courses $16–$34. AE, DC, MC, V. Mon–Fri 11:30am–2:30pm; Sun–Thurs 5:30–10:30pm; Fri–Sat 5:30–11pm. Metro: Metro Center.

MODERATE

Andale ⋆ MEXICAN   Chef Allison Swope's vision of Mexican cuisine and restauranting is uniquely her own. During a visit to the Yucatan peninsula a couple of years ago, Swope was so taken with the cuisine of Oaxaca, Mexico, that upon her return to Washington she set about transforming her "robust American" restaurant, The Mark, into the inventive Mexican Andale (*andale* means "let's go!"). The menu features dishes that combine authentic regional Mexican cuisine with fresh and often non-traditional ingredients: sushi grade tuna marinated with achiote, garlic, Mexican oregano, and sour orange juice; leg of lamb roasted in avocado leaves and presented in a soupy sauce of lamb broth, thickened with garbanzo beans, carrots, and potato, is a standout. Not to miss: the smoky, spicy salsa picante appetizer and the Mexican-style doughnuts with dipping chocolate for dessert. The bar offers 35 brands of tequila and concocts an excellent margarita.

Avoid being shown to the windowless back room, opt instead for seating in either the storefront window for optimum people-watching (Andale is in the middle of downtown), or in the main dining room, where Mexican artwork now hangs. Great deal: Every Monday after 5pm, you can order a bottle of wine or champagne for half price with the order of an entree.

401 7th St. NW. ℂ 202/783-3133. www.andaledc.com. Reservations recommended. Lunch main courses $7–$14; dinner main courses $9–$22. AE, DC, DISC, MC, V. Mon–Sat 11:30am–3pm; Mon 5–9pm; Tues–Thurs 5–10pm; Fri–Sat 5–11pm; Mon–Fri bar stays open but no food is served, 3–5pm. Metro: Gallery Place or Archives/Navy Memorial.

Jaleo ⋆ *Finds* SPANISH   In theater season, Jaleo's dining room fills and empties each evening according to the performance schedule of the Shakespeare Theater, right next door. Lunchtime always draws a crowd from nearby office buildings and the Hill. This restaurant, which opened in 1993, may be credited with initiating the tapas craze in Washington. Though the menu offers a handful of entrees, you really want to consider the tapas, of which there are about 55. These include a very simple but not-to-be-missed grilled bread layered with a paste of fresh tomatoes and topped with anchovies; savory warm goat cheese served with toast points; a skewer of grilled chorizo sausage atop garlic mashed potatoes; a delicious mushroom tart served with roasted red-pepper sauce; and gazpacho. Paella is among the few heartier entrees (it feeds four). Spanish wines, sangrias, and sherries are available by the glass. Finish with a rum-and-butter–soaked apple charlotte in bread pastry or a plate of Spanish cheeses. The casual-chic interior focuses on a large mural of a flamenco dancer inspired by John Singer Sargent's painting *Jaleo*. On Wednesday at 7:45pm and 8:45pm, flamenco dancers perform.

A second and even prettier Jaleo is located in the suburbs, at 7271 Woodmont Ave., Bethesda, Maryland (✆ **301/913-0003**). Though this branch is within walking distance of my house, I prefer the ambience of the original D.C. location.

480 7th St. NW (at E St.). ✆ **202/628-7949**. www.jaleo.com. Reservations accepted until 6:30pm. Lunch main courses $7.50–$11; dinner main courses $11–$28; tapas $3.95–$8. AE, DC, DISC, MC, V. Sun–Mon 11:30am–10pm; Tues–Thurs 11:30am–11:30pm; Fri–Sat 11:30am–midnight. Metro: Archives or Gallery Place.

Les Halles FRENCH/STEAK   We took our French exchange student here, and guess what she ordered: steak *frites*. I did the same. In fact, everyone in the restaurant was devouring the *onglet* (a boneless French cut hangar steak hard to

---

(Kids) Family-Friendly Restaurants

Nearly every restaurant welcomes families these days, starting, most likely, with the one in your hotel. Chinese restaurants are always a safe bet, and so are these:

Austin Grill (p. 163)   An easygoing, good-service joint, with great background music. Kids will probably want to order from their own menu here, and their drinks arrive in unspillable plastic cups with tops and straws.

Legal Sea Foods (p. 143)   Believe it or not, this seafood restaurant has won awards for its kids' menu. It features the usual macaroni and cheese and hot dogs, but also kids' portions of steamed lobster; fried popcorn shrimp; a small fisherman's platter of shrimp, scallops, and clams; and other items, each of which comes with fresh fruit and a choice of baked potato, mashed potatoes, or french fries. Prices range from $3.95 for the hot dog to $16 for the 1-pound lobster (you can also order a half-pound lobster for $8.95).

Famous Luigi's Pizzeria Restaurant (p. 144)   Introduce your kids to pre-Domino's pizza. Luigi's, which has been around since 1943, serves the real thing: big, thick pizza, with fresh toppings. Sit at tables covered in red-checked cloths that have probably withstood countless spilled drinks and splotches of tomato sauce in their time. The restaurant gets noisy, so chances are that loud ones in your party will blend right in.

Old Glory Barbecue (p. 160)   A loud, laid-back place where the waiters are friendly without being patronizing. Go early, since the restaurant becomes more of a bar as the evening progresses. There is a children's menu, but you may not need it—the barbecue, burgers, muffins, fries, and desserts are so good that everyone can order from the main menu.

find outside France), steak au poivre, steak tartare, New York sirloin, and other cuts, all of which come with *frites,* which are a must. (Actually, two diners at our table ordered ravioli and a chicken salad, and boy were they sorry.) The menu isn't all beef, but it is classic French, featuring cassoulet, *confit de canard,* escargots, onion soup, *choucroutte garni,* and an irresistible *frisée aux lardons* (a savory salad of chicory studded with hunks of bacon and toast, smeared thickly with Roquefort). If you spy something on the menu that's not Gallic, ignore it.

Les Halles is big and charmingly French. The banquettes, pressed-tin ceiling, mirrors, wooden floor, and side bar capture the feel of a brasserie. A vast window front overlooks Pennsylvania Avenue and the awning-covered sidewalk cafe, which is enclosed in cold weather and is a superb spot to dine year-round. Every July, from the 4th to the 14th, Les Halles hosts its Liberty Festival, to celebrate America's Independence Day and France's Bastille Day (July 14). Part of the celebration is the annual Bastille Day race, which Les Halles co-sponsors. (Sometimes the event is held close to Bastille Day, if not on the exact day of celebration; see the "Calendar of Events," in chapter 2 for details.) Les Halles is a favorite hangout for cigar smokers, but the smoking area is well ventilated.

1201 Pennsylvania Ave. NW. ℂ 202/347-6848. www.leshalles.net. Reservations recommended. Lunch main courses $9.50–$26; dinner main courses $11–$26. AE, DC, DISC, MC, V. Daily noon–midnight. Metro: Metro Center or Federal Triangle.

Old Ebbitt Grill AMERICAN You won't find this place listed among the city's best culinary establishments, but you can bet it's included in every tour book. It's an institution. The original Old Ebbitt was established in 1856, at 14th and F streets, around the corner. The Grill moved to this location in 1980, bringing much of the old place with it. Among its artifacts are animal trophies bagged by Teddy Roosevelt, and Alexander Hamilton's wooden bears—one with a secret compartment in which it's said he hid whiskey bottles from his wife. The Old Ebbitt is attractive, with Persian rugs strewn on beautiful oak and marble floors, beveled mirrors, flickering gaslights, etched-glass panels, and paintings of Washington scenes. The long, dark mahogany Old Bar area emphasizes the men's saloon ambience.

Tourists and office people fill the Ebbitt during the day, flirting singles take it over at night. You'll always have to wait for a table if you don't reserve ahead. The waiters are friendly and professional in a programmed sort of way; service could be faster. Menus change daily but always include certain favorites: burgers, trout Parmesan (Virginia trout dipped in egg batter and Parmesan cheese, deep-fried), crab cakes, and oysters—Old Ebbitt's raw bar is its saving grace when all else fails; the *Washington Post* food critic claims this is the best raw bar in town, and that's saying something. Aside from the fresh oysters, the tastiest dishes are usually the seasonal ones, with the fresh ingredients making the difference.

675 15th St. NW (between F and G sts.). ℂ 202/347-4801. Reservations recommended. Breakfast $6.95–$9.95; brunch $5.95–$14; lunch main courses $6.95–$14 (as much as $25 when crab cakes are on the menu); dinner main courses $14–$21 (again, up to $25 for crab cakes); burgers and sandwiches $6.95–$11; raw bar $8.95–$19. AE, DC, DISC, MC, V. Mon–Thurs 7:30am–2am; Fri 7:30am–3am; Sat 8:30am–3am; Sun 9:30am–2am (kitchen closes at 1am nightly; raw bar open every night until midnight). Metro: McPherson Square or Metro Center.

Zaytinya ✸✸✸ GREEK/TURKISH/LEBANESE Honest, I would have liked Zaytinya even if my waiter, Isa, hadn't told me I had beautiful eyes. Isa also has beautiful eyes, by the way. All right, down to business. *Conde Nast Traveler* magazine's May 2003 issue named Zaytinya as one of the top 75 new restaurants in the world (the restaurant opened in Oct 2002). Executive chef Jose Andres is behind it all (see reviews of Jaleo, where he continues as the executive chef/partner and of Café Atlantico, where he is the creative director).

Zaytinya is a big restaurant and it stays busy all the time. The place takes reservations only at lunch and for pretheater dinners, 5 to 6:30pm. Zaytinya was hopping on the Sunday night we were there, but fortunately we didn't have a wait. Once seated, we received a basket of hot and billowy thin shells of pita bread, along with a saucer of olive oil swirled with pomegranate syrup. Isa guided us through the menu, explaining that the wine list was almost entirely Greek, that Zaytinya is Turkish for "olive oil," and pointing out which mezze dishes he would recommend. Although the dinner menu lists several entrees, what you want to do here is order lots of little dishes. We savored the zucchini-cheese cakes, which came with a caper and yogurt sauce; the carrot-apricot–pine nut fritters, served with pistachio sauce; sardines; a marinated salmon; *fattoush,* or salad of tomatoes and cucumbers mixed with pomegranate reduction, sumac, and olive oil, with crispy pita bread croutons; and shrimp with tomatoes, onions, ouzo, and kefalograviera cheese. Many of these flavors were new to my palette, but I found everything to be wonderfully delicious. For dessert, we ordered a Turkish coffee chocolate cake, and the more exotic Medjool dates roasted in Vinsanto (a kind of dessert wine), rolled in crushed orange shortbread, with olive oil ice cream. The dates were our favorite. Isa was quite proud of us.

701 9th St. NW (at G St.). (C) 202/638-0800. www.zaytinya.com. Reservations at lunch and pretheater dinner 5–6:30pm. Mezze items $3.75–$8; main courses at dinner $13–$17. AE, DC, DISC, MC, V. Sun–Mon 11:30am–10pm; Tues–Thurs 11:30am–11:30pm; Fri–Sat 11:30am–midnight. Metro: Gallery Place/Chinatown (9th St. exit).

Zola AMERICAN   A lot of people liked Zola right from the start, when it opened in 2002, but I wasn't one of them. But ever since chef Frank Morales took over the kitchen, I've been totally won over. I've had a simple ham and gouda sandwich at lunch and loved it, and I've had seared scallops that tasted delicately sweet, a perfectly done duck breast, an artichoke and goat cheese tart for dinner, and they were each divine. And then there was dessert, the creamsickle: "mandarin orange and vanilla cream layered atop a 'Nilla wafer crust with bitter chocolate sauce"; another hit. Zola is also a cleverly designed restaurant, trading on its location next to the International Spy Museum for a decor that includes backlit panels of coded KGB documents, and a center-pivoted swinging wall/door, that's like something straight out of the TV show, *Get Smart.* We very much liked the red velvet booths in the dining room, and the long curving bar. Zola, in its superb downtown location, has become a popular place for the young and single to hang. Servers are friendly.

800 F St. NW (at 8th St.). (C) 202/654-0999. www.zoladc.com. Reservations recommended. Lunch main courses $7–$17; dinner main courses $7–$24. AE, DC, DISC, MC, V. Mon–Thurs 11:30am–11pm; Fri 11:30am–midnight; Sat 5pm–midnight; Sun 5–9pm. Metro: Gallery Place/Chinatown.

INEXPENSIVE

Haad Thai THAI   The Washington area has lots of Thai restaurants, but not many are downtown. Fewer still offer such good food in such pretty quarters. Haad Thai is a short walk from the MCI Center, and surrounding hotels. Plants and a pink and black mural of a Thai beach decorate the dining room. The standards are the best, including *pad thai, panang gai* (chicken sautéed with fresh basil leaves in curry, with peanut sauce), satays, and deep fried snapper with spicy bean sauce. All dishes are flavorful and only mildly spicy; speak up if you want your food spicier.

1100 New York Ave. NW (entrance on 11th St. NW). (202/682-1111. Reservations recommended. Lunch main courses $5–$9; dinner main courses $8–$17. AE, DC, MC, V. Mon–Fri 11:30am–2:30pm and 5–10:30pm; Sat noon–10pm; Sun 5–10pm. Metro: Metro Center.

Matchbox PIZZA/ITALIAN   This restaurant occupies three floors of a skinny town house in Chinatown, an odd place to find a pizzeria, maybe, but welcome, nonetheless. Matchbox opened in the spring of 2003 and a year later had grown so popular that it won the 2004 Restaurant Association of Metropolitan Washington Award for best new restaurant. The key thing here is the wood-fired brick oven, which bakes the thin pizza crust at temperatures as high as 900°F. You can choose a regularly featured pizza, like the "prosciutto white," which is topped with prosciutto, kalamata olives, fresh garlic, ricotta cheese, fresh mozzarella, and extra-virgin olive oil; or you can request your own set of toppings, from smoked bacon to artichoke hearts. Matchbox is actually a cut above a pizzeria, for it also serves super salads, appetizers, sandwiches, and entrees; its full bar on the first floor is quite the social scene.

713 H St. NW. (202/289-4441. www.matchboxdc.com. Pizzas and sandwiches $8–$17; main courses at lunch and dinner $13–$21. AE, MC, V. Mon–Sat 11:30am–10pm. Metro: Gallery Place-Chinatown.

Tony Cheng's Seafood Restaurant ☛ CHINESE/SEAFOOD   Most of the restaurants in Chinatown look seedy, no matter how good the food might be. Tony Cheng's is the most presentable of Chinatown's eateries, and also a good choice if you like Cantonese specialties and spicy Szechuan and Hunan cuisine. The restaurant is located on the second floor, above Tony Cheng's Mongolian Restaurant, related but not the same eatery. Tony Cheng's Seafood Restaurant has been here for 28 years and has earned a reputation for its Cantonese roast duck (see it for yourself before ordering, since it is displayed in a case at the back of the restaurant); lobster or Dungeness crab, stir-fried and served with either ginger and scallions or black bean sauce; or Szechuan crispy beef, to name just a few. Dim sum is available at lunch weekdays, as well as on the weekend, but you order items off the menu during the week.

619 H St. NW (between 6th and 7th sts.). (202/371-8669. Reservations recommended. Lunch main courses $5–$13; dinner main courses $7–$29. AE, MC, V. Daily 11am–11pm. Metro: Gallery Place-Chinatown.

4 Downtown, 16th Street NW & West
VERY EXPENSIVE

Galileo ☛☛☛ NEAPOLITAN ITALIAN   Food critics mention Galileo as one of the best Italian restaurants in the country and Roberto Donna as one of the nation's best chefs. The likable Donna opened the white-walled grottolike Galileo in 1984; since then, he has opened other restaurants in the area, including Il Radicchio on Capitol Hill (p. 125). He's also written a cookbook, and has established himself as an integral part of Washington culture.

Donna cures his own ham for salami and prosciutto, and his sausages, pastas, mozzarella, marmalades, and breads are all made in-house. Galileo has long featured the cuisine of Donna's native Piedmont region, an area in northern Italy influenced by neighboring France and Switzerland—think truffles, hazelnuts, porcini mushrooms, and veal. But at the time of my research, spring of 2004, Donna was preparing Neapolitan cuisine. Some examples: roasted rack of lamb served with a porcini mushroom tart in a black olive sauce; homemade raviolis filled with buffalo ricotta, ham, and mozzarella in a meat ragu; Mediterranean dorade fish baked in foil with mussels. Whether your menu features Neapolitan or Piedmontese dishes, you will have the choice of ordering a la carte, or from three fixed price menus, $65 for four courses, $75 for five courses, and $85 for six courses. The cellar boasts more than 400 vintages of Italian wine. The atmosphere is relaxed; some diners are dressed in jeans, others in suits. Waiters can be supercilious, though.

For the ultimate dining experience, book a seat at the table in Donna's **Laboratorio del Galileo** ★★★ (② **202/331-0880**), a private dining area and kitchen enclosed by glass, where Donna prepares the 12- to 14-course tasting menu ($98 weekdays, $110 weekends) and entertains you and 29 other lucky diners.

Galileo also has a terrace for warm-weather dining. And last but not least, if you're intrigued but can't afford a dinner here, reserve a seat at the bar for lunch and enjoy something stupendous, say lasagna Bolognese or a bowl of fusilli tossed with asparagus, provolone, and prosciutto, for only $4 to $12.

1110 21st St. NW. ② 202/293-7191. www.robertodonna.com. Reservations recommended. Lunch main courses $14–$20; dinner main courses $24–$40. AE, DC, DISC, MC, V. Mon–Fri 11:30am–2pm, 5:30–10pm; Sat 5:30–10:30pm; Sun 5:30–10pm. Metro: Foggy Bottom.

I Ricchi ★ TUSCAN ITALIAN   Now in its 16th year, I Ricchi remains a popular and convivial place to enjoy Italian food a la Tuscany. An open kitchen with a blazing wood-burning grill creates a warming bustle in the large room. The daily specials are great, especially if you're into fish. Those of hearty appetite will be happy with minestrone; the quill pasta with Tuscan meat sauce; the rolled medallions of pork loin, turkey breast, and veal, each medallion stuffed with spinach and prosciutto; or stuffed baby quail. Start with grilled radicchio.

1220 19th St. NW. ② 202/835-0459. www.iricchi.net. Reservations recommended. Lunch main courses $17–$25; dinner main courses $23–$35. AE, DC, MC, V. Mon–Fri 11:30am–2pm; Mon–Thurs 5:30–10pm; Fri–Sat 5:30–10:30pm. Metro: Dupont Circle.

The Palm ★ *Finds* STEAK   The Palm is one in a chain of 28 locations that started nearly 80 years ago in New York—but here in D.C., it feels like an original. The Washington Palm is 33 years old; its walls, like those in all Palms, are covered with the caricatures of regulars, famous and not-so. (Look for my friend Bob Harris.) If you think you see Tim Russert or Larry King at a table, you're probably right. You can't go wrong with steak, whether it's the 36-ounce dry-aged New York strip, or sliced in a steak salad. Oversize lobsters are a specialty, and certain side dishes are a must: creamed spinach, onion rings, Palm fries (something akin to deep-fried potato chips), and hash browns. You can order half-portions of these, so you have no excuse but to order at least one. Several of the longtime waiters like to kid with you a bit, but the service is always fast.

1225 19th St. NW. ② 202/293-9091. www.thepalm.com. Reservations recommended. Lunch main courses $12–$21; dinner main courses $15–$64 (most items are in the neighborhood of $25–$32). AE, DC, MC, V. Mon–Fri 11:45am–10:30pm; Sat 5:30–10:30pm; Sun 5:30–9:30pm. Metro: Dupont Circle.

The Prime Rib ★★ STEAK/SEAFOOD   The Prime Rib has plenty of competition now, but it makes no difference. Beef lovers still consider this The Place. It's got a definite men's club feel about it, with brass-trimmed black walls, leopard-skin carpeting, and comfortable black-leather chairs and banquettes. Waiters are in black tie, and a pianist at the baby grand plays show tunes and Irving Berlin classics at lunch; at dinner, a bass player joins the pianist.

The meat is from the best grain-fed steers and has been aged for 4 to 5 weeks. Steaks and cuts of roast beef are thick, tender, and juicy. In case you had any doubt, The Prime Rib's prime rib is the best item on the menu, juicy and thick, top-quality meat. For less carnivorous diners, there are about a dozen seafood entrees, including an excellent crab imperial. Mashed potatoes are done right, as are the fried potato skins, but I recommend the hot cottage fries.

2020 K St. NW. ✆ 202/466-8811. www.theprimerib.com. Reservations recommended. Jacket and tie required for men. Lunch main courses $11–$26; dinner main courses $20–$38. AE, DC, MC, V. Mon–Thurs 11:30am–3pm and 5–11pm; Fri 11:30am–3pm and 5–11:30pm; Sat 5–11:30pm. Metro: Farragut West.

Taberna del Alabardero ★★ *Finds* SPANISH   Dress up to visit this truly elegant restaurant, where you receive royal treatment from the Spanish staff, who are accustomed to attending to the real thing—Spain's King Juan Carlos and Queen Sofia have dined here. Not long ago, the Spanish government named the Taberna del Alabardero the best Spanish restaurant outside Spain. The Taberna is also a favorite of dignitaries attending meetings at the nearby World Bank and International Monetary Fund.

The dining room is ornate, with red tufted banquettes, green satin stretched across chairs, and gilded cherubs placed at ceiling corners. Order a plate of tapas to start: lightly fried calamari, shrimp in garlic and olive oil, artichokes sautéed with thin smoky Serrano ham, and marinated mushrooms. Although the a la carte menu changes with the seasons, several paellas (the menu says each feeds two, but you can ask for a single serving) are always available. The lobster and seafood paella served on saffron rice is rich and flavorful. (Ask to have the lobster shelled; otherwise, you do the cracking.) Another signature dish is the stuffed squid sauced in its own ink. The wine list features 250 Spanish wines.

1776 I St. NW (entrance on 18th St. NW). ✆ 202/429-2200. Reservations recommended. Jacket and tie for men suggested. Lunch main courses $18–$24; dinner main courses $26–$37. AE, DC, DISC, MC, V. Mon–Fri 11:30am–2:30pm; Mon–Thurs 5:30–10:30pm; Fri–Sat 5:30–11pm. Metro: Farragut West.

EXPENSIVE

Daily Grill ★ AMERICAN   Talk about retro. In the case of the Daily Grill, retro means revisiting the food favorites of decades past (though the restaurant itself is only a few years old). Step right in and get your Cobb salad, chicken pot-pie, fresh fruit cobbler, and meat and potatoes—all made with high-quality ingredients (and high caloric value).

It's a big space, with a nice bar at the front and windows on three sides. The winding bar offers an extensive selection: good wines, lots of single malts, tequilas, and small-batch bourbons. The Daily Grill is a favorite lunchtime spot—where else can you order eggs Benedict at noon on a weekday?

Don't know about its chain siblings (mostly located in California), but this Daily Grill rightfully claims a reputation for good service and large portions of grilled meats and fish. (The lunch menu boasts a BLT made with "half a pound of bacon.") You might find it hard to choose from the more than 40 menu items, but favorite orders are the short ribs, the chicken potpie, the meatloaf, and the onion rings. If you have a small appetite, look for the half and half combo options, like the $8.95 sandwich and salad entree that my 12-year-old and I both enjoyed recently: Each of us ordered a half sandwich of a BLT, and a Caesar salad. This BLT is not the "half pound of bacon" version that you normally get, which means it's actually the right size, and so is the salad.

1200 18th St. NW. ✆ 202/822-5282. www.dailygrill.com. Reservations recommended. Lunch main courses $8–$18; dinner main courses $10–$26. AE, DC, DISC, MC, V. Mon–Thurs 11:30am–11pm; Fri–Sat

11:30am–midnight; Sun 11:30am–3pm (brunch) and 5–10pm. Metro: Farragut North or Dupont Circle. Another Daily Grill is located in the Georgetown Inn, 1310 Wisconsin Ave. NW (© 202/337-4900).

Equinox ⭐⭐ NEW AMERICAN   Everyone seems to love Equinox. It's not splashy in any way, just a pretty, comfortable restaurant that serves creatively delicious American food. Even if you aren't vegetarian, you'll eat all your vegetables here, because as much care is taken with these garnishes as with the entree itself. And every entree comes with a garnish or two, like the leek fondue or the forest mushrooms with applewood bacon, or the white bean ragout. You can order additional side dishes; consider the macaroni and cheese: Vermont cheddar, Parmesan, and black truffle reduction. The home runs, of course, are the entrees, and the menu is short and to the point: crab cakes made with lump crab mixed with capers, brioche bread crumbs, mayonnaise, and lemon-butter sauce; barbequed wild King salmon with roasted sweet corn; and two or three other dishes, that's it. Equinox has two tasting menus, a $65 four-course and $85 six-course, available at dinner most nights.

818 Connecticut Ave. NW. © 202/331-8118. www.equinoxrestaurant.com. Reservations recommended. Lunch main courses $16–$27; dinner main courses $30–$33. AE, DC, DISC, MC, V. Mon–Fri 11:30am–2pm; Mon–Thurs 5:30–10pm; Fri–Sat 5:30–10:30pm; Sun 5–9pm. Metro: Farragut West.

Olives ⭐ ITALIAN   Olives is a great party place, a restaurant that comes with its own buzz and keeps it going. Big and loud, its dining rooms, on three floors, attempt a Tuscan ambience, with stone walls, earth tones, wood-burning oven, and lots of greenery. The menu is Italian by way of Boston, where chef-owner Todd English's original Olives continues to flourish. Leave your diet at home, for these dishes are decadent, like the five-clam chowder with bacon (not always on the menu, but when it is, get it); the wood-grilled sirloin served over Tuscan bruschetta with caramelized onions, Smithfield ham, Georgian peas, Roquefort cream, and sour shitake glaze, or the whole Atlantic sole on a creamy potato mousseline with toasted almond and confit shrimp sauce. They are all as scrumptious as they sound. (**Note:** Downstairs is not nearly as much fun; upstairs, or on the patio in pleasant weather, is where all the action is.)

1600 K St. NW. © 202/452-1866. www.toddenglish.com. Reservations required. Lunch main courses $11–$19; dinner main courses $20–$32. AE, DC, MC, V. Mon–Fri 11:30am–2:30pm; Mon–Sat 5:30–10pm. Metro: Farragut North.

Oval Room at Lafayette Square ⭐⭐ NEW AMERICAN   The Oval Room is a local favorite, another winner for owner Ashok Bajaj, who also owns the Bombay Club (p. 142) and 701 (p. 133). The Oval Room is a handsome restaurant, with contemporary art hanging on its lettuce-colored walls. Its atmosphere is congenial, not stuffy, no doubt because the bar area separating the restaurant into two distinct rooms sends cheerful sounds in either direction. The quality of the food has always been top-notch: I've liked the pan-roasted Maryland rockfish with tomato confit, while my husband enjoyed the grilled veal chop with potato cake and brandy peppercorn sauce. In case you haven't figured it out, the Oval Room is a short walk from the White House.

800 Connecticut Ave. NW (at Lafayette Square). © 202/463-8700. www.ovalroom.com. Reservations recommended. Lunch main courses $9.75–$23; dinner main courses $16–$26; pretheater dinner (5:30–6:45pm) $25. AE, DISC, MC, V. Mon–Fri 11:30am–3pm; Mon–Sat 5:30–10:30pm. Metro: Farragut West.

Teatro Goldoni ⭐⭐ VENETIAN ITALIAN   In the beginning, around 1997, there was a restaurant named Goldoni, which, when it moved a couple of years later, assumed the new name, Osteria Goldoni, which soon gave birth to a sister restaurant, Teatro Goldoni. Now, the Osteria has closed, leaving Teatro to carry on the Goldoni traditions of festive ambience and superb Venetian Italian cuisine. Teatro's dining room is dramatic, displaying Venetian masks, immense murals, and harlequin colored glass panels. Chef/owner Fabrizio Aielli is on view, performing as if on stage, inside his elevated glass-enclosed kitchen. As dramatic as the decor is the food, which is served with a flourish. Try the lobster risotto or the risotto with chanterelles mushrooms and foie gras, the roasted salmon filet wrapped with prosciutto, the stewed beef in Barolo wine, or the ravioli stuffed with truffle-oil flavored potatoes and leeks. Classic tiramisu is a specialty, but the warm chocolate and almond cake is also very good. Bring a party of people; in true Goldoni tradition, the Teatro is a good spot for a celebration. A $75 tasting menu is available.

1909 K St. NW. (C) **202/955-9494.** www.teatrogoldoni.com. Reservations recommended. Lunch main courses $12–$20; dinner main courses $19–$35. AE, DC, DISC, MC, V. Mon–Fri 11:30am–2pm; Mon–Thurs 5:30–10pm; Fri–Sat 5–11pm. Metro: Farragut North or Farragut West.

Vidalia *Finds* REGIONAL AMERICAN/SOUTHERN   If you're hesitant to dine at a restaurant that's down a flight of steps from the street, your doubts will vanish as soon as you enter Vidalia's tiered dining room. There's a party going on down here. In fact, Vidalia is so popular, you may have to wait a short time in the newly remodeled wine bar, even if you arrive on time for your reservation. But the bar is fun, too, and gives you a jump-start on getting into the mood of the place. And if you don't have a dinner reservation, you might want to check out the bar menu, whose items include devilled eggs and rabbit rillettes, at prices that range from $4.50 to $12.

Executive chef Peter Smith recently revamped the menu to bring a taste of New Orleans to owner/chef Jeff Buben's already Southern cuisine. The new menu features things like a pan-roasted loin of monkfish with crayfish rice fritters, tasso ham, and etouffée sauce; and rockfish filé with succotash and turnip greens. A signature entree remains the scrumptious sautéed shrimp on a mound of creamed grits and caramelized onions in a thyme-and-shrimp cream sauce. Corn bread and biscuits with apple butter are served at every meal. Vidalia is known for its lemon chess pie, which tastes like pure sugar; I prefer the pecan pie. A carefully chosen wine list highlights American vintages.

1990 M St. NW. (C) **202/659-1990.** www.vidaliadc.com. Reservations recommended. Lunch main courses $13–$22; dinner main courses $23–$30. AE, DC, DISC, MC, V. Mon–Fri 11:30am–2:30pm; Sun–Thurs 5:30–10pm; Fri–Sat 5:30–10:30pm. Closed Sun July 4–Labor Day. Metro: Dupont Circle.

MODERATE

Bombay Club *Finds* INDIAN   The Bombay Club is a pleasure, sure to please patrons who know their Indian food as well as those who've never tried it: dishes present an easy introduction to Indian food for the uninitiated, and are sensitive to varying tolerances for spiciness. I'm a wimp in the "heat" department, my husband's the opposite, and we're both happy here.

The spiciest item on the menu is the fiery green chile chicken ("not for the fainthearted," the menu warns—this is the one my husband orders a lot). Most popular are the tandoori salmon and the delicately prepared lobster malabar (that last one is my personal favorite). These two and the other tandoori dishes, like the chicken marinated in a yogurt, ginger, and garlic dressing, are specialties, as is the vegetarian fare—try the black lentils cooked overnight on a slow fire. The Bombay Club is known for its vegetarian offerings (at least nine items are on the menu) and for its Sunday champagne brunch, which offers a buffet of fresh juices, fresh baked breads, and assorted Indian dishes. Patrons are as fond of the service as the cuisine: Waiters seem straight out of *Jewel in the Crown,* attending to your every whim. This is one place where you can linger over a meal as long as you like. Slow-moving ceiling fans and wicker furniture accentuate the colonial British ambience.

815 Connecticut Ave. NW. © 202/659-3727. www.bombayclubdc.com. Reservations recommended. Main courses $7.50–$22; Sun brunch $19. AE, DC, MC, V. Mon–Fri and Sun brunch 11:30am–2:30pm; Mon–Thurs 6–10:30pm; Fri–Sat 6–11pm; Sun 5:30–9pm. Metro: Farragut West.

Legal Sea Foods *★ Kids* SEAFOOD   This famous family-run Boston-based seafood empire, whose motto is "If it's not fresh, it's not Legal," made its Washington debut in 1995. The softly lit dining room is plush, with terrazzo marble floors and rich cherry-wood paneling. Sporting events, especially Boston games, are aired on a TV over the handsome marble bar/raw bar, and you can usually pick up a copy of the *Boston Globe* near the entrance. As for the food, not only is everything fresh, but it's all from certified-safe waters.

Legal's buttery-rich clam chowder is a classic. Other worthy appetizers include garlicky golden-brown farm-raised mussels au gratin and fluffy pan-fried Maryland lump crab cakes served with mustard sauce and greens tossed with asparagus. You can have one of eight or so varieties of fresh fish grilled or opt for one of Legal's specialty dishes, like the Portuguese fisherman's stew, in which cod, mussels, clams, and chorizo are prepared in a saffron-tomato broth. Top it off with a slice of Boston cream pie. Wine lovers will be happy to know that Legal's wine list has received recognition from *Wine Spectator* magazine; parents will be glad that Legal's award-winning kid's menu offers not just macaroni and cheese, but steamed lobster, popcorn shrimp, and other items, each of which comes with fresh fruit and a choice of baked potato, mashed potatoes, or french fries. At lunch, oyster po'boys and the lobster roll are real treats.

You'll find another Legal Sea Foods at National Airport (© 703/413-9810); a third location is at 704 7th St. NW (© 202/347-0007), across from the MCI Center.

2020 K St. NW. © 202/496-1111. www.legalseafoods.com. Reservations recommended, especially at lunch. Lunch main courses $9–$16; sandwiches $9–$17; dinner main courses $12–$30. AE, DC, DISC, MC, V. Mon–Thurs 11am–10pm; Fri 11am–10:30pm; Sat 4–10:30pm. Metro: Farragut North or Farragut West.

INEXPENSIVE

Café Asia ASIAN FUSION   It's easy to miss Café Asia, nestled as it is between hair salons and offices on I St. right near the White House. Inside is a different story. The decor and menu both stand out in really interesting ways. The restaurant has three levels to it, set within an atrium. From street level, walk downstairs to the main dining room, where furniture looks made for child's play, meaning it comes in circular and rectangular shapes and colors of orange, yellow, and white, and these pieces are set closer to the ground than normal. My friend Bill, who is a little over 6 feet, said he was not uncomfortable, though. Upstairs is more of a lounge area, overlooking the lower level; one more flight up is reserved mostly for private parties.

The menu here is pan Asian: Chinese, Indonesian, Japanese, Thai. Our waitress steered my 12-year-old to the Indonesian fried rice, which she said was "more interesting than Chinese," which turned out to mean spicier (it's got chili in it, for one thing). So if you like Americanized, or tamed down, Asian food, you might be happy with the teriyaki and satays. You have many more choices if you want to sample exotic food. I tried the *nasi uduk,* an Indonesian dish which is an Indonesian coconut rice platter with spicy beef, crispy anchovies, pickled vegetables, *emping* (acorn chips), chicken satay, and spicy prawn sauce; I enjoyed it very much, though I was reaching for the water glass after every swallow. My husband and Bill were crazy about the *ikan pepes*, which is Indonesian grilled fish filet with spicy turmeric sauce, fresh basil, and lemon grass, wrapped in banana leaves. Café Asia also serves delicious sushi.

1720 I St. NW. © 202/659-2696. www.cafeasia.com. Reservations accepted. Lunch and dinner main courses $7–$14. AE, DC, DISC, MC, V. Mon–Thurs 11:30am–11pm; Fri 11:30am–midnight; Sat noon–midnight; Sun noon–11pm. Metro: Farragut West

Famous Luigi's Pizzeria Restaurant *Kids* ITALIAN Before there was Domino's or Pizza Hut or Papa John's, there was Luigi's. Make that *way* before— Luigi's opened in 1943. People who grew up in Washington consider Luigi's an essential part of their childhood. I've been here a couple of times with my daughters and they like to reminisce about the place, as if it were Italy we'd visited. The truth is that sometimes the pizzas are a little greasy, but they still taste good. Whether you go at lunch or dinner, you can expect to be among a sea of office folks. At night, the restaurant's atmosphere changes a little, as office workers come in groups to unwind, have a drink, or get a bite; but this isn't a bar, so it doesn't get rowdy. The menu is long, listing all kinds of pastas, sandwiches, grilled dishes, and pizzas (with 44 toppings to choose from). Come here for a little local color, and to please everyone in the family.

1132 19th St. NW (between L and M sts.). © 202/331-7574. www.famousluigis.com. Main courses $5–$17. AE, DC, DISC, MC, V. Mon–Sat 11am–midnight; Sun noon–midnight. Metro: Dupont Circle or Farragut North.

5 U Street Corridor

INEXPENSIVE

Ben's Chili Bowl *Finds* AMERICAN Ben's is a veritable institution, a mom-and-pop place, where everything looks, tastes, and probably even costs the same as when the restaurant opened in 1958. Ben's has won national recognition, too, most recently when it was chosen by the 2004 James Beard Foundation Awards as an "America's Classic," one of four restaurants in the country so named for being "renowned for their timeless appeal."

The most expensive item on the menu is the double turkey burger sub, for $6.25. Formica counters, red bar stools, and a jukebox that plays Motown and reggae tunes—that's Ben's. Ben's continues as a gathering place for black Washington and visitors like Bill Cosby, who's a longtime customer (a chili dog is named after him). Everyone's welcome, though, even the late-nighters who come streaming out of nearby nightclubs at 2 or 3 in the morning on the weekend. Of course, the chili, cheese fries, and half-smokes are great, but so are breakfast items. Try the salmon cakes, grits, scrapple, or blueberry pancakes (available during breakfast hours only, 6–11am).

1213 U St. NW. © 202/667-0909. www.benschilibowl.com. Reservations not accepted. Main courses $2.50–$6.50. No credit cards. Mon–Thurs 6am–2am; Fri–Sat 6am–4am; Sun noon–8pm. Metro: U St.–Cardozo.

Coppi's Organic *Value* ITALIAN Crowded with neighborhood patrons and hungry club-goers headed for one of the nearby music houses, Coppi's is a narrow room decorated with wooden booths and bicycle memorabilia from Italian bike races. The wood-burning oven turns out a mean pizza, a stiff competitor to that of top-dog Pizzeria Paradiso (p. 152). The crust, made of organic dough, is chewy, and your choice of toppings includes quality ham, pancetta, cheeses, and vegetables. Coppi's also makes all its pastas and ice cream in-house. Favorite dishes include pasta topped with baby artichoke pesto, bistecca with porcini mushrooms and pine nuts, and fresh ravioli stuffed and sauced with wine-braised beef. You can count on finding an extensive Italian wine list. Service is friendly but can be spotty; if it seems like your waiter has forgotten you, there's a chance that he has, so speak up before too much time passes.

1414 U St. NW. © 202/319-7773. Reservations accepted. Main courses $11–$20. AE, DC, DISC, MC, V. Sun 5–11pm; Mon–Thurs 6–11pm; Fri–Sat 5pm–midnight. Metro: U St.–Cardozo.

6 Adams-Morgan

EXPENSIVE

Cashion's Eat Place ★★ *Finds* AMERICAN   Cashion's has all the pleasures of a neighborhood restaurant—easy, warm, comfortable—combined with cuisine that is out of this world. Owner/chef Ann Cashion continues to rack up culinary awards as easily as she pleases her patrons; in 2004, Cashion was named "Best Chef/MidAtlantic" by the James Beard Foundation. Her menu changes daily, always featuring about eight entrees, split between seafood and meat: rabbit stuffed with ham and truffles, fritto misto of whole jumbo shrimp and black sea bass filet, served with onion rings and house-made tartar sauce, or pork loin with garlic sauce, fried sweetbreads on a bed of sautéed spinach, and so on. The side dishes that accompany each entree, such as lemon cannelloni bean purée or radish and sprout salad, are equally as appealing. Desserts, like coconut layer cake with huckleberries, or chocolate cinnamon mousse, are worth saving room for. Sunday brunch is popular, too; you can choose from breakfast fare (challah French toast, spinach and Gruyère omelets) or heartier items (grilled rainbow trout, croque-monsieurs).

The charming dining room curves around a slightly raised bar. In warm weather, the glass-fronted Cashion's opens invitingly to the sidewalk, where you can also dine. Tables at the back offer a view of the small kitchen, where Cashion and her staff work away. In winter, ask for a table away from the front door, which lets in a blast of cold air with each new arrival.

1819 Columbia Rd. NW. © 202/797-1819. Reservations recommended. Brunch $8.95–$12; dinner main courses $17–$26. MC, V. Tues 5:30–10pm; Wed–Sat 5:30–11pm; Sun 11:30am–2:30pm and 5:30–10pm.

MODERATE

La Fourchette FRENCH   The nonsmoking section is upstairs, but even if you don't smoke, you'll want to be downstairs, among the French-speaking clientele and Adams-Morgan regulars. The waiters are suitably crusty and the ambience is as Parisian as you'll get this side of the Atlantic—as is the food. The menu lists escargots, onion soup, bouillabaisse, and mussels Provençal, along with specials like the grilled salmon on spinach mousse and the shrimp Niçoise, ever-so-slightly crusted and sautéed in tomato sauce touched with anchovy. Saturday and Sunday brunch offers French toast, omelets, and the like. A colorful mural covers the high walls; wooden tables and benches push up against bare brick walls. In warm weather, you can sit outside at tables set up on the sidewalk.

2429 18th St. NW. © 202/332-3077. Reservations recommended on weekends. Main courses $12–$24. AE, DC, MC, V. Mon–Thurs 11:30am–10:30pm; Fri 11:30am–11pm; Sat 11am–11pm; Sun 10am–10pm.

Lauriol Plaza ★ MEXICAN/SPANISH/LATIN AMERICAN   This place is gigantic—it seats 330—but it's immensely popular—often named as the city's best Mexican restaurant—so you may still have to wait for a table. Lauriol Plaza looks like a factory from the outside, but inside it's stunning. You have a choice of sitting at sidewalk tables, on the rooftop deck, or in the two-tiered dining room with its large mural of a Spanish fiesta on one wall and windows covering another. We had good, though warm, margaritas, the standout carne asada fajitas, and tasty *camarones diablo* (six broiled jumbo shrimp seasoned with spices). Anything mesquite grilled is sure to please. Servings are as large as the restaurant. Sunday brunch, also recommended, is served from 11am to 3pm. With so many people dining here, Lauriol Plaza is a good place to people-watch.

1835 18th St. NW. ① 202/387-0035. www.lauriolplaza.com. Reservations not accepted. Main courses $8–$17. AE, DC, DISC, MC, V. Sun 11am–11pm; Mon–Thurs 11:30am–11pm; Fri–Sat 11:30am–midnight. Metro: Dupont Circle.

INEXPENSIVE

Meskerem ETHIOPIAN Washington has a number of Ethiopian restaurants, but this is probably the best. It's certainly the most attractive; the three-level high-ceilinged dining room has an oval skylight girded by a painted sunburst and walls hung with African art and musical instruments. On the mezzanine level, you sit at *messobs* (basket tables) on low, carved Ethiopian chairs or upholstered leather poufs. Ethiopian music enhances the ambience.

Diners share large platters of food, which they scoop up with a sourdough crepelike pancake called *injera* (no silverware here). You'll notice a lot of *watt* dishes, which refers to the traditional Ethiopian stew, made with your choice of beef, chicken, lamb, or vegetables, in varying degrees of hot and spicy; the *alicha watts* are milder and more delicately flavored. You might share an entree—perhaps *yegeb kay watt* (succulent lamb in thick, hot *berbere* sauce)—along with a platter of five vegetarian dishes served with tomato and potato salads. Some combination platters comprise an array of beef, chicken, lamb, and vegetables. There's a full bar; the wine list includes Ethiopian wine and beer.

2434 18th St. NW. ① 202/462-4100. www.meskeremonline.com. Reservations recommended. Lunch and dinner main courses $7–$13. AE, DC, MC, V. Daily noon–midnight, with bar staying open until 3am Fri–Sat.

Mixtec *Value* REGIONAL MEXICAN This cheerful Adams-Morgan spot attracts a clientele of neighborhood folks, D.C. chefs, and Hispanics from all over, all of whom appreciate the delicious authenticity of the regional Mexican cuisine. The kitchen is open, the dining room colorfully decorated, and the Mexican music lively.

Two items you won't find everywhere are the authentic *menudo,* a stew of tripe and calf's feet (granted, not for everyone); and *tortas,* which are a kind of Mexican sub, layered with grilled pork, chiles, guacamole, and salsa. You will also find delicious small dishes called *antojitos* ("little whims"), in the $2.50 to $4.95 range, which include *queso fundido* (a bubbling hot dish of broiled Chihuahua cheese topped with shredded spicy chorizo sausage flavored with jalapenos and cilantro); and the *enrollados mexicanos,* large flour tortillas wrapped around a variety of fillings, including grilled chicken, beef, vegetables, and salmon. The freshly prepared guacamole is excellent. Wash it all down with a Mexican beer or margarita.

1792 Columbia Rd. ① 202/332-1011. Main courses $3.95–$15. MC, V. Sun–Thurs 10am–10pm; Fri–Sat 10am–11pm.

Pasta Mia *Value* ITALIAN Right next door to Mixtec (see above) is another excellent and inexpensive choice that stays busy all night. You are probably going

Adams-Morgan & Dupont Circle Dining

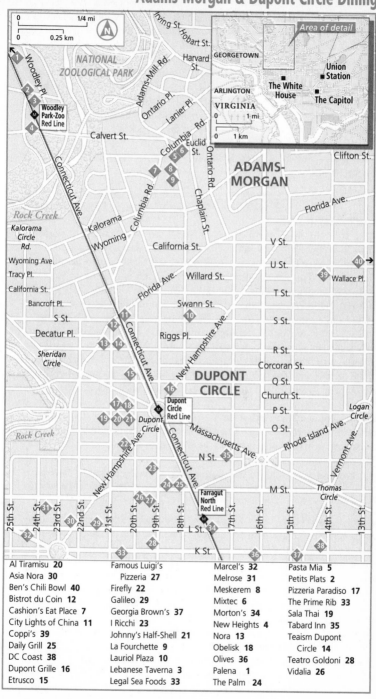

Al Tiramisu **20**
Asia Nora **30**
Ben's Chili Bowl **40**
Bistrot du Coin **12**
Cashion's Eat Place **7**
City Lights of China **11**
Coppi's **39**
Daily Grill **25**
DC Coast **38**
Dupont Grille **16**
Etrusco **15**

Famous Luigi's
   Pizzeria **27**
Firefly **22**
Galileo **29**
Georgia Brown's **37**
I Ricchi **23**
Johnny's Half-Shell **21**
La Fourchette **9**
Lauriol Plaza **10**
Lebanese Taverna **3**
Legal Sea Foods **33**

Marcel's **32**
Melrose **31**
Meskerem **8**
Mixtec **6**
Morton's **34**
New Heights **4**
Nora **13**
Obelisk **18**
Olives **36**
Palena **1**
The Palm **24**

Pasta Mia **5**
Petits Plats **2**
Pizzeria Paradiso **17**
The Prime Rib **33**
Sala Thai **19**
Tabard Inn **35**
Teaism Dupont
   Circle **14**
Teatro Goldoni **28**
Vidalia **26**

to have to wait—sometimes an hour or longer—for a table, too, especially on a Friday or Saturday night, since the restaurant doesn't take reservations. But you may well agree that it's worth it, after you dive into a plate heaped with one of the nearly 25 pasta dishes on the menu. Among the favorites: green fettuccine with creamy porcini-mushroom sauce, cheese tortellini topped with tomato-cream sauce, and penne in tomato sauce with a dollop of pesto. Bread is made in-house, and appetizers, like the Caesar salad or fresh mozzarella and tomatoes, are all flavorful. This place is as low-key as Washington gets, with a simple, brightly lit interior of red-checked covered tables packed together, and dishes served to a table as they are ready.

1790 Columbia Rd. NW. ℂ 202/328-9114. Reservations not accepted. Main courses $9–$13. MC, V. Mon–Sat 6:30–10pm.

7 Dupont Circle

VERY EXPENSIVE

Nora ★★ ORGANIC AMERICAN   Owner-chef Nora Pouillon brings haute panache to organic cookery in this charming restaurant. The cozy paneled bar is an inviting place to wait for your table; up a short flight of stairs lies the main dining room. This converted stable, part of which is skylit, has a weathered-looking beamed pine ceiling, tables lit by shaded paraffin lamps, and a display of Amish and Mennonite patchwork crib quilts on the walls. The atmosphere is relaxed and cozy, and the dress code is anything goes. It's always a full house.

Don't expect brown rice and beans. Instead you'll find chemical-free, organically grown, free-range fare, all extremely healthful. Nightly menus vary with the seasons and everything tastes very fresh. Recent popular dishes included Carolina soft shell crabs with corn sauce and fava beans; roasted smoked pork tenderloin with sweet creamed corn; and pan-roasted Amish chicken breast stuffed with goat cheese and spinach. A vegetarian entree, like green olive risotto, is always an option. Desserts are sinful—for instance, the lemon mousse cheesecake with blueberry compote. An extensive wine list includes, but is not limited to, selections made with organically grown grapes. Nora's offers a $64 tasting menu and a $58 vegetarian tasting menu.

2132 Florida Ave. NW. ℂ 202/462-5143. www.noras.com. Reservations recommended. Main courses $25–$31. AE, MC, V. Mon–Thurs 5:30–10pm; Fri–Sat 5:30–10:30pm. Call if you're planning a visit in late August, since Nora's is often closed 2 weeks at end of Aug/beginning of Sept. Metro: Dupont Circle.

Obelisk ★★★ ITALIAN   Obelisk is the most consistently excellent restaurant in the city. Service and food are simply the best. In this pleasantly spare room that seats only 36, the walls are decorated with 19th-century French botanical prints and Italian lithographs. Here, owner/chef Peter Pastan presents his small fixed-price menus of sophisticated Italian cuisine, using the freshest possible ingredients. Each night diners are offered two or three choices for each of five courses. Dinner might begin with fried soft shell crab with artichoke salad and onion rings, followed by squash blossom ravioli with pesto, and then an artfully arranged dish of pan-cooked grouper with artichokes and thyme, or grilled venison tenderloin with morels and green garlic . . . or whatever Pastan has been inspired to create. Dessert is a choice of cheese or baked specialties, like pear spice cake. Breads and desserts are all baked in-house and are divine. Pastan's carefully crafted wine list represents varied regions of Italy, as well as California vintages. The fixed-price menu is a deal, but the cost of wine and coffees can easily double the price per person.

2029 P St. NW. ℭ **202/872-1180.** Reservations recommended. Fixed-price 5-course dinner $60. DC, MC, V. Tues–Sat 6–10pm. Metro: Dupont Circle.

EXPENSIVE

Al Tiramisu ★★ *finds* ITALIAN   I called last minute for a reservation and the staff was kind enough to squeeze in four of us (*squeeze* being the operative word, as the tables are a little snug in this narrow but intimate restaurant). But the charming servers have time to chat a little without keeping you waiting. It was refreshing to have our waiter, without any discussion, hand the wine list to me, rather than to one of the men at the table. Make sure you give the menu due consideration; this is one place where the mainstays are just as good (and certainly cheaper) than the daily specials. Al Tiramisu is known for its grilled fish and for its black and white truffles. Also exceptional are the grilled squid, housemade spinach-ricotta ravioli with butter and sage sauce, and the osso buco. This is a place to come if you need cheering up. Ebullient chef/owner Luigi Diotaiuti makes his presence known sometimes—check out the restaurant's website for a taste of his personality. A little hokey, perhaps, but fun. The website now features a "celebrity gallery" of photographs of recent diners; take a peek if you admire George Clooney, Michael Douglas, Catherine Zeta-Jones, and others.

2014 P St. NW. ℭ **202/467-4466.** www.altiramisu.com. Reservations required. Lunch main courses $6–$17; dinner main courses $14–$20. AE, DC, MC, V. Mon–Fri noon–2pm; Mon–Thurs 5–10pm; Fri-Sat 5–11pm; Sun 5–9:30pm. Metro: Dupont Circle.

Dupont Grille ★ AMERICAN   Although the Dupont Grille is situated inside the Irish-owned Jurys Washington Hotel, the restaurant is thoroughly American, its chef, Cornell Coulon, hails from New Orleans. The hotel faces Dupont Circle, but the restaurant, which has floor-to-ceiling glass panels that slide open at a slant, sits on 19th Street, which means you get the hustle and bustle of the neighborhood without the full-blown effect of traffic noise. This is a colorful dining spot, both design- and cuisine-wise. Banquettes are pumpkin-toned, and wall panels look like a Mondrian painting—big squares of yellow, black, and white. We followed our waiter's suggestion and ordered a beef confit spring roll with sundried tomato, chutney, and basil dressing; the chopped salad with romaine, radicchio, blue cheese, and tomato topped with a garlicky dressing; and grilled Waluu (a moist and sweet fish found in the Pacific; it's also known as "Hawaiian butterfish"), served on a bed of sautéed snowpeas, daikon radish, preserved ginger, and rock shrimp, with a citrus/soy sauce. A large bar lines the center back wall, and the restaurant opens to a sidewalk cafe in warm weather.

In the Jurys Washington Hotel, 1500 New Hampshire Ave. NW (entrance on 19th St. NW). ℭ **202/939-9596.** Reservations recommended. Breakfast main courses $5.95–$12; lunch main courses $11–$27; brunch $20; dinner main courses $17–$26. AE, DC, DISC, MC, V. Daily 6:30–11am, 11:30am–2:30pm; Sun brunch 11am–2:30pm; Sun–Thurs 5–10pm; Fri–Sat 5:30–11pm. Metro: Dupont Circle.

Firefly ★ CONTEMPORARY AMERICAN   This is an intimate restaurant and popular, which makes for a rollicking experience but also a crowded one—you can feel squeezed in here. A floor-to-ceiling "firefly tree" hung with lanterns heightens this feeling. The food is quite good. We enjoyed the potato gnocchi with smoked trout and sage brown butter and the grilled New York steak with housemade fries, watercress, and Smithfield ham. If fries don't come with your meal, it's worth ordering them as a side, as they're excellent and arrive hot and salty in a paper cone set in its own stand. At lunch, consider the grilled salmon BLT, or the Amish chicken Cobb salad. We had the caramelized apple tart for dessert, which was no good at all, and not even served warm. Firefly lies within the Hotel Madera (see review, chapter 5), but has a separate entrance.

In the Hotel Madera, 1310 New Hampshire Ave. NW. © **202/861-1310.** www.firefly-dc.com. Reservations recommended. Brunch main courses $7.50–$14; lunch main courses $10–$17; dinner main courses $12–$23. AE, DC, DISC, MC, V. Mon–Fri 7–10:30am and 11:30am–2:30pm; Sat–Sun 10am–2:30pm; Sun–Thurs 5:30–10pm; Fri–Sat 5:30–11pm. Metro: Dupont Circle.

Johnny's Half Shell ★ *Finds* SEAFOOD   Whenever a friend visits from out of town and I haven't gotten around to making a restaurant reservation, we usually end up at Johnny's. It's easy, fun, and comfortable; it's open continuously from lunch through the afternoon to closing, and it takes no reservations, so you can usually walk right in and get something fresh from the sea (though weekend nights after 8:30pm, you'll probably have at least a 20-min. wait); and it feels like a hometown restaurant, a rare thing in a city whose residents tend to originate from many other hometowns. Johnny's owners, Ann Cashion and John Fulchino, own another very popular restaurant, Cashion's Eat Place (p. 145) in Adams-Morgan. The restaurant is small, with a decor that features an aquarium behind the long bar, booths along one paneled wall, a tile floor, and a partly open kitchen. The professional yet friendly waiters seem to enjoy themselves.

It's reassuring, too, that the menu seldom changes, since everything is reliably good, from the farm-raised chicken with old-fashioned Eastern Shore slippery dumplings, garden peas, and button mushrooms, to the crab meat imperial with a salad of *haricots verts* (young green beans), tomatoes, and shallots. I recently opted for that crab imperial, which was almost as good as the one my mom used to make. On another visit, I enjoyed the delicious fried oyster po'boy sandwich, while my friend Sue went for the Maryland crab cakes with coleslaw and french fries; we both devoured every morsel. If the sautéed soft-shell crabs with Old Bay and basil beurre blanc and corn pudding are on the menu, get them. My daughter Cait likes the barbecued shrimp appetizer with Asiago cheese grits. Oysters and Wellfleet clams on the half shell are always available, of course. The short wine list includes a few selections by the glass; there are four beers on tap. Desserts are simple but perfect, including homemade ice cream, a choice of hazelnut, almond, pecan, or chocolate tart, and chocolate angel food cake with caramel sauce.

2002 P St. NW. © **202/296-2021.** Reservations not accepted. Lunch main courses $6.95–$20; dinner main courses $16–$22. AE, MC, V. Mon–Thurs 11:30am–10:30pm; Fri–Sat 11:30am–11pm; Sun 5–10pm (Mon–Fri, 3–5pm, a light fare menu of soups and salads is available). Metro: Dupont Circle.

Tabard Inn ★ AMERICAN   The restaurant here is only a shade more conventional than the inn in which it resides (see chapter 5). From the cozy though tattered lounge, where you can enjoy a drink in front of a crackling fire, you enter a narrow room, where hanging plants dangle from skylights and a mural of a ponytailed waiter points the way to the kitchen. A small bar hugs one side of the passage, a series of small tables the other, and both lead to the main space. Or you can head up a set of stairs to another dining room and its adjoining courtyard. The restaurant staff, like the inn staff, is disarmingly solicitous.

The food is fresh and seasonal, making use of the inn's own organically grown vegetables and herbs. Chef Pedro Matamoros changes his menu with the seasons, so sample dishes might include roasted lemon-anchovy-caper halibut served with artichokes, asparagus, grape tomatoes, and olive sauce or grilled Hereford rib-eye steak with fingerling potatoes, baby carrots, mustard greens, and charcuterie sauce. Sunday brunch is an a la carte feast of both breakfast and supper choices from toasted pecan waffles to steamed mussels in an herbed tomato and wine sauce. The Tabard is a favorite spot for Washingtonians.

1739 N St. NW. © 202/833-2668. www.tabardinn.com. Reservations recommended. Breakfast $2.50–$7.50; brunch $10–$14; lunch main courses $10–$16; dinner main courses $19–$27. AE, DC, MC, V. Mon–Fri 7–9:45am and 11:30am–2:30pm; Sat 8–9:45am and 11am–2:30pm; Sun 8–9:15am and 10:30am–2:30pm; daily 6–9pm or 10pm. Metro: Dupont Circle.

MODERATE

Bistrot du Coin ⭐ FRENCH   When Michel Richard, acclaimed chef of Michel Richard Citronelle (p. 156), is homesick, he visits this restaurant, because he thinks it feels like France. I think so, too. The wooden facade that draws your attention from the street, the way the whole glass front of the dining room opens right to the sidewalk, the zinc bar, the moody waiters—everything speaks of a Paris cafe, most of all the food.

But I am not quite the fan of this place that I was when it opened in 2000. Everything is still very much the same: the noise, the inconsistent service, the menu. The first couple of times, Bistrot was charming; now it's less so. Maybe I just need to try the mussels, which I keep hearing about: either curried and creamed, or hiding in a thick gratin of leeks. Other dishes I have chosen have been pleasing. The cassoulet is delicious, and not too hearty; the *tartine baltique* turned out to be an open-faced sandwich with smoked salmon, tamara onions, capers, and olive oil—but it had the look, and a little bit of the taste, of something that had sat out for a while. The steak *frites* are just what you'd hope for, tasty and comforting. The menu presents a limited number of wines, but since these include an $11 glass of Veuve Cliquot champagne, I can't complain. Or select an aperitif from a list of 16, very reasonably priced. I chose the licorice-flavored Ricard, which is similar to pastis, and at less than $5, a delicious deal.

1738 Connecticut Ave. NW. © 202/234-6969. www.bistrotducoin.com. Main courses $13–$27. AE, DISC, MC, V. Sun 11am–11pm; Mon–Wed 11:30am–11pm; Thurs–Sat 11:30am–1am. Metro: Dupont Circle.

City Lights of China CHINESE   One of Washington's best Chinese restaurants outside of Chinatown, City Lights is a favorite of White House workaholics, whatever administration, who frequently order takeout from here. If you are staying at a nearby hotel, you might consider ordering food to go, as well; takeout prices are cheaper for some items. Some of the most popular dishes include crisp fried Cornish hen prepared in a cinnamon-soy marinade and served with a tasty dipping sauce, Chinese eggplant in garlic sauce, stir-fried spinach, crisp fried shredded beef, and Peking duck. The setting, a three-tiered dining room with much of the seating in comfortable leather booths and banquettes, is unpretentious. Neat white-linen tablecloths, cloth flower arrangements in lighted niches, and green neon track lighting complete the picture. There's a full bar.

1731 Connecticut Ave. NW (between R and S sts.). © 202/265-6688. www.citylightsofchina.com. Reservations recommended. Lunch main courses $6.95–$19 (most are about $8.95); dinner main courses $8.95–$19 (most are about $13). AE, DC, DISC, MC, V. Mon–Fri 11:30am–10:30pm; Sat noon–11pm; Sun noon–10:30pm; dinner from 3pm daily. Metro: Dupont Circle.

Etrusco ⭐⭐ ITALIAN   Etrusco is just the sort of place you'd hope to stumble upon as a stranger in town. It's pretty, with a sophisticated but relaxed atmosphere, and the food is excellent. From the slate terrace at street level with umbrella tables, you descend a short flight of steps to the exquisite dining room, which resembles a trattoria with ochre and burnt sienna walls, arched skylight, and tile floor.

On the menu you'll find warm baby octopus salad, *ribollita* (minestrone thickened with bread and Parmesan cheese), pappardelle with shredded duck, grilled scallops, crumb-coated grilled tuna, and the more traditional veal scaloppini and osso buco. It's all very, very good. End with "Grandfather's cake," a light chocolate pie.

1606 20th St. NW. ✆ 202/667-0047. Reservations recommended. Main courses $14–$30. AE, DC, MC. V. Mon–Sat 5:30–10:30pm. Metro: Dupont Circle.

INEXPENSIVE

Pizzeria Paradiso ✻ ITALIAN   This is still the best pizza place in the city, no contest. Peter Pastan, master chef/owner of Obelisk (located right next door and reviewed just above), owns this classy, often crowded, 16-table pizzeria. An oak-burning oven at one end of the charming room produces exceptionally doughy but light pizza crusts. As you wait, you can munch on mixed olives and gaze up at the ceiling painted to suggest blue sky peeking through ancient stone walls. Pizzas range from the plain Paradiso, which offers chunks of tomatoes covered in melted mozzarella, to the robust Siciliano, a blend of nine ingredients including eggplant and red onion. Or you can choose your own toppings from a list of 29. As popular as the pizzas are the *panini* (sandwiches) of homemade focaccia stuffed with marinated roasted lamb and vegetables and other fillings, and the salads, such as tuna and white bean. Good desserts, but a limited wine list. Pizzeria Paradiso has finally opened another location, at 3282 M St. NW (✆ **202/337-1245**), in Georgetown, right next door to Dean & Deluca. This location is larger, has a full bar, and a private party room.

2029 P St. NW. ✆ **202/223-1245.** Reservations not accepted. Pizzas $9.50–$17; sandwiches and salads $4.50–$7.95. DC, MC, V. Mon–Sat 11:30am–11pm; Sun noon–10pm. Metro: Dupont Circle.

Sala Thai THAI   At lunch, you'll see a lot of diners sitting alone and reading newspapers, happy to escape the office. At dinner, the restaurant is filled with groups and couples, plus the occasional family. Among the 53 items to recommend on the menu are no. 41, *nua kra ting tone,* which is spicy beef with onion, garlic, and parsley sauce ("not found at any other Thai restaurant in Washington," said my Thai waitress, sporting multicolored streaks in her hair), and, no. 26, *ka prow,* which is an even spicier dish of either beef, chicken, or pork sautéed with basil leaves and chile. The restaurant lies downstairs from the street; with no windows to watch what's happening on P Street, but you're really here for the food, which is excellent and cheap. Even conventional pad thai doesn't disappoint. Pay attention if your waiter cautions you about the level of spiciness of a dish you order—for some dishes (like no. 38, stir-fried sliced pork in red curry sauce with peppers), you'll need an asbestos tongue.

2016 P St. NW. ✆ **202/872-1144.** www.salathaidc.com. Reservations accepted for 5 or more. Lunch main courses $6.95–$11; dinner main courses $7.95–$17. AE, DC, DISC, MC, V. Mon–Thurs 11:30am–3pm and 4–10:30pm; Fri 11:30am–11pm; Sat noon–11pm; Sun noon–10:30pm. Metro: Dupont Circle.

Teaism Dupont Circle *Finds* ASIAN FUSION   Occupying a turn-of-the-20th-century neoclassic building on a tree-lined street, Teaism has a lovely rustic interior. A display kitchen and tandoor oven dominate the sunny downstairs room, which offers counter seating along a wall of French windows, open in warm weather. Upstairs seating is on banquettes and small Asian stools at hand-crafted mahogany tables.

The impressive tea list comprises close to 30 aromatic blends, most of them from India, China, and Japan. On the menu is light Asian fare served on stainless-steel plates or in lacquer lunch boxes (Japanese "bento boxes," which hold a delicious meal of, for example, teriyaki salmon, cucumber-ginger salad, a scoop of rice with seasoning, and fresh fruit—all $8). Dishes include Thai chicken curry with sticky rice, ostrich burger with Asian slaw, and a portobello and goat cheese sandwich. Baked goods, coconut rice pudding, and lime shortbread cookies are among desserts. At breakfast, you might try ginger scones or cilantro eggs and sausage with fresh tandoor-baked onion nan bread. Everything's available for takeout. Teapots, cups, and other gift items are for sale. *Note:* Teaism has two other locations, both convenient for sightseeing. **Teaism Lafayette Square,** 800 Connecticut Ave. NW (© 202/835-2233), is across from the White House; it's open weekdays from 7:30am to 5:30pm and serves afternoon tea. **Teaism Penn Quarter** ☆, 400 8th St. NW (© 202/638-6010), which is near the MCI Center, the National Gallery, and nightspots, is the only branch that serves beer, wine, and cocktails. Teaism Penn Quarter is open daily, serving all three meals and afternoon tea, and brunch on Saturday and Sunday; its happy hour on Thursday and Friday, from 5:30 to 7:30pm, features free hors d'oeuvres (with purchased drink—try the mango or ginger margaritas) like curries and Asian noodle salads.

2009 R St. NW (between Connecticut and 21st sts.). © 202/667-3827. All menu items $1.50–$8. AE, MC, V. Mon–Thurs 8am–10pm; Fri 8am–11pm; Sat 9am–11pm; Sun 9am–10pm. Metro: Dupont Circle.

8 Foggy Bottom/West End
VERY EXPENSIVE

Marcel's ☆☆ FRENCH   When you walk through the front door, look straight ahead into the exhibition kitchen—chances are you'll be staring directly into the eyes of owner/chef Robert Wiedmaier. He is firmly at the helm here, creating French dishes that include nods to his Belgian training: duck breast with baby turnips, rose lentils, and Calvados sauce, or venison with ragout of winter mushrooms and Madeira sauce. Desserts usually include seasonal tarts such as spring pear tart with raspberry coulis.

Marcel's, named after Wiedmaier's young son, occupies the space that once was home to the restaurant Provence, and Wiedmaier has kept that restaurant's country French decor, including panels of rough-hewn stone framed by rustic shutters and antique hutches displaying Provençal pottery. Stone walls and floors don't do much to buffer all the bustle, however, so you can expect to have a very noisy time of it. To the right of the exhibition kitchen is a spacious bar area. Marcel's offers seating on the patio—right on Pennsylvania Avenue—in warm weather, and live jazz nightly year-round.

2401 Pennsylvania Ave. NW. © 202/296-1166. www.marcelsdc.com. Reservations recommended. Dinner main courses $26–$39; pretheater dinner 5:30–7pm (including round-trip limo to/from Kennedy Center) $48. AE, MC, V. Mon–Thurs 5:30–10pm; Fri–Sat 5:30–11pm; Sun 5:30–9:30pm. Metro: Foggy Bottom.

Melrose ☆☆ AMERICAN   Situated in an upscale hotel, this pretty restaurant offers fine cuisine presented with friendly flourishes. In nice weather, dine outdoors on the beautifully landscaped, sunken terrace whose greenery and towering fountain protect you from traffic noises. The glass-walled dining room overlooks the terrace and is decorated in accents of marble and brass, with more greenery and grand bouquets of fresh flowers.

Brian McBride is the beguiling executive chef who sometimes emerges from the kitchen to find out how you like the angel-hair pasta with mascarpone and lobster, or his pan-seared diver scallops with parsnip purée, or his breast of pheasant stuffed with pistachio mousseline. McBride is known for his use of seafood,

> ## *Value* Pretheater Dinners = Great Deals
>
> Some of Washington's finest restaurants make you an offer you shouldn't refuse: a three-course dinner for just a little bit more than the cost of a typical entree. It's the pretheater dinner, available in early evening on certain nights at certain restaurants; and while your choices may be limited, your meal will undoubtedly be delicious.
>
> At one end of the spectrum is **Marcel's** ☆☆ (p. 153), whose $48 fixed-price includes a starter, an entree (like pan-seared Norwegian salmon), and a dessert of either crème brûlée or chocolate terrine. Marcel's offers this menu nightly from 5:30 to 7pm, and throws in complimentary limo service to and from the Kennedy Center, if you're headed to a show.
>
> **Café Atlantico's** ☆☆ (p. 130) pretheater menu allows you three courses for $22; sample dishes are salmon ceviche as a first course, soft-shell crab with a Veracruz sauce for the main course, and rice-pudding mousse to finish. The restaurant's pretheater menu is available nightly between 5 and 6:30pm.
>
> Other restaurants in this chapter that offer a pretheater menu are **Oval Room at Lafayette Square** ☆☆ (p. 141), **1789** ☆☆ (p. 157), **Melrose** ☆☆ (p. 153), and **701** ☆ (p. 133).

which makes up at least half of the entrees and nearly all of the appetizers. Specialties of the house include shrimp ravioli with sweet corn, black pepper, tomato, and lemongrass beurre blanc, and Melrose crab cakes with grilled vegetables in a rémoulade sauce. Desserts, like the raspberry crème brûlée or the chocolate bread pudding with chocolate sorbet, are excellent. The wine list offers about 25 wines by the glass. Sunday night, the restaurant dispenses with corkage fees; feel free to bring your own bottle. Saturday nights (and sometimes Fri nights) from 7 to 11pm, a quartet plays jazz, swing, and big-band tunes; lots of people get up and dance.

In the Park Hyatt Washington hotel, 1201 24th St. NW. ☎ 202/955-3899. Reservations recommended. Breakfast $9–$19; lunch main courses $18–$34; dinner main courses $20–$38; pretheater dinner $35; Sun brunch $55 ($60 with house champagne, $68 with premium champagne). AE, DC, DISC, MC, V. Mon–Fri 6:30–11am; Sat–Sun 7–11am; daily 11:30am–2:30pm and 5:30–10:30pm (light fare is available daily from 2:30–5:30pm). Metro: Foggy Bottom.

EXPENSIVE

Asia Nora ☆ ASIAN FUSION   This is Nora's Asian offshoot (see the review of Nora on p. 148) and it's just as organic as the original, but with an Asian bent. Literally. Everything's set at a slant here: the tables, the bar, the banquette at the back on the first floor, and the triangular cutaway balcony on the second. Artifacts from Asia—batik carvings, Japanese helmets, and Chinese puppets—decorate the gold-flecked jade walls. It's intimate and exotic, a charged combination. Try sitting at the bar first, on the most comfortable bar stools in town. If you like good bourbons and single-malt scotches, you're in luck.

Waiters dressed in black-satin pajamas serve Asian fusion cuisine, all prepared with organic ingredients, including a salad of baby Asian greens with clementine-sesame vinaigrette, a starter of shu mai dumplings with tender beef short ribs, and a main dish of crispy soft shell crab with spicy tomato line vinaigrette. The menu changes monthly. As at Nora, the desserts here are not to be missed; try the warm chocolate five-spice cake with coconut sorbet.

2213 M St. NW. ⓒ 202/797-4860. www.noras.com. Reservations recommended. Main courses $20–$28. AE, DISC, MC, V. Mon–Thurs 5:30–10pm; Fri–Sat 5:30–10:30pm. Closed at end of Aug/beginning of Sept. Metro: Dupont Circle or Foggy Bottom.

Kinkead's ⋆⋆⋆ AMERICAN/SEAFOOD   When a restaurant has been as roundly praised as Kinkead's, you start to think no place can be *that* good—but Kinkead's really is. After a brief closure in early 2004 for a remodeling of the dining room (purple walls, but otherwise nothing drastic) and a revamping of the menu, Kinkead's re-opened with even more pleasing items on the menu, like the lobster potpie. But most of the favorite dishes are still here: the fried Ipswich clams, cod topped with crab imperial, clam chowder, and pepita-crusted salmon with shrimp, crab, and chiles. And chef Kinkead continues to pile on appetizing garnishes—that crab-crowned cod, for instance, comes with sweet potato purée and ham-laced spoon bread.

Award-winning chef/owner Bob Kinkead is the star at this three-tier, 220-seat restaurant. He orchestrates his kitchen staff in full view of the upstairs dining room, where booths and tables neatly fill the nooks and alcoves of the town house. At street level is a scattering of tables overlooking the restaurant's lower level, the more casual bar and cafe, where a jazz group or pianist performs nearly every evening. *Beware:* If the waiter tries to seat you in the "atrium," you'll be stuck at a table mall-side just outside the doors of the restaurant.

Kinkead's menu (which changes daily for lunch and again for dinner) features primarily seafood, but always includes at least one beef and one poultry entree. The wine list comprises more than 300 selections, and you can trust expert sommelier Michael Flynn to lead you to one you'll enjoy. You can't go wrong with the desserts either, like the chocolate dacquoise with cappuccino sauce. If you're hungry but not ravenous in the late afternoon, stop in for some delicious light fare: fish and chips, lobster roll, soups, and salads.

2000 Pennsylvania Ave. NW. ⓒ 202/296-7700. www.kinkead.com. Reservations recommended. Lunch main courses $15–$25; dinner main courses $26–$35; light fare $6–$23. AE, DC, DISC, MC, V. Daily 11:30am–2:30pm; Sun–Thur 5:30–10pm; Fri–Sat 5:30–10:30pm (light fare served daily 2:30–5:30pm). Metro: Foggy Bottom.

Nectar ⋆⋆ AMERICAN   This tiny place, seating 42, opened in April 2003. Nectar has some intriguing features: Its short menu offers as many appetizers as entrees—six of each. The modest but unusual wine list offers every wine by the glass, half-bottle, or bottle, with prices per glass ranging from $7 to $100, and per bottle ranging from $29 to $450. The decor combines elegant—gilded mirrors and golden sponge-painted walls—with unpretentious: pipes are exposed, though painted. Three friends and I agreed that our meals were winners. For appetizers we chose a fresh and minty pea soup, salad greens topped with sesame dressing, and fresh asparagus; for entrees, we selected veal cheeks with butternut squash purée and Masala spices, pheasant on a bed of ramps, and scallops sautéed with *haricots verts,* chorizo, dried fruit, pistachio, and curry spices. Everything was cooked perfectly and flavored nicely. We found fault only with the service, which was a little slow.

In the George Washington University Inn, 824 New Hampshire Ave. NW. ⓒ 202/298-8085. www.nectardc.com. Reservations recommended. Dinner main courses $25–$28. AE, DC, DISC, MC, V. Tues–Thurs 5–10pm; Fri–Sat 5–11pm. Metro: Foggy Bottom.

MODERATE

Kaz Sushi Bistro JAPANESE   Amiable chef/owner Kazuhiro ("Kaz") Okochi opened his own place after having worked at Sushi-Ko (p. 163) for many years.

This is said to be the best place for sushi in the Washington area, and aficionados vie for one of the six chairs at the bar to watch Kaz and his staff do their thing. Besides sushi, Kaz is known for his napoleon of sea trout and wonton skins, and for his bento boxes, offering exquisite tastings of pan-seared salmon, spicy broiled mussels, and the like. Kaz is one of few chefs in the area trained to handle tora fugu, the blowfish, which can be poisonous if not cleaned properly. The blowfish, if available, is served in winter. This is also the place to come for premium sakes.

1915 I St. NW. ✆ **202/530-5500.** Reservations recommended. www.kazsushi.com. Sushi a la carte $3.25–$6.50; lunch main courses $9.25–$17; dinner main courses $12–$45. AE, DC, DISC, MC, V. Mon–Fri 11:30am–2pm; Mon–Sat 6–10pm. Metro: Farragut West.

9 Georgetown

VERY EXPENSIVE

Michel Richard Citronelle ★★★ INNOVATIVE FRENCH   If Citronelle's ebullient chef/owner Michel Richard is in the kitchen (and you know when he is, since the dining room views the open kitchen), diners in the know decline the menu and ask simply for whatever it is Richard wants to make. Whether you go that route, or choose from the fixed-price or tasting menus, you're in for a (very expensive) treat. Emerging from the bustling kitchen are appetizers like the fricassee of escargots, an egg shell filled with caviar, sweetbreads, porcinis, and crunchy pistachios, and entrees like the crispy lentil-coated salmon or squab leg confit with macaroni gratin and black truffles. But each presentation is a work of art, with swirls of colorful sauce surrounding the main event. If you are passionate about food, you may want to consider dining at the chef's table, which is in the kitchen, so you can watch Richard at work. (This will cost you: $250 per person, with a minimum of six people, is the stated price, but that's to give you a ballpark idea; call for more exact information.)

Citronelle's decor is also breathtaking and includes a wall that changes colors, a state-of-the-art wine cellar (a glass-enclosed room that encircles the dining room, displaying its 8,000 bottles and a collection of 18th- and 19th-century corkscrews), and a Provençal color scheme of mellow yellow and raspberry red.

The dessert of choice: Michel Richard's richly layered chocolate "bar" with sauce noisette (hazelnut sauce). Citronelle's extensive wine list offers about 20 premium by-the-glass selections, but with all those bottles staring out at you from the wine cellar, you may want to spring for one.

In the Latham Hotel, 3000 M St. NW. ✆ **202/625-2150.** www.citronelledc.com. Reservations required. Jacket required, tie optional for men at dinner. Open for dinner only. Fixed-price 6-course dinner $85, fixed price 9-course dinner $125. AE, DC, MC, V. Sun–Wed 6–9pm; Thurs–Sat 6–9:30pm. Closed Sundays in July and August.

Morton's of Chicago ★ STEAK/SEAFOOD   Maybe when the first Morton's opened in 1978, a customer looked at the prices and shouted, "Show me the beef!" and a waiter complied by wheeling out a cart full of slabs of uncooked meat for inspection, thus starting a tradition. Our meal began with this kitschy display of raw meat and vegetable props, and so will yours, too, at this and any other Morton's. It will not be cheap, though—our entrees were each $33, though portions were so large that my children had my leftovers for dinner the next day. Entrees don't come with side dishes; you must pay separately for those.

Although the city is full of steakhouses, this is the only one in Georgetown. Its ambience is less relentlessly masculine than the others, probably because of

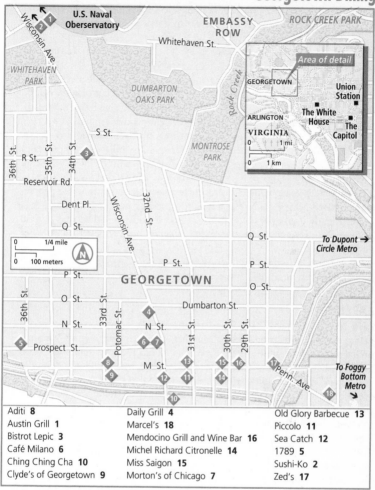

Aditi **8**	Daily Grill **4**	Old Glory Barbecue **13**
Austin Grill **1**	Marcel's **18**	Piccolo **11**
Bistrot Lepic **3**	Mendocino Grill and Wine Bar **16**	Sea Catch **12**
Café Milano **6**	Michel Richard Citronelle **14**	1789 **5**
Ching Ching Cha **10**	Miss Saigon **15**	Sushi-Ko **2**
Clyde's of Georgetown **9**	Morton's of Chicago **7**	Zed's **17**

its varied clientele (couples, businessmen, parents treating their college kid to dinner), and because of a glow emanating from the open kitchen. On a weeknight in winter, the restaurant was not totally full, and we were able to sit in our leather-cushioned booth and talk quietly, pausing only to swallow bites of tender filet mignon, porterhouse steak (both cooked perfectly), oysters on the half-shell, sautéed mushrooms, and asparagus (a tad tough) with hollandaise sauce. End with Godiva chocolate cake, a round derby of chocolate casing, which, when cut, releases a thick stream of melty hot chocolate—heavenly! The other D.C. location of Morton's is downtown, at 1050 Connecticut Ave. NW, at L Street NW (© **202/955-5997**).

3251 Prospect St. NW. © **202/342-6258**. www.mortons.com. Reservations recommended. Main courses $23–$42. AE, DC, MC, V. Mon–Sat 5–11pm; Sun 5–10pm. (Other location open for lunch.)

1789 ★★ AMERICAN In my brown corduroy skirt and tan wool sweater, I felt I'd dressed too casually when I dined here last. The staff never made me feel uncomfortable, it was a quick look around the room that did it, for fellow female diners (of all ages) were dressed in lacey tops, short flouncy dresses, and fancy long skirts.

So put on your best duds for the 1789. The formal but cozy restaurant is housed in a Federal town house near Georgetown University. The best of the five intimate dining rooms is the John Carroll Room, where the walls are hung with equestrian and historical prints and old city maps, a log fire blazes in the hearth, and a gorgeous flower arrangement tops a hunting-themed oak sideboard. Throughout, silk-shaded brass oil lamps provide romantic lighting.

Ris Lacoste varies her menus daily. Appetizers might include lobster tart on puffed pastry with mushrooms, leeks, and tarragon, or grilled quail with barley and mushrooms. Typical entrees range from osso buco with risotto Milanese, to ginger glazed sea scallops with pea shoots, mango, and curried pistachio rice, to roast rack of Colorado lamb with creamy feta potatoes au gratin in red-pepper-purée–infused Merlot sauce. Finish with the decadent hot fudge sundae.

The nightly pretheater menu, 6 to 6:45pm Monday to Friday and 5:30 to 6:45pm Saturday and Sunday, includes appetizer, entree, dessert, and coffee for $30.

1226 36th St. NW. ℂ **202/965-1789.** www.1789restaurant.com. Reservations recommended. Jacket required for men. Main courses $18–$38; fixed-price pretheater menu $30. AE, DC, DISC, MC, V. Mon–Thurs 6–10pm; Fri 6–11pm; Sat 5:30–11pm; Sun 5:30–10pm.

EXPENSIVE

Café Milano ⊛ ITALIAN   The beautiful people factor rises exponentially here as the night wears on. Café Milano has long been a magnet for Washington's famous and attractive, and their visitors. In fact the restaurant stages occasional "fashion brunches," where models strut their stuff while you dine. But this restaurant/nightclub/bar also serves very good food. Salads are big, pasta servings are small, and fish and meat entrees are just the right size. We had the endive, radicchio, and arugula salad topped with thin sheets of Parmesan cheese; a *panzanella* salad of tomatoes, potatoes, red onion, celery, and cucumber basking in basil and olive oil; *cappellacci* (round ravioli) pockets of spinach and ricotta in cream sauce; sautéed sea bass on a bed of vegetables with lemon chive sauce; and the Santa Babila pizza, which has tomatoes, fresh mozzarella, oregano, and basil on a light pizza crust. All were delicious. At Café Milano, it's the nonsmokers who are relegated to the back room, while the smoking section takes over the main part of the restaurant and bar, which opens to the sidewalk cafe. A bevy of good-humored waiters takes care of you.

3251 Prospect St. NW. ℂ **202/333-6183.** www.cafemilano.net. Reservations recommended. Lunch main courses $12–$25; dinner main courses $14–$37. Sun–Wed 11:30am–11pm (bar menu served until midnight); Thurs–Sat 11:30am–midnight (bar menu served until 1am).

Mendocino Grille and Wine Bar ⊛ AMERICAN   As its name suggests, you should come here to enjoy West Coast wine, along with contemporary American cuisine and a California-casual ambience. All of the 125-or-so bottles on the wine list are California vintages, and waiters are knowledgeable about the specifics of each, so don't hesitate to ask questions. California-casual doesn't mean cheap, though: Bottles range from $20 to $500, although most fall in the $50 to $60 range. The restaurant offers 22 wines by the glass, in different sizes, the better for tastings, and most of these run between $7 to $9 each.

Owner Eli Hengst hopes eventually to be using 40% or more organic ingredients in the kitchen. Highlights on the menu include an Amish farmed free-range chicken served with scallion mashed potatoes and grilled vegetables, a New York strip of Kobe beef, and mustard spiced yellowfin tuna presented on orzo with English peas and artichokes.

Rough-textured slate walls alternate with painted patches of Big Sur sky to suggest a West Coast winery in California's wine-growing region. The wall sconces resemble rectangles of sea glass and the dangling light fixtures look like turned-over wineglasses. It's a very pleasant place, where Georgetown neighbors tend to congregate.

2917 M St. NW. © 202/333-2912. www.mendocinodc.com. Reservations recommended. Lunch main courses $8–$15; dinner main courses $20–$29. AE, DC, DISC, MC, V. Mon–Sat 11:30am–3pm; Sun–Thurs 5:30–10pm; Fri–Sat 5:30–11pm.

Sea Catch Restaurant and Raw Bar ⋆ *Finds* SEAFOOD   If you're walking around Georgetown and the crowds are starting to get to you, duck into the brick passageway that lies to the right of a little coffee bar and Mr. Smith's bar on M Street (at 31st St.) and follow it back to the little plaza, where you will find the entrance to the Sea Catch, a true refuge. (Or else you can walk south on 31st St. from M St., and turn right, into the plaza.) Since 1988, the Sea Catch has perched on the bank of the C&O Canal, with an awning-covered wooden deck where you can watch ducks, punters, and mule-drawn barges glide by while you dine. The innlike main dining room has a working fireplace and rough-hewn fieldstone walls from Georgetown quarries. There's also a handsome white Carrara-marble raw bar and a deluxe brasserie. Classic jazz recordings play in the background.

Nothing at the Sea Catch is fried or breaded. For openers, plump farm-raised oysters, clams, house-smoked fish, and other raw-bar offerings merit consideration. Daily fresh fish and seafood specials may include big, fluffy jumbo lump crab cakes served with julienne vegetables in a remoulade sauce or grilled marinated squid with fennel and basil aioli. The kitchen willingly prepares dishes to your specifications, including live lobster from the tanks. An extensive wine list highlights French, Italian, and American selections. Fresh-baked desserts usually include excellent pumpkin pie with pecans.

1054 31st St. NW. © 202/337-8855. www.seacatchrestaurant.com. Reservations recommended. Lunch main courses $7.25–$18; dinner main courses $18–$28. AE, DC, DISC, MC, V. Mon–Sat noon–3pm and 5:30–10pm.

MODERATE

Bistrot Lepic & Wine Bar ⋆⋆ FRENCH   Bistrot Lepic is the real thing—a charming French restaurant that seems plucked right off a Parisian side street. The atmosphere is bustling and cheery, and you hear a lot of French spoken—not just by the waiters, but also by customers. The Bistrot is a neighborhood place, and you'll often see diners waving hellos across the room to each other or even table-hopping. In its 10 years, the restaurant has made some changes to accommodate its popularity, most recently turning the upstairs into a wine bar and lounge; so if you arrive early for your reservation, you now have a place to wait (in the past, one had to hover hungry-eyed at the door). Or you can come just to hang out, sip a glass of wine, and munch on delicious little somethings from the wine bar menu, where the most expensive item is the $12 terrine of homemade foie gras. No need to make a reservation at the wine bar unless you plan to order dinner from the regular menu.

This is traditional French cooking, updated. The seasonal menu offers such entrees as grilled rainbow trout with carrot sauce, beef medallions with polenta and shiitake mushroom sauce, and sautéed sea scallops with ginger broccoli mousse. We opted for specials: rare tuna served on fennel with citrus vinaigrette, and grouper with a mildly spicy lobster sauce upon a bed of spinach.

The modest French wine list offers a fairly good range. The house red wine, Le Pic Saint-Loup, is a nice complement to most menu choices and is $23 a bottle.

1736 Wisconsin Ave. NW. © 202/333-0111. www.bistrotlepic.com. Reservations recommended. Lunch main courses $13–$21; dinner main courses $16–$25. AE, DC, DISC, MC, V. Tues–Sun 11:30am–2:30pm; Tues–Thurs 5:30–10pm; Fri–Sat 5:30–10:30pm; Sun 5:30–9:30pm; wine bar Tues–Thurs and Sun 5:30–11:30pm; Fri–Sat 5:30pm–12:30am ("But if it's not crowded, we close earlier.").

Clyde's of Georgetown AMERICAN   Clyde's has been a favorite watering hole for an eclectic mix of Washingtonians since 1963. You'll see university students, Capitol Hill types, affluent professionals, Washington Redskins, romantic duos, and well-heeled ladies who lunch. A 1996 renovation transformed Clyde's from a saloon to a theme park, whose dining areas include a cherry-paneled front room with oil paintings of sport scenes, and an atrium with vintage model planes dangling from the glass ceiling and a 16th-century French limestone chimney piece in the large fireplace.

Clyde's is known for its burgers, chili, and crab-cake sandwiches. Appetizers are a safe bet, and Clyde's take on the classic Niçoise (chilled grilled salmon with greens, oven-roasted roma tomatoes, green beans, and grilled new potatoes in a tasty vinaigrette) is also recommended. Sunday brunch is a tradition, so popular that the brunch is offered on Saturday, as well. The menu is reassuringly familiar—steak and eggs, omelets, waffles—with variations thrown in. Among bar selections are about 10 draft beers. Wines are half-price on Sundays.

Note: You can park in the underground Georgetown Park garage for $1 per hour for first 2 hours (a deal in Georgetown!). Just show your meal receipt and ask the mall concierge to validate your parking ticket.

3236 M St. NW. © 202/333-9180. www.clydes.com. Reservations recommended. Lunch/brunch $7.95–$16; dinner main courses $11–$24 (most under $12); burgers and sandwiches (except for crab-cake sandwich) $10 or less. AE, DC, DISC, MC, V. Mon–Thurs 11:30am–midnight; Fri 11:30am–1am; Sat 10am–1am; Sun 9am–10:30pm (Sat and Sun brunch runs until 4pm).

Miss Saigon VIETNAMESE   This is a charming restaurant, with tables scattered amid a "forest" of tropical foliage, and twinkly lights strewn upon the fronds of the potted palms and ferns.

The food here is delicious and authentic, though the service can be a trifle slow when the restaurant is busy. To begin, there is the crispy calamari, or the shrimp and pork-stuffed garden rolls. House specialties include steamed flounder, caramel salmon, and "shaking beef" (cubes of tender Vietnamese steak, marinated in wine, garlic, butter, and soy sauce, then sautéed with onions and potatoes and served with rice and salad). There's a full bar. Desserts range from bananas *flambé au rhum* (fried bananas with rum sauce) to ice cream with Godiva liqueur. Not to be missed is drip-pot coffee, brewed table side and served iced over sweetened condensed milk.

3057 M St. NW. © 202/333-5545. Reservations recommended, especially weekend nights. Lunch main courses $4.50–$8.95; dinner main courses $6.50–$23. AE, DC, MC, V. Mon–Fri 11am–10:30pm (lunch menu served until 3pm); Sat–Sun noon–11pm (dinner menu served all day).

Old Glory Barbecue *Kids* BARBECUE   Raised wooden booths flank one side of the restaurant; an imposing, old-fashioned dark-wood bar with saddle-seat stools extends down the other. Recorded swing music during the day, more mainstream music into the night, plays in the background. Old Glory boasts the city's "largest selection of single-barrel and boutique bourbons" and a new rooftop deck with outdoor seating and views of Georgetown.

After 9pm or so, the two-story restaurant becomes packed with the hard-drinkin' young and restless. In early evening, though, Old Glory is prime for anyone—singles, families, or an older crowd—although it's almost always noisy. Come for the messy, tangy, delicious spare ribs; hickory-smoked chicken; tender, smoked beef brisket; or marinated, wood-fired shrimp. Six sauces are on the table, the spiciest being the vinegar-based East Carolina and Lexington. My Southern-raised husband favored the Savannah version, which reminded him of that city's famous Johnny Harris barbecue sauce. The complimentary corn muffins and biscuits; side dishes of collard greens, succotash, and potato salad; and desserts like apple crisp and coconut cherry cobbler all hit the spot.

3139 M St. NW. (C) 202/337-3406. www.oldglorybbq.com. Reservations accepted Sun–Thurs, reservations not accepted Fri–Sat. Main courses $7.95–$25; Sun brunch buffet $14, half-price for children 8–11, free for children under 8. AE, DC, DISC, MC, V. Sun 11am–11:30pm (brunch from 11am–3pm); Mon–Thurs 11:30am–11:30pm; Fri–Sat 11:30am–midnight. Bar stays open later nightly.

Ristorante Piccolo ITALIAN   Couples seem to be drawn to this quaint trattoria, as my husband I were for lunch last Valentine's Day. It's a two-story town house with a porch overlooking busy 31st Street in Georgetown and a little bit of the C&O Canal. Inside feels intimate and romantic, thanks to fireplaces, amber walls, and last but not least, a strolling violinist (Friday and Saturday evenings only). The kitchen turns out admirable versions of traditional Italian fare: freshly made gnocchi with pesto, tomato sauce, and Parmesan; Caesar salad; minestrone; pasta Bolognese. Add a bottle of Italian vino and you're on your way to a good time.

1068 31st. St. NW. (C) 202/342-7414. Reservations accepted. Lunch main courses $7.75–$15; dinner main courses $12–$23. AE, MC, V. Mon–Thurs 11:30am–2:30pm and 4:30–11pm; Fri 11:30am–2:30pm and 4:30–11:30pm; Sat 11:30am–11:30pm; Sun 11:30am–11pm.

INEXPENSIVE

Aditi INDIAN   This charming two-level restaurant provides a serene setting in which to enjoy first-rate Indian cooking to the tune of Indian music. A must here is the platter of assorted appetizers, which features *bhajia* (a deep-fried vegetable fritter) and crispy vegetable samosas stuffed with spiced potatoes and peas. Favorite entrees include lamb biryani, which is basmati rice pilaf tossed with savory pieces of lamb, cilantro, raisins, and almonds; and the skewered jumbo tandoori prawns, chicken, lamb, or beef—all fresh and fork tender—barbecued in the tandoor. Sauces are on the mild side, so if you like your food fiery, inform your waiter. A *kachumber* salad, a medley of chopped cucumber, lettuce, green pepper, and tomatoes, topped with yogurt and spices, is a refreshing accompaniment to entrees. For dessert, try *kheer,* a cooling rice pudding garnished with chopped nuts. There's a full bar.

3299 M St. NW. (C) 202/625-6825. Reservations recommended. Lunch main courses $8–$16; dinner main courses $8–$30. AE, DC, DISC, MC, V. Sun noon–2:30pm; Mon–Sat 11:30am–2:30pm; Sun–Thurs 5:30–10pm; Fri–Sat 5:30–10:30pm.

Ching Ching Cha *Finds* CHINESE   Located just below M Street, this skylit Chinese tearoom offers a pleasant respite from the crowds. You can sit on pillows at low tables or on chairs set at rosewood tables. Choices are simple: individual items like a tea-and-spice boiled egg, puff pastry stuffed with lotus-seed paste, or five-spice peanuts. Most typical is the $11 "tea meal," which consists of miso soup, three marinated cold vegetables, rice, a salad, and tastings of soy-ginger chicken, salmon with mustard-miso sauce, or steamed teriyaki-sauced tofu. Tea

A Spot of Tea

When you think about it, afternoon tea might well have been designed with tourists in mind. At 3 in the afternoon, you may find yourself longing for a break from all the sightseeing, but not wanting to return to your hotel room. The following are some of my favorite teatime stops:

A popular tea is served in the Garden Terrace of the **Four Seasons Hotel,** M Street NW (℃ 202/342-0444), where one wall of windows overlooks the C&O Canal. The Garden Terrace serves drinks and light fare, as well as tea, so expect a mix of businesspeople, couples, and families. This is one place where a children's tea is offered (a choice of tea, milkshake, or soda, with a brownie, peanut-butter-and-jelly sandwich, chocolate-chip cookie, and strawberries dipped in chocolate). Adults get one scone with double Devon cream and both raspberry and blueberry jam, and a variety of finger sandwiches, tartlets, tea cakes, and cookies that change daily. Among the 16 teas are some herbal and decaffeinated brews; champagne and sherries are available at a surcharge. A pianist plays during afternoon tea, Friday through Sunday. Tea is served daily from 2 to 5pm. The price is $28 per adult and $14 per child; reservations suggested. Dress presentably casual.

At **The Jefferson Hotel,** 1200 16th St. NW (at M St.; ℃ **202/833-6206),** scones are baked while you wait—they take about 15 minutes—so they come to you hot and fragrant, served with Devon cream and jam. Afternoon tea is served in the cozy bar/lounge, where original letters and other documents written by Thomas Jefferson hang on the paneled walls. Sink into a red-leather chair and relax as you nibble on those scones; tea sandwiches filled with cucumber and cheese, duck pâté, or

---

choices include several different green, black, medicinal, and oolong teas, plus a Fujian white tea and a ginseng brew.

1063 Wisconsin Ave. NW. ℃ 202/333-8288. Reservations not accepted. All items $4–$11. AE, DISC, MC, V. Tues–Sat 11:30am–9pm; Sun 11:30am–7pm.

Zed's ETHIOPIAN   Though Ethiopian cuisine has long been popular in Washington, few restaurants can match Zed's truly authentic, high-quality fare. Zed's is a charming little place with indigenous paintings, posters, and artifacts adorning pine-paneled walls. Tables are set with fresh flowers, and Ethiopian music enhances the ambience.

Diners use a sourdough crepelike pancake called *injera* to scoop up food. Highly recommended are the *doro watt* (chicken stewed in a tangy, hot red chile–pepper sauce), the *infillay* (strips of tender chicken breast flavored with seasoned butter and honey wine served with a delicious chopped spinach and rice side dish), flavorful lamb dishes, and the deep-fried whole fish. Vegetables have never been tastier. Consider ordering more of the garlicky chopped collard greens, red lentil purée in spicy red-pepper sauce, or a chilled purée of roasted yellow split peas mixed with onions, peppers, and garlic. There's a full bar, and, should you have the inclination, there are Italian pastries for dessert.

1201 28th St. NW (at M St.). ℃ 202/333-4710. www.zeds.net. Reservations accepted for 5 or more. Main courses $9–$15. AE, DC, DISC, MC, V. Daily 11am–11pm.

smoked salmon; and homemade cookies and miniature fruit tarts. You may choose from a selection of 10 to 16 teas. Afternoon tea is served daily from 3 to 5pm for $28 per person. Dress neatly.

Teaism, 400 8th St. NW (© **202/638-6010**), offers a choice of two very different kinds of afternoon teas: the more traditional menu of tea sandwiches, ginger scone, cookies, lime curd tartlets, Swiss chocolates, and a pot of tea; or the Asian menu, which offers you rice balls with pickle and sesame, tea-cured salmon and nori, tofu with ginger, green tea ice cream, mochi, plum truffle, and a pot of tea. Both are delicious, and are served daily from 2:30 to 5:30pm, for $15 each. *Note:* The Lafayette Square branch of Teaism also offers afternoon tea.

The tea at **Washington National Cathedral,** Massachusetts and Wisconsin avenues NW (© **202/537-8993**), begins with a tour of the world's sixth-largest cathedral (see chapter 7), or, in May and September, a choice of either a garden or cathedral tour, winding up on the seventh floor of the West tower, whose arched windows take in a stunning view of the city and beyond to Sugarloaf Mountain in Maryland. Tea consists of scones and jam; sandwich triangles of egg salad or smoked salmon, or maybe pastry cups of tarragon chicken salad; tiny pastries; and brewed tea. During the school year, you can descend from the tower in time to enjoy evensong services performed at 5:30pm by the Youth Choir. Tea is served every Tuesday and Wednesday at 3pm following a 1:30pm tour, for $22 per person. Reserve as far in advance as possible (the cathedral accepts reservations up to 6 months ahead).

10 Glover Park

Buses (the no. 30 series) travel to Glover Park, which is just north of Georgetown, but the easiest thing to do is take a taxi.

EXPENSIVE

Sushi-Ko ⋆ JAPANESE   Sushi-Ko was Washington's first sushi bar when it opened 29 years ago and it remains popular. The sushi chefs are fun to watch—try to sit at the sushi bar. You can expect superb sushi and sashimi standards, but the best items are daily specials, like a sea trout napoleon (diced sea trout layered between rice crackers), flounder sashimi with a black truffle sauce, and the delicately fried soft shell crab (in season, spring and summer). To capture the full range of tastes here order a bunch of the "small dishes," like the grilled baby octopus with mango, or asparagus with smoked salmon and mustard dashi sauce. The tempuras and teriyakis are also excellent. And there's a long list of sakes, as well as burgundy wines and Japanese beer.

2309 Wisconsin Ave. NW. © 202/333-4187. www.sushiko.us. Reservations recommended. Main courses $10–$25. AE, MC, V. Tues–Fri noon–2:30pm; Mon–Thurs 6–10:30pm; Fri 6–11pm; Sat 5:30–11pm; Sun 5:30–10pm.

INEXPENSIVE

Austin Grill *Kids* SOUTHERN/SOUTHWESTERN   Rob Wilder opened his grill in 1988 to replicate the easygoing lifestyle, Tex-Mex cuisine, and music he loved when he lived in Austin. The good food and festive atmosphere make this a great place for the kids, a date, or a group of friends. Austin Grill is loud; as the night progresses, conversation eventually drowns out the sound of the recorded music (everything from Ry Cooder to Yellow Card).

Fresh ingredients are used to create outstanding crabmeat quesadillas, "Lake Travis" nachos (with red onion, refried beans, and cheese), a daily fish special (like rockfish fajitas), Key lime pie, and excellent versions of standard fare (chicken enchiladas, guacamole, pico de gallo, and so on). The margaritas are awesome.

Austin Grill's upstairs overlooks the abbreviated bar area below. An upbeat decor includes walls washed in shades of teal and clay and adorned with whimsical coyotes, cowboys, Indians, and cacti. Arrive by 6pm weekends if you don't want to wait; weekdays are less crowded.

This is the original Austin Grill; another District Austin Grill is located near the MCI Center at 750 E St. NW (© **202/393-3776**). Suburban locations include one in Old Town Alexandria (see chapter 10).

2404 Wisconsin Ave. NW. © 202/337-8080. www.austingrill.com. Reservations not accepted. Main courses $10–$17. AE, DC, DISC, MC, V. Sun–Thurs 11:30am–10pm; Fri–Sat 11:30am–11:30pm.

11 Woodley Park & Cleveland Park

VERY EXPENSIVE

Palena ★★ ITALIAN/FRENCH   One Metro stop past the Woodley Park–Zoo station takes you to the residential neighborhood of Cleveland Park, which is exploding with good restaurants. Palena is one that's worth the trip.

Palena is the creation of two former White House chefs, executive chef Frank Ruta and pastry chef Ann Amernick, who worked together at the White House in the 1980s. As partners in Palena, the two turn out French- and Italian-inspired dishes, such as Portuguese sardines in puff pastry, boudin blanc, Dover sole filet stuffed with porcini and pan roasted with artichokes and endive, a veal chop that *Washington Post* restaurant critic Tom Sietsema calls "the best in the city," and so on. Amernick's contributions range from complimentary caramels at dinner's conclusion, to the fresh sorbets, cheesecake, bread pudding, and other offerings on the dessert menu. This is an elegant restaurant, with an old-world feel (even though it's only about 4 years old). Because of its immediate and sustained success, it's hard to get a reservation, but worth trying for. Or you can dine at the bar and enjoy little plates of things like burgers and fries, Caesar salads, and pastas, perfectly done and everything costing less than $9.

3529 Connecticut Ave. NW. © 202/537-9250. www.palenarestaurant.com. Reservations recommended. Jacket and tie preferred for men. Fixed price menus $53 (3-course), $60 (4-course), and $67 (5- to 6-course). AE, DC, DISC, MC, V. Tues–Sat 5:30–10pm. Metro: Cleveland Park.

EXPENSIVE

New Heights ★ AMERICAN/INTERNATIONAL   This attractive second-floor dining room has a bank of windows looking out over Rock Creek Park, and walls hung with the colorful artwork by local artists. New Heights attracts a casually upscale clientele, which fills the room every night. An Indian influence will always be found in at least one or two items on the menu, to please the palate of owner Amarjeet (Umbi) Singh, as well as those of his patrons. My husband and I have dined at New Heights a lot over the years, our constancy outlasting a number of fine chefs, who seem to come and go here rather quickly. Recent dinners have treated us to horseradish-crusted halibut with crab parsnip purée and au poivre rib-eye steak with lobster hash and roasted garlic butter sauce. In the past, I've found New Heights's innovative cuisine to be too adventurous, but these dishes I can handle. Sunday brunch is heavenly, too: brioche French toast, soup of puréed chestnut with foie gras, and the like.

2317 Calvert St. NW (near Connecticut Ave.). (✆) 202/234-4110. www.newheightsrestaurant.com. Reservations recommended. Brunch $7–$14; dinner main courses $19–$30. AE, DC, DISC, MC, V. Sun–Thurs 5:30–10pm; Fri–Sat 5:30–11pm; Sun brunch 11am–2:30pm. Metro: Woodley Park–Zoo.

Petits Plats ⭐ FRENCH   Petits Plats is another French bistro, and a very pretty one, ensconced in a town house that's situated directly across from the Woodley Park Metro entrance and the Marriott Wardman Park Hotel. You can sit at the sidewalk cafe, on the porch above, or in the front room, back room, or upstairs rooms of the town house. Watching the passersby on busy Connecticut Avenue is a major amusement. Bistro fare includes shrimp bisque with crab meat; five different mussels dishes, like the mussels in a mustard, cream, and white wine sauce (each comes with french fries); Provençal-styled shrimp on an artichoke-bottom dish; Belgian endive salad with apples, walnuts, and Roquefort; and roasted rack of lamb with potatoes au gratin. The reasonably priced Petits Plats becomes even more so Monday through Friday at lunch, when a two-course set menu is available for $14; daily at early dinner, 5:30 to 7pm, and after 9pm, when a three-course set menu is available for $25; and at Saturday and Sunday brunch, when $23 gets you a choice of entree (from eggs Benedict to steak *frites*), a house salad, and all the champagne you like. Since it opened in spring 2000, Petits Plats has gained a loyal following.

2653 Connecticut Ave. NW. (✆) 202/518-0018. www.petits-plats.com. Reservations recommended. Lunch main courses $11–$19; dinner main courses $16–$24. AE, MC, V. Mon–Fri 11:30am–2:30pm; Sat–Sun 11:30am–4:30pm; Tues–Thurs and Sun 5:30–10pm; Fri–Sat 5:30–11pm. Metro: Woodley Park–Zoo.

MODERATE

Lebanese Taverna MIDDLE EASTERN   This family-owned restaurant gives you a taste of Lebanese culture—its cuisine, decor, and music. It's very popular on weekends, so expect to stand in line (reservations are accepted for seating before 6:30pm only). Diners, once seated in the courtyardlike dining room, where music plays and prayer rugs hang on the walls, hate to leave. The wood-burning oven in the back bakes the pita breads and several appetizers. Order mezza dishes for the table: hummus, tabbouleh, baba ghanoush, stuffed grape leaves, cheese pastries, couscous, and pastry-wrapped spinach pies (*fatayer bi sabanikh*), enough for dinner for a couple or as hors d'oeuvres for a table of you. Or consider entrees, such as the roasted half chicken wrapped in bread and served with garlic purée. The wealth of meatless dishes will delight vegetarians, while rotisserie items, especially the chicken and the chargrilled kabobs of chicken and shrimp, will please all others.

There are other Lebanese Tavernas in the area but this is the only one in the District. It continues to win Restaurant Association of Metropolitan Washington awards for "best casual dining" and "neighborhood gathering place."

2641 Connecticut Ave. NW. (✆) 202/265-8681. www.lebanesetaverna.com. Reservations accepted before 6:30pm. Lunch main courses $7.75–$15; dinner main courses $11–$20. AE, DC, DISC, MC, V. Mon–Fri 11:30am–2:30pm; Sat 11:30am–3pm; Mon–Thurs 5:30–10:30pm; Fri–Sat 5:30–11pm; Sun 5–10pm. Metro: Woodley Park–Zoo.

7

Exploring Washington, D.C.

To its scores of "must-see" attractions, the nation's capital in 2004 added several more: the National World War II Memorial, the Marian Koshland Science Museum, and the National Museum of the American Indian. It's an exciting time to visit Washington, D.C., for the city is vibrant with the changes that come in this, an inaugural year, and with the whirl of wonderful new as well as ongoing possibilities for learning about our history, the world, and our culture, awaiting you at museums, memorials, and other landmarks all over town.

I don't envy you having to choose, however. There are too many attractions to visit in one trip. My advice is to consider the whole picture and then decide what it is that really interests you. You don't need to follow the crowd. The National Air and Space Museum continues to be the most visited attraction in Washington, and it is, indeed, marvelous. But if its exhibits don't appeal, don't go. There's plenty else to do.

Here's what I mean. While you are in the neighborhood of the "big name" sights, you may want to pop in to a lesser-known attraction for a different kind of experience. For example, the Capitol, the Supreme Court, and the Library of Congress all dovetail nicely at the intersection of 1st Street and East Capitol Street. But if you crave a fix of something unrelated to government, walk 1 block past the Library of Congress on East Capitol to the Folger Shakespeare Library, where you can admire Tudor architecture and the collection of Renaissance books, paintings, and musical instruments. Take a break and stroll south to Pennsylvania Avenue for some takeout food and return here to picnic in the

---

Head's Up

The September 11, 2001, terrorist attacks, our country's invasion of Iraq in 2003, and other world events have necessitated the implementation of stricter security procedures around the capital. In addition, the U.S. Department of Homeland Security sometimes issues color code warnings, which may affect the operation of attractions. Generally, "Code Red" is the only warning that would close museums and most other attractions. The next level down, "Code Orange," may prompt some sites to close, but not usually. For instance, when a Code Orange was issued during the time our country was at war with Iraq, the Capitol canceled its public tours of the building; once the war ended, the Code Orange was lifted, and the Capitol resumed its public tours. A few weeks later, Homeland Security issued another Code Orange alert, in response to a possible threat from Al Qaeda—this time, the Capitol stayed open for tours.

Call Ahead

If there were only one piece of advice I could give to a visitor, it would be to call ahead to the places you plan to tour each day before you set out. Many of Washington's government buildings, museums, memorials, and monuments are open to the general public nearly all the time—except when they are not.

Because buildings like the Capitol, the Supreme Court, and the White House are "offices" as well as tourist destinations, the business of the day always poses the potential for closing one of those sites, or at least sections, to sightseers. (The White House is probably most vulnerable to this situation.) This caveat is even more important in the wake of the terrorist attack on the Pentagon; touring procedures change and then change again in response to the perceived need for security measures. (See box, "Head's Up," above.)

In addition to security, there's the matter of maintenance. The steady stream of visitors to Washington's attractions necessitates ongoing caretaking which may require closing an entire landmark, or part of it, to the public, or put in place new hours of operation or procedures for visiting. (Construction of the Capitol's Visitor Center is one such example; see information within the Capitol's description in this chapter.)

Finally, Washington's famous museums, grand halls, and public gardens double as settings for press conferences, galas, special exhibits, festivals, and other special events, so you might arrive at, say, the National Air and Space Museum on a Sunday afternoon, as I did not long ago, only to find some of its galleries off limits because caterers were setting up for an event.

Want to avoid frustration and disappointment? Call ahead.

Elizabethan garden. And at night, if the Folger Theatre is staging a production, you owe it to yourself to attend, for these performances are priceless (see chapter 9 for more information). I'm getting carried away, perhaps, but that's what I want you to do: Get carried away by your experiences. Go at your own pace, see what you want to see, and if you don't get to everything, come back for another visit.

As you prepare for sightseeing around the capital, build in some extra time for security procedures, which are in place at most attractions. You'll notice barriers but don't let the sight of them, nor the tighter security precautions, deter you. At many museums,

like the Smithsonian's Air and Space, Natural History, and American History museums, you now must walk past metal detectors, which means that during the busy spring and summer seasons, you may be standing in line outside, as you wait for your turn to pass through security. Other museums have staff search handbags, briefcases, and backpacks. At government buildings, like the Capitol, security procedures run the gamut, including the use of X-ray machines, metal detectors, and hand searches. Make things easy on yourself and everyone else by carrying as little as possible, and certainly no sharp objects. Museums no longer offer the use of lockers.

Washington, D.C., Attractions

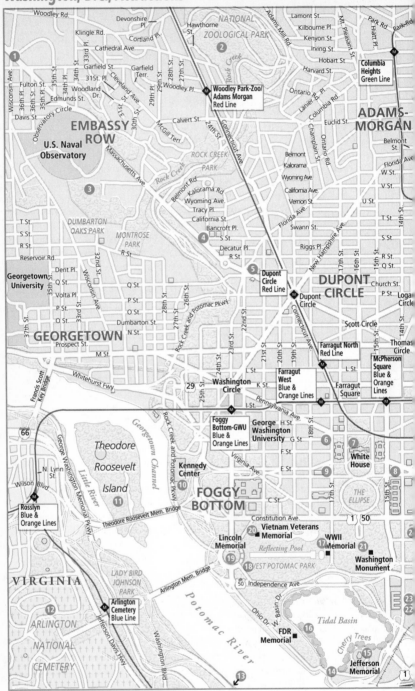

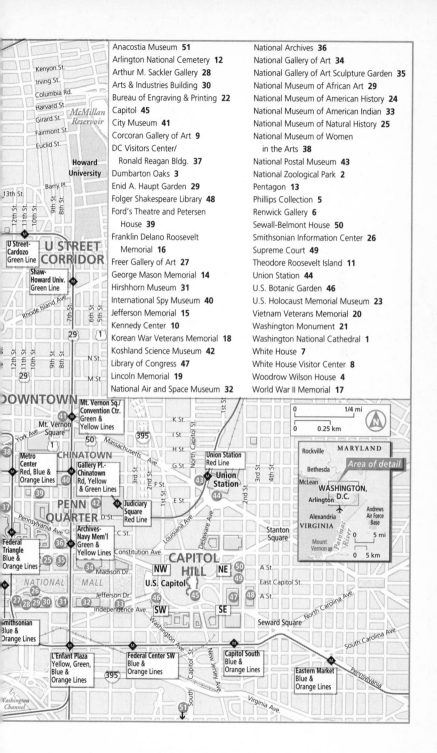

Anacostia Museum **51**
Arlington National Cemetery **12**
Arthur M. Sackler Gallery **28**
Arts & Industries Building **30**
Bureau of Engraving & Printing **22**
Capitol **45**
City Museum **41**
Corcoran Gallery of Art **9**
DC Visitors Center/
  Ronald Reagan Bldg. **37**
Dumbarton Oaks **3**
Enid A. Haupt Garden **29**
Folger Shakespeare Library **48**
Ford's Theatre and Petersen
  House **39**
Franklin Delano Roosevelt
  Memorial **16**
Freer Gallery of Art **27**
George Mason Memorial **14**
Hirshhorn Museum **31**
International Spy Museum **40**
Jefferson Memorial **15**
Kennedy Center **10**
Korean War Veterans Memorial **18**
Koshland Science Museum **42**
Library of Congress **47**
Lincoln Memorial **19**
National Air and Space Museum **32**

National Archives **36**
National Gallery of Art **34**
National Gallery of Art Sculpture Garden **35**
National Museum of African Art **29**
National Museum of American History **24**
National Museum of American Indian **33**
National Museum of Natural History **25**
National Museum of Women
  in the Arts **38**
National Postal Museum **43**
National Zoological Park **2**
Pentagon **13**
Phillips Collection **5**
Renwick Gallery **6**
Sewall-Belmont House **50**
Smithsonian Information Center **26**
Supreme Court **49**
Theodore Roosevelt Island **11**
Union Station **44**
U.S. Botanic Garden **46**
U.S. Holocaust Memorial Museum **23**
Vietnam Veterans Memorial **20**
Washington Monument **21**
Washington National Cathedral **1**
White House **7**
White House Visitor Center **8**
Woodrow Wilson House **4**
World War II Memorial **17**

SUGGESTED ITINERARIES

If You Have 1 Day

Make the Mall your destination, visiting whichever museums appeal to you the most. Then take a breather: If you have young kids, take them for a ride on the carousel across from the Smithsonian's Arts and Industries Building. With or without kids, stroll across the Mall to the National Gallery Sculpture Garden, where you can get a bite to eat in the cafe or relax by the reflecting pool. Rest up, dine in Dupont Circle, stroll Connecticut Avenue, then take a cab to visit the Lincoln Memorial, the Vietnam Veterans Memorial, and the World War II Memorial at night, when these three sites are particularly spectacular.

If You Have 2 Days

On your first day, take a narrated tour of the city (p. 227) for an overview of the city's attractions, stopping at the Jefferson, FDR, Lincoln, Vietnam War Veterans, and World War II memorials, and at the Washington Monument. Use the tour to determine which Mall museums you'll want to visit. After taking in the Washington Monument, walk up 15th Street to F Street, turn right, and walk to Red Sage at 14th and F for some Southwestern fare in the restaurant's open-all-day Border Café. Following lunch, visit your top-pick museums on the Mall.

Start your second day by visiting the Capitol and the Supreme Court. Walk down Pennsylvania Avenue to Seventh Street for lunch at Montmartre, then spend the afternoon visiting the Library of Congress, the Folger Shakespeare Library, and, if you have time, Union Station and the National Postal Museum. Have dinner in Georgetown and browse the shops.

If You Have 3 Days

Spend your first 2 days as described above.

On the morning of your third day, tour the International Spy Museum, followed by the City Museum. Enjoy a late lunch downtown near the MCI Center, such as at Zola or Bistrot D'Oc (see chapter 6), and then visit the National Museum of Women in the Arts. Have a pretheater dinner at one of the many restaurants that offer these good deals (1789 in Georgetown and Marcel's in the West End, are two fine choices; for these and more, see chapter 6). Then head to the Kennedy Center for a performance.

If You Have 4 Days or More

Spend your first 3 days as suggested above.

On the fourth day, visit the U.S. Holocaust Memorial Museum (not recommended for children under 12); this will require most of your day. Have dinner in Adams-Morgan, followed by club-hopping up and down 18th Street. Or take in a salsa lesson at Habana Village, on Columbia Road in Adams-Morgan. See chapter 9 for other suggestions for places to boogie.

If you have a fifth day, consider a day trip to Alexandria, Virginia. Or board a boat for Mount Vernon and spend most of the morning touring the estate (see chapter 10), with the afternoon set aside for seeing sights you've missed. Have dinner in downtown Washington at one of the Seventh Street–district restaurants, then see Shakespeare performed at the Shakespeare Theatre, or head to the Blue Bar at the Henley Park Hotel to sip a drink as you listen to live jazz.

Openings and Closings

Much is happening in D.C. in 2005, a lot of it to do with construction and renovation. But first, what's new: Washington, D.C. has a new science museum, the **Marion Koshland Science Museum,** which debuted in March 2004. In fall 2004, the Smithsonian's much-heralded **National Museum of the American Indian** opened on the National Mall; three permanent exhibit halls display up to 2,000 objects from the museum's 800,000-piece collection. The museum also has a theater and an outdoor performance space. On May 29, 2004, the dedication of the **National World War II Memorial** took place, on the National Mall. See separate entries in this chapter for more information about these attractions.

Throughout 2005, the **Smithsonian's American Art Museum,** the **National Portrait Gallery,** and the **Arts and Industries Building** remain closed for renovation. Scheduled to re-open in 2005 after thorough remodeling are the **FBI Building** and the annex of the **Phillips Collection. The Kennedy Center of the Performing Arts** is going on with all shows, though the place looks like construction-central, as it will for the coming decade while its grand expansion, including a pedestrian plaza, is in production. The new **Newseum** and the **Capitol Visitors Center** are both scheduled to open in 2006. For security reasons, not renovations, the **White House** and the **Pentagon** are both closed to walkup tours, but each allows tours arranged in advance through a senator or congressperson; see their entries in this chapter for details.

1 The Three Houses of Government

Three of the most visited sights in Washington have always been the buildings housing the executive, legislative, and judicial branches of the U.S. government. All three, the Capitol, the White House, and the Supreme Court, are stunning and offer fascinating lessons in American history and government. Although these three landmarks are not as freely open to the public as they once were before the terrorist attacks of September 11, 2001, all three do allow tours.

The Capitol ✶✶✶   The Capitol is as majestic up close at it is from afar. For 135 years it sheltered not only both houses of Congress, but also the Supreme Court and, for 97 years, the Library of Congress as well. When you tour the Capitol, you'll learn about America's history as you admire the place in which it unfolded. Classical architecture, interior embellishments, and hundreds of paintings, sculptures, and other artworks are integral elements of the Capitol.

On the massive bronze doors leading to the **Rotunda** are portrayals of events in the life of Columbus. The Rotunda—a huge 96-foot-wide circular hall capped by a 180-foot-high dome—is the hub of the Capitol. The dome was completed, at Lincoln's direction, while the Civil War was being fought. Ten presidents have lain in state here, with former President Ronald Reagan being the most recent; when Kennedy's casket was displayed, the line of mourners stretched 40 blocks. On the walls are eight immense oil paintings of events in

American history, such as the presentation of the Declaration of Independence and the surrender of Cornwallis at Yorktown. In the dome is an allegorical fresco masterpiece by Constantino Brumidi, *Apotheosis of Washington,* a symbolic portrayal of George Washington surrounded by Roman gods and goddesses watching over the progress of the nation. Brumidi was known as the "Michelangelo of the Capitol" for the many works he created throughout the building. (Take another look at the dome and find the woman directly below Washington; the triumphant *Armed Freedom* figure is said to be modeled after Lola Germon, a beautiful young actress with whom the 60-year-old Brumidi had a child.) Beneath the dome is a *trompe l'oeil* frieze depicting important events in American history. Also in the Rotunda is the sculpture of suffragists Elizabeth Cady Stanton, Susan B. Anthony, and Lucretia Mott. For a long time, the monument had been relegated to the Crypt, one level directly below the Rotunda. Women's groups successfully lobbied for its more prominent position in the Rotunda.

The **National Statuary Hall** was originally the chamber of the House of Representatives. In 1864, it became Statuary Hall, and the states were invited to send two statues each of native sons and daughters to the hall. There are 97 statues in all, since three states, Nevada, New Mexico, and North Dakota, have sent only one. Many of the statues honor individuals who played important roles in American history, such as Henry Clay, Ethan Allen, Daniel Webster, and seven women, including Jeannette Rankin, the first woman to serve in Congress.

You will not see them on your tour, but the **south and north wings** of the Capitol hold the House and Senate chambers, respectively. The House of Representatives chamber is the largest legislative chamber in the world, and the setting for the president's annual State of the Union addresses. (See information further along about watching Senate and House activity.) The Capitol also houses the **Old Supreme Court Chamber,** which has been restored to its mid-19th-century appearance. The Old Supreme Court Chamber is where Chief Justice John Marshall established the foundations of American constitutional law. Allow at least an hour for touring, longer if you plan to attend a session of Congress. Remember to allow time for waiting in line.

At this time, self-guided tours and "VIP" tours (tours reserved in advance by individuals through their congressional offices) have been suspended, for the foreseeable future. The only way now to tour the Capitol Building is in groups of 40. A Capitol Guide Service guide conducts each tour, which is free and lasts about 30 minutes.

You have two options: If you are part of an organized bunch, say a school class on a field trip, you may arrange a tour in advance, putting together groups of no more than 40 each, by contacting your congressional office at least 1 month

---

Under Construction

In mid-2002, construction started on a comprehensive, underground Capitol Visitor Center, with completion scheduled for 2006. Since the Capitol Visitor Center is being created directly beneath the plaza where people traditionally line up for tours on the east side of the Capitol, touring procedures have changed. The best thing to do is to call ahead (© 202/225-6827) to find out the new procedures in place for the time you are visiting, and whether the construction work will temporarily close parts of the building you wish to visit.

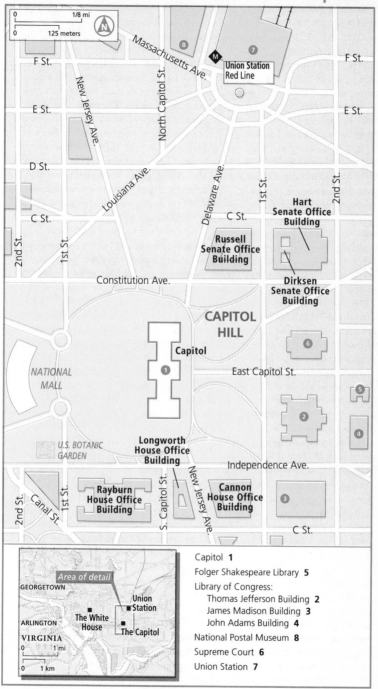

Capitol **1**

Folger Shakespeare Library **5**

Library of Congress:
  Thomas Jefferson Building **2**
  James Madison Building **3**
  John Adams Building **4**

National Postal Museum **8**

Supreme Court **6**

Union Station **7**

ahead, and following the procedures that office outlines for you. If you are on your own, or with family or friends, you will want to get to the Capitol early, by 7:30am, to stand in line for one of a limited number of timed tickets the Capitol distributes daily, starting at 9am. Head to the ticket kiosk at the southwest corner of the Capitol grounds, near the intersection of 1st Street and Independence Avenue SW, across 1st Street from the U.S. Botanic Gardens. It's a first-come, first-served system, with only one ticket given to each person, and each person, including children of any age, must have a ticket. The good news is that once you receive your ticket, you are free to go somewhere nearby to get a bite to eat, or to sightsee, while you wait for your turn to tour the Capitol. The bad news is that all of you, even 1-year-old baby Louie, have to rise early and get to the Capitol by about 7:30am and then stand in line for another hour or more to be sure of touring the Capitol that day. Still, I think this is an improvement over the old touring procedure, which required all of you to stay in the queue until you entered the Capitol—if you left the line, you lost your place. Definitely call the recorded information line (✆ **202/225-6827**) on the morning of your visit to confirm exactly where and how to obtain your ticket.

Now, if you wish to visit either or both the House and Senate galleries, you follow a different procedure. The Senate Gallery is open to visitors only when it is in session, while the House Gallery is open to visitors whether or not it is in session. Try to visit when both the Senate and House are **in session** ★★★. Either way, in session or not, you must have a pass to visit each gallery. (Children under 6 are not allowed in the Senate gallery.) Once obtained, the passes are good through the remainder of the Congress. To obtain visitor passes in advance, contact your representative for a House gallery pass, or your senator for a Senate gallery pass; District of Columbia and Puerto Rico residents should contact their delegate to Congress. If you don't receive visitor passes in the mail, they're obtainable at your senator's office on the Constitution Avenue, or north side, of the building or your representative's or delegate's office on the Independence Avenue, or south side, of the building. (Visitors who are not citizens can obtain a gallery pass by presenting a passport at the Senate or House appointments desk, located on the first floor of the Capitol.) Call the Capitol switchboard at ✆ **202/224-3121** to contact the office of your senator or congressperson. Your congressional office will issue you a pass. You'll know the House and/or the Senate is in session if you see flags flying over their respective wings of the Capitol (House: south side, Senate: north side), or you can check the weekday "Today in Congress" column in the *Washington Post* for details on times of the House and Senate sessions and committee hearings. This column also tells you which sessions are open to the public. Or you can access the Capitol's webpage, www.aoc.gov. Vastly improved in the past year, the website provides lots of good information about the history, art, and construction of the Capitol building; an in-depth education on the legislative process; and schedules of bill debates in the House and Senate, committee markups and meetings, and lots of other good stuff. The aoc.gov (aoc stands for "architect of the capitol") page has links to the individual Senate, www.senate.gov, and House, www.house.gov, pages, or you can go directly to those sites, to connect to your senate or house representative's page.

At the east end of the Mall, entrance on E. Capitol St. and 1st St. NW. ✆ **202/225-6827**. www.aoc.gov, www.house.gov, www.senate.gov. Free admission. Year-round 9am–4:30pm Mon–Sat, with first tour starting at 9:30am and last tour starting at 3:30pm. Closed for tours Sun and Jan 1, Thanksgiving, and Dec 25. Parking at Union Station or on neighborhood streets. Metro: Union Station or Capitol South.

The Supreme Court of the United States ★★★   The highest tribunal in the nation, the Supreme Court is charged with deciding whether actions of Congress, the president, the states, and lower courts are in accord with the Constitution, and with applying the Constitution's enduring principles to novel situations and a changing country. The Supreme Court's chief justice and eight associate justices the authority to invalidate legislation or executive action that conflicts with the Constitution. Out of the 7,000 or so cases submitted to it each year, the Supreme Court hears only about 100 cases, many of which deal with issues vital to the nation. The Court's rulings are final, reversible only by another Supreme Court decision, or in some cases, an Act of Congress or a constitutional amendment.

Until 1935, the Supreme Court met in the Capitol. Architect Cass Gilbert designed the stately Corinthian marble palace that houses the Court today. The building was considered rather grandiose by early residents: One justice remarked that he and his colleagues ought to enter such pompous precincts on elephants.

If you're in town when the Court is in session, try to **see a case being argued** ★★★ (call ℂ **202/479-3211** for details). The Court meets Monday through Wednesday and hears up to four arguments a day, from 10am to noon, and from 1 to 2pm or 3pm, starting the first Monday in October through late April. From mid-May to late June, you can attend brief sessions (about 15 min.) at 10am on Monday, when the justices release orders and opinions. Find out what cases are on the docket by checking the *Washington Post*'s "Supreme Court Calendar." Arrive at least an hour early—earlier for highly publicized cases—to line up for seats, about 150 of which are allotted to the general public.

There are many rituals here. At 10am, the entrance of the justices is announced by the marshal, and all present rise and remain standing while the justices are seated following the chant: "The Honorable, the Chief Justice and Associate Justices of the Supreme Court of the United States. Oyez! Oyez! Oyez! All persons having business before the Honorable, the Supreme Court of the United States, are admonished to draw near and give their attention, for the Court is now sitting. God save the United States and this Honorable Court!" Unseen by the gallery is the "conference handshake"; following a 19th-century tradition symbolizing a "harmony of aims if not views," each justice shakes hands with each of the other eight when they assemble to go to the bench. The Court has a record before it of prior proceedings and relevant briefs, so each side is allowed only a 30-minute argument.

Call the Supreme Court information line to find out days and times that court arguments will take place. You may view these on a first-come, first-served basis, choosing between the 3-minute line, which ushers visitors in and out of the court every 3 minutes, starting at 10am in the morning and at 1pm in the afternoon; or the "regular" line, which admits visitors who wish to stay for the entire argument, starting at 9:30am and 12:30pm (arrive about 90 min. early to snag a spot).

The Supreme Court is cloaked in mystery, purposefully. You can't take cameras or recording devices into the courtroom, and you're not allowed to take notes, either. The justices seldom give speeches and never give press conferences.

When the Court is not in session, you can tour the building and attend a **free lecture** in the courtroom about Court procedure and the building's architecture. Lectures are given every hour on the half-hour from 9:30am to 3:30pm. After the talk, explore the Great Hall and go down a flight of steps to see the **24-minute**

film on the workings of the Court. On the same floor is an exhibit highlighting the "History of High Courts Around the World," on display indefinitely. If you tour the building on your own, you should allow about an hour. You might also consider contacting your senator or congressperson to arrange for a 40-minute guided tour of the building led by a Supreme Court staff member, who will take you places you won't be able to go on your own. There's also a gift shop and a public cafeteria that serves good food.

One 1st St. NE (between E. Capitol St. and Maryland Ave. NE). © **202/479-3000.** www.supremecourtus.gov. Free admission. Mon–Fri 9am–4:30pm. Closed all federal holidays. Metro: Capitol South or Union Station.

The White House ★★   It's amazing when you think about it: This house has served as a residence, office, reception site, and world embassy for every U.S. president since John Adams. The White House is the only private residence of a head of state that has opened its doors to the public for tours, free of charge. It was Thomas Jefferson who started this practice, which is stopped only during wartime. Our war on terrorism caused the administration in 2002 to close the White House for public tours for about 2 years. Thankfully, the White House is once again open for public tours, though not walkup tours. See the box, "How to Arrange a White House Tour," below.

An Act of Congress in 1790 established the city, now known as Washington, District of Columbia, as the seat of the federal government. George Washington and city planner Pierre L'Enfant chose the site for the White House (or "President's House," as it was called before whitewashing brought the name "White House" into use) and staged a contest to find a builder. Although Washington picked the winner—Irishman James Hoban—he was the only president never to live in the White House. The structure took 8 years to build, starting in 1792, when its cornerstone was laid, and its facade is made of the same stone as that used to construct the Capitol. In 1814, during the War of 1812, the British set fire to the White House, gutting the interior; the exterior managed to endure only because a rainstorm extinguished the fire. What you see today is Hoban's basic creation: a building modeled after an Irish country house (in fact, Hoban had in mind the house of the Duke of Leinster in Dublin).

Alterations over the years have incorporated the South Portico in 1824, the North Portico in 1829, and electricity in 1891, during Benjamin Harrison's presidency. In 1902, repairs and refurnishings of the White House cost nearly $500,000. No other great change took place until Harry Truman's presidency, when the interior was completely renovated, after the leg of Margaret Truman's piano cut through the dining room ceiling. The Trumans lived at Blair House across the street for nearly 4 years while the White House interior was shored up with steel girders and concrete. It's as solid as Gibraltar now.

In 1961, Jacqueline Kennedy formed a Fine Arts Committee to help restore the famous rooms to their original grandeur, ensuring treatment of the White House as a museum of American history and decorative arts. "It just seemed to me such a shame when we came here to find hardly anything of the past in the house, hardly anything before 1902," Mrs. Kennedy observed. Presidents through the years have put their own stamp on the White House, the most recent example being President Bush's addition of the T-ball field to the South Lawn.

Highlights of the tour include the **Gold-and-White East Room,** the scene of presidential receptions, weddings (Lynda Bird Johnson, for one), and other dazzling events. This is where the president entertains visiting heads of state and the place where seven of the eight presidents who died in office (all but Garfield) laid in state. It was also where Nixon resigned. The room's early-18th-century

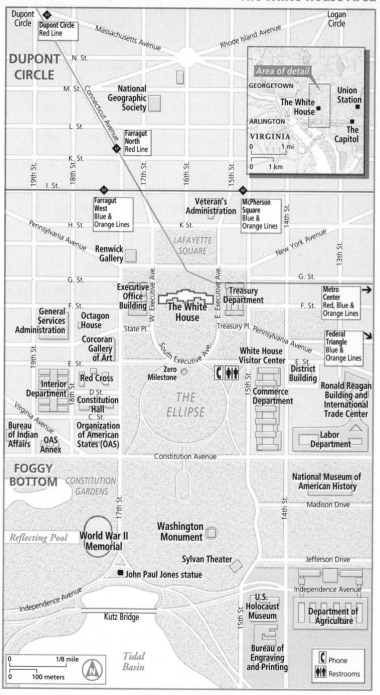

Dupont Circle

Dupont Circle Red Line

Logan Circle

Massachusetts Avenue

Rhode Island Avenue

DUPONT CIRCLE

N. St.

M. St.

National Geographic Society

Area of detail

GEORGETOWN

The White House

Union Station

ARLINGTON

VIRGINIA

The Capitol

0   1 mi

0   1 km

L. St.

Farragut North Red Line

K. St.

Connecticut Avenue

18th St.

19th St.

17th St.

16th St.

15th St.

I. St.

H. St.

Pennsylvania Avenue

Farragut West Blue & Orange Lines

Veteran's Administration

K St.

McPherson Square Blue & Orange Lines

14th St.

LAFAYETTE SQUARE

New York Avenue

13th St.

Renwick Gallery

G. St.

G. St.

Executive Office Building

W. Executive Ave.

The White House

E. Executive Ave.

Treasury Department

Metro Center Red, Blue & Orange Lines

F. St.

General Services Administration

F. St.

Octagon House

State Pl.

Treasury Pl.

Pennsylvania Avenue

F. St.

Federal Triangle Blue & Orange Lines

Corcoran Gallery of Art

E. St.

South Executive Ave.

White House Visitor Center

E. St.

District Building

19th St.

Interior Department

Red Cross

D St.

Zero Milestone

C **††**

15th St.

Commerce Department

Ronald Reagan Building and International Trade Center

18th St.

Constitution Hall

C. St.

THE ELLIPSE

Virginia Avenue

Bureau of Indian Affairs

OAS Annex

Organization of American States (OAS)

Constitution Avenue

Labor Department

FOGGY BOTTOM

CONSTITUTION GARDENS

National Museum of American History

Madison Drive

17th St.

14th St.

Reflecting Pool

World War II Memorial

Washington Monument

■ John Paul Jones statue

Sylvan Theater

Jefferson Drive

Independence Avenue

U.S. Holocaust Museum

15th St.

Independence Avenue

Department of Agriculture

Kutz Bridge

Tidal Basin

Bureau of Engraving and Printing

0   1/8 mile

0   100 meters

C Phone

†† Restrooms

style was adopted during the Theodore Roosevelt renovation of 1902; it has parquet Fontainebleau oak floors and white-painted wood walls with fluted pilasters and classical relief inserts. Note the famous Gilbert Stuart portrait of George Washington that Dolley Madison saved from the British torch during the War of 1812. The portrait is the only object to have remained continuously in the White House since 1800 (except during times of reconstruction).

You'll visit the **Green Room,** which was Thomas Jefferson's dining room but today is used as a sitting room. Mrs. Kennedy chose the green watered-silk-fabric wall covering. In the **Oval Blue Room,** decorated in the French Empire style chosen by James Monroe in 1817, presidents and first ladies have officially received guests since the Jefferson administration. It was, however, Van Buren's decor that began the "blue room" tradition. The walls, on which hang portraits of five presidents (including Rembrandt Peale's portrait of Thomas Jefferson and G. P. A. Healy's of Tyler), are covered in reproductions of early-19th-century French and American wallpaper. Grover Cleveland, the only president to wed in the White House, was married in the Blue Room. This room was also where the Reagans greeted the 52 Americans liberated after being held hostage in Iran for 444 days, and every year it's the setting for the White House Christmas tree.

The **Red Room,** whose satin-covered walls and Empire furnishings are red, is used as a reception room, usually for afternoon teas. Several portraits of past presidents and a Gilbert Stuart portrait of Dolley Madison hang here. Dolley Madison used the Red Room for her famous Wednesday-night receptions.

From the Red Room, you enter the **State Dining Room.** Modeled after late-18th-century neoclassical English houses, this room is a superb setting for state dinners and luncheons. Below G. P. A. Healy's portrait of Lincoln is an inscription written by John Adams on his second night in the White House (FDR had it carved into the mantel): "I Pray Heaven to Bestow The Best of Blessings on THIS HOUSE and on All that shall here-after Inhabit it. May none but Honest and Wise Men ever rule under this Roof."

Note: Even if you have successfully reserved a White House tour for your group, you should still call ℂ **202/456-7041** before setting out in the morning; in case the White House is closed on short notice because of unforeseen events. If this should happen to you, you should make a point of walking by the White House anyway, since its exterior is still pretty awesome. Stroll past it on Pennsylvania Avenue, down 15th Street past the Treasury Building, and along the backside and South Lawn, on E Street.

1600 Pennsylvania Ave. NW (visitor entrance gate at E St. and E. Executive Ave.). ℂ **202/456-7041** or 202/208-1631. www.whitehouse.gov. Free admission. Tours for groups of 10 or more, who have arranged the tour through their congressional offices. Metro: McPherson Square.

The White House Visitor Center ⋆ Even—especially—if you are not able to tour the White House, you should stop here. The Visitor Center opened in 1995 to provide extensive interpretive data about the White House and to serve as a ticket-distribution center (though that function is suspended indefinitely). It is run under the auspices of the National Park Service and the staff is particularly well informed. Try to catch the 30-minute video about the White House, *Where History Lives,* which provides interior views of the presidential precincts (it runs continuously throughout the day). Before you leave the Visitor Center, pick up a copy of the National Park Service's brochure on the White House, which tells you a little about what you'll see in the eight or so rooms you tour and a bit about the history of the White House. The White House Historic

⟨*Tips*⟩ How to Arrange a White House Tour

The White House allows groups of 10 or more to tour the White House, Tuesday through Saturday, from 7:30am to 11:30am. Tours are self-guided and most people take no more than an hour to go through. You must have a reservation to tour the White House. The procedure is simply this: At least 3 or 4 months in advance of your trip, call your senator's or representative's office with the names of the people in your group, and ask for a specific tour date. The tour coordinator passes on this information to the White House, whose staff determines whether there is an availability and then notifies the tour coordinator. The tour coordinator, in turn, contacts you and, if your date is available, obtains the names, birth dates, social security numbers (for those 14 and older), and other information for each of the people in your party. The tour coordinator submits this information to the White House, where the Secret Service reviews the information and clears you for the tour, putting the names of the people in your group on a confirmed reservation list. The White House notifies the congressional tour coordinator, who notifies you, usually about 1 month in advance of your trip. On the day of your White House tour, call ✆ **202/ 456-7041** to make sure that the White House is still open that day to the public. Then off you go, to the south side of East Executive Avenue, near the Southeast Gate of the White House, with photo IDs for everyone in your party who is 15 or older.

Do not bring the following prohibited items: backpacks, bookbags, *handbags or purses*, food and beverages, strollers, cameras, video recorders or any type of recording device, tobacco products, personal grooming items, from cosmetics to hairbrush, any pointed objects, whether a pen or a knitting needle, aerosol containers, guns, ammunition, fireworks, electric stun guns, mace, martial arts weapons/devices, or knives of any description. Cellphones are OK, but not the kind that are also cameras. The White House does not have a coat check facility, so there is no place for you to leave your belongings while you go on the tour. There are no public restrooms or telephones in the White House, and picture-taking and videotaping are prohibited. Best advice: Leave everything but your wallet back at the hotel.

OK, so what do you do if you're a family of four and you want to tour the White House? Groups of fewer than 10 people should call their congressional office and ask whether it might be possible to join with another family to meet the 10-person minimum. The coordinator also emphasizes that you request a reservation at least 4 months in advance.

Association runs a small shop here. The association operates an informative website, **www.whitehousehistory.org.** Before you leave the Visitor Center, take a look at the exhibits, which include:

Architectural History of the White House, including the grounds and extensive renovations to its structure and interior that have taken place since its cornerstone was laid in 1792.

Symbol and Image, showing how the White House has been portrayed by photographers, artists, journalists, political cartoonists, and others.

First Families, with displays about the people who have lived here (such as prankster Tad Lincoln, who once stood in a window above his father and waved a Confederate flag at a military review).

The Working White House, focusing on the vast staff of servants, chefs, gardeners, Secret Service people, and others who maintain this institution.

Ceremony and Celebration, depicting notable White House events, from a Wright Brothers' aviation demonstration in 1911 to a ballet performance by Baryshnikov during the Carter administration.

White House Interiors, Past and Present, including photographs of the ever-changing Oval Office as decorated by administrations from Taft through Clinton.

1450 Pennsylvania Ave. NW (in the Dept. of Commerce Building, between 14th and 15th sts.). ✆ 202/208-1631 for recorded information. Free admission. Daily 7:30am–4pm. Closed Jan 1, Thanksgiving, and Dec 25. Metro: Federal Triangle.

2 The Major Memorials

The capital's major memorials honor esteemed presidents, war veterans, and founding fathers. On May 29, 2004, the American Battle Monuments Commission dedicated the National Mall's newest memorial, the **National World War II Memorial.** Located at the east end of the Reflecting Pool between the Lincoln Memorial and the Washington Monument, the World War II Memorial is the first national memorial dedicated to all who served during World War II, and honors all military veterans of the war, citizens on the home front, and the nation at large. (See the memorial's write-up, below.) In the offing is a memorial to Dr. Martin Luther King Jr.

All of these memorials are located in picturesque **West Potomac Park** (see p. 222 for full details on the park and its famous **cherry blossoms**), which lies at the western end of the National Mall, where it borders the Potomac River and encircles the Tidal Basin. Unfortunately, none of the memorials lie directly on a Metro line, so you can expect a bit of a walk from the specified station.

The easiest thing to do, if you're up to it, is to walk from one monument or memorial to the next. Dress for the weather: light clothing, shades, and sunscreen in summer; a hat, gloves, and warm jacket in winter—these monuments are set in wide open spaces, with little to no protection from the elements. But when the weather is lovely, so is the experience of sauntering around West Potomac Park.

Or, you can go by **Tourmobile** (p. 227), which continually picks up and discharges passengers at each of these sites throughout the day. The National Park Service manages all of these properties and maintains information about each of them, including upcoming events, at **www.nps.gov**; click on "Parks and Recreation," then "Geographic Search," and select "District of Columbia." You click on the name of the individual park to read more about the site.

Some believe the best time to visit the memorials is at night, when they're illuminated in all their imposing white-stone glory and all the crowds are gone. Try it—all of the memorials are safe to visit after dark, with park rangers on hand until midnight year-round, except for the Washington Monument, which closes at 5pm now. You may view the exteriors any time.

Washington Monument 🅐🅐🅐 *(Kids)* The idea of a tribute to George Washington first arose 16 years before his death, at the Continental Congress of 1783. But the new nation had more pressing problems and funds were not readily

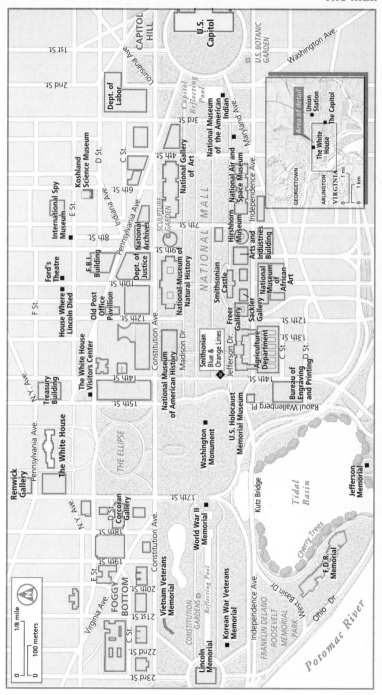

The Mall

U.S. Capitol

CAPITOL HILL

U.S. BOTANIC GARDEN

Washington Ave.

Louisiana Ave.

1st St.

2nd St.

Dept. of Labor

Capitol Reflecting Pool

Area of detail

Union Station

The Capitol

Washington Ave.

The White House

GEORGETOWN

ARLINGTON

VIRGINIA

1 mi

1 km

0

National Museum of the American Indian

Maryland Ave.

3rd St.

D St.

C St.

4th St.

Koshland Science Museum

5th St.

National Gallery of Art

National Gallery of Art

6th St.

Indiana Ave.

E St.

Independence Ave.

National Air and Space Museum

International Spy Museum

Pennsylvania Ave.

7th St.

SCULPTURE GARDEN

Hirshhorn Museum

8th St.

NATIONAL MALL

Arts and Industries Building

Ford's Theatre

9th St.

F.B.I. Building

National Archives

9th St.

Smithsonian Castle

National Museum of African Art

House Where Lincoln Died

10th St.

Dept. of Justice

National Museum of Natural History

Freer Gallery

Sackler Gallery

F St.

Old Post Office Pavilion

11th St.

12th St.

12th St.

13th St.

N.Y. Ave.

The White House Visitors Center

Constitution Ave.

Madison Dr.

Smithsonian Blue & Orange Lines

Agriculture Department

Jefferson Dr.

C St.

D St.

Treasury Building

14th St.

15th St.

National Museum of American History

14th St.

Bureau of Engraving and Printing

Pennsylvania Ave.

The White House

Renwick Gallery

N.Y. Ave.

THE ELLIPSE

Raoul Wallenberg Pl.

U.S. Holocaust Memorial Museum

Washington Monument

Tidal Basin

Kutz Bridge

D St.

Corcoran Gallery

18th St.

17th St.

Jefferson Memorial

Cherry Trees

FRANKLIN DELANO ROOSEVELT PARK

World War II Memorial

19th St.

Constitution Ave.

E St.

FOGGY BOTTOM

Vietnam Veterans Memorial

20th St.

Independence Ave.

West Basin Dr.

F.D.R. Memorial

Virginia Ave.

21st St.

CONSTITUTION GARDENS

Reflecting Pool

Korean War Veterans Memorial

Ohio Dr.

22nd St.

C St.

Lincoln Memorial

Potomac River

23rd St.

N

0   1/8 mile

0   100 meters

available. It wasn't until the early 1830s, with the 100th anniversary of Washington's birth approaching, that any action was taken.

Then there were several fiascoes. A mausoleum was provided for Washington's remains under the Capitol Rotunda, but a grandnephew, citing Washington's will, refused to allow the body to be moved from Mount Vernon. In 1830, Horatio Greenough was commissioned to create a memorial statue for the Rotunda. He came up with a bare-chested Washington, draped in classical Greek garb; a shocked public claimed he looked as if he were "entering or leaving a bath," and so the statue was relegated to the Smithsonian. Finally, in 1833, prominent citizens organized the Washington National Monument Society. Treasury Building architect Robert Mills's design was accepted.

The cornerstone was laid on July 4, 1848, and for the next 37 years, watching the monument grow, or not grow, was a local pastime. Declining contributions and the Civil War brought construction to a halt at an awkward 150 feet (you can still see a change in the color of the stone about halfway up). The unsightly stump remained until 1876, when President Grant approved federal monies to complete the project. Dedicated in 1885, it was opened to the public in 1888.

A major 2-year restoration completed in 2000 repaired the monument's exterior masonry and mortar, refurbished its elevator, installed a new climate-control system, scrubbed the 897 interior steps, and polished the 193 carved commemorative stones.

Visiting the Washington Monument: The Washington Monument is the world's tallest freestanding work of masonry. It stands at the very center of Washington, D.C.; landmarks, and the 360-degree views from the top are spectacular. Due east are the Capitol and Smithsonian buildings; due north is the White House; due west are the World War II and Lincoln Memorials (with Arlington National Cemetery beyond); due south is the Jefferson Memorial, overlooking the Tidal Basin and the Potomac River. "On a clear day, you can see west probably 60 miles, as far as the Shenandoah Mountains," says Bill Line, chief information officer for the National Park Service's National Capital Region. Like being at the center of a compass, it provides a marvelous orientation to the city.

> **Impressions**
>
> *May the spirit which animated the great founder of this city descend to future generations.*
> —John Adams

Climbing the 897 steps is not allowed, but the large elevator whisks visitors to the top in just 70 seconds. As a rule, you are not allowed to walk down the stairs of the monument. If you're absolutely dying to see more of the interior, you must contact the National Park Service at least 1 month ahead of time to arrange for a special walk-down tour. On this tour you'll learn more about the building of the monument and get to see the 193 carved stones inserted into the interior walls. The stones are gifts from foreign countries, all 50 states, organizations, and individuals. The most expensive stone was given by the state of Alaska in 1982—it's pure jade and worth millions. There are stones from Siam (now Thailand), the Cherokee Nation, and the Sons of Temperance.

Allow half an hour here, plus time spent waiting in line. Light snacks are sold at a snack bar on the grounds, where you'll also find a few picnic tables. There's limited but free 2-hour **parking** at the 16th Street Oval.

Ticket Information: Admission to the Washington Monument is free, but you'll still have to get a ticket. The ticket booth is located at the bottom of the hill from the monument, on 15th Street NW between Independence and Constitution avenues. It's open daily from 8am to 4:30pm. Tickets are usually gone by 9am, so plan to get there by 7:30 or 8am, especially in peak season. The tickets grant admission at half-hour intervals between the stated hours, on the day you visit. If you want to get them in advance, call the National Park Reservation Service (© **800/967-2283**) or go to http://reservations.nps.gov; the tickets themselves are free, but you'll pay $1.50 per ticket for shipping and handling, plus a 50¢ service charge per transaction. To make sure that you get tickets for your desired date, reserve these tickets at least 2 weeks in advance.

Directly south of the White House (at 15th St. and Constitution Ave. NW). © **202/426-6841.** Free admission. Daily 9am–5pm. Last elevators depart 15 min. before closing (arrive earlier). Closed Dec 25, open until noon July 4. Metro: Smithsonian, then a 10-min. walk.

National World War II Memorial ★★★   When this memorial was dedicated on May 29, 2004, 150,000 people turned out: President Bush; members of Congress; Marine Corps General (retired) P.X. Kelley, who chaired the American Battle Monuments Commission, the group that spearheaded construction of the memorial; actor Tom Hanks and news anchor Tom Brokaw, both of whom had been active in eliciting support for the memorial; and last but most important, thousands of World War II veterans and their families. These legions of veterans, some dressed in uniform, many wearing a cap identifying the name of the veteran's division, turned out with pride, happy to receive the nation's gratitude, 60 years in the making, expressed profoundly in this memorial.

Designed by Friedrich St. Florian and funded mostly by private donations, the memorial fits nicely into the landscape between the Washington Monument grounds to the east, and the Lincoln Memorial and its reflecting pool to the west. St. Florian purposely situated the 7½-acre memorial so as not to obstruct this long view down the Mall: Fifty-six 17-foot-high granite pillars representing each state and territory stand to either side of a central plaza and the Rainbow pool. Likewise, 24 bas-relief panels divide down the middle so that 12 line each side of the walkway leading from the entrance at 17th Street; the panels to the left, as you walk toward the center of the memorial, illustrate seminal scenes from the war years as they relate to the Pacific theater: Pearl Harbor, amphibious landing, jungle warfare, a field burial, and so on; the panels to the right are sculptured scenes of war moments related to the Atlantic theater: Rosie the Riveter, Normandy

---

Don't Worry, They're Open!

Note: Do not be alarmed or put off if you should see construction surrounding the **Washington Monument,** the **Lincoln Memorial,** or the **Jefferson Memorial.** All three sites remain open to the public 365 days a year. The Washington Monument is in the midst of installing a vehicle barrier security system, a process likely to continue into the fall of 2005; the Jefferson Memorial is also planning to install such a system. The Lincoln Memorial, itself, is not undergoing any changes, it's the roads encircling the memorial: Rock Creek Parkway, Henry Bacon Drive, 23rd Street, and the approach from the Arlington Memorial Bridge, that are being treated for maintenance purposes.

Beach landing, the Battle of the Bulge, the Russians meeting the Americans at the Elbe River. A man named Raymond Kaskey, an architect and sculptor, sculpted these panels based on archival photographs.

Large open pavilions stake out the north and south axes of the memorial, and semicircular fountains create waterfalls on either side. Inscriptions at the base of each pavilion fountain mark key battles. Beyond the center Rainbow Pool is a wall of 4,000 gold stars, one star for every 100 soldiers who died in World War II. People often leave photos and mementoes everywhere around the memorial, which the National Park Service gather up daily (the NPS is currently deciding how best to maintain an archive of these mementoes). If you are lucky, you will see World War II veterans when you visit this memorial. My husband and I saw a man of that certain age, fit looking, very tan, and alone, bend down and touch the word "Okinawa" engraved in the fountain coping at the base of the Pacific pavilion, and start to cry.

From the 17th Street entrance walk south around the perimeter of the memorial to reach a ranger station, where there are brochures and registry kiosks, the latter for looking up names of veterans. Better information and faster service is available online at www.wwiimemorial.com.

17th St. and Constitution Ave. NW. ⒸⓋ 800/639-4WW2 or 202/426-6841. www.wwiimemorial.com. Free admission. Rangers on duty daily 8am–11:45pm, except Dec 25. Metro: Farragut West, Federal Triangle, or Smithsonian.

Lincoln Memorial ★★★ *(Kids*   This beautiful and moving testament to the nation's greatest president attracts millions of visitors annually. Like its fellow presidential memorials, this one was a long time in the making. Although it was planned as early as 1867—2 years after Lincoln's death—Henry Bacon's design was not completed until 1912, and the memorial was dedicated in 1922.

The neoclassical templelike structure, similar in architectural design to the Parthenon in Greece, has 36 fluted Doric columns representing the states of the Union at the time of Lincoln's death, plus two at the entrance. On the attic parapet are 48 festoons symbolizing the number of states in 1922, when the monument was erected. Hawaii and Alaska are noted in an inscription on the terrace. Due east is the Reflecting Pool, lined with American elms and stretching 2,000 feet toward the Washington Monument and the Capitol beyond.

The memorial chamber has limestone walls inscribed with the Gettysburg Address and Lincoln's Second Inaugural Address. Two 60-foot-high murals by Jules Guerin on the north and south walls depict, allegorically, Lincoln's principles and achievements. On the south wall, an Angel of Truth freeing a slave is flanked by groups of figures representing Justice and Immortality. The north-wall mural depicts the unity of North and South and is flanked by groups of figures symbolizing Fraternity and Charity. Most powerful, however, is Daniel Chester French's 19-foot-high seated statue of Lincoln, which disappears from your sightline as you get close to the base of the memorial, then emerges slowly into view as you ascend the stairs.

Lincoln's legacy has made his memorial the site of numerous demonstrations by those seeking justice. Most notable was a peaceful demonstration of 200,000 people on August 28, 1963, at which the Rev. Dr. Martin Luther King Jr. proclaimed, "I have a dream." Look for the words "I have a dream. Martin Luther King, Jr., The March on Washington for Jobs and Freedom, August 28, 1963," inscribed and centered on the granite step, 18 steps down from the chamber. The inscription, which the National Park Service added in July 2003, marks the precise spot where King stood to deliver his famous speech.

An information booth, a small museum, and a bookstore are on the premises. Rangers present 20- to 30-minute programs as time permits throughout the day. Limited free **parking** is available along Constitution Avenue and south along Ohio Drive. Twenty to thirty minutes is sufficient time for viewing this memorial.

Directly west of the Mall in Potomac Park (at 23rd St. NW, between Constitution and Independence aves.). ℭ 202/426-6842. Free admission. Daily 8am–11:45pm. Closed Dec 25. Metro: Foggy Bottom, then a 30-min. walk.

Korean War Veterans Memorial ⭐ This privately funded memorial, founded in 1995, honors those who served in Korea, a 3-year conflict (1950–53) that produced almost as many casualties as Vietnam. It consists of a circular "Pool of Remembrance" in a grove of trees and a triangular "Field of Service," highlighted by lifelike statues of 19 infantrymen, who appear to be trudging across fields. In addition, a 164-foot-long black-granite wall depicts the array of combat and support troops that served in Korea (nurses, chaplains, airmen, gunners, mechanics, cooks, and others); a raised granite curb lists the 22 nations that contributed to the U.N.'s effort there; and a commemorative area honors KIAs, MIAs, and POWs. Plan to spend 15 minutes for viewing. Limited parking is available along Ohio Drive.

Tip: If you don't mind a walk, try to snag a **parking** spot along West Basin Drive near the FDR Memorial; the Korean War and the Vietnam War Veterans memorials, as well as the Lincoln Memorial, are then all within reach.

Just across from the Lincoln Memorial (east of French Dr., between 21st and 23rd sts. NW). ℭ 202/426-6841. Free admission. Rangers on duty daily 8am–11:45pm except Dec 25. Ranger-led interpretive programs are given throughout the day. Metro: Foggy Bottom.

Vietnam Veterans Memorial ⭐⭐ The Vietnam Veterans Memorial is possibly the most poignant sight in Washington: two long, black-granite walls in the shape of a V, each inscribed with the names of the men and women who gave their lives, or remain missing, in the longest war in American history. Even if no one close to you died in Vietnam, it's wrenching to watch visitors grimly studying the directories to find out where their loved ones are listed, or rubbing pencil on paper held against a name etched into the wall. The walls list close to 60,000 people, many of whom died very young.

Because of the raging conflict over U.S. involvement in the war, Vietnam veterans had received almost no recognition of their service before the memorial was conceived by Vietnam veteran Jan Scruggs. The nonprofit Vietnam Veterans Memorial Fund raised $7 million and secured a 2-acre site in tranquil Constitution Gardens to erect a memorial that would make no political statement about the war and would harmonize with neighboring memorials. By separating the issue of the wartime service of individuals from the issue of U.S. policy in Vietnam, the VVMF hoped to begin a process of national reconciliation.

Yale senior Maya Lin's design was chosen in a national competition open to all citizens over 18 years of age. The two walls are angled at 125° to point to the Washington Monument and the Lincoln Memorial. The wall's mirrorlike surface reflects surrounding trees, lawns, and monuments. The names are inscribed in chronological order, documenting an epoch in American history as a series of individual sacrifices from the date of the first casualty in 1959. The National Park Service continues to add names over the years, of those Vietnam veterans who die eventually of injuries sustained during the war.

The wall was erected in 1982. In 1984, a lifesize sculpture of three Vietnam soldiers by Frederick Hart was installed at the entrance plaza. Near the statue, a flag flies from a 60-foot staff. Another sculpture, the *Vietnam Veterans Women's Memorial,* which depicts three servicewomen tending a wounded soldier, was installed on Veterans Day 1993. You should allow about 20 to 30 minutes here.

The park rangers at the Vietnam Veterans Memorial are very knowledgeable and are usually milling about—be sure to seek them out if you have any questions. Limited **parking** is available along Constitution Avenue.

Just across from the Lincoln Memorial (east of Henry Bacon Dr. between 21st and 22nd sts. NW). ℂ 202/ 426-6841. Free admission. Rangers on duty daily 8am–11:45pm except Dec 25. Ranger-led programs are given throughout the day. Metro: Foggy Bottom.

Franklin Delano Roosevelt Memorial ★★★   The FDR Memorial has proven to be one of the most popular of the presidential memorials since it opened in 1997. Its popularity has to do as much with its design as the man it honors. This 7½-acre outdoor memorial stretches out, rather than rising up, across the stone-paved floor. Granite walls define the four "galleries," each representing a different term in FDR's presidency from 1933 to 1945. Architect Lawrence Halprin's design includes waterfalls, sculptures (by Leonard Baskin, John Benson, Neil Estern, Robert Graham, Thomas Hardy, and George Segal), and Roosevelt's own words carved into the stone.

One drawback of the FDR Memorial is the noise. Planes on their way to or from nearby Reagan National Airport zoom overhead, and the many displays of cascading water can sound thunderous. When the memorial first opened, adults and children alike arrived in bathing suits and splashed around on warm days. Park rangers don't allow that anymore, but they do allow you to dip your feet in the various pools. A favorite time to visit is at night, when dramatic lighting reveals the waterfalls and statues against the dark parkland.

Conceived in 1946, the FDR Memorial had been in the works for 50 years. Part of the delay in its construction can be attributed to the president himself. FDR had told his friend Supreme Court Justice Felix Frankfurter, "If they are to put up any memorial to me, I should like it to be placed in the center of that green plot in front of the Archives Building. I should like it to consist of a block about the size [of this desk]." In fact, such a plaque sits in front of the National Archives Building. Friends and relatives struggled to honor Roosevelt's request to leave it at that, but Congress and national sentiment overrode them.

As with other presidential memorials, this one opened to some controversy. Advocates for people with disabilities were incensed that the memorial sculptures did not show the president in a wheelchair, which he used after he contracted polio. President Clinton asked Congress to allocate funding for an additional statue portraying a wheelchair-bound FDR. You will now see a small statue of FDR in a wheelchair, placed at the very front of the memorial, to the right. Step inside the gift shop to view a replica of Roosevelt's wheelchair, as well as one of the rare photographs of the president sitting in a wheelchair. The memorial is probably the most accessible tourist attraction in the city; as at most of the National Park Service locations, wheelchairs are available for free use on-site.

If you don't see a posting of tour times, look for a ranger and request a tour; the rangers are happy to oblige. Thirty minutes is sufficient time to allot here.

In West Potomac Park, about midway between the Lincoln and Jefferson memorials, on the west shore of the Tidal Basin. ℂ 202/426-6841. Free admission. Ranger staff on duty daily 8am–11:45pm. Closed Dec 25. Free parking along W. Basin and Ohio drives. Metro: Smithsonian, with a 30-min. walk; or take the Tourmobile.

George Mason Memorial ★   This memorial honors George Mason, author of the Virginia Declaration of Rights, which had much to do with the establishment of our national Bill of Rights. Dedicated on April 9, 2002, the memorial consists of a bronze statue of Mason, set back in a landscaped grove of trees and flower beds (lots and lots of pansies), arranged in concentric circles around a pool and fountain. Mason appears in 18th-century garb, from buckled shoes to tricorn hat, seated on a marble bench, but leaning backward on one arm and gazing off in the general direction of the Washington Monument. Two stone slabs are inscribed with some of Mason's words, like these, referring to Mason's rejection of slavery, "that slow Poison, which is daily contaminating the Minds & Morals of our People." Wooden benches at the site present a pleasant opportunity to learn about Mason, and take a break, before moving on.

In West Potomac Park, on Ohio Dr. at the Tidal Basin, between the Jefferson and FDR memorials. © 202/426 -6841. Free. Always open, though rangers generally are not posted here. To find out more about George Mason, visit the Jefferson Memorial, a 5-min. walk around the Tidal Basin, where park rangers are on duty 8am–11:45pm. Closed Dec 25. Free parking along W. Basin and Ohio drives. Metro: Smithsonian, with a 2- to 3-min. walk; or take the Tourmobile.

Jefferson Memorial ★★

President John F. Kennedy, at a 1962 dinner honoring 29 Nobel Prize winners, told his guests that they were "the most extraordinary collection of talent, of human knowledge, that has ever been gathered together at the White House, with the possible exception of when Thomas Jefferson dined alone." Jefferson penned the Declaration of Independence and served as George Washington's secretary of state, John Adams's vice president, and America's third president. He spoke out against slavery, although, like many of his countrymen, he kept slaves himself. In addition, he established the University of Virginia and pursued wide-ranging interests, including architecture, astronomy, anthropology, music, and farming.

The site for the Jefferson Memorial was of extraordinary importance. The Capitol, the White House, and the Mall were already located in accordance with architect Pierre L'Enfant's master plan for the city, but there was no spot for such a project that would maintain L'Enfant's symmetry. So the memorial was built on land reclaimed from the Potomac River, now known as the Tidal Basin. Franklin Delano Roosevelt, who laid the cornerstone in 1939, had all the trees between the Jefferson Memorial and the White House cut down so that he could see the memorial every morning.

The memorial is a columned rotunda in the style of the Pantheon in Rome, whose classical architecture Jefferson himself introduced to this country (he designed his home, Monticello, and the earliest University of Virginia buildings in Charlottesville). On the Tidal Basin side, the sculptural group above the entrance depicts Jefferson with Benjamin Franklin, John Adams, Roger Sherman, and Robert Livingston, all of whom worked on drafting the Declaration of Independence. The domed interior of the memorial contains the 19-foot bronze statue of Jefferson standing on a 6-foot pedestal of black Minnesota granite. The sculpture is the work of Rudolph Evans, who was chosen from more than 100 artists in a nationwide competition. Jefferson is depicted wearing a fur-collared coat given to him by his close friend, the Polish general Tadeusz Kosciuszko.

Rangers present 20- to 30-minute programs throughout the day as time permits. Twenty to thirty minutes is sufficient time to spend here.

Spring through fall, a refreshment kiosk at the Tourmobile stop offers snacks. A gift shop, a small museum, and a bookstore are located on the bottom floor of the memorial. There's free 1-hour **parking.**

South of the Washington Monument on Ohio Dr. SW (at the south shore of the Tidal Basin). © 202/ 426-6841. Free admission. Daily 8am–11:45pm. Closed Dec 25. Metro: Smithsonian, with a 20- to 30-min. walk; or take the Tourmobile.

Tips **Parking Near the Mall**

First of all: Don't drive. Use the Metro. But if you're hell-bent on driving on a weekday, set out early to nab one of the Independence or Constitution avenues spots that become legal at 9:30am, when rush hour ends. Arrive about 9:15am and sit in your car until 9:30am (to avoid getting a ticket), then hop out and stoke the meter. So many people do this that if you arrive after 9:30am, you'll find most of the street parking spots gone.

3 The Smithsonian Museums

Wealthy English scientist James Smithson (1765–1829), the illegitimate son of the duke of Northumberland, never explained why he willed his vast fortune to the United States, a country he had never visited. Speculation is that he felt the new nation, lacking established cultural institutions, most needed his bequest. Smithson died in Genoa, Italy, in 1829. Congress accepted his gift in 1836; 2 years later, half a million dollars worth of gold sovereigns (a considerable sum in the 19th century) arrived at the U.S. Mint in Philadelphia. For the next 8 years, Congress debated the best possible use for these funds. Finally, in 1846, James Polk signed an act into law establishing the Smithsonian Institution and authorizing a board to receive "all objects of art and of foreign and curious research, and all objects of natural history, plants, and geological and mineralogical specimens . . . for research and museum purposes."

Since then, private donations have swelled Smithson's original legacy many times over. Although the Smithsonian acquires approximately 70% of its yearly budget from congressional allocations, the institution depends quite heavily on these monies from private donors. Lately, the Smithsonian's pursuit of contributions has been criticized by people both within (some longtime Smithsonian curators and directors have resigned) and without the organization, who fear that donors are given too much say in curatorial matters, that important research is underfunded, and that the institution itself is being crassly commercialized as its new wings and exhibits open bearing the names of the companies and individuals who have paid for them. Stay tuned.

The Smithsonian's collection of nearly 142 million objects spans the entire world and all of its history, its peoples and animals (past and present), and our attempts to probe into the future. The sprawling institution comprises 14 museums (the opening of the National Museum of the American Indian this year brings that number to 15, with 10 of them on the Mall; see "The Mall" map on p. 181), as well as the National Zoological Park in Washington, D.C. (there are two additional museums in New York City). Still, the Smithsonian's collection is so vast that its museums display only about 1% or 2% of the collection's holdings at any given time. Its holdings, in every area of human interest, range from a 3.5-billion-year-old fossil to part of a 1902 Horn & Hardart Automat. Thousands of scientific expeditions sponsored by the Smithsonian have pushed into remote frontiers in the deserts, mountains, polar regions, and jungles.

To find out information about any of the Smithsonian museums, you call the same number: ℂ **202/357-2700** or TTY 202/357-1729. The information specialists who answer are very professional and always helpful. The Smithsonian museums also share the same website, **www.si.edu**, which will help get you to their individual home pages.

Smithsonian Information Center (the "Castle") Make this your first stop, and enter through the Enid A. Haupt Garden (see description further along, in the "Parks & Gardens" section), for a pleasurable experience. Built in 1855, this Norman-style red-sandstone building, popularly known as the "Castle," is the oldest building on the Mall, yet it holds the impressively high-tech and comprehensive Smithsonian Information Center.

The main information area here is the Great Hall, where a 24-minute video overview of the institution runs throughout the day in two theaters. There are two large schematic models of the Mall (as well as a third in Braille), and two large electronic maps of Washington allow visitors to locate nearly 100 popular attractions and Metro and Tourmobile stops. Interactive videos, some at children's heights, offer extensive information about the Smithsonian and other capital attractions and transportation (the menus seem infinite).

The entire facility is accessible to persons with disabilities and information is available in a number of foreign languages. Daily Smithsonian events appear on monitors; in addition, the information desk's volunteer staff can answer questions and help you plan a Smithsonian sightseeing itinerary. Most of the museums are within easy walking distance of the facility.

While you're here, notice the charming vestibule, which has been restored to its turn-of-the-20th-century appearance. It was originally designed to display exhibits at a child's eye level. The gold-trimmed ceiling is decorated to represent a grape arbor with brightly plumed birds and blue sky peeking through the trellis. This is also where the Seattle's Best Coffee kiosk is located, so why not grab a cuppa and a muffin and your guidebook and maps and settle yourself outside on a bench in the Enid A. Haupt Garden and plan your day.

On Sundays, the Castle serves an extensive brunch in its Commons room, from 11am to 2pm, for $33 per adult, $16 for children 12 and under; call ℂ **202/ 371-1083** to make a reservation.

1000 Jefferson Dr. SW. ℂ **202/633-1000.** Daily 8:30am–5:30pm, info desk 9am–4pm. Closed Dec 25. Metro: Smithsonian.

Anacostia Museum and Center for African-American History and Culture
This museum is inconveniently located, but that's because it was initially created in 1967 as a neighborhood museum (which makes it unique among the Smithsonian branches). It's devoted to the African-American experience, focusing on Washington, D.C., and the Upper South. The permanent collection includes about 7,000 items, ranging from videotapes of African-American church services to art, sheet music, historic documents, textiles, glassware, and anthropological objects. In addition, the Anacostia produces a number of shows each year and offers a comprehensive schedule of free educational programs and activities in conjunction with exhibit themes. Allow about an hour here.

1901 Fort Place SE (off Martin Luther King Jr. Ave.). ℂ **202/287-3306.** www.si.edu/anacostia. Free admission. Daily 10am–5pm. Closed Dec 25. Metro: Anacostia, head to the exit marked "Local," turn left after exiting, then take a W2 or W3 bus directly to the museum.

> **Tips Information, Please**
>
> If you want to know what's happening at any of the Smithsonian museums, just get on the phone. **Dial-a-Museum** (ℂ **202/357-2020,** or 202/633-9126 for Spanish), a recorded information line, lists daily activities and special events. For other information, call ℂ 202/357-2700.

Arthur M. Sackler Gallery ⭐ Asian art is the focus of this museum and the neighboring Freer (together, they form the National Museum of Asian Art in the United States). The Sackler opened in 1987, thanks to a gift from Arthur M. Sackler of 1,000 priceless works. Since then, the museum has received 11th- to 19th-century Persian and Indian paintings, manuscripts, calligraphies, miniatures, and book-bindings from the collection of Henri Vever. In spring 2003, art collector Robert O. Muller bequeathed the museum his entire collection of 4,000 Japanese prints and archival materials.

The Sackler's permanent collection displays Khmer ceramics; ancient Chinese jades, bronzes, paintings, and lacquerware; 20th-century Japanese ceramics and works on paper; ancient Near Eastern works in silver, gold, bronze, and clay; and stone and bronze sculptures from South and Southeast Asia. With the addition of Muller's bequest, the Sackler now has a sumptuous graphic arts inventory, covering a century of work by Japanese master printmakers. Supplementing the permanent collection are traveling exhibitions from major cultural institutions in Asia, Europe, and the United States. In the past, these have included such wide-ranging areas as 15th-century Persian art and culture, photographs of Asia, and art highlighting personal devotion in India. A visit here is an education in Asian decorative arts, but also in antiquities.

To learn more, arrive in time for a highlights tour, offered daily, except Wednesday, at 12:15pm. Also enlightening, and more fun, are the public programs that both the Sackler and the Freer Gallery frequently stage, such as performances of contemporary Asian music, tea ceremony demonstrations, and Iranian film screenings. All are free, but you might need tickets; for details, call the main information number or check out the website. Allow at least an hour to tour the Sackler.

The Sackler is part of a museum complex that houses the National Museum of African Art. It shares its staff and research facilities with the adjacent Freer Gallery, to which it is connected via an underground exhibition space.

1050 Independence Ave. SW. ℂ 202/633-4880. www.asia.si.edu. Free admission. Daily 10am–5:30pm; in summer, museum often stays open Thurs until 8pm, but call to confirm. Closed Dec 25. Metro: Smithsonian.

Arts and Industries Building *Kids* The building is closed for (no reopening date given at press time) an extensive renovation, though its children's theater remains open (read below). Completed in 1881 as the first U.S. National Museum, this redbrick and sandstone structure was the scene of President Garfield's Inaugural Ball. (It looks quite similar to the Castle, so don't be confused; from the Mall, the Arts and Industries Building is the one on the left.) From 1976 through the mid-1990s, it housed exhibits from the 1876 U.S. International Exposition in Philadelphia—a celebration of America's centennial that featured the latest advances in technology.

Singers, dancers, puppeteers, and mimes perform in the **Discovery Theater** (open all year except Aug, with performances weekdays and on selected Sat). Call ℂ **202/357-1500** for show times and ticket information; admission of about $5 is charged.

Weather permitting, a 19th-century **carousel** operates across the street, on the Mall.

900 Jefferson Dr. SW (on the south side of the Mall). www.si.edu/ai. Free admission. Daily 10am–5:30pm. Closed Dec 25. Metro: Smithsonian.

Freer Gallery of Art ⭐ Charles Lang Freer, a collector of Asian and American art from the 19th and early 20th centuries, gave the nation 9,000 of these

---

(*Fun Fact* Freeze Frame

About 90% of the American works in the Freer are in their original frames, many of them designed by architect Stanford White or painter James McNeill Whistler.

---

works for his namesake gallery's 1923 opening. Freer's original interest was American art, but his good friend James McNeill Whistler encouraged him to collect Asian works as well. Eventually the latter became predominant. Freer's gift included funds to construct a museum and an endowment to add to the Asian collection, which now numbers more than 28,000 objects. It includes Chinese and Japanese sculpture, lacquer, metalwork, and ceramics; early Christian illuminated manuscripts; Iranian manuscripts, metalwork, and miniatures; ancient Near Eastern metalware; and South Asian sculpture and paintings.

The Freer is mostly about Asian art, but it also displays some of the more than 1,200 American works (the world's largest collection) by **Whistler.** Most remarkable and always on view is the famous **Peacock Room.** Originally a dining room designed for the London mansion of F. R. Leyland, the Peacock Room displayed a Whistler painting called *The Princess from the Land of Porcelain.* But after his painting was installed, Whistler was dissatisfied with the room as a setting for his work. When Leyland was away from home, Whistler painted over the very expensive leather interior and embellished it with paintings of golden peacock feathers. Not surprisingly, a rift ensued between Whistler and Leyland. After Leyland's death, Freer purchased the room, painting and all, and had it shipped to his home in Detroit. It is now permanently installed here. Other American painters represented in the collections are Thomas Wilmer Dewing, Dwight William Tryon, Abbott Henderson Thayer, John Singer Sargent, and Childe Hassam. All in all, you could spend a happy 1 to 2 hours here.

Housed in a grand granite-and-marble building that evokes the Italian Renaissance, the pristine Freer has lovely skylit galleries. The main exhibit floor centers on an open-roof garden court. An underground exhibit space connects the Freer to the neighboring Sackler Gallery, and both museums share the **Meyer Auditorium,** which is used for free chamber-music concerts, dance performances, Asian feature films, and other programs. Inquire about these, as well as children's activities and free tours given daily, at the information desk.

On the south side of the Mall (at 1050 Independence Ave. SW). (202/633-4880. www.asia.si.edu. Free admission. Daily 10am–5:30pm; in summer, gallery often stays open Thurs until 8pm, but call to confirm. Closed Dec 25. Metro: Smithsonian.

Hirshhorn Museum and Sculpture Garden ⭐ This museum of modern and contemporary art is named after Latvian-born Joseph H. Hirshhorn, who, in 1966, donated his vast collection—more than 4,000 drawings and paintings and 2,000 pieces of sculpture—to the United States "as a small repayment for what this nation has done for me and others like me who arrived here as immigrants." At his death in 1981, Hirshhorn bequeathed an additional 5,500 artworks to the museum, and numerous other donors have greatly expanded his legacy.

Constructed 14 feet above ground on sculptured supports, the doughnut-shaped concrete-and-granite building shelters a verdant plaza courtyard where sculpture is displayed. The light and airy interior follows a circular route that makes it easy to see every exhibit without getting lost in a honeycomb of galleries.

Natural light from floor-to-ceiling windows makes the inner galleries the perfect venue for viewing sculpture—second only to the beautiful tree-shaded sunken **Sculpture Garden** ✦ across the street (don't miss it). Paintings and drawings are installed in the outer galleries, along with intermittent sculpture groupings.

A rotating show of about 600 pieces is on view at all times. The collection features just about every well-known 20th-century artist and touches on most of the major trends in Western art since the late 19th century, with particular emphasis on our contemporary period. Among the best-known pieces are Rodin's *Monument to the Burghers of Calais* (in the Sculpture Garden), Hopper's *First Row Orchestra*, de Kooning's *Two Women in the Country*, and Warhol's *Marilyn Monroe's Lips*.

Pick up a free calendar when you enter to find out about free films, lectures, concerts, and temporary exhibits. An outdoor cafe is open during the summer. Free tours of the collection and the Sculpture Garden are given daily; call for information about them.

On the south side of the Mall (at Independence Ave. and 7th St. SW). ℂ **202/633-4674.** http://hirshhorn. si.edu. Free admission. Museum daily 10am–5:30pm; in summer museum often stays open Thurs until 8pm, but call to confirm. Sculpture Garden daily 7:30am–dusk. Closed Dec 25. Metro: L'Enfant Plaza (Smithsonian Museums/Maryland Ave. or Smithsonian exit).

National Air and Space Museum ✦✦ *Kids*   With the opening of the Steven F. Udvar-Hazy Center in December 2003, the National Air and Space Museum now bills itself, "One museum, two locations." It's not realistic, however, to visit both museums in one day: The flagship museum on the National Mall consumes 2 or 3 hours—longer, if you attend an IMAX film or planetarium show; the round trip to the satellite Udvar-Hazy Center, located on the grounds of Washington-Dulles International Airport, takes about 2 hours; and the touring of that museum another 2 or 3 hours. You could do it, but you'd be frantic.

So start with this one, the original, ever-popular Air and Space Museum on the Mall. This museum chronicles the story of the mastery of flight, from Kitty Hawk to outer space. It holds the largest collection of historic aircraft and spacecraft in the world—so many, in fact, that the museum is able to display only about 20% of its artifacts at any one time, hence the opening of the Udvar-Hazy Center.

During the tourist season and on holidays, arrive before 10am to make a beeline for the film ticket line when the doors open. The not-to-be-missed **IMAX films** ✦ shown here are immensely popular, and tickets to most shows sell out quickly. You can purchase tickets up to 2 weeks in advance, but they are available only at the Lockheed Martin IMAX Theater box office on the first floor. Two or more films play each day, most with aeronautical or space-exploration themes; *To Fly* and *Space Station 3D* are two that should continue into 2005. Tickets cost $8 for adults, $6.50 for ages 2 to 12 and 55 or older; they're free for children under 2. You can also see IMAX films most evenings after the museum's closing; call for details (ℂ **202/357-1686**).

You'll also need tickets to attend a show at the **Albert Einstein Planetarium** ✦, which creates "an astronomical adventure" as projectors display blended space imagery upon a 70-foot diameter dome, making you feel as if you're traveling in 3-D through the cosmos. The planetarium's main feature, called "Infinity Express, A 20-Minute Tour of the Universe," gives you the sensation that you are zooming through the solar system, as it explores such questions as "how big is the universe?" and "where does it end?" Tickets are $8 for adults, $6.50 for ages 2 to 12 and 55 or older; you can buy an IMAX film and planetarium combo ticket for $13 per adult, $11 per child.

How Things Fly, a gallery that opened in 1996 to celebrate the museum's 20th anniversary, includes wind and smoke tunnels, a boardable Cessna 150 airplane, and dozens of interactive exhibits that demonstrate principles of flight, aerodynamics, and propulsion. All the aircraft, by the way, are originals.

Kids love the walk-through **Skylab orbital workshop** on the first floor. Other galleries here highlight the solar system, U.S. manned space flights, sea-air operations, and aviation during both world wars. An important exhibit is **Beyond the Limits: Flight Enters the Computer Age,** illustrating the primary applications of computer technology to aerospace. **Explore the Universe** presents the major discoveries that have shaped the current scientific view of the universe; it illustrates how the universe is taking shape, and probes the mysteries that remain. In 2002, the museum added a set of six, two-seat **Flight Simulators** to its first floor galleries (the Udvar-Hazy Center has several more), allowing visitors to climb aboard and use a joystick to pilot an aircraft. For 3 minutes you truly feel as if you are in the cockpit and airborne, maneuvering your craft up, down, and upside-down on a wild adventure, thanks to virtual reality images and high-tech sounds. You must pay $6.50 to enjoy the ride and measure at least 48 inches to go it alone; children under 48 inches must measure at least 42 inches and be accompanied by an adult.

The museum's cafeteria, The Wright Place, offers food from three popular American chains: McDonald's, Boston Chicken, and Donato's Pizza. Best of all, the cafeteria serves up a great view of the Capitol.

Now, to get to the Steven F. Udvar-Hazy Center, you can drive (call © 202/786-2122 for directions, or go to the website, www.nasm.si.edu.), or you can take a shuttle bus from the Air and Space Museum on the Mall. The shuttles run six times a day from both locations, at the same times, starting at 9am with the last shuttle departing at 5pm. You must purchase tickets to take the shuttle, which are sold at the IMAX film box office, for $7 round-trip per person. To purchase shuttle bus tickets in advance, call © 202/633-4629. If you drive to the center, you should be aware that parking is a whopping $12, due to the fact that the center lies on airport property.

At the Udvar-Hazy Center, you'll find two hangars, one for aviation artifacts, the other for space artifacts, and an observation tower for watching planes leave and arrive at Dulles Airport. Eventually, the gallery will hold more than 200 aircraft and 135 spacecraft. The center will also serve as the Air and Space Museum's primary restoration facility, and the public will be able to watch specialists at work. This location also shows IMAX films.

On the south side of the Mall (at 7th and Independence Ave. SW), with entrances on Jefferson Dr. or Independence Ave. © **202/357-2700 (for both locations),** or 202/357-1686 for IMAX ticket information. www.nasm.si.edu. Free admission. Both locations daily 10am–5:30pm. The mall museum often opens at 9am in summer, but call to confirm. Free 1½-hr. highlight tours daily at 10:15am and 1pm. Closed Dec 25. Metro: L'Enfant Plaza (Smithsonian Museums/Maryland Ave. exit) or Smithsonian. The Udvar-Hazy Center is located at 14390 Air and Space Museum Parkway, Chantilly, VA.

National Museum of African Art ⭐ Founded in 1964, and part of the Smithsonian since 1979, the National Museum of African Art moved to the Mall in 1987 to share a subterranean space with the Sackler Gallery (see above) and the Ripley Center. Its aboveground domed pavilions reflect the arch motif of the neighboring Freer Gallery of Art (see above).

Museum Exhibits Scheduled for 2005

The following listing, though hardly comprehensive, is enough to give you an idea about upcoming or current exhibits at major Washington museums. Because schedules sometimes change, it's always a good idea to call ahead. See individual entries in this chapter for phone numbers and addresses.

Corcoran Gallery of Art   "Shomei Tomatsu: After the War" (mid-May to Sept 2005) is a retrospective, mostly from the artist's own collection, and including two hundred black and white photos executed over 30 years, grouped into categories such as "A-Bomb" and "Japan as It Was Before."

Freer Gallery   "The Divine Body in Indian Art" (Oct 16, 2004–June 12, 2005) examines the sculpted body, both divine and human, as illustrated in Jainism, Buddhism, and Hinduism.

Hirshhorn Museum and Sculpture Garden   "Visual Music, 1905-2005" (June 23–Sept 11, 2005). This exhibit explores the impact of music on visual arts and how it influences media art, and visual culture.

National Air and Space Museum   "The Wright Brothers and The Invention of the Aerial Age" (Oct 11, 2003–into 2005), celebrates the 100th anniversary of powered flight. The Wright Brothers' 1903 Wright Flyer is displayed at street level, and the exhibit includes 250 photographs and 150 artifacts related to the lives of the brothers.

National Gallery of Art   "Palace and Mosque, Islamic Art from the Victoria and Albert Museum" (July 18, 2004–Feb 6, 2005). From the London museum with one of the most renowned Islamic art collections, this

The museum collects and exhibits ancient and contemporary art from the entire African continent, but its permanent collection of more than 7,000 objects (shown in rotating exhibits) highlights the traditional arts of the vast sub-Saharan region. Most of the collection dates from the 19th and 20th centuries. Also among the museum's holdings are the *Eliot Elisofon Photographic Archives,* comprising 300,000 photographic prints and transparencies and 120,000 feet of film on African arts and culture. Permanent exhibits include *The Ancient West African City of Benin, a.d. 1300–1897* (cast-metal heads, figures, and architectural plaques that depict kings and attendants); *The Ancient Nubian City of Kerma, 2500–1500 b.c.* (ceramics, jewelry, and ivory animals); *The Art of the Personal Object* (everyday items such as chairs, headrests, snuffboxes, bowls, and baskets); and *Images of Power and Identity* (masks, sculptures and other visual arts from Africa, south of the Sahara).

Inquire at the desk about special exhibits, workshops (including excellent children's programs), storytelling, lectures, docent-led tours, films, and demonstrations. A comprehensive events schedule provides a unique opportunity to learn about the diverse cultures and visual traditions of Africa. Plan on spending a minimum of 30 minutes here.

950 Independence Ave. SW. ☎ **202/357-4600.** www.nmafa.si.edu. Free admission. Daily 10am–5:30pm. Closed Dec 25. Metro: Smithsonian.

exhibit presents 100 works, including Islamic art created for Christian churches. Many of these works have not been exhibited outside the Victoria and Albert Museum.

National Museum of American History   "Taking America to Lunch" (Apr 13, 2004–indefinitely) celebrates the history and endurance of American lunch boxes in this display of 75, created between the 1890s and the 1980s.

Phillips Collection   "Calder Miro: A New Space for the Imagination" (Oct 9, 2004–Jan 23, 2005). Alexander Calder's mobiles are paired with Joan Miro's paintings, to illuminate the works of these two artists, who were also friends.

Renwick Gallery   "High Fiber" (Mar 11–Jul 10, 2005) explores how materials such as metal, plastic, clay, glass, and wood are handled in ways that are commonly used with natural fibers. Everything from quilts to baskets to wallpieces.

Sackler Gallery   "Asian Games: The Art of Contest" (Feb 26–May 15, 2005) exhibits paraphernalia of games and paintings, prints and decorative arts that show people playing games. Also, the exhibit explores the role of games as social and cultural activities in pre-modern Asia.

U.S. Holocaust Memorial Museum   "Deadly Medicine: Creating the Master Race" (Apr 22, 2004–Oct 16, 2005) assembles objects, photographs, documents, and historic film footage from European and American collections, in settings evoking medical and scientific environments.

National Museum of American History ★★★ *Kids*   Well, you could spend days in here (okay, just plan on a few hours). This museum and its neighbor, the National Museum of Natural History, are the behemoths of the Smithsonian, each filled to the gills with artifacts. American History deals with "everyday life in the American past" and the external forces that have helped to shape our national character. It's all very interesting, but since you do have a life to lead, consider this approach to touring.

Start at the top, that is, the third floor, where **The American Presidency** exhibit explores the power and meaning of the presidency by studying those who have held the position. (There's a gift shop just for this exhibit on this floor.) Continue on this floor to an exhibit new to the museum, as of Veterans Day, 2004. Called **The Price of Freedom: Americans at War,** the exhibit examines major American military events and explores the idea that America's armed forces reflect American society. Among the items on display here are George Washington's commission from Congress as commander-in-chief of the Continental Army, and the uniform jacket that Andrew Jackson wore during the Battle of New Orleans in the War of 1812.

Head downstairs to the second floor for the intriguing opportunity of viewing the huge **original Star-Spangled Banner** ★★★, whose 30-by-34-foot expanse has just been painstakingly conserved by expert textile conservators.

This is the very flag that inspired Francis Scott Key to write the poem that eventually became the U.S. national anthem in 1931. Conservation work was completed in August 2004 and now the flag remains on view and outstretched, flat, behind glass, in its specially designed conservation lab.

One of the most popular exhibits on the second floor is **First Ladies: Political Role and Public Image,** which displays the first ladies' gowns and tells you a bit about each of these women. Infinitely more interesting, I think, is the neighboring exhibit, **From Parlor to Politics: Women and Reform in America, 1890–1925,** which chronicles the changing roles of women as they've moved from domestic to political and professional pursuits. Following that, find the exhibit called **Within These Walls . . . ,** which interprets the rich history of America by tracing the lives of the people who lived in this 200-year-old house, transplanted from Ipswich, MA. If this personal approach to history appeals to you, continue on to **Field to Factory,** which tells the story of African-American migration from the South between 1915 and 1940.

Finally, you're ready to hit the first floor, where some exhibits explore the development of farm and power machinery, and timekeeping. A temporary exhibit that opened in August 2002 and ends its popular run in September 2005 is *Bon Appétit!* **Julia Child's Kitchen at the Smithsonian,** a presentation of the famous chef's actual kitchen from her home in Cambridge, Massachusetts. When she moved to California in late 2001, Child donated her kitchen and all that it contained (1,200 items in all) to the museum. Most of these are on display, vegetable peeler to kitchen sink. Also look here for **America on the Move,** which details the story of transportation in America since 1876.

Wind up your visit at the **Palm Court,** where you can stop and have gelato and a sub from Subway restaurant; the Palm Court includes the interior of Georgetown's Stohlman's Confectionery Shop as it appeared around 1900, and part of an actual 1902 Horn & Hardart Automat.

The museum holds many other major exhibits. Inquire at the information desk about highlight tours, films, lectures, concerts, and hands-on activities for children and adults. The museum has four gift shops, and its main one is vast— it's the second largest of the Smithsonian shops (the largest is the one at the National Air and Space Museum).

On the north side of the Mall (between 12th and 14th sts. NW), with entrances on Constitution Ave. and Madison Dr. ✆ 202/357-2700. www.americanhistory.si.edu. Free admission. Daily 10am–5:30pm. Closed Dec 25. Metro: Smithsonian or Federal Triangle.

National Museum of the American Indian ⭐⭐⭐ *(Kids)* Though this museum had not opened at the time of my research, I knew I must include mention of it, for it promises to be a staggeringly handsome and supremely fascinating museum. Consider its exterior: Its burnt sand-colored exterior of kasota limestone wraps around the undulating walls of the museum, making the five-story building a standout among the many white-stone structures on the National Mall. Its interior design incorporates themes of nature and astronomy. For instance, the Potomac (a Piscataway word meaning "where the goods are brought in") is a rotunda that serves as the museum's main gathering place; it is also "the heart of the museum, the sun of its universe" (as noted in the museum's literature). Measuring 120 feet in diameter, with an atrium rising 120 feet to the top of the dome overhead, the Potomac is the central entryway into the museum, a venue for performances, and a hall filled with celestial references, from the equinoxes and solstices mapped on the floor beneath your feet to the sights of sky visible through the oculus in the dome above your head.

The National Museum of the American Indian is very much a "living" museum then, with performances, events, and exhibits that aim at giving Native peoples the chance to tell their own stories. Exhibits explore Native life and history and specific themes, and showcase works of individual artists. Most importantly, the museum is a giant display case for a collection of precious objects representing 1,000 Native communities. A wealthy New Yorker named George Gustav Heyer (1874–1957) assembled the collection of these 800,000 pieces, including wood and stone carvings, masks, pottery, feather bonnets, and so on; the museum displays about 8,000 of these at any given time.

Anticipating that many people will want to visit this museum, the Smithsonian Institution established a same day/timed pass admission procedure. You should arrive no later than 10am to stand in line to obtain a pass, which will be printed with the time you will be able to enter the museum. Your pass is free, but if you want to order yours in advance you can call ② 866/400-6624, or go online to www.tickets.com, to order tickets (the ticket agency, and not the museum, charges you a nominal fee for the service). The National Museum of the American Indian officially opened on September 21, 2004, taking 5 years and $219 million to construct. The museum has two gift shops and a restaurant."

4th St. and Independence Ave. SW. ② 202/633-1000. www.nmai.si.edu. Free admission. Daily 10am–5:30pm. Closed Dec 25. Metro: Federal Center Southwest or L'Enfant Plaza.

National Museum of Natural History ★★ *Kids*   Before you step inside the museum, stop outside first, on the 9th Street side of the building, to visit the **butterfly garden.** Four habitats—wetland, meadow, wood's edge, and urban garden—are on view, designed to beckon butterflies and visitors alike. The garden is at its best in warm weather, but it's open year-round.

Now go inside. Children refer to this Smithsonian showcase as "the dinosaur museum," since there's a dinosaur hall, or sometimes "the elephant museum," since a huge African bush elephant is the first thing you see if you enter from the Mall. Whatever you call it, the National Museum of Natural History is the largest of its kind in the world, and one of the most visited museums in Washington. It contains more than 124 million artifacts and specimens, everything from Ice Age mammoths to the legendary Hope Diamond. The same warning applies here as at the National Museum of American History: You're going to suffer artifact overload, so take a reasoned approach to sightseeing.

If you have children, you might want to make your first stop the first-floor **Discovery Room,** which is filled with creative hands-on exhibits "for children of all ages." Call ahead or inquire at the information desk about hours. Also popular among little kids is the second floor's **O. Orkin Insect Zoo** ★, where they enjoy looking at tarantulas, centipedes, and the like, and crawling through a model of an African termite mound. The Natural History museum, like its sister Smithsonian museums, is struggling to overhaul and modernize its exhibits, some of which are quite dated in appearance, if not in the facts presented. So a renovation of the gems and minerals hall has made the **Janet Annenberg Hooker Hall of Geology, Gems, and Minerals** ★★ worth a stop. You can learn all you want about earth science, from volcanology to the importance of mining. Interactive computers, animated graphics, and a multimedia presentation of the "big picture" story of the earth are some of the things that have moved the exhibit and the museum a bit further into the 21st century.

The **Kenneth E. Behring Hall of Mammals** is an example of an updated section of the museum. Here, visitors can operate interactive dioramas that explain how mammals evolved and adapted to changes in habitat and climate over the course of millions of years. At least 274 models of mammals and a dozen fossils are on display. This exhibit represents the first time the mammal hall has been updated since 1963. Also, don't miss **African Voices Hall,** which presents the people, cultures, and lives of Africa, through photos, videos, and more than 400 objects.

Other Rotunda-level displays include the **fossil collection,** which traces evolution back billions of years and includes a 3.5-billion-year-old stromatolite (blue-green algae clump) fossil—one of the earliest signs of life on Earth—and a 70-million-year-old dinosaur egg. **Life in the Ancient Seas** features a 100-foot-long mural depicting primitive whales, a life-size walk-around diorama of a 230-million-year-old coral reef, and more than 2,000 fossils that chronicle the evolution of marine life. The **Dinosaur Hall** displays giant skeletons of creatures that dominated the earth for 140 million years before their extinction about 65 million years ago. Suspended from the ceiling over Dinosaur Hall are replicas of ancient birds, including a life-size model of the pterosaur, which had a 40-foot wingspan. Also residing above this hall is the jaw of an ancient shark, the *Carcharodon megalodon,* which lived in the oceans 5 million years ago. A monstrous 40-foot-long predator, with teeth 5 to 6 inches long, it could have consumed a Volkswagen Bug in one gulp. In an effort to update this exhibit, the museum in 2001 mounted a digital triceratops (that is, a computerized rendering of that dinosaur); you can manipulate the image to learn more about it.

Don't miss the **Discovery Center,** funded by the Discovery Channel, featuring the Johnson **IMAX theater** with a six-story-high screen for 2-D and 3-D movies (*T-Rex: Back to the Cretaceous* was among those shown in 2004), a six-story Atrium Cafe with a food court, and expanded museum shops. The museum also offers the small **Fossil Café,** located within the dinosaur exhibit on the first floor. In this 50-seat cafe, the tables' clear plastic tops are actually fossil cases that present fossilized plants and insects for your inspection as you munch away on smoked turkey sandwiches, goat cheese quiche, and the like.

The theater box office is on the first floor of the museum; purchase tickets as early as possible, or at least 30 minutes before the screening. The box office is open daily from 9:45am through the last show. Films are shown continuously throughout the day. Ticket prices are $8 for adults and $6.50 for children (2–12) and seniors 55 or older. On Friday nights from 6 to 10pm, the theater stages live jazz nights, starring excellent local musicians ($5 cover).

On the north side of the Mall (at 10th St. and Constitution Ave. NW), with entrances on Madison Dr. and Constitution Ave. ⓒ **202/357-2700,** or 202/633-4629 for information about IMAX films. www.mnh.si.edu. Free admission. Daily 10am–5:30pm. In summer the museum often stays open until 8pm, but call to confirm. Closed Dec 25. Free highlight tours Mon–Thurs 10:30am and 1:30pm, Fri 10:30am. Metro: Smithsonian or Federal Triangle.

National Postal Museum ⍟ This museum is, somewhat surprisingly, a hit, a pleasant hour spent for the whole family. Bring your address book and you can send postcards to the folks back home through an interactive exhibit that issues a cool postcard and stamps it. That's just one feature that makes this museum visitor-friendly. Many of its exhibits involve easy-to-understand activities, like postal-themed video games.

The museum documents America's postal history from 1673 (about 170 years before the advent of stamps, envelopes, and mailboxes) to the present. (Did you know that a dog sled was used to carry mail in Alaska until 1963, when it was replaced by an airplane?) In the central gallery, titled **Moving the Mail,** three planes that carried mail in the early decades of the 20th century are suspended from a 90-foot atrium ceiling. Here, too, are a railway mail car, an 1851 mail/passenger coach, a Ford Model-A mail truck, and a replica of an airmail beacon tower. In **Binding the Nation,** historic correspondence illustrates how mail kept families together in the developing nation. Several exhibits deal with the famed Pony Express, a service that lasted less than 2 years but was romanticized to legendary proportions by Buffalo Bill and others. In the Civil War section you'll learn about Henry "Box" Brown, a slave who had himself "mailed" from Richmond to a Pennsylvania abolitionist in 1856.

The Art of Cards and Letters gallery displays rotating exhibits of personal (sometimes wrenching, always interesting) correspondence taken from different periods in history, as well as greeting cards and postcards. And an 800-square-foot gallery, called **Artistic License: The Duck Stamp Story,** focuses on federal duck stamps (first issued in 1934 to license waterfowl hunters), with displays on the hobby of duck hunting and the ecology of American water birds. In addition, the museum houses a vast research library for philatelic researchers and scholars, a stamp store, and a museum shop. Inquire about free walk-in tours at the information desk.

Opened in 1993, this most recent addition to the Smithsonian complex occupies the lower level of the palatial beaux arts quarters of the City Post Office Building, which was designed by architect Daniel Burnham and is situated next to Union Station.

2 Massachusetts Ave. NE (at 1st St.). ℭ 202/357-2991. www.si.edu/postal. Free admission. Daily 10am–5:30pm. Closed Dec 25. Metro: Union Station.

National Zoological Park ★★ *Kids*   The **giant pandas** are the zoo's biggest draw, but don't stop with Mei Xiang and Tian Tian.

Established in 1889, the National Zoo is home to some 500 species, many of them rare and/or endangered. A leader in the care, breeding, and exhibition of animals, it occupies 163 beautifully landscaped and wooded acres and is one of the country's most delightful zoos. You'll see cheetahs, zebras, camels, elephants, tapirs, antelopes, brown pelicans, kangaroos, hippos, rhinos, giraffes, apes, and, of course, lions, tigers, and bears (oh my).

Consider calling ahead (allow at least 4 weeks and call during weekday business hours) for a **free 90-minute highlights tour** (ℭ 202/673-4671), though it's not recommended for kids under age 4. Tours take place only on weekends. The tour guide will tell you how to look at the animals; where, why, and when to look; and will fill your visit with lots of surprises.

Pointers: Enter the zoo at the Connecticut Avenue entrance; you'll be right by the Education Building, where you can pick up a map and find out about feeding times and any special activities. Note that from this main entrance, you're headed downhill; the return uphill walk can prove trying if you have young children and/or it's a hot day. But the zoo rents strollers, and snack bars and ice-cream kiosks are scattered throughout the park.

The zoo animals live in large, open enclosures—simulations of their natural habitats—along two easy-to-follow numbered paths: **Olmsted Walk** and the **Valley Trail.** You can't get lost and it's hard to miss a thing. Be sure to catch **Amazonia,** where you can hang out for an hour peering up into the trees and still not spy the sloth (do yourself a favor and ask the attendant where it is).

New at the zoo is the Kids' Farm, which offers children ages 3 to 8 a chance to observe farm animals up close. Ducks, chickens, goats, cows, and miniature donkeys are among the animals milling around. Children might also enjoy the vegetable garden and pizza sculpture.

The zoo offers several dining options, including the Mane Restaurant and a number of snack stands scattered around the property. Other facilities include stroller-rental stations, a number of gift shops, a bookstore, and several paid-parking lots. The lots fill up quickly, especially on weekends, so arrive early or take the Metro.

Adjacent to Rock Creek Park, main entrance in the 3000 block of Connecticut Ave. NW. (© 202/673-4800, or 202/673-4717. www.si.edu/natzoo. Free admission. Daily Apr–Oct (weather permitting) grounds 6am–8pm, animal buildings 10am–6pm; daily Oct–Apr grounds 6am–6pm, animal buildings 10am–4:30pm. Closed Dec 25. Metro: Woodley Park–Zoo or Cleveland Park.

Renwick Gallery of the Smithsonian American Art Museum *Finds* A department of the Smithsonian American Art Museum (though located nowhere near it), the Renwick Gallery is a showcase for American creativity in crafts, housed in a historic mid-1800s landmark building of the French Second Empire style. The original home of the Corcoran Gallery, it was saved from demolition by First Lady Jacqueline Kennedy in 1963, when she recommended that it be renovated as part of the Lafayette Square restoration. In 1965, it became part of the Smithsonian and was renamed for its architect, James W. Renwick, who also designed the Smithsonian Castle.

Although the setting—especially the magnificent Victorian Grand Salon with its wainscoted plum walls and 38-foot skylight ceiling—evokes another era, the museum's contents are mostly contemporary. On view on the first floor are temporary exhibits of American crafts and decorative arts. On the second floor, the museum's rich and diverse displays boast changing crafts exhibits and contemporary works from the museum's permanent collection, such as Larry Fuente's *Game Fish,* or Wendell Castle's *Ghost Clock.* The **Grand Salon** on the second floor, styled in 19th-century opulence, is newly refurbished and currently displays 170 paintings and sculptures from the American Art Museum, which is closed for renovation. The great thing about this room, besides its fine art and grand design, is its cushiony, velvety banquettes, perfect resting stops for the weary sightseer. Tour the gallery for about an hour, rest for a minute, then go on to your next destination.

The Renwick offers a comprehensive schedule of crafts demonstrations, lectures, and films. And check out the museum shop near the entrance for books on crafts, design, and decorative arts, as well as craft items, many of them for children. ***Note:*** The main branch of the Smithsonian American Art Museum that is closed for renovation, not this offshoot.

750 9th St. NW (at Pennsylvania Ave. and 17th St. NW). (© 202/357-2700. http://americanart.si.edu. Free admission. Daily 10am–5:30pm. Closed Dec 25. Metro: Farragut West or Farragut North.

4 Elsewhere on the Mall

National Archives The Rotunda of the National Archives displays our country's most important original documents: the Declaration of Independence, the Constitution of the United States, and the Bill of Rights (collectively known as the Charters of Freedom). Until recently, however, it wasn't possible to get a very good look at these documents, and when you did, you had to view the Constitution one page at a time. A superb renovation, known as "The National Archives Experience," has transformed the Rotunda and installed new display cases that allow all visitors, but especially children and those in wheelchairs, much better viewing of the Charters. And, for the first time, you are able to see all four pages of the Constitution in one visit. The renovation adds 14 new document cases that trace the story of the creation of the Charters and the ongoing influence of these fundamental documents on the nation and the world. Further, a restoration of Barry Faulkner's two larger-than-life murals brings the scenes to vivid life. One mural entitled *The Declaration of Independence*, shows Thomas Jefferson presenting a draft of the Declaration to John Hancock, the presiding officer of the Continental Congress; the other, entitled *The Constitution*, shows James Madison submitting the Constitution to George Washington and the Constitutional Convention.

Phase II of the renovation, just completed in late 2004, debuts new exhibition space in the National Archives' public vaults. Exhibits here feature interactive technology and displays of documents and artifacts to explain our country's development in the use of records, from Indian treaties to presidential websites. The new exhibit area includes a theater that, during the day, continually runs dramatic films illustrating the relationship between records and democracy in the lives of real people, and at night, serves as a premier documentary film venue for the city. A special exhibition gallery showcases exhibits of timely topics and sends the exhibits on to other museums.

As a federal institution, the National Archives is charged with sifting through the accumulated papers of a nation's official life—billions of pieces a year—and determining what to save and what to destroy. The Archives' vast accumulation of census figures, military records, naturalization papers, immigrant passenger lists, federal documents, passport applications, ship manifests, maps, charts, photographs, and motion picture film (and that's not the half of it) spans 2 centuries. Anyone is welcome to use the National Archives center for genealogical research—this is where Alex Haley began his work on *Roots*—and it's all available for the perusal of anyone age 16 or over (call for details). If you're interested, visit the building, entering on Pennsylvania Avenue, and head to the fourth floor, where a staff member can advise you about the time and effort that will be involved, and, if you decide to pursue it, exactly how to proceed.

The National Archives building itself is worth an admiring glance. The neoclassical structure, designed by John Russell Pope (also the architect of the National Gallery of Art and the Jefferson Memorial) in the 1930s, is an impressive example of the beaux arts style. Seventy-two columns create a Corinthian colonnade on each of the four facades. Great bronze doors mark the Constitution Avenue entrance and four large sculptures representing the Future, the Past, Heritage, and Guardianship sit on pedestals near the entrances. Huge pediments crown both the Pennsylvania Avenue and Connecticut Avenue entrances to the building.

700 Pennsylvania Ave. NW (between 7th and 9th sts. NW; enter on Pennsylvania Ave.). Ⓒ 866/272-6272 or Ⓒ 202/501-5000 for general information or Ⓒ 202/501-5400 for research information. www.nara.gov. Free admission. Daily 10am–7pm. Call for research hours. Closed Dec 25. Metro: Archives–Navy Memorial.

National Gallery of Art ★★★   Most people don't realize it, but the National Gallery of Art is not part of the Smithsonian complex. Housing one of the world's foremost collections of Western painting, sculpture, and graphic arts, spanning from the Middle Ages through the 20th century, the National Gallery has a dual personality. The original West Building, designed by John Russell Pope (architect of the Jefferson Memorial and the National Archives), is a neoclassic marble masterpiece with a domed rotunda over a colonnaded fountain and high-ceilinged corridors leading to delightful garden courts. It was a gift to the nation from Andrew W. Mellon, who also contributed the nucleus of the collection, including 21 masterpieces from the Hermitage, two Raphaels among them. The ultramodern East Building, designed by I. M. Pei and opened in 1978, is composed of two adjoining triangles with glass walls and lofty tetrahedron skylights. The pink Tennessee marble from which both buildings were constructed was taken from the same quarry; it forms an architectural link between the two structures.

The West Building: On the main floor of the West Building, about 1,000 paintings are on display at any one time. To the left (as you enter off the Mall) is the **Art Information Room,** housing the **Micro Gallery,** where those so inclined can design their own tours of the permanent collection and enhance their knowledge of art via user-friendly computers.

To the right and left of the rotunda are sculpture galleries. On view are more than 800 works from the museum's permanent collection, mostly European sculptures from the Middle Ages to the early 20th century. Among the masterpieces here are Honoré Daumier's entire series of bronze sculptures, including all 36 of his caricatured portrait busts of French government officials.

The **National Gallery Sculpture Garden** ⊛, just across 7th Street from the West Wing, opened to the public in May 1999. The park takes up 2 city blocks and features open lawns; a central pool with a spouting fountain (the pool turns into an ice rink in winter); an exquisite glassed-in pavilion housing a cafe; 17 sculptures by renowned artists like Roy Lichtenstein and Ellsworth Kelly (and Scott Burton, whose *Six-Part Seating* you're welcome to sit upon) and, the latest installment, a Paris Metro sign; and informally landscaped shrubs, trees, and plants. It continues to be a hit, especially in warm weather, when people sit on the wide rim of the pool and dangle their feet in the water while they eat their lunch. Friday evenings in summer, the gallery stages live jazz performances here.

The East Building: Inside this wing is a showcase for the museum's collection of 20th-century art, including works by Picasso, Miró, Matisse, Pollock, and Rothko; this is also the home of the art history research center. Always on display is an exhibit called **Small French Paintings,** which I love.

The National Gallery is in the midst of finishing up a renovation, so some galleries and favorite works of art may not be on view. For instance, the famous, massive aluminum Alexander Calder mobile that usually dangles in the seven-story skylit atrium of the East Building is off being cleaned and won't be re-hung until the summer of 2005. Call ℂ **202/842-6179** for information.

Altogether, you should allow a leisurely 2 hours to see everything here.

Pick up a floor plan and calendar of events at an information desk to find out about National Gallery exhibits, films, tours, lectures, and concerts. Immensely popular is the gallery's Sunday concert series, now in its 63rd year, which take place Sunday evenings at 7pm in the garden court of the West Building. Admission is free and seating is on a first-come basis—people start arriving at 6pm, entering through the 6th Street and Constitution Avenue door, the only entrance open. The concerts feature chamber music, string quartets, pianists and

---

⌒Tips Avoiding the Crowds at the National Gallery of Art

The best time to visit the National Gallery is Monday morning; the worst is Sunday afternoon.

other forms of classical music performances. Call ✆ **202/842-691.** Highly recommended are the free highlight tours (call for exact times) and audio tours. The gift shop is a favorite. The gallery offers several good dining options, among them the concourse-level Cascade Café, which has multiple food stations; the Garden Café, on the ground floor of the West Building; the Terrace Café on the second level of the East Wing (which sometimes tailors its menu to complement a particular exhibit); and the sculpture garden's Pavilion Café.

4th St. and Constitution Ave. NW, on the north side of the Mall (between 3rd and 7th sts. NW). ✆ 202/
737-4215. www.nga.gov. Free admission. Mon–Sat 10am–5pm; Sun 11am–6pm. Closed Jan 1 and Dec 25.
Metro: Archives, Judiciary Square, or Smithsonian.

United States Holocaust Memorial Museum ★★   This museum remains a top draw, as it has been since it opened in 1993. If you arrive without a reserved ticket specifying an admission time, you'll have to join the line of folks seeking to get one of the 1,575 day-of-sale tickets the museum makes available each day (see "Holocaust Museum Touring Tips," below). The museum opens its doors at 10am and the tickets are usually gone by 10:30am. Get in line early in the morning (around 8am).

The noise and bustle of so many visitors can be disconcerting, and it's certainly at odds with the experience that follows. But things settle down as you begin your tour. When you enter, you will be issued an identity card of an actual victim of the Holocaust; at several points in the tour, you can find out the location and status of person on your card—by 1945, 66% of those whose lives are documented on these cards were dead.

The tour begins on the fourth floor, where exhibits portray the events of 1933 to 1939, the years of the Nazi rise to power. On the third floor (documenting 1940–44), exhibits illustrate the narrowing choices of people caught up in the Nazi machine. You board a Polish freight car of the type used to transport Jews from the Warsaw ghetto to Treblinka and hear recordings of survivors telling what life in the camps was like. This part of the museum documents the details of the Nazis' "Final Solution" for the Jews.

The second floor recounts a more heartening story: It depicts how non-Jews throughout Europe, by exercising individual action and responsibility, saved Jews at great personal risk. Denmark—led by a king who swore that if any of his subjects wore a yellow star, so would he—managed to hide and save 90% of its Jews. Exhibits follow on the liberation of the camps, life in Displaced Persons camps, emigration to Israel and America, and the Nuremberg trials. A highlight at the end of the permanent exhibition is a 30-minute film called *Testimony,* in which Holocaust survivors tell their stories. The tour concludes in the hexagonal Hall of Remembrance, where you can meditate and light a candle for the victims. The museum notes that most people take 2 to 3 hours on their first visit; many people take longer.

In addition to its permanent and temporary exhibitions, the museum has a Resource Center for educators, which provides materials and services to Holocaust educators and students; an interactive computer learning center; and a registry of Holocaust survivors, a library, and archives, which researchers may use to retrieve historic documents, photographs, oral histories, films, and videos.

The museum recommends not bringing children under 11; for older children, it's advisable to prepare them for what they'll see. You can see some parts of the museum without tickets, includingtwo special areas on the first floor and concourse: **Daniel's Story: Remember the Children** and the **Wall of Remembrance** (Children's Tile Wall), which commemorates the 1.5 million children

---

⟨ *Tips* **Holocaust Museum Touring Tips**

Because so many people want to visit the museum (it has hosted as many as 10,000 visitors in a single day), tickets specifying a visit time (in 15-min. intervals) are required. Reserve as many as 10 tickets in advance via Tickets. com (② **800/400-9373;** www.tickets.com) for a small fee. If you order well in advance, you can have tickets mailed to you at home. You can also get same-day tickets at the museum beginning at 10am daily (lines form earlier, usually around 8am). Note that same-day tickets are limited, and one person may obtain a maximum of four.

---

killed in the Holocaust, and the **Wexner Learning Center.** There's a cafeteria and museum shop on the premises.

100 Raoul Wallenberg Place SW (formerly 15th St. SW; near Independence Ave., just off the Mall). ② 202/ 488-0400. www.ushmm.org. Free admission. Daily 10am–5:30pm, staying open until 8pm Tues and Thurs mid-Apr to mid-June. Closed Yom Kippur and Dec 25. Metro: Smithsonian.

5 Other Government Agencies

Bureau of Engraving & Printing *(Kids* This is where they will literally show you the money. A staff of 2,600 works around the clock churning it out at the rate of about $700 million a day. Everyone's eyes pop as they walk past rooms overflowing with new greenbacks. But the money's not the whole story. The bureau prints many other products, including 25 billion postage stamps a year, presidential portraits, and White House invitations.

Note: The Bureau of Engraving and Printing responds to Department of Homeland Security "Code Orange" warnings by halting its public tours. Call ahead to confirm that tours are on a normal schedule when you're here.

Many people line up each day to get a peek at all the moola, so arrive early, especially during the peak tourist season.

Consider securing VIP, also called "congressional" tour tickets from your senator or congressperson; VIP tours are offered Monday through Friday at 8:15 and 8:45am, with additional 4, 4:15, 4:30, and 5pm tours added in summer, and last about 45 minutes. Write or call at least 3 months in advance for tickets.

Tickets for general public tours are required every day, and every person taking the tour must have a ticket. To obtain a ticket, go to the ticket booth on the 15th Street side of the building and show a valid photo ID. You will receive a ticket specifying a tour time for that same day, and be directed to the 14th Street entrance of the bureau; you are allowed as many as eight tickets per person. Booth hours are from 8am to 2pm, staying open until 7pm in summer.

The 40-minute guided tour begins with a short introductory film. Then you'll see, through large windows, the processes that go into the making of paper money: the inking, stacking of bills, cutting, and examination for defects. Most printing here is done from engraved steel plates in a process known as *intaglio,* the hardest to counterfeit, because the slightest alteration will cause a noticeable change in the portrait in use. Additional exhibits include bills no longer in use, counterfeit money, and a $100,000 bill designed for official transactions (since 1969, the largest denomination printed for the general public is $100).

After you finish the tour, allow time to explore the **Visitor Center,** open from 8:30am to 3pm (until 7:30pm in summer), where exhibits include informative videos, money-related electronic games, and a display of $1 million. Here, too, you can buy gifts ranging from bags of shredded money—no, you can't tape it back together—to copies of documents such as the Gettysburg Address.

14th and C sts. SW. (C) **800/874-3188** or 202/874-2330. www.moneyfactory.com. Free admission. Mon–Fri 10am–2pm (last tour begins at 1:40pm); in summer, extended hours 5–6:40pm. Closed Dec 25–Jan 1 and federal holidays. Metro: Smithsonian (Independence Ave. exit).

Library of Congress ⚓   The question most frequently asked by visitors to the Library of Congress is: Where are the books? The answer is: on the 532 miles of shelves located throughout the library's three buildings: the **Thomas Jefferson, James Madison Memorial,** and **John Adams** buildings. Established in 1800, "for the purchase of such books as may be necessary for the use of Congress," the library today serves the nation, with holdings for the visually impaired (for whom books are recorded on cassette and/or translated into Braille), research scholars, college students—and tourists. Its first collection of books was destroyed in 1814 when the British burned the Capitol (where the library was then housed) during the War of 1812. Thomas Jefferson then sold the institution his personal library of 6,487 books as a replacement, and this became the foundation of what would grow to become the world's largest library.

Today, the collection contains a mind-boggling 128 million items. Its buildings house more than 29 million catalogued books, 57 million manuscripts, 12 million prints and photographs, 2.7 million audio holdings (discs, tapes, talking books, and so on), about a million movies and videotapes, musical instruments from the 1700s, and the letters and papers of everyone from George Washington to Groucho Marx. The library offers a year-round program of free concerts, lectures, and poetry readings, and houses the Copyright Office.

Just as impressive as the library's holdings is its architecture. Most magnificent is the ornate Italian Renaissance–style **Thomas Jefferson Building,** which was erected between 1888 and 1897 to hold the burgeoning collection and establish America as a cultured nation with magnificent institutions equal to anything in Europe. Fifty-two painters and sculptors worked for 8 years on its interior. There are floor mosaics of Italian marble, allegorical paintings on the overhead vaults, more than 100 murals, and numerous ornamental cornucopias, ribbons, vines, and garlands. The building's exterior has 42 granite sculptures and yards of bas-reliefs. Especially impressive are the exquisite marble **Great Hall** and the **Main Reading Room,** the latter under a 160-foot dome. Originally intended to hold the fruits of at least 150 years of collecting, the Jefferson Building was, in fact, filled up in a mere 13 years. It is now supplemented by the James Madison Memorial Building and the John Adams Building.

On permanent display in the Jefferson Building's Great Hall are several exhibits: The **American Treasures of the Library of Congress** rotates a selection of more than 300 of the rarest and most interesting items from the library's collection—like Thomas Jefferson's rough draft of the Declaration of Independence with notations by Benjamin Franklin and John Adams in the margins, and the contents of Lincoln's pockets when he was assassinated. Be sure to

---

The F.B.I. Gets a Makeover

The Federal Bureau of Investigation has been closed to public tours during its renovation, but it is slated to re-open sometime in 2005. Call (C) **202/ 324-3447** for the latest information.

---

obtain a free audio wand before you view the American Treasures exhibit, so that you can listen to audio treasures: a Duke Ellington recording, an excerpt of Martin Luther King's delivery of his "I have a dream" speech, and so on.

Across the Great Hall from the American Treasures exhibit is one that showcases the **World Treasures of the Library of Congress.** Its multimedia display of books, maps, videos, and illustrations invites visitors to examine artifacts from the library's vast international collections. Tucked away in a corner of the Jefferson Building is another permanent exhibit, the **Bob Hope Gallery of American Entertainment,** which presents on a rotating basis, film clips, memorabilia, and manuscript pages from a collection that the comedian donated to the library in 2000. The **Gershwin Room** houses George and Ira Gershwin memorabilia, including a piano, desk, music manuscripts, and other of the American jazz composers' prized possessions.

If you are waiting for your tour to start (see schedule below), take in the 12-minute orientation film in the Jefferson's visitors' theater or browse in its gift shop. Pick up a calendar of events when you visit. Concerts take place in the Jefferson Building's elegant **Coolidge Auditorium.** The concerts are free but require tickets, which you can obtain through Ticketmaster (© **800/551-7328** or 202/432-7328).

The **Madison Building,** across Independence Avenue from the Jefferson Building, at 10 Independence Ave. SE, offers interesting exhibits and features classic, rare, and unusual films in its **Mary Pickford Theater.** (The theater closed in 2004 for a remodeling that would add accessibility features, but it should be open by 2005.) Find out more about the library's free film and concert series by accessing the LOC website (www.loc.gov), clicking on "Complete News and Events," then "Calendar of Events," and then scrolling down the page to find the postings for the free concert series and the free film series, as well as other events. The Madison Building also houses a cafeteria and the more formal Montpelier Room restaurant; both are open for lunch weekdays.

Anyone over high school age may use the library's collections, but first you must obtain a user card with your photo on it. Go to Reader Registration in Room LM 140 (street level of the Madison Building) and present a driver's license or passport. Then head to the Information Desk in either the Jefferson or Madison buildings to find out about the research resources available to you and how to use them. Most likely, you will be directed to the Main Reading Room. All books must be used on-site.

1st St. SE (between Independence Ave. and E. Capitol St.). © **202/707-8000.** www.loc.gov. Free admission. Madison Bldg. Mon–Fri 8:30am–9:30pm; Sat 8:30am–6pm. Jefferson Bldg. Mon–Sat 10am–5:30pm. Adams Bldg. Mon, Wed, and Thurs 8:30am–9:30pm; Tues, Fri, and Sat 8:30am–5:30pm. Closed federal holidays. Stop at the information desk inside the Jefferson Building's west entrance on 1st St. to obtain same-day free tickets to tour the Library. Tours of the Great Hall: Mon–Fri 10:30 and 11:30am, and 1:30, 2:30, and 3:30pm; Sat 10:30 and 11:30am, and 1:30 and 2:30pm. Contact your congressional representatives to obtain tickets for congressional, or "VIP" tours, a slightly more personal tour given weekdays at 8:30am and 2pm. Metro: Capitol South.

6 More Museums

City Museum ⭐ Long overdue, this museum, which opened in May 2003, presents the story of "the people, events, and communities" of Washington, D.C. A main feature is the 25-minute multimedia show, in which historical figures and contemporary characters come to life, going backwards and forwards in time, as they reveal the main events and personalities that formed this city. "Washington

Stories," as the show is called, runs every 30 minutes and focuses on the early days of D.C. It's a little goofy—the character of Pierre L'Enfant wants to be called "Peter"—and seems designed for viewers with short attention spans, since the presentation of information jumps from bit to bit. But it's successful in conveying certain ideas, for instance, that Washington has always been a city of diversity. An exhibit on the first floor entitled "Washington Perspectives" covers the history of the city through displays of old ticket stubs, photographs, advertisements, and other artifacts, with printed explanations and sometimes recorded voices. The room is divided into four chronological sections, and as you move through each time period, you pick up details, whether it's about the bustle of market life in the 18th century, or segregation in the 1950s. At some point, you'll notice people bent over in the middle of the room, peering at the floor: They're looking at the lit-up map beneath their feet, pieced together from aerial photographs taken in 1999. Your fellow museum-goers are trying to locate specific places on the map. Also on this floor are two galleries that introduce you to two longtime Washington communities: "Chinatown, Place or People?" and "Mount Vernon Square Communities: Generations of Change."

Upstairs are two more exhibits. "Sandlots to Stadiums" basically traces the history of sports and recreation in the city. To me, the much more interesting exhibit is "Taking a Closer Look," which displays old maps, receipts, and drawings; headphones on stands in front of many of the artifacts provide audio recordings of historians giving context to and information about what you are seeing. On the second floor, too, is a reading room and an extensive library of photographs, manuscripts, maps, and books chronicling the city's history. Two flights down, on ground level, is an archaeology lab.

The City Museum resides in the restored and gorgeous Carnegie Library building and its interior is all grand white marble, Palladian windows, and graceful double staircases. The early-20th-century beaux-arts designed structure serves as a fine counterpoint to the brand new, ultramodern and huge D.C. Convention Center, directly across the street.

801 K St. NW (at Mount Vernon Square, between 7th and 9th sts.). ☎ 202/383-1800. www.citymuseumdc. org. Admission exhibits $3 adults, $2 students and seniors; multimedia show $6 adults, $5 students and seniors; combination ticket $8 adults, $6 students and seniors. Tues–Sun 10am–5pm; third Thurs every month until 9pm. Closed Mon and major holidays. Metro: Mount Vernon Square/Convention Center or Gallery Place/Chinatown.

The Corcoran Gallery of Art ★★ This elegant art museum, a stone's throw from the White House, is a favorite party site in the city, hosting everything from inaugural balls to wedding receptions.

The first art museum in Washington, the Corcoran Gallery was housed from 1869 to 1896 in the redbrick and brownstone building that is now the Renwick. The collection outgrew its quarters and was transferred in 1897 to its present beaux arts building, designed by Ernest Flagg.

The collection, shown in rotating exhibits, focuses chiefly on American art. A prominent Washington banker, William Wilson Corcoran was among the first wealthy American collectors to realize the importance of encouraging and supporting this country's artists. Enhanced by further gifts and bequests, the collection comprehensively spans American art from 18th-century portraiture to 20th-century moderns like Nevelson, Warhol, and Rothko. Nineteenth-century works include Bierstadt's and Remington's imagery of the American West; Hudson River School artists; expatriates like Whistler, Sargent, and Mary Cassatt; and two giants of the late 19th century, Homer and Eakins.

> ⸜ **Fun Fact** **The Height of Her Powers**
>
> Displayed on the second floor of the Corcoran Gallery of Art is the white-marble female nude, *The Greek Slave,* by Hiram Powers, considered so daring in its day that it was shown on alternate days to men and women.

The Corcoran is not exclusively an American art museum. On the first floor is the collection from the estate of Sen. William Andrews Clark, an eclectic grouping of Dutch and Flemish masters; European painters; French Impressionists; Barbizon landscapes; Delft porcelains; a Louis XVI *salon dore* transported in toto from Paris; and more. Clark's will stated that his diverse collection, which any curator would undoubtedly want to disperse among various museum departments, must be shown as a unit. He left money for a wing to house it and the new building opened in 1928. Don't miss the small walnut-paneled room known as "Clark Landing," which showcases 19th-century French Impressionist and American art; a room of exquisite Corot landscapes; another of medieval Renaissance tapestries; and numerous Daumier lithographs donated by Dr. Armand Hammer. Allow an hour for touring the collection.

Pick up a schedule of events—temporary exhibits, gallery talks, concerts, art auctions, and more. Families should inquire about the Corcoran's series of Saturday Family Days and Sunday Traditions. (Family Days are especially fun and always feature great live music.) Both programs are free, but you need to reserve a slot for the Sunday events. There is some street parking.

The charming Café des Artistes is open for lunch Wednesday, Friday, and Saturday from 11am to 2pm, on Thursday from 11am to 3pm for lunch and from 4 to 8pm for dinner, and for Sunday brunch from 10:30am to 2pm (reservations accepted for parties of eight or more), which costs $24 per adult, $11 per child (under 12), and includes live gospel music singers; call ⓒ 202/639-1786 for more information. The Corcoran has a nice gift shop.

500 17th St. NW (between E St. and New York Ave.). ⓒ **202/639-1700.** www.corcoran.org. $6.75 adults, $4.75 seniors, $3 students 13–18, $8 families, children under 12 free; admission is free all day Mon, and Thurs after 5pm. Open Wed–Mon 10am–5pm, with extended hours Thurs until 9pm. Free walk-in tours daily (except Tues) at noon, as well as at 7:30pm Thurs and at 2:30pm Sat and Sun. Closed Jan 1 and Dec 25. Metro: Farragut West or Farragut North.

Dumbarton Oaks ⸝*Finds* Many people associate Dumbarton Oaks, a 19th-century Georgetown mansion named for a Scottish castle, with the 1944 international conference that led to the formation of the United Nations. Today the 16-acre estate is a research center for studies in Byzantine and pre-Columbian art and history, as well as landscape architecture. Its yards, which wind gently down to Rock Creek Ravine, are magical, modeled after European gardens. The pre-Columbian museum, designed by Philip Johnson, is a small gem, and the Byzantine collection is a rich one.

This unusual collection originated with Robert Woods Bliss and his wife, Mildred. In 1940, they turned over their estate, their extensive Byzantine collection, a library of works on Byzantine civilization, and 16 acres (including 10 acres of exquisite formal gardens) to Mr. Bliss's alma mater, Harvard, and provided endowment funds for continuing research in Byzantine studies. In the early 1960s, they also donated their pre-Columbian collection and financed the building of a wing to house it, as well as a second wing for Mrs. Bliss's collection of rare books on landscape gardening. The Byzantine collection includes illuminated manuscripts, a 13th-century icon of St. Peter, mosaics, ivory carvings, a 4th-century sarcophagus, jewelry, and more. The pre-Columbian works feature Olmec jade and serpentine figures, Mayan relief panels, and sculptures of Aztec gods and goddesses.

The historic music room, furnished in European antiques, was the setting for the 1944 Dumbarton Oaks Conversations about the United Nations. It has a painted 16th-century French-style ceiling and an immense 16th-century stone fireplace. Among its notable artworks is El Greco's *The Visitation.*

Pick up a self-guiding brochure to tour the staggeringly beautiful **formal gardens,** which include an Orangery, a Rose Garden, wisteria-covered arbors, groves of cherry trees, and magnolias. Unless you're a fan of Byzantine or pre-Columbian art, you're likely to spend more time in the garden, as much as an hour when everything is in bloom. Exit at R Street, turn left, cross an honest-to-goodness Lovers' Lane, and proceed next door to Montrose Park, where you can picnic. There is parking on the street.

1703 32nd St. NW (entrance to collections on 32nd St., between R and S sts.; garden entrance at 31st and R sts.). (C) 202/339-6401. www.doaks.org. Collections suggested donation $1 year-round. Garden Mar 15–Oct $6 adults, $4 children under 12 and seniors; Nov–Mar 15 free. Garden Mar 15–Oct daily 2–6pm; Nov–Mar 2–5pm, weather permitting. Collections year-round Tues–Sun 2–5pm. Gardens and collections are closed national holidays and Dec 24.

Folger Shakespeare Library *(Finds)* "Shakespeare taught us that the little world of the heart is vaster, deeper, and richer than the spaces of astronomy," wrote Ralph Waldo Emerson in 1864. A decade later, Amherst student Henry Clay Folger was profoundly affected by a lecture Emerson gave similarly extolling the bard. Folger purchased an inexpensive set of Shakespeare's plays and went on to amass the world's largest (by far) collection of the bard's works, today housed in the Folger Shakespeare Library. By 1930, when Folger and his wife, Emily, laid the cornerstone of a building to house the collection, it comprised 93,000 books, 50,000 prints and engravings, and thousands of manuscripts. The Folgers gave it all as a gift to the American people.

The building itself has a marble facade decorated with nine bas-relief scenes from Shakespeare's plays; it is a striking example of Art Deco classicism. A statue of Puck stands in the west garden. An **Elizabethan garden** on the east side of the building is planted with flowers and herbs of the period. Inquire about guided tours scheduled at 10am and 11am on every third Saturday from April to October. The garden is also a quiet place to have a picnic.

The facility, which houses some 256,000 books, 116,000 of which are rare (pre-1801), is an important research center not only for Shakespearean scholars, but also for those studying any aspect of the English and continental Renaissance. A multimedia computer exhibition called *The Shakespeare Gallery* offers users a close-up look at some of the Folger's treasures, as well as Shakespeare's life and works. And the oak-paneled **Great Hall,** reminiscent of a Tudor long gallery, is a popular attraction for the general public. On display are rotating exhibits from the permanent collection: books, paintings, playbills, Renaissance musical instruments, and more. Plan on spending at least 30 minutes here.

At the end of the Great Hall is a theater designed to suggest an Elizabethan inn-yard where plays, concerts, readings, and Shakespeare-related events take place (see chapter 9 for details).

201 E. Capitol St. SE. (C) 202/544-7077. www.folger.edu. Free admission. Mon–Sat 10am–4pm. Free walk-in tours daily at 11am, with an extra tour added Sat at 1pm. Closed federal holidays. Metro: Capitol South or Union Station.

Museums of Special Interest

In addition to the many superb museums described within this chapter, there are many wonderful lesser-known ones around the city, usually focusing on very specific interests. They don't appeal to everyone, but if you're a buff of some kind, you might find one of them fascinating. Don't try to drop in without calling, because most of these museums are not open daily and some require appointments.

Anderson House, 2118 Massachusetts Ave. NW (© 202/785-2040): A century-old, 50-room mansion of amazing design and impressive art and furnishings. The mansion is headquarters for the Society of the Cincinnati, which was founded in 1783 by Continental officers (including George Washington) who had served in the American Revolution. Metro: Dupont Circle.

Art Museum of the Americas, 201 18th St. NW, within the Organization of American States (© 202/458-6016): From 80 to 200 works by contemporary Latin and Caribbean artists, on display from the museum's permanent collection. A formal Aztec garden and a second gallery of art in adjoining OAS building. Metro: Farragut West, then walk south about 6 blocks.

Daughters of the American Revolution (DAR) Museum, 1776 D St. NW (© 202/879-3241): Early American furnishings and decorative arts. Metro: Farragut West, then walk south about 5 blocks.

Decatur House , 748 Jackson Place (© 202/842-0920): Historic house museum with permanent collection of Federalist and Victorian furnishings. Metro: Farragut West or McPherson Square.

Dumbarton House, 2715 Q St. NW (© 202/337-2288): Another historic house museum, with a permanent collection of 18th- and 19th-century English and American furniture and decorative arts. Metro: Dupont Circle, with a 20-minute walk along Q Street.

Frederick Douglass National Historic Site, 1411 W St. SE (© 202/426-5961): Last residence of the famous African-American 19th-century abolitionist. Metro: Anacostia, then catch bus no. B2, which stops right in front of the house.

Hillwood Museum and Gardens, 4155 Linnean Ave. NW (© 202/686-8500): Newly renovated estate of Marjorie Merriweather Post, who collected art and artifacts of 18th-century France and Imperial Russia. Formal gardens, grand rooms, high tea. Metro: Van Ness or Cleveland Park.

Interior Department Museum, 1849 C St. NW (© 202/208-4743): Permanent exhibits relating to American historical events and locales, including murals by prominent Native American artists, newly on view on the ninth floor. Metro: Farragut West, then walk about 6 blocks south.

Kreeger Museum, 2401 Foxhall Rd. NW (© 202/338-3552): This museum in a residential neighborhood is a treasure trove of art from the 1850s to 1970s, including Impressionist paintings and the works of many American artists. No Metro; take a cab.

Mary McLeod Bethune Council House National Historic Site, 1318 Vermont Ave. NW (© 202/673-2402): Last residence of African-American activist/educator Bethune, who was a leading champion of black and women's rights during FDR's administration. Metro: McPherson Square.

National Building Museum, 401 F St. NW (✆ **202/272-2448**): Housed within a historic building of mammoth proportions is this fine museum devoted to architecture, building, and historic preservation. Metro: Judiciary Square.

National Geographic Society's Explorers Hall, 17th and M streets NW. (✆ **202/857-7588**): Rotating exhibits related to exploration, adventure, and earth sciences, using interactive programs and artifacts. Metro: Farragut North (Connecticut Ave. and L St. exit).

Octagon ★, 1799 New York Ave. NW (✆ **202/638-3105**): Another historic house museum, it also features exhibits on architecture (its neighbor is the American Institute of Architects headquarters). Metro: Farragut West.

Old Stone House, 3051 M St. NW (✆ **202/426-6851**): 1765 structure said to be the oldest in D.C. still standing on its original foundations. Colonial appearance, English garden. Metro: Foggy Bottom, with a 15-minute walk.

Pope John Paul II Cultural Center, 3900 Harewood Rd. NE (✆ **202/635-5400**): A large multimedia facility that uses interactive presentations to engage visitors of all denominations in exploring issues of religion, world culture, and spirituality in the new millennium. Take a cab.

Sewall-Belmont House, 144 Constitution Ave. NE (✆ **202/546-3989**): A must for those interested in women's history, the historic house displays memorabilia of the women's suffrage movement, which got its start here. Metro: Union Station.

Textile Museum, 2320 S St. NW (✆ **202/667-0441**): Historic and contemporary handmade textile arts, housed in historic John Russell Pope mansion. Metro: Dupont Circle, Q Street exit, then walk a couple of blocks up Massachusetts Avenue until you see S Street.

Tudor Place, 1644 31st St. NW (✆ **202/965-0400**): An 1816 mansion with gardens, home to Martha Washington's descendants until 1984. Metro: Dupont Circle, with a 25-minute walk along Q Street.

United States Navy Memorial and Naval Heritage Center, 701 Pennsylvania Ave. NW (✆ **202/737-2300**): Outside plaza honors men and women of the U.S. Navy; museum features interactive video kiosks used to learn about Navy ships, aircraft, and history. Metro: Archives–Navy Memorial.

Woodrow Wilson House, 2340 S St. NW (✆ **202/387-4062**): The intriguing former home of this president, preserved the way it was when he lived here in the 1920s. Docents guide visitors on hour-long tours, pointing out objects, such as the French Gobelin tapestry given to Wilson by the French ambassador, and the marble mosaic gift from Pope Benedict; telling stories about our 28th president (he liked to whistle the tune "Oh You Beautiful Doll" to his beloved wife, Edith). Metro: Dupont Circle, then walk a couple of blocks up Massachusetts Avenue until you reach S Street.

Ford's Theatre & Lincoln Museum *(Kids)*   On April 14, 1865, President Abraham Lincoln was in the audience at Ford's Theatre, one of the most popular playhouses in Washington. Everyone was laughing at a funny line from Tom Taylor's celebrated comedy, *Our American Cousin,* when John Wilkes Booth crept into the president's box, shot the president, and leapt to the stage, shouting *"Sic semper tyrannis!"* ("Thus ever to tyrants!") With his left leg broken from the vault, Booth mounted his horse in the alley and galloped off. Doctors carried Lincoln across the street to the house of William Petersen, where the president died the next morning.

The theater was closed after Lincoln's assassination and used as an office by the War Department. In 1893, 22 clerks were killed when three floors of the building collapsed. It remained in disuse until the 1960s, when it was remodeled and restored to its appearance on the night of the tragedy. Except when rehearsals or matinees are in progress (call before you go), visitors can see the theater and trace Booth's movements on that fateful night. Free 15-minute talks on the history of the theater and the story of the assassination are given throughout the day. Be sure to visit the Lincoln Museum in the basement, where exhibits—including the Derringer pistol used by Booth and a diary in which he outlines his rationalization for the deed—focus on events surrounding Lincoln's assassination and the trial of the conspirators. Thirty minutes is plenty of time to spend here.

The theater stages productions most of the year (see chapter 9 for information).

517 10th St. NW (between E and F sts.). (C) 202/426-6925. www.nps.gov/foth. Free admission. Daily 9am–5pm. Closed Dec 25. Metro: Metro Center.

The House Where Lincoln Died (the Petersen House) *(Kids)*   After he was mortally wounded at Ford's Theatre, the doctors attending Lincoln had him carried out into the street, where boarder Henry Safford, standing in the open doorway of his rooming house, gestured for them to bring the president inside. So Lincoln died in the home of William Petersen, a German-born tailor. Now furnished with period pieces, the dark, narrow town house looks much as it did on that fateful April night. It takes about 5 minutes to troop through the building. You'll see the front parlor where an anguished Mary Todd Lincoln spent the night with her son, Robert. In the back parlor, Secretary of War Edwin M. Stanton held a cabinet meeting and questioned witnesses. From this room, Stanton announced at 7:22am on April 15, 1865, "Now he belongs to the ages." Lincoln died, lying diagonally because he was so tall, on a bed the size of the one you see here. (The Chicago Historical Society owns the actual bed and other items from the room.) In 1896, the government bought the house for $30,000 and it is now maintained by the National Park Service.

516 10th St. NW. (C) 202/426-6924. Free admission. Daily 9am–5pm. Closed Dec 25. Metro: Metro Center.

International Spy Museum *(★★)*   After several visits to the Spy Museum, my 12-year-old and I like to test each other's powers of observation. We'll be standing in a store or other public place and look around for signs of "hostile surveillance, security systems, and unexpected risk or unlucky breaks." We're putting into practice some tips we picked up at the museum, in a section called "Tricks of the Trade," where interactive monitors teach you what to look for, when it comes to suspicious activity. This tradecraft area is the first you come to in the museum, after you've seen the 5-minute briefing film, and it's easy to spend a lot of time here. In addition to the surveillance games, the section displays trick equipment (such as a shoe transmitter used by Soviets as a listening device and a single-shot pistol disguised as a lipstick tube) and runs film in which spies talk about bugging devices and locks and picks. You can watch a video that shows individuals being made up for disguise, from start to finish, and you can crawl on your belly through ductwork in the ceiling overhead. (The conversations you hear are taped, not floating up from the room of tourists below.)

Try to pace yourself, though, because there's still so much to see, and you can easily reach your limit before you get through the 68,000-square-foot museum. The next section covers the history of spying ("the second oldest profession") and tells about famous spymasters over time, from Moses; to Sun Tzu, the Chinese general, who wrote *The Art of War* in 400 B.C.; to George Washington, whose Revolutionary War letter of 1777 setting up a network of spies in New York, is on view. Learn about the use of codes and code-breaking in spying, with one room of the museum devoted to the Enigma cipher machine used by the Germans (whose "unbreakable" codes the Allied cryptanalysts succeeded in deciphering) in World War II. An actual Enigma machine is displayed, and interactive monitors allow you to simulate the experience of using an Enigma machine, while learning more about its invention and inventor.

Much more follows: artifacts from all over (this is the largest collection of international espionage artifacts ever put on public display); a re-created tunnel beneath the divided city of Berlin during the Cold War; the intelligence-gathering stories of those behind enemy lines and of those involved in planning D-Day in World War II; an exhibit on escape and evasion techniques in wartime; the tales of spies of recent times, told by the CIA and FBI agents involved in identifying them; and a mockup of an intelligence agency's 21st century operations center. You exit the museum directly to its gift shop, which leads to the Spy City Café.

While you may look with suspicion on everyone around you when you leave the museum, you can trust that what you've just learned at the museum is authoritative: The Spy Museum's executive director was with the CIA for 36 years and his advisory board includes two former CIA directors, two former CIA disguise chiefs, and a retired KGB general.

The International Spy Museum has been immensely popular ever since its mid-2002 opening, which often translates into long lines for admission. Consider ordering advance tickets for next-day or future date tours through Ticketmaster (© **202/432-SEAT**), which you can pick up at the Will Call desk inside the museum. You can also purchase advance tickets, including those for tours later in the day, at the box office.

800 F St. NW (at 8th St. NW). © **866/779-6873** or 202/393-7798. www.spymuseum.org. Admission $13 adults (ages 12–65), $12 for seniors and college students, $10 for children ages 5–11. Daily Apr–Aug 9am–8pm; Aug–Oct 10am–7pm; Nov–Mar 10am–5pm; museum closes 1 hour after last admission. Closed Thanksgiving, Dec 25, and Jan 1. Metro: Gallery Place/Chinatown or National Archive/Navy Memorial.

Marian Koshland Science Museum ✮   The National Academy of Sciences operates this museum, which was conceived of by molecular biologist Daniel Koshland, in memory of his wife, the immunologist and molecular biologist, Marian Koshland, who died in 1997. The museum opened in April 2004 in the heart of downtown D.C. Recommended for children over 13, and especially for those with a scientific bent, the museum presents state-of-the-art exhibits that explore the complexities of science. Three exhibits currently on show are the Wonders of Science, which includes animations of groundbreaking research and an introductory film about the nature of science; Global Warming Facts and Our Future; and Putting DNA to Work, which covers the details of current approaches to DNA sequencing, from tracking the origins of SARS to criminal forensics.

6th and E sts. NW. ℂ 202/334-1201. www.koshlandsciencemuseum.org. Admission $5 adults, $3 ages 5-18 and seniors (65+). Wed–Mon 10am–6pm. Closed Tues and Thanksgiving, Christmas, and New Year's Day. Metro: Gallery Place/Chinatown or Judiciary Square.

National Museum of Women in the Arts   Eighteen years after it opened, this stunning collection remains the foremost museum in the world dedicated to celebrating "the contribution of women to the history of art." Founders Wilhelmina and Wallace Holladay, who donated the core of the permanent collection—more than 250 works by women from the 16th through the 20th century—became interested in women's art in the 1960s. After discovering that no women were included in H. W. Janson's *History of Art*, a standard text (which did not address this oversight until 1986!), the Holladays began collecting art by women, and the concept of a women's art museum soon evolved.

Since its opening, the collection has grown to more than 3,000 works by more than 800 artists, including Rosa Bonheur, Frida Kahlo, Helen Frankenthaler, Barbara Hepworth, Georgia O'Keeffe, Camille Claudel, Lila Cabot Perry, Mary Cassatt, Elaine de Kooning, Käthe Kollwitz, and many other lesser-known artists from earlier centuries. You will discover here, for instance, that the famed Peale family of 19th-century portrait painters included a very talented sister, Sarah Miriam Peale. The collection is complemented by an ongoing series of changing exhibits. You should allow an hour here.

The museum is housed in a magnificent Renaissance Revival landmark building designed in 1907 as a Masonic temple by noted architect Waddy Wood. Its sweeping marble staircase and splendid interior make it a popular choice for wedding receptions.

1250 New York Ave. NW (at 13th St.). ℂ **800/222-7270** or 202/783-5000. www.nmwa.org. $8 adults, $6 students over 18 with ID and seniors over 60, youth 18 and under free. Mon–Sat 10am–5pm; Sun noon–5pm. Closed Jan 1, Thanksgiving, and Dec 25. Metro: Metro Center (13th St. exit).

Phillips Collection ★★   Conceived as "a museum of modern art and its sources," this intimate establishment, occupying an elegant 1890s Georgian Revival mansion and a more youthful wing, houses the exquisite collection of Duncan and Marjorie Phillips, avid collectors and proselytizers of modernism. Carpeted rooms with leaded- and stained-glass windows, oak paneling, plush chairs and sofas, and fireplaces establish a comfortable, homelike setting. Today the collection includes more than 2,500 works. Among the highlights: superb Daumier, Dove, and Bonnard paintings; some splendid small Vuillards; five van Goghs; Renoir's *Luncheon of the Boating Party;* seven Cézannes; and six works by Georgia O'Keeffe. Ingres, Delacroix, Manet, El Greco, Goya, Corot, Constable, Courbet, Giorgione, and Chardin are among the "sources" or forerunners of modernism represented. Modern notables include Rothko, Hopper, Kandinsky, Matisse, Klee, Degas, Rouault, Picasso, and many others. It's a collection you'll enjoy viewing for an hour or so, although some of those masterpieces mentioned above may not be on view; 50 of the museum's best loved works, including *Luncheon of the Boating Party,* are on tour to other museums, while the Phillips finishes a renovation. The 50 paintings are due to return by the summer of 2005. Meanwhile, don't be put off by the sight of the construction, which is expanding the Phillips Collection's annex building while keeping the main building open throughout.

A full schedule of events includes temporary shows with loans from other museums and private collections, gallery talks, lectures, and free concerts in the ornate music room. (Concerts take place Sept–May on Sun at 5pm; arrive early.

Although the concert is free, admission to the museum on weekends costs $8.) On Thursday, the museum stays open until 8:30pm for **Artful Evenings** with music, gallery talks, and a cash bar; admission is $8.

On the lower level is a gift shop, which holds clever collectibles tied to the art of the museum.

1600 21st St. NW (at Q St.). © 202/387-2151. www.phillipscollection.org. Admission Sat–Sun $8 adults, $6 students and seniors, free for children 18 and under; contribution accepted Tues–Fri. Special exhibits may require an additional fee. Tues–Sat 10am–5pm year-round (Thurs until 8:30pm); Sun noon–7pm, June–Sept noon–5pm. Free tours Wed and Sat 2pm. Closed Jan 1, July 4, Thanksgiving, and Dec 25. Metro: Dupont Circle (Q St. exit).

7 Other Attractions

John F. Kennedy Center for the Performing Arts ⓖ   Opened in 1971, the Kennedy Center is both the national performing arts center and a memorial to John F. Kennedy. Set on 17 acres overlooking the Potomac, the striking facility, designed by noted architect Edward Durell Stone, encompasses an opera house, a concert hall, two stage theaters, a theater lab, and a film theater. The best way to see the Kennedy Center is to take a free 50-minute guided tour (which takes you through some restricted areas). Tours are offered in English, French, Spanish, and Japanese. You can beat the crowds by writing in advance to a senator or congressperson for passes for a free congressional ("VIP") tour, given year-round Monday through Friday at 9:30am and 4:30pm, and at 9:30am only on Saturday. Call © **202/467-8340** for details.

The tour departs from the parking plaza on level A and takes you to the **Hall of Nations,** which displays the flags of all nations diplomatically recognized by the United States. Throughout the center you'll see gifts from more than 40 nations, including all the marble used in the building (3,700 tons), which Italy donated. First stop is the **Grand Foyer,** scene of many free concerts and programs and the reception area for all three theaters on the main level; the 18 crystal chandeliers are a gift from Sweden. You'll also visit the **Israeli Lounge** (where 40 painted and gilded panels depict scenes from the Old Testament); the **Concert Hall,** home of the National Symphony Orchestra; the newly remodeled **Opera House;** the **African Room** (decorated with beautiful tapestries from African nations); the **Eisenhower Theater;** the **Hall of States,** where flags of the 50 states and four territories are hung in the order they joined the Union; the **Performing Arts Library;** and the **Terrace Theater,** a bicentennial gift from Japan. If there's a rehearsal going on, the tour skips the visits to the theaters.

If you'd like to attend performances during your visit, check out the website or call the toll-free number above and request the current issue of *Kennedy Center News Magazine,* a free publication that describes all Kennedy Center happenings and prices. See chapter 9 for specifics on theater, concert, and film offerings.

Add another 15 minutes after the tour to walk around the building's terrace for a panoramic view of Washington.

The Kennedy Center, like a lot of other places around town, is undergoing a grand renovation. Try not to let it bother you. Eventually, the center will add two new buildings to the 8-acre plaza in front of the center, and better connect the center to the rest of the city. Right now, it's a mess, even though the center's performances, and tours, continue uninterrupted.

The construction affects the parking situation, which is limited. Until construction is completed, you should avoid driving here. If you do, you can expect to pre-pay a flat rate of $15.

2700 F St. NW (at New Hampshire Ave. NW and Rock Creek Pkwy.). ℂ **800/444-1324,** or 202/467-4600 for information or tickets. www.kennedy-center.org. Free admission. Daily 10am–midnight. Free guided tours Mon–Fri 10am–5pm; Sat–Sun 10am–1pm. Metro: Foggy Bottom (free shuttle service between the station and the center, running every 15 min. from 9:45am–midnight weekdays, 10am–midnight Sat, and noon–midnight Sun). Bus: no. 80 from Metro Center.

Union Station ✪ In Washington, D.C., even the very train station where you arrive is an attraction. Union Station, built between 1903 and 1907 in the great age of rail travel, was painstakingly restored in the 1980s at a cost of $160 million. The station was designed by noted architect Daniel H. Burnham, who modeled it after the Baths of Diocletian and Arch of Constantine in Rome.

When it opened in 1907, this was the largest train station in the world. The Ionic colonnades outside were fashioned from white granite. The facade contains 100 eagles. In the front of the building, a replica of the Liberty Bell and a monumental statue of Columbus hold sway. Six carved fixtures over the entranceway represent Fire, Electricity, Freedom, Imagination, Agriculture, and Mechanics. You enter the station through graceful 50-foot Constantine arches and walk across an expanse of white-marble flooring. The **Main Hall** is a massive rectangular room with a 96-foot barrel-vaulted ceiling and a balcony adorned with 36 Augustus Saint-Gaudens sculptures of Roman legionnaires. Off the Main Hall is the **East Hall,** shimmering with scagliola marble walls and columns, a gorgeous hand-stenciled skylight ceiling, and stunning murals of classical scenes inspired by ancient Pompeiian art. Today it's the station's nicest shopping venue.

In its heyday, this "temple of transport" witnessed many important events. President Wilson welcomed General Pershing here in 1918 on his return from France. South Pole explorer Rear Admiral Richard Byrd was also feted at Union Station on his homecoming. And Franklin D. Roosevelt's funeral train, bearing his casket, was met here in 1945 by thousands of mourners.

But after the 1960s, with the decline of rail travel, the station fell on hard times. Rain caused parts of the roof to cave in, and the entire building—with floors buckling, rats running about, and mushrooms sprouting in damp rooms—was sealed in 1981. That same year, Congress enacted legislation to preserve and restore this national treasure.

Today, Union Station is once again a vibrant entity patronized by locals and visitors alike, all 25 million of them yearly. Every square inch of the facility has been cleaned, repaired, and/or replaced according to the original design. About 120 retail and food shops on three levels offer a wide array of merchandise. And you'll be happy to find that most of the offerings in the Food Court are not fast-food joints but an eclectic mix of restaurants. The skylit **Main Concourse,** which extends the entire length of the station, is the primary shopping area as well as a ticketing and baggage facility. A nine-screen **cinema complex** lies on the lower level, across from the Food Court. The remarkable restoration, which involved hundreds of European and American artisans using historical research, bygone craft techniques, and modern technology, is meticulous in every detail. You could spend half a day here shopping, or about 20 minutes touring. Stop by the visitor kiosk in the Main Hall. See chapter 8 for information about Union Station **shops.**

50 Massachusetts Ave. NE. ℂ 202/371-9441. www.unionstationdc.com. Free admission. Daily 24 hr. Shops Mon–Sat 10am–9pm; Sun noon–6pm. Parking: $1 for 2 hr. with store or restaurant's stamped validation; for 2–3 hr., you pay $6 with validated ticket. Without validation, parking rates start at $5 for the 1st hr., and go up from there. Metro: Union Station.

Washington National Cathedral ✧   Pierre L'Enfant's 1791 plan for the capital city included "a great church for national purposes," but possibly because of early America's fear of mingling church and state, more than a century elapsed before the foundation for Washington National Cathedral was laid. Its actual name is the Cathedral Church of St. Peter and St. Paul. The church is Episcopal, but it has no local congregation and seeks to serve the entire nation as a house of prayer for all people. It has been the setting for every kind of religious observance, from Jewish to Serbian Orthodox.

A church of this magnitude—it's the sixth largest cathedral in the world, and the second largest in the U.S.—took a long time to build. Its principal (but not original) architect, Philip Hubert Frohman, worked on the project from 1921 until his death in 1972. The foundation stone was laid in 1907 using the mallet with which George Washington set the Capitol cornerstone. Construction was interrupted by both world wars and by periods of financial difficulty. The cathedral was completed with the placement of the final stone on the west front towers on September 29, 1990, 83 years (to the day) after it was begun.

English Gothic in style (with several distinctly 20th-century innovations, such as a stained-glass window commemorating the flight of *Apollo 11* and containing a piece of moon rock), the cathedral is built in the shape of a cross, complete with flying buttresses and 110 gargoyles. It is, along with the Capitol and the Washington Monument, one of the dominant structures on the Washington skyline. Its 57-acre landscaped grounds have two lovely gardens (the lawn is ideal for picnicking), four schools, a greenhouse, and two gift shops.

Over the years the cathedral has seen much history. Services to celebrate the end of World Wars I and II were held here. It was the scene of President Wilson's funeral (he and his wife are buried here), as well as President Eisenhower's. Helen Keller and her companion, Anne Sullivan, were buried in the cathedral at her request. And during the Iranian crisis, a round-the-clock prayer vigil was held in the Holy Spirit Chapel throughout the hostages' captivity. When they were released, the hostages came to a service here. President Bush's National Prayer and Remembrance service on September 14, 2001, following the cataclysm of September 11, was held here.

The best way to explore the cathedral is to take a 30- to 45-minute **guided tour;** they leave continually from the west end of the nave. You can also walk through on your own, using a self-guiding brochure available in several languages. Call about group and special-interest tours, both of which require reservations and fees (✆ **202/537-5700**). Allow additional time to tour the grounds or "close" and to visit the **Observation Gallery** ✧, where 70 windows provide panoramic views. Tuesday and Wednesday afternoon tours are followed by a high tea in the Observation Gallery for $22 per person; reservations required. Call ✆ **202/537-8993.**

The cathedral hosts numerous events: organ recitals; choir performances; an annual flower mart; calligraphy workshops; jazz, folk, and classical concerts; and the playing of the 53-bell carillon. Check the cathedral's website for schedules.

Massachusetts and Wisconsin Aves. NW (entrance on Wisconsin Ave.). ✆ **202/537-6200.** www.cathedral. org/cathedral. Donation $3 adults, $2 seniors, $1 children. Cathedral Mon–Fri 10am–5:30pm; Sat 10am–4:30pm; Sun 8am–6:30pm; May 1 to Labor Day, the nave level stays open Mon–Fri until 8pm. Gardens daily until dusk. Regular tours Mon–Sat 10–11:30am and 12:45–3:15pm; Sun 12:45–2:30pm. No tours on Palm Sunday, Easter, Thanksgiving, Dec 25, or during services. Services vary throughout the year, but you can count on a weekday Evensong service at 4:30pm, a weekday noon service, and an 11am service every Sun; call for other service times. Metro: Tenleytown, with a 20-min. walk. Bus: Any N bus up Massachusetts Ave. from Dupont Circle or any 30-series bus along Wisconsin Ave. This is a stop on the Old Town Trolley Tour.

8 Just Across the Potomac: Arlington

The land that today comprises Arlington County was originally carved out of Virginia as part of the nation's new capital district. In 1847, the land was returned to the state of Virginia, although it was known as Alexandria County until 1920, when the name was changed to avoid confusion with the city of Alexandria.

The county was named to honor Arlington House, built by George Washington Parke Custis, a descendant of Martha Washington whose daughter married Robert E. Lee. The Lees lived in Arlington House on and off until the onset of the Civil War in 1861. After the first Battle of Bull Run, at Manassas, several Union soldiers were buried here; the beginnings of Arlington National Cemetery date from that time. The Arlington Memorial Bridge leads directly from the Lincoln Memorial to the Robert E. Lee Memorial at Arlington House, symbolically joining these two figures into one Union after the Civil War.

Arlington has long been a residential community, with most people commuting into Washington to work and play. In recent years, however, the suburb has come into its own, booming with business, restaurants, and nightlife, giving residents reasons to stay put and tourists more incentive to visit (see "Arlington Row," in chapter 9). Here are a couple of sites worth seeing:

Arlington National Cemetery ★★ Upon arrival, head over to the **Visitor Center,** where you can view exhibits, pick up a detailed map, use the restrooms (there are no others until you get to Arlington House), and purchase a **Tourmobile ticket** ($6 per adult, $3 for children 3–11), which allows you to stop at all major sites in the cemetery and then reboard whenever you like. Service is continuous and the narrated commentary is informative; this is the only guided tour of the cemetery offered. If you've got plenty of stamina, consider doing part or all of the tour on foot. Remember as you go that this is a memorial frequented not just by tourists but also by those attending burial services or visiting the graves of beloved relatives and friends who are buried here.

This shrine occupies approximately 612 acres on the high hills overlooking the capital from the west side of the Memorial Bridge. It honors many national heroes and more than 260,000 war dead, veterans, and dependents. Many graves of the famous at Arlington bear nothing more than simple markers. Five-star General John J. Pershing's is one of those. Secretary of State John Foster Dulles is buried here. So are President William Howard Taft and Supreme Court Justices Thurgood Marshall and William Brennan. Cemetery highlights include:

The Tomb of the Unknowns, containing the unidentified remains of service members from both world wars, the Korean War, and, until 1997, the Vietnam War. In 1997, the remains of the unknown soldier from Vietnam were identified as those of Air Force 1st Lt. Michael Blassie, whose A-37 was shot down in South Vietnam in 1962. Blassie's family, who had reason to believe that the body was their son's, had beseeched the Pentagon to exhume the soldier's remains and conduct DNA testing to determine if what the family suspected was true. Upon confirmation, the Blassies buried Michael in his hometown of St. Louis. The crypt honoring the dead but unidentified Vietnam War soldiers will remain empty. The entire tomb is an unembellished, massive white-marble block, moving in its simplicity. A 24-hour honor guard watches over the tomb, with the changing of the guard taking place every half-hour April to September, every hour on the hour October to March, and every hour at night.

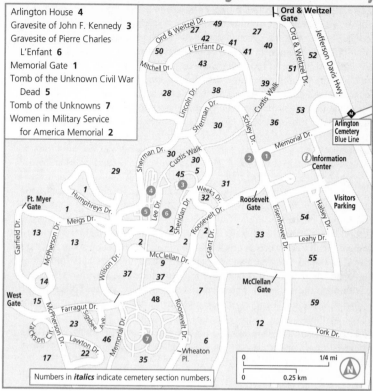

Arlington National Cemetery

Arlington House **4**
Gravesite of John F. Kennedy **3**
Gravesite of Pierre Charles
 L'Enfant **6**
Memorial Gate **1**
Tomb of the Unknown Civil War
 Dead **5**
Tomb of the Unknowns **7**
Women in Military Service
 for America Memorial **2**

Numbers in *italics* indicate cemetery section numbers.

Within a 20-minute walk, all uphill, from the Visitor Center is **Arlington House** (© **703/235-1530;** www.nps.gov/arho), whose structure was begun in 1802, by Martha and George Washington's grandson, George Washington Parke Custis (actually, Custis was George Washington's adopted grandson). Custis's daughter, Mary Anna Randolph, inherited the estate, and she and her husband, Robert E. Lee, lived here between 1831 and 1861. When Lee headed up Virginia's army, Mary fled, and federal troops confiscated the property.

A fine melding of the styles of the Greek Revival and the grand plantation houses of the early 1800s, the house has been administered by the National Park Service since 1933.

You tour the house on your own; park rangers are on-site to answer your questions. About 30% of the furnishings are original. Slave quarters and a small museum adjoin. Admission is free. It's open daily from 9:30am to 4:30pm (closed Jan 1 and Dec 25).

Pierre Charles L'Enfant's grave was placed near Arlington House at a spot that is believed to offer the best view of Washington, the city he designed.

Below Arlington House is the **Gravesite of John Fitzgerald Kennedy.** John Carl Warnecke designed a low crescent wall embracing a marble terrace, inscribed with the 35th president's most famous utterance: "And so my fellow Americans, ask not what your country can do for you, ask what you can do for your country." Jacqueline Kennedy Onassis rests next to her husband, and

Robert Kennedy is buried close by. The Kennedy graves attract streams of visitors. Arrive close to 8am to contemplate the site quietly; otherwise, it's mobbed. Looking north, there's a spectacular view of Washington.

In 1997, the **Women in Military Service for America Memorial** (© 800/ 222-2294 or 703/533-1155; www.womensmemorial.org) was added to Arlington Cemetery to honor the more than 1.8 million women who have served in the armed forces from the American Revolution to the present. The impressive new memorial lies just beyond the gated entrance to the cemetery, a 3-minute walk from the Visitor Center. As you approach the memorial, you see a large, circular reflecting pool, perfectly placed within the curve of the granite wall rising behind it. Arched passages within the 226-foot-long wall lead to an upper terrace and dramatic views of Arlington National Cemetery and the monuments of Washington; an arc of large glass panels (which form the roof of the memorial hall) contains etched quotations from famous people about contributions made by servicewomen. Behind the wall and completely underground is the **Education Center,** housing a **Hall of Honor,** a gallery of exhibits tracing the history of women in the military, a theater, and a computer register of servicewomen, which visitors may access for the stories and information about 250,000 individual military women, past and present. Hours are 8am to 5pm (until 7pm Apr–Sept). Stop at the reception desk for a brochure that details a self-guided tour through the memorial. The memorial is open every day but Christmas.

Plan to spend half a day at Arlington Cemetery and the Women in Military Service Memorial.

Just across the Memorial Bridge from the base of the Lincoln Memorial. © 703/607-8000. www.arlington cemetery.org. Free admission. Apr–Sept daily 8am–7pm; Oct–Mar daily 8am–5pm. Metro: Arlington National Cemetery. If you come by car, parking is $1.25 an hr. for the 1st 3 hrs., $2 an hr. thereafter. The cemetery is also accessible via Tourmobile.

Newseum & Freedom Park ⭐ *Kids*   The Newseum opened in 1997 as the world's first museum dedicated exclusively to news, it's been such a hit that it's already outgrown its location. This location is closed, and a new, larger, and higher-profile headquarters is under construction at 6th Street and Pennsylvania Avenue NW, just off the Mall, though it won't open until 2006. You can visit Freedom Park and the Freedom Forum Journalists Memorial, however.

Adjoining the museum, **Freedom Park,** which opened in the summer of 1996 and sits atop a never-used elevated highway, celebrates the spirit of freedom and the struggle to preserve it. Here, too, are many intriguing exhibits: segments of the Berlin Wall (the largest display of the wall outside of Germany), stones from the Warsaw Ghetto, a bronze casting of a South African ballot box, a headless statue of Lenin (one of many that were pushed over and beheaded when the Soviet Union collapsed in 1991), and a bronze casting of Martin Luther King Jr.'s Birmingham jail-cell door. The glass and steel Freedom Forum Journalists Memorial (honoring, as of 2004, more than 1,528 journalists killed while on assignment; their names are etched in the glass panels) rises above the Potomac, offering views of the Washington Monument, the Lincoln and Jefferson memorials, and the National Cathedral.

1101 Wilson Blvd. (at N. Kent St.). © 888-NEWSEUM or 703/284-3710. www.newseum.org. Freedom Park daily dawn through dusk. Limited parking is available in the building. Metro: Rosslyn.

The Pentagon   Damaged in the shocking September 11, 2001, terrorist attacks in which a hijacked commercial jet crashed into the building, killing 125 people working at the Pentagon, and 64 more people aboard the plane, the Pentagon building has been restored, but at this writing, it remains closed for general public tours, although school and military groups may be able to arrange for tours (call the information number listed below).

The Pentagon is the headquarters of the American military establishment. This immense five-sided structure was built during the early years of World War II. It's one of the world's largest office buildings, housing approximately 23,000 employees. For their convenience, it contains a complete indoor shopping mall, including two banks, a post office, an Amtrak ticket office, a beauty salon, a dry cleaner, and more. It's a self-contained world. There are many mind-boggling statistics to underscore the vastness of the Pentagon—for example, the building contains enough phone cable to circle the globe three times.

Off I-395. © 703/697-1776. www.defenselink.mil/pubs/pentagon. Free admission. Call to find out whether tours are being offered. Metro: Pentagon.

9 Parks & Gardens

Washington is extensively endowed with vast natural areas, all centrally located within the District. Included in all this greenery are thousands of parkland acres, two rivers, the mouth of a 185-mile-long tree-lined canal-side trail, an untamed wilderness area, and a few thousand cherry trees. And there's much more just a stone's throw away.

GARDENS

Enid A. Haupt Garden   Named for its donor, a noted supporter of horticultural projects, this stunning garden presents elaborate flower beds and borders, plant-filled turn-of-the-20th-century urns, 1870s cast-iron furnishings, and lush baskets hung from reproduction 19th-century lampposts. Although on ground level, the garden is actually on a 4¼-acre rooftop above the subterranean Ripley Center and the Sackler and African Art museums. An **"Island Garden"** near the Sackler Gallery, entered via a 9-foot moon gate, has benches backed by English boxwoods set under the canopy of weeping cherry trees.

A **"Fountain Garden"** outside the African Art Museum provides granite seating with walls overhung by hawthorn trees. Three small terraces, shaded by black sourgum trees, are located near the Arts and Industries Building. And five majestic linden trees shade a seating area around the Downing Urn, a memorial to American landscapist Andrew Jackson Downing, who designed the National Mall. Downing's words are inscribed on the base of the urn: "Build halls where knowledge shall be freely diffused among men, and not shut up within the narrow walls of narrower institutions. Plant spacious parks in your cities and unclose their gates as wide as the gates of morning to the whole people." Elaborate cast-iron carriage gates made according to a 19th-century design by James Renwick, flanked by four red sandstone pillars, are placed at the Independence Avenue entrance to the garden.

10th St. and Independence Ave. SW. © 202/357-2700. Free admission. Late May–Aug daily 7am–9:15pm; Sept to mid-May daily 7am–5:45pm. Closed Dec 25. Metro: Smithsonian.

United States Botanic Garden ✦   The Botanic Garden re-opened in late 2001 after a major, 5-year renovation. The grand conservatory devotes half of its space to exhibits that focus on the importance of plants to people, and half to exhibits that focus on ecology and the evolutionary biology of plants. The conservatory holds 4,000 living species; 26,000 plants; a high-walled enclosure, called "The Jungle," of palms, ferns, and vines; an Orchid Room; and, outside the conservatory, a First Ladies Water Garden, formal rose garden, and a lawn terrace. You'll also find a Meditation Garden and gardens created especially with children in mind. Call in advance to arrange for a free, 4-minute tour. The USBG sometimes offers entertainment, like the live music and tours it hosted last summer, staying open until 8pm on the first Tuesday of each month.

Also visit the garden annex across the street, **Bartholdi Park.** The park is about the size of a city block, with a stunning cast-iron classical fountain created by Frédéric Auguste Bartholdi, designer of the Statue of Liberty. Charming flower gardens bloom amid tall ornamental grasses, benches are sheltered by vine-covered bowers, and a touch and fragrance garden contains such herbs as pineapple-scented sage.

245 1st St. ⓒ 202/225-8333. www.usbg.gov. Free admission. Daily 10am–5pm. Metro: Federal Center SW.

PARKS
POTOMAC PARK

West and East Potomac parks, their 720 riverside acres divided by the Tidal Basin, are most famous for their spring display of **cherry blossoms** and all the hoopla that goes with it. So much attention is lavished on Washington's cherry blossoms that the National Park Service devotes a home page to the subject: **www.nps.gov/nacc/cherry**. You can access this site to find out forecasts for the blooms and assorted other details. You can also call the National Park Service (ⓒ **202/485-9880**) for information. In all, there are more than 3,700 cherry trees planted along the Tidal Basin in West Potomac Park, East Potomac Park, the Washington Monument grounds, and in other pockets of the city.

To get to the Tidal Basin by car (*not* recommended in cherry-blossom season), you want to get on Independence Avenue and follow the signs posted near the Lincoln Memorial that show you where to turn to find parking and the FDR Memorial. If you're walking, you'll want to cross Independence Avenue where it intersects with West Basin Drive (there's a stoplight and crosswalk), and follow the path to the Tidal Basin. There is no convenient Metro stop near here.

West Potomac Park encompasses Constitution Gardens; the Vietnam, Korean, Lincoln, Jefferson, and FDR memorials; a small island where ducks live; and the Reflecting Pool (see "The Major Memorials," earlier in this chapter for full listings of the memorials). It has 1,628 cherry trees bordering the Tidal Basin, some of them Akebonos with delicate pink blossoms, but most Yoshinos with white, cloudlike flower clusters. The blossoming of the cherry trees is the focal point of a 2-week-long celebration, including the lighting of the 300-year-old Japanese Stone Lantern near Kutz Bridge, presented to the city by the governor of Tokyo in 1954. (This year's Cherry Blossom Festival is scheduled to run Mar 26–Apr 11, 2005) The trees bloom for a little less than 2 weeks beginning sometime between March 20 and April 17; April 4 is the average date. Planning your trip around the blooming of the cherry blossoms is an iffy proposition, and I wouldn't advise it. All it takes is one good rain and those cherry blossoms are gone. The cherry blossoms are not illuminated at night.

East Potomac Park has 1,681 cherry trees in 11 varieties. The park also has picnic grounds, tennis courts, three golf courses, a large swimming pool, and biking and hiking paths by the water.

ROCK CREEK PARK

Created in 1890, **Rock Creek Park** ✯ (**www.nps.gov/rocr**) was purchased by Congress for its "pleasant valleys and ravines, primeval forests and open fields, its running waters, its rocks clothed with rich ferns and mosses, its repose and tranquillity, its light and shade, its ever-varying shrubbery, its beautiful and extensive

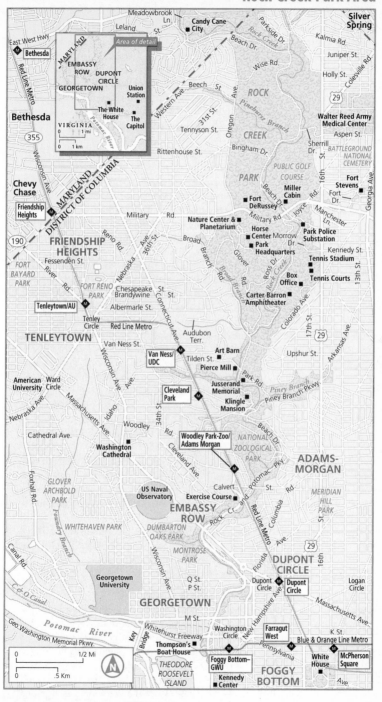

views." A 1,750-acre valley within the District of Columbia, extending 12 miles from the Potomac River to the Maryland border, it's one of the biggest and finest city parks in the nation. Parts of it are still wild; it's not unusual to see a deer scurrying through the woods in more remote sections.

The park's offerings include the Old Stone House, Carter Barron Amphitheater (see chapter 9), playgrounds, an extensive system of beautiful hiking and biking trails, sports facilities, remains of Civil War fortifications, and acres and acres of wooded parklands. See also p. 208 for a description of the formal gardens at **Dumbarton Oaks,** which border Rock Creek Park in upper Georgetown.

For full information on the wide range of park programs and activities, visit the **Rock Creek Nature Center and Planetarium,** 5200 Glover Rd. NW (© **202/ 895-6070**), Wednesday through Sunday from 9am to 5pm; or Park Headquarters, 3545 Williamsburg Lane NW (© **202/895-6015**), Monday through Friday from 7:45am to 4:15pm. To get to the Nature Center by public transportation, take the Metro to Friendship Heights and transfer to bus no. E2 to Military Road and Oregon Avenue/Glover Road, then walk up the hill about 100 yards to the Nature Center. Call © **202/895-6070** to request a brochure that provides details on picnic locations.

The Nature Center and Planetarium is the scene of numerous activities, including weekend planetarium shows for kids (minimum age 4) and adults; nature films; crafts demonstrations; live animal demonstrations; guided nature walks; plus a daily mix of lectures, films, and other events. Self-guided nature trails begin here. All activities are free, but for planetarium shows you need to pick up tickets a half-hour in advance. There are also nature exhibits on the premises. The Nature Center is closed on federal holidays.

Not far from the Nature Center is **Fort DeRussey,** one of 68 fortifications erected to defend the city of Washington during the Civil War. From the intersection of Military Road and Oregon Avenue, you walk a short trail through the woods to reach the fort, whose remains include high earth mounds with openings where guns were mounted, surrounded by a deep ditch/moat.

At Tilden Street and Beach Drive, you can see a water-powered 19th-century gristmill, which normally is grinding corn and wheat into flour (© **202/426- 6908**). It's called **Peirce Mill** (a man named Isaac Peirce built it), but it's currently closed for repairs. Peirce's old carriage house is now the **Rock Creek Gallery** (© **202/244-2482**), where works of local artists are shown; it's open Thursday through Sunday from noon to 6pm (closed federal holidays and 1 month in summer, either July or Aug).

Poetry readings and workshops are held during the summer at **Miller's Cabin,** the one-time residence of High Sierra poet Joaquin Miller, Beach Drive north of Military Road. Call © **202/895-6070** for information.

There's convenient free **parking** throughout the park.

THEODORE ROOSEVELT ISLAND PARK ★★

A serene 91-acre wilderness preserve, Theodore Roosevelt Island is a memorial to the nation's 26th president, in recognition of his contributions to conservation. During his administration, Roosevelt, an outdoor enthusiast and expert field naturalist, set aside a total of 234 million acres of public lands for forests, national parks, wildlife and bird refuges, and monuments.

Native American tribes were here first, inhabiting the island for centuries, until the arrival of English explorers in the 1600s. Over the years, the island passed through many owners before becoming what it is today—an island preserve of swamp, marsh, and upland forest that's a haven for rabbits, chipmunks, great owls, fox, muskrat, turtles, and groundhogs. It's a complex ecosystem in which cattails, arrow arum, and pickerelweed grow in the marshes, and willow, ash, and maple trees root on the mud flats. You can observe these flora and fauna in their natural environs on 2½ miles of foot trails.

In the northern center of the island, overlooking a terrace encircled by a water-filled moat, stands a 17-foot bronze statue of Roosevelt. Four 21-foot granite tablets are inscribed with tenets of his conservation philosophy.

To drive to the island, take the George Washington Memorial Parkway exit north from the Theodore Roosevelt Bridge. The parking area is accessible only from the northbound lane; park there and cross the pedestrian bridge that connects the lot to the island. You can also rent a canoe at Thompson's Boat Center (p. 230) and paddle over, or take the pedestrian bridge at Rosslyn Circle, 2 blocks from the Rosslyn Metro station. You can picnic on the grounds near the memorial; if you do, allow about an hour or two here.

In the Potomac River, between Washington and Rosslyn, VA. See access information above. ℂ 703/ 289-2500. www.nps.gov/this. Free admission. Daily dawn through dusk. Metro: Rosslyn, then walk 2 blocks to Rosslyn Circle and cross the pedestrian bridge to the island.

ACTIVITIES ON THE C&O CANAL

One of the great joys of living in Washington is the **C&O Canal** (**www. nps.gov/choh**) and its unspoiled 184½-mile towpath. You leave urban cares and stresses behind while hiking, strolling, jogging, cycling, or boating in this lush, natural setting of ancient oaks and red maples, giant sycamores, willows, and wildflowers. But the canal wasn't always just a leisure spot for city people. It was built in the 1800s, when water routes were considered vital to transportation. Even before it was completed, the canal was being rendered obsolete by the B&O Railroad, which was constructed at about the same time and along the same route. Today, its role as an oasis from unrelenting urbanity is even more important.

A good source of information about the canal is the National Park Service office at **Great Falls Tavern Visitor Center,** 11710 MacArthur Blvd., Potomac, MD (ℂ **301/767-3714**). At this 1831 tavern, you can see museum exhibits and a film about the canal; there's also a bookstore on the premises. The park charges an entrance fee, $5 per car, $3 per walker or cyclist.

In Georgetown, the **Georgetown Information Center,** 1057 Thomas Jefferson St. NW (ℂ **202/653-5190**), can also provide maps and information.

Hiking any section of the flat dirt towpath or its more rugged side paths is a pleasure (and it's free). There are picnic tables, some with barbecue grills, about every 5 miles on the way to Cumberland, beginning at **Fletcher's Boat House** (ℂ **202/244-0461**), which is about 3¼ miles out of Georgetown and is a good place to rent bikes or boats or to purchase bait, tackle, and a fishing license. Enter the towpath in Georgetown below M Street via Thomas Jefferson Street. If you hike 14 miles, you'll reach **Great Falls,** a point where the Potomac becomes a stunning waterfall plunging 76 feet. Or drive to Great Falls Park on the Virginia side of the Potomac.

Much less strenuous than hiking is a **mule-drawn 19th-century canal boat trip** led by Park Service rangers in period dress. They regale passengers with canal legend and lore and sing period songs. These boats depart from mid-April to mid-September; departure times and tickets are available at the Georgetown Information Center (see above). Both the Georgetown and Great Falls barge rides last about 1 hour and 10 minutes and cost $8 for adults, $6 for seniors over 61, and $5 for children ages 3 to 14.

Call any of the above information numbers for details on riding, rock climbing, fishing, bird-watching, concerts, ranger-guided tours, ice skating, camping, and other canal activities.

10 Especially for Kids

Who knows what kids might enjoy in Washington better than other kids? So I asked my youngest, Lucy (12), and her cousins, Sarah (15) and Nick (10), who offer these suggestions:

Lucy: "I would recommend going to the Spy Museum [International Spy Museum]—for people of all ages. One reason I like it is because the museum has films going on that tell spy stories that are hard to believe, but you know are true. I remember a woman spy who was talking about someone she worked with, a man [Aldrich Ames], who was always sort of quiet and then he went and

---

Kids **Favorite Children's Attractions**

Check for special children's events at museum information desks when you enter. As noted within the listings for individual museums, some children's programs are also great fun for adults. I recommend the programs at the **Corcoran Gallery of Art,** the **Folger Shakespeare Library,** the **Phillips,** and the **Sackler Gallery** in particular. (The gift shops in most of these museums have wonderful toys and children's books.) Call ahead to find out which programs are running. Here's a rundown of the biggest kid-pleasers in town (for details, see the full entries earlier in this chapter):

- **Ford's Theatre & Lincoln Museum and The House Where Lincoln Died** (p. 212): Booth's gun and diary, the clothes Lincoln was wearing the night he was assassinated, and other such grisly artifacts. Kids adore the whole business.

- **International Spy Museum** (p. 212): Both kids and adults enjoy pretending to be spies, testing their powers of observation, and trying to figure out how the Enigma machine works.

- **Lincoln Memorial** (p. 184): Kids know a lot about Lincoln and enjoy visiting his memorial. A special treat is visiting after dark (the same goes for the Washington Monument and Jefferson Memorial).

- **National Air and Space Museum** (p. 192): Spectacular IMAX films (don't miss), planetarium shows, missiles, rockets, a walk-through orbital workshop, and flight simulators.

- **National Museum of Natural History** (p. 197): A Discovery Room just for youngsters, the butterfly garden, an insect zoo, shrunken heads, and dinosaurs, and the IMAX theater showing 2-D and 3-D films.

- **National Zoological Park** (p. 199): Pandas! Kids always love a zoo, and this is an especially good one.

- **Washington Monument** (p. 180): Easy to get them up there, hard to get them down. If only they could use the steps, they'd be in heaven.

worked in Rome and when he came back, all of a sudden he looked different and acted different, like he had a lot of money and he had gotten his teeth fixed and was wearing nice clothes. The man turned out to be a spy against the United States, and the Russians were paying him money for information."

Nick: "I like the ESPN Zone [see chapter 9]. They have really good food, like the ribs, and the games are really fun. I like the kayaking one. I also think it's cool that there are TVs in front of the urinals in the bathrooms."

Sarah: "Go to the Supreme Court, it is really cool. And it's especially really amazing to see all the justices walk in and everyone rises and it's a really cool feeling. And it's also really funny sometimes to see the justices argue with the lawyers. You should know that sometimes for some cases there are really long lines, but otherwise it's really fun and it's a really great experience."

For more ideas, consult the Friday "Weekend" section of the *Washington Post,* which lists numerous activities (mostly free) for kids: special museum events, children's theater, storytelling programs, puppet shows, video-game competitions, and so forth. Call the Kennedy Center, the Lisner, and the National Theatre to find out about children's shows; see chapter 9 for details. Also read the write-up of Discovery Theater, within the Smithsonian's Arts and Industries Building, earlier in this chapter.

I've checked out hotels built with families in mind in chapter 5's "Family-Friendly Hotels"; that hotel pool may rescue your sanity for an hour or two. The "Organized Tours" and "Outdoor Activities" sections below may also be your saving grace when you've run out of steam or need a jump-start to your day.

11 Organized Tours

ON FOOT

A Tour de Force (© 703/525-2948; www.atourdeforce.com) is historian and raconteur Jeanne Fogel's 20-year-old company. She offers a variety of walking and bus tours around the city, revealing little-known anecdotes and facts about neighborhoods, historic figures, and the most visited sites. Fogel's tours are custom designed for groups, not individuals. Call for rates.

TourDC, Walking Tours of Georgetown, Dupont Circle & Embassy Row (© 301/588-8999; www.tourdc.com) conducts 90-minute ($12) walking tours of Georgetown, telling about the neighborhood's history up to the present and taking you past the homes of notable residents.

Guided Walking Tours of Washington (© 301/294-9514; www.dcsightseeing.com) offers 2-hour walks through the streets of Georgetown, Adams-Morgan, and other locations, guided by author/historian Anthony S. Pitch. Inquire about private tours. Rates are $15 per person.

BY BUS

TOURMOBILE Best-known and least expensive, **Tourmobile Sightseeing** (© 888/868-7707 or 202/554-5100; www.tourmobile.com) is a good choice if you're looking for an easy-on/easy-off tour of major sites. The comfortable red, white, and blue sightseeing trams travel to as many as 24 attractions (the company changes its schedule and number of stops, depending on whether sites are open for public tours), including Arlington National Cemetery. Tourmobile is the only narrated sightseeing shuttle tour authorized by the National Park Service. The company offers a number of different tours, but the most popular is the **American Heritage Tour,** which stops at 21 sites on or near the National

Mall and at three sites in Arlington Cemetery. (Again, the number of stops may be fewer than 21, if regularly scheduled stops, like the White House, are not open for public tours due to increased security.) Normally, stops include the memorials and Washington Monument, Union Station, the National Gallery, most of the Smithsonian museums (National Air and Space, National Museum of American History, National Museum of Natural History, and the Arts and Industries Building/Hirshhorn Museum), the Capitol, and several other locations. In Arlington Cemetery, the bus stops at the Kennedy grave sites, the Tomb of the Unknowns, and Arlington House.

You simply hop on a Tourmobile at any of the locations, pay the driver when you first board the bus (you can also purchase a ticket at the booth at the Washington Monument or inside the Arlington National Cemetery Visitor Center, or, for a small surcharge, order your ticket in advance from Ticketmaster at © 800/551-SEAT). Along the route, get off at any stop to visit monuments or buildings. When you finish exploring each area, just show your ticket and climb aboard the next Tourmobile that comes along. The buses travel in a loop, serving each stop about every 15 to 30 minutes. One fare allows you to use the buses all day. The charge for the American Heritage Tour is $20 for anyone 12 and older, $10 for children 3 to 11. For Arlington Cemetery only, those 12 and older pay $6, children $3. Children under 3 ride free. Buses follow circuits from the Capitol to Arlington Cemetery and back. Well-trained narrators give commentaries about sights along the route and answer questions.

Though heated in winter, these trams are not air-conditioned in summer, and though the windows stay open, they can get hot and uncomfortable. Readers also report that Tourmobiles, being the largest trams, take a long time to load and unload passengers, which can be frustrating to those anxious to see the sights.

Tourmobiles operate 9:30am to 4:30pm, daily year-round, except Christmas. (In busy tourist season, Tourmobile sometimes extends its hours.)

Call Tourmobile or access the website for further information and rates for other tours.

OLD TOWN TROLLEY **Old Town Trolley tours** (© 202/832-9800; www. oldtowntrolley.com) offer fixed-price, on-off service as you travel in a loop around the city. You can purchase your ticket at the booth at Union Station, or board without a ticket and purchase it en route. (One exception is the Lincoln Memorial stop. The National Park Service does not allow any tour bus service other than Tourmobile to solicit business on its lands, which means you must have a prepaid ticket to board an Old Town Trolley at the Lincoln Memorial.) Buses operate daily from 9am to 5:30pm year-round. The cost is $26 for adults, $13 for children 4 to 12, free for children under 4. In 2004, Old Town Trolley discounted these prices to $23 and $12, respectively, when you purchased the tickets online. The full tour, which is narrated, takes 2 hours (if you never get off), and trolleys come by every 30 minutes or so. Old Town Trolley tours cost more than Tourmobile tours, but they travel to neighborhoods, like Georgetown, and attractions away from the Mall, like the Washington National Cathedral.

BY BOAT

Since Washington is a river city, why not see it by boat? Potomac cruises allow sweeping vistas of the monuments and memorials, Georgetown, the Kennedy Center, and other Washington sights. Read the information below carefully, since not all boat cruises offer guided tours. Some of the following boats leave from the Washington waterfront and some from Old Town Alexandria:

Spirit of Washington Cruises, Pier 4 at 6th and Water streets SW (© **866/ 211-3811** or 202/554-8000; www.spiritcruises.com; Metro: Waterfront), offers a variety of trips daily, including evening dinner, lunch, brunch, moonlight dance cruises, as well as a half-day excursion to Mount Vernon and back. Lunch and dinner cruises include a 40-minute musical revue. Prices start at $40 for a lunch excursion and $70 for a dinner cruise. Call to make reservations.

The *Spirit of Washington* is a luxury climate-controlled harbor cruise ship with carpeted decks and huge panoramic windows designed for sightseeing. There are three well-stocked bars on board. Mount Vernon cruises are aboard an equally luxurious sister ship, the *Potomac Spirit.*

Potomac Party Cruises (© **703/683-6076;** www.dandydinnerboat.com) operates *The Dandy* and *Nina's Dandy,* both climate-controlled, all-weather, glassed-in floating restaurants that run year-round. Lunch, evening dinner/dance, and special charter cruises are available daily. You board both vessels in Old Town Alexandria, at the Prince Street pier, between Duke and King streets. Trips range from $35 for a 2½-hour weekday lunch cruise to $85 for a 3-hour Saturday dinner cruise.

Odyssey III (© **888/741-0281;** www.odysseycruises.com) was designed specifically to glide under the bridges that cross the Potomac. The boat looks like a glass bullet, with its snub-nosed port and its streamlined 240-foot-long glass body. The wraparound see-through walls and ceiling allow for great views. Like *The Dandy,* the *Odyssey* operates all year. You board the *Odyssey* at the Gangplank Marina, on Washington's waterfront, at 6th and Water streets SW (Metro: Waterfront). Cruises available include lunch, Sunday brunch, and dinner excursions, with live entertainment provided during each cruise. It costs $38 for a 2-hour weekday lunch cruise and $92 for a 3-hour Saturday dinner cruise.

The **Potomac Riverboat Company** ℛ (© **703/548-9000;** www.potomac riverboatco.com) offers three narrated tours April through October aboard the *Matthew Hayes,* on a 90-minute tour past Washington monuments and memorials; the *Admiral Tilp,* on a 40-minute tour of Old Town Alexandria's waterfront; and the *Miss Christin,* which cruises to Mount Vernon, where you hop off and reboard after you've toured the estate. You board the boats at the pier behind the Torpedo Factory in Old Town Alexandria, at the foot of King Street; or, for the Washington monuments and memorials tour, Georgetown's Washington Harbour. *Matthew Hayes* tickets are $16 for adults, $8 for children ages 2 to 12; *Admiral Tilp* tickets are $8 for adults, $5 for children ages 2 to 12; and *Miss Christin* tickets are $27 for adults, $15 for children ages 6 to 10, and include admission to Mount Vernon. A concession stand selling light refreshments and beverages is open during the cruises.

The **Capitol River Cruise's** *Nightingale I* and *Nightingale II* (© **800/405-5511** or 301/460-7447; www.capitolrivercruises.com) are historic 65-foot steel riverboats that can accommodate up to 90 people. The *Nightingale's* narrated jaunts depart Georgetown's Washington Harbour every hour on the hour, from noon to 9pm, April through October (the 9pm outing is offered in summer months only). The 50-minute narrated tour travels past the monuments and memorials to National Airport and back. A snack bar on board sells light refreshments, beer, wine, and sodas; you're welcome to bring your own picnic aboard. The price is $10 per adult, $5 per child ages 3 to 12. To get here, take Metro to Foggy Bottom and then the Georgetown Metro Connection Shuttle or walk into Georgetown, following Pennsylvania Avenue, which becomes M Street. Turn left on 31st Street NW, to the Washington Harbour complex.

A BOAT ON WHEELS Old Town Trolley also operates **DC Ducks** (© 202/ 832-9800; www.dcducks.com), which feature unique land and water tours of Washington aboard the *DUKW,* an amphibious army vehicle (boat with wheels) from World War II that accommodates 30 passengers. Ninety-minute guided tours aboard the open-air canopied craft include a land portion taking in major sights—the Capitol, Lincoln Memorial, Washington Monument, White House, and Smithsonian museums—and a 30-minute Potomac cruise. Purchase tickets inside Union Station at the information desk; board the vehicle just outside the main entrance to Union Station. Hours vary, but departures usually follow a daily 11am and 1 and 3pm schedule (Mar-Oct). Tickets cost $28 for adults, $14 for children 5 to 12, free for children under 5.

BY BIKE

Bike the Sites, Inc. ☆ (© 202/842-2453; www.bikethesites.com) offers a more active way to see Washington. The company has designed several different biking tours of the city, including the popular Capital Sites Ride, which is actually 2 routes, one covering the museums, the other the memorials, and you can do the tour in 2 stints or all at once. If done together, the ride takes 5½ hours and covers more than 55 sites along a 10-mile stretch. Whether ridden in one trip or in separate stages, the tour costs $55 per adult, $45 per child 12 and under. Bike the Sites provides you with a 21-speed Trek Hybrid bicycle fitted to your size, bike helmet, handlebar bag, water bottle, light snack, and two guides to lead the ride. Guides impart historical and anecdotal information as you go. The company will customize bike rides to suit your tour specifications.

12 Outdoor Activities

The Washington area offers plenty of opportunities for outdoor activities. See "Parks & Gardens," earlier in this chapter for complete coverage of the city's loveliest green spaces.

Joggers can enjoy a run on the Mall or along the path in Rock Creek Park.

Rent a bike at **Fletcher's Boat House,** Reservoir and Canal roads (© 202/ 244-0461; www.fletchersboathouse.com), or **Thompson's Boat Center,** 2900 Virginia Ave. at Rock Creek Parkway NW (© **202/333-4861** or 202/333-9543; www.thompsonboatcenter.com; Metro: Foggy Bottom, with a 10-min. walk); both Fletcher's and Thompson's rent bikes from about mid-March to mid-October. At **Big Wheel Bikes,** 1034 33rd St. NW, right near the C&O Canal just below M Street (© **202/337-0254**), you can rent a bike year-round, Tuesday through Sunday. If you need suggested routes or want company, check out Friday's *Washington Post* "Weekend" section listing cycling trips. Rock Creek Park has an **11-mile paved bike route** ☆ from the Lincoln Memorial through the park into Maryland. Or you can follow the bike path from the Lincoln Memorial and go over the Memorial Bridge to pedal to Old Town Alexandria and to Mount Vernon (see chapter 10). On weekends and holidays, a large part of Rock Creek Parkway is closed to vehicular traffic. The C&O Canal and the Potomac parks, described earlier in "Parks & Gardens," also have extended bike paths. A new 7-mile path, the **Capital Crescent Trail,** takes you from Georgetown to the suburb of Bethesda, Maryland, following a former railroad track that parallels the Potomac River for part of the way and passes by old trestle bridges and pleasant residential neighborhoods.

Thompson's Boat Center and **Fletcher's Boat House** (see above for both) rent boats following the same schedule as their bike rental season, basically

March to November. Thompson's has canoes, kayaks, and rowing shells (recreational and racing), and is open for boat and bike rentals daily from 8am to 6pm. Fletcher's is right on the C&O Canal, about 3¼ miles from Georgetown. The same family has owned it since 1850! In addition to renting bikes and canoes, Fletcher's also sells fishing licenses, bait, and tackle. Fletcher's is accessible by car (west on M St. to Canal Rd.) and has plenty of free parking.

From late March to mid-September, you can rent **paddleboats** ☂ on the north end of the Tidal Basin off Independence Avenue (② 202/479-2426). Four-seaters are $16 an hour; two-seaters are $8 an hour, daily from 10am to 6pm.

Washington has numerous **hiking paths.** The C&O Canal offers 184½ miles; Theodore Roosevelt Island has more than 88 wilderness acres to explore; and Rock Creek Park boasts 20 miles of hiking trails (maps are available at the Visitor Information Center or Park Headquarters).

If you're coming to Washington in winter, you can go **ice skating** on the C&O Canal (call ② 301/299-3613 for information on ice conditions), as long as you bring your own skates. For a really fun experience, head to the **National Gallery Sculpture Garden Ice Rink** ☂, on the Mall at 7th Street and Constitution Avenue NW (② 202/289-3360), where you can rent skates, twirl in view of the sculptures, and enjoy hot chocolate and a sandwich in the Pavilion Café, right next to the rink. Another outdoor rink where you can rent skates is **Pershing Park,** at 14th Street and Pennsylvania Avenue NW (② 202/737-6938).

If it's summer and your hotel doesn't have a pool, you might consider one of the neighborhood pools, including a large outdoor pool at 25th and N streets NW (② 202/727-3285); and the Georgetown outdoor pool at 34th Street and Volta Place NW (② 202/282-2366). Keep in mind that these are likely to be crowded.

Tennis lovers will have a hard time finding public courts in Washington. **East Potomac Park** has nine tennis courts, including five indoors (② 202/554-5962). Fees vary with court surface and time of play. **Montrose Park**, right next to Dumbarton Oaks (p. 208) in Georgetown, has several courts available for free on a first-come, first-served basis; but they're often in use.

8

Shopping

Like every other city in America, Washington, D.C., has its fair share of Gaps, Banana Republics, Barnes & Nobles and other chain stores. But have you heard of Olsson's Bookstores? The Zenith Gallery? The Indian Craft Shop? Eastern Market? The Tiny Jewel Box? all about jane? Bet you haven't. Read this chapter for information about these and other beloved homegrown stores, but also to find out where the best shopping opportunities are, and for details, if you must know, about the Washington-area stores with names already so familiar to you.

1 The Shopping Scene

Washington-area stores are usually open daily from 10am to 5 or 6pm Monday through Saturday, with one late night (usually Thurs) when hours extend to 9pm. Sunday hours are usually from noon to 5 or 6pm. Exceptions are the malls, which are open late nightly, and antiques stores and art galleries, which tend to keep their own hours. Be safe and call ahead if there's a store you really want to get to.

Sales tax on merchandise is 5.75% in the District, 5% in Maryland, and 4.5% in Virginia. Most gift, arts, and crafts stores, including those at the Smithsonian museums, will handle shipping for you; clothes stores generally do not.

If you're a true bargain hunter, scope out the *Washington Post* website (**www.washingtonpost.com**) in advance of your trip to see which stores are having sales. Once you get to the *Post*'s home page, hit "Arts and Living" at the top of your screen, click on "Fashion and Beauty," and then click on "Sales and Bargains," a column that's updated weekly.

2 Great Shopping Areas

UNION STATION It's a railroad station, a historic landmark, an architectural marvel, a Metro stop, a shopping mall. Yes, the beauteous Union Station offers some fine shopping opportunities, certainly the best on Capitol Hill: more than 100 specialty shops, and more than 45 eateries.

DOWNTOWN The area bounded east and west by 7th and 14th streets NW, and north and south by New York and Pennsylvania avenues NW, is in a frenzy of development. Stores here include the tony Chanel Boutique, located within the Willard Inter-Continental hotel's courtyard; an ever longer list of "name" stores: Banana Republic, Ann Taylor, H&M, Jos. A. Bank's, and Filene's Basement; and one-of-a-kind places, such as Apartment Zero and Chapters. Look for the huge Borders bookstore at 14th and F streets NW, in the grand old Garfinckel's Building. Hecht's, at 12th and G streets, continues as the sole department store downtown. Metro: Metro Center.

ADAMS-MORGAN   Centered on 18th Street and Columbia Road NW, Adams-Morgan is a neighborhood of ethnic eateries and nightclubs interspersed with the odd secondhand bookshop and eclectic collectibles stores. It's a fun area for walking and shopping. Parking is possible during the day but impossible at night. Closest Metro: You have two choices: Woodley Park/Zoo–Adams Morgan, then walk south on Connecticut Avenue NW until you reach Calvert Street, cross Connecticut Avenue and follow Calvert Street across the bridge until you reach the junction of Columbia Road NW and 18th Street NW. On Saturday, you can catch the no. 98 Adams Morgan–U Street Link shuttle bus, which departs every 15 minutes from the Woodley Park station and takes you to Adams-Morgan. With a Metrorail transfer from the Woodley Park Metro station, the cost is 35¢; with no transfer, you pay $1.20. Second choice: Dupont Circle; exit at Q Street NW and walk up Connecticut Avenue NW to Columbia Road NW.

CONNECTICUT AVENUE/DUPONT CIRCLE   Running from the mini–Wall Street that is K Street north to S Street, Connecticut Avenue NW is a main thoroughfare, where you'll find traditional clothing at Brooks Brothers, Talbots, and Burberry's; casual duds at The Gap; discount items at Filene's Basement and the Ann Taylor Loft; and haute couture at Rizik's. Closer to Dupont Circle are coffee bars and neighborhood restaurants, as well as art galleries; funky boutiques; gift, stationery, book, and record shops; and stores with a gay and lesbian slant. Metro: Farragut North at one end, Dupont Circle at the other.

GEORGETOWN   Georgetown is the city's main shopping area. In the heart of the neighborhood, stores line Wisconsin Avenue and M Street NW, and they also fan out along side streets. You'll find both chain and one-of-a-kind shops, chic as well as thrift. Sidewalks and streets are almost always crowded, and parking can be tough. Weekends, especially, bring out all kinds of yahoos, who are mainly here to drink. Visit Georgetown on a weekday morning, if you can. Weeknights are another good time to visit, for dinner and strolling afterward. Metro: Foggy Bottom, then catch the bright blue Georgetown Metro Connection bus, which runs every 10 minutes, takes only a few minutes to reach Georgetown, and costs 35¢ with a Metrorail transfer, or $1 without a transfer. Metrobuses (the no. 30-series: 30, 32, 34, 36) travel through Georgetown from different parts of the city. Otherwise, consider taking a taxi. If you drive, you'll find parking lots expensive and tickets even more so, so be careful where you plant your car.

UPPER WISCONSIN AVENUE NORTHWEST   In a residential section of town known as Friendship Heights on the D.C. side and Chevy Chase on the Maryland side (7 miles north of Georgetown, straight up Wisconsin Ave.) is a quarter-mile shopping district that extends from Saks Fifth Avenue at one end to Sur La Table at the other. In between lie Lord & Taylor, Neiman Marcus, and Hecht's department stores; a bevy of top shops, such as Tiffany's and Versace; two malls, the Mazza Gallerie and the Chevy Chase Pavilion; and several stand-alone staples, such as Banana Republic. The street is too wide and traffic always too snarled to make this a fun place to stroll, although teenagers do love to loiter here. Drive here if you want; the Hecht's store parking lot offers 2 hours of free parking with validation. Or Metro it; the strip is right on the Red Line, with the "Friendship Heights" exits leading directly into each of the malls and into Hecht's.

OLD TOWN ALEXANDRIA   Old Town, a Virginia neighborhood beyond National Airport, is becomingly increasingly like Georgetown, warts (heavy traffic, crowded sidewalks, difficult parking) and all. Old Town extends from the

Potomac River in the east to the King Street Metro station in the west, and from about First Street in the north to Green Street in the south, but the best shopping is in the center, where King and Washington streets intersect. Weekdays are a lot tamer than weekends. It's always a nice place to visit, though; the drive alone is worth the trip. See chapter 10 for full coverage of Alexandria. Metro: King Street, then take a blue and gold DASH bus (fare $1) to reach the heart of Old Town.

3 Shopping A to Z

ANTIQUES

A few miles north of the city is not too far to go for the good deal or true bonanza you're likely to discover on **Antique Row.** Some 40 antiques and collectible shops line Howard Avenue in Kensington, Maryland, offering every sort of item in a wide variety of styles, periods, and prices. If you don't drive or taxi, you'll have to take the Metro and two buses. From Dupont Circle, board an L2 bus and get a transfer from the driver. Ask him to tell you when you reach the transfer point for the L8 bus. Once there, board the L8 bus and ask to be let off at Connecticut and Knowles avenues. Howard Avenue is 1 block north of Knowles.

Brass Knob Architectural Antiques   When old homes and office buildings are demolished in the name of progress, these savvy salvage merchants spirit away saleable treasures, from chandeliers to wrought-iron fencing. 2311 18th St. NW. ✆ 202/332-3370. www.thebrassknob.com. Metro: Woodley Park or Dupont Circle. There's a second location across the street called the **Brass Knob's Back Doors Warehouse,** 2329 Champlain St. NW (✆ 202/265-0587).

cherry   This is an antiques store, all right, but as its name suggests, a little offbeat. Expect affordable eclectic furnishings and decorative arts, and lots of mirrors and sconces. 1526 Wisconsin Ave. NW. ✆ 202/342-3600. Metro: Foggy Bottom, then walk or take the Georgetown Metro Connection shuttle.

Cherub Antiques Gallery   The Cherub Antiques Gallery specializes in Art Nouveau and Art Deco; signed Tiffany, Steuben, Lalique, and Gallé pieces; Liberty arts and crafts; and Louis Icart etchings. 2918 M St. NW. ✆ 202/337-2224. Metro: Foggy Bottom, then take the Georgetown Metro Connection.

Gore-Dean   Though its offerings include some American pieces, the store specializes in 18th- and 19th-century European furnishings, decorative accessories, paintings, prints, and porcelains. Recently added are a lampshade shop, garden shop, and framing studio. 1525 Wisconsin Ave. NW. ✆ 202/625-9199. www.gore-dean.com. Metro: Foggy Bottom, then take the Georgetown Metro Connection.

Marston-Luce   Stop in here at least to admire, if not buy, a beautiful 18th- or 19th-century French furnishing or two. 1651 Wisconsin Ave. NW. ✆ 202/333-6800. Metro: Foggy Bottom, then take the Georgetown Metro Connection.

Millennium   This is antiques shopping for the TV generation, where anything made between the 1930s and the 1970s is considered collectible. The shop works with nearly a score or so of dealers; stock changes weekly. Funky wares run from Bakelite to Heywood-Wakefield blond-wood beauties to used drinking glasses. 1528 U St. NW. ✆ 202/483-1218. Metro: U St.–Cardozo.

Old Print Gallery   This gallery carries original American and European prints from the 17th through the 19th century, including political cartoons, maps, and historical documents. It's one of the largest antique print and map shops in the United States. 1220 31st St. NW. ✆ 202/965-1818. www.oldprintgallery.com. Metro: Foggy Bottom, then take the Georgetown Metro Connection.

Susquehanna Antiques   This Georgetown store specializes in American, English, and European furniture, paintings, and garden items of the late 18th and early 19th centuries. 3216 O St. NW. (C) 202/333-1511. www.susquehannaantiques.com. Metro: Foggy Bottom, then take the Georgetown Metro Connection.

ART GALLERIES

Art galleries abound in Washington, but especially in the Dupont Circle and Georgetown neighborhoods, and along 7th Street downtown. For a complete listing of local galleries, get your hands on a copy of **"Galleries,"** a monthly guide to major galleries and their shows; the guide is available free at many hotel concierge desks and at many galleries.

DUPONT CIRCLE

For all galleries listed below, the closest Metro stop is Dupont Circle.

Affrica   Authentic and traditional African masks, figures, and artifacts. The gallery's clients include major museums and private collectors from around the world. 2010½ R St. NW. (C) 202/745-7272. www.affrica.com.

Elizabeth Roberts Gallery   A 20-something American University grad opened this gallery in March 2003 to showcase the works of local artists working in different mediums, pottery to prints. The gallery has quickly caught the eye of critics. 2108 R St. NW. (C) 202/328-0828. www.elizabethroberts.net.

Kathleen Ewing Gallery   This gallery features vintage and contemporary photography. 1609 Connecticut Ave. NW. (C) 202/328-0955. www.kathleenewinggallery.com.

The Mansion on O Street   Not an art gallery in the usual sense, H. H. Leonards's Mansion consists of three Victorian town houses joined together and decorated throughout with more than 5,000 antiques and artworks, in styles ranging from Art Deco to avant-garde. H's place is also her home, a special-events spot, and a luxurious B&B to boot. (See the review in chapter 5.) 2020 O St. NW. (C) 202/496-2000. www.omansion.com. Open by appointment only.

GEORGETOWN

For all the galleries listed below, the closest stop is Foggy Bottom, with a transfer to the Georgetown Metro Connection bus to get you the rest of the way.

Addison/Ripley Fine Art   This gallery represents both nationally and regionally recognized artists, from the 19th century to the present; works include paintings, sculpture, photography, and fine arts. 1670 Wisconsin Ave. NW. (C) 202/338-5180. www.addisonripleyfineart.com.

Govinda Gallery   This place, a block from the campus of Georgetown University, generates a lot of media coverage, since it often shows artwork created by famous names and features photographs of celebrities. My husband and I wandered in last winter and we had the gallery to ourselves as we enjoyed the photographs of a young Bob Dylan, taken by the renowned Barry Feinstein. 1227 34th St. NW. (C) 202/333-1180. www.govindagallery.com.

Guarisco Gallery, Ltd.   Its display of 19th- and early-20th-century paintings, watercolors, and sculptures by the likes of Camille Pissarro, T. Robinson, and H. Lebasque make this gallery as much a museum as a shop. 2828 Pennsylvania Ave. NW (in the courtyard of the Four Seasons Hotel). (C) 202/333-8533. www.guariscogallery.com.

Spectrum Gallery   A cooperative venture since 1966, in which 30 professional Washington-area artists, including painters, potters, sculptors, photographers, collagists, and printmakers, share in shaping gallery policy, maintenance,

and operation. The art is reasonably priced. 1132 29th St. NW (just below M St.).
© 202/333-0954. www.spectrumgallery.org.

7TH STREET ARTS CORRIDOR

A couple of these galleries predate the renaissance taking place in this downtown
neighborhood. To get here, take the Metro to either Archives/Navy Memorial
(Blue–Orange Line) or Gallery Place/Chinatown/MCI Center (Red–Yellow Line).

406 Art Galleries   Several first-rate art galleries occupy this historic building,
with its 16-foot-high ceilings and spacious rooms. Look for the **David Adamson
Gallery** (© 202/628-0257; www.adamsoneditions.com), which showcases digital printmaking and photography and the works of contemporary artists, like local
Kevin MacDonald, as well as national and international artists Jim Dine, Chuck
Close, and William Wegman. The **Touchstone Gallery** (© 202/347-2787; www.
touchstonegallery.com), on the second floor, is a self-run co-op of 35 to 40 artists,
each of whom has at least one work on display at all times; and the third floor
Eklektikos Gallery of Art (© 202/783-8444; www.eklektikos.com) represents
regional, national, and international artists. 406 7th St. NW (between D and E sts.).

Zenith Gallery   Across the street from the 406 Group, the 27-year-old Zenith
shows diverse works by contemporary artists, most American, about half of
whom are local. You can get a good deal here, paying anywhere from $50 to
$50,000 for a piece. Among the things you'll find are annual humor shows,
neon exhibits, realism, abstract expressionism, and landscapes. 413 7th St. NW.
© 202/783-2963. www.zenithgallery.com.

BOOKS

Washingtonians are readers, so bookstores constantly pop up throughout the
city. An increasingly competitive market means that chain bookstores do a brisk
business, even though D.C. can claim more general-interest, independent bookstores than any other city. Here are my favorite bookstores in general, used, and
special-interest categories. *Note:* Websites for chain bookstores are for the chain
itself, not individual stores.

GENERAL

Barnes & Noble   This three-story shop in Georgetown has sizable software,
travel book, and children's title sections. A cafe on the second level sometimes
hosts concerts. 3040 M St. NW. © 202/965-9880. www.barnesandnoble.com. Metro: Foggy Bottom, then take the Georgetown Metro Connection shuttle. Other area locations include 555 12th St.
NW (© 202/347-0176) and 4801 Bethesda Ave., in Bethesda, Maryland (© 301/986-1761).

B. Dalton   This is an all-purpose bookstore, heavy on the bestsellers and carrying magazines, too. Union Station. © 202/289-1724. www.barnesandnoble.com. Metro:
Union Station.

Borders   With its overwhelming array of books, records, videos, and magazines, this outpost of the expanding chain has taken over the town. Many hardcover bestsellers are 30% off. The store often hosts performances by local
musicians. 1800 L St. NW. © 202/466-4999. www.borders.com. Metro: Farragut North. Other
Borders stores in the District include 5333 Wisconsin Ave. NW (© 202/686-8270), in upper northwest D.C.; and 600 14th St. NW (© 202/737-1385).

Bridge Street Books   A small, serious shop specializing in politics, poetry,
literature, history, philosophy, and publications you won't find elsewhere. Bestsellers and discounted books are not its specialty. 2814 Pennsylvania Ave. NW (next to

the Four Seasons Hotel). ✆ **202/965-5200.** Metro: Foggy Bottom, then take the Georgetown Metro Connection shuttle.

Chapters, A Literary Bookstore   Chapters is strong in new and backlisted fiction, and is always hosting author readings. Tea is always available, and on Friday afternoons they break out the sherry and cookies. 445 11th St. NW (inside building at 1001 Pennsylvania Ave.). ✆ **202/737-5553.** www.chaptersliterary.com. Metro: Archives-Navy Memorial or Federal Triangle.

Kramerbooks & Afterwords Café *(Finds)*   The first bookstore/cafe in Washington, maybe in this country, this place has launched countless romances. It's jammed and often noisy, stages live music Wednesday through Saturday evenings, and is open all night weekends. Paperback fiction takes up most of its inventory, but the store carries a little of everything. 1517 Connecticut Ave. NW. ✆ **202/387-1400.** www.kramers.com. Metro: Dupont Circle.

Olsson's Books and Records   This 33-year-old independent, quality bookstore chain has about 60,000 to 70,000 books on its shelves. Members of its helpful staff know what they're talking about and will order books they don't have in stock. Some discounts are given on books, tapes, and CDs, and their regular prices are pretty good, too.

Besides this 7th St. NW store, there is one other Olsson's bookstore in the District: at 1307 19th St. NW (✆ 202/785-1133). In the suburbs are five other Olsson's: in Bethesda, Maryland, at 7647 Old Georgetown Rd. (✆ 301/652-3336); in Old Town Alexandria, Virginia, at 106 S. Union St. (✆ 703/684-0077); in Arlington, Virginia, at 2111 Wilson Blvd. (✆ 703/525-4227) and at 1735 N. Lynn St. (✆ 703/812-2103); and at National Airport (✆ 703/417-1087). The stores on 7th Street, in Alexandria, and on Wilson Boulevard in Arlington each have a creditable cafe, known for its loungy atmosphere, made-in-house selections, and artistic crowd. 418 7th St. NW. (✆ **202/638-7610**). www.olssons.com. Metro: Gallery Place or Archive-Navy Memorial.

Politics and Prose Bookstore   Located a few miles north of downtown in a residential area, this much cherished two-story shop may be worth going out of your way for. It has vast offerings in literary fiction and nonfiction alike and an excellent children's department. The store has expanded again and again over the years to accommodate its clientele's love of books, its most recent enlargement in 2002–2003 adding more space and books overall, but especially to the travel and children's sections. The shop hosts author readings nearly every night of the year. A warm, knowledgeable staff will help you find what you need. Downstairs is a cozy coffeehouse. Staff-recommended books are 20% off; otherwise discounts are available only to members. 5015 Connecticut Ave. NW. ✆ **202/364-1919.** www.politics-prose.com. Metro: Van Ness–UDC, and walk, or transfer to an "L" bus to take you the ¾ mile from there.

Trover Shop   This family-owned and -operated shop is close to 50 years old, and is the only general-interest bookstore on Capitol Hill; specializations include political selections and magazines. The store discounts 30% on the *Washington Post* hardcover fiction and nonfiction bestsellers. 221 Pennsylvania Ave. SE. ✆ **202/547-BOOK.** www.trover.com. Metro: Capitol South.

OLD & USED BOOKS

Second Story Books   If it's old, out of print, custom bound, or a small-press publication, this is where to find it. The store also specializes in used CDs and vinyl, and has an interesting collection of antique French and American adver-tising posters. 2000 P St. NW. *C* 202/659-8884. www.secondstorybooks.com. Metro: Dupont Circle. Also at 4836 Bethesda Ave., in Bethesda, MD (*C* 301/656-0170).

SPECIAL-INTEREST BOOKS

ADC Map and Travel Center   Here you'll find street maps and atlases for the East Coast, from Philadelphia to Atlanta, as well as an extensive collection of maps and guidebooks for the entire world. Globes and atlases are also for sale. 1636 I St. NW. *C* 800/544-2659 or 202/628-2608. www.adcmap.com. Metro: Farragut West or Farragut North.

American Institute of Architects Bookstore   This store is geared toward architects, selling mostly theory and history books, although it does carry some coffeetable architectural photograph books and some gifts. 1735 New York Ave. NW. *C* 202/626-7475. Metro: Farragut West.

Back Stage Books and Costumes   Back Stage is headquarters for Washing-ton's theatrical community, which buys its books, scripts, trades, and sheet music here. It's also a favorite costume-rental shop. 545 8th St. SE. *C* 202/544-5744. Metro: Eastern Market.

Franz Bader Bookstore   This store stocks books on art, art history, architec-ture, and photography, as well as exhibition catalogs. 1911 I St. NW. *C* 202/337-5440. Metro: Farragut West or Farragut North.

Lambda Rising   It was a big deal when this gay and lesbian bookstore opened with a plate-glass window revealing its interior to passersby. Now it's an unoffi-cial headquarters for the gay/lesbian/bisexual community, carrying every gay, lesbian, bisexual, and transgender book in print, as well as videos, music, and gifts. 1625 Connecticut Ave. NW. *C* 202/462-6969. Metro: Dupont Circle.

National Museum of American History Giftshop   This museum gift shop carries a wonderful selection of books on American history and culture, includ-ing some for children. Constitution Ave. between 12th and 14th sts. NW. *C* 202/357-1784. www.smithsonianstore.com. Metro: Federal Triangle or Smithsonian.

Reiter's Bookstore   This independent bookstore in the middle of the George Washington University campus is one of the leading scientific, techni-cal, medical, and professional bookshops in the area. It's a great place to stum-ble in to, even if you're not scientifically inclined, because it also has a fine children's science section, some amusing mathematical and scientific toys, and humorous T-shirts ("Hey You, Get Out of the Gene Pool!"). 2021 K St. NW. *C* 202/223-3327. www.reiters.com. Metro: Foggy Bottom.

CAMERAS & FILM DEVELOPING

Photography is a big business in this image-conscious tourist town. A wide range of services and supplies, from inexpensive point-and-shoot cameras to deluxe German and Japanese equipment, is available at competitive prices. Some shops offer repair services and have multilingual staff.

Penn Camera Exchange   Across the street from the FBI Building, Penn Cam-era does a brisk trade with professionals and concerned amateurs. The store offers big discounts on major brand-name equipment, such as Olympus and Canon. Penn has been owned and operated by the Zweig family since 1953; its staff is quite knowledgeable, and its inventory wide-ranging. Their specialty is quality equipment and processing—not cheap, but worth it. 840 E St. NW. *C* 202/347-5777. www.penncamera.com. Metro: Gallery Place or Metro Center. Also at 1015 18th St. NW (*C* 202/785-7366).

Ritz Camera Centers   Ritz sells camera equipment for the average photographer and offers 1-hour film processing. Call for other locations; there are many throughout the area. 1740 Pennsylvania Ave. NW. *C* 202/466-3470. www.ritzpix.com. Metro: Farragut West.

CRAFTS

A mano   Owner Adam Mahr frequently forages in Europe and returns with the unique handmade, imported French and Italian ceramics, linens, and other decorative accessories that you'll covet here. 1677 Wisconsin Ave. NW. *C* 202/298-7200. www.amanoinc.com. Metro: Foggy Bottom, then take the Georgetown Metro Connection shuttle.

American Studio Plus   This store features exquisite contemporary handcrafted American ceramics and jewelry, plus international objets d'art. 2906 M St. NW. *C* 202/965-3273. Metro: Foggy Bottom, then take the Georgetown Metro Connection shuttle.

Appalachian Spring   Country comes to Georgetown. This store sells pottery, jewelry, newly made pieced and appliqué quilts, stuffed dolls and animals, candles, rag rugs, handblown glassware, an incredible collection of kaleidoscopes, glorious weavings, and wooden kitchenware. Everything is made by hand in the United States. 1415 Wisconsin Ave. NW (at P St.). *C* 202/337-5780. Metro: Foggy Bottom, then take the Georgetown Metro Connection shuttle. There's another branch in Union Station (*C* 202/682-0505).

Indian Craft Shop *(Finds*   The Indian Craft Shop has represented authentic Native American artisans since 1938, selling their hand-woven rugs and handcrafted baskets, jewelry, figurines, paintings, pottery, and other items. You need a photo ID to enter the building. Use the C Street entrance, which is the only one open to the public. Department of the Interior, 1849 C St. NW, Room 1043. *C* 202/208-4056. Weekdays and the third Sat of each month. www.indiancraftshop.com. Metro: Farragut West or Foggy Bottom.

The Phoenix   Around since 1955, the Phoenix still sells those embroidered Mexican peasant blouses popular in hippie days; high-end Mexican folk and fine art; handcrafted sterling silver jewelry from Mexico and all over the world; clothing in natural fibers from Mexican and American designers like Eileen Fisher and Flax; collectors' quality masks; and decorative doodads in tin, brass, copper, and wood. 1514 Wisconsin Ave. NW. *C* 202/338-4404. Metro: Foggy Bottom, then take the Georgetown Metro Connection shuttle.

Torpedo Factory Art Center   Once a munitions factory, this three-story building built in 1918 now houses more than 84 working studios and the works of about 165 artists, who tend to their crafts before your very eyes, pausing to explain their techniques or to sell their pieces. Artworks include paintings, sculpture, ceramics, glasswork, and textiles. 105 N. Union St., Alexandria *C* 703/838-4565. www.torpedofactory.org. Metro: King St., then take the DASH bus (AT2, AT5) eastbound to the waterfront.

DISCOUNT SHOPPING

Discount shops in Washington are few and far between. Stores like Wal-Mart and Target are all in the far 'burbs. This list includes the best of the D.C. bunch, followed by a sampling of thrift, secondhand, and consignment stores, where inventory may be eclectic, but the prices are often low. Also check out the listing of flea markets, later in this section.

Filene's Basement *(Value*   This Boston-based store may have gone bankrupt at home but continues to be a hit in Washington, selling designer and famous-name clothes and accessories, and now home furnishings. 1133 Connecticut Ave. NW, Downtown. © 202/872-8430. www.filenesbasement.com. Metro: Farragut North. Also at 529 14th St. NW, in the National Press Club (© 202/638-4110), and in the Mazza Gallerie in upper northwest Washington, 5300 Wisconsin Ave. NW ((© 202/966-0208).

Potomac Mills Mall *(Value)* When you're stuck in the traffic that always clogs this section of I-95, you may wonder if a trip to Potomac Mills is worth it. Believe it or not, this place attracts more visitors than any other site in the Washington area; it's one of the largest indoor outlet malls around, with more than 220 shops such as Old Navy Outlet, Nordstrom Rack, L.L. Bean, and Polo Ralph Lauren. A huge IKEA store, which used to anchor the mall, has seceded, moving to its separate location across the street from Potomac Mills. 30 miles south on I-95 in Prince William, VA. Accessible by car, or by shuttle bus leaving from designated places throughout the area, including Dupont Circle and Metro Center. Call © **800/VA-MILLS** or 703/643-1770 for information about Potomac Mills; call © **703/551-1050** for information about the shuttle-bus service. www.potomacmills.com.

THRIFT/CONSIGNMENT/SECONDHAND SHOPS

Christ Child Opportunity Shop *(Value)* Proceeds from sales go to children's charities. Here you'll find the usual thrift-shop jumble of jewelry, antiques, and collectibles—odds and ends. Most merchandise is left on consignment; if you know antiques, you might find bargains in jewelry, silver, china, quilts, and other items. 1427 Wisconsin Ave. NW (at P St.). © 202/333-6635. Metro: Foggy Bottom, then take the Georgetown Metro Connection shuttle.

Secondhand Rose *(Value)* This upscale second-floor consignment shop specializes in designer merchandise. Creations by Chanel, Armani, Donna Karan, Calvin Klein, Yves Saint-Laurent, Ungaro, Ralph Lauren, and others are sold at about a third of the original price. A stunning Scaasi black-velvet and yellow-satin ball gown might go for $400 (from $1,200 new); Yves Saint-Laurent pumps in perfect condition can be had for as little as $45. Everything is in style, in season, and in excellent condition. Secondhand Rose is also a great place to shop for gorgeous furs, designer shoes and bags, and costume jewelry. 1516 Wisconsin Ave. NW (between P St. and Volta Place). © 202/337-3378. Metro: Foggy Bottom, then take the Georgetown Metro Connection shuttle.

Secondi Inc. On the second floor of a building right above Starbucks is this high-style consignment shop that sells women's clothing and accessories, including designer suits, evening wear, and more casual items—everything from Kate Spade to Chanel. 1702 Connecticut Ave. NW (between R St. and Florida Ave.). © 202/667-1122. Metro: Dupont Circle.

FARMER'S & FLEA MARKETS

Alexandria Farmers' Market The oldest continuously operating farmers' market in the country (since 1752), this market offers locally grown fruits and vegetables, along with delectable baked goods, cut flowers, and plants. Open year-round, Saturday mornings from 5 to 10am. 301 King St. (at Market Square in front of the city hall), in Alexandria. © 703/838-4770. Metro: King St., then take the DASH bus (AT2, AT5) eastbound to Market Square.

Dupont Circle FreshFarm Market *(Kids)* Fresh flowers, produce, eggs, and cheeses are for sale here. The market also features kids' activities and guest appearances by chefs and owners of some of Washington's best restaurants: Bis, Vidalia, Restaurant Nora, Tosca, and 1789. Held Sundays from 9am to 1pm, year-round, rain or shine. The FreshFarm Market organization stages other farmers markets on other days around town; go to the website, www.freshfarm markets.org, for locations, dates, and times. On 20th St. NW, between Q St. and Massachusetts Ave., and in the adjacent Riggs Bank parking lot. © 202/362-8889. Metro: Dupont Circle, Q St. exit.

Eastern Market *Value*   This is the one everyone knows about, even if they've never been here. In continuous operation since 1873, this Capitol Hill institution holds an inside bazaar Tuesday through Sunday, where greengrocers, butchers, bakers, farmers, artists, craftspeople, florists, and other merchants sell their wares. Saturday morning is the best time to go. On Sunday, outside stalls become a flea market. Tuesday through Saturday 7am to 6pm, Sunday 10am to 5pm. 225 7th St. SE (between North Carolina Ave. and C St. SE). © 202/544-0083. www.eastern market.net. Metro: Eastern Market.

Georgetown Flea Market *Finds*   Grab a coffee at Starbucks across the lane and get ready to barter. The Georgetown Flea Market is frequented by all types of Washingtonians looking for a good deal—they often get it—on antiques, painted furniture, vintage clothing, and decorative garden urns. Nearly 100 vendors sell their wares here. Open year-round on Sunday from 9am to 5pm. In the Hardy Middle School parking lot bordering Wisconsin Ave., between S and T sts. NW. © 202/775-FLEA. www.georgetownfleamarket.com. Metro: Foggy Bottom, then take the Georgetown Metro Connection shuttle.

Montgomery County Farm Woman's Cooperative Market   Vendors set up inside every Saturday year-round from 7am to about 3:30pm to sell preserves, homegrown veggies, cut flowers, slabs of bacon and sausages, and mouthwatering pies, cookies, and breads; there's an abbreviated version on Wednesday. Outside, on Saturday, Sunday, and Wednesday, you'll find flea-market vendors selling rugs, tablecloths, furniture, sunglasses—everything. 7155 Wisconsin Ave., in Bethesda. © 301/652-2291. Metro: Bethesda.

FASHION
See also "Discount Shopping," above, and "Shoes," later in this section.

CHILDREN'S CLOTHING
One-of-a-kind children's stores don't do well in downtown Washington. But if your youngster has spilled grape juice all over his favorite outfit and you need a replacement, you can always head to **Hecht's** (p. 231) or to the nearest **Gap Kids:** in Georgetown at 1267 Wisconsin Ave. NW. (© 202/333-2411) or at 2000 Pennsylvania Ave. NW (© 202/429-6862). Also check out these two stores:

April Cornell *Kids*   Too precious for words, this store is almost entirely for girls (and their moms), selling lots of pretty, flowing, flowery dresses, plus linens and nightgowns. Some shirts for little boys. 3278 M St. NW. © 202/625-7887. www.april cornell.com. Metro: Foggy Bottom, then take the Georgetown Metro Connection shuttle.

Kid's Closet *Kids*   Its storefront display of cute kids' clothes stands out among the bank and restaurant facades in this downtown block; inside are clothes and accessories mostly with brand names like OshKosh and Little Me. 1226 Connecticut Ave. NW. © 202/429-9247. Metro: Dupont Circle.

MEN'S CLOTHING
Local branches of **Banana Republic** are at Wisconsin and M streets in Georgetown (© 202/333-2554) and F and 13th streets NW (© 202/638-2724); **The**

Gap has several locations in Washington, including 1120 Connecticut Ave. NW (℗ **202/429-0691**) and 1258 Wisconsin Ave. NW (℗ **202/333-2657**). **Eddie Bauer** has a store at 3040 M St. NW (℗ **202/342-2121**) in Georgetown.

Brooks Brothers Brooks sells traditional men's clothes, as well as the fine line of Peal's English shoes. This store made the news as the place where Monica Lewinsky bought a tie for President Clinton. It also sells an extensive line of women's clothes. 1201 Connecticut Ave. NW. ℗ 202/659-4650. www.brooksbrothers.com. Metro: Dupont Circle or Farragut North. Other locations are at Potomac Mills (p. 240), at National Airport (℗ 703/417-1071), and at 5504 Wisconsin Ave., in Chevy Chase, MD (℗ 301/654-8202).

Burberry's Here you'll find those plaid-lined trench coats, of course, along with well-tailored English clothing for men and women. Hot items include cashmere sweaters and camel's hair duffel coats for men. 1155 Connecticut Ave. NW. ℗ 202/463-3000. www.burberry.com. Metro: Farragut North.

H&M This Swedish-based store sells trendy clothes for the whole family, at reasonable prices. Some designer knockoffs. 1025 F St. NW. ℗ 202/347-3306. www. hm.com. Metro: Metro Center.

Jos. A. Bank Clothiers If you admire the Brooks Brothers line, only wish it were more affordable, look here. This century-old clothier sells suits, corporate casual, weekend casual, and formal attire at prices "20% to 30% lower than competitors." Union Station. ℗ 202/289-9087. www.josbank.com. Metro: Union Station. Two other locations: Lincoln Square, 555 11th St. NW (℗ 202/393-5590) and 1200 19th St. NW (℗ 202/466-2282).

Sherman Pickey Prep to the max is this store, but also a little fey: Think red corduroys. Both men and women's clothes on sale here, including Bill's Khakis and Barbour Outerwear for men, embroidered capris and ribbon belts for women. It's not a chain, though, so it's different in that respect. 1647 Wisconsin Ave. NW. ℗ 202/ 333-4212. www.shermanpickey.com. Metro: Foggy Bottom, then take the Georgetown Metro Connection Shuttle.

Thomas Pink For those who like beautifully made, bright-colored shirts, this branch of the London-based high-end establishment should please. The store also sells ties, boxer shorts, women's shirts, cufflinks, and other accessories. 1127 Connecticut Ave. NW (inside the Mayflower Hotel). ℗ 202/223-5390. www.thomaspink.com. Metro: Farragut North.

Urban Outfitters For the latest in casual attire, from fatigue pants to tube tops. The shop has a floor of women's clothes, a floor of men's clothes, as well as housewares, inflatable chairs, books, cards, and candles. 3111 M St. NW. ℗ 202/342-1012. www.urbn.com. Metro: Foggy Bottom, then take the Georgetown Metro Connection shuttle.

WOMEN'S CLOTHING

Washington women have many more clothing stores to choose from than men. Stores selling classic designs dominate, including **Ann Taylor,** at Union Station (℗ **202/371-8010**), 1140 Connecticut Ave. NW (℗ **202/659-0120**), 600 13th St. NW (℗ **202/737-0325**), and Georgetown Park, 3222 M St. NW (℗ **202/ 338-5290**); and **Talbots,** at 1122 Connecticut Ave. NW (℗ **202/887-6973**) and Georgetown Park, 3222 M St. NW (℗ **202/338-3510**). Beneath their modest apparel, however, Washington women like to wear racy **Victoria's Secret** lingerie—you'll find stores in Union Station (℗ **202/682-0686**) and Georgetown Park (℗ **202/965-5457**), as well as at Connecticut and L streets NW (℗ **202/ 293-7530**).

See "Men's Clothing," immediately above, for locations of Banana Republic, Gap, Sherman Pickey, H&M, Eddie Bauer, Brooks Brothers, and Urban Out-fitters, all of which also sell women's clothes.

Hip boutiques and upscale shops proliferate as well:

all about jane   The independent-minded will enjoy pawing through the ani-mal print, plaid, tweed, and colorful fashions that are making this newcomer a success in Adams-Morgan. 2438½ 18th St. NW. ✆ 202/797-9710. www.allaboutjane.net. Metro: Woodley Park, then a 20-min. walk.

Betsey Johnson   New York's flamboyant flower-child designer personally decorated the bubble-gum-pink walls in her Georgetown shop. Her sexy, offbeat play-dress-up styles are great party and club clothes for the young and the still-skinny young at heart. This is the only Betsey Johnson store in D.C. 1319 Wis-consin Ave. NW. ✆ 202/338-4090. www.betseyjohnson.com. Metro: Foggy Bottom, then take the Georgetown Metro Connection shuttle.

Betsy Fisher   A walk past the store is all it takes to know that this shop is a tad different. Its windows and racks show off whimsically feminine fashions by new American designers. 1223 Connecticut Ave. NW. ✆ 202/785-1975. www.betsyfisher. com. Metro: Dupont Circle.

Chanel Boutique   A modest selection of Chanel's signature designs, acces-sories, and jewelry, at immodest prices. 1455 Pennsylvania Ave. NW (in the courtyard of the Willard Inter-Continental Hotel). ✆ 202/638-5055. Metro: Metro Center.

Commander Salamander   Loud music, young crowd, and funky clothes. Commander Salamander has a little bit of everything, including designer items (Dolce & Gabbana, for instance), some of which are quite affordable. Too cool. 1420 Wisconsin Ave. NW. ✆ 202/337-2265. Metro: Foggy Bottom, then take the Georgetown Metro Connection Shuttle.

French Connection   This outpost of the London-based chain features clothes that are hip but not outrageous. 1229 Wisconsin Ave. NW. ✆ 202/965-4690. www.french connection.com. Metro: Foggy Bottom, then take the Georgetown Metro Connection shuttle.

Nana's   Owner Jackie Flanagan left the world of advertising and publishing to open this store a couple of years ago, naming it after her fashion-wise grand-mother. The shop sells new and vintage styles of work and play clothes, the idea being to mix old and new for a fresh look. Handbags, gifts, and bath products also on sale. 1534 U St. NW (between 15th and 16th sts.). ✆ 202/667-6955. www.nanadc. com. Metro: U St.-Cardozo.

Pirjo   Come here for the funky, baggy, and pretty creations of European designers like Marimekko, Rundholz, and Lillith. Styles range from casual to dressy. Pirjo sells elegant jewelry to boot. 1044 Wisconsin Ave. NW, in Georgetown. ✆ 202/337-1390. Metro: Foggy Bottom, then take the Georgetown Metro Connection shuttle.

Rizik Brothers   In business since 1908, this downtown high-fashion store sells designs by Caroline Herrera (mostly bridal), Rene Lezard, and other Euro-pean and American designers. 1100 Connecticut Ave. NW. ✆ 202/223-4050. www. riziks.com. Metro: Farragut North.

Zara   This cheery store is an outpost of a popular chain started in Spain. Clothes are both dressup and casual, but all trendy. A sprinkling of coats is also found here, when the season calls for it. My 17-year-old loves Zara. 1234-44 Wis-consin Ave. NW. ✆ 202/944-9797. www.zara.com. Metro: Foggy Bottom, then take the George-town Metro Connection Shuttle.

GIFTS/SOUVENIRS

See also "Crafts," earlier in this section. Also check out the gift shops in the museums.

America!   Union Station is full of gift shops, actually, but stop here if you want to pick up a baseball cap with a "DEA," "CIA," or "Police SWAT" insignia on its bill; White House guest towels; and other impress-the-folks-back-home items. Union Station. ✆ **202/842-0540.** www.americastore.com. Metro: Union Station. Or save your shopping for the airport; Made in America has one location at National ((✆ 703/417-1782) and 3 at Dulles (Terminal B: ✆ 703/572-2543; Terminal C: ✆ 703/572-6033; Terminal D: ✆ 703/572-6070).

Chocolate Moose *Finds*   My husband endears himself to me and our daughters when he brings home gifts at Valentine's Day and other occasions from this shop: a Wonder Woman daybook; chunky, transparent, red heart-shaped earrings; wacky cards; paperweight snow globes with figurines inside; candies; eccentric clothing; and other funny, lovely, and useful presents. 1800 M St. NW. ✆ **202/463-0992.** Metro: Farragut North.

GOURMET GOODIES TO GO

Demanding jobs and hectic schedules leave Washingtonians less and less time to prepare their own meals. Or so they say. At any rate, a number of fine-food shops and bakeries are happy to come to the rescue. Even the busiest bureaucrat can find the time to pop into one of these gourmet shops for a movable feast.

See also "Farmer's & Flea Markets," earlier in this section.

Bread Line *Finds*   Owner Mark Furstenberg is credited with revolutionizing bread baking in Washington. He started the Marvelous Market chain (see below), though he has since bowed out. At Bread Line, he concentrates on selling freshly baked loaves of wheat bread, flatbreads, baguettes, and more; sandwiches like the roast pork bun or the muffuletta; tasty soups; and desserts such as bread puddings, pear tarts, and delicious cookies. Seating is available, but most people buy carryout. Open weekdays only, 7:30am to 3:30pm. 1751 Pennsylvania Ave. NW. ✆ **202/822-8900.** Metro: Farragut West or Farragut North.

Dean & Deluca   This famed New York store has set down roots in Washington, in a historic Georgetown building that was once an open-air market. Though it is now closed in, this huge space still feels airy, with its high ceiling and windows on all sides. You'll pay top prices, but the quality is impressive—charcuterie, fresh fish, produce, cheeses, prepared sandwiches and cold pasta salads, hot-ticket desserts, like crème brûlée and tiramisu, and California wines. Also on sale are housewares; on-site is an espresso bar/cafe. 3276 M St. NW. ✆ **202/ 342-2500.** www.deandeluca.com. Metro: Foggy Bottom. There's one other cafe location, at 1299 Pennsylvania Ave. NW (✆ **202/628-8155).**

Firehook Bakery   Known for its sourdough baguettes, apple-walnut bread, fresh fruit tarts, and, at its Farragut Square store, 912 17th St. NW (✆ **202/429- 2253;** Metro: Farragut West), for sandwiches like smoked chicken on sesame semolina bread. 1909 Q St. NW. ✆ **202/588-9296.** www.firehook.com. Metro: Dupont Circle. Also at 3241 M St. NW (✆ 202/625-6247), 3411 Connecticut Ave. NW (✆ 202/362-2253), 215 Pennsylvania Ave. SE (✆ 202/544-7003), 555 13th St. NW (✆ 202/393-0952), 441 4th St. NW (✆ 202/347-1760), and at 2 locations in Alexandria, Virginia.

Lawson's of Dupont   Sitting at Lawson's cluster of outside tables and chairs, you'll see all of Washington pass by, from sharply dressed lawyers to bohemian artistes and panhandlers. You can buy elaborate sandwiches made to order and very nice desserts, wines, breads, and salads. 1350 Connecticut Ave. NW. ⓒ 202/775-0400. Metro: Dupont Circle.

Marvelous Market   First there were the breads: sourdough, baguettes, olive, rosemary, croissants, scones. Now, there are things to spread on the bread, including smoked salmon mousse and tapenade; pastries to die for, from gingerbread to flourless chocolate cake; and prepared foods, such as soups, empañadas, and pasta salads. The breakfast spread on Sunday mornings is sinful, and individual items, like the croissants, are tastier and less expensive here than at other bakeries. The location is grand, with 18th-century chandeliers, an antique cedar bar, and a small number of tables. 1511 Connecticut Ave. NW. ⓒ 202/332-3690. www.marvelousmarket.com. Metro: Dupont Circle. Also at 3217 P St. NW (ⓒ 202/333-2591), 5035 Connecticut Ave. NW (ⓒ 202/686-4040), 1800 K St. NW (ⓒ 202/828-0944), 730 7th St. NW (ⓒ 202/628-0824).

JEWELRY

Beadazzled   The friendly staff helps you assemble your own affordable jewelry from an eye-boggling array of beads and artifacts. The store also sells textiles, woodcarvings, and other crafts from around the world. 1507 Connecticut Ave. NW. ⓒ 202/265-BEAD. www.beadazzled.net. Metro: Dupont Circle.

Chas Schwartz & Son   In business since 1888, Chas Schwartz specializes in diamonds and sapphires, rubies and emeralds, and is one of the few distributors of Hidalgo jewelry (enameled rings and bracelets). The professional staff also repairs watches and jewelry. 1400 F St. NW, or enter through the Willard Hotel, at 1401 Pennsylvania Ave. NW. ⓒ 202/737-4757. Metro: Metro Center. There's another branch at the Mazza Gallerie (ⓒ 202/363-5432); Metro: Friendship Heights.

Keith Lipert Gallery   This decorative arts gallery sells Venetian glassware, high-end costume jewelry by designers such as Oscar de la Renta, and cute little old things, like Art Deco styled handbags. The owner shops in Europe for fashion jewelry and for exquisite gifts suitable for giving to diplomats and international business executives. 2922 M St. NW. ⓒ 202/965-9736. www.keithlipertgallery.com. Metro: Foggy Bottom, then take the Georgetown Metro Connection.

Tiffany & Co.   Tiffany is known for exquisite diamonds and other jewelry that can cost hundreds of thousands of dollars. But you may not know that the store carries less expensive items as well, like $35 candlesticks. Tiffany will engrave, too. Other items include tabletop gifts and fancy glitz: china, crystal, flatware, and a bridal registry service. 5500 Wisconsin Ave., Chevy Chase, MD. ⓒ 301/657-8777. www.tiffany.com. Metro: Friendship Heights.

Tiny Jewel Box   The first place Washingtonians go for estate and antique jewelry, but the six-story store next to the Mayflower Hotel sells the pieces of many designers, from Links of London to Christian Tse, as well as crystal and other house gifts. 1147 Connecticut Ave. NW. ⓒ 202/393-2747. www.tinyjewelbox.com. Metro: Farragut North.

MALLS

Also see the listing for **Potomac Mills** on p. 240.

Chevy Chase Pavilion   This is a manageably sized mall with about 25 stores and restaurants. The inside is unusually pretty, with three levels winding around a skylit atrium. Stores include a two-level Pottery Barn, Hold Everything, Talbots, Georgette Klinger, and J. Crew. The Cheesecake Factory, Starbucks, and a food court are among the dining options. 5335 Wisconsin Ave. NW. ⓒ 202/686-5335. Metro: Friendship Heights.

Fashion Center at Pentagon City   Nordstrom and Macy's are the biggest attractions in this elegant five-story shoppers' paradise. There's also the Ritz-Carlton Hotel where Ken Starr nabbed Monica Lewinsky, multiplex theaters, and a sprawling food court. Williams-Sonoma, Crate & Barrel, and Kenneth Cole are among the more than 170 shops. 1100 S. Hayes St., Arlington, VA. ✆ **703/415-2400**. www.shopsimon.com. Metro: Pentagon City.

Mazza Gallerie   Neiman Marcus anchors this modest-sized though upscale mall, which holds a nine-screen movie theater, a Williams-Sonoma, Saks Fifth Avenue Men's Store, Ann Taylor, Harriet Kassman, and about 18 other stores. 5300 Wisconsin Ave. NW. ✆ **202/966-6114**. www.mazzagallerie.com. Metro: Friendship Heights.

Pavilion at the Old Post Office   Not so much a mall as a tourist trap with souvenir shops and a food court. But you can ride the elevator 315 feet up to the top of the building's clock tower, for a fab view of the city—for free (call ✆ **202/606-8691** for more information from the National Park Service, who operates this service). 1100 Pennsylvania Ave. NW. ✆ **202/289-4224**. www.oldpostofficedc. com. Metro: Federal Triangle.

Ronald Reagan Washington National Airport   Allow extra time before your flight and you can do all of your souvenir shopping here. The 100 stores include Brooks Brothers and Brookstone, and gift shop outlets of the Smithsonian, the National Zoo, and the National Geographic Society. Arlington, VA. ✆ **703/417-8600**. www.mwaa.com/National.

Shops at Georgetown Park   This is a deluxe mall, where you'll see the beautiful people shopping for beautiful things. Ann Taylor, J. Crew, and Polo/Ralph Lauren are just a few of the trendy stores. Sharper Image and Crabtree & Evelyn are here, too.

The Old Town Trolley stops here (see chapter 7) and you can buy trolley tickets from the concierge or from the PretzelMaker vendor stall in the Food Court. There are several restaurants, including Clyde's of Georgetown, gourmet emporium/cafe Dean & Deluca, and the parklike Canal Walk Café Food Court. 3222 M St. NW. ✆ **202/298-5577**. www.shopsatgeorgetownpark.com. Metro: Foggy Bottom, then take the Georgetown Metro Connection shuttle.

Tysons Corner Center and Tysons Corner II, The Galleria   Facing each other across Chain Bridge Road, these two gigantic malls could lead to shopper's overload. Tysons Corner Center, the first and less expensive, has Nordstrom, Bloomingdale's, and L.L. Bean, and specialty stores, such as Abercrombie & Fitch and Crabtree & Evelyn. The Galleria has Macy's, Saks Fifth Avenue, and more than 100 upscale boutiques. Tysons Corner Center, 1961 Chain Bridge Rd., McLean, VA. ✆ **703/893-9400**. www.shoptysons.com. Tysons Corner II, The Galleria, 2001 International Dr., McLean, VA. ✆ **703/827-7700**. www.shoptysonsgalleria.com. Metro: West Falls Church; take shuttle.

Union Station   One of the most popular tourist stops in Washington, Union Station boasts magnificent architecture and more than 120 shops, including the Ann Taylor, Pendleton's, and Appalachian Spring (p. 239). Among the places to eat are America, B. Smith, and an impressive food court. There's also a nine-screen movie-theater complex. 50 Massachusetts Ave. NE. ✆ **202/371-9441** or **202/289-1908**. www.unionstationdc.com. Metro: Union Station.

White Flint Mall   Another Bloomingdale's, another long trip in the car or on the Metro; but once you're there, you can shop, take in a movie, and dine cheaply or well. Notable stores include Lord & Taylor, Borders, and Coach.

11301 Rockville Pike, Kensington, MD. ℂ **301/468-5777**. www.shopwhiteflint.com. Metro: White Flint; then take the free White Flint shuttle, which runs every 15 min.

MISCELLANEOUS

Fahrneys Pens, Inc.   People come from all over to purchase the finest fountain pens, or to have them engraved or repaired. In business since 1929, Fahrneys is an institution, selling Montblanc, Cross, Waterman, the best in the business. 1317 F St. NW (between 13th and 14th sts.). ℂ **800/624-7367** or 202/628-9525. www.fahrneys pens.com. Metro: Metro Center.

Emergency Shopping

You've just arrived in town, but your luggage hasn't—the airline lost it. Or you're about to depart for home or another destination and you notice that the zipper to your suitcase is broken. Or you've arrived at your hotel all in one piece, only to discover you've forgotten something essential: underwear, allergy medicine, an umbrella. What's a lonesome traveler to do? If you find yourself in one of these or a similar situation, one of the following suggestions might be able to come to your rescue.

CVS: This is Washington's main pharmacy and essentials chain. Among the items sold at CVS stores are pantyhose, over-the-counter and prescription medicines, toys, greeting cards, wrapping paper and ribbon, magazines, film and 1-hour photo developing, batteries, candy, some refrigerated food such as milk and orange juice, and office supplies. The stores are ubiquitous, so chances are you'll find one near you. Two centrally located branches are a 24-hour store at 801 7th St. NW (ℂ **202/842-3567**, 202/842-3627 for the pharmacy; www.cvs.com; Metro: Gallery Place/MCI Center), and a store open to 10pm at 435 8th St. NW (ℂ **202/783-4292**, 202/783-4293 for the pharmacy; Metro: Gallery Place/MCI Center or Archives/Navy Memorial).

Doudaklian Leather: Ever since a little shop in Baltimore sewed up my suitcase a few short hours before my husband and I were about to fly to London on our honeymoon (20 years ago), I've had a soft spot for shops like this one, which not only sells major brands of luggage, but repairs them as well, and quickly, if staff are able. Doudaklian is open Monday through Saturday. 921 19th St. NW. (ℂ **202/293-0443**). Metro: Farragut West.

Hecht's: This old reliable is the only department store located downtown. But though it's been around a while, the store continually updates its merchandise to keep up with the times. Run here if you need cosmetics, clothes (for men, women, and children), shoes (but not for children), electronics, appliances, lingerie, luggage, raincoats, and countless other need-immediately goods. Open daily. 1201 G St. NW. (ℂ **202/628-6661**). www.hechts.com. Metro: Metro Center.

Metro Stations: If it starts raining and you're scrambling to find an umbrella, look no further than your closest Metro station, where vendors are at the ready selling umbrellas and other handy things.

Ginza, "for Things Japanese" Everything Japanese, from incense and kimonos to futons to Zen rock gardens. 1721 Connecticut Ave. NW. ⓒ **202/331-7991.** www.ginzaonline.com. Metro: Dupont Circle.

Hats in the Belfry In business for 26 years now, this hat store features designer hats, floppy hats, straw hats, Panama hats, all sorts of hats, for men and women, some for children, and some handbags. Go ahead, try some on. 1237 Wisconsin Ave. NW. ⓒ **202/342-2006.** www.hatsinthebelfry.com. Metro: Foggy Bottom, with a 25-min. walk.

Home Rule ⟨*Value*⟩ Unique housewares; bath, kitchen, and office supplies; and gifts cram this tiny new store. You'll see everything from French milled soap to martini glasses. 1807 14th St. NW (at S St.). ⓒ **202/797-5544.** www.homerule.com. Metro: U St.–Cardozo.

MUSIC

See also the listing for **Olsson's Books and Records** on p. 237.

Borders Besides being a great bookstore, Borders offers the best prices in town for CDs and tapes, and a wide range of music. At 18th and L sts. NW. ⓒ **202/466-4999.** Metro: Farragut North. (See other locations under "Books," earlier in this chapter.)

DJ Hut Everything for lovers of hip-hop, reggae, R&B, and go-go. 2010 P St. NW, 2nd floor. ⓒ **202/659-2010.** www.djhut.com. Metro: Dupont Circle.

Melody Record Shop CDs, cassettes, and tapes, including new releases, are discounted here, plus the shop always has a table of unused but not newly released CDs that sell for about $10 each. Melody offers a wide variety of rock, classical, jazz, pop, show, and folk music, as well as a vast number of international selections. This is also a good place to shop for discounted portable electronic equipment, blank tapes, and cassettes. Its knowledgeable staff is a plus. 1623 Connecticut Ave. NW. ⓒ **202/232-4002.** www.melodyrecords.com. Metro: Dupont Circle, Q St. exit.

Tower Records When you need a record at 10 minutes to midnight on Christmas Eve, you go to Tower. This large, funky store, across the street from George Washington University, has a wide choice of records, cassettes, and CDs in every category—but the prices are high. 2000 Pennsylvania Ave. NW. ⓒ **202/223-3900.** www.tower.com. Metro: Foggy Bottom.

POLITICAL MEMORABILIA

Capitol Coin and Stamp Co. Inc. A museum of political memorabilia—pins, posters, banners—and all of it is for sale. This is also a fine resource for the endangered species of coin or stamp collectors. 1001 Connecticut Ave.NW, Suite 745. ⓒ **202/296-0400.** www.capitolcoin.com. Metro: Farragut North.

SHOES

For men's dress shoes, try **Brooks Brothers** (p. 242). There are local outlets of **Foot Locker** at Union Station (ⓒ **202/289-8364**), 3221 M St. NW (ⓒ **202/333-7640**), and 1934 14th St. NW (ⓒ **202/319-8934**). **Nine West** sells women's shoes from locations at Union Station (ⓒ **202/216-9490**), 1008 Connecticut Ave. NW (ⓒ **202/452-9163**), and 1227 Wisconsin Ave. NW (ⓒ **202/337-7256**).

Comfort One Shoes Despite its unhip name, this store sells a great selection of popular styles for both men and women, including Doc Martens, Birkenstocks, and Ecco. You can always find something that actually feels comfortable. 1636 Connecticut Ave. NW. ⓒ **202/328-3141.** www.comfortoneshoes.com. Metro: Dupont Circle.

Also at 1607 Connecticut Ave. NW (© 202/667-5300), 3222 M St. NW (© 202/333-3399), and other locations.

Steve Madden   The music's so loud, you may not be able to hear a word the salesperson says. This is the city's only Steve Madden location, the women's shoe store that's really popular among the college-age crowd for its chunky platforms, sandals, and thongs. 3109 M St. NW. © 202/342-6195. Metro: Foggy Bottom, then take the Georgetown Metro Connection shuttle.

TOYS

The gift shops at museums and tourist attractions are really your best bets for children's gifts. One other suggestion:

Flights of Fancy *Kids*   Picture books, Playmobil toys, board games, and assorted other toys and amusements cram this small store. Union Station. © 202/371-9800. Metro: Union Station.

WINE & SPIRITS

Barmy Wine and Liquor   Located near the White House, this store sells it all, but with special emphasis on fine wines and rare cordials. 1912 L St. NW. © 202/833-8730. Metro: Farragut North.

Calvert Woodley Liquors   This is a large store with a friendly staff, nice selections, and good cheeses (about 300 to choose from) and other foods to go along with your drinks. 4339 Connecticut Ave. NW. © 202/966-4400. Metro: Van Ness–UDC.

Central Liquor *Value*   This is like a clearinghouse for liquor: Its great volume allows the store to offer the best prices in town on wines and liquor. The store carries more than 250 single-malt scotches. 917 F St. NW. © 800/835-7928 or 202/737-2800. Metro: Gallery Place.

MacArthur Liquor   With a knowledgeable and enthusiastic staff, and an extensive and reasonably priced selection of excellent wines, both imported and domestic, this shop is always busy. 4877 MacArthur Blvd. NW. © 202/338-1433. www. bassins.com. Bus: D4 from Dupont Circle.

9

Washington, D.C., After Dark

Washingtonians can't get enough drama, it seems: All of our major theaters are expanding, big time. The Kennedy Center for the Performing Arts, the Shakespeare Theatre, and Arena Stage—all are undergoing changes so extensive that they won't be complete for years, and in the case of the Kennedy Center, a decade. These theaters remain open throughout the various phases of construction, continuing to draw us, and you, to enjoy high entertainment.

Otherwise, Washington's bars, nightclubs, concert halls, dance clubs, and outdoor amphitheaters proliferate, so read over the listings that follow to see which forms of amusement most appeal. For up-to-date schedules of events, from live music and theater, to children's programs and flower shows, check the Friday "Weekend" section of the *Washington Post,* or go online, and browse the *Post's* nightlife information at **www.washingtonpost.com**. The *City Paper,* available free at restaurants, bookstores, and other places around town, and online at www.washington citypaper.com, is another good source.

TICKETS

TICKETplace, Washington's only discount day-of-show ticket outlet, has one location: at 407 7th St. NW (Metro: Gallery Place/MCI Center or Archives/Navy Memorial). Call ✆ **202/TIC-KETS** (842-5387), for information. You can purchase tickets there, or online at www.ticketplace.org. On the day of performance only (except Sun and Mon; see below), you can buy half-price tickets (with select debit and credit cards: Visa, Master Card, American Express, and Discover—cash and traveler's checks not accepted) to performances with tickets still available at most major Washington-area theaters and concert halls, as well as for performances of the opera, ballet, and other events. TICKETplace is open Tuesday through Friday from 11am to 6pm and Saturday from 10am to 5pm; half-price tickets for Sunday and Monday shows are sold on Saturday. Though tickets are half-price, you have to pay a per-ticket service charge of 12% of the full face value of the ticket.

Tickets are available online Tuesday through Friday, between noon and 4pm. Again, the tickets sold are for same-day performances, at half-price, plus the per-ticket service charge, which for online sales, is 17% of the full face value of the ticket. You must pay by credit card, using MasterCard or Visa, then pick up the tickets at the "Will Call" booth of the theater you're attending; bring your credit card and a photo ID. TICKETplace is a service of the Cultural Alliance of Washington, in partnership with the Kennedy Center, the *Washington Post,* and Ticketmaster.

You can buy full-price tickets for most performances in town through **Ticketmaster** (✆ **202/432-7328;** www.ticketmaster.com), if you're willing to pay a hefty service charge. Purchase tickets to Washington theatrical, musical, and other events before you leave home by going online or by calling ℂ **800/551-SEAT.** Or you can wait until you get here and visit one of Ticketmaster's numerous locations throughout the city, including the TICKETplace outlet on 7th Street (see above); Hecht's Department Store, 12th and G streets NW (Metro: Metro Center); the International Spy Museum (Metro: Gallery Place); the DC Visitor Center in the Ronald Reagan Building, at 1300 Pennsylvania Ave. NW (Metro: Federal Triangle); and the MCI Center (Metro: Gallery Place). When you pay by credit card at TICKETplace and Ticketmaster, you have to show an ID to prove you are the credit card holder.

Another similar ticket outlet is **Tickets.com** (formerly Protix). You can order tickets by calling ℂ **800/955-5566** or 703/218-6500, or by accessing its website at www.tickets.com.

1 The Performing Arts

Washington's performing arts scene has an international reputation. Almost anything on Broadway has either been previewed here or will eventually come here. Better yet, D.C. is home to truly excellent and renowned repertory theater troupes, and to fine ballet, opera, and symphony companies. Rock bands, headliner comedians, and jazz/folk/gospel/R&B/alternative and other musical groups make Washington a must-stop on their tours.

THE TOP THEATERS

Arena Stage   This outpost on the unattractive Washington waterfront is worth seeking out, despite its poor location. (Dine at a downtown restaurant, then drive or take a taxi here; or you can take the Metro, but be careful walking the block or so to the theater.)

Founded by the brilliant Zelda Fichandler in 1950, the Arena Stage is home to one of the oldest acting ensembles in the nation. Several works nurtured here have moved to Broadway, and many graduates have gone on to commercial stardom, including Ned Beatty, James Earl Jones, and Jane Alexander. The excellence of Arena productions has brought the theater much success, to the extent that a major expansion is planned; construction is set to start mid to late 2005, but will not affect the 2005 theater season.

Arena presents eight productions annually on two stages: the **Fichandler** (a theater-in-the-round) and the smaller, fan-shaped **Kreeger.** In addition, the Arena houses the **Old Vat,** a space used for new play readings and special productions.

The 2004–05 September-to-June season includes David Henry Hwang's *M. Butterfly,* Nilo Cruz's *Anna in the Tropics,* Oscar Wilde's *The Importance of Being Earnest,* Edward Albee's *The Goat or Who Is Sylvia?,* August Wilson's *The Piano Lesson,* and Eugene O'Neill's *Anna Christie.* The Arena Stage has always championed new plays and playwrights and is committed to producing works from America's diverse cultures, as well as to reinterpreting the works of past masters. 1101 6th St. SW (at Maine Ave.). ℂ **202/488-3300.** www.arenastage.org. Tickets $40–$66; discounts available for students, people with disabilities, groups, and seniors. Metro: Waterfront.

John F. Kennedy Center for the Performing Arts   This 34-year-old theater complex strives to be not just the hub of Washington's cultural and entertainment scene, but a performing arts theater for the nation. It is constantly evolving, and right now that evolution involves an immense expansion, which will add two buildings to the 8-acre plaza in front of the center, and better connect the center to the rest of the city. The center lies between the Potomac River

Washington, D.C., After Dark

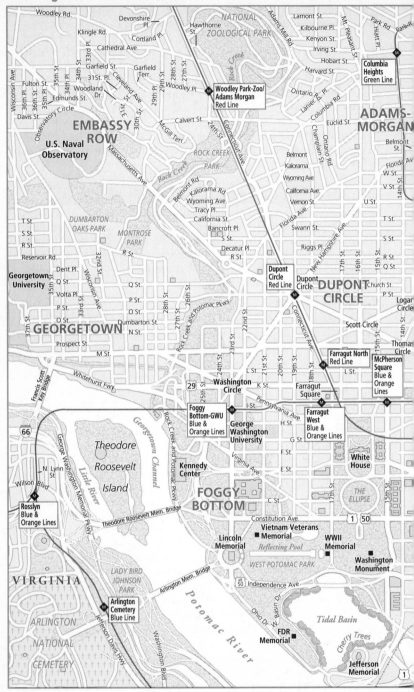

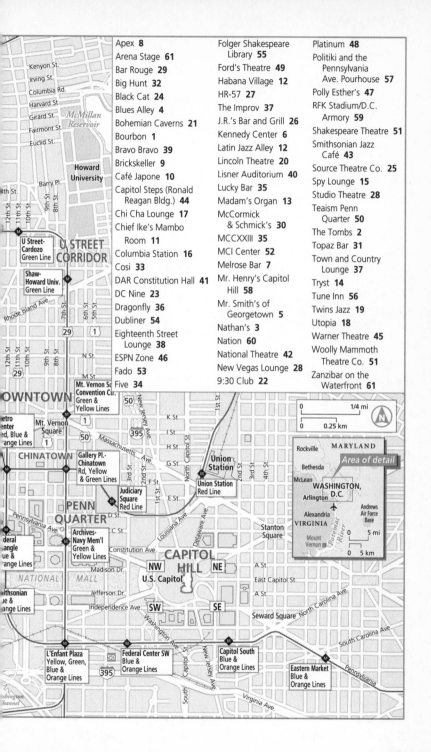

Apex **8**
Arena Stage **61**
Bar Rouge **29**
Big Hunt **32**
Black Cat **24**
Blues Alley **4**
Bohemian Caverns **21**
Bourbon **1**
Bravo Bravo **39**
Brickskeller **9**
Café Japone **10**
Capitol Steps (Ronald Reagan Bldg.) **44**
Chi Cha Lounge **17**
Chief Ike's Mambo Room **11**
Columbia Station **16**
Cosi **33**
DAR Constitution Hall **41**
DC Nine **23**
Dragonfly **36**
Dubliner **54**
Eighteenth Street Lounge **38**
ESPN Zone **46**
Fado **53**
Five **34**

Folger Shakespeare Library **55**
Ford's Theatre **49**
Habana Village **12**
HR-57 **27**
The Improv **37**
J.R.'s Bar and Grill **26**
Kennedy Center **6**
Latin Jazz Alley **12**
Lincoln Theatre **20**
Lisner Auditorium **40**
Lucky Bar **35**
Madam's Organ **13**
McCormick & Schmick's **30**
MCCXXIII **35**
MCI Center **52**
Melrose Bar **7**
Mr. Henry's Capitol Hill **58**
Mr. Smith's of Georgetown **5**
Nathan's **3**
Nation **60**
National Theatre **42**
New Vegas Lounge **28**
9:30 Club **22**

Platinum **48**
Politiki and the Pennsylvania Ave. Pourhouse **57**
Polly Esther's **47**
RFK Stadium/D.C. Armory **59**
Shakespeare Theatre **51**
Smithsonian Jazz Café **43**
Source Theatre Co. **25**
Spy Lounge **15**
Studio Theatre **28**
Teaism Penn Quarter **50**
The Tombs **2**
Topaz Bar **31**
Town and Country Lounge **37**
Tryst **14**
Tune Inn **56**
Twins Jazz **19**
Utopia **18**
Warner Theatre **45**
Woolly Mammoth Theatre Co. **51**
Zanzibar on the Waterfront **61**

and a crisscross of major roadways, which makes it sound like it's easily accessible when, in fact, it is not, for its location actually isolates it from the rest of town. So don't be put off by the unseemly sight of major construction equipment—it's going to be there for quite a while, a decade at least, as the expansion proceeds. The center's performances, meanwhile, continue uninterrupted.

These are top-rated performances by the best ballet, opera, jazz, modern dance, musical, and theater companies in the world. The best costs the most, and you are likely to pay more for a ticket here than at any other theater in D.C.—from $14 for a children's play to more than $285 for a box seat on a Saturday night at the opera, although most ticket prices run in the $50 to $75 range.

The Kennedy Center is committed to being a theater for the people, and toward that end, it continues to stage its **free concert series,** known as "Millennium Stage," which features daily performances by area musicians and sometimes national artists each evening at 6pm in the center's Grand Foyer. (You can check out broadcasts of the nightly performances on the Internet at www.kennedy-center.org/millennium.) During the summer, the Ken-Cen and the Folklore Society of Greater Washington co-sponsor Millennium Stage performances at least once a month at Neptune Plaza in front of the Library of Congress's Thomas Jefferson Building (see the Library of Congress writeup in chapter 7 for more information about its events). The Friday "Weekend" section of the *Washington Post* lists the free performances scheduled for the coming week.

The Kennedy Center is actually made up of six different national theaters: the Opera House, the Concert Hall, the Terrace Theater, the Eisenhower Theater, the Theater Lab, and the American Film Institute (AFI) Film Theater. After a major renovation of the Opera House, the **Washington National Opera** (www.dc-opera.org) returns there for its 2004–05 season to perform Verdi's *Il Trovatore,* Umberto Giordano's *Andrea Chenier,* Benjamin Britten's *Billy Budd,* and Tchaikovsky's *The Maid of Orleans,* to name just some of the upcoming productions. The Washington National Opera's artistic director is Placido Domingo, and tickets often sell out before the season begins.

Among the other productions coming to one of the Kennedy Center stages in the 2004–05 season are **National Symphony Orchestra** concerts, under the direction of Leonard Slatkin, presented in the Concert Hall from September to June; performances by the New York City Ballet, the American Ballet Theatre, and the Joffrey Ballet of Chicago; the musicals *Hairspray* and *Thoroughly Modern Millie;* as well as the drama *Mister Roberts.* A highlight of the season is the Royal Shakespeare Company production of *Hecuba,* by Euripides, starring Vanessa Redgrave. The **Theater Lab** continues by day as Washington's premier stage for children's theater and by night as a cabaret (now in its 17th year) hosting *Shear Madness,* a comedy whodunit (tickets $34–$45).

These are just a smattering of Kennedy Center offerings. 2700 F St. NW (at New Hampshire Ave. NW and Rock Creek Pkwy.). © 800/444-1324 or 202/467-4600 for tickets and information. www.kennedy-center.org. 50% discounts are offered (for select performances) to students, seniors 65 and over, people with permanent disabilities, enlisted military personnel, and persons with fixed low incomes (© 202/416-8340 for details). Garage parking $15. Metro: Foggy Bottom (though it's a fairly short walk, there's a free shuttle between the station and the Kennedy Center, departing every 15 min. 9:45am–midnight, Mon–Sat, noon–midnight Sun). Bus: 80 from Metro Center.

National Theatre The splendid Federal-style National Theatre is the oldest continuously operating theater in Washington (since 1835) and the third oldest in the nation. It's exciting just to see the stage on which Sarah Bernhardt, John Barrymore, Helen Hayes, and so many other notables have performed. The 1,672-seat National is the closest thing Washington has to a Broadway-style playhouse. The 2004–05 season showcases the Twyla Tharp–Billy Joel musical, *Movin' Out,* and yet another tour of *Mamma Mia!*

One thing that has never flagged at The National is its commitment to offering free public-service programs: Saturday-morning children's theater (puppets, clowns, magicians, dancers, and singers) and Monday-night showcases of local groups and performers September through May, plus free summer films. Call ℭ **202/783-3372** for details. 1321 Pennsylvania Ave. NW. ℭ **800/447-7400** or 202/628-6161 to charge tickets. www.nationaltheatre.org. Tickets $30–$75; discounts available for students, seniors, military personnel, and people with disabilities. Metro: Metro Center.

Shakespeare Theatre   This is top-level theater, with superb acting. Try and snag tickets to a play here, for the productions are reliably outstanding. Season subscriptions claim many of the seats and the plays almost always sell out, so if you're interested in attending a play here, you'd better buy your tickets now. This internationally renowned classical ensemble company offers five plays, usually three Shakespearean and two modern classics each September-to-June season. The 2004–05 season includes *Macbeth,* with Kelly McGillis playing Lady Macbeth, *Pericles, The Tempest,* and Oscar Wilde's satire, *Lady Windermere's Fan.*

The company also offers one admission-free 2-week run of a Shakespeare production at the Carter Barron Amphitheater in Rock Creek Park. 450 7th St. NW (between D and E sts.). ℭ **202/547-1122.** www.shakespearetheatre.org. Tickets $20–$66, $10 for standing-room tickets sold 1 hr. before sold-out performances; discounts available for students, seniors, and groups. Metro: Archives–Navy Memorial or MCI Center/Gallery Place.

SMALLER THEATERS

Some of Washington's lesser-known theaters are gaining more recognition all the time. Their productions are consistently professional, and sometimes more contemporary and innovative than those you'll find in the more acclaimed theaters. The **Source Theatre Company,** 1835 14th St. NW, between S and T streets (ℭ **202/462-1073;** www.sourcetheatre.com), is Washington's major producer of new plays. Joy Zinoman, the artistic director of the **Studio Theatre,** 1333 P St. NW, at 14th Street (ℭ **202/332-3300;** www.studiotheatre.org), showcases interesting contemporary plays and nurtures Washington acting talent; the 2004–05 lineup marks the theater's 28th season, in expanded quarters. The **Woolly Mammoth Theatre Company** (ℭ **202/393-3939;** www.woollymammoth.net), offers as many as six productions each year, specializing in new, offbeat, and quirky plays. In the fall of 2004, the Woolly took up residence in its new 265-seat state-of-the-art facility, at 7th and D streets NW, in downtown Washington, just down the street from the Shakespeare Theatre.

In addition, I highly recommend productions staged at the **Folger Shakespeare Library,** 201 E. Capitol St. SE (ℭ **202/544-7077;** www.folger.edu). Plays take place in the library's Elizabethan Theatre, which is styled after the inn-yard theater of Shakespeare's time. The theater is intimate and charming, the theater company is remarkably good, and an evening spent here guarantees an absolutely marvelous experience. The 2004–05 season brings to the stage Shakespeare's *Two Gentlemen of Verona* and *Romeo and Juliet,* as well as a play by David Garrick and George Colman: *The Clandestine Marriage.* The Elizabethan Theatre is also the setting for musical performances, lectures, readings, and other events.

Finally, there's **Ford's Theatre,** 511 10th St. NW, between E and F streets (© **202/347-4833;** www.fordstheatre.org), the actual theater where, on the evening of April 14, 1865, actor John Wilkes Booth shot President Lincoln. Though popular among Washingtonians for its annual holiday performance of Dickens's *A Christmas Carol,* Ford's stages generally mediocre presentations, usually intertwined with American history themes.

INDOOR ARENAS & OUTDOOR PAVILIONS

When Madonna, U2, Britney Spears, or the Dixie Chicks come to town, they usually play at one of the huge indoor or outdoor arenas. The 20,600-seat **MCI Center,** 601 F St. NW, where it meets 7th Street (© **202/628-3200;** www.mci center.com), in the center of downtown, hosts plenty of concerts and also is Washington's premier indoor sports arena (home to the NBA Wizards, the WNBA Mystics, the NHL Capitals, and Georgetown NCAA basketball). Less convenient and smaller is the 10,000-seat **Patriot Center** at George Mason University, 4500 Patriot Circle, Fairfax, VA (© **703/993-3000;** www.patriotcenter.com).

Largest of the outdoor venues is the **Robert F. Kennedy Memorial Stadium,** 2400 E. Capitol St. SE (© **202/547-9077;** www.dcsec.com), packing crowds of 55,000-plus into its seats for D.C. United (men's) and Washington Freedom (women's) soccer games, concerts, and all-day music festivals.

The **Nissan Pavilion at Stone Ridge,** 7800 Cellar Door Dr., off Wellington Road in Bristow, VA (© **703/754-6400** for concert information; www.nissan pavilion.com), has a capacity of 22,500 seats (10,000 under the roof, the remainder on the lawn), is 25 minutes from the Beltway, and features major acts varying from classical to country. The action is enhanced by giant video screens inside the pavilion and on the lawn.

During the summer, there's quality entertainment almost nightly at the **Merriweather Post Pavilion,** 10475 Little Patuxent Pkwy., just off Route 29 in Columbia, MD (© **410/715-5550;** www.merriweathermusic.com), about a 40-minute drive from downtown D.C. There's reserved seating in the open-air pavilion (overhead protection provided in case of rain) and general-admission seating on the lawn (no refunds for rain) to see such performers as Neil Young, Counting Crows, Diana Krall, Blink 182, The Cure, or No Doubt. If you choose the lawn seating, bring blankets and picnic fare (beverages must be bought on the premises).

My favorite summer setting for music is also the closest to D.C. and easiest to get to: **Wolf Trap Farm Park for the Performing Arts,** 1551 Trap Rd., Vienna, VA (© **703/255-1860;** www.wolftrap.org). The country's only national park devoted to the performing arts, Wolf Trap, 30 minutes by car from downtown D.C., offers performances by the National Symphony Orchestra (it's their summer home), and has hosted Lucinda Williams, Shawn Colvin, Lyle Lovett, The Temptations, Ani DiFranco, and many others. Performances take place in the 7,000-seat Filene Center, about half of which is under the open sky. You can also buy cheaper lawn seats on the hill, which is sometimes the nicest way to go. If you do, arrive early (the lawn opens 90 min. before the performance) and bring a blanket and a picnic dinner—it's a tradition. Wolf Trap also hosts a number of very popular **festivals.** The park features a daylong Irish music festival in May; the Louisiana Swamp Romp Cajun Festival and a weekend of jazz and blues in June; and the International Children's Festival each September.

The **Carter Barron Amphitheater,** 16th Street and Colorado Avenue NW (© **202/426-0486**), way out 16th Street, is in Rock Creek Park, close to the

Maryland border. This is the area's smallest outdoor venue, with 4,250 seats. Summer performances include a range of gospel, blues, and classical entertainment. The shows are usually free, but tickets are required. You can always count on Shakespeare: The **Shakespeare Theatre Free For All** takes place at the Carter Barron usually for 2 weeks in June, Tuesday through Sunday evenings; the free tickets are available the day of performance only, on a first-come, first-served basis (call ℂ **202/334-4790** for details). The 2004 Free For All featured *Much Ado About Nothing.*

SMALLER AUDITORIUMS

A handful of auditoriums in Washington are really fine places to catch a performance. The smallest, most clublike auditorium is the 350-seat **Barns of Wolf Trap,** 1635 Trap Rd., Vienna, VA (ℂ **703/938-2404**), which is just up the road from Wolf Trap Farm Park (see above). From late fall until May, the schedule features jazz, pop, country, folk, bluegrass, and chamber musicians. This is the summer home of the Wolf Trap Opera Company, which is the only entertainment booked here May through September.

DAR Constitution Hall, on 18th Street NW, between C and D streets (ℂ **202/628-4780;** www.dar.org), is housed within a beautiful turn-of-the-20th-century beaux arts–style building and seats 3,746. Its excellent acoustics have supported an eclectic (and I mean eclectic) group of performers: Sting, the Buena Vista Social Club, John Hiatt, the Count Basie Orchestra, the Los Angeles Philharmonic, Lil Bow Wow, Ray Charles, Trisha Yearwood, The Strokes, and the O Brother Where Art Thou? tour.

In the heart of happening U Street, the **Lincoln Theatre,** 1215 U St. NW (ℂ **202/328-6000;** www.thelincolntheatre.org), was once a movie theater, vaudeville house, and nightclub featuring black stars like Louis Armstrong and Cab Calloway. The theater closed in the 1970s and reopened in 1994 after a renovation restored it to its former elegance. Today the theater books jazz, R&B, gospel, and comedy acts, and events like the D.C. Film Festival.

At the 1,500-seat **Lisner Auditorium,** on the campus of George Washington University, 21st and H streets NW (ℂ **202/994-6800;** www.lisner.org), you always feel close to the stage. Bookings sometimes include musical groups like Siouxsie and the Banshees, comedians like "Weird Al" Yankovic, and children's entertainers like Raffi, but are mostly cultural shows—everything from a Pakistani rock group to the Washington Revels' annual romp at Christmas.

⌐ *Fun Fact* **Washington Walk of Fame**

If you're going to the Warner Theatre, or are walking by (it's in the heart of downtown), be sure to check out the sidewalk in front of its 13th Street entrance, between E Street and Pennsylvania Avenue NW. Entertainers who have performed here since the theater reopened in 1992 have signed stone "pavers," and these individual blocks, bearing both a signature and a gold star, are on view in the concrete walkway. Look for the signatures of Frank Sinatra, Tony Bennett, Liza Minnelli, Shirley MacLaine, David Copperfield, B. B. King, Mikhail Baryshnikov, Chris Rock, and about 100 others. You'll notice that some performers added their own flourishes: Bonnie Raitt wrote "No Nukes" on hers; Tommy Tune imprinted the soles of his tap shoes in the pavement.

The **Warner Theatre,** 1299 Pennsylvania Ave. NW, with the entrance on 13th Street, between E and F streets (© **202/783-4000;** www.warnertheatre.com), opened in 1924 as the Earle Theatre (a movie/vaudeville palace) and was restored to its original, neoclassical-style appearance in 1992 at a cost of $10 million. It's worth coming by just to see its ornately detailed interior. The 2,000-seat auditorium offers year-round entertainment, alternating dance performances (from Baryshnikov to the Washington Ballet's Christmas performance of *The Nutcracker*) and Broadway/off-Broadway shows *(Grease)* with headliner entertainment (Hanson, Bob Dylan).

2 The Club & Music Scene

If you're looking for a more interactive, tuneful night on the town, Washington offers hip jazz clubs, lively bars, warehouse ballrooms, places where you sit back and listen, places where you can get up and dance, even a roadhouse or two. If you're looking for comic relief, Washington can take care of that, too (the pickings are few but good).

Many nightspots wear multiple hats. For example, the Black Cat is a bar and a dance club, offering food and sometimes poetry readings. So I've listed each nightspot according to the type of music it features. The details are in the description.

The best nightlife districts are Adams-Morgan; the area around U and 14th streets NW, a still-developing district, where it's best to stay on or close to U Street; north and south of Dupont Circle along Connecticut Avenue; downtown streets near the MCI Center, specifically F and G streets, between 7th and 15th streets; and Georgetown. If you don't mind venturing into the suburbs, you should know about Arlington's hot spots (see the "Arlington Row" box on p. 270). As a rule, while club-hopping—even in Georgetown—stick to the major thoroughfares and steer clear of deserted side streets.

The best source of information about what's doing at bars and clubs is a fat weekly, **City Paper,** available free at bookstores, movie theaters, drugstores, and other locations; and online at www.washingtoncitypaper.com. Also check out the monthly *On Tap,* another fat freebie found mostly in bars, but whose website, www.ontaponline.com, is essential reading for carefree 20-somethings. By the way, Thursday night is "College Night" at nearly every club.

Washington's clubs and bars tend to keep their own hours; best to call ahead to make sure the place you're headed is open.

COMEDY

In addition to these two comedy venues, the **Warner Theatre** (see "Smaller Auditoriums," above) also features big-name comedians from time to time.

The Capitol Steps *(Moments*   This musical political satire troupe is made up of former Congressional staffers, equal-opportunity spoofers all, who poke endless fun through song and skits at politicians on both sides of the aisle, and at government goings-on in general. You might catch former president Clinton crooning "Livin' Libido Loca," or U.S. Attorney General John Ashcroft bellowing "Glory Glory Paranoia." Washingtonians have been fans since the Steps got started in 1981. Since then, the troupe has performed more than 5,000 shows and released more than 24 albums, including the latest, "Papa's Got a Brand New Baghdad." Shows take place in the Amphitheater, on the concourse level of the Ronald Reagan Building and International Trade Center, at 7:30pm Friday and

Saturday. 1300 Pennsylvania Ave. NW (in the Ronald Reagan Building). ✆ **202/312-1555.** www. capsteps.com. Tickets $34. Metro: Federal Triangle.

The Improv   The Improv features top performers on the national comedy club circuit as well as comic plays and one-person shows. *Saturday Night Live* performers David Spade, Chris Rock, and Adam Sandler have all played here, as have comedy bigs Ellen DeGeneres, Jerry Seinfeld, and Robin Williams. Shows are about 1½ hours long and include three comics (an emcee, a feature act, and a headliner). Show times are 8pm Sunday, 8:30pm Tuesday through Thursday, 8 and 10:30pm on Friday and Saturday. The best way to snag a good seat is to have dinner here (make reservations), which allows you to enter the club as early as 7pm Sunday through Thursday or after 6:30pm Friday and Saturday. The Friday and Saturday 10:30pm show serves drinks and appetizers only. Dinner entrees (nothing higher than $9.95) include sandwiches and Tex-Mex fare. You must be 18 to get in. 1140 Connecticut Ave. NW (between L and M sts.). ✆ **202/296-7008.** www.dcimprov.com. Cover $15–$35 Sun–Thurs, $15 Fri–Sat, plus a 2-item minimum. Metro: Farragut North.

POP/ROCK/RAVE/ALTERNATIVE

The Birchmere Music Hall and Bandstand   Worth the cab fare from downtown, if you're a fan of live music by varied, stellar performers, such as Garth Brooks, Jonatha Brooke, Jerry Jeff Walker, Crash Test Dummies, Shawn Colvin, Joe Sample, John Hiatt—I could go on and on. The Birchmere is unique in the area for providing a comfortable and relatively small (500-seat) setting, where you sit and listen to the music (there's not a bad seat in the house) and order food and drinks. The Birchmere got started nearly 30 years ago, when it booked mostly country singers. The place has expanded over the years and so has its repertoire; there are still many country and bluegrass artists, but also folk, jazz, rock, gospel, and alternative musicians. The menu tends toward American favorites, such as nachos and burgers; I can recommend the pulled-pork barbecue sandwich and the chili. 3701 Mount Vernon Ave., Alexandria, VA. ✆ **703/549-7500.** www.birchmere.com. Ticket prices range from $17–$50. Take a taxi or drive.

Black Cat   This comfortable, low-key club draws a black-clad crowd to its concert hall, which features national, international, and local indie and alternative groups. The place is made for dancing, accommodating more than 600 people. Adjoining the hall is the Red Room Bar, a large, funky, red-walled living-roomy lounge with booths, tables, a red-leather sofa, pinball machines, a pool table, and a jukebox stocked with a really eclectic collection. A college crowd collects on weekends, but you can count on seeing a 20- to 30-something bunch here most nights, including members of various bands who like to stop in for a drink. Black Cat also hosts film screenings, poetry readings, and other quiet forms of entertainment in its ground floor room called "Backstage," and serves vegetarian food in its smoke-free cafe. Say hello to owner Dante Ferrando while you're here and to his dad, Bobby, who mans the kitchen. The Red Room Bar is open until 2am Sunday through Thursday, and until 3am Friday and Saturday. Concerts take place 4 or 5 nights a week, beginning at about 8:30pm (call for details). 1811 14th St. NW (between S and T sts.). ✆ **202/667-7960.** www.blackcatdc.com. Cover $5–$20 for concerts; no cover in the Red Room Bar. Metro: U St.–Cardozo.

DC 9   This medium-size venue—which holds 250—debuted in spring 2004, with a commitment to offering both live music and DJ shows. Open nightly, DC 9 features indie rock bands Thursday through Saturday nights, 8 to 11pm, and DJs for dancing until 2am or 3am those nights, and from 9:30pm to midnight

Tips **Metro Takes You There**

Recognizing that Washingtonians are keeping later hours these days, Metro not only keeps its trains running until 3am on weekends, but has also inaugurated special shuttle service to Adams-Morgan (home to lots of nightclubs, but no Metro stations).

Here's what you do: Take the Metro to the Red Line's Woodley Park/Zoo–Adams-Morgan Station or to the Green Line's U St.–Cardozo Station, and hop on the no. 98 Adams-Morgan–U St. Link Shuttle, which travels through Adams-Morgan, between these two stations, after 6pm daily, except on Saturday, when service starts at 10am. The U Link Shuttle operates every 15 minutes and costs only 25¢.

other nights. (That schedule may change, however.) The two-story club includes a bar downstairs with couches, booths, bar stools, and a digital jukebox of 130,000 tunes, and the hall upstairs reserved for music. 1940 9th St. NW. ⓒ 202/ 483-5000. www.dcnine.com. No cover downstairs, $5–$10 cover upstairs, depending on show. Metro: U St.–Cardozo.

Eighteenth Street Lounge This place maintains its "hot" status. First you have to find it, and then you have to convince the bouncer to let you in. So here's what you need to know: Look for the mattress shop south of Dupont Circle, then look up. "ESL" (as those in the know call it) sits above the shop, and hangs only a tiny plaque at street level to advertise its existence. Wear something exotic and sexy. If you pass inspection, you may be surprised to find yourself in a restored mansion (Teddy Roosevelt once lived here) with fireplaces, high ceilings, and a deck out back. Or maybe you'll just get right out there on the hardwood floors to dance to acid jazz, hip-hop, reggae, or Latin jazz tunes spun by a deejay. 1212 18th St. NW. ⓒ 202/466-3922. Cover $5–$20 Tues–Sat. Metro: Dupont Circle or Farragut North.

5 This small, three-level space is a reincarnation of what used to be the Garage, a live-music venue. 5 is a deejay-driven dance club, aiming to capture some of the late-night crowd who are too wired to go home. Open Wednesday through Sunday nights, with music starting after 10pm. 1214-B 18th St. NW. ⓒ 202/331-7123. www.fivedc.com. Cover $5–$15. Metro: Dupont Circle or Farragut North.

Nation This concert/dance space has separate areas for live music, dance music, and lounging, and a three-tiered outdoor patio. This is primarily a Gen-X mecca (though some performers attract an older crowd). It's also D.C.'s largest club, accommodating about 2,000 people a night. But Nation is best known for its dance parties. Thursday is Goth night for those addicted to psytrance and darkwave music, black leather, and eyeliner. Saturday is given over to a gay dance party called "Velvet." The game room and state-of-the-art lighting/laser/sound systems are a plus. The Nation is in a pretty bad neighborhood, so make sure you have good directions to get there; the building itself is very secure. 1015 Half St. SE (at K St.). ⓒ 202/554-1500. www.nationdc.com. Cover $7–$30. Metro: Navy Yard.

9:30 Club Housed in yet another converted warehouse, this major live-music venue hosts frequent record-company parties and features a wide range of top performers. You might catch Sheryl Crow, Simple Minds, The Clarks, Luna, The Tragically Hip, Lucinda Williams, or even Tony Bennett. It's only open when there's a show on, which is almost every night (but call ahead), and, obviously,

D.C. Boogie

Dance clubs used to be hard to find in Washington, but now they proliferate. Salsa, swing, rave, rock, disco, freak . . . you name it, it's happening here. Strictly speaking, many dance spots are not "clubs," but restaurants, bars, or concert halls that feature live or recorded music on certain days or at certain times. But so what? The choices are here and varied. So read on, and then put on your dancing shoes and get on out there.

For clubs not already listed within this chapter, I've provided an address and phone number; otherwise, refer back to full entries within the main text to find out information.

For dinner and romantic dancing in the old-fashioned way, you might want to try the **Blue Bar** at the Henley Park Hotel, 926 Massachusetts Ave. NW (© **202/638-5200**), a delightful cocktail lounge with live jazz and dancing Friday and Saturday nights; or the **Melrose Bar,** at the Park Hyatt Hotel, 1201 24th St. NW (© **202/955-3899**), for dinner and swing dancing to live jazz Saturday nights (and sometimes Fri nights, too—call).

Latin jazz continues to be popular in Washington and one of the best places to salsa and merengue is Adams-Morgan's **Habana Village,** which is open Wednesday through Saturday evenings, with salsa lessons offered Wednesday through Friday and tango lessons on Saturday. Other choices for lessons and dancing include **Latin Jazz Alley,** also in Adams-Morgan, **Zanzibar** on the Waterfront, **Lucky Bar,** near Dupont Circle, and **Bravo Bravo,** downtown at Connecticut and K streets.

Adams-Morgan, in general, is a convenient neighborhood to travel if you're in a dancing mood. Among the top spots are **Chief Ike's Mambo Room,** 1725 Columbia Rd. NW (© **202/332-2211**), where dance maniacs of all ages and races rock out to a mix of deejay tunes, hip-hop to R&B; and **Madam's Organ,** which is technically not a dance club, but becomes one pretty quickly when its excellent live jazz, blues, or R&B musicians take the (tiny, windowfront) stage—the place gets so packed that you'll probably end up dancing where you stand.

Just south of Adams-Morgan and Dupont Circle lies one of D.C.'s hottest clubs, the **Eighteenth Street Lounge.** Known as "ESL," the club is so hip, it scarcely announces itself. (Look for a tiny bronze plaque.) The two-level club keeps its dance floors dark, and crowded with fashionably dressed men and women moving to the deejay-driven acid jazz, hip-hop, and instrumental reggae tunes.

Dance venues, where the emphasis is on live bands playing current music, include **Black Cat, DC9, IOTA,** in Arlington (see the "Arlington Row" box later in this chapter, for more selections there), and **State Theatre,** in Falls Church. Alas, the live rock-dance scene is a category that remains woefully underrepresented in Washington.

Most places offer deejay-spun dance music. In addition to those mentioned above, you might consider the **New Vegas Lounge,** for sexy twisting and turning to the blues; the waterfront **Zanzibar,** for choices ranging from alternative to hip-hop; **Polly Esther's** for '70s and '80s retro; and **Nathans,** for a combination of international, Euro, and Top 40.

the crowd (as many as 1,200) varies with the performer. Best to buy tickets ($10-$50) in advance, whether at the box office or online. The sound system is state of the art and the sightlines are excellent. There are four bars: two on the main dance-floor level, one in the upstairs VIP room (anyone is welcome here unless the room is being used for a private party), and another in the distressed-looking cellar. The 9:30 Club is a standup place, literally—there are few seats. 815 V St. NW (at Vermont Ave.). ℂ 202/393-0930. www.930.com. Metro: U St.–Cardozo, 10th St. exit.

Platinum   Housed in a great old building that still has its original marble floor, sweeping staircase, and high ceilings, this nightclub is the exclusive domain of the young and good-looking who like to dance. Music is described as progressive, but it's really just contemporary disco played by deejays. Four levels, three dance floors, a VIP lounge, smoke machines, balconies, high-tech sound systems—it's all here. Open Thursday to Saturday. 915 F St. NW. ℂ 202/393-3555. www.platinumclubdc.com. Cover $10, $15 after midnight Sat. Metro: MCI Center–Gallery Place.

Polly Esther's   This is a three-dance-clubs-in-one emporium with '70s disco music (think the Village People, ABBA, the BeeGees) blaring from the sound system on the "Polly Esther's" dance floor, '80s tunes by artists like Madonna and Prince playing in the "Culture Club," and current radio hits blasting throughout "Club Expo." Decor for each floor matches the music of that era, so, for instance, you'll see such artifacts as a John Travolta memorial and Brady Bunch memorabilia in the Polly Esther's club. Open Thursday through Saturday. 605 12th St. NW. ℂ 202/737-1970. www.pollyesthers.com. Cover $7 Thurs, $8 Fri, $10 Sat. Metro: Metro Center.

State Theatre   This is another club that's located outside the city ("7 minutes from Key Bridge") and not near a Metro station, but it offers reasonably priced live shows featuring great local and national bands (and lots of names from the past, such as Jefferson Starship and Dave Mason). This relatively small hall (holds 800) was once a movie house, and its renovation has endowed it with a superb sound system and good sightlines. The theater has a dance floor, and seats 160 at tables and another 200 theater style in the balcony, with everyone else standing. It's first-come, first-served for the seats, so if you really want one, get here by the time the box office opens at 6:30pm, if not earlier. The State offers a full menu and bar; table dwellers pay an extra $8 minimum per person for food. Most people don't mind standing, since the music featured is pretty danceable. Dr. John, Marcia Ball, Beausoleil, The Radiators, and Blame It on Jane are some of the acts you might catch here. 220 N. Washington St., Falls Church, VA. ℂ 703/237-0300. www.thestatetheatre.com. Tickets cost anywhere from $5–$45, depending on the act. Metro: East Falls Church, with a 4-min. cab ride from there.

JAZZ & BLUES

A calendar of jazz gigs for these and other clubs is posted at **www.dcjazz.com**, including free performances, such as those at the **Four Seasons Garden Terrace lounge,** 2800 Pennsylvania Ave. NW (ℂ **202/342-0444**), where a pianist plays jazz standards Thursday through Saturday nights, and often on other nights.

Blues Alley   Blues Alley, in Georgetown, has been Washington's top jazz club since 1965, featuring such artists as Nancy Wilson, McCoy Tyner, Sonny Rollins, Wynton Marsalis, Rachelle Ferrell, and Maynard Ferguson. There are usually two shows nightly at 8 and 10pm; some performers also do midnight shows on weekends. Reservations are essential (call after noon); since seating is on a first-come, first-served basis, it's best to arrive no later than 7pm and have dinner. Entrees on the steak and Creole seafood menu are in the $17 to $23 range, snacks and sandwiches are $5.25 to $10, and drinks are $5.35 to $9. The decor is classic jazz club: exposed brick walls, beamed ceiling, and small, candlelit tables. Sometimes well-known visiting musicians get up and jam with performers. 1073 Wisconsin Ave. NW (in an alley below M St.). ✆ 202/337-4141. www.bluesalley. com. Cover $16–$40, plus $9 food or drink minimum, plus $2.25 surcharge. Metro: Foggy Bottom, then take the Georgetown Metro Connection Shuttle.

Bohemian Caverns   Rising from the ashes on the very spot where jazz greats such as Duke Ellington, Billie Holiday, and so many others performed decades ago, Bohemian Caverns hopes to establish that same presence and host today's jazz stars. The club's decor is cavelike, as it was in the '20s. Musicians you might catch here include Shirley Horn and Marshall Keyes. Name artists appear on Friday and Saturday nights, usually for two shows, at 9:30pm and 1:30am. Performances on other nights range from poetry readings to blues groups. The Caverns is also a restaurant, whose entrees are named after jazz legends and range in price from $7 to $19. 2001 11th St. NW (at U St). ✆ 202/299-0801. www.bohemiancaverns. com. Cover $5–$20. Metro: U St.–Cardozo.

Columbia Station *(Value)*   This fairly intimate club in Adams-Morgan showcases live blues and jazz nightly. The performers are pretty good, which is amazing, considering there's no cover. Columbia Station is also a bar/restaurant, with the kitchen usually open until midnight, serving pastas, seafood, and Cajun-influenced cuisine. 2325 18th St. NW. ✆ 202/462-6040. Metro: U St.–Cardozo or Woodley Park–Zoo–Adams-Morgan and catch the U Link Shuttle.

HR-57   This cool club is named for the House Resolution passed in 1987 that designated jazz "a rare and valuable national American treasure." More than a club, HR-57 is also the Center for the Preservation of Jazz and Blues. Step inside Wednesday through Saturday evenings, for a jazz jam session or star performance. 1610 14th St. NW. ✆ 202/667-3700. www.hr57.org. Cover $6–$10. Metro: U St.–Cardozo or Woodley Park–Zoo–Adams-Morgan and catch the U Link Shuttle.

Madam's Organ Restaurant and Bar *(Finds)*   This beloved Adams-Morgan hangout fulfills owner Bill Duggan's definition of a good bar: great sounds and sweaty people. The great sounds feature One Night Stand, a jazz group, on Monday; bluesman Ben Andrews on Tuesday; bluegrass with Bob Perilla & the Big Hillbilly Bluegrass Band on Wednesday; and the salsa sounds of Patrick Alban and Noche Latina on Thursday, which is also Ladies' Night. On Friday and Saturday nights, regional blues groups pack the place. The club includes a wide-open bar decorated eclectically with a 150-year-old gilded mirror, stuffed fish and animal heads, and paintings of nudes. The second-floor bar is called Big Daddy's Love Lounge & Pick-Up Joint, which tells you everything you need to know. Other points to note: You can play darts, and redheads pay half-price for drinks. For what it's worth, *Playboy's* May 2000 issue named Madam's Organ one of the 25 best bars in America. Food is served, but I'd eat elsewhere. 2461 18th St. NW. ✆ 202/667-5370. www.madamsorgan.com. Cover $3–$7. Metro: U St.–Cardozo or Woodley Park–Zoo–Adams-Morgan and catch the Adams-Morgan/U St. Link Shuttle.

Mr. Henry's Capitol Hill   Almost every Friday night, at 8pm, Mr. Henry's features a jazz group—maybe the Kevin Cordt Quartet—who play on the second floor of this cozy restaurant. There's no cover, but it's expected that you'll order something off the menu (perhaps a burger or gumbo). Mr. Henry's has been around for at least 30 years and has always attracted a gay and lesbian clientele, though it's a comfortable place for everyone. 601 Pennsylvania Ave. SE. ℂ 202/546-8412. Minimum food/drink charge of $8. Metro: Eastern Market.

New Vegas Lounge   This small club closed for a time to clean up its act, reopening in November 2003, much improved in appearance: exposed brick walls, slate fireplace, hardwood dance floor, L-shaped bar. The music, thank God, is the same: blues and more blues, mostly played by the Out of Town Blues Band, who favor soulful hits by the likes of Otis Redding. The word is, though, that service is bad. 1415 P St. NW. ℂ 202/483-3971. www.vegaslounge.biz. $15 cover most nights. Metro: Dupont Circle.

Smithsonian Jazz Café *Value*   What a treat! The museum that's a must during the day is also a must Friday evenings, when the Atrium Café features performances of local jazz pros. Food and drink are also available. In the National Museum of Natural History, 10th St. NW and Constitution Ave. NW. ℂ 202/357-2700. www.si.edu/imax. $5 cover. Metro: Federal Triangle or Smithsonian.

Twins Jazz   This intimate jazz club offers live music nearly every night—it's closed on Monday. On weeknights, you'll hear local artists; weekends are reserved for out-of-town acts, such as Bobby Watson, Gil Scott Heron, and James William. Musicians play two shows on Friday and Saturday nights, at 9pm and 11pm. Sunday night is a weekly jam session attended by musicians from all over town. The menu features American, Ethiopian, and Caribbean dishes. The age group of the crowd varies. 1344 U St. NW. ℂ 202/234-0072. www.twinsjazz.com. Cover $10–$30, with a $10–$20 table minimum, plus a 2-drink-per-person minimum. Metro: U St.–Cardozo.

Late-Night Bites

If your stomach is grumbling after the show is over, the dancing has ended, or the bar has closed, you can always get a meal at one of a growing number of late-night or all-night eateries.

In Georgetown, the **Bistro Francais**, 3128 M St. NW (ℂ 202/338-3830), has been feeding night owls for years; it even draws some of the area's top chefs after their own establishments close. Open until 4am Friday and Saturday, until 3am every other night, the Bistro is thoroughly French, serving steak frites, omelets, and pâtés.

On U Street, **Ben's Chili Bowl**, 1213 U St. NW (ℂ 202/667-0909), serves up chili dogs, turkey subs, and cheese fries until 4am on Friday and Saturday nights. (See review, chapter 6.)

In Adams-Morgan one all-night dining option is the **Diner**, 2453 18th St. NW (ℂ 202/232-8800), which serves some typical (eggs and coffee, grilled cheese) and not-so-typical (a grilled fresh salmon club sandwich) diner grub.

Finally, in Dupont Circle, stop in at **Kramerbooks & Afterwords Café**, 1517 Connecticut Ave. NW (ℂ 202/387-1400), for big servings of everything, from quesadillas to french fries to French toast. The bookstore stays open all night on weekends, and so does its kitchen.

Utopia   Unlike most music bars, the arty New York/SoHo–style Utopia is serious about its restaurant operation. A moderately priced international menu features entrees ranging from lamb couscous to blackened shrimp with Creole
cream sauce, not to mention pastas and filet mignon with béarnaise sauce.
There's also an interesting wine list and a large selection of beers and single-malt
scotches. The setting is cozy and candlelit, with walls used for a changing art
gallery show (the bold, colorful paintings in the front room are by Moroccan
owner Jamal Sahri). The eclectic crowd here varies with the music, ranging from
early 20s to about 35, for the most part, including South Americans and Europeans. There's live music each night it's open, with Thursday always featuring
live Brazilian jazz and Wednesday the bluesy jazz singer Pam Bricker. There's no
real dance floor, but people find odd spaces to move to the tunes. 1418 U St. NW
(at 14th St.). ✆ 202/483-7669. You must order drink or food. Metro: U St.–Cardozo.

INTERNATIONAL SOUNDS

Bravo Bravo *Finds*   Wildly popular among Latin music fans, this club has
been open for more than a decade. In fact, the crowd itself is mostly Latin and
Spanish-speaking, including the DJs. The club holds 500 people, all of whom
stay to dance until 4am on Friday and Saturday nights. The club offers salsa lessons on Wednesday nights, when the action is a little tamer. 1001 Connecticut Ave.
NW. ✆ 202/223-5330. www.bravobravo.com. Cover $15 (minimum). Metro: Farragut West or
Farragut North.

Chi Cha Lounge *Finds*   You can sit around on couches, eat Ecuadorian tapas,
and listen to live Latin music, which is featured Sunday through Thursday. Or
you can sit around on couches and smoke Arabic tobacco through a 3-foot-high
arguileh pipe. Or you can just sit around. This is a popular neighborhood place.
1624 U St. NW. ✆ 202/234-8400 (call after 4:30pm). Sometimes a $15 minimum. Metro:
U St.–Cardozo.

Habana Village   This three-story nightclub has a bar/restaurant on the first
floor, a bar/dance floor with deejay on the second level, and a live music space
on the third floor. Salsa and merengue lessons are given Wednesday through Friday evenings, $10 per lesson. Otherwise, a deejay or live band plays danceable
Latin jazz tunes. 1834 Columbia Rd. NW. ✆ 202/462-6310. Cover $5 Fri–Sat after 9:30pm
(no cover for women). Metro: U St.–Cardozo or Woodley Park–Zoo–Adams-Morgan, and catch the
Adams-Morgan/U St. Link Shuttle.

Latin Jazz Alley   This Adams-Morgan hot spot is another place to get in on
Washington's Latin scene. At the Alley, you can learn to salsa and merengue
Wednesday and Thursday nights; each lesson $5 to $10. The club features live
Brazilian music Thursday nights, 10pm to 1am. Friday and Saturday nights,
from about 10pm to 2am, a deejay plays Latin jazz. Dinner is served until mid-
night. 1721 Columbia Rd. NW, on the 2nd floor of the El Migueleno Cafe. ✆ 202/328-6190.
$5–$10 for salsa dance lessons; 2-drink minimum. Metro: U St.–Cardozo or Woodley
Park–Zoo–Adams-Morgan and catch the Adams-Morgan/U St. Link Shuttle.

Zanzibar on the Waterfront   One day Washington will get its act together
and develop the waterfront neighborhood in which you find Zanzibar. In the
meantime, this area is pretty deserted at night, except for a handful of restaurants and Arena Stage. It really doesn't matter, though, because inside the nightclub you're looking out at the Potomac. Yes, this is a club with actual windows.
In keeping with current trends, Zanzibar has lots of couches and chairs arranged

just so. A Caribbean and African menu is available, and you can dine while listening to both live and deejay music. Open Wednesday through Sunday, Zanzibar offers something different each night, from jazz and blues to oldies. Wednesday is salsa night, with free lessons from 7 to 8pm, though a cover still applies: $5 to get in before 10pm and $10 after. An international crowd gathers here to dance or just hang out. 700 Water St. SW. ✆ 202/554-9100. www.zanzibar-otw. com. Cover typically $5–$15 (the club has an elaborate pricing structure). Metro: Waterfront.

GAY CLUBS

Dupont Circle is the gay hub of Washington, D.C., with at least 10 gay bars within easy walking distance of one another. Here are two from that neighborhood; also refer back to **Nation** (p. 260), whose Saturday night "Velvet" party is a gay event, and to **Mr. Henry's Capitol Hill** (p. 263), whose live jazz on Friday night pleases every persuasion, though the restaurant itself has long been a popular spot for gays and lesbians.

Apex   Apex (used to be called "Badlands") is an institution and still going strong as a favorite dance club for gay men. In addition to the parquet dance floor in the main room, the club has at least six bars throughout the first level. Upstairs is the Annex bar/lounge/pool hall, and a show room where karaoke performers commandeer the mike Friday night. 1415 22nd St. NW (near P St.). ✆ 202/296-0505. www.apex-dc.com. Sometimes a cover of $3–$12, depending on the event. Metro: Dupont Circle.

J.R.'s Bar and Grill   This casual and intimate all-male Dupont Circle club draws a crowd that is friendly, upscale, and very attractive. The interior—not that you'll be able to see much of it, because J.R.'s is always sardine-packed—has a 20-foot-high pressed-tin ceiling and exposed brick walls hung with neon beer signs. The big screen over the bar area is used to air music videos, showbiz sing-alongs, and favorite TV shows. Thursday is all-you-can-drink for $8 from 5 to 8pm; at midnight, you get free shots. The balcony, with pool tables, is a little more laid back. Food is served daily, until 5pm Sunday and until 7pm all other days. 1519 17th St. NW (between P and Q sts.). ✆ 202/328-0090. Metro: Dupont Circle.

3 The Bar Scene

Washington has a thriving and varied bar scene. But just when you think you know all the hot spots, a spate of new ones pop up. Travel the triangle formed by the intersections of Connecticut Avenue, 18th Street, and M Street, in the Dupont Circle neighborhood, and you'll find the latest bunch. (The triangle is also a nightclub mecca—see the write-ups for the Eighteenth Street Lounge and 5, in "The Club & Music Scene" section of this chapter.)

If you're in the mood for a sophisticated setting, seek out a bar in one of the nicer hotels, like **the Jefferson, the Willard,** the **Sofitel Lafayette Square,** the **Ritz-Carlton** (either one, in Georgetown or in the West End), or **the St. Regis** (see chapter 5 for more information and suggestions). If you want a convivial atmosphere and decent grub, try establishments that are equal parts restaurant and bar. Refer to chapter 6 for details about **Clyde's of Georgetown, Old Ebbitt Grill,** and **Old Glory Barbeque.**

Otherwise, here are a range of options for you, from upscale to low-key, but each with its own character.

Bar Rouge   Hopping, popping Bar Rouge lies just inside the Hotel Rouge (see chapter 5), but also has its own entrance from the street—you must pass under the watchful eyes of the stone Venuses arrayed in front to reach it. As acid jazz or modern international music pulses throughout the narrow room, a large flat-screen monitor on the back wall of the bar presents evolving visions of flowers blooming, snow falling, and other photographically engineered scenes. The place is full of attitude-swaggering patrons tossing back drinks with names like the Brigitte Bardot Martini. A lucky few have snagged seats on the white leather-cushioned barstools at the deep red mahogany bar. Others lounge on the 20-foot-long tufted banquette and munch on little dishes of scallop ceviche sopapillas, roasted pumpkin ravioli, and other Latin-inspired tastings served by waitresses in patent leather go-go boots and seductive black attire. Bar Rouge aims to be a scene, and succeeds. But be forewarned: If it looks crowded, you'll probably want to go elsewhere. 1315 16th St. NW (at Massachusetts Ave. and Scott Circle). © 202/232-8000. Metro: Dupont Circle.

Big Hunt   This casual and comfy Dupont Circle hangout for the 20- to 30-something crowd bills itself as a "happy hunting ground for humans" (read: meat market). It has a kind of *Raiders of the Lost Ark*/jungle theme. A downstairs room (where music is the loudest) is adorned with exotic travel posters and animal skins; another area has leopard skin–patterned booths under canvas tenting. Amusing murals grace the balcony level, which adjoins a room with pool tables. The candlelit basement is the spot for quiet conversation. The menu offers typical bar food, and the bar offers close to 30 beers on tap, most of them microbrews. An outdoor patio lies off the back poolroom.

Note: This place and the Lucky Bar might be the perfect antidotes to their exclusive neighbors down the block, the Eighteenth Street Lounge, Dragonfly, and MCCXXIII. If you're rejected there, forget about it and come here. 1345 Connecticut Ave. NW (between N St. and Dupont Circle). © 202/785-2333. Metro: Dupont Circle.

Bourbon *Finds*   North of Georgetown, in the homey area known as "Glover Park" is this neighborhood bar that has a comfortable feel to it, even though it's only about a year old. The owners have invited their regulars to bring in black and white family photos, so that's what are on the walls. Downstairs is a narrow room and long bar, upstairs is a dining room with leather booths. Fifty bourbons are on offer, along with 12 wines on draft, 10 beers on tap, as well as the usual complement of bar beverages. Another plus is the rooftop deck of theirs. 2348 Wisconsin Ave. NW. © 202/625-7770. Take a taxi.

Brickskeller *Value*   If you like beer and you like choices, head for Brickskeller, which has been around for just about 50 years and offers more than 1,000 beers from around the world. If you can't make up your mind, ask one of the waiters, who tend to be knowledgeable about the brews. The tavern draws students, college professors, embassy types, and people from the neighborhood. Brickskeller is a series of interconnecting rooms filled with gingham tableclothed tables; upstairs rooms are open only weekend nights. The food is generally okay—and the burgers are more than okay, especially the excellent Brickburger, topped with bacon, salami, onion, and cheese. 1523 22nd St. NW. © 202/293-1885. Metro: Dupont Circle or Foggy Bottom.

Café Japone   This place is a hoot. The upstairs is a karaoke bar, where locals and tourists seem to be competing for most humorous performance. The downstairs is a respectable restaurant, serving sushi and Japanese fusion dishes. Beyond the restaurant is a club, featuring loud DJ music. Take your pick. 2032 P St. NW. © 202/223-1573. Metro: Dupont Circle or Foggy Bottom.

Cosi   Popular from the start, when it was called "XandO" (pronounced "zando"), Cosi by any name is a welcoming place in the morning for a coffee drink, and even more inviting for a cocktail later in the day—cocktails are not served until 5pm. But for dessert drinks, the place can't be beat. Men: You'll see a lot of cute women hanging out here, drawn perhaps by the make-your-own s'mores and other delicious desserts. Cosi also serves sandwiches and soups. The music is loud; the decor a cross between bar and living room, with Internet hookups available. Not every Cosi is open late, but the ones I include here are: The Connecticut Avenue and 20th Street Cosi's are open until 1am, the Pennsylvania Avenue Cosi stays open until 11pm. 1350 Connecticut Ave. NW ✆ **202/296-9341.** Metro: Dupont Circle, 19th St. exit. Other locations include those at 1647 20th St. NW, at Connecticut Ave. NW (✆ 202/332-6364), and 301 Pennsylvania Ave. SE (✆ 202/546-3345).

Dragonfly   Expect to wait in line to get in here and the other hip clubs along this stretch of Connecticut Avenue. Dragonfly is a club, with music playing, white walls glowing, white-leather chairs beckoning, and people in black vogueing. And Dragonfly is a restaurant, with serious aspirations to please sushi-lovers. 1215 Connecticut Ave. NW. ✆ **202/331-1775.** Metro: Dupont Circle or Farragut North.

The Dubliner   This is your typical old Irish pub, the port you can blow into in any storm, personal or weather-related. It's got the dark-wood paneling and tables, the etched and stained glass windows, an Irish-accented staff from time to time, and, most importantly, the Auld Dubliner Amber Ale. You'll probably want to stick to drinks here, but you can grab a burger, grilled chicken sandwich, or roast duck salad; the kitchen is open until 1am. The Dubliner is frequented by Capitol Hill staffers and journalists who cover the Hill. Irish music groups play nightly. In the Phoenix Park Hotel, 520 N. Capitol St. NW, with its own entrance on F St. NW. ✆ **202/737-3773.** www.dublinerdc.com. Metro: Union Station.

ESPN Zone   This is not a date place, unless your date happens to be Anna Kournikova. It's three levels of sports mania, in the form of interactive sports games, a restaurant, 200 televisions throughout the place tuned to sporting events, a bar area, and the most popular attraction, the Screening Room. This last venue offers a giant 16-foot video screen flanked by six 36-inch screens, each showing a different event. Seats with special headphones are arrayed in front of the screen, and you control what you listen to. ESPN Zone is also a sports bar/restaurant serving American staples: burgers, fries, huge salads, chicken tenders, and yes, ribs. 555 12th St. NW. ✆ **202/783-3776.** www.espnzone.com. Metro: Metro Center.

Fadó   Another Irish pub, but this one is Ireland as a theme park. The odd thing about it is its location: in the heart of Chinatown. Fadó was designed and built by the Irish Pub Company of Dublin, which shipped everything—the stone for the floors, the etched glass, the milled wood—from Ireland. The pub has separate areas, including an old Irish "bookstore" alcove and a country cottage bar. Authentic Irish food, like potato pancakes, is served with your Guinness. *Fadó*, Gaelic for "long ago," doesn't take reservations, which means that hungry patrons tend to hover over your table waiting for you to finish. 808 7th St. NW. ✆ **202/789-0066.** www.fadoirishpub.com. Metro: Gallery Place–Chinatown.

Lucky Bar   Lucky Bar is a good place to kick back and relax. But, in keeping with the times, it also features free salsa dance lessons on Monday night. Sometimes the music is live, but mostly it's courtesy of a deejay. Other times the jukebox plays, but never so loud that you can't carry on a conversation. The bar has a front room overlooking Connecticut Avenue and a back room decorated with good-luck signs, couches, hanging TVs, booths, and a pool table. Lucky Bar is known in the area as a "soccer bar," with its TVs turned to soccer matches going

(*Value*   **Cheap Eats: Happy Hours to Write Home About**

Even the diviest of bars puts out some free nibbles to complement your drink—peanuts or pretzels at the very least. And good-value promotions are increasingly popular at area bars and nightclubs, such as **Whitlow's on Wilson** in Arlington (see the "Arlington Row" box on p. 270), where you can chow down on a half-price burger every Monday night. A step above these are certain fine restaurants and hotels around town that set out gourmet food during happy hour, either for free or an astonishingly low price. Here are three that you might like. But be forewarned: when it comes to free food, Washingtonians can be aggressive.

In the bar area only, **McCormick & Schmick's,** 1652 K St. NW, at the corner of 17th Street NW (© 202/861-2233), offers a choice of giant burger, fried calamari, quesadillas, fish tacos, and more, for only $1.95 each. The offer is good Monday through Friday from 3:30 to 6:30pm and 10:30pm to midnight. Friendly bartenders make you feel at home as they concoct mixed drinks with juice they squeeze right at the bar (the drinks, alas, are not discounted).

Teaism Penn Quarter, 400 8th St. NW (© 202/638-6010), which is near the MCI Center, the FBI Building, the National Gallery, and nightspots, features happy hour Thursday and Friday from 5:30 to 7:30pm, with free hors d'oeuvres like Thai chicken and Indian curries, Asian noodle salads, sticky white rice, green salad—make a meal of it! Drinks are not discounted, but they are unusual: sakes, Asian beers, gingery margaritas, and the like.

The clubby, mahogany-paneled **Town and Country Lounge,** in the Renaissance Mayflower Hotel, 1127 Connecticut Ave. NW (© 202/347-3000), is the setting weeknights from 5:30 to 7:30pm for complimentary cocktail-hour hors d'oeuvres that change from night to night: slices of roast beef on toasts, chicken/beef fajitas, pastas, and so on. Here, you also have the pleasure of watching the personable bartender Sambonn Lek at work, whether mixing drinks, performing magic tricks, or matchmaking. Drinks are regular price.

on around the world. 1221 Connecticut Ave. NW. © 202/331-3733. Metro: Dupont Circle or Farragut North.

MCCXXIII   This is about as swank and New York as Washington gets: Hipsters lined up at the velvet rope, a dress code (but really an excuse for the doorman to decide whether you measure up for admittance), outrageously high prices (drink and food charges are written in Roman numerals, so some people are taken aback when settling up), a soaring ceiling, and opulent interior, beautiful women servers who purr at you, and more beautiful people milling about. 1223 Connecticut Ave. NW. © 202/822-1800. www.1223.com. Cover $10 after 10pm. Metro: Dupont Circle or Farragut North.

Mr. Smith's of Georgetown   Mr. Smith's bills itself as "The Friendliest Saloon in Town," but the truth is that it's so popular among regulars, you're in danger of being ignored if the staff doesn't know you. The bar, which opened

Arlington Row

As unlikely as it seems, one of the hottest spots for Washington nightlife is a stretch of suburban street in Arlington, Virginia. I'm talking about a section of Wilson Boulevard in the Clarendon neighborhood, roughly between Highland and Danville streets. People used to refer to this area as "Little Vietnam," for the many Vietnamese cafes and grocery stores that have flourished here. But more recently, this specific patch of Arlington has gained renown as a musical mecca, because of the profusion of live music venues that have sprung up.

Let's get one thing straight: Arlington is not Adams-Morgan. Adams-Morgan is urban, ethnic, and edgy, full of the requisite black clothes, body piercings, colorful hair, tattoos, and bad attitudes. Arlington Row is a lot tamer, attracting, so far anyway, a crowd of all ages, usually dressed for comfort. You don't feel like your presence has to make a statement. Certainly, the clubs are more accessible: Metro stops are nearby, parking is easier, streets are safer, and clubs front the streets with picture windows and aren't as exclusive.

I wouldn't recommend that you visit Arlington Row if it weren't for one key element: the music. It's live, it's good (most of the time), and it's here almost nightly. So take the Metro to the Clarendon stop and walk down Wilson, or drive up Wilson from Key Bridge, turn left on Edgewood Road or another side street, and park on the street. Then walk to these spots, all of which serve food:

If you're a teetotaler, or just in the mood for the mellowest of experiences, head to **Common Grounds Coffeehouse**, 3211 Wilson Blvd., which is 1 block west of the Clarendon Metro station (✆ **703/312-0427**; www.cgespresso.com). The coffeehouse serves up yummy comfort food and live music Thursday to Saturday. The atmosphere is folksy, the music usually country, acoustic guitar, or indie. Cover ranges from $6 to $9.

The smallest of the bunch, **Galaxy Hut**, 2711 Wilson Blvd. (✆ **703/525-8646**; www.galaxyhut.com), is a comfortable bar with far-out art on

about 37 years ago, has a front room with original brick walls, wooden seats, and a long bar, at which you can count on finding pairs of newfound friends telling obscene jokes, loudly. At the end of this room is a large piano around which customers congregate each night to accompany the pianist. An interior light-filled garden room adjoins an outdoor garden area. 3104 M St. NW. ✆ 202/333-3104. www.mrsmiths.com. Metro: Foggy Bottom, then take the Georgetown Metro Connection shuttle.

Nathans   Nathans is in the heart of Georgetown. If you pop in here in mid-afternoon, it's a quiet place to grab a beer or glass of wine and watch the action on the street. Visit at night, though, and it's a more typical bar scene, crowded with locals, out-of-towners, students, and a sprinkling of couples in from the 'burbs. That's the front room. The back room at Nathans is a civilized, candlelit restaurant serving classic American fare. After 11:30pm on Friday and Saturday, this room turns into a dance hall, playing deejay music and attracting the 20-somethings Friday night, an older crowd Saturday night. 3150 M St. NW (at the corner of Wisconsin Ave.). ✆ 202/338-2600. Metro: Foggy Bottom, then take the Georgetown Metro Connection shuttle.

the walls and a patio in the alley. Look for live alternative rock most nights.

At **IOTA,** 2832 Wilson Blvd. (© **703/522-8340;** iotaclubandcafe.com), up-and-coming local bands take the stage nightly in a setting with minimal decor (cement floor, exposed brick walls, and a wood-beamed ceiling); there's a patio in back. There's live music nightly. If there's a cover, it's usually $8 to $18.

Whitlow's on Wilson, 2854 Wilson Blvd. (© **703/276-9693;** www.whitlows.com), is the biggest spot on the block, spreading throughout four rooms, the first showcasing the music (usually blues, with anything from surfer music to rock thrown in). The place has the appearance of a diner, from Formica table-booths to a soda fountain, and serves retro diner food. (Mon half-price burger nights are a good deal.) The other rooms hold coin-operated pool tables, dartboards, and air hockey. Cover is usually $3 to $5 Thursday through Saturday after 9pm.

Clarendon Grill, 1101 N. Highland St. (© **703/524-7455;** www.cgrill.com), wins a best decor award for its construction theme: murals of construction workers, building materials displayed under the glass-covered bar, and so forth. Music is a mix of modern rock, jazz, and reggae. Cover is $3 to $5 Wednesday through Saturday.

Now, get in your car, hop the Metro, or get out your rambling shoes to visit one other place, about a mile south of this stretch of Wilson:

Rhodeside Grill, 1836 Wilson Blvd. (© **703/243-0145;** www.rhodeside grill.com), 3 blocks from the Courthouse Metro stop, is a well-liked American restaurant on its first floor. The rec-room-like bar downstairs features excellent live bands playing roots rock, jazz funk, Latin percussion, country rock, reggae—you name it. Cover averages $5 or more Thursday through Saturday starting at 9:30pm.

Politiki, Top of the Hill, and the Pour House   This is three separate bars in one, hardly the traditional approach favored by other pubs along this stretch of Capitol Hill. The Pour House, on the first floor, plays on a Pittsburgh theme (honoring the owner's roots), displaying Steeler and Penguin paraphernalia, and drawing Iron City drafts from its tap and pierogis from the kitchen. Downstairs is Politiki, a tiki bar: Think Scorpion Bowl and piña colada drinks, pupu platters, and hula dancer figurines. The basement has pool tables, a bar, and a lounge area (behind beaded curtains); the street level has booths and a bar. On the top floor is "Top of the Hill," promoted as "hip and upscale," but not really, although you will find leather chairs, art, and chandeliers here. 319 Pennsylvania Ave. SE. © 202/546-1001. Metro: Capitol South.

Spy Lounge   You enter this cool bar through the Felix Restaurant and Lounge, and that's because Alan Popowsky owns them both. The Spy attempts a modern European feel, with metal stools and white walls, and builds upon a spy theme, showing scenes from James Bond movies continually on its TV screens. Popowsky keeps the place from getting too crowded, or riffraffy, by allowing only a certain number of people in at a time (and only those who are dressed attractively). 2406 18th St. NW. © **202/483-3549.** Metro: U St.–Cardozo or Woodley Park–Zoo–Adams-Morgan, and catch the Adams-Morgan/U St. Link Shuttle.

The Tombs Housed in a converted 19th-century Federal-style home, The Tombs, which opened in 1962, is a favorite hangout for students and faculty of nearby Georgetown University. (Bill Clinton came here during his college years.) They tend to congregate at the central bar and surrounding tables, while local residents head for "the Sweeps," the room that lies down a few steps and has red-leather banquettes.

Directly below the upscale 1789 restaurant (see chapter 6 for a review), The Tombs benefits from 1789 chef Riz Lacoste's supervision. The menu offers burgers, sandwiches, and salads, as well as more serious fare. 1226 36th St. NW. © **202/337-6668.** Metro: Foggy Bottom, then take the Georgetown Metro Connection shuttle into Georgetown, with a walk from Wisconsin Ave.

Topaz Bar This is Bar Rouge's sister (they are owned and managed by the same company) and also lies within a hotel, the Topaz. The decor here emphasizes cool sensuality, hence the Philippe Starck bar stools, blue velvet settees, zebra-patterned ottomans, and leopard-print rugs. A lighting scheme fades into and out of colors: blue to pink to black, and so on. Everyone here is drinking the Blue Nirvana, a combo of champagne, vodka, and a touch of blue curacao liqueur—a concoction that tends to turn your tongue blue, by the way. The Topaz Bar serves small plates of delicious Asian-inspired tastes, like shrimp and pork dumplings and chicken satays. 1733 N St. NW. © **202/393-3000.** Metro: Dupont Circle or Farragut North.

Tryst This is the most relaxed of Washington's lounge bars. The room is surprisingly large for Adams-Morgan, and it's jam-packed with worn armchairs and couches, which are usually occupied, no matter what time of day. People come here to have coffee or a drink, get a bite to eat, read a book, meet a friend. The place feels almost like a student lounge on a college campus, only alcohol is served. A bonus: Tryst offers free wireless Internet service. 2459 18th St. NW. © **202/232-5500.** www.trystdc.com. Metro: U St.–Cardozo or Woodley Park–Zoo–Adams-Morgan and catch the Adams-Morgan/U St. Link Shuttle.

Tune Inn *Finds* Capitol Hill has a number of bars that qualify as institutions, but the Tune Inn is probably the most popular. Capitol Hill staffers and their bosses, apparently at ease in dive surroundings, have been coming here for cheap beer and greasy burgers since it opened in 1955. (All the longtime Capitol Hillers know that Friday is crab cake day at the Tune Inn, and they all show up.) 33½ Pennsylvania Ave. SE. © **202/543-2725.** Metro: Capitol South.

10

Side Trips from Washington, D.C.

Just across the Potomac River from Washington, D.C., is the picturesque enclave of Old Town Alexandria, where George Washington dined and hung out with friends. In fact, in Washington's day, the city of Alexandria fell within the boundaries of the nation's capital. (Congress retroceded the Virginia territory back to the state of Virginia in 1847.)

It's easy enough—and recommended —to tour certain historic areas of Old Town Alexandria, which is a mere 8 miles from the capital, and George Washington's plantation, Mount Vernon, which is 8 miles beyond Alexandria. Plan to visit Mount Vernon first, then stop in Old Town on your return. At Mount Vernon, you'll be able to tour

our first president's exquisite estate and gardens, as you learn fascinating facts about the man/soldier/hero/statesman. In Old Town Alexandria, you'll discover a charming waterfront village full of historic attractions, good restaurants and shops, lively bars and nightclubs, and streets for strolling.

But don't expect to find these spots any less crowded than the capital's attractions; their unique appeal, suburban locations, and proximity to downtown make them popular to local tourists and out-of-towners alike.

If you'd like to explore farther afield, consider picking up a copy of *Frommer's Virginia* or *Frommer's Maryland & Delaware* (both Wiley Publishing, Inc.).

1 Mount Vernon

Only 16 miles south of the capital, George Washington's Southern plantation dates from a 1674 land grant to the president's great-grandfather.

ESSENTIALS
GETTING THERE   If you're going by car, take any of the bridges over the Potomac River into Virginia and follow the signs pointing the way to National Airport/Mount Vernon/George Washington Memorial Parkway. You travel south on the George Washington Memorial Parkway, the river always to your left, passing by National Airport on your right, continuing through Old Town Alexandria, where the parkway is renamed "Washington Street," and heading 8 miles farther, until you reach the large circle that fronts Mount Vernon.

You might also take a bus or boat to Mount Vernon. These bus and boat tour prices include the price of admission to Mount Vernon.

Gray Line Buses (© **800/862-1400,** also 303/386-8300 or, at Union Station 202/289-1995; www.graylinedc.com) go to Mount Vernon daily (except Christmas, Thanksgiving, and New Year's Day), leaving from the bus's terminal at Union Station at 8:30am and returning by 1:30pm. The cost is $30 per adult and $15 per child. (AAA members show your membership card to receive a 10% discount.) From mid-June through October, Gray Line operates a second tour to Mount Vernon, leaving Union Station at 2pm. Ticket prices are the same. Gray Line offers several other tours, so call for further information.

(*Fun Fact* **The George Washington Memorial Parkway**

Though few people realize it, the George Washington Memorial Parkway is actually a national park. The first section was completed in 1932 to honor the bicentennial of George Washington's birth. The parkway follows the Potomac River, running from Mount Vernon, past Old Town and the nation's capital, ending at Great Falls, Virginia. Today, the parkway is a major commuter route leading into and out of the city. Even the most impatient driver, however, can't help but notice the beautiful scenery and views of the Jefferson and Lincoln memorials and the Washington Monument that you pass along the way.

The Spirit of Washington Cruises's (© **202/554-8000;** www.spiritcruises. com) *Potomac Spirit* leaves from Pier 4 (6th and Water sts. SW; 3 blocks from the Green Line Metro's Waterfront Station) every day except Monday, from mid-March to mid-October at 8:30am, returning by 3pm; cost is $34 per adult, $23 per child (ages 6–11; younger children free). The Potomac Riverboat Company's (© **703/684-0580** or 703/548-9000; www.potomacriverboatco.com) *Miss Christin* operates Tuesday through Sunday May through August (weekends only Apr and Sept–Oct), departing at 11am for Mount Vernon from the pier adjacent to the Torpedo Factory, at the bottom of King Street in Old Town Alexandria, and costing $27 per adult, $15 per child (ages 6–10; free for children under 6). Arrive 30 minutes ahead of time at the pier, to secure a place on the boat. The trip takes 50 minutes each way. The boat departs Mount Vernon at 4pm to return to Old Town.

If you're in the mood for exercise in a pleasant setting, rent a **bike** (see the box called "Biking to Old Town Alexandria & Mount Vernon" on p. 281 for rental locations and other information).

Finally, it is possible to take **public transportation** to Mount Vernon by riding the Metro to the Yellow Line's Huntington Station and proceeding to the lower level, where you catch the Fairfax Connector bus (no. 101) to Mount Vernon. The connector bus is a 20-minute ride and costs 75¢. Call © **703/339-7200** for schedule information.

TOURING THE ESTATE

Mount Vernon Estate and Gardens If it's beautiful out, and you have the time, you could easily spend half a day or more soaking in the life and times of George Washington at Mount Vernon. The centerpiece of a visit to this 500-acre estate is a tour through 14 rooms of the mansion, whose oldest part dates from the 1740s. The plantation was passed down from Washington's great-grandfather, who acquired the land in 1674, eventually to George in 1754. Washington proceeded over the next 45 years to expand and fashion the home to his liking, though the American Revolution and his years as president kept Washington away from his beloved estate much of the time.

What you see today is a remarkable restoration of the mansion, displaying many original furnishings and objects used by the Washington family. The rooms have been repainted in the original colors favored by George and Martha. There's no formal guided tour, but attendants stationed throughout the house and grounds provide brief orientations and answer questions; when there's no line, a walk-through takes about 20 minutes. You can also rent an audio tour for

$4 that provides a 40-minute plantation overview narration. Maps of the property are available at the entrance, including an adventure map for children.

But don't stop there. After leaving the house, you can tour the outbuildings: the kitchen, slave quarters, storeroom, smokehouse, overseer's quarters, coach house, and stables. A 4-acre exhibit area called "George Washington, Pioneer Farmer" includes a replica of Washington's 16-sided barn and fields of crops that he grew (corn, wheat, oats, and so forth). Docents in period costumes demonstrate 18th-century farming methods. At its peak, Mount Vernon was an 8,000-acre working farm, reminding us that, more than anything, Washington considered himself first and foremost a farmer.

A museum on the property exhibits Washington memorabilia, and details of the restoration are explained in the museum's annex; there's also a gift shop. You'll want to walk around the grounds (especially in nice weather) and see the wharf (and take a 30-min. narrated excursion on the Potomac, offered three times a day, seasonally, Tues–Sun, $8 per adult, $4 per child ages 6–11), the slave burial ground, the greenhouse, the lawns and gardens, and the tomb containing George and Martha Washington's sarcophagi (24 other family members are also interred here). Celebrations are held at the estate every year on the third Monday in February, the date commemorating Washington's birthday; admission is free to anyone who shares Washington's birthday, February 22.

Mount Vernon belongs to the Mount Vernon Ladies' Association, which purchased the estate for $200,000 in 1858, from John Augustine Washington, great-grandnephew of the first president. Without the group's purchase, the estate might have crumbled and disappeared, for neither the federal government nor the Commonwealth of Virginia had wanted to buy the property when it was earlier offered for sale.

Today more than a million people tour the property annually. The best time to visit is off season; during the heavy tourist months (especially in spring), avoid weekends and holidays if possible, and arrive early year-round to beat the crowds.

Southern end of the George Washington Memorial Pkwy. (mailing address: P.O. Box 110, Mount Vernon, VA 22121). © 703/780-2000. www.mountvernon.org. Admission $11 adults, $11 seniors, $5 children 6–11, free for children under 6. Apr–Aug daily 8am–5pm; Mar and Sept–Oct daily 9am–5pm; Nov–Feb daily 9am–4pm.

DINING & SHOPPING

Mount Vernon's comprehensive **gift shop** offers a wide range of books, children's toys, holiday items, Mount Vernon private-labeled food and wine, and Mount Vernon licensed furnishings.

A **food court** features indoor and outdoor seating and a menu of baked goods, deli sandwiches, coffee, grilled items, Pizza Hut pizza, and Mrs. Fields cookies. You can't **picnic** on the grounds of Mount Vernon, but you can drive a mile north on the parkway to Riverside Park, where there are tables and a lawn overlooking the Potomac.

Meanwhile, the Mount Vernon Inn restaurant is still the option I'd recommend.

Tips **Special Activities at Mount Vernon**

There's an ongoing schedule of events at Mount Vernon, especially in summer. These might include tours focusing on 18th-century gardens, slave life, Colonial crafts, or archaeology; and, for children, hands-on history programs and treasure hunts. Call or check the website to find out whether anything is on during your visit.

Mount Vernon Inn AMERICAN TRADITIONAL   Lunch or dinner at the inn is an intrinsic part of the Mount Vernon experience. It's a quaint and charming Colonial-style restaurant, complete with period furnishings and three working fireplaces. The waiters are all in 18th-century costumes. Be sure to begin your meal with the homemade peanut and chestnut soup (usually on the lunch menu). Lunch entrees range from Colonial turkey "pye" (a sort of Early American quiche served in a crock with garden vegetables and a puffed pastry top) to a pulled pork barbecue sandwich. There's a full bar, and premium wines are offered by the glass. At dinner, tablecloths and candlelight make this a more elegant setting. Choose from soups (perhaps broccoli cheddar) and salads, entrees such as Maryland crab cakes or roast venison with peppercorn sauce, homemade breads, and dessert (like whiskey cake or English trifle).

Near the entrance to Mount Vernon Estate and Gardens. ℂ **703/780-0011.** Reservations recommended for dinner. Lunch main courses $5.50–$8.50; dinner main courses $13–$25; fixed-price dinner $16. AE, DISC, MC, V. Daily 11am–3:30pm and Mon–Sat 5–9pm.

2 Alexandria

Old Town Alexandria is about 8 miles south of Washington.

Founded by a group of Scottish tobacco merchants, the seaport town of Alexandria was born in 1749 when a 60-acre tract of land was auctioned off in half-acre lots. Colonists came from miles around, in ramshackle wagons and stately carriages, in sloops, brigantines, and lesser craft, to bid on land that would be "commodious for trade and navigation and tend greatly to the ease and advantage of the frontier inhabitants." The auction took place in Market Square (still intact today), and the surveyor's assistant was a capable lad of 17 named George Washington. (Market Square, by the way, is the site of the oldest continually operating farmers' market in the country; go there on a Sat between 5 and 10am and you'll be participating in a 253-year-old tradition.)

Today, the original 60 acres of lots in George Washington's hometown (also Robert E. Lee's) are the heart of Old Town, a multimillion-dollar urban renewal historic district. Many Alexandria streets still bear their original Colonial names (King, Queen, Prince, Princess, Royal—you get the drift), while others, like Jefferson, Franklin, Lee, Patrick, and Henry, are obviously post-Revolutionary.

In this "mother lode of Americana," the past is being restored in an ongoing archaeological and historical research program. And though the present can be seen in the abundance of shops, boutiques, art galleries, and restaurants that capitalize on the tourist traffic, it's still easy to imagine yourself in Colonial times by listening for the rumbling of horse-drawn vehicles over cobblestone (portions of Prince and Oronoco streets are still paved with cobblestone); dining on Sally Lunn bread and other 18th-century grub in the centuries-old Gadsby's Tavern; and learning about the lives of the nation's forefathers during walking tours that take you in and out of their houses.

ESSENTIALS

GETTING THERE   If you're driving, take the Arlington Memorial or the 14th Street Bridge to the George Washington Memorial Parkway south, which becomes Washington Street in Old Town Alexandria. Washington Street intersects with King Street, Alexandria's main thoroughfare. Turn left from Washington Street onto one of the streets before or after King Street (southbound left turns are not permitted from Washington St. onto King St.) and you'll be heading toward the waterfront and the heart of Old Town. If you turn right from

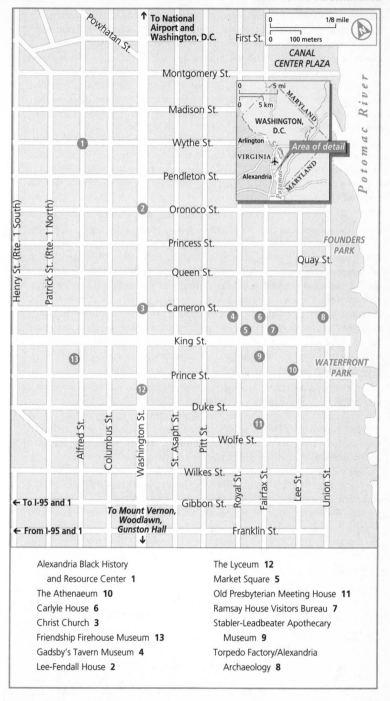

Old Town Alexandria

To National Airport and Washington, D.C.

First St.

CANAL CENTER PLAZA

0 — 1/8 mile
0 — 100 meters

Powhatan St.

Montgomery St.

Madison St.

Wythe St.

Pendleton St.

Oronoco St.

Princess St.

Queen St.

Cameron St.

King St.

Prince St.

Duke St.

Wolfe St.

Wilkes St.

Gibbon St.

Franklin St.

Henry St. (Rte. 1 South)

Patrick St. (Rte. 1 North)

Alfred St.

Columbus St.

Washington St.

St. Asaph St.

Pitt St.

Royal St.

Fairfax St.

Lee St.

Union St.

Potomac River

FOUNDERS PARK

Quay St.

WATERFRONT PARK

← To I-95 and 1

← From I-95 and 1

To Mount Vernon, Woodlawn, Gunston Hall

WASHINGTON, D.C.

MARYLAND

Arlington

VIRGINIA

Alexandria

Area of detail

MARYLAND

0 — 5 mi
0 — 5 km

Alexandria Black History
   and Resource Center **1**
The Athenaeum **10**
Carlyle House **6**
Christ Church **3**
Friendship Firehouse Museum **13**
Gadsby's Tavern Museum **4**
Lee-Fendall House **2**

The Lyceum **12**
Market Square **5**
Old Presbyterian Meeting House **11**
Ramsay House Visitors Bureau **7**
Stabler-Leadbeater Apothecary
   Museum **9**
Torpedo Factory/Alexandria
   Archaeology **8**

Washington Street onto King Street, you'll find an avenue of shops and restaurants. You can obtain a free parking permit from the Visitors Center (see information about parking in the Visitors Center paragraph, below), or park at meters or in garages. The town is compact, so you won't need a car once you arrive.

The easiest way to make the trip may be the Metro's Yellow and Blue lines to the King Street station. From the King Street station, you can catch an eastbound AT2 or AT5 blue-and-gold DASH bus (℘ **703/370-DASH**), marked either "Old Town" or "Braddock Metro," which will take you up King Street. Ask to be dropped at the corner of Fairfax and King streets, which will put you right across the street from Ramsay House, the visitor center. The fare is $1 most of the time, but free weekends, from Friday evening through Sunday night. Or you can walk into Old Town, although it's about a mile from the station into the center of Old Town.

VISITOR INFORMATION The **Alexandria Convention and Visitors Association,** located at Ramsay House Visitors Center, 221 King St., at Fairfax Street (℘ **800/388-9119** or 703/838-4200; www.funside.com), is open daily from 9am to 5pm (closed Jan 1, Thanksgiving, and Dec 25). Here you can obtain a map/self-guided walking tour and brochures about the area; learn about special events that might be scheduled during your visit and get tickets for them; and receive answers to any questions you might have about accommodations, restaurants, sights, or shopping. The center supplies materials in five languages.

If you come by car, get a free 1-day parking permit here for any 2-hour meter for up to 24 hours; when you park, put money in the meter to cover yourself until you post your permit. The permit can be renewed for a second day.

ORGANIZED TOURS Though it's easy to see Alexandria on your own by putting yourself in the hands of Colonial-attired guides at individual attractions, you might consider taking a comprehensive walking tour. The Visitors Center offers 1½-hour architectural and history tours, leaving from the Visitors Center garden, weather permitting, at least once a day, at 10:30am, with additional tours added during busy seasons. The tour costs $10 per person (free for age 6 and under) and you pay the guide when you arrive at the Visitors Center.

Alexandria Colonial Tours (℘ **703/519-1749;** www.alexcolonialtours.com) conducts tours March through November (again, weather permitting) at 7:30 and 9pm Friday and Saturday, 7:30pm only on Sunday, with a 7:30pm tour offered Wednesday and Thursday evenings in the summer. This 1-hour tour departs from Ramsay House and costs $7 for adults, $5 for children ages 7 to 12, free for children under 7. You purchase tickets from the guide, who will be dressed in Colonial attire and standing in front of the Visitors Center.

CITY LAYOUT Old Town is very small and laid out in an easy grid. At the center is the intersection of Washington Street and King Street. Streets change from North to South when they cross King Street. For example, North Alfred Street is the part of Alfred north of King Street. Guess where South Alfred Street is.

SPECIAL EVENTS

Two organizations publish helpful calendars of key Alexandria events: the **Alexandria Convention and Visitors Association** (℘ **800/388-9119** or 703/838-4200; www.funside.com), which covers Alexandria at large; and the City of Alexandria's **Office of Historic Alexandria** (℘ **703/838-4554;** www.ci.alexandria.va.us: Click on "Historic Alexandria," then "Tourism and History,"

(Value Very Important Patriot (VIP) Pass

Money-saving tickets are on sale at the **Ramsay House Visitors Center.** One example is the **Very Important Patriot (VIP) Pass,** costing $26 for an adult, $14 for children ages 11 to 17. The pass admits you to the Carlyle House, Gadsby's Tavern Museum, and the Lee-Fendall House and reserves your place on a guided walking tour of Old Town, as well as a ride aboard a riverboat that cruises the Potomac River along the Alexandria waterfront. The VIP Pass can save you about $7 per adult and $8 per child. Unfortunately, it can be hard to coordinate the timed tours of the historic sights and the scheduled departures of the walking tour and boat excursion within the framework of a single day. The pass makes the most sense if you're staying more than 1 day. You should also know that the pass is available April through October and only on weekends during the months of April, September, and October. Ask about other passes.

then "Historic Events Calendar"), which focuses on the historic sights. You can call and ask them to mail you information, or you can access their separate and continually updated websites. Event highlights include:

JANUARY The **birthdays of Confederate General Robert E. Lee and his father,** Revolutionary War hero "Light Horse Harry" Lee, are celebrated together at the Lee-Fendall House the third Sunday of the month. The party features period music, refreshments, and house tours. Admission in 2004 was $5 per adult, $2 for children 11 to 17, and free for children under 11.

FEBRUARY Alexandria celebrates **George Washington's Birthday** over the course of several days, including Presidents' Weekend, which precedes the federal holiday, usually the third Monday in February. Festivities typically include a Colonial costume or black-tie banquet, followed by a ball at Gadsby's Tavern, a 10-kilometer race, special tours, a Revolutionary War encampment at Fort Ward Park (complete with uniformed troops engaging in skirmishes), the nation's largest George Washington Birthday Parade (50,000–75,000 people attend each year), and 18th-century comic opera performances. Most events, such as the parade and historical reenactments, are free. The Birthnight Ball at Gadsby's Tavern requires tickets, which cost $60 per person in 2004.

MARCH On the first Saturday in March, King Street is the site of a popular **St. Patrick's Day Parade.**

APRIL Alexandria celebrates **Historic Garden Week in Virginia** with tours of privately owned local historic homes and gardens the third Saturday of the month. Call the Visitors Center (© 703/838-4200) in early 2005 for more information about tickets and admission prices for the tour.

JUNE The **Red Cross Waterfront Festival,** the second weekend in June, honors Alexandria's historic importance as a seaport and the vitality of its Potomac shoreline today with a display of historic tall ships, ship tours, boat rides and races, nautical art exhibits, waterfront walking tours, fireworks, children's games, an arts and crafts show, food booths, and entertainment. Admission is charged.

JULY Alexandria's birthday (its 256th in 2005) is celebrated with a concert performance by the Alexandria Symphony Orchestra, fireworks, birthday cake, and other festivities. The Saturday following the Fourth of July. All events are free.

SEPTEMBER   This year is the 63rd Annual Tour of Historic Alexandria Homes, which takes you to some of the city's most beautifully restored and decorated private homes. Third Saturday in September. Tickets and information from the Visitors Center.

OCTOBER   October celebrations include the **Alexandria Arts Safari,** which takes place on the first Saturday in October and features archaeological and arts tours, and interactive events. Torpedo Factory. Free.

   Halloween Walking Tours take place toward the end of October. A lantern-carrying guide in 18th-century costume describes Alexandria's ghosts, graveyards, legends, myths, and folklore as you tour the town and graveyards. Call the Visitors Center for information.

NOVEMBER   There's a **Christmas Tree Lighting** in Market Square the Friday after Thanksgiving; the ceremony, which includes choir singing, puppet shows, dance performances, and an appearance by Santa and his elves, begins at 7pm. The night the tree is lit, thousands of tiny lights adorning King Street trees also go on.

DECEMBER   Holiday festivities continue with the **Annual Scottish Christmas Walk** on the first Saturday in December. Activities include kilted bagpipers, Highland dancers, a parade of Scottish clans (with horses and dogs), caroling, fashion shows, storytelling, booths (selling crafts, antiques, food, hot mulled punch, heather, fresh wreaths, and holly), and children's games. Admission is charged for some events.

   The **Historic Alexandria Candlelight Tour,** the second week in December, visits seasonally decorated historic Alexandria homes and an 18th-century tavern. There is Colonial dancing, string quartets, madrigal and opera singers, and refreshments, too. Purchase tickets at the Ramsay House Visitors Center.

   There are so many holiday-season activities that the Visitors Association issues a special brochure about them each year. Pick one up to learn about decorations, workshops, walking tours, tree lightings, concerts, bazaars, bake sales, craft fairs, and much more.

WHAT TO SEE & DO

Colonial and post-Revolutionary buildings are Old Town Alexandria's main attractions. My favorites are the Carlyle House and Gadsby's Tavern Museum, but they are all worth a visit.

   Except for the Alexandria Black History and Resource Center, whose closest Metro stop is the Braddock Street station, and Fort Ward, to which you should drive or take a taxi, these sites are most easily accessible via the King Street Metro station, combined with a ride on the DASH bus to the center of Old Town.

   Old Town has hundreds of charming boutiques, antiques stores, and gift shops selling everything from souvenir T-shirts to 18th-century reproductions. Some of the most interesting are at the sites, but most are clustered on King and Cameron streets and their connecting cross streets. A guide to antiques stores is available at the Visitors Center. Also see chapter 8, which includes some Alexandria shops.

Alexandria Black History Resource Center   In a 1940s building that originally housed the black community's first public library, the center exhibits historical objects, photographs, documents, and memorabilia relating to black citizens of Alexandria from the 18th century forward. In addition to the permanent collection, the museum presents rotating exhibits and other activities. If you're interested in further studies, check out the center's Watson Reading Room. A half-hour is really enough time to spend at the center.

The center is actually on the outskirts of Old Town, and not in the best neighborhood. From here, it makes sense to walk, rather than to take the Metro or even a taxi, into Old Town. Have a staff person point you in the direction of Washington Street, where you will turn right and be only 2 blocks from the Lee-Fendall House, at Oronoco and Washington streets (see below).

638 N. Alfred St. (at Wythe St.). ✆ 703/838-4356. http://oha.ci.Alexandria.va.us/bhrc. Free admission (donations accepted). Tues–Sat 10am–4pm. Metro: Braddock Rd. From the station, walk across the parking lot and bear right until you reach the corner of West and Wythe sts., where you'll proceed 5 blocks east along Wythe until you reach the center.

The Athenaeum   This grand building, with its Greek Revival architecture-style, stands out among the narrow old town houses on the cobblestone street. Built in 1851, the Athenaeum has been many things: the Bank of the Old Dominion, where Robert E. Lee kept his money prior to the Civil War; a commissary for the Union Army during the Civil War; a church; a triage center where wounded Union soldiers were treated; and a medicine warehouse. Now the hall serves as an art gallery and performance space for the Northern Virginia Fine Arts Association. So pop by to admire the Athenaeum's imposing exterior, including the four soaring Doric columns, and its interior hall: 24-foot-high ceilings, enormous windows, and whatever contemporary art is on display. This won't take you more than 20 minutes, tops.

201 Prince St. (at South Lee St.). ✆ **703/548-0035**. www.Alexandria-athenaeum.org. Free admission (donations accepted). Wed–Fri 11am–3pm; Sat noon–4pm; Sun noon–5pm.

⌒ *Moments*   Biking to Old Town Alexandria & Mount Vernon

One of the nicest ways to see Washington is on a bike ride in Virginia. Rent a bike at Fletcher's Boat House or some other location listed under "Outdoor Activities" in chapter 7, then hop on the pathway that runs along the Potomac River, heading toward the monuments and the Arlington Memorial Bridge. In Washington, this is the Rock Creek Park Trail; once you cross Memorial Bridge (near the Lincoln Memorial) into Virginia, the name changes to the Mount Vernon Trail, which, as it sounds, is a straight shot to Mount Vernon.

As you tool along, you have a breathtaking view of the Potomac and of Washington's grand landmarks: the Kennedy Center, Washington Monument, Lincoln Memorial, Jefferson Memorial, the National Cathedral off in one direction, and the Capitol off in the other.

Of course, this mode of transportation is also a great way to see Old Town Alexandria and Mount Vernon, too. The trail carries you past Reagan National Airport, via two pedestrian bridges that take you safely through the airport's roadway system. Continue on to Old Town, where you really should dismount for a walk around, a tour of some of the historic properties listed in this chapter, or take in some refreshment from one of the restaurants, before you proceed to Mount Vernon. The section from Memorial Bridge to Mount Vernon is about 19 miles in all.

Carlyle House Historic Park   One of Virginia's most architecturally impressive 18th-century homes, Carlyle House also figured prominently in American history. In 1753, Scottish merchant John Carlyle completed the mansion for his bride, Sarah Fairfax of Belvoir, a daughter of one of Virginia's most prominent families. It was designed in the style of a Scottish/English manor house and lavishly furnished. Carlyle, a successful merchant, had the means to import the best furnishings and appointments available abroad for his new Alexandria home.

When it was built, Carlyle House was a waterfront property with its own wharf. A social and political center, the house was visited by the great men of the day, including George Washington. But its most important moment in history occurred in April 1755, when Maj. Gen. Edward Braddock, commander-in-chief of His Majesty's forces in North America, met with five Colonial governors here and asked them to tax colonists to finance a campaign against the French and Indians. Colonial legislatures refused to comply, one of the first instances of serious friction between America and Britain. Nevertheless, Braddock made Carlyle House his headquarters during the campaign, and Carlyle was less than impressed with him. He called the general "a man of weak understanding . . . very indolent . . . a slave to his passions, women and wine . . . as great an Epicure as could be in his eating, tho a brave man." Possibly these were the reasons his unfinanced campaign met with disaster. Braddock received, as Carlyle described it, "a most remarkable drubbing."

> **Tips Planning Note**
>
> Many Alexandria attractions are closed on Monday.

Tours are given on the hour and half-hour and take about 40 minutes; allow another 10 or 15 minutes if you plan to tour the tiered garden of brick walks and boxed parterres. Two of the original rooms, the large parlor and the adjacent study, have survived intact; the former, where Braddock met the governors, still retains its original fine woodwork, paneling, and pediments. The house is furnished in period pieces; however, only a few of Carlyle's possessions remain. In an upstairs room, an architecture exhibit depicts 18th-century construction methods with hand-hewn beams and hand-wrought nails.

121 N. Fairfax St. (between Cameron and King sts.). ✆ 703/549-2997. www.carlylehouse.org. Admission $4 adults, $2 children 11–17, free for children under 11. Tues–Sat 10am–4:30pm, Sun noon–4:30pm; winter hours 10am–4pm.

Christ Church   This sturdy redbrick Georgian-style church would be an important national landmark even if its two most distinguished members had not been Washington and Lee. It has been in continuous use since 1773, the town of Alexandria growing up around the building that was once known as the "Church in the Woods."

Over the years, the church has undergone many changes, adding the bell tower, church bell, galleries, and organ by the early 1800s, the "wine-glass" pulpit in 1891. For the most part, the original structure remains, including the hand-blown glass in the windows.

Christ Church has had its historic moments. Washington and other early church members fomented revolution in the churchyard, and Robert E. Lee met here with Richmond representatives to discuss assuming command of Virginia's military forces at the beginning of the Civil War. You can sit in the pew where George and Martha sat with her two Custis grandchildren, or in the Lee family pew.

It's traditional for U.S. presidents to attend a service here on a Sunday close to Washington's birthday and sit in his pew. One of the most memorable of these visits took place shortly after Pearl Harbor, when Franklin Delano Roosevelt attended services with Winston Churchill on the World Day of Prayer for Peace, January 1, 1942.

Of course, you're invited to attend a service (Sun at 8, 9, and 11:15am and 5pm; Wed at 7:15am and 12:05pm; and Thurs at 7pm). There's no admission, but donations are appreciated. A guide gives brief lectures to visitors. A gift shop is open Tuesday through Saturday 10am to 4pm, and the first and third Sunday 8:45am to 1pm. Twenty minutes should do it here.

118 N. Washington St. (at Cameron St.). (C) **703/549-1450.** www.historicchristchurch.org. Suggested donation $5 adults, $3 children. Mon–Sat 9am–4pm; Sun 2–4pm. Closed all federal holidays.

Fort Ward Museum & Historic Site (Kids)

A short drive from Old Town is a 45-acre museum and park that transport you to Alexandria during the Civil War. The action here centers, as it did in the early 1860s, on an actual Union fort that Lincoln ordered erected. It was part of a system of Civil War forts called the "Defenses of Washington." About 90% of the fort's earthwork walls are preserved, and the Northwest Bastion has been restored with six mounted guns (originally there were 36). A model of 19th-century military engineering, the fort was never attacked by Confederate forces. Self-guided tours begin at the Fort Ward ceremonial gate.

Visitors can explore the fort and replicas of the ceremonial entrance gate and an officer's hut. There's a museum of Civil War artifacts on the premises where changing exhibits focus on subjects such as Union arms and equipment, medical care of the wounded, and local war history.

There are picnic areas with barbecue grills in the park surrounding the fort. Living-history presentations take place throughout the year. This is a good stop if you have young children, in which case you could spend an hour or two here (especially if you bring a picnic).

4301 W. Braddock Rd. (between Rte. 7 and N. Van Dorn St.). (C) **703/838-4848.** www.fortward.org. Free admission (donations welcome). Park daily 9am–sunset. Museum Tues–Sat 9am–4pm; Sun noon–5pm. Call for information regarding special holiday closings. From Old Town, follow King St. west, go right on Kenwood Ave., then left on West Braddock Rd.; continue for ¾ mile to the entrance on the right.

Friendship Firehouse

Alexandria's first firefighting organization, the Friendship Fire Company, was established in 1774. In the early days, the company met in taverns and kept its firefighting equipment in a member's barn. Its present Italianate-style brick building dates from 1855; it was erected after an earlier building was, ironically, destroyed by fire. Local tradition holds that George Washington was involved with the firehouse as a founding member, active firefighter, and purchaser of its first fire engine, although research does not confirm these stories. The museum displays an 1851 fire engine, and old hoses, buckets, and other firefighting apparatus. This is a tiny place, which you can easily "do" in 20 minutes.

107 S. Alfred St. (between King and Prince sts.). (C) **703/838-3891.** http://oha.ci.Alexandria.va.us/friendship. Free admission. Fri–Sat 10am–4pm; Sun 1–4pm.

Gadsby's Tavern Museum (★)

Alexandria was at the crossroads of 18th-century America, and its social center was Gadsby's Tavern, which consisted of two buildings (one Georgian, one Federal) dating from around 1785 and 1792, respectively. Innkeeper John Gadsby combined them to create "a gentleman's tavern," which he operated from 1796 to 1808; it was considered one of the finest in the country. George Washington was a frequent dinner guest; he and Martha danced in the second-floor ballroom, and it was here that Washington celebrated his last birthday. The tavern also welcomed Thomas Jefferson, James Madison, and the Marquis de Lafayette, the French soldier and statesman who served in the American army under Washington during the Revolutionary War and remained close to Washington. It was the scene of lavish parties, theatrical performances, small circuses, government meetings, and concerts. Itinerant merchants used the tavern to display their wares, and traveling doctors and dentists treated a hapless clientele (these were rudimentary professions in the 18th century) on the premises.

The rooms have been restored to their 18th-century appearance. On the 30-minute tour, you'll get a good look at the Tap Room, a small dining room; the Assembly Room, the ballroom; typical bedrooms; and the underground icehouse, which was filled each winter from the icy river. Tours depart 15 minutes before and after the hour. Inquire about living-history programs, such as "Gadsby's Time Travels," geared toward children, and "Candlelight Tours" (by group reservation), which take you through the museum in the evening, and may include music and entertainment along the way. Cap off the experience with a meal at the restored Colonial-style restaurant (see "Dining," below).

134 N. Royal St. (at Cameron St.). ☏ 703/838-4242. www.gadsbystavern.org. Admission $4 adults, $2 children 11–17, free for children under 11. Tours Apr–Oct Tues–Sat 10am–5pm, Sun–Mon 1–5pm; Nov–Mar Wed–Sat 11am–4pm, Sun 1–4pm. Closed most federal holidays.

Lee-Fendall House Museum   This handsome Greek Revival–style house is a veritable Lee family museum of furniture, heirlooms, and documents. "Light Horse Harry" Lee never actually lived here, though he was a frequent visitor, as was his good friend George Washington. He did own the original lot, but sold it to Philip Richard Fendall (himself a Lee on his mother's side), who built the house in 1785. Fendall married three Lee women, including Harry's first mother-in-law, and, later, Harry's sister.

Thirty-seven Lees occupied the house over a period of 118 years (1785–1903), and it was from this house that Harry wrote Alexandria's farewell address to George Washington, delivered when he passed through town on his way to assume the presidency. (Harry also wrote and delivered, but not at this house, the famous funeral oration to Washington that contained the words: "First in war, first in peace, and first in the hearts of his countrymen.") During the Civil War, the house was seized and used as a Union hospital.

Thirty-minute guided tours interpret the 1850s era of the home and provide insight into Victorian family life. You'll also see the Colonial garden with its magnolia and chestnut trees, roses, and boxwood-lined paths. Much of the interior woodwork and glass is original.

614 Oronoco St. (at Washington St.). ☏ 703/548-1789. www.leefendallhouse.org. Admission $4 adults, $2 children 11–17, free for children under 11. Tues–Sat 10am–4pm; Sun 1–4pm. Call ahead to make sure the museum is open, since it often closes for special events. Tours on the hour 10am–3pm. Closed Thanksgiving and mid-Dec to Feb.

The Lyceum   This Greek Revival building houses a museum depicting Alexandria's history from the 17th through the 20th century. It features changing exhibits and an ongoing series of lectures, concerts, and educational programs.

You can obtain maps and brochures about Virginia state attractions, especially Alexandria attractions. The knowledgeable staff will be happy to answer questions. But even without its many attractions, the brick and stucco Lyceum merits a visit.

Built in 1839, it was designed in the Doric temple style to serve as a lecture, meeting, and concert hall. It was an important center of Alexandria's cultural life until the Civil War, when Union forces appropriated it for use as a hospital. After the war it became a private residence, and still later it was subdivided for office space. In 1969, however, the city council's use of eminent domain prevented the Lyceum from being demolished in favor of a parking lot. Allow about 20 minutes here.

201 S. Washington St. (off Prince St.). ℭ **703/838-4994.** www.alexandriahistory.org. Free admission. Mon–Sat 10am–5pm; Sun 1–5pm. Closed Jan 1, Thanksgiving, and Dec 25.

Old Presbyterian Meeting House   Presbyterian congregations have worshipped in Virginia since the Rev. Alexander Whittaker converted Pocahontas in Jamestown in 1614. This brick church was built by Scottish pioneers in 1775. Although it wasn't George Washington's church, the Meeting House bell tolled continuously for 4 days after his death in December 1799, and memorial services were preached from the pulpit here by Presbyterian, Episcopal, and Methodist ministers. According to the Alexandria paper of the day, "The walking being bad to the Episcopal church the funeral sermon of George Washington will be preached at the Presbyterian Meeting House." Two months later, on Washington's birthday, Alexandria citizens marched from Market Square to the church to pay their respects.

Many famous Alexandrians are buried in the church graveyard, including John and Sarah Carlyle, Dr. James Craik (the surgeon who treated—some say killed—Washington, dressed Lafayette's wounds at Brandywine, and ministered to the dying Braddock at Monongahela), and William Hunter Jr., founder of the St. Andrew's Society of Scottish descendants, to whom bagpipers pay homage on the first Saturday of December. It is also the site of a Tomb of an Unknown Revolutionary War Soldier. Dr. James Muir, minister between 1789 and 1820, lies beneath the sanctuary in his gown and bands.

The original Meeting House was gutted by a lightning fire in 1835, but parishioners restored it in the style of the day a few years later. The present bell, said to be recast from the metal of the old one, was hung in a newly constructed belfry in 1843, and a new organ was installed in 1849. The Meeting House closed its doors in 1889, and for 60 years it was virtually abandoned. But in 1949 it was reborn as a living Presbyterian U.S.A. church, and today the Old Meeting House looks much as it did following its first restoration. The original parsonage, or manse, is still intact. There's no guided tour, but there is a recorded narrative in the graveyard. Allow 20 minutes for touring.

321 S. Fairfax St. (between Duke and Wolfe sts.). ℭ **703/549-6670.** www.opmh.org. Free admission, but you must obtain a key from the office to tour the church. Sun services at 8:30 and 11am, except in summer, when a service is held at 10am.

Stabler-Leadbeater Apothecary Museum   When its doors closed in 1933, this landmark drugstore was the second oldest in continuous operation in America. Run for five generations by the same Quaker family (beginning in 1792), the store counted Robert E. Lee (who purchased the paint for Arlington House here), George Mason, Henry Clay, John C. Calhoun, and George Washington among its famous patrons. Gothic Revival decorative elements and Victorian-style doors were added in the 1840s. Today the apothecary looks much as it did in Colonial times, its shelves lined with original handblown gold-leaf–labeled bottles (actually the most valuable collection of antique medicinal bottles in the country), old scales stamped with the royal crown, patent medicines, and equipment for bloodletting. The clock on the rear wall, the porcelain-handled mahogany drawers, and two mortars and pestles all date from about 1790. Among the shop's documentary records is this 1802 order from Mount Vernon: "Mrs. Washington desires Mr. Stabler to send by the bearer a quart bottle of his best Castor Oil and the bill for it."

A 5-minute audio tour will guide you around the displays. The adjoining gift shop uses its proceeds to maintain the apothecary. Allow 15 minutes.

Note: The Apothecary closed for renovation in 2004, but should be open by the time you read this; call ahead to be sure.

105–107 S. Fairfax St. (near King St.). (✆ 703/836-3713. www.apothecarymuseum.org. Admission $2.50 adults, $2 children 11–17, free for children under 11. (Prices may increase in 2005, following the renovation.) Mon–Sat 10am–4pm; Sun 1–5pm. Closed major holidays.

Torpedo Factory   This block-long, three-story building was built in 1918 as a torpedo shell-case factory, but now accommodates some 165 professional artists and craftspeople who create and sell their own works on the premises. Here you can see artists at work in their studios: potters, painters, printmakers, photographers, sculptors, and jewelers, as well as those who create stained-glass windows and fiber art.

On permanent display are exhibits on Alexandria history provided by Alexandria Archaeology (✆ **703/838-4399;** www.alexandriaarchaeology.org), which is headquartered here and engages in extensive city research. A volunteer or staff member is on hand to answer questions. Art lovers could end up browsing for an hour or two.

105 N. Union St. (between King and Cameron sts. on the waterfront). (✆ 703/838-4565. www.torpedofactory. org. Free admission. Daily 10am–5pm; archaeology exhibit area Tues–Fri 10am–3pm, Sat 10am–5pm, Sun 1–5pm. Closed Easter, July 4, Thanksgiving, Dec 25, and Jan 1.

ACCOMMODATIONS

It is simply not possible to find inexpensive lodging within, or close by, Old Town Alexandria. In fact, Historic Old Town proper has only one hotel inside its boundaries. That one, the **Holiday Inn Select Old Town,** 480 King St. (✆ **800/ 368-5047** or 703/549-6080; www.hiselect.com/axe/oldtown), and another just outside the Historic District, **Morrison House,** 116 S. Alfred St. (✆ **866/834-6628** or 703/838-8000; www.morrisonhouse.com), are the two I'd recommend, if you're interested in staying overnight on this side of the Potomac. Expect to pay for their fine accommodations.

Rates at the Holiday Inn range from $188 to $289; suites start at $400. Rooms feature 18th-century-style furnishings; king, queen, or double beds; and sitting areas. Amenities at this hotel include complimentary continental breakfast on weekdays, bike rentals, a fitness center, and an indoor pool. Ask about discounts for AAA, AARP, government, and any other groups to which you may belong.

Morrison House is an elegant small hotel recently inducted as a member into the elite Relais & Châteaux. The hotel has only 45 rooms, each appointed in high style with canopied four-poster beds, mahogany armoires, decorative fireplaces, and the like. Rates start at $175 for the smallest room off season, and at $299 for a deluxe room in season. Morrison House is known for its restaurant, **Elysium,** which presents award-winning contemporary American cuisine.

For other recommendations, check the **Alexandria Convention and Visitors Association** website, **www.funside.com,** where you can book an online reservation and also read about various promotions that hotels are offering.

DINING

There are so many fine restaurants in Alexandria that Washingtonians often drive over just to dine here and stroll the cobblestone streets.

EXPENSIVE

Geranio ⊛ REGIONAL ITALIAN   Many folks think this is the best restaurant in Old Town. After a dinner in front of the log fire, including a fine bottle of Chianti, an appetizer of potted duck with garlic confit and olive oil crostini (or maybe the lobster risotto), entree of grilled salmon with pancetta and red-wine sauce (or maybe the osso buco), followed by dessert of tiramisu (or maybe lemon parfait), you might agree. Excellent service.

722 King St. (between Washington and Columbus sts.). ✆ 703/548-0088. www.geranio.net. Reservations recommended. Lunch items $8–$15; dinner main courses $15–$30. AE, DC, MC, V. Mon–Fri 11:30am–2:30pm; Mon–Sat 6–10:30pm; Sun 5:30–9:30pm.

La Bergerie ⊛ CLASSIC FRENCH   This restaurant has been here forever and is ever popular, even though its longtime owners sold La Bergerie in 2002. Waiters are tuxedoed and entrees are updated traditional: escargots sprinkled with hazelnuts, smoky foie gras, lobster bisque with lobster and its coral, tournedos of beef with wild mushrooms and béarnaise sauce. The restaurant is known for its dessert soufflés, which you must request when you order your entrees. You'll want to dress up here.

218 N. Lee St. ✆ 703/683-1007. www.labergerie.com. Reservations required. Lunch main courses $13–$17; dinner main courses $17–$29. AE, DC, DISC, MC, V. Mon–Sat 11:30am–2:30pm; Mon–Thurs 5:30–9:30pm; Fri–Sat 5:30–10:30pm; Sun 5–9pm.

MODERATE

Gadsby's Tavern COLONIAL AMERICAN   George Washington often came here to dine and dance, and this is where he reviewed his troops for the last time. Gadsby's Tavern tends toward the touristy, but it does evoke the 18th century authentically, with period music, wood-plank floors, hurricane-lamp wall sconces, and a rendition of a Hogarth painting over the fireplace (one of several).

Servers are dressed in traditional Colonial attire. A strolling violinist entertains Tuesday and Wednesday nights, an "18th-century gentleman" regales guests with song and tells the news of the day (200 years ago, on the day you are there). When the weather's nice, you can dine in a flagstone courtyard edged with flower beds.

The fare is adequate. It's all homemade, including the sweet Sally Lunn bread, which is baked daily. You might start with soup from the stockpot served with homemade sourdough crackers, followed by baked ham and cheese pie (a sort of Early American quiche), hot roast turkey with giblet gravy and bread-and-sage stuffing on Sally Lunn bread, or George Washington's favorite: slow-roasted crisp duckling served with fruit dressing and Madeira sauce. For dessert, try the English trifle or creamy buttermilk-custard pie with a hint of lemon. Colonial "coolers" are also available: scuppernong, Wench's Punch, and such. The Sunday brunch menu adds such items as thick slices of toast dipped in a batter of rum and spices, with sausage, hash browns, and hot cinnamon syrup. And a desserts and libations menu highlights such favorites as Scottish apple gingerbread and bourbon apple pie, along with a wide selection of beverages.

138 N. Royal St. (at Cameron St.). ✆ 703/548-1288. Reservations recommended at dinner. Lunch/brunch items $8–$15; dinner main courses $15–$25. Half-price portions available on some items for children 12 and under. AE, DC, MC, V. Mon–Sat 11:30am–3pm; Sun 11am–3pm; daily 5:30–10pm.

Taverna Cretekou ⭐ GREEK   There aren't many truly Greek (as opposed to Mediterranean or Middle Eastern) restaurants in the Washington area, and this is undeniably the best. The Taverna has been open since 1973, and is only gaining in popularity, for its traditional dishes of spanakopita and moussaka, as well as contemporary items, such as grilled red snapper with oregano and lemon, or rainbow trout stuffed with spinach and feta. The ouzo flows and, on Thursday nights, Greek music and dancing breaks out, usually ending up with diners and waiters joining the musicians.

818 King St. (at Alfred St.). © **703/548-8688**. www.tavernacretekou.com. Reservations recommended. Lunch and dinner items $11–$18; Sun brunch $16. AE, MC, V. Tues–Fri 11:30am–2:30pm and 5–10pm; Sat noon–11pm; Sun brunch 11am–3pm and dinner 5–9:30pm.

INEXPENSIVE

La Madeleine *Kids* FRENCH CAFE   It may be part of a self-service chain, but this place is charming nonetheless. Its French country interior has a beamed ceiling, bare oak floors, a wood-burning stove, and maple hutches displaying crockery and pewter mugs. Its range of affordable menu items makes this a good choice for families with finicky eaters in tow.

Come in the morning for fresh-baked croissants, Danish, scones, muffins, and brioches, or a heartier bacon-and-eggs plate. Throughout the day, there are delicious salads (such as roasted vegetables and rigatoni), sandwiches (including a traditional croque-monsieur), and hot dishes ranging from quiche and pizza to rotisserie chicken with a Caesar salad. After 5pm, additional choices include pastas and specials such as beef tenders en merlot or herb-crusted pork tenderloin, both served with garlic mashed potatoes and green beans almondine. Conclude with a yummy fruit tart or chocolate, vanilla, and praline triple-layer cheesecake with graham-cracker crust. Wine and beer are served.

500 King St. (at S. Pitt St.). © **703/739-2854**. www.lamadeleine.com. Reservations not accepted. Breakfast main courses $3.30–$6.50; lunch and dinner main courses $5–$10. AE, DISC, MC, V. Sun 7am–10pm; Mon–Thurs 6:30am–10:30pm; Fri–Sat 6:30am–11:30pm.

South Austin Grill SOUTHERN/SOUTHWESTERN   One of seven Austin Grills in the area, this one offers the same menu, music, and ambience as other links in the chain. See p. 163 for a review of the Glover Park location.

801 King St. (at S. Columbus St.). © **703/684-8969**. www.austingrill.com. Reservations not accepted. Main courses $8–$17. AE, DC, DISC, MC, V. Mon 11:30am–10:30pm; Tues–Thurs 11:30am–11pm; Fri 11:30am–midnight; Sat 11am–midnight; Sun 11am–10:30pm.

Union Street Public House AMERICAN/SEAFOOD   You might have to wait in line to be seated, but the line usually moves fast, since the restaurant has lots of pubby rooms. The laid-back atmosphere and comfortable decor make this a natural stop for families, groups, informal dates, and anyone who's just hopped off the bike trail to Mount Vernon. Window seats upstairs are coveted for their views of King Street. Downstairs rooms tend to emphasize the *pub* in public house—this is where singles mingle. The menu offers burgers, po'boys, oysters, fried calamari, salads, and so on.

121 S. Union St. © **703/548-1785**. www.usphalexandria.com. Reservations accepted for groups of 8 or more, except on Fri–Sat nights. Main courses $7–$20. AE, DISC, MC, V. Mon–Thurs 11:30am–10:30pm; Fri–Sat 11:30am–11:30pm; Sun 11am–10:30pm.

Appendix:
Washington, D.C., in Depth

Two hundred and fifteen years ago, the world wondered why America had chosen this swampy locale as its capital. It took its first 100 years for Washington to evolve from bumpkin backwater status to an international hub of power, diplomacy, and beauty, and the city has been coming into its own ever since. Today, Washington, D.C., fully commands center stage.

And people from all over the world do come to see the capital. Tourism contributes to the bustle of this city that serves as the seat of the nation's government, as well as home to more than 572,000 people, scores of vibrant neighborhoods, countless historic landmarks and other tourist attractions, a thriving cultural and arts scene, many beautiful parks, and loads of terrific restaurants. The capital is the centerpiece of a metropolitan region that extends into the suburbs of Virginia and Maryland. This Greater Washington area has a population of 5.5 million people, making it one of the most rapidly expanding metropolitan areas, as well as the fastest growing job base, in the nation.

Just a few short years ago, Washington wasn't so attractive; visitors came to tour federal buildings, like the Capitol, the White House, and the Smithsonian museums, but stayed away from the downtown and nontouristy areas. A revitalizing and steady change has taken place as elected government officials, like Mayor Anthony A. Williams, his city council, and Congresswoman Eleanor Holmes Norton, have joined efforts with entrepreneurs and nonprofit agencies to revive the economy, add attractions throughout town, and provide better services to both residents and visitors. D.C.'s success has attracted the attention of national and international investors, happy to do business in the capital's profitable marketplace. Notable among Washington's most recent developments are: the opening of the truly luxurious Mandarin Oriental Hotel and an explosion of new restaurants, the debut of the Smithsonian's National Museum of the American Indian, the dedication of the National World War II Memorial on the National Mall, and the grand expansions taking place at D.C.'s major theaters, from the Kennedy Center to the Shakespeare Theatre.

All of this undeniable progress continues to force Congress to contemplate handing over more control of the District to the District itself. Since D.C. is not a state, Congress oversees the city's budget and legislation. Residents elect a mayor and council, who govern the nonfederal responsibilities of the city, but Congress's micromanagement of these local issues tends to impede planning and progress. Residents also elect a delegate to Congress (Norton is the current representative), who introduces legislation and votes in committees, but who cannot vote on the House floor. This unique situation, in which residents of the District pay federal income taxes but don't have a vote in Congress, is a matter of local concern—you may notice D.C. license plates bearing the inscription "Taxation without Representation." Congresswoman Norton and others have begun to push for D.C.'s statehood or, at the very least, a true vote in Congress. For more information about the history, politics, and local lore of the city of Washington, check out the website, www.dc.gov, which provides a lot of good information and also links you to many other helpful sources.

Whether or not Washington eventually wins voting rights and statehood, its dual roles as nation's capital and independent city have always been and will ever be intertwined with American history, as the following section makes clear.

1 History 101

A WANDERING CONGRESS It all began in 1783, when 250 Revolutionary War soldiers, understandably angered because Congress was ignoring their petitions for back pay, stormed the temporary capitol in Philadelphia to demand justice. The citizens of Philadelphia sympathized with the soldiers and ignored congressional pleas for protection; as the soldiers rioted outside, lawmakers huddled inside the State House behind locked doors. When the soldiers finally calmed down and returned to their barracks, Congress decided it would be prudent to move itself to Princeton. Lawmakers also decided they needed a capital city whose business was government and the protection thereof.

This decision to relocate was not a new one. Congress had been so nomadic during its first decade that when a statue of George Washington was commissioned in 1783, satirist Francis Hopkinson suggested putting it on wheels. Before permanently settling in Washington, Congress convened in New York, Baltimore, Philadelphia, Lancaster, Princeton, Annapolis, York, and Trenton.

A DEAL MADE OVER DINNER When Congress proposed that a city be designed and built for the sole purpose of housing the government of the new nation, fresh difficulties arose. There was a general feeling that wherever the capital might be built, a great commercial center would blossom; therefore, many cities vied for the honor. Then, too, northerners were strongly opposed to a southern capital—and vice versa. Finally, after 7 years of bickering, New Yorker Alexander Hamilton and Virginian Thomas Jefferson worked out a compromise over dinner one night in

Dateline

- 1608 Capt. John Smith sails up Potomac River from Jamestown; for the next 100 years, Irish-Scottish settlers colonize the area.
- 1783 Continental Congress proposes new "Federal Town"; both North and South vie for it.
- 1790 A compromise is reached: If the South pays off the North's Revolutionary War debts, the new capital will be situated in its region.
- 1791 French engineer Pierre Charles L'Enfant designs the capital city but is fired within a year.
- 1792 Cornerstone is laid for Executive Mansion.
- 1793 Construction begins on the Capitol.
- 1800 First wing of the Capitol completed; Congress moves from Philadelphia; President John Adams moves into Executive Mansion.
- 1801 Library of Congress established.
- 1812 War with England.
- 1814 British burn Washington.
- 1817 Executive Mansion rebuilt, its charred walls painted white; becomes known as White House.
- 1822 Population reaches 33,000.
- 1829 Smithsonian Institution founded for the "increase and diffusion of knowledge."
- 1861 Civil War; Washington becomes North's major supply depot.
- 1865 Capitol dome completed; Lee surrenders to Grant on April 8; Lincoln assassinated at Ford's Theatre on April 14.
- 1871 Alexander "Boss" Shepherd turns Washington into a showplace, using many of L'Enfant's plans.
- 1900 Population reaches about 300,000.
- 1901 McMillan Commission plans development of Mall from Capitol to Lincoln Memorial.
- 1907 Union Station opens, largest train station in country.

New York. The North would support a southern site for the capital in return for the South's assumption of debts incurred by northern states during the Revolutionary War. As a further sop to the North, it was agreed that the seat of government would remain in Philadelphia through 1800 to allow time for surveying, purchasing land, and constructing government buildings.

ENTER L'ENFANT TERRIBLE An act passed in 1790 specified a site "not exceeding 10 miles square" to be located on the Potomac. President George Washington, an experienced surveyor charged with selecting the exact site, chose a part of the Potomac Valley where the river becomes tidal and is joined by the Anacostia. Maryland gladly provided 69¼ square miles and Virginia 30¾ square miles for the new Federal District. (In 1846, Virginia's territorial contribution was returned to the state. The District today covers about 67 square miles.) Washington hired Andrew Ellicott and Benjamin Banneker, a free black and self-taught mathematician and astronomer, to lay out the boundaries of the city.

President Washington commissioned French military engineer Pierre Charles L'Enfant to design the federal city. It has since been said that "it would have been hard to find a man better qualified artistically and less fitted by temperament" for the job. L'Enfant arrived in 1791 and immediately declared Jenkins Hill (today Capitol Hill) "a pedestal waiting for a monument." He surveyed every inch of the designated Federal District and began creating his vision by selecting dominant sites for major buildings. He designed 160-foot-wide avenues radiating from squares and circles centered on monumental sculptures and fountains. The Capitol, the "presidential palace," and an equestrian statue—the last to be erected where the Washington Monument stands today—were to be the city's focal

- 1912 Cherry trees, a gift from Japan, planted in Tidal Basin.
- 1914 World War I begins.
- 1922 Lincoln Memorial completed.
- 1941 First plane lands at National Airport; United States declares war on Japan.
- 1943 Pantheon-inspired Jefferson Memorial and Pentagon completed.
- 1960 Population declines for first time, from 800,000 to 764,000.
- 1963 More than 200,000 March on Washington, hear Martin Luther King Jr.'s "I Have a Dream" speech supporting civil rights.
- 1971 John F. Kennedy Center for Performing Arts opens.
- 1976 Metro, city's first subway system, opens in time for bicentennial.
- 1982 Vietnam Veterans Memorial erected in Constitution Gardens.
- 1993 U.S. Holocaust Memorial Museum opens near Mall.
- 1994 Marion Barry is elected to a fourth term as mayor after serving time in prison.
- 1995 Korean War Veterans Memorial is dedicated. Pennsylvania Avenue closed to vehicular traffic in front of the White House on security grounds.
- 1997 Federal government offers aid package to save D.C. from bankruptcy. Franklin Delano Roosevelt Memorial is dedicated.
- 1998 White House beset by sex scandal. In December, the House of Representatives impeaches President Clinton.
- 1999 Washington, D.C., inaugurates Mayor Anthony Williams. In February, the Senate acquits President Clinton.
- 2001 While thousands protest, President George W. Bush takes office in January after the most controversial election in modern U.S. history. In September, 180 people die when terrorists hijack a commercial airliner and crash it into the Pentagon.
- 2002 The city recovers from the aftermath of September 11, 2001, terrorist attacks, rebuilds the destroyed section of the Pentagon, and imposes tighter security at federal buildings and airports. An elusive pair of snipers terrorizes the

continues

points. Pennsylvania Avenue would be the major thoroughfare, and the Mall was conceived as a bustling ceremonial avenue of embassies and other distinguished buildings.

L'Enfant's plan dismayed landowners who were promised $67 per acre for land donated for buildings, while land for avenues was to be donated free; of the 6,661 acres to be included in the boundaries of the federal city, about half would comprise avenues and the 2-mile-long Mall.

D.C. area, killing 10 people and wounding three, before capture in October. D.C. Mayor Anthony Williams wins re-election.

- 2003 The U.S. invades Iraq. D.C.'s own City Museum of Washington opens, to tell the story of Washington, from a non-federal perspective.
- 2004 The U.S. stays involved in Iraq but turns over control to an interim Iraqi government. WWII Memorial dedicated, Smithsonian National Indian Museum opens, both on the Mall.

A more personable man might have won over the reluctant landowners and commissioners, inspiring them with his dreams and his passion, but L'Enfant exhibited only a peevish and condescending secretiveness that alienated one and all. A year after he had been hired, L'Enfant was fired. Congress offered him $2,500 compensation for his year of work, and James Monroe urged him to accept a professorship at West Point. Insulted, he spurned all offers, suing the government for $95,500 instead. He lost and died a pauper in 1825. In 1909, in belated recognition of his services, his remains were brought to Arlington National Cemetery. Some 118 years after he had conceived it, his vision of the federal city finally had become a reality.

HOME NOT-SO-SWEET HOME   In 1800, government officials (106 representatives and 32 senators) arrived according to schedule, ready to settle into their new home. What they found bore little resemblance to a city. "One might take a ride of several hours within the precincts without meeting with a single individual to disturb one's meditation," commented one early resident. Pennsylvania Avenue was a mosquito-infested swamp, and there were fewer than 400 habitable houses. Disgruntled Secretary of the Treasury Oliver Wolcott wrote his wife, "I do not perceive how the members of Congress can possibly secure lodgings, unless they will consent to live like Scholars in a college or Monks in a monastery." The solution was a boom in boardinghouses.

Abigail Adams was dismayed at the condition of her new home, the presidential mansion. The damp caused her rheumatism to act up, the main stairs had not yet been constructed, not a single room was finished, and there were not even enough logs for all the fireplaces. And since there was "not the least fence, yard, or other convenience," she hung the presidential laundry in the unfinished East Room. To attend presidential affairs or to visit one another, Washington's early citizens had to drive through mud and slush, their vehicles often becoming embedded in bogs and gullies—not a pleasant state of affairs, but one that would continue for many decades.

There were many difficulties in building the capital. Money was in short supply, as were materials and labor, with the result that the home of the world's most enlightened democracy was built largely by slaves. In the background, there was talk of abandoning the city and starting over elsewhere.

REDCOATS REDUX   Then came the War of 1812. At first, fighting centered on Canada and the West—both too far away to affect daily life in the capital. (In the early 1800s, it was a 33-hr. ride from Washington, D.C., to Philadelphia—if you made good time.) In May 1813, the flamboyant British Rear

Admiral Cockburn sent word to the Executive Mansion that "he would make his bow" in the Madisons' drawing room shortly. On August 23, 1814, alarming news reached the capital: The British had landed troops in Maryland. On August 24, James Madison was at the front, most of the populace had fled, and Dolley Madison created a legend by refusing to leave the president's mansion without Gilbert Stuart's famous portrait of George Washington. As the British neared her gates, she calmly wrote a blow-by-blow description to her sister:

"Our kind friend, Mr. Carroll, has come to hasten my departure, and is in a very bad humour with me because I insist on waiting until the large picture of General Washington is secured, and it requires to be unscrewed from the wall. This process was found too tedious for these perilous moments; I have ordered the frame to be broken, and the canvas taken out; it is done . . . And now, dear sister, I must leave this house, or the retreating army will make me a prisoner in it, by filling up the road I am directed to take."

When the British arrived early that evening, they found dinner set up on the table (Dolley had hoped for the best until the end), and, according to some accounts, ate it before torching the mansion. They also burned the Capitol, the Library of Congress, and newly built ships and naval stores. A thunderstorm later that night saved the city from total destruction, while a tornado the next day added to the damage but daunted the British troops.

The new capital seemed doomed. Margaret Bayard Smith, wife of the owner of the influential *National Intelligencer,* privately lamented, "I do not suppose the Government will ever return to Washington. All those whose property was invested in that place, will be reduced to general poverty . . . The consternation about us is general. The despondency still greater." But the *Intelligencer* was among the printed voices speaking out against even a temporary move. Editorials warned that it would be a "treacherous breach of faith" with those who had "laid out fortunes in the purchase of property in and about the city." To move the capital would be "kissing the rod an enemy has wielded."

Washingtonian pride rallied and the city was saved once again. Still, it was a close call; Congress came within nine votes of abandoning the place!

In 1815, leading citizens erected a brick building in which Congress could meet in relative comfort until the Capitol was restored. The Treaty of Ghent, establishing peace with Great Britain, was ratified at Octagon House, where the Madisons were temporarily ensconced. And Thomas Jefferson donated his own books to replace the destroyed contents of the Library of Congress. Confidence was restored and the city began to prosper. When the Madisons moved into the rebuilt presidential mansion, its exterior had been painted gleaming white to cover the charred walls. From then on, it would be known as the White House.

THE CITY OF MAGNIFICENT INTENTIONS   Between the War of 1812 and the Civil War, few people evinced any great enthusiasm for Washington. European visitors in particular looked at the capital and found it wanting. It was still a provincial backwater, with Pennsylvania Avenue and the Mall remaining muddy messes inhabited by pigs, goats, cows, and geese. Many were repelled by the slave auctions openly taking place in the backyard of the White House. The best that could be said—though nobody said it—was that the young capital was picturesque. Meriwether Lewis kept the bears he captured during his 4,000-mile expedition up the Missouri in cages on the president's lawn. Native American chiefs in full regalia were often seen negotiating with the white man's government. Matching them in visual splendor were magnificently attired European court visitors.

The only foreigner who praised Washington was Lafayette, who visited in 1825 and was feted with lavish balls and dinners throughout his stay. Charles Dickens gave the city the raspberry in 1842:

"It is sometimes called the City of Magnificent Distances, but it might with greater propriety be termed the City of Magnificent Intentions . . . Spacious avenues, that begin in nothing and lead nowhere; streets, miles long, that only want houses, roads, and inhabitants; public buildings that need but a public to be complete; and ornaments of great thoroughfares, which only lack great thoroughfares to ornament—are its leading features."

Tobacco chewing and sloppy senatorial spitting particularly appalled him:

"Both houses are handsomely carpeted, but the state to which these carpets are reduced by the universal disregard of the spittoon with which every honorable member is accommodated, and the extraordinary improvements on the pattern which are squirted and dabbled upon it in every direction, do not admit of being described. I will merely observe, that I strongly recommend all strangers not to look at the floor; and if they happen to drop anything . . . not to pick it up with an ungloved hand on any account."

But Dickens's critique was mild when compared with Anthony Trollope's, who declared Washington in 1860 "as melancholy and miserable a town as the mind of man can conceive."

A NATION DIVIDED   During the Civil War, the capital became an armed camp. It was the principal supply depot for the Union Army and an important medical center. Parks became campgrounds, churches became hospitals, and forts ringed the town. The population doubled from 60,000 to 120,000, including about 40,000 former slaves who streamed into the city seeking federal protection. More than 3,000 soldiers slept in the Capitol building, and a bakery was set up in the basement. The streets were filled with the wounded, and Walt Whitman became a familiar figure, making daily rounds to comfort the ailing soldiers. In spite of everything, Lincoln insisted that work on the incomplete Capitol be continued. "If people see the Capitol going on, it is a sign we intend the Union shall go on," he said. When the giant dome was finished in 1863 and a 35-star flag was flown overhead, Capitol Hill's field battery fired a 35-gun salute, honoring the Union's then 35 states.

There was joy in Washington and an 800-gun salute in April 1865, when news of the fall of the Confederacy reached the capital. The joy was short-lived. Five days after Appomattox, President Lincoln was shot at Ford's Theatre while attending a performance of *Our American Cousin*. Black replaced the festive tricolored draperies adorning the town, and Washington went into mourning.

The war had enlarged the city's population while doing nothing to improve its facilities. Agrarian, uneducated ex-slaves stayed on, and poverty, unemployment, and disease were rampant. A red-light district remained, the parks were trodden bare, and tenement slums mushroomed within a stone's throw of the Capitol.

LED BY A SHEPHERD   Whereas L'Enfant had been aloof and introverted, his glorious vision was not forgotten, finally being implemented 70 years later by Alexander "Boss" Shepherd, a swashbuckling and friendly man. A real estate speculator who had made his money in a plumbing firm, Shepherd shouldered a musket in the Union Army and became one of Gen. Ulysses S. Grant's closest intimates. When Grant became president, he wanted to appoint Shepherd governor, but blue-blooded opposition ran too high. Washington high society considered him a parvenu and feared his ambitions for civic leadership. In response,

Grant named the more popular Henry D. Cooke (a secret Shepherd ally) governor and appointed Shepherd vice president of the Board of Public Works. No one was fooled. Shepherd made all the governor's decisions, and a joke went around the capital: "Why is the new governor like a sheep? Because he is led by A. Shepherd." He became the official governor in 1873.

Shepherd vowed that his "comprehensive plan of improvement" would make the city a showplace. An engineer he wasn't—occasionally, newly paved streets had to be torn up because he had forgotten to install sewers. But he was a first-rate politician who knew how to accomplish his goals. He began by hiring an army of laborers and starting them on projects all over town. Congress would have had to halt work on half-finished sidewalks, streets, and sewers throughout the District in order to stop him. The press liked and supported the colorful Shepherd; however, people forced out of their homes because they couldn't pay the high assessments for improvements hated him. Between 1871 and 1874, he established parks, paved and lighted the streets, installed sewers, filled in sewage-laden Tiber Creek, and planted more than 50,000 trees. He left the city bankrupt—more than $20 million in debt. But he got the job done.

L'ENFANT REBORN Through the end of the 19th century, Washington continued to make great aesthetic strides. The Washington Monument, long a truncated obelisk and major eyesore, was finally dedicated in 1885. Pennsylvania Avenue was becoming the ceremonial thoroughfare L'Enfant had envisioned, and important buildings were completed one after another. Shepherd had done a great deal, but much was still left undone. In 1887, L'Enfant's "Plan for the City of Washington" was resurrected. In 1900, Michigan Senator James McMillan—a retired railroad mogul with architectural and engineering knowledge—determined to complete the job L'Enfant had started a century earlier. A tireless lobbyist for government-sponsored municipal improvements, he persuaded his colleagues to appoint an advisory committee to create "the city beautiful." At his personal expense, McMillan sent this illustrious committee—landscapist Frederick Law Olmsted (designer of New York's Central Park), sculptor Augustus Saint-Gaudens, and noted architects Daniel Burnham and Charles McKim—to Europe for 7 weeks to study the landscaping and architecture of that continent's great capitals. Assembled at last was a group that combined L'Enfant's artistic genius and Shepherd's political savvy.

"Make no little plans," counseled Burnham. "They have no magic to stir men's blood, and probably themselves will not be realized. Make big plans, aim high in hope and work, remembering that a noble and logical diagram once recorded will never die, but long after we are gone will be a living thing, asserting itself with ever growing insistency."

The committee's big plans—almost all of which were accomplished—included the development of a complete park system, selection of sites for government buildings, and the designing of the Lincoln Memorial, the Arlington Memorial Bridge, and the Reflecting Pool (the last inspired by Versailles). They also got to work on improving the Mall; their first step was to remove the tracks, train sheds, and stone depot constructed there by the Baltimore and Potomac Railroad. In return, Congress authorized money to build the monumental Union Station, whose design was inspired by Rome's Baths of Diocletian.

Throughout the McMillan Commission years, the House was under the hostile leadership of Speaker "Uncle Joe" Cannon of Illinois, who, among other things, swore he would "never let a memorial to Abraham Lincoln be erected in that goddamned swamp" (West Potomac Park). Cannon caused some problems and delays, but on the whole the committee's prestigious membership added weight to their usually accepted recommendations. McMillan, however, did not live to see most of his dreams accomplished. He died in 1902.

By the 20th century, Washington was no longer an object of ridicule. The capital was coming into its own as a finely designed city of sweeping vistas studded with green parks and grand architecture. Congress's 1899 mandate limiting building heights in downtown Washington ensured the prominence of landmarks in the landscape. As the century progressed, the city seamlessly incorporated additional architectural marvels, including the Library of Congress, Union Station, and the Corcoran Gallery, which were all built around the turn of the century; several more Smithsonian museums and the Lincoln Memorial were completed in 1922. A Commission of Fine Arts was appointed in 1910 by President Taft to create monuments and fountains, and, thanks to Mrs. Taft, the famous cherry trees presented to the United States by the Japanese in 1912 were planted in the Tidal Basin.

During the Great Depression in the 1930s, FDR's Works Progress Administration (WPA) put the unemployed to work erecting public buildings and artists to work beautifying them. By the 1930s, too, increasing numbers of automobiles—nearly 200,000—were traversing Washington's wide avenues, joining the electric streetcars that had been in use since about 1890.

Washington's population, meanwhile, continued to grow, spurred by the influx of workers remaining after each of the world wars. In 1950, the city's population reached a zenith of more than 800,000 residents, an estimated 60% of whom were black. At the same time that Washington was establishing itself as a global power, the city was gaining renown among African Americans as a hub of black culture, education, and identity. From the 1920s to the 1960s, Washington drew the likes of Cab Calloway, Duke Ellington, and Pearl Bailey, who performed at speakeasies and theaters along a stretch of U Street called the Black Broadway. (The reincarnated "New U," as it is dubbed, now attracts buppies, yuppies, and restless youth to its nightclubs and bars.) Howard University, created in 1867, distinguished itself as the nation's most comprehensive center for the higher education of blacks. And when the Civil Rights movement gained momentum throughout the country in the 1960s and 1970s, Washington's large black presence (nearly 75% of the city's overall population) and activist spirit were instrumental in furthering the cause.

On August 28, 1963, black and white Washingtonians joined the ranks of the more than 200,000 who "Marched on Washington" to ensure passage of the Civil Rights Act. It was at this event that Rev. Martin Luther King Jr. delivered his stirring "I Have a Dream" speech at the Lincoln Memorial, where 41 years earlier, during the memorial's dedication ceremony, black officials were required to stand and watch from across the road. When King was assassinated on April 4, 1968, rioting erupted here as it did in many U.S. cities. Ever since, black and white Washingtonians have continued to thrash out race relations in a city whose population has stabilized at 572,000, about 60% of which now is African-American, including the city's mayor and congressional representative. Mayor Anthony A. Williams, whose second term expires at the end of 2006, and Congresswoman Eleanor Holmes Norton, who is now in her eighth term in office, continue to focus their efforts on improving the city.

Washington, the federal city, proceeds apace, adding more jewels to its crown. In 1989, renovation of the city's magnificent Union Station was completed.

Architect Daniel Burnham designed the palatial City Post Office Building, which, in 1993, became part of the Smithsonian complex as the National Postal Museum. The same year saw the opening of the U.S. Holocaust Memorial Museum. In 1995, the Korean War Veterans Memorial was dedicated. Washington's fourth presidential monument—and the first in more than half a century—was dedicated in May 1997, to honor Franklin Delano Roosevelt; it is the first memorial in Washington designed to be totally wheelchair accessible. The Women in Military Service Memorial, next to Arlington Cemetery, was inaugurated in October 1997, followed, in June 1998, by a Civil War memorial recognizing the efforts of African-American soldiers who fought for the Union.

The year 2003 saw the opening of a huge, new convention center, a City Museum of Washington (across the street from the convention center), and the National Air and Space Museum's large auxiliary building, the Steven F. Udvar-Hazy Center, at the Washington-Dulles International Airport. In 2004, huge crowds turned out for the opening of the Smithsonian's National Museum of the American Indian and the dedication of the National World War II Memorial, both on the National Mall. Changes are sure to abound in 2005, starting with the presidential inauguration and the convening of the 109th session of Congress.

If the city's optimism about its prosperity and growth was profoundly shaken by the September 11, 2001, terrorist attacks, it has been largely restored in the years since. The economy continues to rebound, and tourists are returning to Washington. Today, as always, the capital of the United States gladly welcomes to town visitors from around the world.

Index

See also Accommodations and Restaurant indexes, below.

GENERAL INDEX

A AA (American Automobile Association), 46, 57, 65
AARP, 31
Above and Beyond Tours, 31
Access America, 26
Accessible Journeys, 30
Access Information, 28
Accommodations, 80–117.
  See also Accommodations
  Index
  Adams-Morgan, 101–104
  Alexandria, VA, 286
  best, 7–9
  Capitol Hill, 82–88
  Downtown
    East of 16th Street
      NW, 88–96
    16th Street NW and
      West, 96–101
  Dupont Circle, 104–109
  family-friendly, 89
  Foggy Bottom, 109–112
  Georgetown, 112–115
  landing the best room, 82
  The Mall, 82–88
  money-saving tips, 81–82
  packages, 117
  reservations, 82
  surfing for, 34–35
  West End, 109–112
  what's new in, 2
  Woodley Park, 115–117
Acela trains, 47
Adams, Abigail, 292
Adams-Morgan, 70
  accommodations, 101–104
  restaurants, 145–148
  shopping, 233
ADC Map and Travel Center,
  238
Addison/Ripley Fine Art, 235
Addresses, finding, 69
Aer Lingus, 56
Aeroflot, 56
Affrica, 235
African-American Family Day
  at the National Zoo, 23

African-Americans, 296
  Alexandria Black History
    Resource Center,
    280–281
  Anacostia Museum and
    Center for African-
    American History and
    Culture, 189
  Frederick Douglass
    National Historic
    Site, 210
  Mary McLeod Bethune
    Council House National
    Historic Site, 210–211
  special events, 21, 23, 25
Afternoon tea, 4, 162
Air Canada, 56
Airfares
  discounts for international
    visitors, 56
  getting the best, 45–46
Airlines, 1, 37–38
  bankruptcy and, 38
  international, 56
Airports, 38–43
  information centers at,
    62–63
  security procedures, 43–45
Air Tickets Direct, 45
Alamo car rentals, 43, 77
Albert Einstein Planetarium,
  192–193
Alexandria, VA, 5, 276–288.
  See also Old Town
  Alexandria
  accommodations, 286
  layout of, 278
  restaurants, 287–288
  special events, 278–280
  traveling to, 276, 278
  visitor information, 278
Alexandria Arts Safari, 280
Alexandria Black History
  Resource Center, 280–281
Alexandria Colonial Tours,
  278
Alexandria Convention and
  Visitors Association, 278
Alexandria Farmers' Market,
  240

Alitalia, 56
All about jane, 243
A mano, 239
America!, 244
American Automobile Asso-
  ciation (AAA), 46, 57, 65
American Express, 78
  traveler's checks, 17
American Foundation for
  the Blind, 30
American Institute of Archi-
  tects Bookstore, 238
American Studio Plus, 239
Amtrak, 47
ANA Airways, 56
Anacostia Museum and Cen-
  ter for African-American
  History and Culture, 189
Anderson House, 210
Ann Taylor, 242
Annual Scottish Christmas
  Walk (Alexandria, VA), 280
Antique Row, 234
Antiques, 234–235
Apex, 266
Appalachian Spring, 239
April Cornell, 241
Area codes, 78
Arena Stage, 251
  accessibility information, 29
Arlington, VA, sights and
  attractions, 218–221
Arlington House, 219
Arlington National Ceme-
  tery, 218–220
Arlington Row, 270–271
Artful Evenings, 215
Art galleries, 235–236
Arthur M. Sackler Gallery,
  190, 195
Art Museum of the
  Americas, 210
Art museums and exhibits
  Arthur M. Sackler Gallery,
    190
  Art Museum of the
    Americas, 210
  Corcoran Gallery of Art,
    194, 207–208
  Dumbarton Oaks, 208–209

exhibits scheduled for
2005, 194–195
Freer Gallery of Art,
190–191, 194
Hillwood Museum and
Gardens, 210
Hirshhorn Museum and
Sculpture Garden,
191–192, 194
Kreeger Museum, 210
National Gallery of Art,
194–195, 201–203
National Museum of
African Art, 193–194
National Museum of
Women in the Arts, 214
Phillips Collection,
214–215
Renwick Gallery of the
Smithsonian American
Art Museum, 200
Rock Creek Gallery, 224
Arts and Industries Building,
190
The Athenaeum (Alexandria,
VA), 281
ATMs (automated teller
machines), 17, 54
A Tour de Force, 227
Avis car rentals, 43

B ack Stage Books and
Costumes, 238
Baltimore-Washington
International Airport
(BWI), 40–41
transportation to/from, 43
visitor information, 62–63
Banana Republic, 241
Barmy Wine and Liquor, 249
Barnes & Noble, 236
Barns of Wolf Trap (Vienna,
VA), 257
Bar Rouge, 266–267
Bars, 266–272
Bartholdi Park, 222
Bastille Day, 25
B. Dalton, 236
Beadazzled, 245
Bed & Breakfast Accommo-
dations, 82
Betsey Johnson, 243
Betsy Fisher, 243
Bicycling, 5, 230
to Old Town Alexandria
and Mount Vernon, 281
tours, 230
Big Hunt, 267
Big Wheel Bikes, 230
Bike the Sites, 230

The Birchmere Music Hall
and Bandstand, 259
Black Cat, 259
Black Family Reunion, 25
Black History Month, 21
Blue Bar, 261
Blues Alley, 262–263
Boat rentals, 230–231
Boat tours and cruises,
6, 228–230
mule-drawn 19th-century
canal boat trip, 225–226
Bohemian Caverns, 263
Boingo, 37
Bon Appétit! Julia Child's
Kitchen at the Smithson-
ian, 196
Books, recommended, 48
Bookstores, 236–238
Borders, 236, 248
Bourbon, 267
Brass Knob Architectural
Antiques, 234
Brass Knob's Back Doors
Warehouse, 234
Bravo Bravo, 261, 265
Bread Line, 244
Brickskeller, 267
Bridge Street Books,
236–237
British Airways, 56
Brooks Brothers, 242, 248
Bucket shops, 45
Budget car rentals, 43, 77
Burberry's, 242
Bureau of Engraving &
Printing, 204–205
Burnham, Daniel, 199, 216,
295, 297
Business hours, 57
Bus travel, 75–76

C abs, 77–78
to/from airports, 41
Café Japone, 267
Calendar of events, 21–26
Alexandria, VA, 278–280
Calvert Woodley Liquors, 249
Cameras and film
developing, 238–239
C&O Canal, 225
Cannon, Joe, 295–296
Capital Beltway, 46
Capital Crescent Trail, 230
The Capitol, 2–3
sightseeing, 171–174
accessibility informa-
tion, 29
Capitol Coin and Stamp Co.
Inc., 248

Capitol Hill, 69
accommodations, 82–88
restaurants, 121–125
Capitol Reservations, 82
Capitol River Cruise, 229
The Capitol Steps, 258–259
Capitol Visitor Center, 3, 172
Carlyle House Historic Park
(Alexandria, VA), 282
Carousel, 190
Car rentals, 76–77
at Baltimore-Washington
International Airport
(BWI), 43
at Dulles airport, 42
at National Airport, 42
surfing for, 35
Carter Barron Amphitheater,
256–257
Car travel
to/from airports, 42, 43
driving safety for interna-
tional visitors, 55
to Washington, D.C., 46–47
within Washington, D.C., 76
Cellphones, 37
Central Liquor, 249
Chanel Boutique, 243
Chapters, A Literary Book-
store, 237
Chas Schwartz & Son, 245
Cherry, 234
Cherry Blossom Events,
23, 222
Cherub Antiques Gallery, 234
Chevy Chase Pavilion, 245
Chi Cha Lounge, 265
Chief Ike's Mambo Room,
261
Child, Julia: *Bon Appétit!*
Julia Child's Kitchen at
the Smithsonian, 196
Children, families with
information and resources,
32–33
shopping
clothing, 241
toys, 249
sights and attractions,
226–227
Children's Hospital National
Medical Center, 78
Chinese New Year Celebra-
tion, 22
Chocolate Moose, 244
Christ Child Opportunity
Shop, 240
Christ Church (Alexandria,
VA), 282–283
Christmas Pageant of
Peace/National Tree
Lighting, 26

Christmas Tree Lighting (Alexandria, VA), 280
Circulator shuttle bus system, 1
City Museum, 206–207
City Paper, 258
Civil War, 294
Clarendon Grill (Arlington, VA), 271
Cleveland Park restaurants, 164–165
Climate, 20–21
Club and music scene, 258–266
Columbia Station, 263
Comedy clubs, 258–259
Comfort One Shoes, 248–249
Commander Salamander, 243
Common Grounds Coffee-house (Arlington, VA), 270
Congress, U.S., tours, 19
Congresspersons, locating, 78
Connecticut Avenue, 68
    shopping, 233
Consolidators, 45
Constitution Avenue, 68
Coolidge Auditorium, 206
The Corcoran Gallery of Art, 194, 207–208
Cosi, 267–268
Crafts, 239
Credit cards, 18, 54
    lost or stolen, 19
Currency and currency exchange, 53–54
Custis, George Washington Parke, 218, 219
Customs regulations, 51–53
CVS, 247
Cyberstop Cafe, 79

D ance clubs, 261
DAR Constitution Hall, 257
DASH bus, 278
Daughters of the American Revolution (DAR) Museum, 210
David Adamson Gallery, 236
Daylight savings time, 61
DC Ducks, 230
DC 9, 259–260
Dean & Deluca, 244
Decatur House, 210
Delta Shuttle, 38
Dial-a-Museum, 189
Diamond Cab Company, 78
Dickens, Charles, 294
Dinosaur Hall (National Museum of Natural History), 198

Disabilities, travelers with, 28–30
Discount shopping, 239–240
Discovery Center (National Museum of Natural History), 198
Discovery Theater, 190
DJ Hut, 248
Dollar car rentals, 43
Doudaklian Leather, 247
Downtown, 70
    accommodations
        East of 16th Street NW, 88–96
        16th Street NW and West, 96–101
    restaurants
        East of 16th Street NW, 125–138
        16th Street NW and West, 138–144
    shopping, 232
Dragonfly, 268
Driver's licenses, foreign, 50–51
Driving safety, 55
Drugstores, 78
The Dubliner, 268
Dumbarton House, 210
Dumbarton Oaks, 208–209, 224
Dupont Circle, 6, 70
    accommodations, 104–109
    art galleries, 235
    gay clubs, 266
    restaurants, 148–153
    shopping, 233
Dupont Circle FreshFarm Market, 240–241
Dupont-Kalorama Museum Walk Day, 24

E astern Market, 6, 241
East Potomac Park, 222, 231
Eddie Bauer, 242
Eighteenth Street Lounge, 260, 261
Eklektikos Gallery of Art, 236
Elderhostel, 32
Electricity, 57
Elizabeth Roberts Gallery, 235
Embassies and con-sulates, 57
Embassy Row, 6, 68, 70, 227
Emergencies, 58
Enid A. Haupt Garden, 221
Enterprise, 77
Entry requirements, 49–51
ESPN Zone, 268

Europ Assistance, 53
Expedia, 33, 34

F adó, 268
Fahrneys Pens, Inc., 247
Families with children
    information and resources, 32–33
    shopping
        clothing, 241
        toys, 249
    sights and attractions, 226–227
Family Travel Files, 33
Family Travel Forum, 32
Family Travel Network, 32
Farmer's markets, 240–241
Fashion Center at Pentagon City, 246
Fashions (clothing), 241–243
Fax machines, 60
Federal Bureau of Investigation, 205
Festivals and special events, 21–26
    Alexandria, VA, 278–280
Fichandler stage, 251
Filene's Basement, 239–240
Film, flying with, 46
Filmfest DC, 23
Firehook Bakery, 244
Fletcher's Boat House, 225, 230–231
Flights.com, 45
Flight Simulators (National Air and Space Museum), 193
Flights of Fancy, 249
Fly-Cheap, 45
Flying Wheels Travel, 30
Foggy Bottom, 70–71
    accommodations, 109–112
    restaurants, 153–156
Folger Shakespeare Library, 209, 255
Foot Locker, 248
Ford's Theatre, 226, 256
Ford's Theatre & Lincoln Museum, 212
Foreign visitors, 49–61
    customs regulations, 51–53
    entry requirements, 49–51
    safety suggestions for, 54–55
    traveling around the United States, 56–57
    traveling to the United States, 56
Fort DeRussey, 224

Fort Ward Museum & Historic Site (Alexandria, VA), 283
406 Art Galleries, 236
Four Seasons Garden Terrace lounge, 262
Franklin Delano Roosevelt Memorial, 186
Franz Bader Bookstore, 238
Frederick Douglass National Historic Site, 210
Freedom Park (Arlington), 220
Freer Gallery of Art, 190–191, 194
French Connection, 243
Frequent-flier clubs, 45
Friendship Firehouse (Alexandria, VA), 283
Frommers.com, 35

Gadsby's Tavern Museum (Alexandria, VA), 283–284
Galaxy Hut (Arlington, VA), 270–271
The Gap, 241–242
Gap Kids, 241
Gardens, 221–222
    Dumbarton Oaks, 209
    Elizabethan garden at Folger Shakespeare Library, 209
    Enid A. Haupt Garden, 221
    Hillwood Museum and Gardens, 210
    United States Botanic Garden, 221–222
Gasoline, 58
Gay and lesbian travelers
    bookstore, 238
    clubs, 266
    information and resources, 30–31
George Mason Memorial, 186–187
Georgetown, 71
    accommodations, 112–115
    art galleries, 235–236
    restaurants, 156–162
    shopping, 233
    transportation to, 75
Georgetown Flea Market, 6, 241
Georgetown Garden Tour, 24
Georgetown Information Center, 225
Georgetown University Medical Center, 79
George Washington Memorial Parkway, 274

George Washington University Hospital, 78
Gifts and souvenirs, 244
Ginza, 248
Glover Park, 71
    restaurants, 163–164
Gold-and-White East Room (The White House), 176, 178
Gore-Dean, 234
GoToMyPC, 36
GO 25 card, 33
Gourmet food, 244
Govinda Gallery, 235
Grant, Ulysses S., 294–295
Gray Line Buses, 273
Great Falls, 225
Great Falls Tavern Visitor Center (Potomac, MD), 225
The Greek Slave, 208
Green Room (The White House), 178
GSM (Global System for Mobiles) wireless network, 37
Guarisco Gallery, 235
Guided Walking Tours of Washington, 227

Habana Village, 261, 265
Hall of Nations, 215
Halloween, 25–26
Halloween Walking Tours (Alexandria, VA), 280
H&M, 242
Happy hours, 269
Hats in the Belfry, 248
Health concerns, 27
Health insurance, 26–27
    for international visitors, 53
Hecht's, 241, 247
Hertz car rentals, 43, 77
Hiking, 231
Hillwood Museum and Gardens, 210
Hirshhorn Museum and Sculpture Garden, 191–192, 194
Hispanic Heritage Month, 25
Historic Alexandria Candlelight Tour, 280
Historic Garden Week in Virginia (Alexandria, VA), 279
History of Washington, D.C., 290–297
Holidays, 58
Holocaust Memorial Museum, United States, 195, 203–204
Home Rule, 248

Hospitals, 78–79
Hotels, 80–117. *See also* Accommodations Index
    Adams-Morgan, 101–104
    Alexandria, VA, 286
    best, 7–9
    Capitol Hill, 82–88
    Downtown
        East of 16th Street NW, 88–96
        16th Street NW and West, 96–101
    Dupont Circle, 104–109
    family-friendly, 89
    Foggy Bottom, 109–112
    Georgetown, 112–115
    landing the best room, 82
    The Mall, 82–88
    money-saving tips, 81–82
    packages, 117
    reservations, 82
    surfing for, 34–35
    West End, 109–112
    what's new in, 2
    Woodley Park, 115–117
Hot lines, 79
Hotwire, 34
The House Where Lincoln Died (the Petersen House), 212, 226
Howard University Hospital, 79
HR-57, 263

I Can, 30
Ice skating, 7, 231
IMAX films
    National Air and Space Museum, 192, 193
    National Museum of Natural History, 198
The Improv, 259
Independence Air, 38
Independence Day, 24–25
Indian Craft Shop, 239
Insurance, 26–27
Interior Department Museum, 210
International Gay & Lesbian Travel Association (IGLTA), 31
International Spy Museum, 212–213, 226
International Tourist Guide Day, 22
International visitors, 49–61
    customs regulations, 51–53
    entry requirements, 49–51
    safety suggestions for, 54–55

International visitors (cont.)
traveling around the
United States, 56–57
traveling to the United
States, 56
Internet access, 35–37, 79
InTouch USA, 37, 55
IOTA (Arlington, VA), 271
IPass network, 36
I2roam, 36

J azz and blues clubs,
262–265
Jefferson, Thomas, 176, 201,
205, 290–291, 293
Birthday, 23
Jefferson Memorial,
183, 187
Jewelry, 245
John F. Kennedy Center for
the Performing Arts. See
Kennedy Center for the
Performing Arts
Jos. A. Bank Clothiers, 242
J.R.'s Bar and Grill, 266

K athleen Ewing Gallery,
235
Keith Lipert Gallery, 245
Kennedy, John Fitzgerald,
Gravesite of, 219–220
Kennedy, Robert, 220
Kennedy Center for the
Performing Arts, 3
free concert series, 254
Millennium Stage free
performances, 5, 254
Open House Arts
Festival, 25
restaurants, 123
sightseeing and tours,
215–216
theaters, 251, 254
Kenneth E. Behring Hall
of Mammals, 197–198
Kids
information and resources,
32–33
shopping
clothing, 241
toys, 249
sights and attractions,
226–227
Kid's Closet, 241
Kite Festival, Smithsonian,
22–23
KLM, 56
Korean War Veterans
Memorial, 185

Kramerbooks & Afterwords
Café, 79, 237
Kreeger Museum, 210
Kreeger stage, 251

L abor Day Concert, 25
Lambda Rising, 31, 238
Language aid, 58–59
Latin Jazz Alley, 261, 265
Latin music, 265–266
Lawson's of Dupont,
244–245
Lee, Robert E., birthday of
(Alexandria, VA), 279
Lee-Fendall House Museum
(Alexandria, VA), 284
Legal aid, 59
L'Enfant, Pierre Charles, 176,
187, 207, 217, 291–292
grave, 219
Library of Congress,
5, 205–206
Limousines, to/from airports,
41, 43
Lincoln, Abraham
Birthday, 22
Ford's Theatre & Lincoln
Museum, 212, 226
The House Where Lincoln
Died (the Petersen
House), 212
Lincoln Memorial, 4, 183,
184–185, 226
Lincoln Theatre, 257
Liquor laws, 59
Lisner Auditorium, 257
Lockheed Martin IMAX
Theater (National Air
and Space Museum), 192
Lost-luggage insurance, 27
Lucky Bar, 261, 268–269
Lufthansa, 56
Luggage Express, 44
Luggage-service
companies, 44
The Lyceum (Alexandria, VA),
284–285

M acArthur Liquor, 249
Madam's Organ Restaurant
and Bar, 261, 263
Madison Building, 206
Mail, 59
Mail2web, 36
The Mall, 5–6, 69–70
accommodations, 82–88
parking near, 188
Malls, 245–247

The Mansion on O Street,
235
Maps, 79
Marathon, Marine Corps, 25
Marian Koshland Science
Museum, 3, 213–214
Marine Corps Marathon, 25
Marston-Luce, 234
Martin Luther King Jr.'s
Birthday, 21
Marvelous Market, 245
Mary McLeod Bethune
Council House National
Historic Site, 210–211
Mary Pickford Theater, 206
Mason, George, Memorial,
186–187
Massachusetts Avenue, 68
Mazza Gallerie, 246
MCCXXIII, 269
MCI Center, 256
McCormick & Schmick's, 269
McMillan, James, 295
MEDEX International, 27
Medic Alert Identification
Tag, 27
Medical insurance, 26–27
Melody Record Shop, 248
Melrose Bar, 261
Memorial Day, 24
Merriweather Post Pavilion
(Columbia, MD), 256
Metro, to night spots, 260
Metrobus system, 75–76
Metroliner, 47
Metrorail, 71, 74–75
from National Airport,
41–42
Meyer Auditorium, 191
Millennium, 234
Miller's Cabin, 224
Money matters, 17–20
for international visitors,
53–54
Montgomery County Farm
Woman's Cooperative
Market, 241
Montrose Park, 231
Moss Rehab Hospital, 30
Mount Vernon, 273–276
Mr. Henry's Capitol Hill,
263–264
Mr. Smith's of Georgetown,
269–270
Music stores, 248

N ana's, 243
Nation, 260
National Air and Space
Museum, 192–194, 226

National Airport, Ronald Reagan Washington, 40
  getting into town from, 41–42
  visitor information, 63
  shopping at, 246
National Archives, 200–201
National Building Museum, 211
National car rentals, 43, 77
National Gallery of Art, 194–195, 201–203
  Sculpture Garden, 7, 202
National Gallery Sculpture Garden Ice Rink, 231
National Geographic Society's Explorers Hall, 211
National Museum of African Art, 193–194
National Museum of American History, 195–196
  Giftshop, 238
National Museum of Natural History, 197–198, 226
National Museum of the American Indian, 3, 196–197
National Museum of Women in the Arts, 214
National Park Service
  telephone numbers and websites, 65
  visitor information, 64
National Postal Museum, 198–199
National Statuary Hall (The Capitol), 172
National Symphony Orchestra, 254
National Theatre, 254–255
  accessibility information, 30
National World War II Memorial, 3, 180, 183–184
National Zoological Park, 199–200, 226
  African-American Family Day at, 23
Naval Heritage Center, 211
Neighborhoods, 69–71
Newseum (Arlington), 220
New Vegas Lounge, 264
Nightlife and entertainment, 250–272
  Arlington, 270–271
  bar scene, 266–272
  club and music scene, 258–266
  comedy clubs, 258–259
  dance clubs, 261
  jazz and blues clubs, 262–265
  performing arts, 251–258

pop/rock/rave/alternative clubs, 259
  schedules of events, 250
  tickets, 250–251
9:30 Club, 260–262
Nine West, 248
Nissan Pavilion at Stone Ridge (Bristow, VA), 256
Now, Voyager, 31

O ctagon, 211
Odyssey III, 229
Old Presbyterian Meeting House (Alexandria, VA), 285
Old Print Gallery, 234
Old Stone House, 211
Old Supreme Court Chamber (The Capitol), 172
Old Town, 276
Old Town Alexandria. See also Alexandria, VA
  shopping, 233–234
  sights and attractions, 280–286
Old Town Trolley tours, 228
Old Vat, 251
Olsson's Books and Records, 237
Onassis, Jacqueline Kennedy, 176, 200, 219
On Tap, 258
O. Orkin Insect Zoo (National Museum of Natural History), 197
Orbitz, 33, 34
Outdoor activities, 230–231
Oval Blue Room (The White House), 178

P addleboats, 231
Parking, near the Mall, 188
Parks and gardens, 221–226
Passport information, 51
Patriot Center (Fairfax, VA), 256
Pavilion at the Old Post Office, 246
Peirce Mill, 224
Penn Camera Exchange, 238
Penn Quarter, 70
Pennsylvania Avenue, 68
The Pentagon (Arlington), 220–221
Performing arts, 251–258
Pershing Park, 231
Petrol, 58
Phillips Collection, 6, 195, 214–215
The Phoenix, 239

Pirjo, 243
Planetarium
  Albert Einstein (National Air and Space Museum), 192–193
  Rock Creek Nature Center and, 224
Platinum, 262
Poison-control hot line, 79
Political memorabilia, 248
Politics and Prose Bookstore, 237
Politiki, Top of the Hill, and the Pour House, 271
Polly Esther's, 262
Pope John Paul II Cultural Center, 211
Potomac Mills Mall, 240
Potomac Park, 222
Potomac Party Cruises, 229
Potomac Riverboat Company, 229
Prescription medications, 27
Presidential Inauguration, 21
Priceline, 34

Q uadrants, 65

R ail SALE, 47
Rainfall, average, 21
Red Cross Waterfront Festival (Alexandria, VA), 279
Red Room (The White House), 178
Red Top Executive Sedan, 41, 43
Reiter's Bookstore, 238
Renwick Gallery of the Smithsonian American Art Museum, 195, 200
Reservations
  accommodations, 82
  restaurants, 118
Restaurants, 118–165. See also Restaurant Index
  Adams-Morgan, 145–148
  Alexandria, VA, 287–288
  best, 10–12
  Capitol Hill, 121–125
  Cleveland Park, 164–165
  by cuisine, 119–121
  Downtown
    East of 16th Street NW, 125–138
    16th Street NW and West, 138–144
  Dupont Circle, 148–153
  family-friendly, 135
  Foggy Bottom, 153–156

Restaurants *(cont.)*
  Georgetown, 156–162
  Glover Park, 163–164
  late-night, 264
  pretheater, 154
  prices, 119
  reservations, 118
  at sightseeing attractions, 122–123
  U Street Corridor, 144–145
  vegetarian, 130
  West End, 153–156
  what's new in, 2
  Woodley Park, 164–165
Restrooms, 61
Rhodeside Grill (Arlington, VA), 271
Ritz Camera Centers, 239
Rizik Brothers, 243
Robert F. Kennedy Memorial Stadium, 256
Rock Creek Gallery, 224
Rock Creek Nature Center and Planetarium, 224
Rock Creek Park, 5, 222–224
Ronald Reagan Washington National Airport, 40
  getting into town from, 41–42
  visitor information, 63
  shopping at, 246
Roosevelt, Franklin Delano, Memorial, 186
The Rotunda (The Capitol), 171–172

S ackler Gallery, 190, 195
Safety, 27–28
  for international visitors, 54–55
Saint-Gaudens, Augustus, 216, 295
St. Patrick's Day Parade, 22
St. Patrick's Day Parade (Alexandria, VA), 279
Saudi Arabian Airlines, 56
Science Museum, Marian Koshland, 3, 213–214
Sculpture Garden
  Hirshhorn Museum, 192
  National Gallery of Art, 7, 202
Seasons, 20–21
Secondhand Rose, 240
Secondi Inc., 240
Second Story Books, 237–238
Security procedures
  at airports, 43–45
  around the capital, 166

Senior travelers, 31–32
7th Street Arts Corridor, 236
Sewall-Belmont House, 211
Shakespeare, William
  Birthday Celebration, 23
  Folger Shakespeare Library, 209
Shakespeare Theatre, 255
Shakespeare Theatre Free For All, 24, 257
Shepherd, Alexander "Boss," 294–295
Sherman Pickey, 242
Shipping your luggage, 44
Shoes, 248–249
Shopping, 232–249
  areas for, 232–234
  discount, 239–240
  emergency, 247
Shops at Georgetown Park, 246
Side-Step, 33
Sights and attractions, 166–230
  Arlington, 218–221
  for kids, 226–227
  major memorials, 180–187
  openings and closings, 171
  suggested itineraries, 170
  what's new in, 2–3
SkyCap International, 44
Sky Terrace, 6–7
The Smithsonian
  accessibility information, 29
  Information Center (the "Castle"), 65, 189
  museums, 188–200
Smithsonian Craft Show, 23–24
Smithsonian Festival of American Folklife, 24
Smithsonian Jazz Café, 264
Smithsonian Kite Festival, 22–23
Society for Accessible Travel and Hospitality, 30
Source Theatre Company, 255
Southwest Airlines, 38
Special events and festivals, 21–26
  Alexandria, VA, 278–280
Spectrum Gallery, 235–236
Spirit of Washington Cruises, 229, 274
Spy Lounge, 271–272
Spy Museum, International, 212–213, 226
Stabler-Leadbeater Apothecary Museum (Alexandria, VA), 285–286

Star-Spangled Banner, original, 195–196
State Dining Room (The White House), 178
State Theatre, 262
STA Travel, 33, 45
Steve Madden, 249
Steven F. Udvar-Hazy Center, 192, 193
Student travelers, 33
Studentuniverse.com, 33
Studio Theatre, 255
Supreme Court of the United States, 5, 175–176
Susquehanna Antiques, 235

T albots, 242
Taxes, 59
Taxis, 77–78
  to/from airports, 41
Teaism Penn Quarter, 269
Ted Airlines, 38
Telegraph and telex services, 60
Telephone, 59–60
Telephone directories, 60–61
Temperatures, average, 21
Textile Museum, 211
Theater, 251–256
Theater Lab, 254
Theodore Roosevelt Island Park, 224–225
Thomas Jefferson Building, 205
Thomas Pink, 242
Thompson's Boat Center, 230–231
Thrifty car rentals, 43, 77
Ticketmaster, 250–251
TICKETplace, 250
Tickets.com, 251
Tiffany & Co., 245
Time zones, 61
Tiny Jewel Box, 245
Tipping, 61
T-Mobile Hotspot, 37
Toilets, 61
The Tomb of the Unknowns (Arlington), 218
The Tombs, 272
Topaz Bar, 272
Torpedo Factory (Alexandria, VA), 286
Torpedo Factory Art Center, 239
Touchstone Gallery, 236
TourDC, 227

Tourmobile, 180
    accessibility informa-
        tion, 29
Tourmobile Sightseeing,
    227–228
Tours
    advance reservations
        for, 18–19
    Alexandria, VA, 278
    by bike, 230
    boat, 6, 228–230
        mule-drawn 19th-
            century canal boat
            trip, 225–226
    bus, 227–228
    Old Town Trolley, 228
    walking, 227
    The White House, 179
Tower Records, 248
Town and Country Lounge,
    269
Toys, 249
Train travel
    from Baltimore-
        Washington Interna-
        tional Airport (BWI), 43
    for international visitors,
        56–57
    to Washington, 47
Transportation, 1–2, 71–78
    accessibility information,
        28–29
    by bus, 75–76
    by car, 76–77
    by Metrorail, 71, 74–75
    from National Airport,
        41–42
    by taxi, 77–78
Travel Assistance Interna-
    tional, 27
TravelAxe, 34
Traveler's Aid Society
    International, 58
Traveler's checks, 17–18, 54
    lost or stolen, 19–20
Travelex Insurance
    Services, 26
Travel Guard International, 26
Travel insurance, 26–27
Travel Insured
    International, 26
Travelocity, 33, 34, 81
Trip-cancellation insur-
    ance, 26
Trollope, Anthony, 294
Trover Shop, 237
Tryst, 272
Tudor Place, 211
Tune Inn, 272
Twins Jazz, 264

Tysons Corner Center, 246
Tysons Corner II, The
    Galleria, 246

Udvar-Hazy Center, 192,
    193
Union Station, 6, 47
    shopping, 232, 236, 239,
        242, 244, 246, 248, 249
    sightseeing, 216
    visitor information, 63–64
United States Botanic
    Garden, 221–222
United States Holocaust
    Memorial Museum, 195,
    203–204
United States Navy Memo-
    rial and Naval Heritage
    Center, 211
Upper Wisconsin Avenue
    Northwest, shopping
    on, 233
Urban Outfitters, 242
USA Groups, 82
US Airways Shuttle, 38
USA Railpass, 56
U.S. Capitol, 2–3
    sightseeing, 171–174
    accessibility informa-
        tion, 29
U Street Corridor, 70
    restaurants, 144–145
Utopia, 265

Very Important Patriot
    (VIP) Pass, 279
Veterans Day, 26
Victoria's Secret, 242
Video, flying with, 46
Vietnam Veterans Memorial,
    185–186
Vietnam Veterans Women's
    Memorial, 186
Virgin Atlantic, 56
Virtual Bellhop, 44
Visas, 49–50
Visitor information, 16–17,
    62–65

Walking tours, 4–5
Warner Theatre, 257, 258
War of 1812, 292–293
Washington, D.C., Visitor
    Information Center, 64
Washington, D.C. Convention
    and Tourism Corporation
    (WCTC), 16

Washington, George, 176,
    178, 195, 213, 217, 291
    Birthday
        Alexandria, VA, 279
        Washington, D.C., 22
    Mount Vernon Estate and
        Gardens, 274–275
Washington D.C. Accommo-
    dations, 82. See also
    Accommodations Index
Washington Dulles Interna-
    tional Airport (Dulles), 40
    transportation to/from,
        42–43
    visitor information, 63
Washington Flyer Express
    Bus, 42
Washington Metropolitan
    Transit Authority, accessi-
    bility information, 28
Washington Monument, 180,
    182–183, 226
Washington National
    Cathedral, 4
    Annual Flower Mart, 24
    Open House, 25
    sightseeing and tours, 217
    tea at, 163
Washington National Opera,
    254
Wayport, 37
Weather, 20–21
    information, 79
Websites
    for airfares, 33–34
    best, 12–13
    for hotels, 34
    for rental cars, 35
    travel-planning and
        booking, 33–35
West End
    accommodations, 109–112
    restaurants, 153–156
Western Union, 20
West Potomac Park, 180, 222
Wheelchair accessibility,
    28–30
Whistler, James McNeill, 191
White Flint Mall, 246–247
The White House, 2, 176–178
    accessibility information,
        29
    Easter Egg Roll, 23
    Fall Garden Tours, 25
    Spring Garden Tours, 23
    tours, 179
The White House Visitor
    Center, 64, 178–180
Whitlow's on Wilson (Arling-
    ton, VA), 269, 271

Wilson, Woodrow, House, 211
Wine and spirits, 249
Wisconsin Avenue, 68–69
Wolf Trap Farm Park for the Performing Arts (Vienna, VA), 256
Women
   National Museum of Women in the Arts, 214
   Sewall-Belmont House, 211
   Vietnam Veterans Women's Memorial, 186
Women in Military Service for America Memorial, 220
Women's History Month, 22
Woodley Park, 71
   accommodations, 115–117
   restaurants, 164–165
Woodrow Wilson House, 211
Woolly Mammoth Theatre Company, 255
Worldwide Assistance Services, 53

Yahoo! Mail, 36
Yellow Cab, 78

Zanzibar, 261
Zanzibar on the Waterfront, 265–266
Zara, 243
Zenith Gallery, 236
Zoo, National, 199–200, 226
   African-American Family Day at, 23

ACCOMMODATIONS
Butterfield 9, 10, 125, 128
Capital Hilton, 99
Capitol Hill Suites, 87
Courtyard by Marriott Northwest, 101–102
Embassy Suites Hotel Downtown, 2, 8, 89, 106–107
Four Points Sheraton, Washington, D.C. Downtown, 9, 94
Four Seasons Hotel, 8, 9, 112
Georgetown Suites, 114
George Washington University Inn, 110–111
Grand Hyatt Washington, 88–89
Hamilton Crowne Plaza Washington, DC, 92
Hampton Inn, 2
Hay-Adams, 10, 96–97
Henley Park, 92–93

Hilton Garden Inn, Washington, DC, Franklin Square, 95
Hilton Washington, 89, 101
Holiday Inn on the Hill, 86
Holiday Inn Select Old Town (Alexandria, VA), 286
The Hotel George, 82–83
Hotel Helix, 95
Hotel Madera, 107–108
Hotel Monaco Washington DC, 7, 89
Hotel Monticello of Georgetown, 114–115
Hotel Rouge, 7, 99–100
Hotel Tabard Inn, 108–109
Hotel Washington, 93
The Jefferson, a Loews Hotel, 8, 9, 97
Jurys Normandy Inn, 8, 9, 102
Jurys Washington Hotel, 109
JW Marriott Hotel on Pennsylvania Avenue, 90
Kalorama Guest House, 102, 104, 116
Lincoln Suites Downtown, 100–101
The Madison, 90–91
Mandarin Oriental, Washington DC, 2, 8–10, 83, 86
The Mansion on O Street, 104
Morrison-Clark Historic Inn, 8, 94
Morrison House (Alexandria, VA), 286
Omni Shoreham Hotel, 10, 89, 116
One Washington Circle Hotel, 111–112
Park Hyatt Washington, 109–110
Phoenix Park Hotel, 86–87
Renaissance Mayflower, 7, 97–98
Residence Inn Capitol, 2, 87–88
The Ritz-Carlton, Washington, D.C., 8, 10, 110
The Ritz-Carlton Georgetown, 112–113
St. Gregory Luxury Hotel and Suites, 10, 105
The St. Regis, 8, 98–99
Sofitel Lafayette Square, Washington, D.C., 91
Swann House, 8, 105–106
Topaz Hotel, 7–8, 106
Wardman Park Marriott Hotel, 115

Washington Terrace Hotel, 96
Willard Inter-Continental Washington, 7, 91–92
Woodley Park Guest House, 116–117

RESTAURANTS
Aditi, 161
Al Tiramisu, 15, 149
Andale, 14, 134
Asia Nora, 154–155
Austin Grill, 163–164
Ben's Chili Bowl, 14–15, 144, 264
Bistro Bis, 124
Bistro Francais, 264
Bistrot D'Oc, 13, 129–130
Bistrot du Coin, 14, 151
Bistrot Lepic & Wine Bar, 2, 159–160
Bombay Club, 14, 130, 142–143
B. Smith's, 123–124
Café 15, 128
Café Asia, 143–144
Café Atlantico, 11, 130–131, 154
Café des Artistes, 208
Café Milano, 158
Cashion's Eat Place, 11, 145
The Caucus Room, 11, 128–129
Charlie Palmer Steak, 11, 121–123
Ching Ching Cha, 161–162
City Lights of China, 11, 151
Clyde's of Georgetown, 160
Coppi's Organic, 144–145
Daily Grill, 140–141
DC Coast, 131
Diner, 264
Dirksen Senate Office Building South Buffet Room, 123
Dupont Grille, 149
Equinox, 141
Etrusco, 151–152
Famous Luigi's Pizzeria Restaurant, 11, 14, 100, 135, 144
15 Ria, 131–132
Firefly, 149–150
Fossil Café, 198
Gadsby's Tavern (Alexandria, VA), 287
Galileo, 2, 14, 138–139
Garden Terrace (Four Seasons Hotel), 162
Georgetown Inn, 113
Georgia Brown's, 15, 130, 132

Geranio (Alexandria, VA), 287
Gerard's Place, 11–12, 129
Haad Thai, 137–138
House of Representatives Restaurant, 122
Il Radicchio, 125
I Ricchi, 139
Jaleo, 2, 134–135
The Jefferson Hotel, 162–163
Johnny's Half Shell, 150
Kaz Sushi Bistro, 155–156
Kinkead's, 11, 14, 155
Kramerbooks & Afterwords Café, 264
La Bergerie (Alexandria, VA), 287
Laboratorio del Galileo, 15, 139
La Colline, 11, 124
La Fourchette, 145
La Madeleine (Alexandria, VA), 288
Lauriol Plaza, 14, 145–146
Lebanese Taverna, 130, 165
Legal Sea Foods, 14, 135, 143
Les Halles, 11, 135
Library of Congress's Cafeteria, 123
Longworth Building Cafeteria, 123
Marcel's, 15, 153, 154
Matchbox, 138
Melrose, 9, 109, 153–154

Mendocino Grille and Wine Bar, 158–159
Meskerem, 130, 146
Michel Richard Citronelle, 9, 11, 12, 156
Miss Saigon, 160
Mixtec, 146
The Monocle, 15, 124–125
Montmartre, 125
Morton's of Chicago, 156–157
Mount Vernon Inn (VA), 276
Nectar, 155
New Heights, 164–165
Nora, 130, 148
Obelisk, 14, 148–149
Occidental Grill, 132
Oceanaire Seafood Room, 132–133
Old Ebbitt Grill, 14, 136
Old Glory Barbecue, 135, 160–161
Olives, 141
Oval Room at Lafayette Square, 141, 154
Palena, 2, 164
The Palm, 14, 139
Pasta Mia, 130, 146, 148
Petits Plats, 165
Pizzeria Paradiso, 14, 152
The Prime Rib, 14, 139–140
Rayburn House Office Building Cafeteria, 122–123
Red Sage Grill/Red Sage Border Café, 129

Ristorante Piccolo, 161
Sala Thai, 152
Sea Catch Restaurant and Raw Bar, 159
Senate Dining Room, 122
701, 15, 133
South Austin Grill (Alexandria, VA), 288
Supreme Court's Cafeteria, 123
Sushi-Ko, 163
Tabard Inn, 150–151
Taberna del Alabardero, 11, 14, 140
Taverna Cretekou (Alexandria, VA), 288
Teaism, 163
Teaism Dupont Circle, 152–153
Teaism Lafayette Square, 153
Teaism Penn Quarter, 153
Teatro Goldoni, 11, 141–142
TenPenh, 133
Tony Cheng's Seafood Restaurant, 11, 138
Tosca, 14, 133–134
Union Street Public House (Alexandria, VA), 288
Vidalia, 14, 142
Washington National Cathedral, 163
Zaytinya, 136–137
Zed's, 162
Zola, 137

Great Trips Like Great Days Begin with a Plan

FranklinCovey and Frommer's Bring You *Frommer's Favorite Places*® Planner

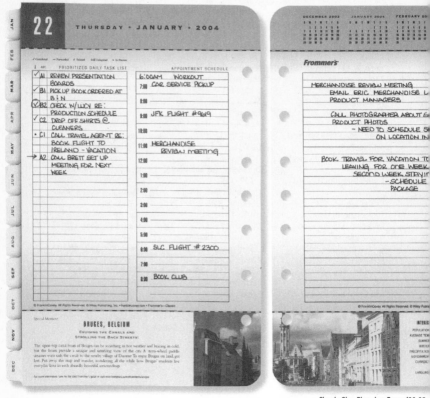

Classic Size Planning Pages $39.95

The planning experts at FranklinCovey have teamed up with the travel experts at Frommer's. The result is a full-year travel-themed planner filled with rich images and travel tips covering fifty-two of Frommer's Favorite Places.

- Each week will make you an expert about an intriguing corner of the world
- New facts and tips every day
- Beautiful, full-color photos of some of the most beautiful places on earth
- Proven planning tools from FranklinCovey for keeping track of tasks, appointments, notes, address/phone numbers, and more

Save 15%

when you purchase Frommer's Favorite Places travel-themed planner and a binder.

Order today before your next big trip.

www.franklincovey.com/frommers
Enter promo code 12252 at checkout for discount. Offer expires June 1, 2005.

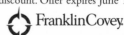

FranklinCovey.

Frommer's is a trademark of Arthur Frommer.

FROMMER'S® NATIONAL PARK GUIDES

Algonquin Provincial Park
Banff & Jasper
Family Vacations in the National
Parks

Grand Canyon
National Parks of the American
West
Rocky Mountain

Yellowstone & Grand Teton
Yosemite & Sequoia/Kings
Canyon
Zion & Bryce Canyon

FROMMER'S® MEMORABLE WALKS

Chicago
London

New York
Paris

San Francisco

FROMMER'S® WITH KIDS GUIDES

Chicago
Las Vegas
New York City

Ottawa
San Francisco
Toronto

Vancouver
Walt Disney World® & Orlando
Washington, D.C.

SUZY GERSHMAN'S BORN TO SHOP GUIDES

Born to Shop: France
Born to Shop: Hong Kong,
Shanghai & Beijing

Born to Shop: Italy
Born to Shop: London

Born to Shop: New York
Born to Shop: Paris

FROMMER'S® IRREVERENT GUIDES

Amsterdam
Boston
Chicago
Las Vegas
London

Los Angeles
Manhattan
New Orleans
Paris
Rome

San Francisco
Seattle & Portland
Vancouver
Walt Disney World®
Washington, D.C.

FROMMER'S® BEST-LOVED DRIVING TOURS

Austria
Britain
California
France

Germany
Ireland
Italy
New England

Northern Italy
Scotland
Spain
Tuscany & Umbria

THE UNOFFICIAL GUIDES®

Beyond Disney
California with Kids
Central Italy
Chicago
Cruises
Disneyland®
England
Florida
Florida with Kids
Inside Disney

Hawaii
Las Vegas
London
Maui
Mexico's Best Beach Resorts
Mini Las Vegas
Mini Mickey
New Orleans
New York City
Paris

San Francisco
Skiing & Snowboarding in the
West
South Florida including Miami &
the Keys
Walt Disney World®
Walt Disney World® for
Grown-ups
Walt Disney World® with Kids
Washington, D.C.

SPECIAL-INTEREST TITLES

Athens Past & Present
Cities Ranked & Rated
Frommer's Best Day Trips from London
Frommer's Best RV & Tent Campgrounds
in the U.S.A.
Frommer's Caribbean Hideaways
Frommer's China: The 50 Most Memorable Trips
Frommer's Exploring America by RV
Frommer's Gay & Lesbian Europe
Frommer's NYC Free & Dirt Cheap

Frommer's Road Atlas Europe
Frommer's Road Atlas France
Frommer's Road Atlas Ireland
Frommer's Wonderful Weekends from
New York City
The New York Times' Guide to Unforgettable
Weekends
Retirement Places Rated
Rome Past & Present

Travel Tip: He who finds the best hotel deal has more to spend on facials involving knobbly vegetables.

Hello, the Roaming Gnome here. I've been nabbed from the garden and taken round the world. The people who took me are so terribly clever. They find the best offerings on Travelocity. For very little cha-ching. And that means I get to be pampered and exfoliated till I'm pink as a bunny's doodah.

travelocity

Travel Tip: Make sure there's customer service for any change of plans — involving friendly natives, for example.

One can plan and plan, but if you don't book with the right people you can't seize le moment and canoodle with the poodle named Pansy. I, for one, am all for fraternizing with the locals. Better yet, if I need to extend my stay and my gnome nappers are willing, it can all be arranged through the 800 number at, oh look, how convenient, the lovely company coat of arms.

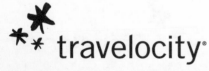

Travel Tip: He who finds the best hotel deal has more to spend on facials involving knobbly vegetables.

Hello, the Roaming Gnome here. I've been nabbed from the garden and taken round the world. The people who took me are so terribly clever. They find the best offerings on Travelocity. For very little cha-ching. And that means I get to be pampered and exfoliated till I'm pink as a bunny's doodah.

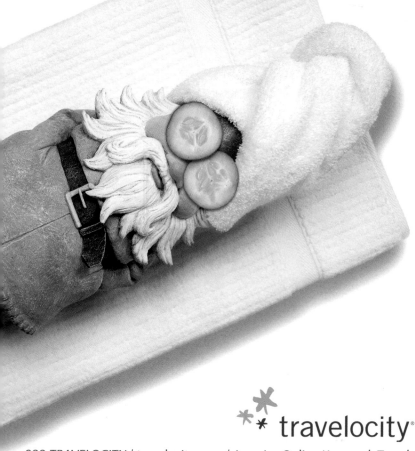

travelocity®

1-888-TRAVELOCITY / travelocity.com / America Online Keyword: Travel

Now that you

know where to go...

how ya gonna

get there?

Our lowest rates.